U^{the}nofficial Guide® to
Las Vegas 2005

Also available from John Wiley & Sons, Inc.:

Beyond Disney: The Unofficial Guide to Universal, Sea World, and the Best of Central Florida

Inside Disney: The Incredible Story of Walt Disney World and the Man Behind the Mouse

Mini Las Vegas: The Pocket-Sized Unofficial Guide to Las Vegas

Mini-Mickey: The Pocket-Sized Unofficial Guide to Walt Disney World

The Unofficial Guide to California with Kids

The Unofficial Guide to Central Italy: Florence, Rome, Tuscany, and Umbria

The Unofficial Guide to Chicago

The Unofficial Guide to Cruises

The Unofficial Guide to Disneyland

The Unofficial Guide to England

The Unofficial Guide to Florida

The Unofficial Guide to Florida with Kids

The Unofficial Guide to Hawaii

The Unofficial Guide to London

The Unofficial Guide to Maui

The Unofficial Guide to Mexico's Best Beach Resorts

The Unofficial Guide to New Orleans

The Unofficial Guide to New York City

The Unofficial Guide to Paris

The Unofficial Guide to San Francisco

The Unofficial Guide to Skiing and Snowboarding in the West

The Unofficial Guide to South Florida

The Unofficial Guide to Walt Disney World

The Unofficial Guide to Walt Disney World for Grown-Ups

The Unofficial Guide to Walt Disney World with Kids

The Unofficial Guide to Washington, D.C.

the Unofficial Guide® to Las Vegas

2005

Bob Sehlinger

with Deke Castleman, Muriel Stevens,
and Chris Mohney

WILEY

Please note that prices fluctuate in the course of time, and travel information changes under the impact of many factors that influence the travel industry. We therefore suggest that you write or call ahead for confirmation when making your travel plans. Every effort has been made to ensure the accuracy of information throughout this book, and the contents of this publication are believed correct at the time of printing. Nevertheless, the publishers cannot accept responsibility for errors or omissions or for changes in details given in this guide or for the consequences of any reliance on the information provided by the same. Assessments of attractions and so forth are based upon the author's own experience, and, therefore, descriptions given in this guide necessarily contain an element of subjective opinion, which may not reflect the publisher's opinion or dictate a reader's own experience on another occasion. Readers are invited to write the publisher with ideas, comments, and suggestions for future editions.

Published by:
John Wiley & Sons, Inc.
111 River Street
Hoboken, NJ 07030

Produced by Menasha Ridge Press
Cover design by Michael J. Freeland
Interior design by Michele Laseau
Photo credit: Robert Young Pelton/Corbis

For information on our other products and services or to obtain technical support please contact our Customer Care Department within the United States at (800) 762-2974, outside the U.S. at (317) 572-3993, or fax (317) 572-4002

Wiley also publishes its books in a variety of electronic formats. Some content that appears in print may not be available in electronic formats.

ISBN 0-7645-5971-0

Manufactured in the United States of America
5 4 3 2

Contents

List of Maps, Charts and Illustrations

Acknowledgments

The people of Las Vegas love their city and spare no effort to assist a writer trying to dig beneath the facade of flashing neon. It is important to them to communicate that Las Vegas is a city with depth, diversity, and substance. "Don't just write about our casinos," they demand, "take the time to get to know us."

We made every effort to do just that, enabled each step of the way by some of the most sincere and energetic folks a writer could hope to encounter. Cam Usher of the Las Vegas Convention and Visitors Authority also spared no effort in offering assistance and contacts. Thanks to Nevada expert Deke Castleman for his contributions to our entertainment, nightlife, and buffet coverage, and to gambling pro Anthony Curtis for his tips on the best places to play.

Restaurant critic Muriel Stevens ate her way through dozens of new restaurants but drew the line when it came to buffet duty. Jim McDonald of the Las Vegas Police Department shared his experiences and offered valuable suggestions for staying out of trouble. Larry Olmsted evaluated Las Vegas golf courses, and forest ranger Debbie Savage assisted us in developing material on wilderness recreation. New to our field research team was Russell Helms, who reviewed shows, checked out nightclubs, and inspected hotels.

Purple Hearts to our field research team, who chowed down on every buffet and $2 steak in town, checked in and out of countless hotels, visited tourist attractions, and stood for hours in show lines:

K'-Lynne Cotton	Shirley Gutke	Chris Mohney
Marty Newey	Dan Cotton	Nathan Lott
Julie Newey	Leslie Cummins	Russell Helms
Holly Cross	Grace Walton	

Much gratitude to Gabbie Oates, Mopsy Gascon, Annie Long, and Steve Jones, the pros who turned all this effort into a book.

Introduction

<u>On a Plane to Las Vegas</u>

I never wanted to go to Las Vegas. I'm not much of a gambler and have always thought of Las Vegas as a city dedicated to separating folks from their money. As it happens, however, I have some involvement with industries that hold conventions and trade shows there. For some years I was able to persuade others to go in my place. Eventually, of course, it came my turn to go, and I found myself aboard a Delta jumbo jet on my first trip to Las Vegas.

Listening to the banter of those around me, I became aware that my fellow passengers were divided into two distinct camps. Some obviously thought themselves on a nonstop flight to Nirvana and could not have been happier. Too excited to remain seated, they danced up and down the aisles clapping one another on the back in anticipation. The other passengers, by contrast, groused and grumbled, swore under their breath, and wore expressions suggesting a steady diet of lemons. These people, as despondent as Al Capone en route to a tax audit, lamented their bad luck and cursed those who had made a trip to such a place necessary.

To my surprise, I thoroughly enjoyed Las Vegas. I had a great time without gambling and have been back many times with never a bad experience. The people are friendly, the food is good, hotels are a bargain, it's an easy town to get around in, and there is plenty to do (24 hours a day, if you are so inclined).

It's hard to say why so many folks have such strong feelings about Las Vegas (even those who have never been there). Among our research team we had people willing to put their kids in boarding school for a chance to go, while others begged off to have root canal surgery or prune their begonias. A third group wanted to go very badly but maintained the pretense of total indifference. They reminded me of people who own five TVs yet profess never to watch television; they clearly had not mustered the courage to come out of the closet.

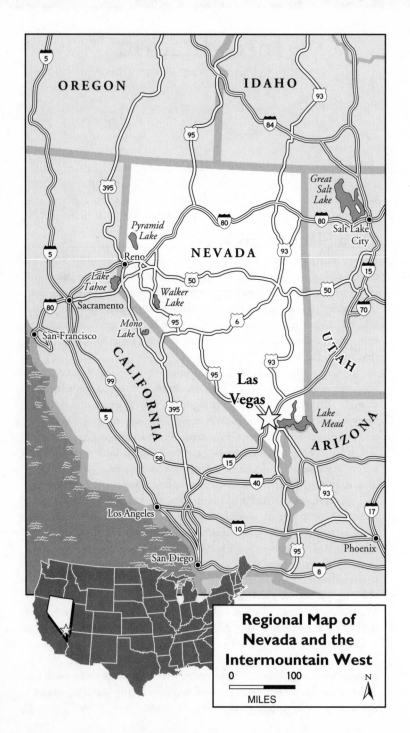

Regional Map of Nevada and the Intermountain West

0   100

MILES

N

What I discovered during my first and subsequent visits is that the nongambling public doesn't know very much about Las Vegas. Many people cannot see beyond the gambling, cannot see that there could possibly be anything of value in Las Vegas for nongamblers or those only marginally interested in gambling.

When you ask these people to describe their ideal vacation, they wax eloquent about lazy days relaxing in the sun, playing golf, enjoying the luxury of resort hotels, eating in fine restaurants, sight-seeing, shopping, and going to the theater. Outdoor types speak no less enthusiastically about fishing, boating, hiking, and, in the winter, skiing. As it happens, Las Vegas offers all of these diversions and probably at the most reasonable prices available anywhere. Gambling is just the tip of the iceberg in Las Vegas, but it's all many people can see.

Las Vegas is, of course, about gambling, but there's so much more. Las Vegas has sunny, mild weather two-thirds of the year, some of the finest hotels and restaurants in the world, the most diversified celebrity and production-show entertainment to be found, unique shopping, internationally renowned golf courses, and numerous attractions. For the outdoor enthusiast, Red Rock Canyon National Conservation Area, Lake Mead National Recreation Area, and Toiyabe National Forest offer some of the most exotic and beautiful wilderness resources in North America.

This guide is designed for those who want to go to Las Vegas and for those who have to go to Las Vegas. If you are a recreational gambler and/or enthusiastic vacationer, we will show you ways to have more fun, make the most of your time, and spend less money. If you are one of the skeptics, unwilling spouses or companions of gamblers, business travelers, or people who think they would rather be someplace else, we will help you discover the seven-eighths of the Las Vegas iceberg that is hidden. We will demonstrate that you can have the time of your life in this friendly city and never bet that first nickel.

Looking Back, Looking Ahead

In 1946, Bugsy Siegel opened the Flamingo Hotel, kicking off the metamorphosis that changed three miles of mostly barren desert into what is now the Las Vegas Strip. The original Flamingo was an eyepopper in its day and established a baseline that all subsequent casinos had to at least match, if not improve upon.

As new hotels appeared in the neon Valhalla, each contributed something different, and occasionally something better, raising the bar (to use a high-jumping metaphor) incrementally. Two properties, the Desert Inn and Caesars Palace, advanced the standard significantly, but because they catered to an exclusive clientele, their competitors chose not to follow suit.

Then, in 1989, came the Mirage, a large hotel and casino offering the spectacle of Caesars and the refined taste of the Desert Inn (almost) but, more importantly, targeting not the carriage trade but rather the average tourist. The Mirage was equal parts tourist attraction, hotel, and casino, and each part was executed with imagination and flair. Not many Las Vegas tourists could afford the Mirage's expensive guest rooms, but the place was nonetheless a must-see on every visitor's touring itinerary.

The Mirage's success demonstrated that gamblers, contrary to prevailing opinion, actually paid attention to their gaming environment and, if given a choice, preferred an interesting, dynamic, and attractive setting to the cramped, noisy, monochromatic boiler room that was the norm. Beyond a doubt, the Mirage was in a class by itself. Observers waited impatiently to see if any competitor would challenge the Mirage, though most believed the standard was impossibly high.

The answer was not long in coming. A veritable explosion of new developments was rushed from the drawing board to the construction zone. First was the Excalibur in 1990. It was big, plastic, gaudy, and certainly no direct competitor to the Mirage, but its Knights-of-the-Round-Table theme played exceptionally well with the blue-collar and family markets. Next came the Class of 1993, which included the pyramid-shaped Luxor, Treasure Island (sister property to the Mirage), and the MGM Grand Hotel and Theme Park. Though the MGM Grand Theme Park was a bust, the hotel and casino were immediately successful. Likewise, the Luxor and Treasure Island (T. I.), with their knockout themes, rocketed up the pop chart.

In the three years before the next wave of new hotels opened in 1996, the vital signs of the newer and older properties were monitored closely. The MGM Grand was the largest hotel-casino in the world, Excalibur was a close second, and the other new hotels offered more than 2,500 rooms each. As with the bull stock market in the late 1990s, there was endless speculation and debate about how long the building boom could last. But the preliminary data seemed to indicate that the new properties were responsible for increasing the aggregate market. Room occupancy rates remained high.

Though more visitors were coming to Las Vegas, the lion's share of the business was going to the newer, high-profile hotels. Older properties, including some of the Strip's most established casinos, found themselves increasingly in the margins. So too, downtown Las Vegas was in a tailspin, with gaming revenues down, or flat, year after year. The new marching orders, avoided or ignored for so long, were crystal clear: if you want to play in the big league, you have to upgrade. And upgrading meant approximating the Mirage standard.

The response of downtown Las Vegas was to combine the Fremont Street casinos into a mega-gaming venue, a new Glitter Gulch, tied together by a pedestrian plaza under the canopy of the Fremont Street Experience electric light show. Back on the Strip, older properties, including Bally's, the Desert Inn, the Flamingo, Harrah's, the Sahara, the Boardwalk, Circus Circus, and the Riviera, scrambled to upgrade. One property, Vegas World, was razed to make room for a whole new hotel-casino. The venerable Caesars Palace alone managed to stay ahead of the game, making improvements each year to maintain its position at or near the top of the Strip food chain.

In 1996, the Stratosphere Hotel and Casino, which has the tallest observation tower in the United States, opened at the old Vegas World site. Farther south on the Strip, the Monte Carlo hit the scene, a joint venture between then-Circus Circus Enterprises and Mirage Resorts. Then, in 1997, New York–New York opened its doors. With more than 100,000 people a day visiting during its first weeks of operation, New York–New York quickly dispelled the notion that the Strip was overbuilt. In typical Las Vegas go-for-broke style, the Dunes, the Sands, and the Hacienda were blown up to make room for yet more gargantuan gambling palaces.

The boom proceeded at warp speed, with a construction frenzy that through 2001 added a whopping 23,000 new rooms to Las Vegas's inventory (now totaling roughly 130,000). Bellagio (opened in 1998) draws its inspiration from Italy's Lake Como, adding 3,000 rooms to the Mirage Resorts galaxy and catering to the upscale market. Across the street is the 2,900-room Paris Casino Resort with its own 50-story Eiffel Tower. Just south is the new Aladdin, a 2,600-room complex with an ancient desert kingdom theme. On the site of the old Sands is the Venetian. An all-suite property with 3,000 suites in its first building phase and 1,013 in its second, the Venetian features a shopping complex in a Venice canal setting complete with gondola rides. And at the southern end of the Strip on the old Hacienda property, the 3,700-room Mandalay Bay, a Mandalay Resort Group (formerly Circus Circus Enterprises) hotel-casino for an adult clientele, opened in early 1999.

Not all of the new development is on the Strip or downtown. More and more new casinos are being built around town in an effort to cater to the local population and visitors who don't want to battle the traffic of the Strip. In just the past ten years, we have witnessed the opening of the Fiestas (Henderson and Rancho), Texas Station, Silverton, the Hard Rock, the Orleans, Arizona Charlie's East, Green Valley Ranch, Tuscany, the Cannery, and Sunset Station. To the west of the Strip is the Suncoast and the JW Marriott, a 550-room spa and golf resort in the Summerlin residential area of Las Vegas that was built in 1999. In late 1999, Hyatt completed its 500-room hotel-casino, the Hyatt Las Vegas, in nearby Henderson. The development is surrounded by a man-made lake and a Jack Nicklaus–designed golf course.

Both the Hyatt and the JW Marriott Las Vegas have had a tough time luring visitors away from the Strip. In a marketing flip-flop, the Marriott's Rampart Casino gave up on out-of-towners and began targeting the locals. The Hyatt is trying (fairly successfully) to fill its rooms with meeting attendees and golfers.

Then there are the mergers and acquisitions. In 2000, Steve Wynn, the visionary behind the Mirage (and the Las Vegas transformation it started), sold the Mirage, Bellagio, T. I., Golden Nugget, and half of Monte Carlo to MGM Grand for $6.4 billion. Wynn, meanwhile, purchased the Desert Inn, where he is building a 3,000-room nonthemed resort called Wynn Las Vegas, stating ironically that "themes are a thing of the past." Wynn always seems to be a step ahead of the pack and might be correct about themes. Still, it's like Dr. Spock saying that children are a thing of the past.

Only months earlier, Hilton's casino subsidiary, Park Place Entertainment, bought Caesars Palace and O'Shea's, adding them to a line-up that already included the Las Vegas Hilton, Bally's, Paris, and the Flamingo. In 2004, Park Place changed its name to Caesars Entertainment to reflect the prestige of its flagship properties. The Mandalay Resort Group owns a good chunk of what's left (but maybe not for long), including Luxor, Mandalay Bay, Excalibur, Circus Circus, and half of the Monte Carlo. In June of 2004, MGM Mirage signed an agreement under which MGM Mirage acquired Mandalay Resort Group for a whopping $7.9 billion, leaving MGM Mirage with control of 36,000 Strip hotel rooms. In an even bigger (not to mention surprising) deal, Harrah's bought Caesars' Entertainment making it the largest casino-gambling company in the world. The deal requires the approval of the state and the Gaming Control Board. In other mergers, Harrah's acquired the Rio, and Station Casinos bought the Fiesta and the Reserve. In the Phoenix-rising department, the long dormant Maxim was resurrected as the Westin Casuarina.

Also in 2004, MGM-Mirage sold its downtown plum, the Golden Nugget, to 30-somethings Tim Poster and Tom Breitling, who leveraged their youthful story into a 13-episode reality TV show for Fox called *The Casino*. Also downtown, the Plaza, Gold Spike, and Western were purchased from Gaughan Properties by Barrick Gambling. To complete the downtown fruit basket turnover, the Four Queens was sold to a local slot bar owner. The new owner immediately alienated Four Queens regulars by closing downtown's best show lounge.

The biggest deal was on the Strip, where Planet Hollywood and Starwood Hotels landed the financially troubled Aladdin for a bargain price. The Desert Passage Mall at the Aladdin, also on the block, sold to a German holding company. *Sehr gut!*

If you wonder where it will all end, you're not alone. Critics point out that the city's infrastructure is not keeping pace with the new development. The Strip is the most sclerotic traffic artery imaginable, making

45-minute slogs out of a one-mile trip. Some relief came in 2004 in the form of a monorail, which runs along the east side of the Strip and loops over to the Las Vegas Convention Center, then on to the Sahara. Water also is a problem (look around, it's a desert out there!). Casino owners duck the blame for spiraling water consumption by insisting that it's the expanding local population that accounts for most of the usage. This is a bit disingenuous, given that the ten-year building boom and new casinos are what's driving population growth. New properties currently under construction will create almost 14,500 new jobs. That's a lot of thirsty people, dogs to bathe, and lawns to water.

For you, the Las Vegas visitor, the news is mixed. The good news is that most of the new hotels and casinos that opened in 2004 were very upscale. The bad news is that most of the new hotels and casinos that opened in 2004 were very upscale. You're free to visit ritzy joints and gawk, and they will gleefully separate you from your stake, but at the end of the day it's only the fat cats who can afford a bed. For the moment you can buy a luxury hotel room in Las Vegas for less than you'd pay at a lot of other places, but Vegas rooms are a bargain in only a relative sense. There's no more Courvoisier on a jug wine budget in America's gambling Mecca.

If you're wondering, the Class (no pun intended) of 2004 included THEhotel at Mandalay Bay, the Ritz-Carlton Lake Las Vegas, and the Westin Casuarina. Coming in 2005 is Wynn Las Vegas, rising on the hallowed ground of the historic Desert Inn. Sired by Steve Wynn, the father of the Mirage and the Bellagio, Wynn Las Vegas will no doubt be yet another transformational project. For the visionary Wynn, the head of the pack is the only place to be.

The most important development by far, however, and one unthinkable only a couple of years ago, is quietly taking place at these same top-of-the-line Strip properties. Simply put, sales revenues from hotel rooms, food and beverages, shows and events, and ancillary sales (shopping, spa services, etc.) are surpassing gaming revenues. The Mirage demonstrated that a hotel could be positioned as a luxury product and charge accordingly. Though most strip properties hedged their bets with various incentives to attract patrons, they learned they didn't have to offer loss-leader buffets, restaurants, and shows to get people through the door. From the establishment of the Mirage until the present, the upscale casinos and hotels have discovered, through experimenting with various pricing models, that there's apparently much less price sensitivity than previously thought. This sea change in the prevailing revenue model has paved the way for such prestige brands as Four Seasons, Ritz-Carlton, Hyatt Regency, and JW Marriott to enter the market with luxury resorts where gaming is almost an afterthought. Facilitating the process is an upsurge in meeting, convention, and trade-show business, especially in events that can be accommodated by a single hotel.

Though your business is welcome at any Las Vegas property, the new revenue model has created a caste system. You can play quarter slots anywhere (at least for the moment), but if you want to see a big-name show, or dine at upscale hotel restaurants, you'd better be pretty well-heeled. For the other hotel casinos, the Saharas, Rivieras, Stratospheres, Imperial Palaces, Excaliburs, and others, attracting guests and players requires offering bargains and discounts. If the Strip was an airliner, you could stroll up the aisle from your economy seat and see what's going on in First Class, but you won't be able to stay or eat there.

The dining scene is another plus. Buffets continue to improve as competition sharpens, and there is now a branch of seemingly every big-name restaurant in Las Vegas (Four Seasons, Le Cirque, Aqua, Delmonico Steak House, Lawry's, Morton's, The Palm, Wolfgang Puck, Brennan's, Commander's Palace, and on and on). Although theme dining continues to proliferate, the public has weeded out the weak sisters. It's fine to have a theme, but patrons are appropriately voting their palate. Proprietary restaurants are holding their own, but just barely. The bad news is that, aside from buffets, it costs more to dine in Las Vegas now, especially in the new, brand-name joints. As an extreme example, the Mandalay Bay Burger Bar features a $60 hamburger! Still, compared to other cities with dynamic restaurant scenes, Las Vegas remains a relative bargain, especially if you're willing to venture away from the Strip.

Production and celebrity-headliner shows are not the bargain they once were. In fact, the average price of a ticket has increased by 100% in the last ten years, and several shows cost more than $100. On the other side of the coin, the quality of the average show has also trended up. Las Vegas promoters claim prices are a bargain compared to entertainment elsewhere, but that's wishful thinking. Probably half of the shows in town are overpriced. Coming to the rescue, however, are afternoon shows. These historically low-budget and often amateurish productions have given way to a litter of new, high-quality afternoon selections that offer a bargain alternative to the mortgage-the-farm-priced shows playing the major showrooms. Another happy development is the return of downtown shows, a species that came perilously close to extinction.

A few years back, the big buzz was Las Vegas as a family destination. Insiders understood, however, that all the talk was just that. At most, the family thing was a PR exercise to make Las Vegas appear more wholesome. It was tacitly understood that the big dogs would never allow theme parks and other family-oriented attractions to actually compete with the casinos for a visitor's time. Lost in the backwash of this hollow debate, however, was the exponential burgeoning of theme shopping. Although undoubtedly there will be some retail casualties, the case can be made that shopping is almost as potent an attraction in Las Vegas as gambling. On the Strip alone are three huge themed shopping venues (Forum Shops, Grand Canal Shops, and Desert Passage) and a comparatively white-bread mall, but one that's buttressed with every big-name department store in North America. Not to be left in the wake, downtown launched the Las Vegas Premium Outlets shopping complex, which features 120 stores, all flogging upmarket brands. For the first time, there is something powerful enough to suck the players right out of the casinos, and it arrived on the scene as stealthily as a Trojan horse.

The economic downturn in 2002 through 2004, coupled with the fallout from 9/11, cast a shadow over the entire Las Vegas tourism environment, causing a number of big projects to be put on, at least, temporary hold. Meanwhile, occupancy rates remained high, spurred by an uptick in convention business. Even so, developers worry that hotel-room supply is outpacing demand and that maybe there won't be enough visitors to fill all those new malls and designer restaurants. Simply put, the bull in Las Vegas was every bit as headstrong as the bull in the 1990s stock market and, if anything, even more difficult to corral. Today, for the first time in more than a decade, casino companies are managing their growth, and, in an economic climate that's uncharted waters for many, are behaving more like an IBM than a runaway dotcom. Whether high-ticket shows, expense-account restaurants, boutique retailers, and $200 room rates will survive the shakedown is a toss-up, even for the handicappers. The only certainty is that the casinos have placed huge bets in a game of economic roulette. Now, like every sweaty-palmed player in their casinos, they wait anxiously to see where the roulette ball will fall.

About This Guide

Why "Unofficial"?

Most guides to Las Vegas tout the well-known sights, promote the local casinos, restaurants, and hotels indiscriminately, and leave out a lot of good stuff. This guide is different.

Instead of pandering to the tourist industry, we'll tell you if a well-known restaurant's mediocre food is not worth the wait. We'll complain loudly about overpriced hotel rooms that aren't convenient to the places you want to be, and we'll guide you away from the crowds and congestion for a break now and then.

We send in a team of evaluators who tour the casinos and popular attractions, review the production shows, eat in the area's best restaurants, perform critical evaluations of its hotels, and visit the best nightclubs. If a restaurant serves bad food or a show is not worth the admission price, we can say so—and, in the process, make your visit more fun, efficient, and economical.

Building a Guidebook

We got into the guidebook business because we were unhappy with the way travel guides make the reader work to get any usable information. Wouldn't it be nice, we thought, to make guides that are easy to use?

Most guidebooks are compilations of lists. This is true regardless of whether the information is presented in list form or artfully distributed through pages of prose. There is insufficient detail in a list, and prose can present tedious helpings of nonessential or marginally useful information. Not enough wheat, so to speak, for nourishment in one instance, and too much chaff in the other. Either way, these types of guides provide little more than departure points from which readers initiate their own quests.

Many guides are readable and well researched, but they tend to be difficult to use. To select a hotel, for example, a reader must study several pages of descriptions with only the boldface hotel names breaking up large blocks of text. Because each description essentially deals with the same variables, it is difficult to recall what was said concerning a particular hotel. Readers generally must work through all the write-ups before beginning to narrow their choices. The presentation of restaurants, shows, and attractions is similar except that even more reading is required. To use such a guide is to undertake an exhaustive research process that requires examining nearly as many options and possibilities as starting from scratch. If any recommendations are actually made, they lack depth and conviction. These guides compound rather than solve problems by failing to boil travelers' choices down to a thoughtfully considered, well-distilled, and manageable few.

How Unofficial Guides Are Different

Readers care about the authors' opinions. The authors, after all, are *supposed* to know what they are talking about. This, coupled with the fact that the traveler wants quick answers (as opposed to endless alternatives), dictates that authors should be explicit, prescriptive, and above all, direct. This *Unofficial Guide* tries to do just that. It spells out alternatives and recommends specific courses of action. It simplifies complicated destinations and attractions and helps the traveler feel in control in the most unfamiliar environments. The objective of an *Unofficial Guide* is not to have the most information or all of the information; it aims to have the most accessible, useful information, unbiased by affiliation with any organization or industry.

An *Unofficial Guide* is a critical reference work that focuses on a travel destination that appears to be especially complex. Our authors and research team are completely independent from the attractions, restaurants, and hotels we describe. *The Unofficial Guide to Las Vegas* is designed for individuals and families traveling for the fun of it, as well as for business travelers and convention-goers, especially those visiting Las Vegas for the first time. The guide is directed at value-conscious adult consumers who seek a cost-effective, though not Spartan, travel style.

How This Guide Was Researched and Written

While much has been written about Las Vegas, very little has been evaluative. Some guides practically regurgitate the hotels' and casinos' own promotional material. In preparing this work, we took nothing for granted. Each casino, hotel, restaurant, show, and attraction was visited at different times throughout the year by a team of trained observers. They conducted detailed evaluations and rated properties and entertainments according to formal, tested rating criteria. Interviews were conducted to determine what tourists of all ages enjoyed most *and least* during their Las Vegas visit.

While our observers are independent and impartial, they do not claim to have special expertise. Like you, they visited Las Vegas as tourists or business travelers, noting their satisfaction or dissatisfaction. However, the primary differences between the average tourist and the trained evaluator are the evaluator's skills in organization, preparation, and observation. The trained evaluator is responsible for much more than simply observing and cataloging. While the average tourist is being entertained by the magic of Lance Burton, for instance, the professional is rating the performance in terms of theme, pace, continuity, and originality. The evaluator also checks out the physical arrangements: Is the sound system clear without being overpowering? Is seating adequate? Can everyone in the audience easily see the staging area? And what about the performers: are they competent and professional? Are they compelling and engaging? Does the performance begin and end on time? Does the show contain the features described in the hotel's promotional literature? These and many other considerations figure prominently in the rating of any staged performance. Observer teams use detailed checklists to analyze casinos, attractions, hotel rooms, buffets, and restaurants. Finally, evaluator ratings and observations are integrated with tourist reactions and the opinions of patrons for a comprehensive quality profile of each feature and service.

In compiling this guide, we recognize that tourists' ages, backgrounds, and interests will strongly influence their taste in Las Vegas offerings and will account for a preference for one show or casino over another. Our sole objective is to provide the reader with sufficient description, critical evaluation, and pertinent data to make knowledgeable decisions according to individual tastes.

Letters, Comments, and Questions from Readers

We expect to learn from our mistakes, as well as from the input of our readers, and to improve with each book and edition. Many of those who use the *Unofficial Guides* write to us to ask questions, make comments, or share their own discoveries and lessons learned in Las Vegas. We appreciate all such input, both positive and critical, and encourage our readers to continue writing. Readers' comments and observations will be frequently incorporated in revised editions of the *Unofficial Guide* and will contribute immeasurably to its improvement.

How to Write the Author:

Bob Sehlinger
The Unofficial Guide to Las Vegas
P.O. Box 43673
Birmingham, AL 35243
UnofficialGuides@menasharidge.com

If you write us or return our reader-survey form, you can rest assured that we won't release your name and address to any mailing-list companies, direct-mail advertisers, or other third parties. Unless you instruct us otherwise, we will assume that you do not object to being quoted in the *Unofficial Guide.* When you write, be sure to put your return address on your letter as well as on the envelope—sometimes envelopes and letters get separated. And remember, our work takes us out of the office for long periods of time, so forgive us if our response is delayed.

Reader Survey

At the back of this guide, you will find a short questionnaire that you can use to express opinions concerning your Las Vegas visit. Clip the questionnaire out along the dotted line and mail it to the above address.

How Information Is Organized:
By Subject and by Geographic Zones

To give you fast access to information about the *best* of Las Vegas, we've organized material in several formats.

Hotels   Because most people visiting Las Vegas stay in one hotel for the duration of their trip, we have summarized our coverage of hotels in charts, maps, ratings, and rankings that allow you to quickly focus your decision-making process. We do not go on page after page describing lobbies and rooms which, in the final analysis, sound much the same. Instead, we concentrate on the specific variables that differentiate one hotel from another: location, size, room quality, services, amenities, and cost.

Restaurants   We provide a lot of detail when it comes to restaurants. Since you will probably eat a dozen or more restaurant meals during your stay, and since not even you can predict what you might be in the mood for on Saturday night, we provide detailed profiles of the best restaurants in Las Vegas.

Entertainment and Nightlife   Visitors frequently try several different shows or nightspots during their stay. Because shows and nightspots, like restaurants, are usually selected spontaneously after arriving in Las Vegas, we believe detailed descriptions are warranted. All continuously running

Las Vegas
Touring Zones

N

0   3
MILES

stage shows, as well as celebrity showrooms, are profiled and reviewed in the entertainment section of this guide. The best nightspots and lounges in Las Vegas are profiled alphabetically under nightlife in the same section.

Geographic Zones   Though it's easy to get around in Las Vegas, you may not have a car or the inclination to venture far from your hotel. To help you locate the best restaurants, shows, nightspots, and attractions convenient to where you are staying, we have divided the city into geographic zones:

- Zone 1   The Las Vegas Strip and Environs
- Zone 2   Downtown Las Vegas
- Zone 3   Southwest Las Vegas
- Zone 4   North Las Vegas
- Zone 5   Southeast Las Vegas and the Boulder Highway

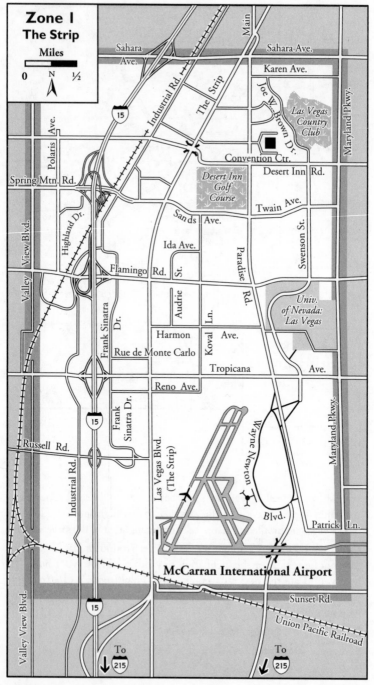

Zone 1
The Strip

Miles

0   N   ½

Sahara Ave.

Sahara Ave.

Karen Ave.

Main

The Strip

Industrial Rd.

Joe W. Brown Dr.

Las Vegas Country Club

Maryland Pkwy.

15

Convention Ctr.

Desert Inn Rd.

Desert Inn Golf Course

Polaris Ave.

Spring Mtn. Rd.

Twain Ave.

Swenson St.

Valley View Blvd.

Highland Dr.

Sands Ave.

Ida Ave.

Flamingo Rd.

St.

Paradise Rd.

Univ. of Nevada: Las Vegas

Frank Sinatra Dr.

Audrie

Koval Ln.

Harmon

Ave.

Rue de Monte Carlo

Tropicana

Ave.

Reno Ave.

Frank Sinatra Dr.

Las Vegas Blvd. (The Strip)

Wayne Newton

Maryland Pkwy.

15

Russell Rd.

Industrial Rd.

Blvd.

Patrick Ln.

McCarran International Airport

Valley View Blvd.

Sunset Rd.

Union Pacific Railroad

15

To
↓ 215

To
↓ 215

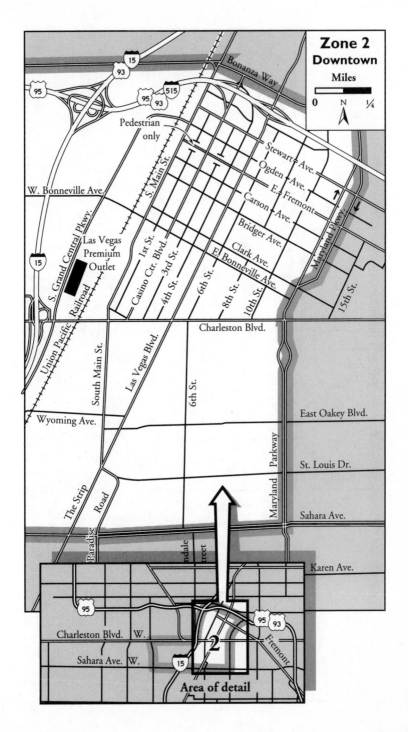

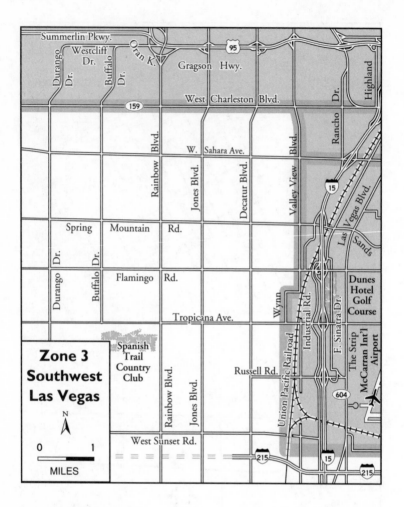

Zone 3
Southwest
Las Vegas

N

0   1

MILES

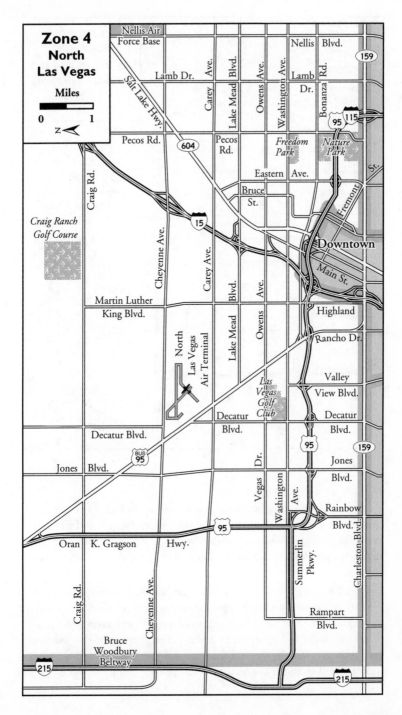

Zone 4
North
Las Vegas

Miles

0   1

Zone 5
Southeast
Las Vegas and the
Boulder Highway

N

    All profiles of hotels, restaurants, and nightspots include zone numbers. For example, if you are staying at the Golden Nugget and are interested in Italian restaurants within walking distance, scanning the restaurant profiles for restaurants in Zone 2 will provide you with the best choices.

Comfort Zones   Because every Las Vegas hotel-casino has its own personality and attracts a specific type of customer, for each property we have created a profile that describes the casino's patrons and gives you a sense of how it might feel to spend time there. The purpose of the comfort-zone section is to help you find the hotel-casino where you will feel most welcome and at home. Comfort-zone descriptions begin on page 82.

Las Vegas: An Overview

Gathering Information

Las Vegas has the best selection of complementary visitor guides of any American tourist destination we know. Available at the front desk or concierge table at almost every hotel, the guides provide a wealth of useful information on gaming, gambling lessons, shows, lounge entertainment, sports, buffets, meal deals, tours and sight-seeing, transportation, shopping, and special events. Additionally, most of the guides contain coupons for discounts on dining, shows, attractions, and tours.

What's On is the most comprehensive of the visitor guides. *Today in Las Vegas* is also very comprehensive, but is organized somewhat differently. Because both formats come in handy, we always pick up a copy of each.

The guides are published weekly or biweekly and are distributed on a complementary basis in Las Vegas. If you want to see a copy before you leave home, subscriptions or single issues are available as follows:

Today in Las Vegas	*What's On Magazine*
Lycoria Publishing Company	4425 Industrial Road
3626 Pecos McLeod Drive, Suite 14	Las Vegas, NV 89103
Las Vegas, NV 89121	(702) 891-8811
(702) 385-2737	www.ilovevegas.com
www.todayinlv.com	

Other publications include *Showbiz Magazine,* published by the *Las Vegas Sun* newspaper, and *Where Las Vegas.* Both have much of the same information discussed above, plus feature articles.

The *Las Vegas Advisor* is a 12-page monthly newsletter containing some of the most useful consumer information available on gaming, dining, and entertainment, as well as taking advantage of deals on rooms, drinks, shows, and meals. With no advertising or promotional content, the newsletter serves its readers with objective, prescriptive, no-nonsense advice, presented with a sense of humor. The *Advisor* also operates a dynamite Web site at **www.lasvegasadvisor.com.** At a subscription rate of $50 a year, the *Las Vegas Advisor* is the best investment you can make if you plan to spend four or more days in Las Vegas each year. If you are a one-time visitor but wish to avail yourself of all this wisdom, single copies of the *Las Vegas Advisor* can be purchased for $5 at the Gambler's Book Club store at 630 South 11th Street, (call (702) 382-7555, (800) 522-1777, or visit **www.gamblersbook.com**). To speed delivery of the first issue (which includes discount coupons), send a self-addressed, legal-sized envelope with $1.06 postage along with your request. For additional information:

Las Vegas Advisor
Huntington Press
3687 South Procyon Avenue, Suite A
Las Vegas, NV 89103
(702) 252-0655 or (800) 244-2224
www.lasvegasadvisor.com

Las Vegas and the Internet

The explosive growth of Las Vegas is not only physical, but also virtual. The following are the best places to go on the web to launch yourself into Las Vegas cyberspace:

The site of the *Las Vegas Advisor,* **www.lasvegasadvisor.com,** is a great source of information on recent and future developments, dining, entertainment, and gambling. The site features a nifty trip planner as well as a miniature vacation guide.

The official Web site of the Las Vegas Convention and Visitors Authority is **www.lasvegas24hours.com.** This comprehensive site has hundreds of links to hotels, casinos, the airport, and area transportation, as well as information on the convention center, sight-seeing, and dining. To pull up the menu of categories (hotels, entertainment, etc.), click "Search."

The largest Las Vegas Web site is **www.lasvegas.com,** a travel site sponsored by the *Las Vegas Review-Journal.* The newspaper's own Web site is **www.lvrj.com.** Another big Las Vegas travel Web site, with an excellent listing of hotels and their dining and entertainment options, is **www.vegas.com.** Try *What's On* magazine's **www.ilovelasvegas.com** for shows and nightspots. Another good site for entertainment information is *Showbiz* magazine's **www.lvshowbiz.com.**

The best site for finding discounts on hotels is **www.travelaxe.com.** Travelaxe allows you to download a free software program that compares room rates offered by a wide range of discounters. You can also access Travelaxe from the *Las Vegas Advisor* site.

An extensive site aimed at people relocating to Las Vegas or interested in investing in Las Vegas real estate is at **www.lasvegas4sale.com.**

When to Go to Las Vegas

The best time to go to Las Vegas is in the spring or fall, when the weather is pleasant. If you plan to spend most of your time indoors, it doesn't matter what time of year you choose. If you intend to golf, play tennis, run, hike, bike, or boat, try to go in March, April, early May, October, November, or early December.

Because spring and fall are the nicest times of year, they are also the most popular. The best time of year for special deals and bargain room rates is in December (after the National Finals Rodeo in early December and excluding the week between Christmas and New Year's), January, and during the scorching months of the summer, particularly July and August.

Las Vegas Weather and Dress Chart				
Month	Average a.m. Temp.	Average p.m. Temp.	Pools O=Open	Recommended Attire
January	57	32		Coats and jackets are a must.
February	50	37		Dress warmly: jackets and sweaters.
March	69	42	O	Sweaters for days, but a jacket at night.
April	78	50	O	Still cool at night—bring a jacket.
May	88	50	O	Sweater for evening, but days are warm.
June	99	68	O	Days are hot; evenings are moderate.
July	105	75	O	Bathing suits.
August	102	73	O	Dress for the heat—spend time at a pool!
September	95	65	O	Days warm, sweater for evening.
October	81	53	O	Bring a jacket or sweater for afternoon.
November	67	40		Sweaters and jackets, coats for night.
December	58	34		Coats and jackets a must. Dress warmly!

Weather in December, January, and February can vary incredibly. While high winds, cold, rain, and snow are not unheard of, chances are better that temperatures will be mild and the sun will shine. Though the weather is less dependable than in spring or fall, winter months are generally well suited to outdoor activities. We talked to people who in late February water-skied on Lake Mead in the morning and snow-skied the same afternoon at Lee Canyon up in the mountains. The winter months provide an unbeatable combination of good value and choice of activities. From mid-May through mid-September, however, the heat is blistering. During these months, it's best to follow the example of the gambler or the lizard—stay indoors or under a rock.

Crowd Avoidance

In general, weekends are busy and weekdays are slower. The exceptions are holiday periods and when large conventions or special events are being held. Most Las Vegas hotels have a lower guest-room rate for weekdays than for weekends. For a stress-free arrival at the airport; good availability of rental cars; and a quick, easy hotel check-in, try to arrive Monday afternoon through Thursday morning (Tuesday and Wednesday are best).

Las Vegas hosts huge conventions and special events (rodeos, prize fights) that tie up hotels, restaurants, transportation, showrooms, and traffic for a week at a time. If you prefer to schedule your visit at a time when things are a little less frantic, we provide a calendar that lists the larger citywide conventions and regularly scheduled events—to help you avoid the crowds. Note that two or three medium-sized conventions meeting at the same time can impact Las Vegas as much as one big citywide event.

Because conventions of over 12,000 attendees can cause problems for the lone vacationer, the list of conventions and special events on pages 24–27 will help you plan your vacation dates. Included are the convention date, the number of people expected to attend, and the convention location (with hotel headquarters, if known at the time of publication). If you would like to have a more complete convention calendar mailed to you, call the Las Vegas Convention and Visitors Authority at (702) 892-0711 or (702) 892-7576. The convention calendar is also available online at **www.lasvegas24hours.com.**

Arriving and Getting Oriented

If you drive, you will have to travel through the desert to reach Las Vegas. Make sure your car is in good shape. Check your spare tire and toss a couple gallons of water in the trunk, just in case. Once en route, pay attention to your fuel and temperature gauges.

Virtually all commercial air traffic into Las Vegas uses McCarran International Airport. At McCarran, a well-designed facility with good, clear signs, you will have no problem finding your way from the gate to the baggage claim area, though it is often a long walk. Fast baggage handling is not the airport's strongest suit, so don't be surprised if you have to wait a long time on your checked luggage. If you are renting a car from a rental company with a counter at the airport, you can often complete the paperwork before your checked baggage arrives. Once you have picked up your bags, you will have to produce the baggage claim check before you're allowed to exit the building.

Even if you do not intend to rent a car, getting from the airport to your hotel is no problem. Shuttle services are available at a cost of $4–$6 one-way and $9 round-trip. Sedans and "stretch" limousines cost about $25–$40 one-way or $3 trip fee with $1.80 per mile thereafter. Cab fare to Las Vegas Strip locations ranges from $9–$18 one-way plus tip. One-way taxi fares to downtown run about $15–$20. Fares are regulated and should not vary from company to company. The limo service counters are in the hall just outside the baggage claim area. Cabs are at the curb. Additional information concerning ground transportation is available on the McCarran International Airport Web site, **www.mccarran.com.**

TAXI OPERATORS	
Off the Airport	
A-North Las Vegas Cab (702) 643-1041	Nellis Cab Co. (702) 248-1111
ABC (702) 736-8444	Vegas Western Cab (702) 736-8000
Ace Cab Co. (702) 736-8383	Yellow Checker and Star
Henderson Taxi (702) 384-2322	Transportation (702) 873-2227

If you rent a car, you will need to catch your rental company's courtesy vehicle at the middle curb of the authorized vehicle lanes. These ground-level lanes are between the baggage claim building and the main terminal.

If someone is picking you up, go to ground level on the opposite side of the baggage claim building (away from the main terminal) to the baggage claim/arrivals curb. If the person picking you up wants to park and meet you, hook up on the ground level of the baggage claim building near the car-rental counters where the escalators descend from the main terminal.

There are two ways to exit the airport by car. You can depart via the old route, Swenson Street, which runs north-south roughly paralleling the Strip; or you can hop on the new spur of Interstate 215. Dipping south from the airport, I-215 connects with I-15. We recommend using I-215 if you are headed downtown or to any of the hotels west of the Strip. Swenson Street is a better route if you are going to the Las Vegas Convention Center, to UNLV, or to hotels on or east of the Strip.

Convenience Chart   To give you an idea of your hotel's convenience to local, popular destinations such as the Strip, downtown, the Las Vegas

CONVENTIONS/SPECIAL EVENTS CALENDAR

Dates	Convention/Event	Number of Attendees	Location
2004			
Sept. 9–11	International Vision Expo	20,000	Venetian
Sept. 9–12	North American Bridal Association	5,000	LVCC/TBD
Sept. 10–13	ABC Kids Expo	3,500	LVCC/TBD
Sept. 11–15	National Association of Insurance and Financial Advisors	3,000	Mandalay Bay Resort/Casino
Sept. 12–15	GenMar. Holdings, Inc.	4,000	LVCC/Caesars Palace
Sept. 14–16	National Guard Association of the U.S.	4,500	LVCC/LV Hilton
Sept. 16–18	Amusement & Music Operators Assoc.	5,500	LVCC/LV Hilton
Sept. 16–18	Intl. Assn. for the Leisure & Entertainment Industry/Fun Expo	4,500	LVCC/LV Hilton
Sept. 22–23	Western Nursery and Garden Expo	9,000	LVCC/Hard Rock Hotel/Casino
Sept. 22–23	World Wide Pet Supply Assn./Super Zoo	10,000	LVCC/TBD
Sept. 26–29	Electronic Retailing Association	3,000	Paris Las Vegas
Sept. 27–30	National Mining Assn./Minexpo Intl. 2004	35,000	LVCC/TBD
Oct. 3–7	American Trucking Associations	3,300	LV Hilton
Oct. 5–7	G2E: Global Gaming Expo	25,000	LVCC/TBD
Oct. 6–8	Interbike Expo	23,000	Sands Expo Ctr./Multiple
Oct. 6–9	Latin American Studies Association	4,000	Riviera Hotel & Casino
Oct. 9–13	U.S. Telecom Association	2,700	Venetian
Oct. 12–14	National Business Aviation Assn., Inc.	30,000	LVCC/Paris Las Vegas
Oct. 14–16	AARP	20,000	Sands Expo Ctr../Venetian
Oct. 18–20	National Assn. of Convenience Stores	25,000	LVCC/LV Hilton
Oct. 20–22	Metalcon International	8,500	LVCC/LV Hilton
Oct. 23–27	American Society of Anesthesiologists	16,000	LVCC/LV Hilton
Oct. 28–30	Las Vegas Antique Arms Show	3,000	Riviera Hotel & Casino
Oct. 29–Nov. 1	Automotive Parts Rebuilders Assn. International Big R Show	4,000	LV Hilton
Nov. 2–5	Automotive AfterMarket Products Week and Expo (AAPEX)	100,000	Sands Expo Ctr. Multiple
Nov. 2–5	Specialty Equipment Market Assn.	100,000	LVCC/LV Hilton
Nov. 3–6	Intl. Autobody Congress and Exposition NACE Expo	35,000	Mandalay Bay Resort/Casino.
Nov. 8–11	International Spa Association	2,500	Sands Expo Ctr./Venetian
Nov. 10–12	California Rental Association	4,500	LVCC/LV Hilton
Nov. 15–18	Comdex Las Vegas 2004	50,000	LVCC/TBD
Nov. 17–18	Bank Administration Institute Retail Delivery Conference and Expo	10,000	LVCC/LV Hilton

Dates	Convention/Event	Number of Attendees	Location
2004			
Nov. 23–26	Sports Network International, Inc.	4,500	Cashman Ctr./ Wellesley Inn
Dec. 1–3	International Pool and Spa Expo	15,000	LVCC/LV Hilton
Dec. 9–12	Assn. for Career and Technical Education	12,000	LVCC/LV Hilton
Dec. 12–15	National Ground Water Association	6,000	LVCC
2005			
Jan. 6–9	2005 International CES	115,000	LVCC/LV Hilton
Jan. 6–9	Adult Entertainment Expo	15,000	Sands Expo Ctr./Venetian
Jan. 13–15	Las Vegas Antique Arms Show	5,000	Riviera Hotel & Casino
Jan. 17–21	World of Concrete Expo	75,000	LVCC/LV Hilton
Jan. 19–20	AEC Systems	5,000	LVCC/TBD
Jan. 26–28	Surfaces	41,000	Sands Expo Ctr./Venetian
Jan. 28–31	Shooting, Hunting and Outdoor Trade Show and Conference/Shot Show	33,000	LVCC/TBD
Feb. 3–5	Vacuum Dealers Trade Association	4,000	LVCC/LV Hilton
Feb. 14–17	Magic Marketplace	90,000	LVCC/Sands Expo/LV Hilton
Feb. 21–24	Western Veterinary Conference	11,500	Mandalay Bay Resort/Casino
Feb. 27–Mar. 3	Associated Surplus Dealers/Associated Merchandise Dealers	52,000	LVCC/Sands Expo/LV Hilton
Feb. 28–Mar. 2	Nightclub and Bar Convention and Trade Show	38,000	LVCC/LV Hilton
Mar. 3–5	Awards and Recognition Association	5,000	LVCC/LV Hilton
Mar. 15–19	Conexpo–CON/AGG	135,000	LVCC/TBD
Mar. 30–31	National Association of Tobacco Outlets (NATO) Conference and Expo	4,000	LVCC/TBD
Mar. 30–Apr. 1	National Association of Pizzeria Operators–International Pizza Expo	13,000	LVCC/LV Hilton
Mar. 31–Apr. 2	North American Bridal Association	5,000	LVCC/TBD
Apr. 5–6	Medtrade Spring	4,000	LVCC/LV Hilton
Apr. 6–8	Intl. Wireless Communications Expo	13,000	LVCC/LV Hilton
Apr. 7–8	National Automatic Merchandising Assn.	4,500	LVCC/LV Hilton
Apr. 7–9	Billiard Congress of America	8,000	LVCC/LV Hilton
Apr. 18–21	National Association of Broadcasters	125,000	LVCC/LV Hilton
Apr. 28–30	Automotive Engine Rebuilders Assn.	5,000	LVCC/LV Hilton
Apr. 30–May 2	Las Vegas Hair and Nail Conference	11,000	LVCC/LV Hilton
Apr. 30–May 5	Intl. Aesthetics Cosmetics and Spa Conf.	30,000	LVCC/LV Hilton
May 3–5	Networld and Interop	27,500	LVCC/Multiple
May 5–7	Hospitality Design Exposition	20,000	Sands Expo Ctr./ Venetian

CONVENTIONS/SPECIAL EVENTS CALENDAR *(cont'd)*

Dates	Convention/Event	Number of Attendees	Location
2005			
May 10–12	Kitchen/Bath Industry Show	44,000	LVCC/TBD
May 22–25	Intl. Council of Shopping Centers	34,000	LVCC/LV Hilton
May 24–26	Aviation Industry Week GSE AS3	5,000	LVCC/LV Hilton
un. 3–7	JCK Show	40,000	Venetian
Jun. 5–7	Las Vegas Merchandise Expo	6,000	LVCC/LV Hilton
Jun. 5–7	Las Vegas Merchandise Expo	6,000	LVCC/LV Hilton
Jun. 8–10	Infocomm/Intl. Communications Industries Association	20,000	LVCC/TBD
Jun. 16–18	The Truck Show—Western Addition	27,000	LVCC/LV Hilton
Jun. 21–23	Las Vegas Intl. Hotel Restaurant Show	10,000	LVCC Multiple
Jun. 26–30	Healthcare Financial Management Association National Institute	3,000	Bally's Las Vegas
Jul. 5–9	Idea: Intl. Assn. of Fitness Professionals	9,000	LVCC/LV Hilton
Jul. 15	National Nutritional Foods Association	8,000	Sands Expo Ctr./ Venetian
Jul. 20–22	Icast/American Sportfishing Association	6,000	LVCC/LV Hilton
Jul. 24–26	Cosmoprof North America	30,000	Mandalay Bay Resort/Casino
Aug. 14–18	Associated Surplus Dealers/Associated Merchandise DealersExpo	52,000	LVCC/Sands/ LV Hilton
Aug. 22–26	United Brotherhood of Carpenters and Joiners of America	4,000	Bally's Las Vegas
Aug. 29–Sept. 1	Magic Marketplace	90,000	LVCC/Sands Expo/LV Hilton

Convention Center, UNLV, and the airport, we have pro vided a section on getting around. Included in that chapter is a "convenience chart" that lists estimated times by foot and cab from each hotel to the destinations outlined above (see pages 48–51). In the same section are tips for avoiding traffic congestion and for commuting between the Strip and downtown.

Rental Cars   All of the national car-rental companies have operations in Las Vegas, and there are also a few local companies. Each year we observe how long it takes each of the Las Vegas rental-car agencies to process customers' paperwork and send them on their way. Interestingly, the car rental agencies with counters at the airport are much faster than agencies located outside the airport. At the airport, most companies complete the paperwork and have you on your way in a zippy five to ten minutes. Outside the airport, processing time ranges from 12 to 20 minutes. For those customers using the off-airport agencies, the processing time is in addition to any time spent waiting for the agency's courtesy vehicle and

Dates	Convention/Event	Number of Attendees	Location
Sept. 8–11	North American Bridal Association	5,000	LVCC/TBD
Sept. 11–14	National Postal Forum	5,000	LVCC/LV Hilton
Sept. 12–14	G2E: Global Gaming Expo	27,000	LVCC/TBD
Sept. 26–28	Pack Expo Las Vegas/Sponsored by Packaging Machinery Manufacturers Inst.	27,000	LVCC/LV Hilton
Sept. 27–29	Western Nursery and Garden Expo	10,000	LVCC/Hard Rock Hotel/ Casino
Oct. 4–7	Diving Equipment and Marketing	16,000	LVCC/LV Hilton Assn./DEMA Show
Oct. 16–19	American Health Care Association	3,500	LVCC/LV Hilton
Oct. 18–20	California Rental Association	4,500	LVCC/LV Hilton
Oct. 19–21	Interbike Expo	13,000	Sands Expo Ctr./ Venetian
Oct. 19–21	Intl. Sanitary Supply Association	17,500	LVCC/TBD
Nov. 1–4	Automotive After Market Products Week & Expo (AAPEX)Expo	130,000	LVCC/Sands/ LV Hilton
Nov. 14–17	Comdex Las Vegas 2005	50,000	LVCC/TBD
Dec. 4–8	American Society of Health-System Pharmacists	25,000	LVCC Multiple
Dec. 13–15	Power-gen	20,000	LVCC/TBD

commuting to the off-airport location. (Courtesy vehicles pick up passengers at the center curb outside the baggage claim building about every 10 to 15 minutes.) The processing time also excludes time spent waiting in line at the rental agency before being served. If rental cars are comparatively cheap in Las Vegas, taxes and fees are not. If you rent your car at the airport (includes both terminal and off-terminal locations on airport property) here's what you can expect to pay:

State Sales Tax	7.5%
Nevada Rental Service Fee	6.0%
Airport Concession Recovery Fee	10.0%
Reimbursement of Registration and License Fee	4.0%
Total	27.0%

Had enough? Powers at the airport don't think so. In addition to the above you are charged a $3 per day Consumer Facility Charge. You can avoid the 10% fee and the three bucks per day by renting the car at a non-airport location like your hotel. Be advised, however, that it's not unusual for agencies to bump up the rental price at such locations.

At the airport, the process of disembarking from the plane, walking to the baggage area, waiting for and claiming luggage, and proceeding to the car-rental counter has the effect of evenly distributing car-rental customers. Lines at the airport car-rental counters ebb and flow, but almost never exceed six to eight customers. The longest airport lines are at the Avis and Hertz counters, but these move quickly, with enough agents to keep waiting time to a minimum.

RENTAL CAR AGENCIES

At the Terminal

Alamo/National (702) 261-5391	Hertz (702) 736-4900
All State Car Rental (702) 736-6147	Payless 702) 736-6147
Avis (702) 261-5591	Sav-mor (702) 736-1234
Budget (702) 736-1212	Thrifty (702) 896-7600
Enterprise (702) 261-4435	

Off the Airport

Alamo/National (702) 261-5391	Enterprise (800) 261-7331
Dollar (888) 205-3315	Rent-a-Vette (702) 736-2592
Dream Car Rentals (702) 731-6452	US Rent-a-Car (702) 798-6100

In contrast to agencies in the airport, customers of agencies outside the airport mass into groups as they are picked up by the shuttle buses. Therefore, instead of arriving in a more or less continuous, manageable flow (as at the airport), customers of off-airport agencies frequently descend in veritable platoons. In a recent development, Dollar moved its rental-processing operations out of the terminal, turning one of the most efficient rental operations at the airport into nightmare of long lines and slow processing.

In the dollar-and-cents department, prices fluctuate so much from week to week that it's anyone's guess who will offer the best deal during your visit. Usually the best deals are on the company's Web site, but **www.expedia.com, www.travelocity.com,** and **www.orbitz.com** are often worth checking, especially if you're visiting during a particularly busy time, such as during a citywide convention. On rental company sites, counterintuitively, you can often get a better deal if you don't indicate that you're a member of AAA, AARP, etc. After you get your quote, see if you can improve the deal by trying again, entering your organizational or age information.

Be aware that Las Vegas is a feast-or-famine city when it comes to rental-car availability. On many weekends, or when a citywide convention is in town, it may be impossible to get a rental car unless you reserved way advance. If, on the other hand, you come to town when business is slow, the rental agencies will practically give you a car. We have been able to rent from the most expensive companies for as little as $22 a day under these circumstances. If you are visiting during a slow time, reserve a car in advance to cover yourself, and then, on arrival, ask each rental company to quote you its best price. If you can beat the price on your reserved car, go for it.

Improbably, the best place for finding rental car deals is **www.mouse savers.com,** a site dedicated to finding deals at Disneyland and Walt Disney World. The site lists rental car codes that you can use to get great discounts. Some of the codes are for Orlando and southern California only, but many others you can use anywhere in the United States The site also offers some great tips on how to compare different codes and deals.

Another way to score a deal on a rental car is to bid on **www.price line.com.** We've used Priceline to get cars at less than $20 per day. Understand, however, that if your bid is accepted, the entire rental cost will be non-refundably charged to your credit card. In other words, no backing out for any reason. Before placing your bid, check our conventions and special events calendar on pages 24–27. If there's a big convention in town, demand will be high and a lowball bid might not work.

When you (or your travel agent) call to reserve a rental car, ask for the smallest, least expensive car in the company's inventory, even if you ultimately intend to rent a larger vehicle. It's possible that you will be upgraded without charge when you arrive. If not, rental agencies frequently offer on-site upgrade incentives that beat any deals you can make in advance. Always compare daily and weekly rates.

If you decline insurance coverage on the rental car because of protection provided by your credit card, be aware that the coverage provided by the credit card is secondary to your regular auto insurance policy. In most situations the credit-card coverage only reimburses you the deductible on your regular policy. Also be aware that some car-rental contracts require that you drive the car only in Nevada. If you, like many tourists, visit Hoover Dam or trek out to the Grand Canyon, you will cross into Arizona. Another item to check in advance, if applicable, is whether your rental agency charges for additional drivers.

When you rent your car, make sure you understand the implications of bringing it back empty of fuel. Some companies will charge $4 or more per gallon if they have to fill the tank on return. At one agency, we returned a car with between a third and a half tank of gas remaining and were charged $36, the same as if we had coasted in with a completely empty tank. Also, beware of signs at the car-rental counters reading "Gas today—$2.17–$2.55 per gallon" or some such. That usually applies to the price of the gas already in the car when you rent it,

gallon of a fill-up should you return the car empty.
on for a fill-up on return will be somewhere in the fine
al contract.

car problem we encountered involved a pinhead-sized chip on the windshield. Understanding the fine print of rental car contracts, and because we always decline the insurance offered by the agencies, we inspect our cars thoroughly for any damage before accepting the car and leaving the lot. In this instance, as always, we inspected the car thoroughly and did not notice any windshield flaws. When we returned the car after three days, we were requested to remain at the counter to complete an "accident report." Insisting that we were unaware of any damage, we requested that the car be retrieved for our inspection. Still unable to find the alleged damage, we asked the counter agent to identify it for us. The agent responsible for the accident report then had to scrutinize the windshield before she could find the mark, even though she knew its exact location from the employee who checked the car in. The conclusion to be drawn here is that if you decline coverage, the rental agency may hold you responsible for even the tiniest damage, damage so slight that you may never notice it. Before you leave the lot, inspect your rental car with care, examining every inch, and have the agency record anything you find. This will not inhibit them from charging you for damage sustained while the car is in your possession, but at least you will have the peace of mind of knowing that they are not putting one over on you.

Some rental companies will charge you for "loss of use" if you have an accident that takes the car out of use. Because some car insurance policies do not pay loss-of-use charges, check your coverage with your insurance agent before you rent. Finally, if you use a credit card to pay for your rental car, be aware that Diner's Club offers the best supplemental insurance coverage.

Las Vegas Customs and Protocol

In a town where the most bizarre behavior imaginable is routinely tolerated, it is ironic that so many visitors obsess over what constitutes proper protocol. This mentality stems mainly from the myriad customs peculiar to gaming and the *perceived* glamour of the city itself. First-timers attach a great deal of importance to "fitting in." What makes this task difficult, at least in part, is that half of the people with whom they are trying to fit in are first-timers too.

The only hard rules for being accepted downtown or on the Strip are to have a shirt on your back, shoes on your feet, some manner of clothing below the waist, and a little money in your pocket. Concerning the latter, there is no maximum. The operational minimum is bus fare back to wherever you came from.

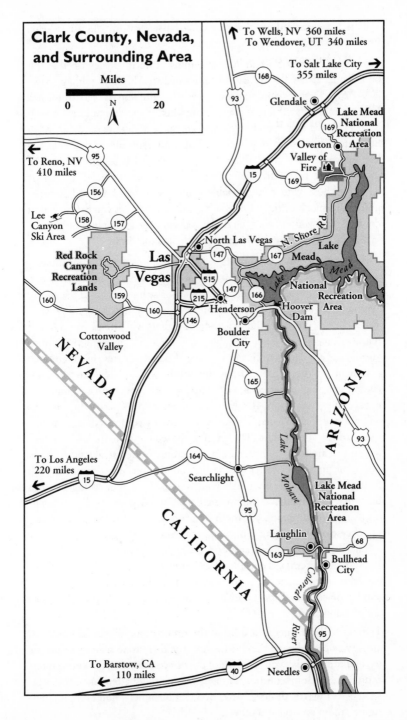

Clark County, Nevada, and Surrounding Area

Miles

0   N   20

To Wells, NV 360 miles
To Wendover, UT 340 miles

To Salt Lake City
355 miles

168

93

Glendale

Lake Mead
National
Recreation
Area

169

Overton
Valley of
Fire

15

169

To Reno, NV
410 miles

95

156

158

Lee
Canyon
Ski Area

157

N. Shore Rd.

Lake
Mead

Red Rock
Canyon
Recreation
Lands

North Las Vegas

147

167

Lake Mead

Las
Vegas

515

National
Recreation
Area

147

160

159

215

166

Henderson

Hoover
Dam

160

146

Boulder
City

Cottonwood
Valley

NEVADA

165

ARIZONA

To Los Angeles
220 miles

15

164

93

Searchlight

95

Lake
Mohave

Lake Mead
National
Recreation
Area

CALIFORNIA

Laughlin

68

163

Bullhead
City

Colorado

To Barstow, CA
110 miles

40

Needles

95

River

This notwithstanding, there are three basic areas in which Las Vegas first-timers tend to feel especially insecure:

Gambling   The various oddities of gaming protocol are described in this book under the respective casino games in Part Three: Gambling (pages 279–325). Despite appearances, however, gambling is very informal. While it is intelligent not to play a game when/if you do not know how, it is unwarranted to abstain because you are uncertain of the protocol. What little protocol exists (things like holding your cards above the table and keeping your hands away from your bet once play has begun) has evolved to protect the house and honest players from cheats. Dealers (a generic term for those who conduct table games) are not under orders to be unfriendly, silent, or rigid. Observe a game that interests you before you sit down. Assure yourself that the dealer is personable and polite. Never play in a casino where the staff is surly or cold; life's too short.

Eating in Gourmet Restaurants   These are a lot of meat-and-potatoes places with fancy names, so there is no real reason to be intimidated. Men will feel more comfortable in sport coats, but ties are rarely worn. Women turn up in everything from slacks and blouses to evening wear. When you sit down, a whole platoon of waiters will attend you. Do not remove your napkin from the table. In gourmet rooms, only the waiters are allowed to place napkins in the laps of patrons. After the ceremonial placement of the napkin, the senior waiter will speak. When he concludes, you may order cocktails, consider the menu, sip your water, or engage in conversation. If there are women in your party, their menus will not have prices listed. If your party is totally comprised of women, a menu with prices listed will be given to the woman who looks the oldest. When you are ready to order, even if you only want a steak and fries, do not speak until the waiter has had an opportunity to recite in French from the menu. To really please your waiters, order something that can be prepared tableside with dramatic flames and explosions. If your waiters seem stuffy or aloof, ask them to grind peppercorns or grate Parmesan cheese on something. This will usually loosen them up.

There will be enough utensils on the table to perform a triple bypass. Because these items are considered expendable, use a different utensil for each dish, surrendering it to the waiter along with the empty plate at the end of the course. If there are small yellow sculptures on the table, they are probably butter.

Tipping   Because about a third of the resident population of Las Vegas are service providers in the tourist industry, there is no scarcity of people to tip. From the day you arrive until the day you depart, you will be interacting with redcaps, porters, cabbies, valet-parking attendants, bellhops, waiters, maître d's, dealers, bartenders, keno runners, housekeeping personnel, room service, and others.

Tipping is an issue that makes some travelers very uncomfortable. How much? When? To whom? Not leaving a tip when one is customary makes you feel inexperienced. Not knowing how much to tip makes you feel vulnerable and out of control. Is the tip you normally leave at home appropriate in Las Vegas?

The most important thing to bear in mind is that a tip is not automatic, nor is it an obligation. A tip is a reward for good service. The following suggestions are based on traditional practices in Las Vegas:

Porters and Redcaps   A dollar a bag.

Cab Drivers   A lot depends on the service and the courtesy. If the fare is less than $8, give the cabbie the change and $1. In other words, on a $4.50 fare give him the 50 cents change plus a buck. If the fare is more than $8, give the cabbie the change and $2. If you are asking the cabbie to take you only a block or two, the fare will be small, but your tip should be large ($3–$5) to make up for his wait in line and to partially compensate him for missing a better-paying fare. Add an extra dollar to your tip if the cabbie does a lot of luggage handling.

Valet Parking   Two dollars is correct if the valet is courteous and demonstrates some hustle. A dollar will do if the service is just OK. Only pay when you take your car out, not when you leave it. Because valet attendants pool their tips, both of the individuals who assist you (coming and going) will be taken care of.

Bellmen   When a bellhop greets you at your car with one of those rolling carts and handles all of your bags, $5 is about right. The more of your luggage that you carry, of course, the less you should tip. Sometimes bellhops who handle only a small bag or two will put on a real performance when showing you your room. I had a bellhop in one Strip hotel walk into my room, crank up the air conditioner, turn on the television, throw open the blinds, flick on all the lights, flush the commode, and test the water pressure in the tub. Give me a break. I tipped the same as if he had simply opened the door and put my luggage in the room.

Waiters   Whether in a coffee shop, a gourmet room, or ordering from room service, the standard gratuity for acceptable service is 15–20% of the total tab, before sales tax. At a self-serve buffet or brunch, it is customary to leave $2 for the folks who bring your drinks and bus your dishes.

Cocktail Waiters/Bartenders   Tip by the round. For two people, $1 a round; for more than two people, $2 a round. For a large group, use your judgment: Is everyone drinking beer, or is the order long and complicated? In casinos where drinks are sometimes on the house, it is considered good form to tip the server $1 per round or per every couple of rounds.

Dealers and Slot Attendants   If you are winning, it is a nice gesture to tip the dealer or place a small bet for him. How much depends on your winnings and on your level of play. With slot attendants, tip when they perform a specific service or you hit a jackpot. In general, unless other services are also rendered, it is not customary to tip change makers or cashiers.

Keno Runners Tip if you have a winner or if the runner really provides fast, efficient service. How much to tip will vary with your winnings and with your level of play.

Showroom Maître d's, Captains, and Servers There is more to this than you might expect. If you are planning to take in a show, see our suggestions for tipping in the chapter on entertainment (see pages 195–197).

Hotel Maids On checking out, leave $2–$4 for each day you stayed (more if you're really messy), providing the service was good.

Does Anyone Know What's Going on at Home? (Does Anyone Really Care?)

If you are more interested in what you are missing at home than what is going on in Las Vegas, **Borders Book Shop,** at 2323 South Decatur Boulevard, stocks Sunday papers from most major cities. To find out whether Borders stocks your favorite newspaper, call (702) 258-0999.

Las Vegas as a Family Destination

Occasionally the publisher sends me around to promote the *Unofficial Guide* on radio and television, and every year I am asked the same question: is Las Vegas a good place for a family vacation?

Objectively speaking, Las Vegas is a great place for a family vacation. Food and lodging are a bargain, and there are an extraordinary number of things, from swimming at Wet 'n' Wild to rafting through the Black Canyon on the Colorado River, that the entire family can enjoy together. If you take your kids to Las Vegas *and forget gambling,* Las Vegas compares favorably with every family tourist destination in the United States. The rub, of course, is that gambling in Las Vegas is pretty hard to ignore.

The marketing gurus, as you may have observed, have tried mightily to recast the town's image and to position Las Vegas as a family destination. The strategy no doubt attracts some parents already drawn to gambling but previously unwilling to allocate family vacation time to a Las Vegas trip. Excepting these relatively few families, however, it takes a lot more than hype to convince most parents that Las Vegas is a suitable destination for a family vacation.

For years, Las Vegas has been touted as a place to *get away* from your kids. For family tourism to succeed in Las Vegas, that characterization has to be changed, or at least minimized. Next, and much more unlikely, gambling must be relegated to a position of secondary importance. There is gambling on cruise ships, for example, but gambling is not the primary reason people go on cruises. Las Vegas, similarly, cannot develop as a bona fide family destination until something supersedes gambling as the main draw. Not very likely. Wet 'n' Wild and Adventuredome at Circus Circus represent a start, but they are only a fraction of what Las Vegas will require to achieve critical mass as a family vacation venue.

To legitimately appeal to the family travel market, the city must consider the real needs of children and parents. Instead of banishing children to midway and electronic-games arcades, hotels need to offer substantive, educational, supervised programs or "camps" for children. The Station casinos are breaking some new ground in this area. Additionally, and equally important, Las Vegas must target and sell the family tourist trade in nontraditional geographic markets. Though Southern California is Las Vegas's largest and most lucrative market, it's not reasonable to expect families with Disneyland, SeaWorld, and Universal Studios in their backyard to travel to Las Vegas to visit a theme park.

Taking Your Children to Las Vegas Today

Las Vegas today is a predominantly adult tourist destination. As a city (including the surrounding area), however, it has a lot to offer children. What this essentially means is that the Strip and downtown have not been developed with children in mind, but if you are willing to make the effort to venture away from the gambling areas, there are a lot of fun and wholesome things for families to do. As a rule, however, people do not go to Las Vegas to be continually absent from the casinos.

Persons under age 21 are not allowed to gamble, nor are they allowed to hang around while *you* gamble. If you are gambling, your children have to be somewhere else. On the Strip and downtown, the choices are limited. True, most Las Vegas hotels have nice swimming pools, but Las Vegas summer days are much too hot to stay out for long. While golf and tennis are possibilities, court or greens fees are routinely charged, and you still must contend with limitations imposed by the desert climate.

After a short time, you will discover that the current options for your children's recreation and amusement are as follows:

1. You can simply allow your children to hang out. Given this alternative, the kids will swim a little, watch some TV, eat as much as their (or your) funds allow, throw water balloons out of any hotel window that has not been hermetically sealed, and cruise up and down the Strip (or Fremont Street) on foot, ducking in and out of souvenir stores and casino lobbies.

2. If your children are a mature age ten or older, you can turn them loose at the Adventuredome at Circus Circus or at the Wet 'n' Wild swimming park. The kids, however, will probably cut bait and go cruising after two hours at the Adventuredome and about four hours of Wet 'n' Wild.

3. You can hire a babysitter to come to your hotel room and tend your children. This works out pretty much like option 1, without the water balloons and the cruising.

4. You can abandon the casino (or whatever else you had in mind) and "do things" with your kids. Swimming and eating (as always) will figure prominently into the plan, as will excursions to places that have engaged the children's curiosity. You can bet that your kids will want to go to the Adventuredome at Circus Circus and probably to the Wet 'n' Wild swimming park. The white tigers, dolphins, and exploding volcano at the Mirage; the naval battle at T. I.; the MGM Grand Lion Habitat; the high-tech attractions at the Luxor, the Sahara, the Forum Shops, and the Las Vegas Hilton; and the Stratosphere Tower are big hits with kids. The Excalibur offers a sort of movie/ride in which you feel as if you are riding a real roller coaster. New York–New York and the Sahara each feature a real roller coaster. If you have two children and do a fraction of all this stuff in one day, you will spend $80 to $250 for the four of you, not counting meals and transportation.

   If you have a car, however, there are lots of great, inexpensive places to go— enough to keep you busy for days. We recommend Red Rock Canyon and Hoover Dam for sure. On the way to Hoover Dam, you can stop for a tour of the Ethel M. Chocolate Factory.

   A great day excursion (during the spring and fall) is a guided raft trip through the Black Canyon on the Colorado River. This can easily be combined with a visit to Hoover Dam. Trips to the Valley of Fire State Park (driving, biking, hiking) are also recommended during the more temperate months.

   Around Las Vegas there are a number of real museums and museums/tourist attractions. The Lied Discovery Children's Museum (just north of downtown) is worthwhile, affordable, and a big favorite with kids age 14 and younger. While you are in the neighborhood, try the Natural History Museum directly across the street.

5. You can pay someone else to take your kids on excursions. Some in-room sitters (bonded and from reputable agencies) will take your kids around as long as you foot the bill. For recommendations, check with the concierge or front desk of your hotel. If your kids are over age 12, you can pack them off on one of the guided tours advertised by the handful in the various local visitor magazines.

Hotels That Solicit Family Business

Only Circus Circus and the Excalibur actively seek the family trade with carnival game midways where children and adults can try to win stuffed animals, foam-rubber dice, and other totally dispensible objects. A great setup for the casinos, the midways turn a nice profit while innocuously introducing the youngsters to games of chance. In addition, Circus Circus operates the Adventuredome theme park and offers free circus acts each evening, starring top-notch talent, including aerialists (flying trapeze artists). The Excalibur provides family-oriented production shows, as well as impromptu magic, puppet, and comedy shows in its second-floor Medieval Village. Both hotels offer reasonably priced rooms and inexpensive food and drink. The Excalibur has the better swimming pool of the two, but Circus Circus offers the nicer guest rooms (Excalibur bathrooms are equipped with a shower only, i.e. no tub).

Parents traveling with children are grudgingly welcome at all of the larger hotels, though certain hotels are better equipped to deal with children than others. If your children are water puppies and enjoy being in a swimming pool all day, Mandalay Bay, Venetian, Aladdin, Flamingo, Monte Carlo, MGM Grand, Mirage, Rio, Tropicana, Caesars Palace, Bellagio, and T. I. have the best pools in town. The Las Vegas Hilton, the Palms, and Hard Rock Hotel, among others, also have excellent swimming facilities.

If your kids are older and into sports, the MGM Grand, Caesars Palace, the Las Vegas Hilton, and Bally's, offer the most variety.

When it comes to childcare and special programs, the MGM Grand, Sunset Station, Venetian, Orleans, Suncoast, Green Valley Ranch, and Gold Coast, along with the Hampton Inn, provide childcare facilities.

Our personal favorite hotel for a family vacation is the Green Valley Ranch, a Station casino and resort about 15 minutes southeast of the Strip. Its location is convenient to Lake Mead, Hoover Dam, the Black Canyon of the Colorado, and Red Rock Canyon, for starters. It has a great swimming areas, good restaurants, and lovely guest rooms. And when you want to sneak into the casino or have an adults-only meal, there's on-site childcare. Best of all, Green Valley Ranch is isolated. There's no place nearby where your kids can get into trouble.

Tours and Excursions

For the most part, the various bus sight-seeing tours available in Las Vegas offer two things: transportation and drivers who know where they're going. In our opinion, if you have a car and can read a map, you will save both money and hassle by going on your own.

Special Events

There is almost always something fun going on in Las Vegas outside of gambling. Among other things, there are minor league baseball, rodeos, concerts, UNLV basketball and football, and, of course, movies. If you are traveling with children, it's worth the effort to pick up a local newspaper and check out what's going on.

Part One

Lodging and Casinos

Where to Stay: Basic Choices

The Las Vegas Strip and Downtown

From a visitor's perspective, Las Vegas is more or less a small town that's fairly easy to get around. Most of the major hotels and casinos are in two areas: downtown and on Las Vegas Boulevard, known as the Strip.

The downtown hotels and casinos are often characterized as older and smaller than those on the Strip. While this is true in a general sense, there are both large and elegant hotels downtown. What really differentiates downtown is the incredible concentration of casinos and hotels in a relatively small area. Along Fremont Street, downtown's main thoroughfare, the casinos present a continuous, dazzling galaxy of neon and twinkling lights for more than four city blocks. Known as Glitter Gulch, these several dozen gambling emporiums are sandwiched together in colorful profusion in an area barely larger than a parking lot at a good-sized shopping mall.

Contrast in the size, style, elegance, and presentation of the downtown casinos provides a varied mix, combining extravagant luxury and cosmopolitan sophistication with an Old West boom-town decadence. Though not directly comparable, downtown Las Vegas has the feel of New Orleans's Bourbon Street: alluring, exotic, wicked, sultry, foreign, and above all, diverse. It is a place where cowboy, businessperson, showgirl, and retiree mix easily. And like Bourbon Street, it is all accessible on foot.

If downtown is the French Quarter of Las Vegas, then the Strip is Plantation Row. Here, huge resort hotel-casinos sprawl like estates along a four-mile section of Las Vegas Boulevard South. Each hotel is a vacation destination unto itself, with casino, hotel, restaurants, pools, spas, landscaped grounds, and even golf courses. While the downtown casinos are fused into a vibrant, integrated whole, the huge hotels on the Strip demand individual recognition.

While the Strip is literally a specific length of Las Vegas Boulevard South, the large surrounding area is usually included when discussing hotels, casinos, restaurants, and attractions. East and parallel to the Strip is Paradise Road, where the Las Vegas Convention Center and several hotels are located. Also included in the Strip area are hotels and casinos on streets intersecting Las Vegas Boulevard, as well as properties positioned to the immediate west of the Strip (on the far side of I-15).

Choosing a Hotel

The variables that figure most prominently in choosing a hotel are price, location, your itinerary, and your quality requirements. There is a wide selection of lodging with myriad combinations of price and value. Given this, your main criteria for selecting a hotel should be its location and your itinerary.

The Strip versus Downtown for Leisure Travelers

Though there are some excellent hotels on the Boulder Highway and elsewhere around town, the choice for most vacation travelers is whether to stay downtown or on (or near) the Strip. Downtown offers a good choice of hotels, restaurants, and gambling, but only a limited choice of entertainment, and fewer amenities such as swimming pools and spas. There are no golf courses and only four tennis courts downtown. If you have a car, the Strip is an 8- to 15-minute commute from downtown via I-15. If you do not have a car, public transportation from downtown to the Strip is as efficient as Las Vegas traffic allows and quite affordable.

If you stay on the Strip, you are more likely to need a car or require some sort of transportation. There are more hotels to choose from on the Strip, but they are spread over a much wider area and are often (but not always) pricier than downtown. On the Strip, one has a sense of space and elbow room, as many of the hotels are constructed on a grand scale. The selection of entertainment is both varied and extensive on the Strip, and Strip recreational facilities rival those of the world's leading resorts.

Downtown is a multicultural, multilingual melting pot with an adventurous, raw, robust feel. Everything in this part of town seems intense and concentrated, an endless blur of action, movement, and light. Diversity and history conspire in lending vitality and excitement to this older part of Las Vegas, an essence more tangible and real than the monumental, plastic themes and fantasies of many large Strip establishments.

Though downtown caters to every class of clientele, it is less formal and, with exceptions, more of a working man's gambling town. Here the truck driver and welder gamble alongside the secretary and the rancher. The Strip, likewise, runs the gamut but tends to attract more high rollers, middle-class suburbanites, and business travelers going to conventions.

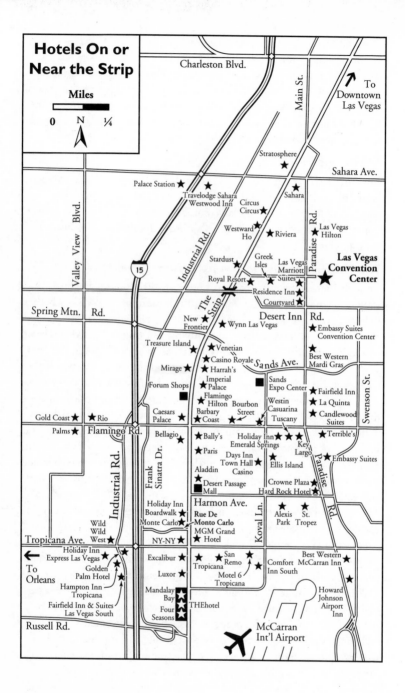

Hotels On or Near the Strip

Miles

0   N   ¼

Charleston Blvd.

Main St.

To Downtown Las Vegas

Sahara Ave.

Stratosphere

Palace Station ★
Travelodge Sahara
Westwood Inn
Circus Circus ★
Sahara ★

Westward Ho ★
Riviera ★

Las Vegas Hilton

Valley View Blvd.

Industrial Rd.

15

Stardust ★
Greek Isles ★
Las Vegas Marriott Suites ★

Las Vegas Convention Center ★

Paradise Rd.

Royal Resort ★

Residence Inn ★
Courtyard ★

Spring Mtn. Rd.

The Strip

New Frontier ★
Wynn Las Vegas ★

Desert Inn Rd.

Embassy Suites ★
Convention Center

Treasure Island ★
Venetian ★
Casino Royale ★
Harrah's ★

Sands Ave.

Best Western ★
Mardi Gras

Mirage ★
Imperial Palace ★

Forum Shops ■
Flamingo
Hilton
Bourbon
Street

Sands Expo Center ■

Swenson St.

Fairfield Inn ★

Gold Coast ★   ★ Rio

Caesars Palace ★
Barbary Coast ★

Westin Casuarina ★
Tuscany ★

La Quinta ★
Candlewood Suites ★

Palms ★

Flamingo Rd.

Bellagio ★

Bally's ★
Holiday Inn ★★★
Emerald Springs
Key Largo ★

Terrible's ★

Frank Sinatra Dr.

Paris ★

Days Inn ★
Town Hall ★
Casino

Ellis Island ★

Embassy Suites ★

Aladdin ■

Paradise Rd.

Industrial Rd.

Desert Passage ■
Mall

Crowne Plaza ★
Hard Rock Hotel ★

Harmon Ave.

Koval Ln.

Alexis ★   St. ★
Park   Tropez

Holiday Inn Boardwalk ★
Monte Carlo ★

Rue De Monto Carlo
MGM Grand Hotel ★

Tropicana Ave.

Wild Wild West ★

NY-NY ★

To Orleans

Holiday Inn ★
Express Las Vegas ★★
Golden Palm Hotel ★
Hampton Inn Tropicana
Fairfield Inn & Suites Las Vegas South

Excalibur ★
Luxor ★

San Remo ★
Tropicana ★
Motel 6 Tropicana

Comfort Inn South ★

Best Western ★
McCarran Inn

Howard Johnson Airport Inn ★

Russell Rd.

Mandalay Bay ★★
Four Seasons ★★

THEhotel

McCarran Int'l Airport

40

The Fremont Street Experience

For years, downtown casinos watched from the sidelines as Strip hotels turned into veritable tourist attractions. There was nothing downtown, for example, to rival the exploding volcano at the Mirage, the theme parks at Circus Circus, the pirate battle at Treasure Island (T. I.), or the view from the Stratosphere Tower. As gambling revenue dwindled and more customers defected to the Strip, downtown casino owners finally got serious about mounting a counterattack.

The counterattack, known as the Fremont Street Experience, was launched at the end of 1995. Its basic purpose was to transform downtown into an ongoing event, a continuous party, a happening. Fremont Street through the heart of Glitter Gulch was forever closed to vehicular traffic and turned into a park, with terraces, street musicians, and landscaping. By creating an aesthetically pleasing environment, Las Vegas–style, the project united all of the casinos in a sort of diverse gambling mall.

Transformative events on the ground aside, however, the main draw of the Fremont Street Experience is up in the air. Four blocks of Fremont Street are covered by a 1,400-foot-long, 90-foot-high "space frame"—an enormous, vaulted, geodesic matrix. This futuristic structure totally canopies Fremont Street. In addition to providing nominal shade from the blistering sun, the space frame serves as the stage for a nighttime attraction that has definitely improved downtown's fortune. Set into the inner surface of the space frame are 12.5 million LEDs which come to life in a computer-driven, multisensory show. The LEDs are augmented by 40 speakers on each block, booming symphonic sound in syncopation with the lights.

We at the *Unofficial Guide* enjoy and appreciate downtown Las Vegas, and all of us hope that the Fremont Street Experience will continue to have a beneficial effect. We are amazed and appalled, however, by the city's general lack of commitment to improving its infrastructure, particularly the traffic situation. The market, in terms of aggregate numbers of gamblers, is undeniably located out on the Strip. To create an attraction sufficiently compelling to lure this market downtown is to fight only half the battle. The other half of the battle is to make it easy for all those folks on the Strip to get downtown. There are plans to extend the monorail with a downtown station as the northern terminus. The gestation for this much-needed addition to the public transportation mix is fuzzy. Our guess is that we'll be lucky to see the monorail by 2010.

If You Visit Las Vegas on Business

If you are going to Las Vegas for a trade show or convention, you will want to lodge as close as possible to the meeting site (ideally within easy walking distance), or alternatively, close to a monorail station. Many Strip hotel-casinos—including the Riviera, Stardust, Flamingo, Venetian,

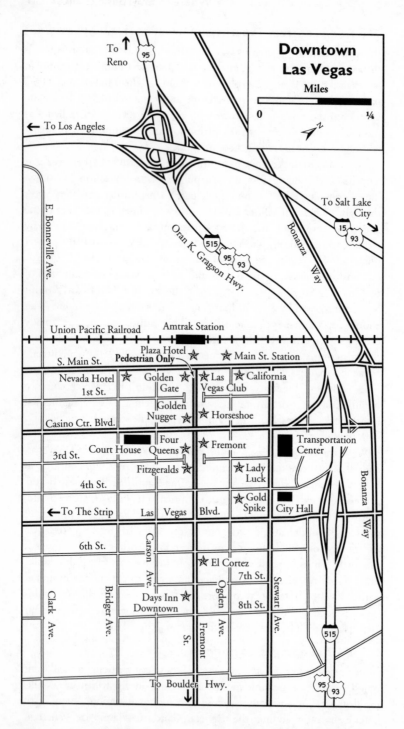

Downtown Las Vegas

Miles

0   ¼

Paris, Bellagio, Mandalay Bay, Aladdin, Las Vegas Hilton, MGM Grand, T. I., Tropicana, Sahara, Mirage, Caesars Palace, Harrah's, and Bally's—host meetings of from 100 to 2,000 attendees, offer lodging for citywide shows and conventions held at the Las Vegas Convention Center and the Sands Expo and Convention Center, and have good track records with business travelers.

Our maps should provide some assistance in determining which hotels and motels are situated near your meeting site.

Because most large meetings and trade shows are headquartered at the Convention Center or on the Strip, lodging on the Strip is more convenient than staying downtown. Citywide conventions often provide a shuttle service from the major hotels to the Las Vegas Convention Center, and, of course, cabs and the monorail are available, too. Las Vegas traffic is a mess, however, particularly in the late afternoon, and there are a finite number of cabs. One alternative to staying near your meeting site or on the monorail route is to find a good deal on a room elsewhere around town and commute to your meeting in a rental car. Often the savings on the room will pay for your transportation.

Large Hotel-Casinos versus Small Hotels and Motels

Lodging properties in Las Vegas range from tiny motels with a dozen rooms to colossal hotel-casino resort complexes of 5,000 rooms. As you might expect, there are advantages and drawbacks to staying in either a large or small hotel. Determining which size is better for you depends on how you plan to spend your time in Las Vegas.

If your leisure or business itinerary calls for a car and a lot of coming and going, the big hotels can be a real pain. At the Luxor, Excalibur, and Las Vegas Hilton, to name a few, it can take as long as 15 minutes to get from your room to your car if you use the self-parking lot. A young couple staying at the Las Vegas Hilton left their hotel room 40 minutes prior to their show reservations at the Mirage. After trooping to their van in the Hilton's distant self-parking lot, the couple discovered they had forgotten their show tickets. By the time the husband ran back to their room to retrieve the tickets and returned to the van, only five minutes remained to drive to the Mirage, park, and find the showroom. As it turned out, they missed the first 15 minutes of the performance.

Many large hotels have multistory, self-parking garages that require lengthy and dizzying drives up and down ramps. Post-9/11 security likewise has complicated coming and going at some large, multistory parking garages. Hotel guests are asked to show their room key and sometimes must submit to having their car searched. Nonguests visiting the hotel are occasionally required to answer a string of questions regarding the purpose of their visit. If you plan to use the car frequently and do not want to deal with the hassle of remote parking lots, big garages, or the tipping associated

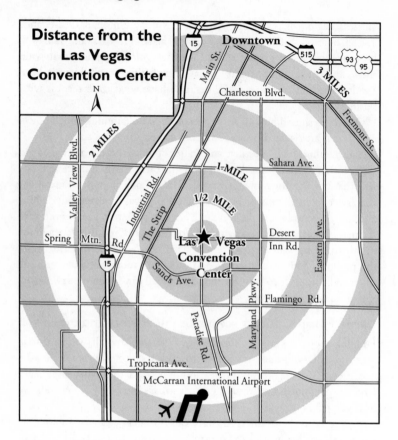

Distance from the Las Vegas Convention Center

N

Downtown · 15 · 515 · 93 · 95 · 3 MILES

Main St. · Charleston Blvd. · Fremont St.

2 MILES · Valley View Blvd. · Industrial Rd. · The Strip · 1-MILE · Sahara Ave.

1/2 MILE

Spring · Mtn. · Rd. · 15 · Las Vegas Convention Center · Sands Ave. · Desert Inn Rd. · Eastern Ave.

Maryland Pkwy. · Flamingo Rd.

Paradise Rd.

Tropicana Ave. · McCarran International Airport

with valet parking, we recommend that you stay in a smaller hotel or motel that provides quick and convenient access to your car.

Quiet and tranquillity can also be reasons for choosing a smaller hotel. Many Las Vegas visitors object to passing through a casino whenever they go to or leave their room. Staying in a smaller property without a casino permits an escape from the flashing lights, the never-ending clanking of coins, and the unremitting, frenetic pace of an around-the-clock gambling town. While they may not be as exciting, smaller hotels tend to be more restful and homelike.

The ease and simplicity of checking in and out of smaller properties has its own appeal. To be able to check in or pay your bill without standing in a line, or to unload and load the car directly and conveniently, significantly diminishes the stress of arriving and departing. When we visited the registration lobby of one of the larger hotels on a Friday afternoon, for example, it reminded us of Kennedy International Airport shut down by a winter storm. Guests were stacked dozens deep in the check-in lines. Others, having abandoned any hope of registering in the near future, slept curled up around their luggage or sat reading on the floor. The whole lobby was awash in suitcases, hanging bags, and people milling about. Though hotel size and check-in efficiency are not always inversely related, the sight of a registration lobby fitted out like the queuing area of Disneyland's Jungle Cruise should be enough to make a sane person think twice.

Along similar lines, a large hotel does not ensure more comfortable or more luxurious accommodations. In Las Vegas there are exceptionally posh and well-designed rooms in both large and small hotels, just as there are threadbare and poorly designed rooms in properties of every size. A large establishment does, however, usually ensure a superior range of amenities, including on-site entertainment, room service, spas or exercise rooms, concierge services, bell services, valet parking, meeting rooms, babysitting, shoe shining, dry cleaning, shopping, 24-hour restaurants, copy and fax services, check cashing, and, of course, gambling.

If you spill a cosmopolitan on your khakis, you may want to think twice before ponying up for the hotel/casino in-house laundry service. You'll pay by the piece, and you'll pay dearly. After a couple of days of laundry pile up on the bed, do like we do and take advantage of an area wash-and-fold service. Our favorite is **Wizard of Suds** (4275 Arville Street) where the courteous staff will wash and fold your dirties for cheap. At a dollar a pound, and with quick turnaround if you drop off before noon, you can't beat the Wizard; (702) 873-8653.

If you plan to do most of your touring on foot or are attending a convention, a large hotel in a good location has its advantages. There will be a variety of restaurants, entertainment, shopping, and recreation close at hand. In case you are a night owl, you will be able to eat or drink at any hour, and there will always be lots going on. Many showrooms offer 11 p.m. or midnight shows, and quite a few hotels (Sam's Town, Suncoast, Gold Coast, Orleans, and Santa Fe Station) have 24-hour bowling.

For visitors who wish to immerse themselves in the atmosphere of Las Vegas, to live in the fast lane, and to be where the action is, a large hotel is recommended. These people feel they are missing something unless they stay in a large hotel-casino. For them, it is important to know that the excitement is only an elevator ride away.

Getting Around: Location and Convenience

Las Vegas Lodging Convenience Chart

The following chart will give you a feel for how convenient specific hotels and motels are to common Las Vegas destinations. Both walking and cab commuting times are figured on the conservative side. You should be able to do a little better than the times indicated, particularly by cab, unless you are traveling during rush hour or attempting to navigate the Strip on a weekend evening.

Regarding the monorail, times listed include loading and unloading as well as the actual commuting time. The Strip monorail stations are located in the far rear of the host casinos, so, for example, the walk from the Strip entrance of the MGM Grand to the station is about five minutes. The MGM Grand station is the closest station to the Bellagio on the west side of the Strip. From your guest room at the Bellagio it will take 10 to 12 minutes to walk to the MGM Grand station. In our experience, because of the walking required to reach the nearest monorail station from casinos on the Strip's west side, you might want to consider a cab if you're in a hurry. Always check traffic conditions before you hop in a cab. If the Strip is gridlocked (very common), head for the monorail.

Commuting to Downtown from the Strip

Commuting to downtown from the Strip is a snap on I-15. From the Strip you can get on or off I-15 at Tropicana Avenue, Flamingo Road, Spring Mountain Road, or Sahara Avenue. Once on I-15 heading north, stay in the right lane and follow the signs for downtown and US 95 South. If you exit onto Casino Center Boulevard, you will be right in the middle of downtown with several large parking garages conveniently at hand. Driving time to downtown varies from about 16 minutes from the south end of the Strip (I-15 via Tropicana Avenue) to about 6 minutes from the north end (I-15 via Sahara Avenue).

Commuting to the Strip from Downtown

If you are heading to the Strip from downtown, you can pick up US 95 (and then I-15) by going north on either Fourth Street or Las Vegas Boulevard. Driving time from downtown to the Strip takes 6 to 16 minutes, depending on your destination.

Free Connections

Traffic on the Strip is so awful that the hotels, both individually and in groups, are creating new alternatives for getting around.

1. An elevated tram links the Bellagio and Monte Carlo on the west side. Farther south on the west side, a shuttle tram serves the Excalibur, Luxor, Mandalay Bay, Four Seasons, and THEhotel.

2. The Rio operates a shuttle from the Rio Visitor's Center, just south of Paris Las Vegas on the Strip, to the Rio, about half a mile west of the Strip on West Flamingo Road. Shuttles are also available linking the Barbary Coast on the northeast corner of the Strip and Flamingo to the Gold Coast about a mile west.

3. Free shuttle service from the nongaming Polo Towers near the Aladdin to the Stratosphere runs on the hour northbound to the Stratosphere and on the half hour for the southbound return from 9 a.m. until 11 p.m.

Las Vegas Monorail

The long-awaited $650 million Las Vegas Monorail began service in 2004 with nine trains running the three-mile route between the MGM Grand and the Sahara. The route parallels the Strip between Tropicana and Sands Avenue and then cuts east to the Las Vegas Convention Center and the Las Vegas Hilton before continuing to the last stop at the Sahara. Trains run approximately every five minutes between 8 a.m. and midnight. From one end of the line to the other takes about 18 minutes and includes seven stops. The fare is $3 one way. Because the stations are located at the extreme rear of the casinos served, you're better off walking if you're going less than a mile. The monorail is a godsend, however, to convention and tradeshow attendees commuting from Strip hotels to the Las Vegas Convention Center and the Sands Exposition Center; (702) 699-8200; **www.lvmonorail.com.**

COMMONLY USED PUBLIC TRANSPORTATION ROUTES				
	Round-trip from/to	Hours of Operation	Frequency of Service	Fare
Monorail	MGM Grand/ Sahara	8 a.m.–midnight	Every 5 minutes	$3
Citizen's Area Transit Bus # 301	Vacation Village*/ Downtown Transportation Center	24 hours	Every 15 minutes	$2
Citizen's Area Transit Bus # 302 (Strip Express) Northbound	Vacation Village*/ Downtown Transportation Center	10 a.m.–1 a.m.	Every 20 minutes	$2
Citizen's Area Transit Bus # 302 (Strip Express) Southbound	Downtown Transportation Center/Vacation Village*	10 a.m.–1 a.m.	Every 20 minutes	$2
Citizen's Area Transit Bus # 303 (Mall Circulator)	Vacation Village*/ Las Vegas Factory Outlet Stores	8:30 a.m.– 10:30 a.m.	Once an hour on the half hour	$2
Las Vegas Strip Trolley Route	Luxor/Stratosphere	9:30–1:30 a.m.	Every 15 minutes	$1.65

Vacation Village is closed, but remains a landmark.

Buses and Trolleys

Las Vegas's Citizen's Area Transit (CAT) provides reliable bus service at reasonable rates. Although one-way fares along the Strip are $2, one-way fares in residential areas are only $1.25. Children ages five and under

COMMUTING TIMES IN MINUTES

From Hotel	To Las Vegas Strip	Convention Center	Down- town	McCarran Airport	UNLV Thomas & Mack Center
Aladdin	on Strip	8/cab	15/cab	7/cab	8/cab
Alexis Park	5/cab	8/cab	15/cab	5/cab	6/cab
Ambassador Strip Travelodge	3/cab	9/cab	15/cab	4/cab	6/cab
AmeriSuites	4/cab	5/walk	15/cab	10/cab	9/cab
Arizona Charlie's Boulder	12/cab	18/cab	12/cab	20/cab	22/cab
Arizona Charlie's Decatur	19/cab	18/cab	12/cab	21/cab	20/cab
Bally's	on Strip	8/mono	15/cab	7/cab	7/cab
Barbary Coast	on Strip	7/mono	15/cab	8/cab	9/cab
Bellagio	on Strip	11/mono	15/cab	11/cab	12/cab
Best Western Mardi Gras	6/cab	10/walk	15/cab	9/cab	7/cab
Best Western McCarran Inn	6/cab	9/cab	15/cab	4/cab	7/cab
Boardwalk Holiday Inn	on Strip	11/mono	15/cab	11/cab	12/cab
Boulder Station	19/cab	18/cab	12/cab	21/cab	20/cab
Bourbon Street	4/walk	7/mono	15/cab	7/cab	7/cab
Caesars Palace	on Strip	7/mono	12/cab	10/cab	10/cab
California	13/cab	15/cab	downtown	19/cab	19/cab
Cannery	23/cab	26/cab	20/cab	30/cab	30/cab
Casino Royale	on Strip	7/mono	14/cab	10/cab	10/cab
Circus Circus	on Strip	5/cab	13/cab	14/cab	13/cab
Comfort Inn Paradise Road	4/cab	5/walk	15/cab	10/cab	9/cab
Courtyard	4/cab	5/walk	15/cab	9/cab	8/cab
Courtyard, Las Vegas South	4/cab	14/cab	15/cab	8/cab	12/cab
El Cortez	11/cab	15/cab	6/walk	16/cab	17/cab
Ellis Island	4/cab	6/cab	14/cab	8/cab	8/cab
Emerald Suites	18/cab	21/cab	15/cab	23/cab	24/cab
Excalibur	on Strip	13/cab	14/cab	7/cab	8/cab
E-Z 8 Motel	4/cab	9/cab	12/cab	9/cab	10/cab
Fairfield Inn Las Vegas Airport	5/cab	5/cab	15/cab	9/cab	8/cab
Fairfield Inn & Suites Las Vegas South	4/cab	14/walk	15/cab	8/cab	12/cab
Fiesta Henderson	18/cab	17/cab	19/cab	17/cab	15/cab
Fiesta Rancho	18/cab	18/cab	10/cab	22/cab	22/cab
Fitzgeralds	14/cab	15/cab	downtown	17/cab	17/cab
Flamingo Hilton	on Strip	7/mono	13/cab	8/cab	8/cab

mono = monorail

From	To				UNLV Thomas
Hotel	Las Vegas Strip	Convention Center	Down-town	McCarran Airport	& Mack Center
Four Queens	15/cab	15/cab	downtown	19/cab	17/cab
Four Seasons	on Strip	14/cab	15/cab	7/cab	13/cab
Fremont	15/cab	15/cab	downtown	19/cab	17/cab
Frontier	on Strip	8/cab	13/cab	11/cab	10/cab
Gold Coast	4/cab	13/cab	14/cab	10/cab	10/cab
Gold Spike	14/cab	15/cab	4/walk	18/cab	17/cab
Golden Gate	14/cab	15/cab	downtown	19/cab	18/cab
Golden Nugget	14/cab	15/cab	downtown	18/cab	19/cab
Golden Palm Hotel	4/cab	14/cab	14/cab	9/cab	11/cab
Greek Isles	7/walk	5/walk	14/cab	9/cab	11/cab
Green Valley Ranch Station	15/cab	18/cab	16/cab	15/cab	14/cab
Hampton Inn Tropicana	10/walk	6/cab	9/cab	10/cab	6/cab
Hard Rock Hotel	4/cab	6/cab	15/cab	6/cab	6/cab
Harrah's	on Strip	5/mono	15/cab	10/cab	10/cab
Holiday Inn Crowne Plaza	5/cab	5/cab	14/cab	8/cab	6/cab
Holiday Inn Emerald Springs	4/cab	8/cab	15/cab	7/cab	7/cab
Holiday Inn Express	4/cab	14/cab	15/cab	8/cab	12/cab
Horseshoe	14/cab	15/cab	downtown	19/cab	19/cab
Howard Johnson Airport	5/cab	7/cab	15/cab	3/cab	5/cab
Hyatt Regency Lake Las Vegas	45/cab	49/cab	43/cab	37/cab	46/cab
Imperial Palace	on Strip	5/mono	15/cab	10/cab	10/cab
JW Marriott Las Vegas	18/cab	21/cab	15/cab	23/cab	24/cab
Key Largo/Quality Inn	5/cab	5/cab	14/cab	8/cab	10/cab
King 8	4/cab	13/cab	14/cab	8/cab	10/cab
La Quinta Tropicana	5/cab	13/cab	14/cab	10/cab	10/cab
Lady Luck	14/cab	15/cab	3/walk	19/cab	18/cab
Las Vegas Club	14/cab	15/cab	downtown	19/cab	18/cab
Las Vegas Hilton	5/mono	5/walk	13/cab	10/cab	8/cab
Las Vegas Marriott Suites	14/cab	5/walk	15/cab	10/cab	9/cab
Luxor	on Strip	13/cab	15/cab	8/cab	10/cab
Main Street Station	14/cab	15/cab	downtown	19/cab	19/cab
Mandalay Bay	on Strip	14/cab	16/cab	7/cab	13/cab
Manor Suites	10/cab	17/cab	20/cab	12/cab	17/cab
Marriott Renaissance	6/mono	4/walk	13/cab	10/cab	8/cab
MGM Grand	on Strip	11/mono	15/cab	9/cab	9/cab
Mirage	on Strip	6/mono	15/cab	11/cab	10/cab

COMMUTING TIMES IN MINUTES *(continued)*

From Hotel	To Las Vegas Strip	Convention Center	Down- town	McCarran Airport	UNLV Thomas & Mack Center
Monte Carlo	on Strip	11/mono	15/cab	11/cab	12/cab
Montelago Village Lake Las Vegas Resort	45/cab	49/cab	43/cab	37/cab	46/cab
Motel 6 Tropicana	3/cab	12/cab	15/cab	6/cab	8/cab
Nevada Hotel	14/cab	15/cab	downtown	19/cab	18/cab
Nevada Palace	21/cab	26/cab	21/cab	19/cab	18/cab
New York– New York	on Strip	11/mono	15/cab	11/cab	12/cab
Orleans	4/cab	15/cab	14/cab	11/cab	11/cab
Palace Station	5/cab	10/cab	10/cab	14/cab	15/cab
Palms	5/cab	13/cab	14/cab	10/cab	10/cab
Paris	on Strip	9/mono	15/cab	8/cab	8/cab
Plaza Hotel	14/cab	15/cab	downtown	19/cab	18/cab
Quality Inn	5/walk	8/cab	15/cab	8/cab	8/cab
Red Rock Station	18/cab	21/cab	15/cab	23/cab	24/cab
Residence Inn	4/cab	6/cab	15/cab	12/cab	12/cab
Residence Inn Las Vegas South	4/cab	14/cab	15/cab	8/cab	12/cab
Rio	5/cab	14/cab	13/cab	10/cab	10/cab
Ritz-Carlton	45/cab	49/cab	43/cab	37/cab	46/cab
Riviera	on Strip	4/cab	14/cab	11/cab	10/cab
Royal Resort	3/walk	5/cab	14/cab	13/cab	11/cab
Sahara	on Strip	6/mono	13/cab	13/cab	11/cab
St. Tropez	5/cab	6/cab	15/cab	7/cab	6/cab

mono = monorail

ride all routes for free. All public transportation requires exact fare. Transfers are free on all routes but must be used within two hours of issue. All CAT buses are equipped with wheelchair lifts and bicycle racks, both of which are provided at no extra charge. Handicapped persons requiring door-to-door service should call ahead for reservations. For general route and fare information, to request a schedule through the mail, or to make reservations for door-to-door service, call (702) 228-7433, or visit **www.catride.com.**

The Las Vegas Strip Trolley Company is privately owned and provides transportation along the Strip and between the Strip and downtown. These vehicles are styled to look like San Francisco cable cars, and a ride costs $1.65 (exact change). The transit runs from 9:30 a.m. to 1:30 a.m., making trips on the half hour. Children ages four and under ride free. Call (702) 382-1404 for more information. *Note:* Fare collection on the trolleys is inefficient; it's quicker to take a regular transit bus.

From	To				UNLV Thomas
Hotel	Las Vegas Strip	Convention Center	Down-town	McCarran Airport	& Mack Center
Sam's Town	20/cab	25/cab	20/cab	18/cab	17/cab
San Remo	5/walk	11/mono	15/cab	6/cab	8/cab
Santa Fe Station	27/cab	30/cab	23/cab	33/cab	36/cab
Silverton	10/cab	17/cab	20/cab	12/cab	17/cab
Stardust	on Strip	4/cab	13/cab	12/cab	10/cab
Stratosphere	3/cab	7/cab	9/cab	14/cab	14/cab
Suncoast	18/cab	21/cab	15/cab	23/cab	24/cab
Sunrise Suites	19/cab	24/cab	19/cab	17/cab	16/cab
Sunset Station	18/cab	17/cab	18/cab	16/cab	15/cab
Terrible's	5/cab	6/cab	15/cab	6/cab	6/cab
Texas Station	17/cab	16/cab	13/cab	22/cab	22/cab
THEhotel at Mandalay Bay	on Strip	14/cab	15/cab	7/cab	13/cab
T. I.	on Strip	6/mono	14/cab	11/cab	10/cab
Tropicana	on Strip	11/mono	15/cab	6/cab	9/cab
Tuscany	5/cab	5/cab	14/cab	8/cab	10/cab
Venetian	on Strip	6/mono	14/cab	8/cab	8/cab
Westin Casuarina	4/walk	11/mono	15/cab	7/cab	7/cab
Westward Ho	on Strip	5/cab	15/cab	13/cab	12/cab
Wild, Wild, West	3/cab	13/cab	14/cab	8/cab	11/cab
Wynn Las Vegas	on Strip	8/cab	13/cab	10/cab	9/cab

What's in an Address?

Downtown

The heart of the downtown casino area is Fremont Street between Fourth Street (on the east) and Main Street (on the west). Hotel-casinos situated along this quarter-mile four-block stretch known as Glitter Gulch include the Plaza Hotel, Golden Gate, Las Vegas Club, Binion's Horseshoe, Golden Nugget, Fremont, Four Queens, and Fitzgeralds. Parallel to Fremont and one block north is Ogden Avenue, where the California, Lady Luck, and the Gold Spike are located. Main Street Station is situated on Main Street at the intersection of Ogden.

All of the downtown hotel-casinos are centrally positioned and convenient to the action, with the exception of the El Cortez, which sits three blocks to the east. While there is a tremendous difference in quality and price among the downtown properties, the locations of all the hotels (except the El Cortez) are excellent. When you stay downtown, everything is within a five-minute walk. By comparison, on the Strip it takes longer to walk from the entrance of Caesars Palace to the entrance of the Mirage, next door, than to cover the whole four blocks of the casino center downtown.

The Strip

While location is not a major concern when choosing from among the downtown hotels, it is of paramount importance when selecting a hotel on the Strip.

We once received a promotional flyer from a Las Vegas casino proudly proclaiming that it was located "right on the Strip." It supported the claim with a color photo showing its marquee and those of several other casinos in a neat row with their neon ablaze. What recipients of this advertisement (except those familiar with Las Vegas) never would have guessed was that the photo had been taken with a special lens that eliminated all sense of distance between the casinos. While the advertised casino appeared to be next door to the other casinos in the picture, it was in reality almost a mile away.

A common variation on the same pitch, but without the photo, is "Stay Right on the Las Vegas Strip at Half the Price." Once again, the promoter is attempting to deceive by taking advantage of the recipient's ignorance of Strip geography. As it happens, the Las Vegas Strip (Las Vegas Boulevard South) starts southwest of the airport and runs all the way downtown, a distance of about seven miles. Only the four-mile section between Mandalay Bay and the Stratosphere contains the large casinos and other attractions of interest to visitors. South of Mandalay Bay "on the Strip" is the airport boundary, some small motels, discount shopping, and some nice desert. North of the Stratosphere en route to downtown, the Strip runs through a recently resurgent commercial area sprinkled with wedding chapels, fast-food restaurants, and small motels.

The Best Locations on the Strip

Beware of hotels and motels claiming to be on the Strip but not located between Mandalay Bay and the Stratosphere. They might be nice properties, but chances are you will be disappointed with the location.

If you stay on the Strip, you want to be somewhere in the Four Seasons to Stratosphere stretch, and even there, some sections are much more desirable than others. The Mandalay Bay basically anchors the south end of the Strip, about a quarter mile from the Luxor, its closest neighbor. Likewise, at the other end, the Stratosphere and the Sahara are somewhat isolated. In between, there are distinct clusters of hotels and casinos.

esting and diversified upscale shopping centers in the United States. There are also some very good restaurants in this section. Finally, this cluster is a four-minute cab ride (or a 16-minute walk) from the Las Vegas Convention Center.

Strip Cluster 4 The next cluster up the Strip is between Convention Center Drive and Riviera Boulevard. Arrayed along a stretch just over a half-mile long are the Stardust, Westward Ho, Riviera, and Circus Circus with its Adventuredome theme park. Great for people-watching and enjoying the lights, this area contains the third largest concentration of major hotels and casinos. Casinos and hotels in this cluster are considerably less upscale than those in the "grand cluster" but offer acceptable selections for dining and entertainment, as well as proximity to the Las Vegas Convention Center.

Strip Cluster 5 Finally, near the intersection of Las Vegas Boulevard and Sahara Avenue there is a relatively isolated cluster that contains Wet 'n' Wild (a water theme park), the Sahara, and, about a third of a mile toward town, the Stratosphere. Though fairly isolated if you intend to walk, for visitors with cars or monorail riders this cluster provides convenient access to the Strip, the Convention Center, and downtown.

Just off the Strip

If you have a car, and if being right on the Strip is not a big deal to you, there are some excellent hotel-casinos on Paradise Road, and to the east and west of the Strip on intersecting roads. The Rio, Palms, and Gold Coast on Flamingo Road, Palace Station on Sahara Avenue, and Orleans on Tropicana Avenue offer exceptional value; they are all less than a half mile west of the Strip and are situated at access ramps to I-15, five to ten minutes from downtown. To the east of the strip are the Hard Rock on Harmon Avenue, the Tuscany on Flamingo, and the Las Vegas Hilton on Paradise, among others.

Boulder Highway, Green Valley, Summerlin, and North Las Vegas

Twenty minutes from the Strip in North Las Vegas are Texas Station, the Fiesta Rancho, the Cannery, and, on the edge of civilization, Santa Fe Station. All four have good restaurants, comfortable guest rooms, and lively, upbeat themes. Hotel-casinos on Boulder Highway southeast of town include Boulder Station, Sam's Town, Arizona Charlie's Boulder, and Nevada Palace. Also to the southeast are Sunset Station, Fiesta Henderson, and Green Valley Ranch. Like the North Las Vegas trio, the Boulder Highway and Green Valley properties cater primarily to locals. Northwest of town is the posh JW Marriott Las Vegas, with two upscale hotels and the Tournament Player's Club (TPC) at the Canyons Golf Course.

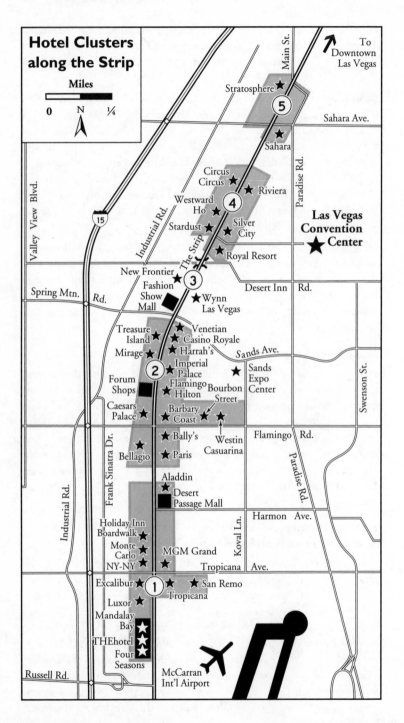

Hotel Clusters along the Strip

Miles

0   N   ¼

To Downtown Las Vegas

Main St.

Stratosphere ★

⑤

Sahara Ave.

Sahara ★

Paradise Rd.

Circus Circus ★

Riviera ★

Westward Ho ★

④

Las Vegas Convention Center ★

Stardust ★

Silver City ★

The Strip

Royal Resort ★

New Frontier ★

③

Desert Inn Rd.

Spring Mtn. Rd.

Fashion Show Mall ■

Wynn Las Vegas ★

Treasure Island ★

Venetian ★

Casino Royale ★

Sands Ave.

Mirage ★

Harrah's ★

②

Imperial Palace ★

Sands Expo Center ★

Forum Shops ■

Flamingo Hilton ★

Bourbon Street

Caesars Palace ★

Barbary Coast ★

Swenson St.

Bally's ★

Westin Casuarina

Flamingo Rd.

Bellagio ★

Paris ★

Frank Sinatra Dr.

Paradise Rd.

Aladdin ★

Desert Passage Mall ■

Industrial Rd.

Harmon Ave.

Holiday Inn Boardwalk ★

Monte Carlo ★

MGM Grand ★

Koval Ln.

NY-NY ★

Tropicana Ave.

Excalibur ★

①

★ San Remo

Tropicana ★

Luxor ★

Mandalay Bay ★★

THEhotel ★★

Four Seasons ★

McCarran Int'l Airport

Russell Rd.

Valley View Blvd.

Industrial Rd.

15

Nearby is the Suncoast and Red Rock Station. Also northwest of the Strip is Arizona Charlie's Decatur.

The Lights of Las Vegas: Traffic on the Strip

During the past decade, Las Vegas has experienced exponential growth—growth that unfortunately has not been matched with the development of necessary infrastructure. If you imagine a town designed for about 300,000 people being inundated by a million or so refugees (all with cars), you will have a sense of what's happening in Las Vegas.

The Strip, where a huge percentage of the local population works and where more than 80% of tourists and business travelers stay, has become a clogged artery in the heart of the city. The heaviest traffic on the Strip is between Tropicana and Sahara Avenues, where most of the larger hotels are located. Throughout the day and night, local traffic combines with gawking tourists, shoppers, and cruising teenagers to create a three-mile-long, bumper-to-bumper bottleneck.

When folks discuss the "lights of Las Vegas," it used to be that they were talking about the marquees of the casinos. More recently, however, the reference is to the long, multifunctional traffic lights found at virtually every intersection on the Strip. These lights, which flash a different signal for every possible turn and direction, combine with an ever-increasing number of vehicles to ensure that nobody goes anywhere very fast. Also affected are the major traffic arteries that cross the Strip east to west; the worst snarls occur at the intersection of the Strip and Flamingo Avenue.

Strip traffic is the Achilles heel of Las Vegas development and growth. It is sheer lunacy to believe you can plop a litter of megahotels on the Strip without compounding an already horrific traffic situation. While city government and the hospitality industry dance around the issue, traffic gets worse and worse. Approximately 48,000 hotel rooms were added along the Strip during the 1990s, and about 30,000 more came on line since the millennium, with another 8,000 or more under construction or on the drawing board. The monorail along the east side of the Strip represents a great alternative to driving, but it hasn't noticeably mitigated gridlock on the Strip. Also, stations are positioned so far to the rear of the casinos that walking is faster than taking the train for distances up to one mile. In another effort, I-15 between downtown and the I-215 junction to the south has been widened and the interchanges improved. While certainly welcome, the project has done little to alleviate Strip traffic. Interestingly, the only initiative that has really worked is the construction of elevated pedestrian bridges over the major Strip intersections. In addition to markedly improving safety, the bridges remove pedestrians from the street level mayhem, leaving the battlefield to vehicles.

Sneak Routes

Fortunately, most of the large hotels along the Strip have back entrances that allow you to avoid the insanity of the main drag. Industrial Road, Frank Sinatra Drive, and I-15 run parallel to the Strip on the west side, providing backdoor access to hotels situated on the west side of Las Vegas Boulevard. Paradise Road and Koval Lane run parallel to the Strip on the east side.

SNEAK ROUTES

Hotels on the East Side of the Strip

The *Aladdin* is accessible from westbound Harmon Road.

Bally's and *Paris* can be reached by turning north off Harmon Avenue onto an isolated section of Audrie Street.

The *Barbary Coast* is the only major hotel on the east side of the Strip that is truly stuck. If you want to go to the Barbary Coast, park somewhere else and walk over. Don't even think about arriving at or departing from the Barbary Coast's parking lot between 3:30 p.m. and 8 p.m.

The *Flamingo Hilton, Harrah's Las Vegas,* the *Imperial Palace,* and *O'Shea's* each have a back entrance off Audrie Street, a small thoroughfare branching off of Flamingo Road. Audrie Street can also be reached by turning west on Albert or Ida avenues from Koval Lane.

The *MGM Grand* is accessible by heading west (toward the Strip) on Tropicana Avenue or by turning west off Koval Lane.

The Riviera can be reached by turning west on Riviera Boulevard from Paradise.

The Sahara has an entrance on Paradise Road.

The *Tropicana* is accessible by turning south off Tropicana Avenue onto Koval Lane and then turning right onto Reno Avenue.

The Venetian is accessible from Koval Lane.

Hotels on the West Side of the Strip

Bellagio has an entrance off Flamingo Road (heading east).

Caesars Palace can be accessed from Frank Sinatra Drive.

Circus Circus, Westward Ho, and the *Stardust* can be reached via Industrial Road.

Excalibur, Luxor, and *Mandalay Bay* can be reached by turning south off Tropicana onto Koval Lane and then turning right onto Reno Avenue. Reno Avenue intersects the Strip at a traffic light, allowing you to cross to Excalibur and Luxor. You can also access all three hotels via Frank Sinatra Drive.

The Holiday Inn Boardwalk is accessed from the Strip.

The Mirage and *T.I.* are accessible by taking Industrial Road or I-15 and then turning east on Spring Mountain Road.

The Monte Carlo can be reached from Frank Sinatra Drive.

The New Frontier has an entrance off Fashion Show Drive, which connects to Industrial Road.

New York–New York can be reached via Tropicana Avenue or from Frank Sinatra Drive.

The Stratosphere's self-park garage is off Baltimore Street, which connects to Las Vegas Boulevard.

A hallmark development in 2004 was the construction of Frank Sinatra Drive between the Strip and I-15. The new road runs from south of Mandalay Bay to the intersection with Industrial Road and serves as backdoor entrance to T. I., the Mirage, Caesar's Palace, Monte Carlo, New York–New York, Excalibur, Luxor, Mandalay Bay, THEhotel, and Four Seasons. Frank Sinatra Drive also runs behind the Bellagio and the Boardwalk, but there is no access to either's self-parking lot.

Though a real boon for those in the know, the road is primarily used by casino employees and by truckers making deliveries. It is congested only during the 3:30–5:30 p.m. shift change period.

Room Reservations:
Getting a Good Room, Getting a Good Deal

Because Las Vegas is so popular for weekend getaways, weekend occupancy averages an astounding 92% of capacity for hotels and 70% of capacity for motels. Weekday occupancy for hotels is a respectable 83%, and for motels, 63%. What these figures mean, among other things, is that you want to nail down your lodging reservations before you leave home.

Also, consider that these occupancy percentages are averages. When a large convention is in town or when Las Vegas hosts a championship prizefight, the National Finals Rodeo, or any other major event, rooms become hard to find. If you are heading to Las Vegas purely for fun and relaxation, you may want to avoid going when the town is packed. For more information about dates to avoid, see pages 48–51.

The Wacky World of Las Vegas Hotel Reservations

Though there are almost 130,000 hotel rooms in Las Vegas, getting one is not always a simple proposition. In the large hotel-casinos there are often five or more separate departments that have responsibility for room allocation and sales. Of the total number of rooms in any given hotel, a number are at the disposal of the casino; some are administered by the reservations department at the front desk; some are allocated to independent wholesalers for group and individual travel packages; others are blocked for special events (fights, Super Bowl weekend, etc.); and still others are at the disposal of the sales and marketing department for meetings, conventions, wedding parties, and other special groups. Hotels that are part of a large chain (Holiday Inn, Hilton, etc.) have some additional rooms administered by their national reservations systems.

At most hotels, department heads meet each week and review all the room allocations. If rooms blocked for a special event, say a golf tournament, are not selling, some of those rooms will be redistributed to other departments. Since special events and large conventions are scheduled far in advance, the decision makers have significant lead time. In most hotels, a major reallocation of rooms takes place 40–50 days prior to the dates for which the rooms are blocked, with minor reallocations made right up to the event in question.

If you call the reservations number at the hotel of your choice and are informed that no rooms are available for the dates you've requested, it does not mean the hotel is sold out. What it does mean is that the front desk has no more rooms remaining in their allocation. It is a fairly safe assumption that all the rooms in a hotel have not been reserved for guests. The casino will usually hold back some rooms for high rollers, the sales department may have some rooms reserved for participants in deals they are negotiating, and some rooms will be in the hands of tour wholesalers or blocked for a citywide convention. If any of these remaining rooms are not committed by a certain date, they will be reallocated. So a second call to the reservations department may get you the room that was unavailable when you called two weeks earlier.

Getting the Best Deal on a Room

Compared to hotel rates in other destinations, lodging in Las Vegas is so relatively inexpensive that the following cost-cutting strategies may seem gratuitous. If you are accustomed to paying $120 a night for a hotel room, you can afford 60% of the hotels in town, and you may not be inclined to wade through all the options listed below to save $20 or $30 a night. If, on the other hand, you would like to obtain top value for your dollar, read on.

Beating Rack Rates

The benchmark for making cost comparisons is always the hotel's standard rate, or rack rate. This is what you would pay if, space available, you just walked in off the street and rented a room. In a way, the rack rate is analogous to an airline's standard coach fare. It represents a straight, nondiscounted room rate. In Las Vegas, you assume that the rack rate is the most you should have to pay and that with a little effort you ought to be able to do better.

To learn the standard room rate, call room reservations at the hotel(s) of your choice. Do not be surprised if there are several standard rates, one for each type of room in the hotel. Have the reservationist explain the difference in the types of rooms available in each price bracket. Also ask which of the described class of rooms you would get if you came on a wholesaler, tour operator, or airline tour package. This information will allow you to make meaningful comparisons among various packages and rates.

The Season

December and January are roller-coaster months for Las Vegas. In December, the town is empty except for National Finals Rodeo week in early December and Christmas/New Year's week. Similarly, in January, the town is packed during the Consumer Electronics Show and Super Bowl weekend, and pretty much dead the rest of the time. During the slow parts of these months, most of the hotels offer amazing deals on lodging. Also, hotels sometimes offer reduced rates in July and August. While the list below stands up pretty well as a general guide, one type of deal or package might beat another for a specific hotel or time of year.

Sorting Out the Sellers and the Options

To book a room in a particular hotel for any given date, there are so many different in-house departments, as well as outside tour operators and wholesalers selling rooms, that it is almost impossible to find out who is offering the best deal. This is not because the various deals are so hard to compare but, rather, because it is so difficult to identify all the sellers.

Though it is only a rough approximation, here is a list of the types of rates and packages available, ranked from the best to the worst value.

Room Rates and Packages	Sold or Administered By
1. Gambler's rate	Casino or hotel
2. December, January, and summer specials	Hotel room reservations or marketing department
3. Wholesaler packages	Independent wholesalers
4. Tour operator packages	Tour operators
5. Reservation service discounts	Independent wholesalers and consolidators
6. Internet discounts	Internet travel vendors
7. Half-price programs	Half-price program operators
8. Commercial airline packages	Commercial airlines
9. Hotel packages	Hotel sales and marketing
10. Corporate rate	Hotel room reservations
11. Hotel standard room rate	Hotel room reservations
12. Convention rate	Convention sponsor

The room-rate ranking is subject to some interpretation. A gambler's rate may, at first glance, seem to be the least expensive lodging option available, next to a complementary room. If, however, the amount of money a guest is obligated to wager (and potentially lose) is factored in, the gambler's rate might be by far the most expensive.

Complementary and Discounted Rooms for Gamblers

Most Las Vegas visitors are at least peripherally aware that casinos provide complementary or greatly discounted rooms to gamblers. It is not unusual, therefore, for a business traveler, a low-stakes gambler, or a nongambling tourist to attempt to take advantage of these deals. What they quickly discover is that the casino has very definite expectations of any guest whose stay is wholly or partially subsidized by the house. If you want a gambler's discount on a room, they will ask what game(s) you intend to play, the amount of your average bet, how many hours a day you usually gamble, where (at which casinos) you have played before, and how much gambling money you will have available on this trip. They may also request that you make an application for credit or provide personal information about your occupation, income, and bank account.

If you manage to bluff your way into a comp or discounted room, you can bet that your gambling (or lack thereof) will be closely monitored after you arrive. If you fail to give the casino an acceptable amount of action, you will probably be charged the nondiscounted room rate when you check out.

Even for those who expect to do a fair amount of gambling, a comp or discounted room can be a mixed blessing. By accepting the casino's hospitality, you incur a certain obligation (the more they give you, the bigger the obligation). You will be expected to do most (if not all) of your gambling in the casino where you are staying, and you will also be expected to play a certain number of hours each day. If this was your intention all along, great. On the other hand, if you thought you would like to try several casinos or take a day and run over to Hoover Dam, you may be painting yourself into a corner.

Taking Advantage of Special Deals

When you call, always ask the reservationist if the hotel has any package deals or specials. If you plan to gamble, be sure to ask about "gambling sprees" or other gaming specials. If you do not anticipate gambling enough to qualify for a gambling package, ask about other types of deals. If the reservationist is not knowledgeable, don't conclude that the hotel offers no packages or special deals of its own. Instead, have the reservationist transfer your call to the sales and marketing department and ask them.

If you have a lot of lead time before your trip, write or call the hotel and ask about joining their slot club. Though only a few hotels will send you a membership application, inquiring about the slot club will get you categorized as a gambler on the hotel's mailing list. Once in Las Vegas, sign up for the slot clubs of hotel-casinos that you like. This will ensure that you receive notification of special deals that you can take advantage of on subsequent visits. Being a member of a hotel's slot club can also come in handy when rooms are scarce. Once, trying to book a room, we were told the hotel was sold out. When we mentioned that we had a slot card, the reservationist miraculously found us a room. If you are a slot club member, it is often better to phone the slot club member services desk instead of the hotel reservations desk.

If you enjoy window shopping on the Internet, log onto the home page of hotels that interest you. As far as rooms go, however, it's rare in our experience to find a deal on the hotel's Web site that's better than the ones they quote you on the phone. A reservationist on the phone knows she has a good prospect on the line and will work with you within the limits of her authority. On the Web there's no give or negotiation: it's a take-it-or-leave-it deal. Finally, most hotels, including many of the new super properties, really haven't learned how to merchandise rooms through their Web site.

Having shopped the hotel for deals, start checking out tour operator and wholesaler packages advertised in your local newspaper, and compare what you find to packages offered in the Sunday edition of the *Los Angeles Times*. Next, check out packages offered by the airline tour services (American Airlines Fly-Away, Delta Vacations, etc.). When working with the airline tour services, always ask if they have any special deals going on with particular hotels.

Take the better deals and packages you discover, regardless of the source, and discuss them with a travel agent. Explain which one(s) you favor and ask if he or she can do any better. After your travel agent researches the options, review the whole shooting match and select the deal that best fits your schedule, requirements, and budget.

Since Las Vegas room rates are among the most reasonable in the country, you may not want to go to all of this effort. If you are working with a restricted budget, or plan to visit Las Vegas once or more each year, it is probably worth the hassle to check the rate and package options. If, conversely, you are used to paying $85–$140 a night for a hotel room, you may prefer to choose a hotel and leave it to your travel agent to get you the best deal available.

Timing Is Everything

Timing is everything when booking a guest room in Las Vegas. If a particular hotel has only a few rooms to sell for a specific date, it will often bounce up the rate for those rooms as high as it thinks the market will bear. Conversely, if the hotel has many rooms available for a certain date, it will lower the rate accordingly. The practice remains operative all year, although the likelihood of hotels having a lot of rooms available is obviously greater during "off-peak" periods. As an example, we checked rates at an upscale nongaming hotel during two weeks in October. Depending on the specific dates, the rate for the suite in question ranged from $75 (an incredible bargain) to $200 (significantly overpriced) per night.

Which day of the week you check in can also save or cost you some money. At some hotels a standard room runs 20% less if you check in on a Monday through Thursday (even though you may stay through the weekend). If you check into the same room on a weekend, your rate will be higher and may not change if you keep your room into the following week. A more common practice is for the hotel to charge a lower rate during the week and a higher rate on the weekend.

Helping Your Travel Agent to Help You

A travel agent friend told me once, "Las Vegas is our least favorite destination." What she meant, essentially, is that travel agents cannot make much money selling trips to Las Vegas. Airfares to Las Vegas are among the lowest in the country, and hotel rooms frequently go for less than $50 a night. On top of this, the average stay in Las Vegas is short. To a travel agent, this adds up to a lot of work with little potential for a worthwhile commission. Because an agent derives only a small return for booking travel to Las Vegas, there isn't much incentive for the travel agent to become product knowledgeable.

Except for a handful of agents who sell Las Vegas travel in volume (usually in Las Vegas's primary markets), there are comparatively few travel agents who know much about Las Vegas. This lack of information translates into travelers not getting reservations at their preferred hotel, paying more than is necessary, or being placed in out-of-the-way or otherwise undesirable lodging.

When you call your travel agent, ask if he or she has been to Las Vegas. Firsthand experience means everything. If the answer is no, either find another agent or be prepared to give your travel agent a lot of direction. Do not accept any recommendations at face value. Check out the location and rates of any suggested hotel and make certain that the hotel is suited to your itinerary.

Because travel agents tend to be unfamiliar with Las Vegas, your agent may try to plug you into a tour operator's or wholesaler's preset package. This essentially allows the travel agent to set up your whole trip with a single phone call and still collect an 8–10% commission. The problem with this scenario is that most agents will place 90% of their Las Vegas business with only one or two wholesalers or tour operators. In other words, path of least resistance for them, and not much choice for you.

Often, travel agents will use wholesalers who run packages in conjunction with airlines. Because of the wholesaler's exclusive relationship with the carrier, these trips are easy for travel agents to book. However, they will probably be more expensive than a package offered by a high-volume wholesaler who works with a number of airlines in a primary Las Vegas market.

To help your travel agent get you the best possible deal, do this:

1. Determine where you want to stay in Las Vegas (the Strip, downtown, Boulder Highway, etc.), and if possible choose a specific hotel. This can be accomplished by reviewing the hotel information provided in this guide, by writing or calling hotels that interest you, or by checking out your selected hotels on the Internet.

2. Check out the Las Vegas travel ads in the Sunday travel section of your local newspaper and compare them to ads running in the newspapers of one of Las Vegas's key markets (i.e., Los Angeles, San Diego, Phoenix, Chicago). See if you can find some packages that fit your plans and that include a hotel you like.

3. Call the wholesalers or tour operators whose ads you have collected. Ask any questions you might have concerning their packages, but do not book your trip with them directly.

4. Check out deals available on the Internet. Start with **www.travelaxe.com**, a site that provides a comparative overview of rates offered by the primary Internet discount sellers.

5. Tell your travel agent about the packages and Internet deals you find and ask if he or she can get you something better. The packages in the paper will serve as a benchmark against which to compare alternatives proposed by your travel agent.

6. Choose from among the options uncovered by you and your travel agent. No matter which option you elect, have your travel agent book it. Even if you go with one of the packages in the newspaper, it will probably be commissionable (at no additional cost to you) and will provide the agent some return on the time invested on your behalf. Also, as a travel professional, your agent should be able to verify the quality and integrity of the package.

No Room at the Inn (Maybe) If you are having trouble getting a reservation at the hotel of your choice, let your travel agent assist you. As discussed, the agent might be able to find a package with a wholesaler or tour operator that bypasses the hotel reservations department. If this does not work, he or she can call the sales and marketing department of the hotel and ask them, as a favor, to find you a room. Most hotel sales reps will make a special effort to accommodate travel agents, particularly travel agents who write a lot of Las Vegas business. Do not be shy or reluctant about asking your travel agent to make a special call on your behalf. This is common practice in the travel industry and affords the agent an opportunity to renew contacts in the hotel's sales department.

If your travel agent cannot get you a room through a personal appeal to the sales department and does not know which tour operators and wholesalers package the hotel you want, have the agent call hotel room reservations and:

1. Identify him- or herself as a travel agent.

2. Inquire about room availability for your required dates; something might have opened up since their (or your) last call.

3. If the reservationist reports that there are still no rooms available, have your travel agent ask for the reservations manager.

4. When the reservations manager comes on the line, have your agent identify him- or herself and ask whether the hotel is holding any space for wholesalers. If the answer is yes, have your agent request the wholesalers' names and phone numbers. This is information the reservations manager will not ordinarily divulge to an individual but will release to your travel agent. Armed with the names and numbers of wholesalers holding space, your agent can start calling the listed wholesalers to find you a package or a room.

No Room at the Inn (for Real) More frequently than you would imagine, Las Vegas hotels overbook their rooms. This happens when guests do not check out on time, when important casino customers arrive on short notice, and when the various departments handling room allocations get their signals crossed. When this occurs, guests who arrive holding reservations are told that their reservations have been canceled.

To protect yourself, always guarantee your first night with a major credit card (even if you do not plan to arrive late), send a deposit if required, and insist on a written confirmation of your reservation. When you arrive and check in, have your written confirmation handy.

Precautions notwithstanding, the hotel still might have canceled your reservation. When a hotel is overbooked, for whatever reason, it will take care of its serious gambling customers first, its prospective gambling customers (leisure travelers) second, and business travelers last. If you are informed that you have no room, demand that the hotel honor your reservation by finding you a room or by securing you a room at another hotel of comparable or better quality. Should the desk clerk balk at doing this, demand to see the reservations manager. If the reservations manager stonewalls, go to the hotel's general manager. Whatever you do, do not leave until the issue has been resolved to your satisfaction.

Hotels understand their obligation to honor a confirmed reservation, but they often fail to take responsibility unless you hold their feet to the fire. We have seen convention-goers, stunned by the news that they have no room, simply turn around and walk out. Wrong. The hotel owns the problem, not you. You should not have to shop for another room. The hotel that confirmed your reservation should find you a room comparable to or better than the one you reserved, and for the same rate.

Where the Deals Are

Hotel room marketing and sales is confusing even to travel professionals. Sellers, particularly the middlemen, or wholesalers are known by a numbing array of different and frequently ill-defined terms. Furthermore, roles overlap, making it difficult to know who, specifically, is providing a given service. Below we try to sort all of this out for you and encourage you to slog through it. Understanding the system will make you a savvy consumer and will enable you to get the best deals regardless of your destination.

Tour Operators and Wholesalers

Las Vegas hotels have always had a hard time filling their rooms from Sunday through Thursday. On the weekends, when thousands of visitors arrive from Southern California, Phoenix, and Salt Lake City, the town comes alive. But on Sunday evening, as the last of the Los Angelenos retreat over the horizon, Las Vegas lapses into the doldrums. The Las Vegas Convention and Visitors Authority, along with hotel sales departments, seek to fill the rooms on weekday nights by bringing meetings, conventions, and trade shows to town. While collectively they are successful, on many weekdays there remain a lot of empty hotel rooms.

Recognizing that an empty hotel room is a liability, various travel entrepreneurs have stepped into the breach, volunteering to sell rooms for the hotels and casinos. These entrepreneurs, who call themselves tour operators, inbound travel brokers, travel wholesalers, travel packagers, Internet retailers, or receptive operators, require as a quid pro quo that the hotels provide them a certain number of rooms at a significantly reduced nightly rate, which they in turn resell at a profit. As this arrangement extends the sales outreach of the hotels, and as the rooms might otherwise go unoccupied, the hotels are only too happy to cooperate with this group of independent sales agents. Though a variety of programs have been developed to sell the rooms, most are marketed as part of group and individual travel packages.

This development has been beneficial both to the tourist and the hotel. Predicated on volume, some of the room discount is generally passed along to consumers as an incentive to come to Las Vegas during the week or, alternatively, to stay in town beyond the weekend. Wholesalers have made such a positive contribution to the Las Vegas hotel occupancy rate that rooms are now made available to them for weekends as well as weekdays.

By purchasing your room through a tour operator or wholesaler, you may be able to obtain a room at the hotel of your choice for considerably less than if you went through the hotel's reservations department. The hotel commits rooms to the wholesaler at a specific deep discount, usually 18–30% or more off the standard quoted rate, but makes no effort to control the price the wholesaler offers to his customers.

Wholesalers holding space at a hotel for a specific block of time must surrender that space back to the hotel if the rooms are not sold by a certain date, usually 7–14 days in advance. Since the wholesaler's performance and credibility is determined by the number of rooms filled in a given hotel, the wholesaler is always reluctant to give rooms back. The situation is similar to when the biology department at a university approaches the end of the year without having spent all of its allocated budget. The department head reasons that if the remaining funds are not spent (and the surplus is returned to the university), the university might reduce the budget for the forthcoming year. Tour wholesalers depend on the hotels for their inventory. The more rooms the hotels allocate, the more inventory they have to sell. If a wholesaler keeps returning rooms unsold, it is logical to predict that the hotel will respond by making fewer accommodations available in the future. Therefore, the wholesaler would rather sell rooms at a bargain price than give them back to the hotel unsold.

TOUR OPERATORS AND TRAVEL WHOLESALERS

Some of the following businesses will deal directly with consumers; have your travel agent call the wholesalers.

A & P Tours
East McKeesport, Pennsylvania
(412) 351-4800
(Deals directly with consumers)

America West Vacations
Tempe, Arizona
(800) 235-9298
www.americawestvacations.com
(Deals directly with consumers)

Edison Travel
Kansas City, Kansas
(913) 788-7997 or
(800) 875-2228
(Deals directly with consumers)

Funjet Vacations
Milwaukee, Wisconsin
(800) 558-3050
Southfield, Michigan
(248) 827-4050
www.funjet.com
(Deals directly with consumers)

Kingdom Vacations
Plains, Pennsylvania
(800) 626-8747
www.kingdomvacations.com

Mile High Tours
Denver, Colorado
(303) 758-8246 or
(800) 777-TOUR
www.milehightours.com
(Deals directly with consumers)

MLT Vacations
Minnetonka, Minnesota
(952) 474-2540 or
(800) 328-0025
www.mltvacations.com

Sunquest Vacations
Toronto, Ontario
(416) 485-1700
www.sunquest.net

Sunquest Vacations West
Richmond, British Columbia
(604) 714-5141

Taking Advantage of Tour Operator and Travel Wholesaler Deals
There are several ways for you to tap into the tour operator and wholesaler market. First, check the travel sections of your Sunday paper for travel packages or tours to Las Vegas. Because Las Vegas hotels work with tour operators and wholesalers from all over the country, there will undoubtedly be someone in your city or region running packages to Las Vegas. Packages generally consist of room, transportation (bus or air), and often other features, such as rental cars, shows, etc. Sometimes the consumer can buy the package for any dates desired; other times the operator or wholesaler will specify the dates. In either event, if a particular package fits your needs, you (or your travel agent) can book it directly by calling the phone number listed in the ad.

If you cannot find any worthwhile Las Vegas packages advertised in your local paper, go to a good newsstand and buy a Sunday paper, preferably from Los Angeles, but alternatively from San Diego, Phoenix, Salt Lake City, Denver, or Chicago. These cities are hot markets for Las Vegas, and their newspapers will almost always have a nice selection of packages advertised. Because the competition among tour operators and wholesalers in these cities is so great, you will often find deals that beat the socks off anything offered in your part of the country.

Find a package that you like and call for information. Do not be surprised, however, if the advertised package is not wholly available to you. If you live, say, in Nashville, Tennessee, a tour operator or wholesaler in Los Angeles may not be able to package your round-trip air or bus to Las Vegas. This is because tour operators and wholesalers usually work with bus and air carriers on a contractual basis, limiting the transportation they sell to round trips originating from their market area. In other words, they can take care of your transportation if you are flying from Southern California but most likely will not have a contract with an airline that permits them to fly you from Nashville. What they sometimes do, however, and what they will be delighted to do if they are sitting on some unsold rooms, is sell you the "land only" part of the package. This means you buy the room and on-site amenities (car, shows, etc.), if any, but will take care of your own travel arrangements.

Buying the "land only" part of a package can save big bucks because the wholesaler always has more flexibility in discounting the "land" part of the package than in discounting the round-trip transportation component. One of the sweetest deals in travel is to purchase the "land only" part of a package at a time when the airlines are running a promotion. We combined a two-for-one air special from Delta with a "land only" package from a wholesaler and chalked up a savings of 65% over separate quoted rates and a 22% savings over the full air/land package offered by the wholesaler.

Finding Deals on the Internet

Wholesalers, packagers, and many of the other players discussed operate on the Internet, as do specialized Web travel vendors. By far the easiest way to scout room deals on the Internet is through **www.travelaxe.com.** At Travelaxe, you can download free software (only runs on PCs) that scans the better Internet sites selling discounted rooms. You enter your proposed check-in and check-out dates (required) as well as preferences concerning location and price (optional), and click "Search." The program scans a dozen or more seller sites and presents the discounted rates for all hotels in a chart for comparison. The prices listed in the chart represent the *total* you'll pay for your entire stay. To determine the rate per night, divide the total by the number of nights you'll be staying. If you decide to book, you deal directly with the site offering the best price. The software doesn't scan the individual hotel Web sites, so if you have a specific hotel in mind, you might want to check the hotel's site and call the hotel's reservation desk to ask about specials. We've run a number of tests on the Travelaxe program and found that it usually delivers the best prices available on the Internet.

Finally, for Internet shopping, consider **www.priceline.com.** There you can tender a bid for a room. You can't bid on a specific hotel, but you can specify location ("Convention Center, UNLV Area, Las Vegas Strip Area," etc.) and the quality rating expressed in stars. If your bid is accepted, you will be assigned to a hotel consistent with your location and quality requirements, and your credit card will be charged in a non-refundable transaction for your entire stay. Notification of acceptance usually takes less than an hour. We recommend bidding $30 to $45 per night for a three-star hotel and $60 to $85 per night for a four-star. To gauge your chances of success, check to see if any major conventions or trade shows are scheduled during your preferred dates. Note that Price-line lists "Las Vegas Strip Area" as opposed to "Las Vegas Strip." Thus you might be booked into a hotel close to, but not on the Strip.

Reservation Services

When wholesalers and consolidators deal directly with the public, they frequently represent themselves as "reservation services." When you call, you can ask for a rate quote for a particular hotel, or alternatively, ask for their best available deal in the area where you prefer to stay. If there is a maximum amount you are willing to pay, say so. Chances are the service will find something that will work for you, even if they have to shave a dollar or two off their own profit.

The discount available (if any) from a reservation service depends on whether the service functions as a consolidator or a wholesaler. Consolidators are strictly sales agents who do not own or control the room inventory they are trying to sell. Discounts offered by consolidators are determined by the hotels with rooms to fill. Consolidator discounts vary enormously depending on how desperate the hotel is to unload the rooms. When you deal with a room reservation service that operates as a consolidator, you pay for your room as usual when you check out of the hotel.

Wholesalers, as we discussed above, have long-standing contracts with hotels that allow the wholesaler to purchase rooms at an established deep discount. Some wholesalers hold purchase options on blocks of rooms while others actually pay for rooms and own the inventory. Because a wholesaler controls the room inventory, it can offer whatever discount it pleases consistent with current demand. In practice, most wholesaler reservation-service discounts fall in the 10–40% range. When you reserve a room with a reservation service that operates as a wholesaler, you must usually pay for your entire stay in advance with your credit card. The service then sends you a written confirmation and usually a voucher (indicating prepayment) for you to present at the hotel.

Our experience has been that the reservation services are more useful in finding rooms in Las Vegas when availability is scarce than in obtaining deep discounts. Calling the hotels ourselves, we were often able to beat the reservation services' rates when rooms were generally available. When the city was booked, however, and we could not find a room by calling the hotels ourselves, the reservation services could almost always get us a room at a fair price.

RESERVATION SERVICES	
Hotel Reservations Network	(800) 96-HOTEL
	www.hotelreservationsnetwork.com
Reservations Plus	(800) 733-6644
	www.resplus.com
RMC Travel Center	(800) 245-5738
Accommodations Express	(800) 444-7666
	www.accomodationsexpress.com

Hotel-Sponsored Packages

In addition to selling rooms through tour operators, consolidators, and wholesalers, most hotels periodically offer exceptional deals of their own. Sometimes the packages are specialized, as with golf packages, or are offered only at certain times of the year, for instance December and January. Promotion of hotel specials tends to be limited to the hotel's primary markets, which for most properties is Southern California, Arizona, Utah, Colorado, Hawaii, and the Midwest. If you live in other parts of the country, you can take advantage of the packages but probably will not see them advertised in your local newspaper.

Some of the hotel packages are unbelievable deals. Once, for instance, one hotel offered three nights' free lodging, no strings attached, to any adult from Texas; and the Stardust ran a $32 special that included a room, a show, and a buffet for two people. On certain dates in November, December, and January, the Flamingo offered a deal that included a room for two or more nights at $35 per night (tax inclusive), with two drinks and a show thrown in for good measure. In July of 2004, 27 hotels offered rates less than $40. Look for the hotel specials in Southern California newspapers, or call the hotel and ask.

An important point regarding hotel specials is that the hotel reservationists do not usually inform you of existing specials or offer them to you. In other words, *you have to ask.*

Travelers Discount Guide

A company called Travelers Discount Guide publishes a book of discount coupons for bargain rates at hotels throughout California and Nevada. These books are available free of charge in many restaurants and motels along the main interstate highways. Since most folks make reservations prior to leaving home, picking up the coupon book en route does not help much. For $3 ($5 Canadian), however, TDG will mail you a copy (third class) before you make your reservations. Properties listed in the guide for Las Vegas are generally smaller, nongaming hotels. If you call and use a credit card, TDG will send the guide first class for an additional charge. Write or call:

Travelers Discount Guide
4205 N.W. Sixth Street
Gainesville, FL 32609
(352) 371-3948
www.roomsaver.com or www.travelersdiscountguide.com

How to Evaluate a Travel Package

Hundreds of Las Vegas package trips and vacations are offered to the public each year. Almost all include round-trip transportation to Las Vegas and lodging. Sometimes room tax, transportation from the airport, a rental car, shows, meals, welcome parties, and/or souvenirs are also included.

In general, because the Las Vegas market is so competitive, packages to Las Vegas are among the best travel values available. Las Vegas competes head-to-head with Atlantic City for Eastern travelers and with Reno, Lake Tahoe, Laughlin, and other Nevada destinations for Western visitors. Within Las Vegas, downtown competes with the Strip, and individual hotels go one-on-one to improve their share of the market. In addition to the fierce competition for the destination traveler, the extraordinary profitability of gambling also works in the consumer's behalf to keep Las Vegas travel economical. For a large number of hotels, amazing values in dining and lodging are used to lure visitors to the casino.

Packages should be a win/win proposition for both the buyer and the seller. The buyer (or travel agent) only has to make one phone call and deal with a single salesperson to set up the whole trip: transportation, lodging, rental car, show admissions, and even golf, tennis, and sightseeing. The seller, likewise, only has to deal with the buyer one time, eliminating the need for separate sales, confirmations, and billings. In addition to streamlining selling, processing, and administration, some packagers also buy airfares in bulk on contract like a broker playing the commodities market. Buying or guaranteeing a large number of airfares in advance allows the packager to buy them at a significant savings from posted fares. The same practice is also applied to hotel rooms. Because selling packaged trips is an efficient way of doing business, and the packager can often buy individual components (airfare, lodging) in bulk at a discount, savings in operating expenses realized by the seller are sometimes passed on to the buyer. So the package is not only convenient but an exceptional value. In any event, that is the way it is supposed to work.

In practice, the seller occasionally realizes all of the economies and passes none of the savings along to the buyer. In some instances, packages are loaded with extras that cost the packager next to nothing but run the retail price sky-high. While this is not as common with Las Vegas packages as those to other destinations, it occurs frequently enough to warrant some comparison shopping.

When considering a package, choose one that includes features you are sure to use. Whether you use all the features or not, you will most certainly pay for them. Second, if cost is of greater concern than convenience, make a few phone calls and see what the package would cost if you booked its individual components (airfare, lodging, rental car) on your own. If the package price is less than the à la carte cost, the package is a good deal. If the costs are about the same, the package is probably worth it for the convenience.

An Example   My niece and her husband were looking at a package they found with Delta Vacations. The package included round-trip airfare (on Delta) from Atlanta, four nights' lodging (Friday through Monday) at the Luxor, airport transfers (transportation to and from the airport), and about 20 "bonus features," including:

- 2-for-1 admission to Hoover Dam tours
- Free admission to the Imperial Palace Auto Collection
- 2-for-1 cocktails at New York–New York
- A free Planet Hollywood souvenir
- Discounted Lake Mead Boat Cruises

The price, tax included, was $548 per person, or $1,096 all together. Checking the Luxor and a number of airlines, they found the following:

Same room at the Luxor, 2 people to a room, for 4 nights with room tax included	$519
Transportation to and from the airport	$14
Subtotal	$533

Subtracting the $533 (lodging and airport transfers) from the cost of Delta's package total of $1,096, they determined that the air and "bonus features" portion of the package was worth $563 ($1,096 – $533 = $563). If they were not interested in using any of the bonus features, and they could fly to Las Vegas for less than $563, they would be better off turning down the package.

Scouting around, the lowest fare they could find was $320 on American Airlines with an advance purchase ticket. This piece of information completed their analysis as follows:

Option A: Delta Vacation package for 2	$1,096
Option B: Booking their own air and lodging	
Lodging, including tax	$519
Airfare on American Airlines for 2	$640
Transportation to and from hotel	$14
Total	$1,173

In this example, the package saves money and is also more convenient. Most of the two-fers and other deals bundled into the package are available through freebie Las Vegas visitor magazines, but you might not have discovered them. Be aware that it doesn't always work out this way. We analyze dozens of packages each year, and there are as many bad deals as good deals. The point is, always do your homework.

For Business Travelers

Convention Rates: How the System Works

Business travelers, particularly those attending trade shows or conventions, are almost always charged more for their rooms than leisure travelers. For big meetings, called citywide conventions, huge numbers of rooms are blocked in hotels all over town. These rooms are reserved for visitors attending the meeting in question and are usually requested and coordinated by the meeting's sponsoring organization in cooperation with the Las Vegas Convention and Visitors Authority.

Individual hotels negotiate a nightly rate with the convention sponsor, who then frequently sells the rooms through a central reservations system of its own. Since the hotels would rather have gamblers or leisure travelers than people attending conventions (who usually have limited time to gamble), the negotiated price tends to be high, often $10 to $50 per night above the rack rate.

Meeting sponsors, of course, blame convention rates on the hotels. Meanwhile the hotels maintain a stoic silence, not wishing to alienate meeting organizers. Following the publication of an earlier edition of this guide, the publisher received the following irate letter from a major convention sponsor:

Mr. Sehlinger writes that the convention sponsors often charge what they think the market will bear. Therefore, if the convention-goer gets gouged on a room, it is the doing of the convention sponsor, not the hotel. This statement is completely false and misleading and puts [convention sponsors] in a false light. [Our organization] does not make any profit on hotel rooms....The general practice is to charge our members exactly what the hotel charges us. Each member pays his or her own hotel bill when leaving Las Vegas, and [we] receive no commission, kickback, or other payment from the hotel.

To be fair, convention sponsors should be given some credit simply for having their meeting in Las Vegas. Even considering the inflated convention rates, meeting attendees will pay 15–40% less in Las Vegas for comparable lodging than in other major convention cities. As for the rest, well, let's take a look.

Sam Walton taught the average American that someone purchasing a large quantity of a particular item should be able to obtain a better price (per item) than a person buying only one or two. If anyone just walking in off the street can buy a single hotel room for $50, why then must a convention sponsor, negotiating for 900 rooms for five nights in the same hotel (4,500 room-nights in hotel jargon), settle for a rate of $60 per night?

Many Las Vegas hotels take a hardline negotiating position with meeting sponsors because (1) every room occupied by a convention-goer is one less room available for gamblers, and (2) they figure that most business travelers are on expense accounts. In addition, timing is a critical factor in negotiating room rates. The hotels do not want business travelers occupying rooms on weekends or during the more popular times of the year. Convention sponsors who want to schedule a meeting during high season (when hotels fill their rooms no matter what) can expect to pay premium rates. In addition, and regardless of the time of year, many hotels routinely charge stiff prices to convention-goers as a sort of insurance against lost opportunity. "What if we block our rooms for a trade show one year in advance," a sales manager asked, "and then a championship prizefight is scheduled for that week? We would lose big-time."

A spokesman for the Las Vegas Convention and Visitors Authority indicated that the higher room rates for conventioneers are not unreasonable given a hotel's commitment to the sponsor to hold rooms in reserve. But reserved rooms, or room blocks as they are called, fragment a hotel's inventory of available rooms, and often make it harder, not easier, to get a room in a particular hotel. The bottom line is that convention-goers pay a premium price for the benefit of having rooms reserved for their meeting—rooms that would be cheaper, and often easier to reserve, if the sponsor had not reserved them in the first place. For a major, citywide convention, it is not unusual for attendees to collectively pay in excess of $1 million for the peace of mind of having rooms reserved.

Whether room blocking is really necessary is an interesting question. The Las Vegas Convention and Visitors Authority works with convention sponsors to ensure that there is never more than one citywide meeting in town at a time and to make sure that sponsors do not schedule their conventions at a time when Las Vegas hotels are otherwise normally sold out (National Finals Rodeo week, Super Bowl weekend, New Year's, and so on). Unfortunately for meeting planners, some major events (prizefights, tennis matches) are occasionally scheduled in Las Vegas on short notice. If a meeting planner does not block rooms and a big fight is announced for the week the meeting is in town, the attendees may be unable to find a room. This is such a nightmare to convention sponsors that they cave in to exorbitant convention rates rather than risk not having rooms. The actual likelihood of a major event being scheduled at the same time as a large convention is small, though the specter of this worst-case scenario is a powerful weapon in the bargaining arsenal of the hotels.

On balance, meeting sponsors negate their volume-buying clout by scheduling meetings during the more popular times of year or, alternatively, by caving in to the hotels' "opportunity cost" room pricing. Conversely, hotels play unfairly on the sponsor's fear of not having enough rooms, and they charge premium rates to cover improbable, ill-defined opportunity losses. Is there collusion here? Probably not. The more likely conclusion is that both hotels and sponsors have become comfortable with an inflexible negotiating environment, but one that permits meeting sponsors to distribute the unreasonable charges pro rata to their attendees.

Working through the Maze

If you attempt to bypass the sponsoring organization and go directly through the hotel, the hotel will either refer you to the convention's central reservations number or quote you the same high price. Even if you do not identify yourself as a convention-goer, the hotel will figure it out by the dates you request. In most instances, even if you lie and insist that you are not attending the convention in question, the hotel will make you pay the higher rate or claim to be sold out.

By way of example, we tried to get reservations at the Riviera for a major trade show in the spring, a citywide convention that draws about 30,000 attendees. The show runs six days plus one day for setting up, or seven days total, Saturday through Friday. Though this example involves the Riviera, we encountered the same scenario at every hotel we called.

When we phoned reservations at the Riviera and gave them our dates, they immediately asked if we would be attending a convention or trade show. When we answered in the affirmative, they gave us the official sponsor's central reservations phone number in New York. We called the sponsor and learned that a single room at the Riviera (one person in one room) booked through them would cost $91 per night, including room tax. The same room (we found from other sources) booked directly through the Riviera would cost $80 with tax included.

We called the Riviera back and asked for the same dates, this time disavowing any association with the trade show, and were rebuffed. Obviously skeptical of our story, the hotel informed us that they were sold out for the days we requested. Unconvinced that the hotel was fully booked, we had two different members of our research team call. One attempted to make reservations from Wednesday *of the preceding week* through Tuesday of the trade show week, while our second caller requested a room from Wednesday of the trade show week through the following Tuesday. These respective sets of dates, we reasoned, would differ sufficiently from the show dates to convince the Riviera that we were not conventioneers. In each case we were able to make reservations for the dates desired at the $80-per-night rate.

It should be stressed that a hotel treats the convention's sponsoring organization much like a wholesaler who reserves rooms in a block for a negotiated price. What the convention, in turn, charges its attendees is out of the hotel's control. Once a hotel and convention sponsor come to terms, the hotel either refers all inquiries about reservations to the sponsor or accepts bookings at whatever nightly rate the sponsor determines. Since hotels do not want to get in the way of their convention sponsors (who are very powerful customers) or, alternatively, have convention attendees buying up rooms intended for other, nonconvention customers, the hotel reservations department carefully screens any request for a room during a convention period.

Strategies for Beating Convention Rates

There are several strategies for getting around convention rates:

1. Check the Internet Unlike packagers and wholesalers, Internet sellers serve as a communications nexus and can often point you to a hotel you had not considered that still has rooms available, or to a property that unexpectedly has some last-minute rooms because of cancellations. Try the aforementioned **www.travelaxe.com,** which facilitates comparing rates offered by more than a dozen online sellers.

2. Buy a package from a tour operator or a wholesaler This tactic makes it unnecessary to deal with the convention's central reservations office or with an individual hotel's reservations department. Many packages allow you to buy extra days at a special discounted room rate if the package dates do not coincide perfectly with your meeting dates.

Packages that use air charter services operate on a fixed, inflexible schedule. As a rule these packages run three nights (depart Thursday, return Sunday; or depart Friday, return Monday) or four nights (depart Monday, return Friday; or depart Sunday, return Thursday). Two-night, five-night, and seven-night charter packages can also be found. Charter air packages offer greater savings, but usually less flexibility, than packages that use commercial carriers.

Since the Riviera would not give us their standard rate for the tradeshow dates, our remaining alternatives were to either find a package or book through the sponsor's central reservations. We wanted to travel from Birmingham, Alabama, and stay at the Riviera for the seven nights of the show. For one person, the options were as follows:

Option A: Reservations through show's official sponsor

Riviera for 7 nights at $91 per night (tax included)	$637
plus round-trip airfare from Birmingham, Alabama	$344
Total	$981

Option B: Charter package

Riviera for 7 nights, all taxes, round-trip direct flights, 2 breakfasts, 2 dinner buffets, and 3 shows

Total	$798

Option C: Airline tour service's package
American's Fly-Away Vacations offered round-trip airfare, 7 nights' lodging, taxes
included, to the Riviera for $789 but were sold out for the required dates when we
called 6 weeks in advance. They were able to offer the same package for the Las
Vegas Hilton at $873. The Las Vegas Hilton is within easy walking distance of both
the Riviera and the Convention Center.

Total	$789 or $873

Delta Vacations did not use the Riviera but had a package with round-trip airfare
and 7 nights' lodging, all taxes included, available for the desired dates at 2 hotels
not within walking distance of the Riviera or the Las Vegas Convention Center:

Flamingo	$769
Harrah's	$879

United's Vacation Planning Center, whose wholesaler is Funway Holidays, had a package with round-trip airfare, 7 nights' lodging at the Riviera, taxes, and airport transfers available for the dates of the show.

Total	$851

If you are able to beat the convention rate by booking a package or getting a room from a wholesaler, don't blow your cover when you check in.
If you walk up to the registration desk in a business suit and a convention
ID badge, the hotel will void your package and charge you the full convention rate. If you are supposed to be a tourist, act like one, particularly
when you check in and check out.

3. Find a hotel that does not participate in the convention room blocks
Many of the downtown, North Las Vegas, and Boulder Highway hotels,
as well as a few of the Strip hotels, do not make rooms available in blocks
for conventions. If you wish to avoid convention rates, obtain a list of
your convention's "official" hotels from the sponsoring organization and
match it against the hotels listed in this guide. Any hotel listed in this
book that does not appear on the list supplied by the meeting sponsors is
not participating in blocking rooms for your convention. This means
you can deal with the nonparticipating hotels directly and should be able
to get their regular rate.

Strip Hotels that Rarely Participate in Room Blocks

Circus Circus	Excalibur	Luxor	Westward Ho

Downtown Hotels that Seldom Participate in Room Blocks

Binion's Horseshoe	Fitzgeralds	Lady Luck
California	Four Queens	
El Cortez	Fremont	

Most citywide trade shows and conventions are held at the Las Vegas
Convention Center. Of all the nonparticipating hotels, only Circus Circus and Westward Ho are within a 15-minute walk. If you stay at any of

the other hotels, you will have to commute to the Convention Center by shuttle, cab, or car.

4. Reserve late Thirty to sixty days prior to the opening of a citywide convention or show, the front desk room reservations staff in a given hotel will take over the management of rooms reserved for the meeting from the hotel's sales and marketing department. "Room Res," in conjunction with the general manager, is responsible for making sure that the hotel is running at peak capacity for the dates of the show. The general manager has the authority to lower the room rate from the price negotiated with the sponsor. If rooms are not being booked for the convention in accordance with the hotel's expectations, the general manager will often lower the rate for attendees and, at the same time, return a number of reserved rooms to general inventory for sale to the public. A convention-goer who books a room at the last minute might obtain a lower rate than an attendee who booked early through the sponsor's central housing service. Practically speaking, however, do not expect to find rooms available at the convention headquarters hotel or at most of the hotels within easy walking distance. As a rule of thumb, the farther from the Convention Center or headquarters a hotel is, the better the chances of finding a discounted room at the last minute.

The Las Vegas Convention Center

The Las Vegas Convention Center is the largest single-level convention and trade show facility in the United States. Almost 3.2 million square feet of exhibit space are divided into two main buildings: the brand new South Hall and the older North Hall. A pedestrian bridge over Desert Inn Road connects the halls. Trade shows that crowd facilities in Washington, San Francisco, and New York fit with ease in this immense Las Vegas complex. In addition to the exhibit areas, the Center has a new lobby and public areas, a kitchen that can cater a banquet for 12,000 people, and 144 meeting rooms. Serving as headquarters for shows and conventions drawing as many as 250,000 delegates, the Convention Center is on Paradise Road, one very long block off the Las Vegas Strip and three miles from the airport.

For both exhibitors and attendees, the Las Vegas Convention Center is an excellent site for a meeting or trade show. Large and small exhibitors can locate and access their exhibit sites with a minimum of effort. Numerous loading docks and huge bay doors make loading and unloading quick and simple for large displays arriving by truck. Smaller displays transported in vans and cars are unloaded on the north side of the main hall and can be carried or wheeled directly to the exhibit area without climbing stairs or using elevators. The exhibit areas and meeting rooms are well marked and easy to find.

The Las Vegas Convention and Visitors Authority also operates Cashman Field Center, home of Las Vegas's AAA baseball team. In addition to a baseball stadium, the Center contains a 2,000-seat theater and 100,000 square feet of meeting and exhibit space. For more information, call (702) 892-0711.

Lodging within Walking Distance of the Las Vegas Convention Center

Although participants in citywide conventions lodge all over town, a few hotels are within easy walking distance of the Convention Center. Next door, and closest, is the huge Las Vegas Hilton, with over 3,100 rooms. The Hilton routinely serves as headquarters for meetings and shows in the Convention Center and provides, if needed, an additional 220,000 square feet of exhibit, ballroom, banquet, special event, and meeting room space. Many smaller conventions conduct all their meetings, including exhibits, at the Hilton. The walk from the lobby of the Hilton to the Convention Center is about five minutes for most people.

Also nearby is the new 548-room Marriott Renaissance (opens February 2005), a non-gaming hotel targeting business travelers. A long half-block away (to its rear entrance) is the 2,075-room Riviera Hotel. Like the Las Vegas Hilton, the Riviera is often the headquarters for large shows and meetings at the Convention Center. With 158,000 square feet of meeting and banquet space, the Riviera, like the Hilton, hosts entire meetings and provides supplemental facilities for events at the Convention Center. The walk from the rear (eastern) entrance of the Riviera to the Convention Center takes about ten minutes.

HOTELS WITHIN A 20-MINUTE WALK OF THE CONVENTION CENTER

AmeriSuites	202 suites	7-minute walk
Circus Circus	3,741 rooms	15-minute walk
Greek Isles	212 rooms	7-minute walk
Las Vegas Courtyard (Marriott)	149 rooms	6-minute walk
Las Vegas Hilton	3,174 rooms	5-minute walk
Mardi Gras Inn (Best Western)	314 suites	12-minute walk
Marriott Renaissance	548 rooms	4-minute walk
Las Vegas Marriott Suites	255 suites	9-minute walk
New Frontier	988 rooms	20-minute walk
Residence Inn (Marriott)	192 suites	7-minute walk
Riviera Hotel	2,075 rooms	10-minute walk
Stardust	2,500 rooms	15-minute walk

Cabs and Shuttles to the Convention Center

Large, citywide conventions often provide complementary bus service from major hotels to the Convention Center. If you are staying at a smaller hotel and wish to use the shuttle bus, walk to the nearest large hotel on the shuttle route. Though cabs are plentiful and efficient in Las Vegas, they are sometimes in short supply at convention or trade show daily opening and closing times. Public transportation—CAT buses ($2) and the Las Vegas Strip Trolley ($1.65)—is also available from the larger hotels. Exact fare is required.Your best bet is to stay within walking distance of the Convention Center. If you end up staying too far away to walk, a car is often less trouble than depending on cabs and shuttle buses.

Monorail to the Convention Center

If you are staying at a hotel in the section of the Strip between Tropicana and Sands (Spring Valley Road), the best way to commute to the Convention Center is via the monorail. It's a no brainer for guests in hotels on the east side of the strip. For convention-goers' lodging on the west side of the Strip, it's often a long walk to nearest station. If traffic on the Strip isn't snarled, west-siders may want to consider taking a cab.

Lunch Alternatives for Convention and Trade-Show Attendees

The Convention Center food service provides a better-than-average lunch and snack selection. As at most convention centers, however, prices are high. Outside of the Convention Center, but within walking distance, are the buffet and coffee shop at the Hilton restaurants, at the Marriott Renaissance, and Nippon, a Japanese restaurant and sushi bar (a ten-minute walk). The better restaurants at the Las Vegas Hilton are not open for lunch.

The restaurants mentioned above provide decent food and fast service but are bustling eateries not particularly conducive to a quiet business lunch. At 3900 Paradise Road, however, there is a small shopping center (only three minutes from the Convention Center by cab) that has several quiet, high-quality ethnic restaurants. Also located in the shopping center is a sandwich shop. If you're up for a monorail ride, you can commute to Harrah's in about five minutes. There are dozens of fast-serve and full-service restaurants within a five-minute walk of Harrah's.

Parking at the Las Vegas Convention Center

In all, there are 5,500 parking spaces for cars in nine color-coded parking lots. The most convenient parking is in the Silver Lots right in front of the main entrance. The largest and third most convenient parking is in the Gold Lots across Paradise Road north of Convention Center Drive. On the east side of the convention center are the Blue, Orange, Red, and Green lots. The Blue Lot, tucked into the northeast corner of the property, is second only to the Silver Lots in convenience, but is used extensively by convention center employees. The Orange Lot on the southeast side is likewise convenient, but is largely reserved for tractor-trailer parking during large trade shows. The Red Lot is adjacent to the new South Hall and is a good choice if the South Hall is where you'll spend most of your time. Finally, the Green Lot is the most remote of all, though more acceptable if your primary business is in the South Hall.

Though access to the exhibit floor varies from meeting to meeting, attendees are often required to enter through the Convention Center's main entrance off Paradise Road. If not parked in the Gold or Silver lots, convention-goers must hike around the complex in order to reach the front door, a seven- to ten-minute walk. For other meetings, properly credentialed attendees (i.e., those with registration badges) are permitted to enter the exhibit halls by one of several doors along the sides of the Convention Center halls. As a rule, getting out is not as hard as getting in, and attendees are usually permitted to exit through the side doors.

Comfort Zones:
Matching Guests with Hotels

I remember a good friend, a single woman of 32, who, in search of a little romance, decided to take a Caribbean cruise. Thinking that one cruise was pretty much like any other, she signed up for a cruise without doing much shopping around. She ended up on a boat full of retired married folks who played bingo or bridge every evening and were usually in the sack by 10:30 p.m. My friend mistakenly assumed, as have many others, that cruises are homogeneous products. In fact, nothing could be farther from the truth. Each cruise provides a tailored experience to a specific and narrowly defined market. If my friend had done her homework, she could have booked passage on a boat full of young single people and danced and romanced into the night.

In Las Vegas, it is likewise easy to assume that all the hotels and casinos are fairly similar. True, they all have guest rooms, restaurants, and the same mix of games in the casino, but each property molds its offerings to appeal to a well-defined audience. This concerted effort to please a specific population of guests creates what we call a "comfort zone." If you are among the group a hotel strives to please, you will feel comfortable and at home and will have much in common with the other guests. However, if you fail to determine the comfort zone before you go, you may end up like my friend—on the wrong boat.

Visitors come to Las Vegas either to vacation and play or to attend a meeting or convention. While these reasons for coming to Las Vegas are not mutually exclusive, there is a marked difference between a recreational visitor and a business traveler. The vacationer is likely to be older (45 years and up), retired, and from the Midwest, Southern California, Arizona, Colorado, or Hawaii. The business traveler is younger on average and comes from just about anywhere. Individual hotels and casinos pay close attention to these differences and customize their atmosphere, dining, and entertainment to satisfy a specific type of traveler.

The California Hotel, downtown, for example, targets Hawaiians and maintains a food store and restaurants that supply their clientele with snacks and dishes from the islands. On the Boulder Highway, Sam's Town is geared toward cowboys and retired travelers. Entertainment at Sam's Town consists of bowling and country-western dancing. Circus Circus on the Strip attracts the RV crowd (with its own RV park) but also offers large, low-priced rooms, buffets, free circus acts, and an amusement park to lure families. The Las Vegas Hilton and the Venetian, both next door to the convention centers, go the extra mile to make business travelers feel at home.

Some hotels are posh and exclusive, while others are more spartan and intended to appeal to younger or more frugal visitors. Each property, however, from its lounge entertainment to its guest-room decor or the dishes served in its restaurants, is packaged with a certain type of guest in mind.

Because Las Vegas is basically a very informal town, you will not feel as out of place as my friend did on her cruise if you happen to end up in the wrong hotel. In any given property, there is a fairly broad range of clientele. There always will be hotels where you experience a greater comfort level than at others, however. In a place as different as Las Vegas, that added comfort can sometimes mean a lot.

Democracy in the Casinos

While Las Vegas hotels and casinos continue to be characterized as appealing to "high rollers" or "grinds," the distinction has become increasingly blurred. High rollers, of course, are wealthy visitors who come to gamble in earnest, while grinds are less affluent folks who grudgingly bet their money a nickel or quarter at a time. For many years, the slot machine was symbolic of the grinds. Unable to join the action of the high-stakes table games, these blue-collar gamblers would sit for hours pumping the arms of the slots. More recently, however, the slots are the symbol of casino profitability, contributing anywhere from 40–100% of a given casino's bottom line.

The popularity of the slot machine among gamblers of all types has democratized the casino. The casinos recognize that the silver-haired lady at the quarter slots is an extremely valuable customer and that it is good business to forego the impression of exclusivity in order to make her comfortable. In Las Vegas there are casinos that maintain the illusion of an upper-crust clientele while quietly practicing an egalitarianism that belies any such pretense. By virtue of its economic clout, the slot machine has broadened the comfort zone of the stuffiest casinos and made Las Vegas a friendlier, more pleasant (albeit noisier) place.

The Feel of the Place

Las Vegas's hotel-casinos have distinctly individual personalities. While all casinos contain slot machines, craps tables, and roulette wheels, the feel of each particular place is unique, a product of the combined characteristics of management, patrons, and design. This feel, or personality, determines a hotel-casino's comfort zone, the peculiar ambience that makes one guest feel totally at home while another runs for the exit.

The Author's Bias Openly Admitted   As you read the hotel-casino descriptions that follow, you will perhaps intuit that the author is a little claustrophobic. I do not understand why so many casinos are dark, noisy, and confining; they are more like submarines than places of recreation. Why, I'd like to know, isn't there a casino in a nice, rooftop atrium where you can watch the sun set and the birds fly over? Is there a reason why we should be blinded by blinking lights or deafened by clanking coins in gloomy, red-Naugahyde-upholstered tunnels?

Apparently there is some casino marketing theory which postulates that customers will gamble longer and more aggressively if their circadian rhythms are disturbed, their natural clocks unplugged. Zoos confuse nocturnal animals this way to make them rummage around when they should be sleeping. Casino customers, like these animals, are never supposed to know if it is day or night. This is patently ridiculous, of course, because unlike bats and lemurs, almost every gambler has a watch or can tell what time it is by the type of food on the buffet.

Why do I worry about this, you ask? Isn't doubling down on any two cards and re-splitting pairs in blackjack more important than how low the ceiling is? Maybe to you, my friend, but not to me. I want to gamble where I can breathe, stand up straight, and not smell the person playing at the next machine. I'd like for my pupils to be the same size for more than three consecutive seconds, and I'd like to be able to conduct a conversation without using a megaphone. I'd even like to know whether or not it's raining outside. And while I'm aware that it is perfectly possible to play craps in an alley, that's not why I go to Las Vegas. We've got plenty of alleys at home.

This is not to imply that I gamble in the departure concourse at the airport but to warn you about my natural bias against hotels and casinos that feel like velveteen U-boats. If, in the following descriptions, I talk about "ceiling height" a lot, I hope you will understand.

Hotels with Casinos

How to Avoid Reading the Hotel-Casino Descriptions   If you don't care how a place "feels" but just want to know whether it has room service and tennis courts, or when check-out time is, you can skip to the alphabetically arranged Hotel Information Chart at the end of this chapter.

Aladdin Resort and Casino   (www.aladdincasino.com)

With the distinction of being the only Strip hotel to be imploded and then rebuilt on the same site, the Aladdin Resort and Casino was the Las Vegas version of Phoenix rising. The question for the moment, however, is how high can this bird fly?

From its bungled opening to the present, the Aladdin has missed the mark. Not by much, mind you, but enough to precipitate a bankruptcy filing in 2002. Its location is a little too remote, its theme a little too average, its self-parking a little too inconvenient, its shopping venue a little too confusing, and on and on. In 2004, the Aladdin was acquired by Planet Hollywood and Starwood Hotels & Resorts, who plan to correct many of Aladdin's chronic problems. However, it took the new owners a long time to obtain their gaming license, so it will probably be late 2005 before major changes are noticeable. In the meantime, the Aladdin will continue to be one the of the best values for the money on the Strip.

The Aladdin's theme, of course, draws its inspiration from the *Arabian Nights* tales, which in turn are based on the Islamic culture and folklore of North Africa and the eastern Mediterranean. The casino and hotel present the theme in whimsical storybook fashion with some Las Vegas neon and glitter tossed in for good measure. A two-story, football-field-long mural over the Strip entrance, for example, twinkles with fiber-optic flowers, not something you'd likely see in the desert, even with a good buzz. The size of the mural typifies the oversize proportions of the casino and hotel public areas, where scale dominates detail. The hotel lobby occupies the lower level, with the casino on the second floor. Continuing upward, there is a mezzanine level and third floor overlooking the entire gaming area. The casino's more interesting details include ebony Pegasus flying horse sculptures at the entrance to the sports book and an Aladdin's lamp the size of a small locomotive atop the Lamp Bar. Another attention getter, the Roc Bar, sits beneath the watchful eye of a mammoth, raven-like bird from the Sinbad story.

Ringing the casino except on the west is the Desert Passage shopping venue. Built to human scale and more realistically rendered than the fanciful casino, Desert Passage consists of 130 upscale stores and restaurants situated along the streets of a mythical Arabian city. Incorporating the icons and architecture of the Arab world from Istanbul to Marrakech, Desert Passage streets reside in perpetual twilight beneath sky murals painted on an arched ceiling. The overall effect is well done, much in the image of the Forum Shops at Caesars Palace and the Grand Canal Shops at the Venetian. You can enter Desert Passage from the Strip or from two entrances connecting the shopping complex with the casino.

Guest rooms at the Aladdin are roomy and come equipped with two phone lines and a complete computer set up that allows guests to go online without bringing along their own computers. The lobby for the hotel is on the lowest level and can be accessed from Harmon Avenue. Elevators serving the guest-room floors are adjacent to the lobby, eliminating the usual inconvenient trek through the casino with all of your luggage.

The swimming complex, situated six floors up, is spacious and offers the usual amenities, but visually is not very interesting.

Entertainment at the Aladdin includes the Aladdin Theatre for the Performing Arts, a huge venue that hosts headliners, concerts, and theater productions, and the smaller CenterStage showroom.

Dining at the Aladdin is good, with something for every budget. The Aladdin Spice Market buffet is one of the best in town. Altogether there are 21 restaurants on site. They range from national chains such as P. F. Chang's to clones of celebrated eateries in other cities like Anasazi, IBIZA, Commander's Palace, and Todai, a sushi buffet. During our last visit, however, some of the restaurants were struggling (as were a number of the Desert Passage retailers) so expect a few changes in the line-up.

The Aladdin targets the Southwestern United States, European, Middle Eastern, and Asian markets as well as convention and business visitors.

Arizona Charlie's Boulder and Decatur (www.arizonacharlies.com)

Patronized primarily by locals, Arizona Charlie's are working person's casinos with a Southwestern ranch flavor. Everything is informal, a sort of shirtsleeves place. And it's busy. There is an energy, a three-ring circus feel of much going on at once—lots of slots, some table games, a sports book, burgers and beer, and a lounge that often features big-name (OK, medium-name) entertainment. The hotel rooms are passable, but the real reason to patronize Arizona Charlie's is the video poker—they're among the best machines in town, and considering what town you're in, this means they're among the best machines anywhere. The original Arizona Charlie's is on Decatur, west of the Strip. The newer Arizona Charlie's Boulder is situated on the Boulder Highway.

Bally's   (www.ballyslv.com)

A complete resort, Bally's is blessed with exceptional restaurants, one of the better buffets in Las Vegas, and a groundbreaking Sunday champagne brunch. Entertainment likewise is top-quality, with an outstanding production show, *Jubilee!* Guest rooms are large and comfortable, and the hotel, although quite spread out, is easy to navigate. Amenities include a health club and spa and a large, diversified shopping arcade.

The casino is immense, open, and elegantly modern—sophisticated in a formal, understated way, like a tuxedo. Active without being claustrophobic, and classy without being stiff, Bally's captures the style of Continental casinos without sacrificing American informality.

Bally's caters to meetings and conventions and is one of the few hotels where you will not feel out of place in a business suit. Guests are frequently under age 40 here and come from all over, but particularly Southern California, Chicago, and elsewhere in the Midwest. Bally's also has a loyal Spanish-speaking clientele.

Demonstrating legitimate concern about the traffic congestion on the Strip, Bally's joined with the MGM Grand in constructing a monorail that was the first link in the Las Vegas Monorail line. Subsequently, the monorail was extended north along the Strip all the way to the Sahara, with a loop over to the Las Vegas Convention Center and the Las Vegas Hilton. In a separate project, Bally's has built a series of moving walkways to transport guests from Las Vegas Boulevard into the casino. In a Las Vegas first, Bally's also offers moving walkways *out* of the casino. Maybe this is the only way, short of a forklift, that Bally's could get the bulk loaders out of the buffet.

Barbary Coast   (www.coastcasino.com)

The Barbary Coast is an old-fashioned casino for real gamblers. Appointed in dark wood embellished with murals in stained glass, this small hotel-casino serves a loyal clientele of locals and serious gamblers. With the feel of an exclusive and tasteful gentleman's club, the Barbary Coast's offerings are straightforward and simple. Table games still reign supreme in the casino, and its two gourmet restaurants, Michael's and Drai's, are regarded by many locals as the most dependable in town. There is no showroom, no swimming pool, no sauna or whirlpool, and most of the 200 hotel rooms (decorated in a San Francisco-turn-of-the-century style) are reserved for regular customers. The Barbary Coast is centrally located if you're on foot, but just about the worst hotel on the Strip to get into and out of by car.

Bellagio   (www.bellagio.com)

It's no secret that Steve Wynn established a new standard for Las Vegas hotel-casinos when he opened the Mirage in 1989. While it's doubtful that Wynn foresaw the impact the Mirage would have on Las Vegas, it's certain that he relishes his role as an instrument of change. Like an author trying to build on the success of an earlier work, Wynn took another shot at bumping up the standard in 1999. The vehicle for Wynn's aspirations this time was the Bellagio, on the site of the old Dunes hotel and golf course. Quite simply, Wynn intended for it to be the best hotel in the world, a hotel intended to rewrite the concept of hospitality. In 2000, however, in a move that took everyone by surprise, Wynn sold the Bellagio, along with his other casino properties, to MGM Grand for $6.4 billion in cash. Wynn's latest attempt to rock the Las Vegas status quo is Wynn Las Vegas, opening in 2005 on the site of the venerable Desert Inn. For now, though, back to the Bellagio.

With its main entrance off the Strip just south of Flamingo Road, the Bellagio is inspired by an Italian village overlooking Lake Como in the sub-Alpine north of Italy. The facade of the Bellagio will remind you somewhat of the themed architecture Wynn employed at T. I., only this time it's provincial Italian instead of Caribbean. The Bellagio village is arrayed along the west and north sides of a man-made lake, where dancing fountains provide allure and spectacle, albeit more dignified than the Mirage's exploding volcano or T. I.'s buccaneer carnage.

Rising behind the village facade in a gentle curve is the 3,925-room hotel, complete with casino, restaurants, shopping complex, spa, and pool. Imported marble is featured throughout, even in the guest rooms and suites, as are original art, traditionally styled furnishings, and European antiques. Guest rooms and meeting rooms also feature large picture windows affording views of lushly landscaped grounds and formal gardens.

Surprisingly, the Italian village theme of Bellagio's lakefront facade is largely abandoned in the hotel's interior. Though a masterpiece of integrated colors, textures, and sightlines, the interior design reflects no strong sense of theme. In two steps, passing indoors, you go from a provincial village on a very human scale to a monumentally grand interior with proportions reminiscent of national libraries. You've heard it's lovely, and naturally it is, but somehow in a very different way than you might have anticipated. The vast spaces are exceedingly tasteful and unquestionably sophisticated, yet they fail to evoke the fun, whimsy, and curiosity so intrinsic to the Mirage and T. I.

Perhaps because Las Vegas has conditioned us to a plastic, carnival sort of stimulation, entering the Bellagio is like stepping from the midway into the basilica. The surroundings impress but do not engage our emotions—except, of course, for the art, and that is exactly the point. Seen as a rich, neutral backdrop for the extraordinary works of art displayed throughout Bellagio, the lapse of thematic continuity is understandable. No theme could compete, and none should.

Truly the art is everywhere, even on the ceiling of the registration lobby, where a vibrantly colorful blown glass piece by Dale Chihuly hangs. Some wonderful works are showcased in the Bellagio's restaurants. Thirteen original Picassos, for example, are on exhibit in the restaurant of the same name.

Architecturally, Bellagio's most creative and interesting spaces are found in its signature conservatory and botanical gardens (where the flowers and plants are changed regularly) and in its restaurants. If you spend time at the Bellagio, visit each of the restaurants for a moment, if only to take in their stunning design. All Bellagio's restaurants, including a Las Vegas branch of Le Cirque, feature panoramic views. Some offer both indoor and outdoor dining experiences. In addition to the restaurants, Bellagio serves one of Las Vegas's best—and not unexpectedly one of the city's most expensive—buffets. With the exception of the buffet and coffee shop, Bellagio's restaurants require reservations, preferably made a month to six weeks before you leave home.

The Bellagio's showroom hosts a production of the justly acclaimed *Cirque du Soleil.* Though terribly expensive, the show is *Cirque's* most challenging production yet, featuring a one-of-a-kind set that transforms seamlessly from hard surface to water. Like Bellagio itself, the *Cirque* production *"O"* (from the pronunciation of the French word *eau* for water) lacks the essential humor and humanness of *Cirque's Mystere* at T. I., but is nonetheless heartrendingly beautiful.

Meant to be luxurious, the Bellagio seeks to establish itself as the prestige address of Las Vegas. Retailers in the shopping venue include Chanel, Hermes, Tiffany, Gucci, and Fred Leighton. Rates for guest rooms and suites are among the highest ever seen on the Strip, and its purported target market includes high rollers and discriminating business travelers who often eschew gaming properties. It's hard, however, to discuss exclusivity and personal service in the same breath with 3,000 rooms. Also, there's a lot of both new and old competition for the upscale market, including Caesars, the Venetian, and Mandalay Bay, to name a few. What's more, Bellagio guests do not have to look far to make comparisons: All north-facing guest rooms peer directly down on the stunning pool complex at Caesars Palace.

Room rates have bounced all over the place in recent years and in the future may bounce to a level that you find acceptable. If you stay at the Bellagio you will find the same basic informality typical of the rest of the Strip, and, surprisingly, you will encounter in the hotel more people like you than super rich. Expressed more directly, Bellagio is a friendly place to stay and gamble and not at all pretentious. I did have a funny experience, however, in one of its retail shops. For three days I passed the same men's clothing shop and never saw a soul in it. Suspecting that it was being avoided because of the Bellagio's reputation for expensive boutique shopping, I ventured in. As a test I chose a cotton shirt-jacket almost identical in appearance to one I had seen in a Banana Republic catalog for $68. Not finding a price tag, I inquired of the helpful salesperson and was informed that this garment sold for $1,490. When I laughed out loud, he explained in all seriousness that the shirt was made in Italy. Indeed, and no doubt hand-delivered via the Concorde!

Boardwalk   (www.hiboardwalk.com)

The Boardwalk, though completely upgraded, remains a modest casino by Las Vegas standards. Blessed with a good location next to the Monte Carlo, the Boardwalk is a jumping-off place for guests heading to more imposing surroundings up and down the Strip. Acquired in 1994 by Holiday Inn, the casino was expanded and rebuilt from scratch with a light, airy, Coney Island–boardwalk theme. In 1998, the Boardwalk was bought by Mirage, and in summer 2000 was acquired by MGM Grand. Though all table games are represented, the emphasis is definitely on slots. A newish hotel tower (built while under Holiday Inn's ownership) offers guest rooms that live up to the Holiday Inn standard, but won't quite meet that of MGM. On the down side, at present dining is limited to counter service, a buffet, and a small coffee shop. Because the only entrance to the Boardwalk is via the Strip, auto accessibility is also a problem. Owing to the former Holiday Inn connection, guests at the Boardwalk run the gamut.

Boulder Station   (www.boulderstation.com)

Boulder Station is a clone of Palace Station, sharing its railroad theme and emphasis on good food and lounge entertainment. Located on Boulder Highway not far from the Arizona Charlie's Boulder, Boulder Station features a roomy casino with a Western town motif (more in the image of turn-of-the-century Denver than of Dodge City). Tastefully done, with much attention to detail, the casino includes one of the nicest sports books in Las Vegas. Thirty-three big-screen, high-resolution monitors make the Boulder Station sports book a superb place for spectators. Like its sister properties, Boulder Station is an oasis for the hungry, with a great buffet, several good full-service restaurants, and possibly the best selection of fast food found in any casino. Guest rooms in the 300-room hotel tower are modest but comfortable, with good views. There is a swimming pool, but it is small and stark. Clientele consists primarily of locals and Southern Californians.

Comparing Boulder Station to Palace Station, we like the casino much better at Boulder Station but prefer the guest rooms at Palace Station's tower. The buffets and restaurants run pretty much a dead heat, but Boulder Station is less crowded.

Bourbon Street   (www.bourbonstreethotel.com)

Bourbon Street is located a block east of the Strip on Flamingo. Known locally as an "overflow" joint, Bourbon Street offers a small casino, a lounge, a totally bizarre lineup on live entertainment, a coffee-shop-quality restaurant, and inexpensive guest rooms within easy walking distance of the Strip.

Caesars Palace   (www.caesars.com)

Of Las Vegas's theme hotels and casinos, Caesars Palace was the first to fully realize its potential. As an exercise in whimsical fantasy and excess, Caesars' Roman theme has been executed with astounding artistry and attention to detail. Creating an atmosphere of informality in surroundings too pretentious to believe is hard to pull off, but that is exactly what Caesars Palace has done. Somehow the vaulted ceilings, classic statuary, and graceful arches accommodate the clanking of coins and the activity of the pits. Gambling at Caesars feels a little like pitching horseshoes in the Supreme Court, but, incredibly, it works.

Caesars Palace provides three spacious and luxurious casinos, excellent restaurants, beautiful landscaping, top celebrity entertainment, exquisite guest rooms, and all of the services and amenities of a world-class resort. The adjoining Forum Shops, opened in 1992 and expanded in 1997 and again in 2004, give Caesars Palace the distinction of offering one of the most unique themed shopping complexes in the United States.

In 2003, Caesars finished a complete renovation and face-lift of its original hotel towers. The year 2004 saw the opening of the Roman Plaza, a shopping, dining, and entertainment venue reaching from Caesars' new Flamingo Road entrance to the hotel lobby and casino. A 26-story luxury hotel tower opening in 2005 will bring Caesars' total room count to 3,370. Besides nine-foot ceilings, the new tower rooms will feature spa tubs and televisions in the bathrooms. Another swimming pool will be added as well to the enormous Gardens of the Gods complex. All of this is on the heels of a late-1990s expansion that included a new 29-floor hotel tower with a 20,000-square-foot health spa and fitness center. Guest rooms in the new towers (floors five and up) offer some of the best views on the Strip. Outside there is an elaborate new "Roman bath" swimming complex with four large pools and two outdoor whirlpool spas. Caesars Palace offers a broad assortment of entertainment options, from Celine Dion in the eyepopping Coliseum showroom, to live jazz at the Terraza Lounge, to modern rock and disco at Cleopatra's Barge, to silhouetted dancers and DJ-spun hip-hop at Shadow. For the less energetic, there is the daunting Forum Shops themed shopping venue.

Dining at Caesars has been totally revamped with the addition of 808 (Pacific Rim cuisine) and Bradley Ogden serving "fresh farm" American cuisine. Among other upscale choices are authentic Chinese and Japanese (including a sushi bar), Italian, and steak and seafood. For casual dining, there's the 24-hour Café Lago featuring both menu service and buffet, and Cypress Street Marketplace, an all-hours gourmet deli and food court.

Originally designed for high-rollers, Caesars is now enjoyed by a broad range of clientele from the East, the Midwest, and Southern California. Popular with Asian and Hispanic visitors, Caesars also hosts meetings and caters to business travelers.

California   (www.thecal.com)

The California is a pleasant, downtown hotel-casino with excellent, moderately priced restaurants and a largely Hawaiian and Filipino clientele. It is a friendly, mellow place to stay or gamble—unpretentious, and certainly comfortable. The casino rambles but, like most downtown casinos, does not allow much elbowroom. The decor is subdued and tasteful, with wood paneling and trim. The shops, menus, and services work to make visiting Pacific Islanders feel as much at home as visitors from Kansas City or Tampa. While some hotel-casinos are spectacles or happenings, the California is simply a nice, relaxed place to spend some time.

Cannery

Four miles north of downtown on Craig Road, the Cannery opened in 2002 and expanded in 2004 with the usual locals' formula: big casino, small hotel. The theme has nothing to do with Steinbeck or fish, though the industrial, 1940s-style structure of corrugated metal and steal beams would be right at home on Cannery Row. Instead, produce, specifically vegetables and fruit, take center stage with murals and paintings of colossal berries, apples, and veggies. Even the red, patterned carpet is festooned with oranges, apples, and pears.

The roomy, uncluttered casino is roughly circular, surrounding a slightly elevated lounge decorated with World War II–era, Betty Grable–style pin-ups. Restaurants, including a good Mexican eatery, a steakhouse, fast-food court, and a respectable buffet, are arrayed around the periphery. For entertainment, a 14-screen movie theater opens in 2005.

Guest rooms are smallish, with oak-finish furniture, and brightly colored soft goods. Views from guest-room windows are about as uninspiring as it gets.

Casino Royale   (www.casinoroyalehotel.com)

Located across the Strip from the Mirage, the diminutive Casino Royale has about 150 guest rooms. Small, accessible, and unpretentious, Casino Royale provides bargain lodging in the Strip's high-rent district. While the crowded and slot-heavy casino will make downtown gamblers feel right at home, the Casino Royale's newest feature is its second-floor Outback Steakhouse. The property's clientele runs the gamut from tour groups to convention-goers on a tight budget to folks who could not get rooms at other hotels on the block.

Castaways

Closed in January 2004, the Castaways was purchased at a foreclosure sale by casino veteran Randy Miller and partners and expected to reopen before the end of 2004.

Circus Circus   (www.circuscircus.com)

Circus Circus was the first hotel on the Strip to actively pursue family trade. Children, young adults, retirees, and the novice (or modest) gambler are welcome here. The labyrinthine casino has low ceilings and is frenetic, loud, and always busy. On a positive note, it was redecorated in lighter colors in 1998, and is now a much more pleasant place to gamble. Dollar blackjack and nickel slots abound. The circus theme, both exciting and wholesome at the same time, is extended to every conceivable detail of the hotel's physical space and operation. Entertainment consists of live, top-quality circus acts (free) and a games midway.

Circus Circus has a very good steak house (the only escape from the circus theme); a huge, inexpensive buffet; an RV park; and a monorail shuttle that connects the property's two main buildings. And, to give credit for great innovation, Circus Circus was the first casino to set aside a nonsmoking gaming area. In 1993, Circus Circus launched what is now the Adventuredome, formerly Grand Slam Canyon, a desert canyon–themed amusement park totally enclosed in a giant pink dome. Here guests can enjoy a roller coaster, a flume ride, robotic dinosaurs, and more. A detailed description of Adventuredome can be found in Part Five, "Shopping and Seeing the Sights," on page 413.

In 1997, Circus Circus opened a hotel tower as well as a shopping and restaurant arcade adjoining Adventuredome. The arcade restaurants provide Circus Circus with much-needed alternatives to the steak house and the buffet.

El Cortez   (www.elcortezhotelcasino.com)

Several blocks east of the central downtown casino area, El Cortez caters to seniors, motor-coach tours, and blue-collar locals. The large, rambling casino is congested and bustling; the slots are the major draw. The oldest original casino in Las Vegas, El Cortez has the aesthetic appeal of a garment factory, with narrow aisles, low ceilings, and slot machines packed into every conceivable crevice. Food and drink are bargains, however, and the loose slots give patrons a lot of play for their money. Also, there is considerable Las Vegas history in El Cortez; one section of the original building appears just as it did when the casino opened in 1941. Guest rooms at El Cortez are quite nice, and an exceptional value.

Excalibur   (www.excaliburcasino.com)

The Excalibur is owned by Mandalay Resort Group (formerly Circus Circus Enterprises) and is designed to attract an upscale family business. By combining a Knights of the Round Table theme, restaurants with giant portions, family-oriented entertainment, and moderate costs, the Excalibur "packs 'em in," especially on weekends. A Las Vegas rendition of a medieval realm, the Excalibur is oversized, garish, and more in the image of K-mart than of King Arthur.

The Excalibur's restaurants and shops are part of a medieval village theme area on the top floor of three levels. On the lower floor is a midway-type games arcade, the Excalibur's showroom (where jousting tournaments are featured), and a now-primitive motion simulator (it was the Wrst virtual ride in Las Vegas, and it's never been upgraded). The cavernous middle level contains the casino, a roomy and festive place with a

1950s art deco decor, meant no doubt to approximate the best in Dark Ages interior design. The atmosphere is supposed to be courtly and regal but has more the feel of an aircraft hangar decorated by Ozzie and Harriet.

The Excalibur is the sixth-largest hotel in the world and the fifth-largest in Las Vegas, and it certainly features the world's largest hotel parking lot (so far removed from the entrance that trams are dispatched to haul in the patrons). If you can get past the parking lot commute, the plastic execution of its medieval theme, the fact that most guest rooms have showers only (no tubs), and you do not object to joining the masses, there is good value to be had at the Excalibur. The food is good and economically priced, as is the entertainment. The staff is friendly and accommodating, and you won't go deaf or blind, or become claustrophobic, in the casino. A spa and workout facility round out Excalibur's product mix. If you need a change of pace, a covered walkway connects the Excalibur with the Luxor next door, pedestrian bridges provide direct access to New York–New York and the Tropicana, and an overhead train runs to Luxor and Mandalay Bay.

Fiesta Henderson   (www.casinofiesta.com)

Fiesta Henderson was formerly the Reserve, an African safari–themed casino. In an effort to convert the property to a Mexican theme, its parent company, Station Casinos, has created a most peculiar melange (even for Las Vegas). The casino, stripped of its stuffed monkeys and lions, is now southwestern/Mexican in flavor, but the guest rooms still sport the safari motif with African prints and dark-wood furniture. Located southeast of Las Vegas at the intersection of I-515 and West Lake Mead Drive, Fiesta Henderson offers a 37,000-square-foot casino, two restaurants, and three up-and-coming bars. As is the case with all Station casinos, the Fiesta Henderson caters primarily to locals.

Fiesta Rancho   (www.stationcasinos.com)

The Fiesta Rancho, which opened in 1994, was the first of two casinos to be situated at the intersection of Rancho Drive and Lake Mead Boulevard in North Las Vegas (the other is Texas Station). With 100 guest rooms and a video poker–packed, 40,000-square-foot casino (including the Spin City annex), the Fiesta features an Old Mexico theme. Entertainment includes a country dance hall. Restaurants specializing in southwestern food and steaks are the Fiesta's major draw. An excellent buffet features a mesquite grill. On Sunday there is a good Margarita Brunch. In 1997, the Fiesta finally got around to putting in a swimming pool, and in 1999, it expanded the casino and added a food court. The food court allowed them to expand the southwestern restaurant, add an oyster bar and a tequila bar (300 different margaritas, olé!), and open one of the best pizza parlors in town. Not only does the parlor serve excellent pizza, but it houses the 16-ton pipe organ rescued from the Roxy Theater in New York and restored, which a world-class organist plays every night. How's *that* for atmosphere? The Fiesta, acquired by rival Station Casinos, depends primarily on local clientele.

Fitzgeralds (www.fitzgeralds.com)

Located downtown, Fitzgeralds anchors the east end of the Glitter Gulch section of Fremont Street. After filing for bankruptcy in 2002, the hotel was purchased by Don Barden, which make him Nevada's first African American casino owner. The casino is large and compartmentalized with gold press-metal ceilings, mirrored columns, and print carpet with little Irish hats. Completely renovated, the casino has largely abandoned its signature "luck of the Irish" theme. While the new look is more consistent with the clean, polished style pioneered by the Golden Nugget, Fitzgeralds has sacrificed much of its traditional warmth and coziness.

Rooms on the upper floors of the Fitz afford some of the best views in town, and corner rooms with hot tubs are a great bargain. Recently, the Fitz added a streetside swimming pool. The Fitzgeralds's registered guests tend to be older travelers and retirees from the Midwest. In the casino, the crowd is a mixed bag of regulars and bargain hunters lured by ads for free gifts in the local visitor guides.

Flamingo (www.flamingolv.com)

Built with gangster money in the 1940s and acquired by the Hilton Hotel chain in 1970, and more recently by Caesars Entertainment, the Flamingo is a curious blend of Las Vegas hyperbole and corporate pragmatism. Once a tourist attraction in itself, this venerable hotel was the first super-resort on the Strip. Today, with its 3,642 rooms, four towers, and prime location, it is the Queen Mother of the Strip's most prestigious block, surrounded by Bally's, the Barbary Coast, the Imperial Palace, Caesars Palace, Harrah's, and the Mirage. In 1995, the Flamingo renovated its guest rooms and added a stunning central swimming and garden complex complete with rock grottoes and wildlife habitats. In 1997, the Flamingo's Strip facade was face-lifted and a large, comfortable sports book was opened in the inner casino.

Hilton, as you might expect, curbed the excesses of the colorful previous owners and transformed the Flamingo from a Las Vegas exaggeration into a very dependable chain hotel. Flashier than the Las Vegas Hilton and Bally's (its sister properties), the Flamingo is also less formal, offering an ambience comfortable to leisure and business travelers alike. The large, bustling casino retains the bright Miami pinks, magentas, and tangerines that established the Flamingo's identity more than four decades ago, but the hotel lobby, rooms, and services are standard Hilton. The Flamingo has consistent restaurants, a pretty good seafood buffet, varied showroom productions, truly creative lounge entertainment, and one of the top swimming areas in town.

Thanks to the Hilton national reservations system, the hotel's clientele comes in all colors and sizes, and from all over the country (but especially Southern California). The Flamingo actively cultivates the Japanese market and also does a strong business with tour wholesalers. Because it has one of the most diverse customer bases of any Las Vegas hotel, the Flamingo likewise has a very broad comfort zone.

Four Queens   (www.fourqueens.com)

The Four Queens, situated in the heart of downtown, offers good food, respectable hotel rooms, and a positively cheery casino. Joining its neighbor, the Golden Nugget, as a member of the "All Right to Be Bright Club," the Four Queens casino was among the first to abandon the standard brothel red in favor of a glistening, light decor offset by a tropical print carpet. The result, as at the Golden Nugget, is a gaming area that feels fun, upbeat, and clean. Loyal Four Queens hotel guests tend to be middle-aged or older and come from Southern California, Texas, Hawaii, and the Midwest. The Four Queens also caters to the motor-coach tour market. In the casino there is a mix of all ages and backgrounds. Locals love Hugo's Cellar restaurant, but the Four Queens' top-quality lounge has been closed by the property's new owner, a local slot bar operator.

Four Seasons   (www.fourseasons.com/lasvegas)

Four Seasons Hotels and Mandalay Resort Group have combined to introduce a new concept to Las Vegas: the hotel within a hotel. The Four Seasons is an exclusive, 424-room, noncasino hotel contained by the greater Mandalay Bay megaresort.

You can get to Four Seasons from within Mandalay Bay, but just barely: You walk almost behind the Mandalay Bay front desk, pass through two sets of double service doors, climb down a spiral staircase, and blunder into the Four Seasons lobby. Signs are few and small. This is the "back" entrance; Four Seasons prefers you to use the main, front, valet entrance, which is right off the Strip, a little south of Mandalay Bay's entrance.

You can access Mandalay Bay from Four Seasons by backtracking or by taking the private elevator to the casino level. You can also walk up the stairs at the Four Seasons elevator bay (the elevators are a pretty long hike from the front desk).

The lobby area has a plush feel, decorated with wood, Victorian sofas and easy chairs, a grand piano, and even a fireplace—a 1930s, New York atmosphere that's very different (and pleasingly so) from Las Vegas in the new millennium. Off the lobby is a 60-seat sitting area and a second lounge that fronts the First Floor Grill gourmet room. There's also the Verandah Café, the most exclusive coffee shop in town—giant French doors open onto the Four Seasons' private pool area, where you can also dine al fresco. The pool has lush foliage, a spa, and cabanas, which are kept cool and refreshing by misters.

Four Seasons' 424 rooms are on the 35th–39th floors of the Mandalay Bay tower. Private express elevators deliver guests to the Four Seasons' floors. Rates start at $350 for a superior king, but if you haggle a little, you can land a moderate king for less. However, it will still come at a hefty premium over Mandalay Bay's rooms, which are nearly identical. The main difference between the two standard rooms is the Four Seasons' fully stocked "private bar" (you'll pay $2.75 for a can of Coke, $4 for a pack of Lifesavers, $6 for an airline-sized bottle of liquor, and $19 for a small bottle of wine). Clear out the beverages from the mini-refrigerator and store your own drinks and snacks. Housekeepers provide turn-down service before bedtime.

Four Seasons will appeal to ultra-upscale travelers looking for a mini-oasis that insulates them from the hullabaloo of Las Vegas. But it doesn't come cheaply. You're paying for the brandness as much as the grandness, and there's plenty of better values nearby (even in the same building).

Fremont   (www.fremontcasino.com)

The Fremont is one of the landmarks of downtown Las Vegas. Acquired by the Boyd family in 1985, the Fremont offers good food, budget lodging, and a robust casino. Several years ago they redecorated and considerably brightened up the casino, which is noisy and crowded. The table games are roomily accommodated beneath a high ceiling ringed in neon, while the slots are crammed together along narrow aisles like turkeys on their way to market. Locals love the Fremont, as do Asians, Hawaiians, and the inevitable Southern Californians. The Fremont, like all Boyd properties, is friendly, informal, and comfortable.

Gold Coast   (www.goldcoastcasino.com)

The Gold Coast, a half mile west of the Strip on Flamingo, is a favorite hangout for locals. A casual inspection of the Gold Coast reveals nothing unique: No fantasy theme, no special decor or atmosphere. But the Gold Coast does pay attention to detail and has the local market wired. The Gold Coast serves one of the best breakfast specials in town, has one of the top buffets for quality and value, provides lounge entertainment at all hours of the day, offers headliners and modest production shows in its showroom, and makes sure it has the locals' favorite kind of slots. To top things off, there is also a two-screen movie complex and a huge bowling alley. Free transportation is provided throughout the day to the casino's sister property, the Barbary Coast, on the Strip.

Gold Spike   (www.goldspikehotelcasino.com)

Situated downtown and about a four-minute walk from the heart of Fremont Street, the Gold Spike is basically a slot joint. Congested, loud, and smoky, with all the ambience of a boiler room, the Gold Spike lures customers with low minimums, cheap food, and $25 rooms.

Golden Gate   (www.goldengatecasino.net)

Another downtown casino devoted primarily to slots, the Golden Gate is crowded and dingy but redeems itself in part by offering one of the best shrimp cocktail specials in Las Vegas. Incongruously, the Golden Gate has a piano player performing mellow standards. Although odd, his presence takes the edge off the ever-frenetic casino and shrimp cocktail bar. On the western end of Glitter Gulch on Fremont Street, the Golden Gate has 106 budget hotel rooms.

Golden Nugget   (www.goldennugget.com)

The undisputed flagship of the downtown hotels and one of the most meticulously maintained and managed properties in Las Vegas, the Golden Nugget is smack in the middle of Glitter Gulch. The hotel offers bright, cheery rooms with tropical decor, a first-rate showroom, plus lounge entertainment, excellent restaurants, a large pool, a first-rate spa, a shopping arcade, and a workout room. The casino is clean and breezy, with white enameled walls and white lights. The feel here is definitely upscale, though comfortable and informal. There is breathing room at the Golden Nugget, and an atmosphere that suggests a happy, more fun-filled approach to gambling. In 2003, previous owners sold the Golden Nugget to MGM Mirage 30-somethings Tim Poster and Tom Breitling. The new kids on the block immediately inked a deal with Fox for a 13-episode reality TV series called *The Casino* starring, who else, themselves!

If you stay or gamble at the Golden Nugget, you are likely to meet people from New York, Dallas, Chicago, Los Angeles, and San Diego, as well as visitors from Taiwan, Hong Kong, and Japan. Younger travelers (ages 28–39) like the Golden Nugget, as do older tourists and retirees, many of whom arrive on motor-coach tours.

Greek Isles   (www.greekislesvegas.com)

The Greek Isles is located on Convention Center Drive within five to seven minutes of the Las Vegas Convention Center by foot. Originally the Paddlewheel, it was purchased by Debbie Reynolds and completely renovated. So extensive were Debbie's improvements that she couldn't pay the mortgage and sold the place to, get this, the World Wrestling Federation (now known as World Wrestling Entertainment). WWF turned out to be (big surprise) clueless about running a hotel and sold it to the current owners, who have turned it into the Greek Isles. Operating with a small, slots-only casino, a combination Greek restaurant/coffee shop, a pool, and a designed-by-Debbie showroom with bizarrely eclectic entertainment, the property offers nice guest rooms at great rates to convention and trade-show attendees.

Green Valley Ranch   (www.greenvalleyranchresort.com)

The newest of the Station casinos, Green Valley Ranch Station is located about 15 minutes southeast of the Strip at the intersection of Green Valley Parkway and the I-215 Beltway in an upscale residential area. The property offers a 496-room hotel, a casino with 40 table games and almost 2,500 slot and video poker machines, six restaurants (including a buffet), a spa, and a 10-screen cinema complex. Like all Station casinos, Green Valley Ranch Station provides locals with high-pay slots, good dining value, an excellent slot club, and high-quality lounge entertainment.

Unlike most Station casinos, however, Green Valley Ranch is very upscale. The restaurants are trendy, featuring some of Las Vegas's best-known chefs, and the unique Whiskey Sky dance club rivals the best nightspots on the Strip. The hotel and its guest rooms are in the Spanish mission–style and are truly luxurious. The pool complex is lovely, more resembling a country club pool than that of a Las Vegas hotel. The hotel is perched on a hill overlooking the Strip. Unfortunately, few of the guest rooms enjoy the knockout view, and none have balconies.

Located within easy striking distance of Lake Mead, Hoover Dam, the Black Canyon of the Colorado, and Red Rock Canyon, Green Valley Ranch offers a super option for families and the outdoor oriented.

Hard Rock Hotel   (www.hardrockhotel.com)

Located off the Strip on Harmon near Paradise, the Hard Rock is billed as the world's first rock-and-roll hotel and casino. Like the adjoining Hard Rock Café, the 668-room hotel and domed casino are loaded to the gills with rock memorabilia and artifacts. Everywhere it's rock, rock, rock, from lounge music to the casino, which features piano-shaped roulette tables and chandeliers made from gold saxophones. The guest rooms, which offer a nice view, are surprisingly tasteful, with a Danish-modern European feel. The pool area is comfortable, nicely designed, and was recently enlarged. Other strengths include five restaurants, an upscale nightclub, and The Joint, Las Vegas's most intimate venue for live rock. The Hard Rock Hotel targets baby boomers and younger folks from Southern California as well as from the Midwest and the big Northeastern cities.

Harrah's Las Vegas   (www.harrahslasvegas.com)

Harrah's occupies the middle of the Strip's most prestigious block and is within easy walking distance of Bally's, the Flamingo, the Mirage, Caesars Palace, Paris, Bellagio, the Venetian, and T. I. Unpretentious and upbeat, Harrah's offers tasteful guest rooms as well as a beautiful show-room, a comedy club, above-average restaurants and buffet, a hot dance club, a pool, an exercise room, and a spa. The L-shaped casino is bright and roomy, and there is a feeling of lightheartedness and fun that is missing in far too many gambling halls. Best of all, the staff at Harrah's, from dealers to desk clerks, is exceptionally friendly and helpful. Though it is hard to imagine anyone not feeling comfortable at Harrah's, its clientele tends to be older visitors from the Midwest and Southern California, as well as business and convention travelers.

Harrah's elected to forego its highly successful riverboat theme for a new theme celebrating carnival and Mardi Gras. An ambitious expansion accompanied the re-theming, including a new hotel tower and a totally new facade featuring two giant gold-leaf court jesters hefting a 10-ton, 22-foot-diameter globe. The casino has been enlarged by 30% and redecorated with brightly colored confetti-patterned carpet, ceiling murals, and jazzy fiber-optic lighting. Other additions include a renovated swimming area, a new bar/restaurant with an outdoor patio, a steak house with a view of the Strip, and Carnival Court, an outdoor plaza with fountains, street entertainment and a covered amphitheater.

Horseshoe   (www.binions.com)

The Horseshoe, or more correctly Binion's Horseshoe, is one of the anchors of Glitter Gulch. The casino is large and active, with row upon row of slots clanking noisily under a suffocatingly low ceiling. The table games are less congested, occupying an extended vertical space canopied by mirrors. With an Old West theme executed in the obligatory reds and lavenders, the Horseshoe is dark, but not dark enough to slow the enthusiasm of the locals and "real gamblers" who hang out there. One of the city's top spots for poker and craps, the Horseshoe is famous for not having any maximum bet limitations. You can bet $1 million dollars on a single roll of the dice if you wish.

On the lower (basement) level is the coffee shop and what may be one of the most pleasant bars in the city; it, too, is dark but for once is paneled in rich woods. Twenty or so stories up from the cellar is the Ranch Steak House restaurant and lounge, offering a great view of the city. Also offering a great view is the Horseshoe's rooftop pool. The Horseshoe washed ashore on the banks on insolvency in 2004 and shut down for several months, something unthinkable for one of Nevada's most storied casinos. To the rescue came Harrah's, who paid off the Horseshoe's creditors and managed to get the joint open just in time for its signature World Series of Poker.

Hyatt Regency Lake Las Vegas   (www.lakelasvegas.hyatt.com)

The Hyatt Regency, along with the Ritz-Carlton and the Montelago Village Resort, are at the heart of the Lake Las Vegas golf and meeting venue 17 miles east of the Strip. The guest rooms and public spaces are decorated in a wood-, tile-, and stucco-rich Mediterranean Moroccan style that's both restful and exotic. The casino is small, almost an afterthought, but offers sweeping views of the surrounding lake and mountains. If you've ever wanted to play in a casino where you could keep an eye on the weather, this is your place. There is Japengo, an Asian fusion restaurant for fine dining, and Café Tajine, an informal café serving breakfast and lunch. There are no grand showrooms—in fact, not much entertainment in general. There are, however, excellent golf, water activities at the pool and lake, and remarkable views from the guest rooms. The Hyatt targets business travelers and small meetings, as well as golfers.

Imperial Palace   (www.imperialpalace.com)

The Imperial Palace has a large, active casino lavishly executed with mammoth chandeliers and carved beams. There is a lovely swimming and sunbathing area complete with waterfall, and a Nautilus-equipped exercise room and spa. *Legends in Concert,* one of the hottest shows in Las Vegas, plays nightly at the Imperial Palace's showroom, and the on-site auto museum is a first-rate tourist attraction in its own right. No hotel in Las Vegas has a better location than the Imperial Palace, which is situated just south of Harrah's.

Most of the guest rooms at the Imperial Palace are modern and of Holiday Inn–level quality. The food is on a par with most neighboring hotels. Imperial Palace owner Ralph Engelstad died in November of 2003. Though most Vegas watchers expected the 27-year-old resort to go on the auction block, Engelstad's plucky wife, Betty, not only decided to keep plugging away, but also ordered a major renovation. The ambitious project includes a new facade for the building, a sidewalk café, a glass-walled upscale restaurant, a pedestrian corridor for monorail passengers, and a redo of all the resort's guest rooms in a new design. It's about time that Imperial Palace rallied to meet the competition.

JW Marriott Las Vegas/Rampart Casino (www.gowestmarriott.com)

The JW Marriott Las Vegas is the Wrst of several new upscale properties to offer a Scottsdale/Palm Beach resort experience as an alternative to the madness of the Strip. Situated west of town near Red Rock Canyon, the JW Marriott Las Vegas consists of two Southwestern-style hotels built around the TPC golf course. The JW Marriott officially opened as The Resort at Summerlin in 1999, and a year or so later changed its name to The Regent Las Vegas. Marriott acquired the property in late 2001 and the name changed again. As an added twist, the classy, circular casino has yet another name, Rampart Casino (after the road on which the casino is located). The JW Marriott is operated primarily as a meeting venue with secondary emphasis on golf and the resort's exceptional spa. The casino, operated by an independent contractor, targets the local market.

Standard hotel rooms are huge at 560 square feet. In many rooms, French doors open onto a balustrade overlooking the pools and gardens (11 acres of palms and pines tower over the winding pools, waterfalls, and walkways), or better yet, the mountains to the west, a stirring alternative to the usual neon. Baths feature a whirlpool tub, separate shower, bathrobes, and telephone.

Restaurants serve Italian, continental, and beef fare. The buffet here is one of the better spreads in town. Although the lounges, including an "Irish Pub," offer live entertainment, there is no showroom. Though pricey, the JW Marriott is perfect for those who come to enjoy the beauty and recreational resources of the mountains and valleys west of Las Vegas. Only minutes away are world-class hiking, rock climbing, mountain biking, and road biking.

Key Largo Casino and Quality Inn (www.keylargocasino.com)

The Quality Inn is a great compromise property. Though small, it has all the essentials (mini-casino, restaurant, gift shop, lounge, pool). The Quality Inn offers quiet and simplicity with most of the amenities of a large resort; a wet bar and a refrigerator are standard in every room. The Quality's crowning glory is a green and extraordinarily peaceful central courtyard and pool complex. Its location permits easy access to the Strip and the airport.

Lady Luck Park Plaza Las Vegas   (www.ladylucklv.com)

The Lady Luck is located downtown a block north of Fremont Street. It offers nice rooms (or small suites) at a great price, and it has an excellent restaurant (the Burgundy Room), a large, uncomplicated casino, and a modest showroom. Not afraid to be different, the Lady Luck is one of the few casinos anywhere to have wall-sized plate-glass windows. If you are claustrophobic and looking for a casino where you won't feel cooped up, the Lady Luck might be your place. The staff is personable and the atmosphere informal. If you want variety, Glitter Gulch is a four-minute walk away. The Lady Luck appeals to a diverse clientele, including Filipinos, Asian Americans, Californians, motor-coach tourists, and locals. In 2002, the Lady Luck was sold to AMX Nevada, who announced that part of the hotel would be converted to timeshares. Stay tuned.

Las Vegas Club   (www.vegasclubcasino.net)

The Las Vegas Club is a downtown hotel-casino with a sports theme. The corridor linking the casino with the sports bar is a veritable sports museum and has dozens of vintage photos of boxing, baseball, and basketball legends. The casino itself, with its high, mirrored ceilings, is modest but feels uncrowded. It also has some of the more player-friendly blackjack rules around. If you plan on staying at the Las Vegas Club, ask for a room in the new North Tower. The food is good and consistent. The Las Vegas Club draws from Hawaii and the Midwest but also does a big business with bus groups and seniors.

Las Vegas Hilton   (www.lv-hilton.com)

Next door to the Las Vegas Convention Center, the Hilton does more meeting, trade show, and convention business than any other hotel in town. There are days at the Hilton when it's rare to see someone not wearing a convention badge. As you might expect, the Hilton is accommodating but not glitzy and provides a comfortable, neutral environment for its business clientele.

A 10- to 12-minute walk from the Strip, the Hilton operates under the valid assumption that many of its guests may never leave the hotel during their Las Vegas stay (except to go to the Convention Center). Thus the Hilton is an oasis of self-sufficiency and boasts lounges, a huge pool, an exercise room, a shopping arcade, a buffet, and a coffee shop.

The Las Vegas Hilton has some of the best restaurants in town and features enough ethnic and culinary variety to keep most guests happy. The showroom at the Hilton hosts big-name headliners. *Star Trek: The Experience,* an interactive video and virtual reality amusement center featuring a space-flight simulation ride and a 3-D theater presentation, is one of the top casino-based attractions in the city.

The casino, like the hotel itself, is huge and tastefully businesslike in its presentation but by no means formal or intimidating. The Hilton sports book is one of the largest in Las Vegas. If you can afford it, the Hilton is the most convenient place to stay in town if you are attending a trade show or convention at the Las Vegas Convention Center. If, however, you are in Las Vegas for pleasure, staying at the Hilton is like being in exile. Anywhere you go, you will need a cab, the new monorail, or your own car. If you park in one of the Hilton's far-flung, self-parking lots, it will take you as long as 15 minutes to reach your car from your guest room.

Luxor   (www.luxor.com)

The Luxor is on the Strip south of Tropicana Road next to the Excalibur. Representing Mandalay Resort Group's first serious effort to attract a more upscale, less family-oriented clientele, the Luxor is among the more tasteful of Las Vegas's themed hotels. Though originally not believed to be on a par with T. I. and the MGM Grand, the Luxor may well be the most distinguished graduate of the much-publicized hotel class of 1993. While the MGM Grand is larger and T. I. more ostentatious, the Luxor demonstrates an unmatched creativity and architectural appeal.

Rising 30 stories, the Luxor is a huge pyramid with guest rooms situated around the outside perimeter from base to apex. Guest-room hallways circumscribe a hollow core containing the world's largest atrium.

Inside the atrium, inclinators rise at a 39-degree angle from the pyramid's corners to access the guest floors. While the perspective from inside the pyramid is stunning, it is easy to get disoriented. Stories about hotel guests wandering around in search of their rooms are legion. After reviewing many complaints from readers, we seriously recommend carrying a small pocket compass.

The Luxor's main entrance is from the Strip via a massive sphinx. From the sphinx, guests are diverted into small entryways designed to resemble the interior passages of an actual pyramid. From these tunnels, guests emerge into the dramatic openness of the Luxor's towering atrium. Rising imposingly within the atrium is an ancient Egyptian city.

Proceeding straight ahead at ground level from the main entrance brings you into the casino. Open and attractive, the 100,000-square-foot casino is tasteful by any standard.

One level below the casino and the main entrance is the Luxor's main showroom. One floor above entry level, on a mezzanine of sorts, is an array of structures that reach high into the atrium. These dramatic elaborate buildings and facades transform the atrium. They are styled and themed to conjure up an Egyptian bazaar or town center. Here you'll find an attraction designed by Douglas Trumbull, creator of the *Back to the Future* ride at Universal Studios Florida, and an IMAX theater. In addition to the attractions, on this level are three restaurants, a huge electronic games arcade, and a collection of retail shops.

Flanking the pyramid are two hotel towers that were part of a $300-million expansion completed in 1997; the expansion included a new health spa and fitness center, and additional meeting and conference space.

The biggest surprise of all (to anyone who has ever stayed in a Mandalay Resort Group property) are the Luxor's large, tasteful guest rooms. Decorated in an understated Egyptian motif with custom-made furniture, the standard guest rooms are among the most nicely appointed in town. The only disappointment is that many of the guest rooms do not have tubs. In all, the Luxor offers 4,474 guest rooms, which makes it the second largest hotel in Las Vegas.

The Luxor's large, attractive pool complex, surrounded by private cabanas, desperately needs some additional plants and trees. Self-parking is not as much a problem at the Luxor as at most large properties. Valet parking is quick and efficient, however, and well worth the $1 or $2 tip. The Luxor is within a 5- to 12-minute walk of the Excalibur, the Tropicana, and the MGM Grand. A moving walkway connects the Luxor to the Excalibur and an overhead "cable liner" (a monorail propelled by a cable à la San Francisco cable cars) connects it with Mandalay Bay.

Main Street Station   (www.mainstreetcasino.com)

Situated on Main Street between Ogden and Stewart in downtown Las

Vegas, Main Street Station originally opened in 1992 as a paid-admission nighttime entertainment complex with a casino on the side. Owned and managed by an Orlando, Florida, entrepreneur with no casino experience, it took Main Street Station less than a year to go belly-up. The property was acquired several years later by Boyd Gaming, which used Main Street Station's hotel to accommodate overflow guests from the California across the street. In 1997, the Boyds reopened the casino, restaurants, and shops, adding a brew pub in the process.

The casino is one of the most unusual in town (thanks largely to the concept of the original owner), with the feel of a turn-of-the-century gentleman's club. Though not as splendid now as in its original incarnation, the casino still contains enough antiques, original art, and oddities to furnish a museum. With its refurbished guest rooms, brew pub, steak house, excellent buffet, and unusual casino, Main Street Station is both interesting and fun, adding some welcome diversity to the downtown hospitality mix.

Mandalay Bay   (www.mandalaybay.com)

Mandalay Resort Group's Mandalay Bay opened on March 1, 1999, on the site of the old Hacienda, imploded on New Year's Day 1998. It completes the Mandalay Bay "Miracle Mile," which stretches along the Strip south from Monte Carlo, bypassing New York–New York, and continuing with Excalibur and Luxor. A cable liner connects Excalibur, Luxor, and Mandalay Bay every 15 minutes, 24 hours a day (it stops at Luxor on the northbound leg only).

Mandalay Bay, with over 4,800 rooms (including the on-site Four Seasons Hotel and THEhotel), is a megaresort in the true sense of the overworked word. Within the sprawling complex are the 43-story, three-wing tower; a 12,000-seat arena; an 1,800-seat theater; a 1,700-seat concert venue; a dozen restaurants; an 11-acre water park; three large lounges; and the third-largest convention facility in Las Vegas. Mandalay Bay has Las Vegas's only actual hotel-within-a-hotel on the property: the 400-room Four Seasons. The whole schmear cost a cool billion plus. Adjoining the main casino is, yet another on-site hotel, THEhotel at Mandalay Bay, with 1,120 suites. Both the Four Seasons and THEhotel are profiled in this section under their own names.

But that's not the half of it, because Mandalay Bay isn't your standard megaresort. It's clear that the planners and designers set out to take a few risks and appeal to a young, hip, fun-seeking market—as opposed to Bellagio, which has targeted a more refined, sophisticated, older clientele. If Bellagio is the crowning culmination of the Las Vegas of the twentieth century, Mandalay Bay might be Las Vegas's first foray into the twenty-first. All the different ideas jammed into Mandalay Bay might not always add up to a cohesive whole, but so many parts of the sum are unique that you can't help being intrigued.

The signature spectacle is the four-story wine tower at Manhattan celebrity chef Charlie Palmer's restaurant, Aureole. This nearly 50-foot-tall glass-and-stainless-steel structure stores nearly 10,000 bottles of wine. Lovely, athletic women dressed all in black—spandex tights, racing gloves, hard hats—manipulate the motorized cable, one on each of the four sides, that raises them up to retrieve a selected bottle and lowers them back down to deliver it.

The China Grill Café, the bar-and-grill annex to Mandalay Bay's Oriental room, China Grill, has a centerpiece 34-seat bar, which is circled by a rubber conveyor. The belt goes round and round between the bar sitters and the open kitchen, carrying plates of "Zen Sum" appetizers.

Red Square Russian restaurant has a one-of-a-kind refrigerated walk-in showcase, open to the public, which stores 150 different varieties of vodka at 15 degrees. Drinks are served on a long bar top that has a thick strip of ice running its length (basically it keeps the bottom of the glasses chilled and provides a great medium for leaving fingerprints). Red Square also has a 16-foot-tall statue of Vladimir Lenin out front; the howl of criticism over the questionable taste of such a display prompted Mandalay to lop off Lenin's head, and the statue now has a big hole at the neck. Inside, Red Square sports a curious Communist theme, a paean to the Soviet 1930s when Joe Stalin was slaughtering his nation's civilians. Huge heroic posters of Russian intellectuals and professionals carrying shovels and pipe and automatic weapons fill the walls, and plentiful hammer-and-sickles symbolize the former Soviet Union no less than a swastika represents the Third Reich.

Rumjungle, a Polynesian dining and nightclub combo, is fronted by a huge "wall of fire": 80 small gas-fed flames surround two big flames at the entrance. The House of Blues restaurant and entertainment complex serves food (Southern style and Creole/Cajun), has the world's largest collection of Deep South folk art, as well as a strange dark bar with a crucifix theme. House of Blues also puts on a Sunday gospel brunch and holds rock and pop concerts in its 1,800-seat theater. Wolfgang Puck's Trattoria del Lupo (serving Italian fare), a Mexican restaurant, a noodle room, a coffee shop, a buffet, and ice cream and coffee counters round out the dining possibilities at Mandalay Bay. A main attraction at Mandalay Bay is Shark Reef, a 90,000-square-foot aquarium exhibit with a walk-through acrylic tunnel. The aquarium is home to about 2,000 marine species, including Nile crocodiles, moray eels, stingrays, and, of course, sharks.

The Coral Reef Lounge is one of the largest and most interesting bars in Las Vegas. Taking up a good part of an acre of the property, the Coral Reef is surrounded by lush tropical "foliage" (though fake, it's very effective) and has three distinct sitting areas: the 25-seat marble video-poker bar; the lounge itself, with a big stage and good enough acoustics that the bands can crank it up; and a wooden deck away from the main noise, where you sit amongst the virtual vegetation, rock waterfalls, and lily ponds.

Speaking of acreage, the casino is typically monumental, with plenty of elbow room between machines and tables. The race and sports book boasts the largest screen in town, which is only right, since the book is so big the screen must be seen from long distances. The 80-seat (each one an oversized, velour-covered easy chair) Turf Lounge and the large poker room are connected.

The pool area is also imaginative. The 11-acre Mandalay Beach has a lazy river, a placid pool, a beachfront café and bar, and a wedding chapel. The centerpiece, however, is a huge wave pool. The surf can be cranked up from one to eight feet, but there seems to be a little problem with the big water—it floods the sandy beach! Apparently, even machine-made seas can get too high. For the surfing lessons, the beach area is cleared so sunbathers don't get drenched.

Mandalay Bay's only weakness, until 2004 that is, was its miniscule number of shopping opportunies. This was corrected with the opening of the Mandalay Place Mall. In the pedestrian passage that connects Mandalay Bay with the Luxor, the mall features 40 boutiques and restaurants, including a superb wine shop, a bookstore with the best selection of titles on Las Vegas we've seen, and a burger joint where you can purchase a $60 hamburger.

All in all, Mandalay Bay accomplishes what every new mega-casino-hotel sets out to do—deliver an inventive and hip experience that sets a new standard for all the megajoints that follow.

MGM Grand Hotel and Casino   (www.mgmgrand.com)

When Steve Wynn opened the Mirage, he combined the amenities of a world-class resort with the excitement and visual appeal of a tourist attraction. At the Mirage, T. I., and Bellagio, however, the attraction component is rendered in terms of nonparticipatory visual spectacle: at the Mirage, an exploding volcano; at T. I., a pirate battle; and at Bellagio, dancing fountains. The attraction is peripheral, no more or no less than a powerful and eye-popping way to generate traffic for the casino.

At Kirk Kerkorian's MGM Grand, the evolutionary combination of gambling resort and attraction was carried to the next logical stage, the development of a theme park ostensibly, if not actually, on an equal footing with the casino. This elevation of a nongaming attraction to a position of prominence signaled the first significant tourism product diversification in Las Vegas since the dawn of the luxury resort hotel-casinos in the 1950s. Make no mistake, the purpose of the theme park was to funnel patrons into the casino. But the theme park offered a recreation alternative intended to attract nongamblers as well as gamblers. As it happened, however, the highly publicized theme park was pitifully designed. In 2000, after seven years of limping along, the MGM (not so) Grand Adventures park closed. Probably, in retrospect, the park served its purpose, that is, to draw attention to the MGM Grand Hotel and Casino in its opening year.

The MGM Grand claims the distinction of being both the largest hotel in the United States (with 5,034 rooms) and the world's largest casino. Within the 112-acre complex, there is a 15,200-seat special-events arena; 380,000 square feet of convention space; an enormous swimming area; four tennis courts; a health spa; and a multilevel parking facility.

There's a small casino outside the lobby of the Mansion, MGM's ultra-upscale whale digs, and a 6.6-acre pool-and-spa complex took over a chunk of the now-defunct amusement park along with the dedicated convention center. The MGM Grand is on the northeast corner of Tropicana Avenue and the Strip. The Strip entrance passes beneath a 45-foot-tall MGM Lion atop a 25-foot pedestal, all surrounded by three immense digital displays. The lion entrance leads to a domed rotunda with table games and a Rainforest Café, and from there to the MGM Grand's four larger casinos. All of the casinos are roomy and plush, with high ceilings and a comfortable feeling of openness.

A second entrance, with a porte-cochere 15 lanes wide, serves vehicular traffic from Tropicana Avenue. For all practical purposes, this is the main entrance to the MGM Grand, permitting you to go directly to the hotel lobby and its 53 check-in windows without lugging your belongings through the casinos. Just beyond the registration area is the elevator core, with 35 elevators servicing 30 guest floors.

Beyond the elevator core, a wide passageway leads toward five of the MGM Grand's eight distinct restaurants (not counting theme-park restaurants or fast food). Among the upscale restaurants are Craftsteak, offering beef and seafood; Nob Hill, serving California-style cuisine; Emeril's, offering Creole/Cajun dishes; SEABLUE, a Mediterranean tapas restaurant; Fiamma, an Italian trattoria; Grand Wok, featuring Asian specialties from a half-dozen countries; and Pearl, a Chinese restaurant. More informal dining is available at the Rainforest Café and the Studio Café. The MGM Grand's buffet (disappointing), and pizza kitchen adjoin the casinos between the porte-cochere and lion entrances. For fast food there is a food court housing McDonald's, Mamma Ilardo's, and Hamada's Oriental Express.

There are three showrooms at the MGM Grand. The 630-seat Hollywood Theater features headliners, the larger (1,700-seat) Grand Theater is home to a high-energy production show, and the La Femme Theatre is home to the saucy Frency cabaret show of the same name. Entertainment is also offered in the casino's four lounges. In addition, the MGM Grand's special-events arena can accommodate boxing, tournament tennis, rodeo, and basketball, as well as major exhibitions.

Amenities at the MGM Grand, not unexpectedly, are among the best in Las Vegas. The swimming complex is huge—23,000 square feet of pool area, with five interconnected pools graced with bridges, fountains, and waterfalls. Other highlights of the complex include a floating stream, a poolside bar, and luxury cabanas. Adjoining the swimming area are a complete health club and spa and four lighted tennis courts. For those to whom recreation means pumping quarters into a machine, there is an electronic games arcade supplemented by a "games of skill" midway. The most exotic addition to the entertainment mix is Lion Habitat, where you can watch live lions. In the transportation department, the MGM Grand is the southern terminus of the Las Vegas monorail.

A first at the MGM Grand is a youth center that provides supervised programs for children (ages 3–12) of hotel guests both day and night. Only 50 or so children can be accommodated in the center, with a maximum five-hour stay.

Guest rooms at the MGM Grand are comfortable, with large baths. Almost all of the rooms have a small sitting area positioned by a large window. Rooms on the higher floors have exceptional views. Part of the old MGM Marina Hotel was incorporated into the new MGM Grand. Rooms in the old structure have been renovated but are not comparable in size or quality to the new rooms.

Drawing from a wide cross-section of the leisure market, the MGM Grand derives the majority of its business from individual travelers and tour and travel groups, but with a rising percentage coming from trade show and convention attendees. Room rates in the $90–$160 range make the MGM Grand accessible to a broad population. Geographically, the MGM Grand targets Southern California, Phoenix, Denver, Dallas, Houston, Chicago, and the Midwest.

Mirage   (www.themirage.com)

The Mirage has had an impact on the Las Vegas tourist industry that will be felt for years to come. By challenging all the old rules and setting new standards for design, ambience, and entertainment, the Mirage precipitated the development of a class of superhotels in Las Vegas, redefining the thematic appeal and hospitality standard of hotel-casinos.

Exciting and compelling without being whimsical or silly, the Mirage has demonstrated that the public will respond enthusiastically to a well-executed concept. Blending the stateliness of marble with the exotic luxury of tropical greenery and the straightforward lines of polished bamboo, the Mirage has created a spectacular environment that artfully integrates casino, showroom, shopping, restaurants, and lounges. Both lavish and colorful, inviting and awe-inspiring, the Mirage has avoided cliché. Not designed to replicate a famous palace or be the hotel version of "Goofy Golf," the Mirage makes an original statement.

An atrium rainforest serves as a central hub from which guests can proceed to all areas of the hotel and casino. Behind the hotel's front desk, a

60-foot-long aquarium contains small sharks, stingrays, and colorful tropical fish. In the entranceway from Las Vegas Boulevard is a natural-habitat zoological display housing rare white Bengal tigers. Outside, instead of blinking neon, the Mirage has a 55-foot-tall erupting volcano that disrupts traffic on the Strip every half hour. There is also a live dolphin exhibit and a modern showroom that is among the most well-designed and technologically advanced in Las Vegas.

The restaurants at the Mirage are special, especially Kokomo's, with its seafood specialties; Renoir, a Mobil Five-star winner; and Samba, a Brazilian steakhouse. For bulk eaters, there is an excellent and affordable buffet. Illusionists Siegfried and Roy were the headliners in one of two showrooms until Roy was attacked and disabled by one of his tigers. Impressionist Danny Gans performs in the other. Amenities at the Mirage include a stunning swimming and sunning complex with waterfalls, inlets, and an interconnected series of lagoons; a stylish shopping arcade; and a spa with exercise equipment and aerobics instruction. The casino is huge and magnificently appointed, yet informal, with its tropical motif and piped-in Jimmy Buffett music. Guest rooms at the Mirage have been completely renovated and are now among the nicest in town.

Though registered guests pay premium prices (by Las Vegas standards) for the privilege of staying at the Mirage, the hotel is not an exclusive retreat of the wealthy. With its indoor jungle, live tigers and sharks, and traffic-snarling volcano, the Mirage remains one of Clark County's top tourist attractions. Whether by foot, bus, trolley, cab, or bicycle, every Las Vegas visitor makes at least one pilgrimage. The Mirage has become the Strip's melting pot and hosts the most incredible variety of humanity imaginable. Visitors wander wide-eyed through the casino at all hours of the day and night.

Monte Carlo   (www.monte-carlo.com)

The Monte Carlo opened on June 21, 1996. With 3,002 guest rooms, the Monte Carlo ranks as the tenth largest hotel in Las Vegas (and eleventh in the world). The megaresort is modeled after the Place du Casino in Monte Carlo, Monaco, with ornate arches and fountains, marble floors, and a Gothic glass registration area. If the Monte Carlo fails as a resort, the building will be a perfect place to relocate the Nevada State Capitol.

On the surface, it's yet another huge hotel in the Las Vegas Age of the Megaresort. But scratch the surface just a little and you glimpse the future of Monopoly-board Las Vegas and the gambling business in general. Monte Carlo is a joint venture between Mirage Resorts, now owned by MGM Grand (which put up the land and a small amount of cash) and Mandalay Resort Group (which put up the rest of the cash and runs the joint), two of the largest casino competitors in the world. By combining their resources, Mirage and Mandalay were able to finance, design, and construct a monumental hotel-casino in record time (15 months from start to finish) and can operate it without taxing their individual infrastructures.

The guest rooms, furnished with marble entryways and French period wall art, are mid- to upper-priced (to compete with MGM Grand). There is an elaborate swimming complex with slides, a wave pool, and a man-made stream. There is also an exceptional health and fitness center, an interesting shopping arcade, and a brewpub with live entertainment. The casino, about a football field long and similarly shaped, is capped with simulated skylights and domes. The showroom is designed especially for illusionist Lance Burton, who signed a long-term contract to perform there. Restaurants cover the usual bases, offering steak, Italian, and Asian specialties, with the brewpub thrown in for good measure.

Compared to the powerful themes of New York–New York, T. I., and the Luxor, the Monte Carlo's turn-of-the-century Monacan theme fails to stimulate much excitement or anticipation. Besides being beyond the tourist's frame of reference, the theme lacks any real visceral dimension. The word grand comes to mind, but more in the context of a federal courthouse or the New York Public Library. Simply put (and this may be a big plus), the Monte Carlo is an attractive hotel-casino as opposed to a crowd-jammed tourist attraction.

Montelago Village Resort at Lake Las Vegas (www.montelagovillage.com)

Part of the Lake Las Vegas development 17 miles east of the Strip, Montelago Village Resort took its place in 2004 alongside the Ritz-Carlton and the Hyatt Regency. An Intrawest Resort real estate property, Montelago Village brings a Mediterranean village ambience, with winding cobblestone streets, to complement the neighboring golf and meeting hotels. Specialty shops, galleries, small cafés, and restaurants line the plazas and narrow avenues. Como's Steakhouse, the flagship eatery when Monetelago Village opened, will be joined by additional restaurants during 2005. The Tuscan-inspired casino, adjacent to the village, offers the usual, plus a large number of penny, two-cent, and nickel slot machines. Tennuta, located in the casino, serves as the resort's 24-hour restaurant.

The resort offers one-, two-, and three-bedroom condominiums, all with DVDs and high-speed Internet access. Light carpets and wall colors contrast with rich burgundy upholstery and dark hardwoods in the rooms. The full kitchens offer countertop dining. Lower units provide patios, most upper units balconies. Resort amenities include a marina, a fitness center, two swimming pools, and a games room.

The New Frontier   (www.frontierlv.com)

If ever a Las Vegas hotel has been through the wringer, it's the Frontier . . . oops, make that the NEW Frontier. Though mostly forgotten, this is the hotel that essentially launched *Siegfried & Roy* in Las Vegas, the hotel with a super location smack in the middle of the Strip, and the hotel with owners, the Elardi family, who allowed the Frontier to get embroiled in a labor dispute and strike that lasted six and one-half years. In 1998, the Elardis sold the Frontier to Phil RuYn, who quickly settled the strike and christened the property the New Frontier. RuYn poured a couple million into repairs and improvements. Some, like the new roof, you probably won't notice, but others, such as the new Chinese and Italian restaurants and the addition of a Gilley's Saloon (the bar with the mechanical bull from the film Urban Cowboy), stand out proudly. However, RuYn wants to tear the whole place down and build San Francisco, a $500-million Bay Area–themed megaresort. He faces an uphill battle, though, since the designer is suing RuYn and will probably win.

In the meantime, the New Frontier stands, and may yet survive for some time. It is easily accessed from Fashion Show Drive or the Strip and is within easy walking distance of some of the best shopping in town. Through the improvements, the New Frontier has retained that unpretentious feel that has made it popular with both visitors and locals for more than 40 years.

New York–New York   (www.nynyhotelcasino.com)

When it opened in December 1996, this architecturally imaginative hotel-casino set a new standard for the realization of Las Vegas megaresort themes. It's a small joint by megaresort standards ("only" around 2,000 rooms), but the triumph is in the details. The guest rooms are in a series of distinct towers reminiscent of a mini–Big Apple skyline, including the Empire State, Chrysler, and Seagrams buildings. Though the buildings are connected, each offers a somewhat different decor and ambiance.

A half-size Statue of Liberty and a replica of Grand Central Station lead visitors to one entrance, while the Brooklyn Bridge leads to another. The interior of the property is broken into themed areas such as Greenwich Village, Wall Street, and Times Square. The casino, one of the most visually interesting in Las Vegas, looks like an elaborate movie set. Table games and slots are sandwiched between shops, restaurants, and a jumble of street facades.

The street scenes are well executed, conveying both a sense of urban style and tough grittiness. New York–New York sacrificed much of its visual impact, however, by not putting in an imitation sky. At Sunset Station, by way of contrast, the Spanish architecture is augmented significantly by vaulted ceilings, realistically lighted and painted with clouds. This sort of finishing touch could have done wonders for New York–New York.

Like its namesake, New York–New York is congested in the extreme, awash day and night with curious sightseers. There are so many people just wandering around gawking that there's little room left for hotel guests and folks who actually came to gamble. Because aisles and indoor paths are far too narrow to accommodate the crowds, New York–New York succumbs periodically to a sort of pedestrian gridlock.

Manhattan rules, however, do not apply at New York–New York: It's OK here to make eye contact and decidedly rude to shove people out of the way to get where you want to go. If you find yourself longing for the thrill of a New York cab ride, go hop on the roller coaster. New York–New York's coaster is the fourth one on the Strip, but it's the only one where you can stand on the street and hear the riders scream.

In the entertainment department, there are two showrooms, one featuring *Cirque du Soliel's Zumanity* and one hosting comedienne Rita Rudner. Lounges include a raucous Irish pub, a dueling pianos club, and a Coyote Ugly bar. Based on the movie of the same name, the bar features a platoon of dancing female bartenders with enough attitude to stop a real New Yorker dead in his tracks.

Guest rooms at New York–New York approximate the Holiday Inn standard but are somewhat disappointing for a hotel with such a strong, resonant theme. Likewise, the swimming area and health and fitness center are just average. Full-service restaurants are a little better than average, though Gallagher's Steakhouse, a real Big Apple import, can hold its own with any beef place, in or out of Las Vegas. Counter-service fast food is quite interesting, if not altogether authentic New York.

Nevada Palace   (www.nvpalace.com)

The Nevada Palace is a small, recently renovated Boulder Highway property patronized primarily by locals and by seniors who take advantage of its 168-space RV park. Pleasant, with a new pool, spa facilities, two decent restaurants, and fair room rates, the Nevada Palace is a friendly, less hectic alternative to staying downtown or on the Strip.

Orleans   (www.orleanscasino.com)

Opened in 1997, Orleans is just west of I-15 on Tropicana Avenue and owned by Coast Resorts, which also run the Barbary Coast, the Suncoast, and the Gold Coast. Marketed primarily to locals, Orleans has a New Orleans/bayou theme executed in a hulking cavern of a building. The casino is festive with bright carpets, high ceilings, a two-story replication of a French Quarter street flanking the table games, and a couple of nifty bars. Orleans has a celebrity showroom that is attracting great musical talent (The Doobie Brothers, Willie Nelson) and several restaurants that have little to do with the Louisiana theme. The buffet, which does serve Creole/Cajun dishes, has come a long way but can't quite match Louisiana standards. Upstairs, over the slots and buffet area, is a 70-lane bowling complex. In 2004, the Orleans arena the 9,000-seat facility and home to the Las Vegas Wranglers pro hockey team premiered. Two hotel towers with a total of 1,426 large guest rooms complete the package.

Orleans has expanded steadily since its first year, adding restaurants, a movie complex, more casino space, the arena, a games arcade, and a child-care center.

Palace Station   (www.palacestation.com)

Located four minutes off the Strip on West Sahara, Palace Station is a local favorite that also attracts tourists. With great lounge acts, a first-rate buffet, dependable restaurants that continuously offer amazing specials, a tower of handsome guest rooms, good prices, and a location that permits access to both downtown and the Strip in less than ten minutes, Palace Station is a standard setter for locals' casinos. Decorated in a railroad theme, the casino is large and busy and places heavy emphasis on the slots (which are supposedly loose—i.e., having a high rate of payoff). There is also first-rate lounge entertainment.

The Palms   (www.thepalmslasvegas.com)

Located west of the Strip on Flamingo roughly across the street from the Gold Coast, Palms opened in late 2001. Though it primarily targets a youthful local market, Palms offers the size and amenities of many Strip casinos, including a roomy 95,000-square-foot casino, a 42-story hotel tower, several entertainment venues, and a 14-screen cinema. The pool complex that is ground zero for hip, younger guests. Ghostbar, a nightclub on top of the hotel tower, along with the hip, ground-floor dance club, Rain, also attracts under-30s and keeps the Palms jumping until the wee hours, seven days a week. The restaurant line-up, equally impressive, leads off with Alize, serving gourmet French cuisine, and Nine, a steakhouse imported from Chicago. Rounding out the dining mix are an Asian fusion restaurant, a Mexican restaurant, a good buffet, a 24-hour coffee shop, and a food court. Guest rooms are solid four-star and offer exceptional views of the Strip on both sides of the building through floor-to-ceiling windows.

The Palms is too far from the Strip for most guests to feel comfortable walking. For those with a car, however, the coming and going is easy, and the hotel location on West Flamingo facilitates accessing Strip casinos via alternate routes rather than joining the gridlock on Las Vegas Boulevard. Both in design and target market, the Palms is very much like the Hard Rock Hotel. You can bet that the two will compete head to head for the trend-conscious, affluent, young adult market. Older guests may feel like relics at the Palms' nightspots, but will otherwise find the property friendly, accessible, and convenient.

Paris Las Vegas   (www.paris-lv.com)

On the Strip next to Bally's and across from Bellagio, Paris trots out a French Parisian theme in much the same way New York–New York caricatures the Big Apple. Paris has its own 50-story Eiffel Tower (with a restaurant halfway up), and an Arc de Triomphe. Thrown in for good measure are the Champs Elysée, Parc Monceau, and the Paris Opera House.

Like New York–New York, Paris presents its iconography in a whimsical way, contrasting with the more realistic Venetian or the Forum Shops at Caesars Palace. The casino resides in a park-like setting roughly arrayed around the base of the Eiffel Tower, three legs of which protrude through the roof of the casino. There's no live poker at Paris, and the video-poker schedules are lackluster, but the casino offers all of the usual table games and features the only authentic French roulette game in the country.

Flanking the tower and branching off from the casino are dining and shopping venues designed to re-create Parisian and rural petit-village street scenes. Though spacious, the casino and other public areas at Paris are exceedingly busy, bombarding the senses with color, sound, and activity. While at the Venetian you have the sense of entering a grand space, at Paris the feeling is more of envelopment.

The hotel towers, with their almost 3,000 guest rooms, rise in an L shape framing the Eiffel Tower. The rooms are quite stunning, and rank along with the dining as one of Paris's most outstanding features.

Like at the Venetian, the pool complex is on the roof. The facility is spacious but rather plain and underdeveloped in comparison with the rest of the property. One of the better spas and health clubs in Las Vegas connects both to the pool area and to the hotel.

The dining scene at Paris is a work in progress, though most of the property's restaurants opened to great acclaim. The flagship restaurant, French, of course, is situated 11 stories above the Strip in the Eiffel Tower. Several other restaurants, closer to the ground, and including the buffet, also feature French cuisine. A Chinese restaurant, a "new world Caribbean," the Italian/French La Provençal, and what passes for a coffee shop and late-night restaurant round out the dining offerings. This last, called Mon Ami Gabi, serves until 2 a.m. on an outdoor terrace overlooking the Strip.

Back inside, there's the Rue de la Paix shopping venue, not as large or impressive as the Canal Shops or the Forum Shops, but offering exclusive boutique shopping. The showroom hosts headliners. Risavé, with balconies overlooking the Strip, is the happening nightspot. And, of course, if you don't mind a little waiting, you can take an elevator ride to the top of the Eiffel Tower for a knockout view of the Strip.

Plaza (www.plazahotelcasino.com)

The Plaza has the distinction of being the only hotel in Las Vegas with its own railroad station (though the passenger trains no longer run on this stretch of track). Not too long ago, the hotel was run-down and about what you would expect for a downtown property attached to a train terminal. However, the Plaza renovated its tower rooms and now offers nice accommodations at very good prices. The only downtown hotel to provide on-site tennis, the Plaza also has one of only two downtown Las Vegas showrooms featuring production shows and, periodically, live theater (invariably comedy). The property houses a domed restaurant with a view straight down the middle of Glitter Gulch and the Fremont Street Experience. The view is the main attraction here, but the food has improved as of late. If you go, reserve a table by the window.

The casino's table gaming area is dated but pleasant, with a high, dark-green ceiling punctuated by crystal chandeliers. Patrons include downtown walk-ins, attendees of small meetings and conventions, and Southern Californians.

Red Rock Station (www.redrockstation.com) Opens late 2005

The newest of the Station casinos, Red Rock Station opens its doors in late 2005 or early 2006. The 400-room hotel and casino will be situated west of the Strip, five miles from the entrance of Red Rock Canyon and a stone's throw from several top golf courses. There will be 10 restaurants including a buffet and a gourmet room, six lounges, a 16-screen movie arcade, and a childcare center. Catering primarily to locals, the 87,000-square-foot casino will include 2,700 slot/video poker machine and 60 table games, an ultramodern sports book, a poker room, and a bingo parlor. The hotel rooms will afford excellent views of the nearby Spring Mountains. Rounding out the amenities are a workout room, a full-service spa, and a three-acre pool and beach area. According to the master development plan, an adjacent shopping venue will be added later. Red Rock Station should prove to be a great choice for those wanting to take advantage of biking, hiking, horseback riding, and rock climbing at nearby Red Rock Canyon.

Rio (www.harrahs.com)

The Rio is one of Las Vegas's great treasures. Vibrantly decorated in a Latin American carnival theme, the Rio offers resort luxury at local prices. The guest rooms (all plush one-room suites) offer exceptional views and can be had for the price of a regular room at many other Las Vegas hotels. The combination of view, luxury, and price makes the Rio a great choice for couples on romantic getaways or honeymoons.

On Flamingo Road, three minutes west of the Strip, the Rio also allows easy access to downtown via I-15. With over a dozen excellent restaurants (including the only Indian restaurant in a casino), two great buffets, high-energy nightclubs, a huge shopping arcade, a workout room, and an elaborate multipool swimming area, the Rio offers exceptional quality in every respect. The Rio is a one-stop entertainment destination, with five showrooms offering everything from stand-up comedy to topless production shows to a vocal group trumpeting God and America. Festive and bright without being tacky or overdone, the enlarged casino offers a comfortable sports book.

In a phased expansion over the past eight years, the Rio has quadrupled its guest-room inventory, doubled the size of its swimming complex, beefed up its lineup of restaurants, and in the process turned into a true destination resort. Masquerade Village—a retail, restaurant, and specialty shopping venue that rings the casino—is home to the *Masquerade in the Sky*, a parade featuring floats and performers suspended from tracks high above the casino floor.

The Rio staff ranks very high in terms of hospitality, warmth, and an eagerness to please. The Rio is one of the few casinos to successfully target both locals and out-of-towners, particularly Southern Californians.

The Ritz-Carlton, Lake Las Vegas (www.ritzcarlton.com/resorts/lake_las_vegas)

Opened in early 2003, this is the first Ritz-Carlton in Nevada. The Mediterranean-themed hotel is set on Lake Las Vegas across from the Hyatt Regency (accessible by boat or gondola). Both hotels are part of the larger Lake Las Vegas hotel-golf-residential-retail development, though the Ritz-Carlton is, of course, on the ritzier side. Geared primarily to golf, spa, and corporate business, this resort area is a pleasant change from the frenetic pace of the Strip. Emphasis is placed on relaxation rather than frenzied activity. The hotel's public spaces are sumptuously comfortable without being intimidatingly ornate (even though a Florentine high tea takes place in the lobby).

The hotel's 349 guest rooms include 35 suites and 64 Club Level concierge rooms. Warm colors, premium fabrics and furnishings, and oversized marble bathrooms meet and exceed the luxurious standards established by the chain at large. A decent percentage of the rooms sport terraces or balconies with views of the lake or pool area. One arm of the hotel, modeled after the Pontevecchio bridge in Florence, spans a corner of the lake and does in fact serve as a transit across the water (reaching a future retail development zone). The upper levels of the bridge host the Club Level rooms.

The Spa Vita di Lago offers the full-court press of pampering, including a dizzying array of massages, baths, beauty treatments, and therapies.

Private spas and saunas, a state-of-the-art fitness center, and an upscale salon round out the possibilities. Resort packages are available, combining various spa regimens with local touring and excursions, golfing arrangements, or water recreation on the lake. The hotel has a sheltered pool area as well as a sand beach on the lake itself. With 33,000 square feet of reconfigureable meeting space, this property has the most meeting space per guest room of any Ritz-Carlton.

Dining options include the "elegant yet relaxed" (let's not say casual) Medici Café and Terrace, which offers Mediterranean and Italian cuisine for breakfast, lunch, dinner, and Sunday brunch. Health-oriented and "spa" cuisine can also be had poolside or in the spa. The adjacent Monte Lago Village continues the prevalent Florentine theme and decor, with shops and restaurants nestled along cobblestone streets. The Village also features a casino that is modest in size but opulent in appointments, modeled after those found in the French Riviera. Set under an Italianate bell tower and decorated to match its surroundings, the casino has the inevitable slots, plus craps, roulette, blackjack, and mini-baccarat, among other games.

Riviera   (www.theriviera.com)

Extending from the Strip halfway to Paradise Road (and the Las Vegas Convention Center), the Riviera is well positioned to accommodate both leisure and business travelers. Though not isolated, the Riviera provides so much in the way of gambling, entertainment, and amenities that many guests never feel the need to leave the property. The Riviera has more long-running shows (four) than any other hotel in Las Vegas except the Rio, and offers a highly varied entertainment mix. These include a production show, a comedy club, a striptease show, a female impersonator show, as well as celebrity entertainers and lounge acts.

While some hotels may serve better food, there are few that offer more variety to the informal diner. Guests on the move can choose from a number of fast-food restaurants in the Food Court or go for the Riviera's buffet. Upscale restaurants round out the package and supply ethnic diversity. As for amenities, the Riviera provides a spacious pool and sunbathing area, tennis courts, a shopping arcade, and a wedding chapel. Guest rooms, particularly in the towers, are more comfortable than the public areas suggest.

The casino is large (big enough for guests to get lost in on the way to the rest room) and somewhat of a maze. There is always a lot of noise and light, and a busy, unremitting flurry of activity. Walk-in traffic mixes with convention-goers, retirees on "gambling sprees," and tourists on wholesaler packages. Asians, Asian Americans, and Southern Californians also patronize the Riviera.

Sahara   (www.saharahotelandcasino.com)

The Sahara, sporting a Moroccan theme after an extensive renovation, is at the far north end of the Strip (toward downtown). A complex of buildings and towers, the Sahara offers a casino, a convention hall, two showrooms, a decent buffet, a shopping arcade, two upscale restaurants, and a swimming pool. Fronting the building along the Strip are two attractions worth noting: Speedworld, a virtual reality racecar "ride," and Speed, a roller coaster. The Sahara is a little remote for anyone who wants to walk, but if you have a car or take the Las Vegas Monorail (station on-site), it is nicely positioned in relation to the Strip, downtown, and the Convention Center.

The Sahara is comfortable, but not flashy. Guest rooms are modern, and the new casino, with its Moroccan styling, is both tasteful and visually appealing. For the most part, the Sahara caters to businesspeople attending meetings or conventions and to leisure travelers from Southern California and the Southwest.

Sam's Town   (www.samstownlv.com)

About 20 minutes east of the Strip on Boulder Highway, Sam's Town is a long, rambling set of connected buildings with an Old West mining-town motif. In addition to the hotel and casino, there are a bowling alley, a very good buffet, one of Las Vegas's better Mexican eateries, a steakhouse, a great 1950s-style diner, and two RV parks. The lounge is popular with both locals and visitors and features live country-Western music and dancing. An events center and an 18-screen movie theater were added in 2000.

Other pluses include a free-form pool, a sand volleyball court, a childcare center, and a spa. Joining the "let's be an attraction" movement, Sam's Town offers an atrium featuring plants, trees, footpaths, waterfalls, and even a "mountain." A waterfall in the atrium is the site of a free but very well done fountains-and-light show (keep your eye on the robotic wolf). Frequent customers, besides the locals, include seniors and cowboys.

San Remo   (www.sanremolasvegas.com)

The San Remo sits next door to the Tropicana and across Tropicana Avenue from the MGM Grand Hotel. Because it is close to the airport and the southern end of the Strip, the San Remo's traditional market has been business travelers as well as Southern Californians, Southwestern leisure travelers, and Japanese "package tourists."

The San Remo has a chandeliered casino, an OK restaurant, an average buffet, decent prime-rib specials, and a good sushi bar. Dark hardwood furniture contrasts pleasantly with light wallpaper and patterned accessories in the guest rooms, some of which are in need of refurbishing. A central courtyard and pool complete the package. Self parking is easy and convenient at the San Remo making it a good choice for those who want to lodge close to the action but plan to use their cars to sight-see.

Santa Fe Station   (www.stationcasinos.com)

Santa Fe Station is about 20 minutes northwest of Las Vegas, just off US 95. Like Sam's Town, the Rio, and the Suncoast, Santa Fe Station targets both locals and tourists. Acquired by Station Casinos in 2000, the name was changed from Santa Fe to Santa Fe Station. Bright and airy, with a warm Southwestern decor, Santa Fe Station is one of the more livable hotel-casinos in Las Vegas.

Santa Fe Station offers a spacious casino, a better-than-average buffet, and an all-purpose restaurant featuring steak, prime rib, and Mexican specialties. Santa Fe Station doesn't have a showroom, but live entertainment is provided in the lounge. In addition to a pool, there is a bowling alley. There is also a movie theater. Guest rooms, also decorated in a southwestern style, are nice and a good value.

Silverton   (www.silvertoncasino.com)

Southwest of Las Vegas at the Blue Diamond Road exit off I-15, Silverton opened in 1994 as Boomtown, with a nicely executed Old West mining-town theme. The casino has since removed or replaced much of the mining paraphernalia, however. The Silverton just might be the best kept secret in Las Vegas. Its newly remodeled guest rooms feature dark hardwood furniture, leather couches, pillow-top matresses, and tile bathrooms. Thick drapes and good soundproofing insulate the rooms from nearby highway noise. At rack rates of about $50, Silverton hotel rooms are among the best values going.

As concerns dining, the Twin Creeks Steakhouse can hold its own with any chophouse in town, and the 24-hour Sundance Grill, aside from serving excellent food, is a gorgeous room, reminiscent in décor of the celebrity chef restaurants at Bellagio or Mandalay Bay. On the quirky side is the Shady Grove Lounge, with a 1967 Airstream trailer and a couple of bowling lanes worked into the theme. There's also an excellent buffet. The comfy Hideaway showroom features celebrity bands and headliners, and good lounge entertainment is a Silverton's tradition.

In 2004, the casino was doubled in size and designed around $5 million worth of freshwater and saltwater aquariums. And speaking of fish, an adjacent retail development includes a 145,000-square foot Pro Bass Shops Outdoor World mega-store with an indoor archery, a putting range, and a driving range.

Ten minutes from the Strip, Silverton is in a great position to snag Southern Californians. Silverton also targets the RV crowd with a large, full-service RV park.

Stardust   (www.stardustlv.com)

On the Strip at the intersection with Convention Center Drive, the Stardust caters to the tour and travel market, meeting and trade-show attendees, and locals. With a location that affords easy access to the Riviera and Circus Circus, the Stardust is well placed for Strip action and is about a 15-minute walk from the Las Vegas Convention Center. A high-rise tower with handsome guest rooms has doubled the number of rooms available at the Stardust, while new meeting facilities have elevated the property's status with business travelers. Amenities include a shopping arcade and a heated pool. The Stardust has consistent, high-quality restaurants such as William B's, which features some of Las Vegas's better prime rib.

The lounge entertainment is better than average at the Stardust, and Wayne Newton signed a contract with the Stardust guaranteeing he will perform there exclusively. The casino was renovated to the tune of $24 million in 1999 and is much more livable but just as spread out as ever.

Stratosphere (www.stratlv.com)

The Stratosphere Tower is the brainchild of Vegas World owner Bob Stupak, the quintessential Las Vegas maverick casino owner. Vegas World had been one of the last sole-proprietorship casinos in Las Vegas, but the lack of financing to complete the tower forced Stupak to sell 75% of his company to Lyle Berman and Grand Casinos of Minnesota and Mississippi (not to be confused with Las Vegas's MGM Grand). Stupak's original idea was to attach a tourist attraction (the tower) to Vegas World. Berman, however, ultimately realized that such a juxtaposition would be like locating the Washington Monument next to a Texaco station and insisted that Vegas World be bulldozed. The resort that has risen from the rubble happily combines Stupak's vision with Berman's taste.

The Stratosphere hotel-casino opened on April 30, 1996, and Las Vegas hasn't been the same since. At 1,149 feet, Stratosphere Tower is the tallest building west of the Mississippi—taller than the Eiffel Tower (the real one). It houses indoor and outdoor observation decks, a 360-seat revolving restaurant, and meeting rooms. The 360-degree view is breathtaking day (a life-size relief map of Las Vegas Valley and beyond) and night (the shimmering blaze of a billion bulbs).

Also at the top (hang on to your hats!) are three thrill rides. The world's highest roller coaster is also the world's slowest and shortest. It's a yawner, barely worth the 50 seconds of your time. However, if you try it, be sure to step out to the right! New to the lineup is a vacuous ride that essentially lifts the gondola-thingy you're in over the side of the tower and pretends it's going to drop you. The third ride, however, a gravity/thrill experience called The Big Shot, is a monster: It rockets you straight up the tower's needle with a force of four Gs, then drops you back down with no Gs. And it all happens, mind you, at 1,000 feet in the air!

A second construction phase, including another 1,000 rooms and a new pool area, were completed in 2001.

Suncoast   (www.suncoastcasinos.com)

Like most of the Coast casinos, Suncoast is designed to attract locals. Located west of Las Vegas in Summerlin near some of the area's best golf courses, Suncoast offers high-return slots and video poker, a surprisingly good (for a locals joint) fitness center, 64 lanes of bowling, and a 16-screen movie complex. In the food department, there's a decent buffet as well as restaurants serving Italian, Mexican, and big wads of meat respectively. The casino is open and uncrowded, rendered in a Southwestmission style. A showroom that features name bands, a new pool, and a childcare center round out the offerings. For its size (440 rooms/78,000-square-foot casino), the Suncoast offers a pretty amazing array of attractions and amenities. Perhaps the Suncoast's most extraordinary yet unheralded feature is the breathtaking view of the mountains to the west as seen through floor-to-ceiling windows in every guest room. And speaking of mountains, the Suncoast is a perfect location for anyone interested in hiking, rock climbing, mountain biking, or road biking in the nearby cayons and valleys.

Sunset Station   (www.sunsetstation.com)

Sunset Station opened in June 1997, the fourth Station Casino (after Palace, Boulder, and Texas), just off I-215 in far southeast Las Vegas Valley about a 20-minute drive from the Strip (depending on traffic). Known as the "Henderson highrise," the 21-story tower presides over a fast-growing residential neighborhood; with 457 rooms, Sunset is large for a locals' casino. It's also the classiest, most highly themed and architecturally realized of the Station Casinos, decorated to replicate a Spanish village. The casino's centerpiece is the Gaudi Bar; with its tiled floors and stained-glass ceilings, it reflects the eccentric vision of Barcelona architect Antoni Gaudi.

Station's formula of good food, lounge entertainment and movies, childcare, and extra touches prevails. It boasts a steakhouse, Italian, Mexican, and seafood (with oyster bar) restaurants, the Feast Buffet and 24-hour coffee shop, a microbrewery, and fast food galore. There's also a Kid's Quest childcare center, the 500-seat Club Madrid lounge, and a 13-screen movie theater. The extras include a pool and plaza area featuring two sandy volleyball courts, a badminton court, and a 5,000-seat outdoor concert amphitheater (Alice Cooper performed there recently).

All in all, it's worth staying in the slightly oversized and moderately priced rooms at Sunset Station if you're visiting friends and relatives in Henderson or want, for some reason, to be close to Hoover Dam, Lake Mead, or Valley of Fire.

Terrible's
(www.terribleherbst.com/ett-gaming/casino-hotel)

Terrible's is the product of a well-done $65 million renovation of the dilapidated old Continental Hotel and Casino. Located a couple of blocks off the Strip at the intersection of Paradise and Flamingo Roads, Terrible's offers excellent value with totally refurbished guest rooms, a good buffet, and a casino that's clean, bright, and busy. Terrible, by the way, is a person, Terrible Herbst to be exact. The Herbst family is well known locally for their gas stations and for auto racing. Terrible's targets locals but is a good choice, by virtue of its location and easy parking, for anyone who has a car and intends to use it.

Texas Station   (www.stationcasinos.com)

Owned by Station Casinos, which also owns and operates Palace Station, Sunset Station, Boulder Station, and the two Fiestas, Texas Station has a single-story full-service casino with 91,000 square feet of gaming space, decorated with black carpet sporting cowboy designs such as gold, boots, ropes, revolvers, covered wagons, etc. The atmosphere is contemporary Western, a subtle blend of Texas ranch culture and Spanish architecture. This property offers seven restaurants, one of Las Vegas's better buffets, two bars, a dance hall called the Armadillo Honky Tonk, a 60-lane bowling center, childcare facilities, and a 12-screen theater showing first-run movies. Texas Station caters to locals and cowboys and is at the intersection of Rancho Drive and Lake Mead Boulevard in North Las Vegas.

THEhotel at Mandalay Bay   (www.mandalaybay.com)

Like the Four Seasons at Mandalay Bay, THEhotel is another "hotel-within-a-hotel." Situated on the west side of the main casino, THEhotel can be accessed through a connecting corridor or through a dedicated porte-cochere. While the Four Seasons is designed to blend with and reinforce the general style of Mandalay Bay, THEhotel, very much a boutique property, offers a starkly contrasting experience. THEhotel is clubby and masculine with rich dark woods, modern furnishings, and a style that mixes empire, art deco, and Asian influences. The public areas achieve a feeling of both spaciousness and intimacy, while the suites are cozy in the way of a private library or reading room. Elegant and sophisticated, descriptors often applied indiscriminately, fit THEhotel perfectly.

Though multi-bedroom suites are available, the standard one-bedroom suite at 725 square feet is the largest of any hotel in Las Vegas. The suites offer a separate sitting room with slate-colored walls and oversized upholstered couch and side chair. These are complemented by a polished-wood contemporary desk and side tables. The overall effect is totally congruent and extremely striking. A large flatplasma television, a wet bar, and simple, yet arresting, Asian wall art complete the picture. The bedroom is more conventional with earth-tone soft goods, but includes a dark-colored accent wall behind the bed. The bathrooms, appointed in granite, marble, and chrome, are large with separate glass-enclosed tub and shower. Because THEhotel targets business travelers, all suites are equipped with high-speed Internet connections and a fax/printer/copier.

On the top, 43rd floor of the hotel tower is THErestaurant (no kidding), offering fine dining and panoramic views of the Strip. Adjoining THErestaurant is a lounge. An informal 24-hour restaurant on the ground floor rounds out the dining options. Also on the ground floor is THEbar. One floor up is a full-service spa and a fitness center.

T. I.   (www.treasureisland.com)

In 2004, Treasure Island became the hipper T. I. It's one of three megacasino resorts that opened during the fall of 1993. On the southwest corner of the Strip at Spring Mountain Road next door to the Mirage, T. I. is Caribbean in style. Management thought the original buccaneer theme was juvenile and Disney-esque, and further believed that it was responsible for luring thousands of unwanted families with children to the resort. So down came all the pirate hats, sabres, skulls, and crossed bones, and all the other grisly skeletal parts that were the—shall we say—backbone, of the joint's decor. The new adult version is fine, but a little dull by comparison. The only vestige of the buccaneer days is the streetside battle where pirates now fight very adult, full-bosomed "sirens" instead of the English Navy. As you would expect, all the cleavage and leg ensures about twice as many kids in the audience. Though similar in amenities and services, T. I. targets a younger, more middle-class family clientele than the Mirage.

T. I. is an attraction as well as a hotel and casino. Crossing the Sirens' Cove from the Strip on a plank bridge, guests enter a seaside village. Colorful and detailed, the village (which serves as the main entrance to the hotel and casino) is sandwiched between rocky cliffs and landscaped with palms. Every 90 minutes a pirate ship sails into the harbor and engages the sirens in a raging battle (firing over the heads of tourists on the bridge). Exceptional special effects, pyrotechnics, and a cast of almost two dozen pirates and sirens per show ensure that any Strip traffic not snarled by the Mirage's volcano (next door) will most certainly be stopped dead by T. I.'s battle of the sexes. The pirates are always defeated, of course, but have a lot more fun losing to the sirens than they ever did beating the British.

Passing through the main sally port, you enter the commercial and residential area of the village, with shops, restaurants, and, of course, the casino. The casino continues the old Caribbean theme, with carved panels and whitewashed, beamed ceilings over a black carpet, punctuated with fuschia, sapphire blue, and emerald green. The overall impression is one of tropical comfort: exciting, but easy on the eye and spirit. In addition to the usual slots and table games, a comfortable sports book is provided.

The main interior passageway leads to a shopping arcade, a steakhouse, and the buffet. T. I.'s most upscale restaurant is the Buccaneer Bay overlooking the Sirens' Cove. Here you can enjoy a quiet, relaxing meal while watching the sirens administer a good lap dance to the pirates before heaving them overboard. Only in America.

T. I. amenities include a beautifully landscaped swimming area with slides, waterfalls, grottoes, and tranquil pools. The Caribbean theme gives way to luxury and practicality in the well-equipped health club and spa. Larger than that of the Mirage, the facility features weight machines, free weights, a variety of aerobic workout equipment, large whirlpools, steam rooms, and saunas.

T. I. is home to the extraordinary *Cirque du Soleil*, which performs in a custom-designed 1,500-seat theater. The hottest T. I. nightspot is Tangerine with an indoor lounge and an outdoor deck where "seductive" barmaids augmented by "burlesque dancers" work the crowd into a hormonal frenzy for the DJ. For the less arousable, there's Kahunaville, a Jimmy Buffet Margaritaville clone, and Mist, a chic, alluring, intimate lounge where the music is usually too loud to permit conversation (yeah, you're right, this is an old fart talking).

Guest rooms at T. I. are situated in a Y-shaped, coral-colored tower that rises directly behind the pirate village. Decorated in soft, earth-tone colors, the rooms provide a restful retreat from the bustling casino. Additionally, the rooms feature large windows affording a good view of the Strip or (on the east side) of the mountains and sunset. The balconies that are visible in photos of T. I. are strictly decorative and cannot be accessed from the guest rooms. Self-parking is easier at T. I. than at most Strip hotels. Valet parking is fast and efficient. An elevated tram connects T. I. to the Mirage next door.

Tropicana   (www.tropicanalv.com)

At the southern end of the Strip, the Tropicana sits across Las Vegas Boulevard from the Excalibur and opposite MGM Grand on Tropicana Avenue. With its Paradise and Island Towers and 1,910 rooms, the Tropicana is the oldest of the four hotels at the intersection of the Strip and Tropicana. It offers a full range of services and amenities, including tennis, an exercise room, meeting and convention space, and a shopping arcade. The Tropicana is also home to one of Las Vegas's most celebrated swimming and sunbathing complexes. This facility, a system of lagoons and grottos em-bellished with flowing water, is less a swimming pool than a water park.

The Tropicana has four restaurants of merit that specialize, respectively, in steak and prime rib, Italian food, and Japanese teppan grill combinations. Entertainment offerings consist of a comedy club, a long-running production show, and lounge acts. The Tropicana's casino is bustling and bright, with multicolored floral carpeting and a stunning, 4,000-square-foot stained-glass canopy over the table games. Both festive and elegant, the Tropicana casino is an attraction in its own right and ranks as one of the city's more pleasant places to gamble, especially for table players.

Guest rooms in the Island Tower are furnished in an exotic, tropical bamboo motif. Guest rooms in the Paradise Tower are more conventional, with bright tropical yellow soft goods and blond furniture. Views from the upper rooms of both towers are among the best in town.

The Tropicana does a thriving business with the travel wholesalers and motor-coach tours, and also aggressively targets the Japanese and Hispanic markets. In the casino, you will find a more-youthful-than-average clientele, including a lot of guests from the nearby Excalibur enjoying the Trop's more luxurious and sophisticated style. The Tropicana's domestic market draws, not unexpectedly, from Southern California. It is particularly popular with slot players.

Tuscany (www.tuscanylasvegas.com)

Opened in 2003, the Tuscany is an Italian-themed hotel and casino located on East Flamingo between Koval and Paradise, just far enough from the Strip to make commuting on foot problematic. After years of railing against low-ceiling, noisy, claustrophobic casinos and big, hyper-themed, whimsical megaresorts, you'd think the open, sedate, and tasteful Tuscany would be the answer to a travel writer's prayer. Wrong. The Tuscany is none of the things we hate, and at least physically embodies all of the features we admire, but . . . it's B-O-R-I-N-G! Wide aisles in the casino, multiple shades of decorator beige, tasteful carpet, and shiny tile floors (also beige) combine to send you yawning back to your room (more about that in a minute). It's the quietest casino we've ever experienced by far, and there's nothing, repeat nothing, to excite you or even catch your eye.

The casino markets primarily to locals and has succeeded in pleasing them with its choice of slots and good video-poker schedules. Table games, like most everything else, are understated. As for restaurants, there's a nice Italian restaurant in the adjoining hotel, a modest buffet, a coffee shop with good 24-hour steak specials, and in the future the casino will add a food court.

Now speaking of the adjoining hotel, it's what saves the Tuscany. A beautiful exposed-beam lobby with an inviting hearth leads to a cozy lounge/showroom and the aforementioned Italian eatery. Guest rooms are large, with a plush sofa and armchair, pine-finish furniture, round dining table with chairs, wet bar, and fridge. The bath offers a separate, glass-door shower, a roomy tub, large vanity, and a private toilet enclosure. The windows are small, which is fine because there's not much of a view. Two framed prints, one of an Italian village, and the other . . . can it be? Yes, the second print is an exact copy of the first! Oh well, who notices wall art in hotel rooms anyway? Hotel parking (easy and conveniently adjoining the various guest-room buildings) coupled with comfy guest rooms, makes the Tuscany a nice place to stay and an easy place to leave when you want to go somewhere more exciting.

Venetian   (www.venetian.com)

On the site of the fabled Sands Hotel across the Strip from T. I., the Venetian is a gargantuan development constructed in two phases. The first phase, the Venetian, drawing its theme from the plazas, architecture, and canals of Venice, Italy, opened in spring 1999. The second phase, including a 1,000-guest-room tower opened in the summer of 2003. The Venetian follows the example of New York–New York, Mandalay Bay, Luxor, and Paris Las Vegas in bringing the icons of world travel to Las Vegas.

Visiting the Venetian is like taking a trip back to the artistic, architectural, and commercial center of the world in the sixteenth century. You cross a 585,000-gallon canal on the steep-pitched Rialto Bridge, shadowed by the Campanile Bell Tower, to enter the Doge's Palace. Inside, reproductions of famous frescoes, framed by 24-karat-gold molding, adorn the 65-foot domed ceiling at the casino entrance. The geometric design of the flat-marble lobby floor provides an M.C. Escher–like optical illusion that gives the sensation of climbing stairs—a unique and thoroughly delightful touch. Behind the front desk is a large illustrated map of the island city, complete with buildings, landmarks, gondolas, and ships. Characters in period costumes from the twelfth to seventeenth centuries roam the public areas, singing opera, performing mime, and jesting.

Although the Venetian claims that its bread-and-butter customers are business travelers and shoppers, it hasn't neglected to include a casino in its product mix. In fact, the Venetian casino, at 116,000 square feet, is larger than that of most Strip competitors. When the Lido Casino came on line with the completion of Phase II, the overall resort topped out at more than 200,000 square feet of casino; the MGM Grand weighs in at 175,000 square feet. The Venetian Casino is styled to resemble a Venetian palace with architecture and decor representative of the city's Renaissance era. Period frescoes on recessed ceilings over the table games depict Italian villas and palaces. The huge and stupifyingly ornate casino offers 110 table games and 2,500 slot machines. The perimeter of the casino houses a fast-food court, along with French, Italian, and Southwestern restaurants, and what could be the fanciest coffee shop in town.

Upstairs is the Grand Canal Shoppes, with 54 stores, mostly small boutiques. The Escher-like floor design continues throughout the shopping venue, with different colors and shapes providing variations on the theme. The centerpiece of the mall is the quarter-mile Grand Canal itself, enclosed by brick walls and wrought-iron fencing and cobbled with small change. Gondolas ply the waterway, steered and powered by gondoliers who serenade the four passengers in each ($13 adults, $5 children). Passing beneath arched bridges, the canal ends at a colossal reproduction of St. Marks Square. Like The Forum Shops, the Grand Canal Shoppes are arranged beneath a vaulted ceiling painted and lighted to simulate the sky.

The Venetian's 17 restaurants, most designed by well-known chefs, provide a wide range of dining environments and culinary choice. Wolfgang Puck's Postrio, Joachim Splichal's Pinot Brasserie, Emeril Lagasse's Delmonico Steakhouse, Eberhard Müller's Lutéce, Thomas Keller's Bouchon, and Kevin Wu's Royal Star are some of the culinary power-hitters represented.

An all-suite hotel, the Venetian offers guest accommodations averaging 700 square feet and divided into sleeping and adjoining sunken living areas. The living-room area contains adequate space for meetings, work, or entertaining, and is equipped with combination fax machine/copiers with a dedicated phone line. The development plan calls for two Y-shaped hotel towers, each with 3,000 suites and connected directly to the Sands Expo and Convention Center.

The five-pool swimming complex and spa area are situated on the rooftop over the shopping venue and are well insulated from the bustle of the Strip. One of the largest of its kind in the country, the ultra-upscale bi-level Canyon Ranch Spa offers fitness equipment and classes, therapies, and sauna and steam, as well as a 40-foot indoor rock-climbing wall, medical center, beauty salon, and café.

The Venetian targets the convention market with its mix of high-end business lodging, power restaurants, unique shopping, and proximity to Sands Expo and Convention Center (with 1.7 million square feet, the Sands has more convention space than the Las Vegas Convention Center). The Venetian will certainly welcome tourists and gamblers, who come mostly on the weekend, but the other five days will be monopolized by the trade-show crowds.

Westin Casuarina (www.westin.com/lasvegas)

Talk about phoenix rising. Westin acquired the old Maxim hotel, a place where business travelers reluctantly stayed when they couldn't get into Bally's, and transformed it into a high-end boutique hotel. Both the casino and showroom are modest by Las Vegas standards, and the Westin was still working out the kinks in its restaurant when we went to press, but its guest rooms are exceptionally nice. The Westin caters to business travelers, so each room is equipped with dual-line telephones, cordless phone, and high-speed Internet access by request. There is ample meeting space for small meetings and conventions. If you travel with Fido, he's welcome at the Westin (they even supply a special dog bed). Travelers with some downtime can enjoy the pool, full-service spa, and fitness center. Situated about a block from the heart of the Strip, dozens of shows and hundreds of restaurants are within easy walking distance. If you have a car, the Westin has ample parking and is easy to enter and exit. Finally, in case you're interested, a "casuarina" is a type of tree that is native to the Cayman Islands. If you want to see one, the Cayman Islands is where you'll have to go: there are no causarina trees at the Causarina.

Westward Ho   (www.westwardho.com)

A sprawling motel next to the Stardust, Westward Ho offers a slot-oriented casino decorated in the usual dark colors. There are lounge entertainment, a couple of pools, palatable but undistinguished dining, good deals on drinks and snacks, and easy foot access to a number of nearby casinos.

Wild Wild West (www.wwwesthotelcasino.com)

Located just west of the Strip at Exit 37 off I-15 at Tropicana Avenue, Wild Wild West is a small, 261-room hotel and casino that is convenient to the Strip, downtown, and the airport. Its guest rooms are very basic but clean and comfortable. For east-facing rooms especially, however, there is a lot of road noise from I-15. The casino offers mostly slots and video poker, with a few table games and a sports book thrown in to keep up appearances. There is a lounge, a 24-hour bar and restaurant serving a half-pound burger and fries for $1.99, a pool and jacuzzi, and in case you're packing a pig, a barbecue pit. The adjacent Wild Wild West Truck Plaza offers over 15 acres of paved and lighted parking, designated drop pads, security patrol, and easy access from I-15. Also available are diesel and unleaded fuel, a truck wash, convenience store, and weigh station. Wild Wild West markets to locals and truckers.

Wynn Las Vegas (www.wynnlasvegas.com)

Well, here we go again. Steve Wynn of Mirage and Bellagio fame is developing yet another cutting edge, standard-setting property on the site of the historic Desert Inn. This time around, however, the competition is savvier, better financed, and more sophisticated than the last time around. In fact, there's been so much innovation since Wynn's last big play (Bellagio) that the fabled visionary will have to come up with something truly amazing to go one up. The stakes are stupendous. The new Wynn Las Vegas, due to open in spring 2005, will cost upwards of $2.5 billion. And get this: no theme. Somewhat out of character for the man whose hotels based their identity on exploding volcanoes, pirate battles, and dancing fountains. There will be, however, an artificial "mountain" with waterfalls sculptured around several small lakes.

Wynn Las Vegas will be a 2,716-room hotel, including 350 suites. Most of the rooms will be in the sleek, gently curving, 50-story glass tower, with the remainder flanking the Desert Inn Golf Course, which will be retained. All of the tower rooms will feature floor-to-ceiling windows with views either overlooking the Strip or the golf course. Room amenities include customized plasma and LCD televisions, European linens, and high-speed, wireless Internet access.

A 2,100-seat showroom will host a production created by Wynn and *Cirque du Soleil* mastermind Franco Dragone. Leaks to the press (pun intended) suggest that the theater will project a water theme where water surrounds guests literally. Think of a clear glass theater suspended in a giant fishbowl. Another showroom will be a permanent home for *Avenue Q*, the Tony Award winner for best musical. The new $40-million theater will be built especially for the show. Wynn Las Vegas will be the only place except on Broadway where you can see *Avenue Q*.

In the dining department, Wynn Las Vegas will showcase 18 restaurants under the creative supervision of executive chef Grant MacPherson. Other features will include a 100,000-square-foot casino with a sports book, a swimming complex, a full-service spa, and an upscale shopping venue flogging brands such as Chanel, Cartier, Gaultier, Ferrari, and Maserati. If you lose your plane ticket, you can pick up a nice Ferrari convertible at the Wynn Las Vegas full-service dealership.

Definitely targeting the business traveler and convention attendees, Wynn Las Vegas will offer 200,000 square feet of meeting space, including 18 meeting rooms with full patios and views of the golf course.

Navigating the Land of the Giants

The grand hotels of Las Vegas are celebrated on television, in film, and, of course, in countless advertisements. These are the prestige properties in a town that counts more hotel rooms than any other city in the world. Located along the center and southern end of the Strip, these hyper-themed mammoths beckon with their glamour and luxury. Specifically we're talking about:

Aladdin	Bay/Four Seasons	New York–New York
Bellagio	MGM Grand	Paris Las Vegas
Caesars Palace	Mirage	T. I.
LuxorMandalay	Monte Carlo	Venetian

But can so many hotels actually mean less choice? From a certain perspective, the answer is yes. The Strip, you see, is suffering a paroxysm of homogeneity. After you've chosen your preferred icon (Statue of Liberty, Eiffel Tower, pyramid, pirate ship, volcano, etc.), you've done the heavy lifting. Aside from theme, the big new hotels are pretty much the same. First, they're all so large that walking to the self-park garage is like taking a hike. Second, there are high-quality guest rooms in all of the new properties, as well as at Caesars Palace, an older hotel that has kept pace. This is a far cry from ten years ago, say, when only a handful of hotels offered rooms comparable to what you'd find at a garden variety Hyatt or Marriott. Third, all of the megahotels are distinguished by designer restaurants, each with its big-name chef, that are too expensive for the average guest to afford. Ditto for most of the showrooms.

So let's say you're a person of average means and you want to stay in one of the new, glitzy superhotels. Location is not important to you as long as it's on the Strip. How do you choose? If you have clear preference for gondolas over pirate ships, or sphinx over lions, simply select the hotel with the theme that fires your fantasies. If, however, you're pretty much indifferent when it comes to the various themes, make your selection on the basis of price. Using the Internet, your travel agent, and the resources provided in this guide, find the colossus that offers the best deal. Stay there and venture out on foot to check all the other hotels. Believe us, once you're ensconced, having the Empire State Building outside your window instead of a statue of Caesar won't make any difference.

As it happens, there are also a number of livable, but more moderately priced, hotels mixed in among the giants, specifically:

Bally's	Casino Royale	Harrah's
Barbary Coast	Excalibur	Imperial Palace
Boardwalk	Flamingo	Tropicana

Many of these hotels were the prestige addresses of the Strip before the building boom of the past decade. They are still great places, however, and properties where you can afford to eat in the restaurants and enjoy a show. Best of all, they are located right in the heart of the action. It's cool, of course, to come home and say that you stayed at Bellagio, but you could camp at the Excalibur for a week for what a Bellagio weekend would cost.

Suite Hotels

Suites

The term *suite* in Las Vegas covers a broad range of accommodations. The vast majority of suites are studio suites consisting of a larger-than-average room with a conversation area (couch, chair, and coffee table) and a refrigerator added to the usual inventory of basic furnishings. In a one-bedroom suite the conversation area is normally in a second room separate from the sleeping area. One-bedroom suites are not necessarily larger than studio suites in terms of square footage but are more versatile. Studio and one-bedroom suites are often available in Las Vegas for about the same rate as a standard hotel room.

Larger hotels, with or without casinos, usually offer roomier, more luxurious multiroom suites. Floor plans and rates for these premium suites can be obtained for the asking from the hotel sales and marketing department.

There are some suite hotels that do not have casinos. Patronized primarily by business travelers and nongamblers, these properties offer a quiet alternative to the glitz and frenetic pace of the casino hotels. Because there is no gambling to subsidize operations, however, suites at properties without casinos are usually (but not always) more expensive than suites at hotels with casinos.

While most hotels with casinos offer suites, only the Rio, the Tuscany, THEhotel at Mandalay Bay, and the Venetian are all-suite properties. The basic studio suite is a plush, one-room affair with wet bar and sitting area but no kitchen facilities. The Rio, on Flamingo Road just west of the I-15 interchange, sometimes makes its suites available at less than $110 per night and is one of the best lodging values in town. Suites at the Venetian average about 700 square feet, divided into a sunken living room, an adjacent sleeping area, and a bathroom. The suite configuration at the Venetian is rectangular, while the suites at the Rio and Tuscany are more square in layout. In both cases the sleeping area is open to the living area. THEhotel offers suites with a sitting room and a separate bedroom.

Suite Hotels without Casinos

AmeriSuites (www.amerisuites.com)

At Paradise and Harmon, AmeriSuites offers tidy, but not luxurious, one-room suites at good prices. In addition to a small fitness center, an outdoor pool, and a few small meeting rooms, the AmeriSuites serves a complementary breakfast buffet. By taxi, the AmeriSuites is about four minutes from the Strip and five minutes from the Las Vegas Convention Center.

Alexis Park (www.alexispark.com)

The Alexis Park is the best known of the Las Vegas one- and two-room suite properties. Expensive, and therefore relatively exclusive, the Alexis offers most of the amenities of a large resort hotel, including a lovely pool, lighted tennis courts, and an exercise room. Pegasus, a continental restaurant at the Alexis, has been rated in past years by Mobil and others (though not by us) as the best gourmet restaurant in Las Vegas. Suites are upscale and plush, with a Southwestern decor. The hotel's staff is extremely friendly and not at all pretentious. Alexis Park's clientele includes executive-level business travelers and a good number of Southern California young professionals.

Crowne Plaza Holiday Inn (www.sixcontinentshotels.com)

The Crowne Plaza is four minutes by cab to both the Strip and the Las Vegas Convention Center. There is a pool and a café, and a fine selection of ethnic restaurants is within easy striking distance. Suites are mostly of the two-room variety and are nicely, but not luxuriously, appointed.

Holiday Inn Emerald Springs (www.holidayinnlasvegas.com)

The Holiday Inn, formerly the Emerald Springs Inn, two blocks east of the Strip on Flamingo Road, is a newer property offering moderately priced one- and two-room suites. Featuring pink stucco, marble, and large fountains both inside and out, the lobby, common areas, and rooms are tranquil and sedate by Las Vegas standards. The Veranda Café is the in-house coffee shop and serves a breakfast buffet. There is a lounge, heated pool, and spa.

Mardi Gras Inn Best Western   (www.mardigrasinn.com)

The Mardi Gras offers spartan suites at good rates. Quiet, with a well-manicured courtyard and a pool, the Mardi Gras is only a short walk from the Las Vegas Convention Center. There is a coffee shop on the property, and a number of good restaurants are less than half a mile away. Though a sign in front of the property advertises a casino, there is only a small collection of slot machines.

Las Vegas Marriott Suites   (www.marriott.com)

With an outdoor pool and hot tub, a fitness center, a full-service restaurant, and room service, the Marriott Suites offers the amenities you would expect from a Marriott. And the small building and easy access to parking make the Marriott Suites easy to navigate. Suites are tastefully decorated, though not as plush as some Marriott properties. At the southwest corner of Desert Inn and Paradise Roads, the Marriott Suites is about a five-minute walk to the Convention Center and a five-minute cab ride to the Strip.

Residence Inn   (www.residenceinn.com)

Across from the Las Vegas Convention Center, the Residence Inn by Marriott offers comfortable one- and two-bedroom suites with full kitchens. Patronized primarily by business travelers on extended stays, the Residence Inn provides a more homelike atmosphere than most other suite properties. While there is no restaurant at the hotel, there is an excellent selection within a half-mile radius. Amenities include a pool, hot tubs, and a coin laundry. A second Residence Inn is about a mile away at the Hughes Center.

St. Tropez   (www.sttropezlasvegas.com)

The St. Tropez offers beautifully decorated one- and two-room suites at rates often less than $100 per night. Adjoining a small shopping mall, the St. Tropez provides a heated pool, a fitness center, VCRs in the suites, and a complementary continental breakfast. The St. Tropez is within five minutes of the Strip and the airport, and about seven minutes from the Convention Center. Most guests are upscale business and convention travelers.

Las Vegas Motels

Because they must compete with the huge hotel-casinos, many Las Vegas motels offer great rates or provide special amenities such as a complementary breakfast. Like the resorts, motels often have a very specific clientele. La Quinta Motor Inn, for instance, caters to government employees, while the Best Western on Craig Road primarily serves folks visiting Nellis Air Force Base.

For the most part, national motel chains are well represented in Las Vegas. We have included enough chain and independent motels in the following ratings-and-rankings section to give you a sense of how these properties compare with hotel-casinos and all-suite hotels. Because chain hotels are known entities to most travelers, no descriptions are provided beyond the room quality ratings and summary charts. After all, a Comfort Inn in Las Vegas is pretty much like a Comfort Inn in Louisville, and we are all aware by now that Motel 6 leaves the light on for you.

Hotel-Casinos and Motels: Rated and Ranked

What's in a Room?

Except for cleanliness, state of repair, and decor, most travelers do not pay much attention to hotel rooms. There is, of course, a discernible standard of quality and luxury that differentiates Motel 6 from Holiday Inn, Holiday Inn from Marriott, and so on. In general, however, most hotel guests fail to appreciate that some rooms are better engineered than other rooms.

Contrary to what you might suppose, designing a hotel room is (or should be) a lot more complex than picking a bedspread to match the carpet and drapes. Making the room usable to its occupants is an art, a planning discipline that combines both form and function.

Decor and taste are important, certainly. No one wants to spend several days in a room where the decor is dated, garish, or even ugly. But beyond the decor, there are variables that determine how "livable" a hotel room is. In Las Vegas, for example, we have seen some beautifully appointed rooms that are simply not well designed for human habitation. The next time you stay in a hotel, pay attention to the details and design elements of your room. Even more than decor, these are the things that will make you feel comfortable and at home.

Here are a few of the things we check that you may want to start paying attention to:

Room Size   While some smaller rooms are cozy and well designed, a large and uncluttered room is generally preferable, especially for a stay of more than three days.

Temperature Control, Ventilation, and Odor   The guest should be able to control the temperature of the room. The best system, because it's so quiet, is central heating and air-conditioning, controlled by the room's own thermostat. The next best system is a room module heater and air conditioner, preferably controlled by an automatic thermostat, but usually by manually operated button controls. The worst system is central heating and air without any sort of room thermostat or guest control.

The vast majority of hotel rooms have windows or balcony doors that have been permanently secured shut. Though there are some legitimate safety and liability issues involved, we prefer windows and balcony doors that can be opened to admit fresh air. Hotel rooms should be odor-free and smoke-free and not feel stuffy or damp.

Room Security   Better rooms have locks that require an encoded plastic card instead of the traditional lock and key. Card and slot systems allow the hotel, essentially, to change the combination or entry code of the lock with each new guest who uses the room. A burglar who has somehow acquired a room key to a conventional lock can afford to wait until the situation is right before using the key to gain access. Not so with a card and slot system. Though larger hotels and hotel chains with lock and key systems usually rotate their locks once each year, they remain vulnerable to hotel thieves much of the time. Many smaller or independent properties rarely rotate their locks.

In addition to the entry lock system, the door should have a deadbolt, and preferably a chain that can be locked from the inside. A chain by itself is not sufficient. Doors should also have a peephole. Windows and balcony doors, if any, should have secure locks.

Safety   Every room should have a fire or smoke alarm, clear fire instructions, and preferably a sprinkler system. Bathtubs should have a nonskid surface, and shower stalls should have doors that either open outward or slide side-to-side. Bathroom electrical outlets should be high on the wall and not too close to the sink. Balconies should have sturdy, high rails.

Noise   Most travelers have occasionally been kept awake by the television, partying, amorous activities of people in the next room, or by traffic on the street outside. Better hotels are designed with noise control in mind. Wall and ceiling construction are substantial, effectively screening routine noise. Carpets and drapes, in addition to being decorative, also absorb and muffle sounds. Mattresses mounted on stable platforms or sturdy bed frames do not squeak even when challenged by the most passionate and acrobatic lovers. Televisions enclosed in cabinets, and with volume governors, rarely disturb guests in adjacent rooms.

In better hotels, the air-conditioning and heating system is well maintained and operates without noise or vibration. Likewise, plumbing is quiet and positioned away from the sleeping area. Doors to the hall, and to adjoining rooms, are thick and well fitted to better keep out noise.

Darkness Control   Ever been in a hotel room where the curtains would not quite come together in the middle? In Las Vegas, where many visitors stay up way into the wee hours, it's important to have a dark, quiet room where you can sleep late without the morning sun blasting you out of bed. Thick, lined curtains that close completely in the center and extend beyond the dimensions of the window or door frame are required. In a well-planned room, the curtains, shades, or blinds should almost totally block light at any time of day.

Lighting   Poor lighting is an extremely common problem in American hotel rooms. The lighting is usually adequate for dressing, relaxing, or watching television but not for reading or working. Lighting needs to be bright over tables and desks and alongside couches or easy chairs. Since so many people read in bed, there should be a separate light for each person. A room with two queen beds should have an individual light for four people. Better bedside reading lights illuminate a small area so that if you want to sleep and someone else prefers to stay up and read, you will not be bothered by the light. The worst situation by far is a single lamp on a table between beds. In each bed, only the person next to the lamp will have sufficient light to read. This deficiency is often compounded by light bulbs of insufficient wattage.

In addition, closet areas should be well lit, and there should be a switch near the door that turns on lights in the room when you enter. A seldom seen, but desirable, feature is a bedside console that allows a guest to control all or most lights in the room from bed.

Furnishings   At bare minimum, the bed(s) must be firm. Pillows should be made with nonallergenic fillers and, in addition to the sheets and spread, a blanket should be provided. Bedclothes should be laundered with a fabric softener and changed daily. Better hotels usually provide extra blankets and pillows in the room or on request, and sometimes use a second top sheet between the blanket and the spread.

There should be a dresser large enough to hold clothes for two people during a five-day stay. A small table with two chairs, or a desk with a chair, should be provided. The room should be equipped with a luggage rack and a three-quarter- to full-length mirror.

The television should be color and cable-connected and, ideally, should have a volume governor and remote control. It should be mounted on a swivel base and preferably enclosed in a cabinet. Local channels should be posted on the set and a local TV program guide should be supplied.

The telephone should be TouchTone, conveniently situated for bedside use, and on it or nearby there should be easy-to-understand dialing instructions and a rate card. Local White and Yellow Pages should be provided. Better hotels have phones in the bath and equip room phones with long cords.

Well-designed hotel rooms usually have a plush armchair or a sleeper sofa for lounging and reading. Better headboards are padded for comfortable reading in bed, and there should be a nightstand or table on each side of the bed(s). Nice extras in any hotel room include a small refrigerator, a digital alarm clock, and a coffee maker.

Bathroom Two sinks are better than one, and you can't have too much counter space. A sink outside the bath is great when two people bathe and dress simultaneously. Sinks should have drains with stoppers.

Better bathrooms have both tub and shower with a nonslip bottom. Tub and shower controls should be easy to operate. Adjustable shower heads are preferred. The bath needs to be well lit and should have an exhaust fan and a guest-controlled bathroom heater. Towels should be large, soft, fluffy, and provided in generous quantities, as should hand towels and washcloths. There should be an electrical outlet for each sink, conveniently and safely placed.

Complementary shampoo, conditioner, and lotion are a plus, as are robes and bathmats. Better hotels supply their bathrooms with tissues and extra toilet paper. Luxurious baths feature a phone, a hair dryer, sometimes a small television, or even a hot tub.

Vending There should be complementary ice and a drink machine on each floor. Welcome additions include a snack machine and a sundries (combs, toothpaste) machine. The latter are seldom found in large hotels that have 24-hour restaurants and shops.

Rating the Hotels and Casinos

To help you select your Las Vegas hotel, we offer three different ratings:

1. Room Rating
2. Value Rating
3. Leisure, Recreation, and Services Rating

Although all three ratings will be defined in the following section, we should pause here to explain some changes from previous editions of this guide. The addition of so many luxury hotels in Las Vegas has necessitated an adjustment of our rating scales to allow for more meaningful comparison of the better hotels. Expressed differently, to make more room at the top, we had to adjust the entire scale. In terms of net effect, most hotels' ratings dropped slightly from last year. Generally speaking, however, this drop is the result of our adjustment as opposed to a shortcoming of the hotel.

Room Ratings

To separate properties according to the relative quality, tastefulness, state of repair, cleanliness, and size of their standard rooms, we have grouped the hotels and motels into classifications denoted by stars. Star ratings in this guide apply to Las Vegas properties only and do not necessarily correspond to ratings awarded by Mobil, AAA, or other travel critics. Because stars have little relevance when awarded in the absence of commonly recognized standards of comparison, we have tied our ratings to expected levels of quality established by specific American hotel corporations.

WHAT THE RATINGS MEAN		
★★★★★	*Superior Rooms*	Tasteful and luxurious by any standard
★★★★	*Extremely Nice Rooms*	What you would expect at a Hyatt Regency or Marriott
★★★	*Nice Rooms*	Holiday Inn or comparable quality
★★	*Adequate Rooms*	Clean, comfortable, and functional without frills—like a Motel 6
★	*Super Budget*	

Star ratings apply to *room quality only* and describe the property's standard accommodations. For almost all hotels and motels, a "standard accommodation" is a hotel room with either one king bed or two queen beds. In an all-suite property, the standard accommodation is either a studio or one-bedroom suite. Also, in addition to standard accommodations, many hotels offer luxury rooms and special suites, which are not rated in this guide. Star ratings for rooms are assigned without regard to whether a property has a casino, restaurant(s), recreational facilities, entertainment, or other extras.

In addition to stars (which delineate broad categories), we also employ a numerical rating system. Our rating scale is 0–100, with 100 as the best possible rating, and zero (0) as the worst. Numerical ratings are presented to show the difference we perceive between one property and another. Rooms at the Luxor, Flamingo Hilton, and the Stardust, for instance, are all rated as ★★★½ (three-and-a-half stars). In the supplemental numerical ratings, the Luxor and the Flamingo Hilton are rated 82 and 80, respectively, while the Stardust is rated 76. This means that within the three-and-a-half-star category, the Luxor and the Flamingo Hilton are comparable, and both have somewhat nicer rooms than the Stardust.

How the Hotels Compare

Here is a comparison of the hotel rooms in town. We've focused strictly on room quality and excluded any consideration of location, services, recreation, or amenities. In some instances, a one- or two-room suite can be had for the same price or less than that of a hotel room.

If you used an earlier edition of this guide, you will notice that many of the ratings and rankings have changed. These changes are occasioned by such positive developments as guest-room renovation, improved maintenance, and improved housekeeping. Failure to properly maintain guest rooms and poor housekeeping affect the ratings negatively. Finally, some ratings change as a result of enlarging our sample size. Because we cannot check every room in a hotel, we inspect a number of randomly chosen rooms. The more rooms we inspect in a particular hotel, the more representative our sample is of the property as a whole. Some of the ratings in this edition have changed as a result of extended sampling.

The guest rooms in many Las Vegas hotels can vary widely in quality. In most hotels the better rooms are situated in high-rise structures known locally as "towers." More modest accommodations, called "garden rooms," are routinely found in one- and two-story outbuildings. It is important to understand that not all rooms in a particular hotel are the same. When you make inquiries or reservations, always define the type of room you are talking about.

Finally, before you begin to shop for a hotel, take a hard look at this letter we received from a couple in Hot Springs, Arkansas:

We canceled our room reservations to follow the advice in your book [and reserved a hotel room highly ranked by the Unofficial Guide]. We wanted inexpensive, but clean and cheerful. We got inexpensive, but [also] dirty, grim, and depressing. I really felt disappointed in your advice and the room. It was the pits. That was the one real piece of information I needed from your book! The room spoiled the holiday for me aside from our touring.

Needless to say, this letter was as unsettling to us as the bad room was to our reader. Our integrity as travel journalists, after all, is based on the quality of the information we provide to our readers. Even with the best of intentions and the most conscientious research, however, we cannot inspect every room in every hotel. What we do, in statistical terms, is take a sample: We check out several rooms selected at random in each hotel and base our ratings and rankings on those rooms. The inspections are conducted anonymously and without the knowledge of the management. Although it would be unusual, it is certainly possible that the rooms we randomly inspect are not representative of the majority of rooms at a particular hotel. Another possibility is that the rooms we inspect in a given hotel are representative but that by bad luck a reader is assigned a room that is inferior. When we rechecked the hotel our reader disliked, we discovered that our rating was correctly representative, but that he and his wife had unfortunately been assigned to one of a small number of threadbare rooms scheduled for renovation.

The key to avoiding disappointment is to snoop around in advance. We recommend that you ask for a photo of a hotel's standard guest room before you book, or at least get a copy of the hotel's promotional brochure. Be forewarned, however, that some hotel chains use the same guest room photo in their promotional literature for all hotels in the chain; a specific guest room may not resemble the brochure photo. When you or your travel agent call, ask how old the property is and when your guest room was last renovated. If you arrive and are assigned a room inferior to that which you had been led to expect, demand to be moved to another room deserving of your expectations.

Cost estimates are based on the hotel's published rack rates for standard rooms, averaged between weekday and weekend prices. Each "$" represents $50. Thus a cost symbol of "$$$" means a room (or suite) at that hotel will cost about $150 a night.

HOW THE HOTELS COMPARE			
Hotel	**Star Rating**	**Quality Rating**	**Cost ($=$50)**
Ritz-Carlton Lake Las Vegas	★★★★★	97	$$$$
THEhotel at Mandalay Bay	★★★★½	96	$$$$$$-
Caesars Palace	★★★★½	95	$$$-
Bellagio	★★★★½	95	$$$$-
JW Marriott Las Vegas	★★★★½	95	$$$$$-
The Venetian	★★★★½	94	$$$$-
Four Seasons at Mandalay Bay	★★★★½	94	$$$$$$$-
Mandalay Bay	★★★★½	92	$$$$$-
Paris	★★★★½	91	$$+
Mirage	★★★★½	90	$$$-
Montelago Village Lake Las Vegas	★★★★	90	$$$$-
Alexis Park	★★★★	88	$$-
Embassy Suites Convention Center	★★★★	88	$$-
St. Tropez	★★★★	88	$$
Hyatt Regency Lake Las Vegas	★★★★	88	$$$$-
Las Vegas Hilton (East, North Towers)	★★★★	87	$-
MGM Grand	★★★★	87	$$
Aladdin	★★★★	87	$$+
Hard Rock Hotel	★★★★	86	$$$$$$-
Bally's	★★★★	85	$$-
Rio	★★★★	85	$$
Westin Casuarina	★★★★	85	$$$$$$$-
T. I.	★★★★	84	$$-
Tuscany	★★★★	84	$$-
Palms	★★★★	84	$$+
Las Vegas Marriott Suites	★★★★	84	$$$+
Green Valley Ranch	★★★★	84	$$$$+
Golden Nugget	★★★★	83	$$-
Crowne Plaza	★★★★	83	$$+
Residence Inn by Marriott	★★★★	83	$$$-
Silverton	★★★½	82	$-

HOW THE HOTELS COMPARE (continued)

Hotel	Star Rating	Quality Rating	Cost ($=$50)
Sunset Station	★★★½	82	$+
Harrah's	★★★½	82	$$-
Suncoast	★★★½	82	$$-
Luxor	★★★½	82	$$
AmeriSuites	★★★½	82	$$+
Emerald Suites Tropicana	★★★½	81	$+
Monte Carlo	★★★½	81	$$
Palace Station (Tower)	★★★½	81	$$$+
Flamingo Hilton	★★★½	80	$+
Stratosphere	★★★½	79	$+
Candlewood Suites	★★★½	79	$$-
Manor Suites	★★★½	79	$$-
Courtyard by Marriott	★★★½	79	$$-
Embassy Suites in Las Vegas	★★★½	79	$$+
Sam's Town	★★★½	78	$+
Fairfield Inn & Suites Las Vegas South	★★★½	78	$$-
Stardust	★★★½	76	$+
New Frontier (Atrium Tower)	★★★½	75	$
Main Street Station	★★★½	75	$+
Orleans (New Tower)	★★★ ½	75	$+
Arizona Charlie's Boulder	★★★	75	$-
Riviera (Monaco Tower)	★★★	75	$+
New York–New York	★★★	75	$$-
Clarion Hotel and Suites	★★★	74	$$+
Holiday Inn Express Las Vegas	★★★	74	$$$-
Las Vegas Club (North Tower)	★★★	73	$-
Tropicana	★★★	73	$+
Riviera	★★★	73	$+
Greek Isles	★★★	73	$$-
Santa Fe Station	★★★	73	$$-
Circus Circus	★★★	72	$+
Fiesta Henderson	★★★	72	$+
Barbary Coast	★★★	71	$+
Texas Station	★★★	70	$$-
San Remo	★★★	69	$-
Sahara	★★★	69	$+
Four Queens	★★★	69	$+
Comfort Inn Paradise Road	★★★	68	$$+
California	★★★	67	$+

HOW THE HOTELS COMPARE (continued)

Hotel	Star Rating	Quality Rating	Cost ($=$50)
Boulder Station	★★★	67	$$+
Ambassador Strip Travelodge	★★★	67	$$$+
Fairfield Inn Las Vegas Airport	★★★	66	$$+
Boardwalk	★★★	66	$+
Excalibur	★★★	66	$+
Arizona Charlie's Decatur	★★★	65	$-
Imperial Palace	★★★	65	$-
Fremont, Sam Boyd's	★★★	65	$
Lady Luck (East Tower)	★★★	65	$+
Best Western Mardi Gras Inn	★★★	65	$+
Royal Resort	★★½	76	$$-
Hampton Inn Tropicana	★★½	73	$+
La Quinta	★★½	69	$$+
Casino Royale	★★½	65	$-
Horseshoe (East Wing)	★★½	64	$-
Key Largo Casino and Quality Inn	★★½	64	$-
Bourbon Street	★★½	64	$-
Cannery	★★½	64	$+
Terrible's	★★½	63	$-
Fitzgeralds	★★½	63	$+
El Cortez	★★½	62	$+
Fiesta Rancho	★★½	62	$+
Plaza	★★½	60	$-
Nevada Palace	★★½	59	$+
Gold Coast	★★½	58	$+
La Quinta Tropicana	★★½	58	$+
Best Western McCarran Inn	★★½	57	$-
Westward Ho	★★½	55	$
Travelodge Sahara Westwood Inn	★★	56	$-
Days Inn Town Hall Casino Hotel	★★	55	$$-
Days Inn Downtown	★★	53	$-
Motel 6 Tropicana	★★	52	$-
Howard Johnson Airport	★★	52	$-
Super 8	★★	52	$+
Wild Wild West	★★	51	$-
Golden Palm Hotel	★★	50	$-
Palace Station (Garden)	★★	74	$$$$-

The Top 30 Best Deals in Las Vegas

Having listed the nicest rooms in town, let's reorder the list to rank the best combinations of quality and value in a room. As before, the rankings are made without consideration of location or the availability of restaurant(s), recreational facilities, entertainment, and/or amenities. Once again, each lodging property is awarded a value rating on a 0–100 scale. The higher the rating, the better the value.

A reader recently complained to us that he had booked one of our top-ranked rooms in terms of value and had been very disappointed in the room. We noticed that the room the reader occupied had a quality rating of ★★½. We would remind you that the value ratings are intended to give you some sense of value received for dollars spent. A ★★½ room at $30 may have the same value rating as a ★★★★ room at $85, but that does not mean the rooms will be of comparable quality. Regardless of whether it's a good deal or not, a ★★½ room is still a ★★½ room.

Listed below are the best room buys for the money, regardless of location or star classification, based on averaged rack rates. Note that sometimes a suite can cost less than a hotel room.

THE TOP 30 BEST DEALS IN LAS VEGAS				
Hotel	Value Rating	Star Rating	Quality Rating	Cost ($=$50)
1. Las Vegas Hilton	99	★★★★	87	$-
2. Las Vegas Club	90	★★★	73	$-
3. Silverton	89	★★★½	82	$-
4. New Frontier	85	★★★	82	$-
5. Arizona Charlie's Boulder	78	★★★	75	$-
6. Horseshoe	77	★★½	64	$-
7. Key Largo and Quality Inn	74	★★½	64	$-
8. Arizona Charlie's Decatur	68	★★★	65	$-
9. Stardust	64	★★★½	76	$+
10. San Remo	64	★★★	69	$-
11. Terrible's	64	★★½	63	$-
12. Alexis Park	62	★★★★	88	$$-
13. Main Street Station	61	★★★½	75	$+
14. Orleans	61	★★★½	75	$+
15. Bally's	60	★★★★	85	$$-
16. Golden Nugget	58	★★★★	83	$$-
17. Sam's Town	58	★★★½	78	$+
18. Sunset Station	57	★★★½	82	$+
19. Emerald Suites Tropicana	57	★★★½	81	$+
20. Stratosphere	55	★★★½	79	$+
21. Imperial Palace	55	★★★	65	$-

THE TOP 30 BEST DEALS IN LAS VEGAS *(continued)*

Hotel	Value Rating	Star Rating	Quality Rating	Cost ($=$50)
22. Fremont, Sam Boyd's	54	★★★	65	$
23. Harrah's	53	★★★½	82	$+
24. Paris	52	★★★★½	91	$$+
25. Treasure Island	52	★★★★	84	$$-
26. Tuscany	52	★★★★	84	$$-
27. Flamingo Hilton	52	★★★½	80	$+
28. Tropicana	51	★★★	73	$+
29. Suncoast	50	★★★½	82	$$-
30. Embassy Suites Convention Ctr.	49	★★★★	88	$$-

Leisure, Recreation, and Services Rating of Hotel-Casinos

Many Las Vegas visitors use their hotel rooms only as a depository for luggage and a place to take a quick nap or shower. These folks are far more interested in what the hotel has to offer in terms of gambling, restaurants, live entertainment, services, and recreational pursuits.

Ranked on pages 145–146 in terms of the breadth and quality of their offerings, are Las Vegas hotels with full casinos. Using a weighted model, we have calculated a composite Leisure, Recreation, and Services Rating. The rating is designed to help you determine which properties provide the best overall vacation or leisure experience.

Interpreting the LR&S Ratings

Room quality is not considered in the Leisure, Recreation, and Services Rating (LR&S). Therefore a hotel with ordinary rooms may attain a high LR&S score. A casino could have very ordinary guest rooms, for example, but score high in the LR&S rankings because it has a beautiful casino, excellent restaurants, a highly regarded buffet, shopping, and a good showroom.

Some hotels may score low because they offer little in the way of entertainment, recreation, or food service. If the property is somewhat isolated, like El Cortez, these deficiencies pose serious problems. If, on the other hand, a hotel is situated in a prime location, the shortcomings hardly matter. The Barbary Coast does not have a showroom, but is within easy walking distance of showrooms at Caesars Palace, Bally's, the Mirage, Harrah's, the Imperial Palace, and the Flamingo. Likewise, the Four Queens, downtown, doesn't have a buffet but is within a three-minute walk of buffets at the Golden Nugget, Fremont, and Lady Luck.

Because the LR&S is a composite rating, its primary value is in identifying the properties that offer the highest quality and greatest variety of restaurants, diversions, and activities. The rating does not, however, indicate what those restaurants, diversions, or activities are. Bellagio and Caesars Palace have the highest LR&S ratings, but neither has a golf course. If you want to walk right out your door and tee off, you would do well to stay at the JW Marriott Las Vegas. When you have identified several properties that seem interesting, check the alphabetized profiles in the Hotel Information Chart (pages 150–181) to make sure your preliminary selections offer the features that are important to you.

	LR&S RATING FOR HOTELS WITH FULL CASINOS	
Rank	**Hotel**	**Leisure, Recreation, & Services Rating**
1.	Mandalay Bay (THEhotel, Four Seasons)	97
2.	Bellagio	94
3.	Caesars Palace	93
4.	Mirage	93
5.	MGM Grand	91
6.	Rio	90
7.	Venetian	90
8.	Aladdin	88
9.	T. I.	88
10.	Luxor	87
11.	Paris	87
12.	Flamingo Hilton	83
13.	Las Vegas Hilton	83
14.	New York–New York	83
15.	Ritz-Carlton	82
16.	Monte Carlo	81
17.	Bally's	79
18.	Harrah's	79
19.	Hard Rock Hotel	78
20.	Stratosphere	78
21.	Tropicana	78
22.	Hyatt Regency Lake Las Vegas	**78**
23.	Green Valley Ranch	77
24.	Palms	77
25.	Excalibur	76
26.	JW Marriott Las Vegas/Rampart Casino	76
27.	Golden Nugget	75
28.	Montelago Village Lake Las Vegas	75
29.	Orleans	75
30.	Sunset Station	74

LR&S RATING FOR HOTELS WITH FULL CASINOS *(continued)*

Rank	Hotel	Leisure, Recreation, & Services Rating
31.	Imperial Palace	72
32.	Riviera	72
33.	Sahara	71
34.	Sam's Town	70
35.	Texas Station	69
36.	Main Street Station	68
37.	Palace Station	67
38.	Santa Fe Station	67
39.	Silverton	67
40.	New Frontier	66
41.	Stardust	65
42.	Boulder Station	65
43.	Fiesta Rancho	65
44.	Suncoast	65
45.	Gold Coast	64
46.	Lady Luck	62
47.	Fiesta Henderson	61
48.	Four Queens	61
49.	Westin Casuarina	61
50.	Barbary Coast	59
51.	California	59
52.	Cannery	59
53.	San Remo	59
54.	Plaza	58
55.	Arizona Charlie's Boulder	57
56.	Arizona Charlie's Decatur	56
57.	Horseshoe	56
58.	Fremont	55
59.	Tuscany	55
60.	Las Vegas Club	54
61.	Boardwalk	53
62.	Fitzgeralds	51
63.	Nevada Palace	51
64.	Terrible's	51
65.	Westward Ho	51
66.	Casino Royale	46
67.	Greek Isles	46
68.	Wild Wild West	46
69.	Bourbon Street	45
70.	El Cortez	31
71.	Key Largo and Quality Inn	30

When Only the Best Will Do

The trouble with profiles is that details and distinctions are sacrificed in the interest of brevity and information accessibility. For example, while dozens of properties are listed as having swimming pools, we've made no qualitative discriminations. In the alphabetized profiles, a pool is a pool.

In actuality, of course, though most pools are quite basic and ordinary, a few (Mirage, Tropicana, Flamingo, Monte Carlo, MGM Grand, Aladdin, Mandalay Bay, Bellagio, Venetian, JW Marriott Las Vegas, and the Rio) are pretty spectacular. To distinguish the exceptional from the average, we provide this best-of list.

Best Dining (Expense No Issue)
1. Bellagio
2. Venetian
3. MGM Grand
4. Mandalay Bay
5. Caesar's Palace
6. Paris
7. Palms
8. Mirage

Best Dining (For Great Value)
1. Orleans
2. Suncoast
3. Main Street Station
4. Palace Station
5. Gold Coast
6. Excalibur
7. California
8. Fiesta Rancho
9. Boulder Station
10. Sam's Town

Best Sunday Brunches
1. Sterling Brunch, Bally's
2. Commander's Palace Jazz Brunch—Desert Passage
3. The Steakhouse at Circus Circus
4. Bellagio Sunday Champagne Brunch
5. Green Valley Ranch Station

Best Buffets
1. Aladdin Spice Market Buffet
2. Bellagio Buffet
3. Paris Le Village Buffet
4. Mirage Cravings Buffet
5. Rio Carnival World
6. Green Valley Ranch Feast Buffet
7. Texas Station Feast Buffet
8. Palms Fantasy Market Buffet
9. Orleans French Market Buffet
10. Sam's Town Firelight Buffet

Most Visually Interesting Casinos
1. Venetian
2. Caesars Palace
3. Mandalay Bay
4. Luxor
5. Mirage
6. New York–New York
7. Aladdin
8. Sunset Station
9. Main Street Station
10. Rio

Best for Bowling
1. Gold Coast
2. Sam's Town
3. Orleans
4. Santa Fe Station

Best Spas
1. Venetian
2. Caesars Palace
3. Bellagio
4. Mandalay Bay/THEhotel/
   Four Seasons
5. Mirage
6. Paris
7. MGM Grand
8. Monte Carlo
9. T. I.

Best for Golf
1. JW Marriott Las Vegas
2. Ritz-Carlton Lake Las Vegas
3. Hyatt Regency Lake Las Vegas
4. Montelago Village Lake Las Vegas

Best for Tennis
1. MGM Grand
2. Bally's
3. Caesars Palace
4. JW Marriott Las Vegas
5. Las Vegas Hilton

Best for Shopping On-Site or within a Four-Minute Walk
1. Caesars Palace
2. Venetian
3. Mirage
4. T. I.
5. Aladdin
6. New Frontier

**Best for Weight Lifting, Nautilus, Stationary Cycling, Stair Machines,
and Other Indoor Exercise Equipment**
1. Venetian
2. Caesars Palace
3. Mandalay Bay
4. Bellagio

5. MGM Grand
6. Mirage
7. Paris
8. T. I.
9. Luxor
10. JW Marriott Las Vegas
11. Monte Carlo

Best for Jogging or Running
1. Mandalay Bay
2. Las Vegas Hilton

Best Swimming and Sunbathing
1. Mandalay Bay
2. Bellagio
3. Caesars Palace
4. Mirage
5. MGM Grand
6. Venetian
7. Tropicana
8. Flamingo
9. T. I.
10. Monte Carlo
11. Hard Rock Hotel
12. Rio
13. Palms
14. Las Vegas Hilton

Hotel	Star Rating	Zone	Street Address
Aladdin	★★★★	1	3667 Las Vegas Boulevard South Las Vegas, 89109
Alexis Park	★★★★	1	375 East Harmon Avenue Las Vegas, 89109
Ambassador Strip Travelodge	★★★	1	5075 Koval Lane Las Vegas, 89109
AmeriSuites	★★★½	1	4520 Paradise Road Las Vegas, 89109
Arizona Charlie's Boulder	★★★	5	4575 Boulder Highway Las Vegas, 89121
Arizona Charlie's Decatur	★★★	4	740 South Decatur Boulevard Las Vegas, 89107
Bally's	★★★★	1	3645 Las Vegas Boulevard South Las Vegas, 89109
Barbary Coast	★★★	1	3595 Las Vegas Boulevard South Las Vegas, 89109
Bellagio	★★★★½	1	3600 Las Vegas Boulevard South Las Vegas, 89177
Best Western Mardi Gras Inn	★★★	1	3500 Paradise Road Las Vegas, 89109
Best Western McCarran Inn	★★½	1	4970 Paradise Road Las Vegas, 89119
Boardwalk	★★★	1	3750 Las Vegas Boulevard South Las Vegas, 89109
Boulder Station	★★★	5	4111 Boulder Highway Las Vegas, 89121
Bourbon Street	★★½	1	120 East Flamingo Road Las Vegas, 89109
Caesars Palace	★★★★½	1	3570 Las Vegas Boulevard South Las Vegas, 89109
California	★★★	2	12 East Ogden Avenue Las Vegas, 89101
Candlewood Suites	★★★½	1	4034 South Paradise Road Las Vegas, 89109
Cannery	★★½	4	2121 East Craig Road Las Vegas, 89032
Casino Royale	★★½	1	3411 Las Vegas Boulevard South Las Vegas, 89109
Circus Circus	★★★/ ★★★	1	2880 Las Vegas Boulevard South Las Vegas, 89109
Clarion Hotel and Suites	★★★	1	325 East Flamingo Road Las Vegas, 89109

Local Phone	Fax	Toll-Free Reservations	Discount Available	Number of Rooms
(702) 736-0111	(702) 785-5511	(877) 333-9474		2,600
(702) 796-3300	(702) 796-3354	(800) 582-2228	Government, military	500
(702) 736-3600	(702) 736-0726	(800) 221-2222	Senior, military	106
(702) 369-3366	(702) 369-0009	(800) 833-1516	Senior, AAA	139
(702) 951-9000	(702) 951-9201	(877) 951-8002		300
(702) 258-5111	(702) 258-5192	(800) 342-2695	Government	225
(702) 739-4111	(702) 739-4405	(800) 634-3434	Government, AAA, senior	2,814
(702) 737-7111	(702) 693-8546	(888) BARBARY		200
(702) 693-7444	(702) 693-8546	(888) 987-6667		3,000
(702) 731-2020	(702) 731-4005	(800) 634-6501	Senior, military AAA, AARP	314
(702) 798-5530	(702) 798-7627	(800) 626-7575	Senior, military	100
(702) 735-1167	(702) 739-8152	(800) HOLIDAY	Senior, military, AAA, government	654
(702) 432-7777	(702) 432-7730	(800) 683-7777		300
(702) 737-7200	(702) 734-3490	(800) 634-6956	Senior	166
(702) 731-7110	(702) 731-7172	(800) 634-6661	Senior, military government	3,009
(702) 385-1222	(702) 388-2670	(800) 634-6255		781
(702) 836-3660	(702) 836-3661	none		160
(702) 507-5700	(702) 507-5750	(866) 999-4899	Government, racer, trucker, corporate	201
(702) 737-3500	(702) 650-4743	(800) 854-7666		152
(702) 734-0410	(702) 734-0410	(800) 634-3450	Senior	3,770
(702) 732-9100	(702) 731-9784	(800) 732-7889	Senior, AAA, government, military	150

Hotel	Check Out Time	Non-Smoking	Rack Rate	Room Quality	Room Value
Aladdin	11		$$+	87	44
Alexis Park	11	3	$$-	88	62
Ambassador Strip Travelodge	11	✓	$$$+	67	17
AmeriSuites	11	Floors	$$+	82	37
Arizona Charlie's Boulder	11		$-	75	78
Arizona Charlie's Decatur	11	3	$-	65	68
Bally's	11	Floors	$$-	85	60
Barbary Coast	Noon	3	$+	71	40
Bellagio	Noon	3	$$$$-	95	30
Best Western Mardi Gras Inn	Noon	3	$+	65	39
Best Western McCarran Inn	Noon	3	$-	57	40
Boardwalk	Noon	3	$+	66	40
Boulder Station	Noon	3	$$+	67	24
Bourbon Street	Noon	3	$-	64	45
Caesars Palace	Noon	Floors	$$$-	95	46
California	Noon	3	$+	67	47
Candlewood Suites	Noon	3	$$-	79	43
Cannery	Noon	3	$+	64	40
Casino Royale	Noon	3	$-	65	46
Circus Circus	11	Floors	$+/ $+	59/ 72	45/ 43
Clarion Hotel and Suites	Noon	Floors	$$+	74	25

Concierge	Convention Facilities	Meeting Rooms	Valet Parking	RV Park	Room Service	Free Breakfast
✓	✓	✓	✓			✓
✓	✓	✓	✓			✓
						✓
	✓	✓				✓
					✓	✓
✓			✓			
✓	✓	✓	✓			✓
✓	✓	✓	✓			✓
✓	✓	✓	✓		✓	✓
		✓				Monday–Friday
						✓
		✓	✓			✓
✓	✓	✓	✓			✓
	✓	✓				✓
✓	✓	✓	✓			✓
		✓	✓		✓	Breakfast
		✓	✓		✓	✓
	✓	✓	✓		✓	Limited
		✓			✓	✓

Hotel	Fine Dining/ Type of Food	Coffee Shop	24-hr. Café	Buffet	Casino
Aladdin	International, Steak	✓	✓	✓	✓
Alexis Park	Continental	✓			
Ambassador Strip Travelodge		Adjacent			
AmeriSuites					
Arizona Charlie's East	American			✓	
Arizona Charlie's Decatur	Chinese, Steak	✓	✓	✓	✓
Bally's	Continental, Steak	✓	✓	✓	✓
Barbary Coast	Continental	✓	✓		✓
Bellagio	Continental	✓	✓	✓	✓
Best Western Mardi Gras Inn	American		✓		Slots
Best Western McCarran Inn					
Boardwalk	American, Italian	✓	✓	✓	✓
Boulder Station	Steak/Seafood, Italian, Mexican, Chinese	✓	✓	✓	✓
Bourbon Street	Continental		✓		Slots
Caesars Palace	Asian, French, Italian, Continental, Japanese, Steak	✓	✓	✓	✓
California	Pasta, Seafood, Steak	✓	✓	Breakfast	✓
Candlewood Suites					
Cannery	American, Mexican, Steak		✓	✓	✓
Casino Royale	American, Italian		✓		✓
Circus Circus	Steak, Italian, Mexican	✓	✓	✓	✓
Clarion Hotel and Suites	American	✓			

Lounge	Showroom Entertainment	Gift Shop Drugs/News	Pool	Exercise Rooms	Tennis & Racquet Games
✓	Headliners	✓	✓		
✓		✓	✓		
			✓ Heated		
			✓	✓	
	Live music	✓	✓		
✓	Headliner	✓	✓ Seasonal		
✓	Production show, celebrity headliners	✓	✓	Health spa	Tennis
✓	Live music	✓	✓		
✓	Production show	✓	✓	✓	
		✓	✓		
			✓		
✓	Variety shows, live music	✓	✓	✓	
✓	Country-western performers	✓	✓		
✓	Comedy, live music		Privileges		
✓	Celebrity headliner	✓	✓ Heated	Health spa	✓
		✓	✓		
			✓	✓	
✓		✓	✓		
			✓		
✓	Circus acts, free theme park	✓	✓		
		✓	✓ Heated	✓	

Hotel	Star Rating	Zone	Street Address
Comfort Inn Paradise Road	★★★	1	4350 East Paradise Road Las Vegas, 89109
Courtyard Las Vegas South	★★★½	1	5845 Industrial Road Las Vegas, 89118
Courtyard by Marriott	★★★½	1	3275 Paradise Road Las Vegas, 89109
Crowne Plaza	★★★★	1	4255 Paradise Road Las Vegas, 89109
Days Inn Downtown	★★	2	707 East Fremont Street Las Vegas, 89101
Days Inn Town Hall Casino Hotel	★★	1	4155 Koval Lane Las Vegas, 89109
El Cortez	★★½	2	600 East Fremont Street Las Vegas, 89101
Embassy Suites Convention Center	★★★★	1	3600 South Paradise Road Las Vegas, 89109
Embassy Suites in Las Vegas	★★★½	1	4315 Swenson Street Las Vegas, 89119
Emerald Suites Tropicana	★★★½		8930 Graphic Center Drive Las Vegas, 89118
Excalibur	★★★	1	3850 Las Vegas Boulevard South Las Vegas, 89109
Fairfield Inn Las Vegas Airport	★★★	1	3850 Paradise Road Las Vegas, 89109
Fairfield Inn & Suites Las Vegas	★★★½	1	5775 Industrial Road Las Vegas, 89118
Fiesta Henderson	★★★	5	777 West Lake Mead Drive Henderson, 89015
Fiesta Rancho	★★½	3	2400 North Rancho Drive Las Vegas, 89130
Fitzgeralds	★★½	2	301 Fremont Street Las Vegas, 89101
Flamingo Hilton	★★★½	1	3555 Las Vegas Boulevard South Las Vegas, 89109
Four Queens	★★★	2	202 Fremont Street Las Vegas, 89101
Four Seasons at Mandalay Bay	★★★★½	1	3960 Las Vegas Boulevard South Las Vegas, 89119
Fremont, Sam Boyd's	★★★	2	200 East Fremont Street Las Vegas, 89101
Gold Coast	★★½	1	4000 West Flamingo Road Las Vegas, 89103

Local Phone	Fax	Toll-Free Reservations	Discount Available	Number of Rooms
(702) 938-2000	(702) 938-2001	(866) 847-2001		199
(702) 895-7519	(702) 895-7658	(800) 321-2211	Government, corporations	146
(702) 791-3600	(702) 796-7981	(800) 321-2211	Government, military	149
(702) 369-4400	(702) 369-3770	(800) 2-CROWNE	Senior, AARP	201
(702) 388-1400	(702) 388-9622	(800) 325-2344		147
(702) 731-2111	(702) 731-1113	(800) 634-6541	Senior, government, military, corporate	360
(702) 385-5200	(702) 385-1554	(800) 634-6541		401
(702) 893-8002	(702) 893-0378	(800) EMBASSY	AAA, senior, government	286
(702) 795-2800	(702) 795-1520	(800) EMBASSY	AAA, senior, government	220
(702) 507-9999	(702) 507-9998	(800) 695-8284	AAA, AARP	225
(702) 597-7777	(702) 597-7040	(800) 937-7777		4,008
(702) 791-0899	(702) 895-9810	(800) 228-2800	AAA, AARP government	129
(702) 895-0910	(702) 895-9310	(800) 228-9290	AAA, AARP government	218
(702) 558-7777	(702) 567-7373	(800) 844-9593		224
(702) 631-7000	(702) 631-6588	(800) 731-7333		100
(702) 388-2400	(702) 388-2181	(800) 274-LUCK	Senior	638
(702) 733-3111	(702) 733-3353	(800) 732-2111	AAA, AARP	3,642
(702) 385-4011	(702) 387-5122	(800) 634-6045	Military, government	690
(702) 632-5000	(702) 632-5222	(877) 632-5200		424
(702) 385-3232	(702) 388-2660	(800) 634-6182		447
(702) 367-7111	(702) 367-8419	(888) 402-6278	Senior	711

Hotel	Check Out Time	Non-Smoking	Rack Rate	Room Quality	Room Value
Comfort Inn Paradise Road	11	✓	$$+	68	24
Courtyard Las Vegas South	Noon	Floors	$$-	75	40
Courtyard by Marriott	Noon	Floors	$$-	79	39
Crowne Plaza	Noon	✓	$$+	83	38
Days Inn Downtown	11	✓	$-	53	33
Days Inn Town Hall Casino Hotel	Noon	✓	$$-	55	17
El Cortez	11	✓	$+	62	36
Embassy Suites Convention Center	11	✓	$$-	88	49
Embassy Suites in Las Vegas	11	✓	$$+	79	32
Emerald Suites Tropicana	Noon	✓	$+	81	57
Excalibur	11	Floors	$+	66	39
Fairfield Inn Las Vegas Airport	Noon	✓	$+	66	43
Fairfield Inn & Suites Las Vegas South	Noon	✓	$$-	78	42
Fiesta Henderson	Noon	Floors	$+	72	43
Fiesta Rancho	Noon	✓	$+	62	31
Fitzgeralds	Noon	Floors	$+	63	41
Flamingo Hilton	Noon	Floors/ Portion of casino	$+	80	52
Four Queens	Noon	Floors	$+	69	38
Four Seasons at Mandalay Bay	Noon	✓	$$$$$$$-	94	18
Fremont, Sam Boyd's	Noon	✓	$	65	54
Gold Coast	Noon	Floors	$+	58	34

Concierge	Convention Facilities	Meeting Rooms	Valet Parking	RV Park	Room Service	Free Breakfast
						✓
	No [business ctr.., boardrooms]	Yes	Yes, complementary		✓	Free breakfast
✓	✓	✓			Dinner	Coffee
✓		✓			✓	Coffee
						✓
		✓	✓			✓
✓	✓	✓				✓ ✓
		✓	✓			✓ ✓
		✓	✓	✓		✓
		✓			Limited	✓
		Conference rooms	Free			✓
			✓			
		✓	✓			
✓		✓	✓			✓
	✓	✓	✓			✓
	✓	✓	✓			✓
✓	✓	✓	✓			✓
	✓	✓	✓			Breakfast only
	✓	✓	✓			✓

Hotel	Fine Dining/ Type of Food	Coffee Shop	24-hr. Café	Buffet	Casino
Comfort Inn Paradise Road					
Courtyard Las Vegas South	American, breakfast only		No (24-hr. food market)	Breakfast	
Courtyard by Marriott		✓		✓	
Crowne Plaza	American	✓			
Days Inn Downtown	American		✓		
Days Inn Town Hall Casino Hotel			✓		✓
El Cortez	Family/Steak	✓	✓		✓
Embassy Suites Convention Center	American				
Embassy Suites in Las Vegas					
Emerald Suites Tropicana					
Excalibur	Continental, Italian, Prime Rib, Steak	✓	✓	✓	✓
Fairfield Inn Las Vegas Airport					
Fairfield Inn & Suites Las Vegas South		✓			
Fiesta Henderson	Italian, Steak, Mexican		✓	✓	✓
Fiesta Rancho	Mexican, Seafood, Italian, Steak, Chinese	✓	✓	✓	✓
Fitzgeralds	Steak, American, International	✓	✓	✓	✓
Flamingo Hilton	Italian, Asian, Seafood, Continental	✓	✓	✓	✓
Four Queens	American, Chinese	✓	✓		✓
Four Seasons at Mandalay Bay	American, Continental	✓			
Fremont, Sam Boyd's	Ribs, Chinese, American, Pacific Rim	✓	✓	✓	✓
Gold Coast	Steak, Italian, Seafood	✓	✓	✓	✓

Lounge	Showroom Entertainment	Gift Shop Drugs/News	Pool	Exercise Rooms	Tennis & Racquet Games
				✓	
✓		✓	✓		
		✓	✓ Heated		Tennis
✓		✓	✓ Heated		Privileges
✓			✓		
✓	Nightly, live entertainment	✓	✓ Heated		
✓					
✓		✓	✓	✓	
✓			✓	✓	
			✓	✓	
✓	Production show, King Arthur's Tournament	✓	✓ Heated		
			✓		
✓		✓	✓	✓	
✓	Live music	✓	✓		
✓	Live music	✓	✓ Heated		
			✓		
✓	Production show, musical comedy	✓	✓ Heated	Health spa	Tennis
		✓			
✓			✓ Heated	Health & fitness spa	
✓	Headliners Wayne Newton, T–F	✓			
✓	Dancing	✓	✓ Heated		✓

Hotel	Star Rating	Zone	Street Address
Golden Nugget	★★★★	2	129 East Fremont Street Las Vegas, 89101
Golden Palm Hotel	★★	1	3111 West Tropicana Avenue Las Vegas, 89103
Greek Isles	★★★	1	305 Convention Center Drive Las Vegas, 89109
Green Valley Ranch	★★★★	5	2300 Paseo Drive Henderson, 89012
Hampton Inn Tropicana	★★½	1	4975 South Industrial Road Las Vegas, 89118
Hard Rock Hotel	★★★★	1	4455 Paradise Road Las Vegas, 89109
Harrah's	★★★½	1	3475 Las Vegas Boulevard South Las Vegas, 89109
Holiday Inn Express Las Vegas	★★★	1	5760 Polaris Las Vegas, 89118
Horseshoe	★★½/ ★★½	2	128 East Fremont Street Las Vegas, 89101
Howard Johnson Airport	★★	1	5100 Paradise Road Las Vegas, 89119
Hyatt Regency at Lake Las Vegas	★★★★	5	101 Montelago Boulevard Henderson, 89011
Imperial Palace	★★★	1	3535 Las Vegas Boulevard South Las Vegas, 89109
JW Marriott Las Vegas	★★★★½		221 North Rampart Boulevard Las Vegas, 89128
Key Largo Casino and Quality Inn	★★½	1	377 East Flamingo Road Las Vegas, 89109
La Quinta	★★½	1	3970 Paradise Road Las Vegas, 89109
La Quinta Tropicana	★★½		4975 South Valley View Boulevard Las Vegas, 89118
Lady Luck	★★★/ ★★½	2	206 North Third Street Las Vegas, 89101
Las Vegas Club	★★★/ ★★½	2	18 East Fremont Street Las Vegas, 89101
Las Vegas Hilton	★★★★	1	3000 Paradise Road Las Vegas, 89109
Las Vegas Marriott Suites	★★★★	1	325 Convention Center Drive Las Vegas, 89109
Luxor	★★★½	1	3900 Las Vegas Boulevard South Las Vegas, 89119

Local Phone	Fax	Toll-Free Reservations	Discount Available	Number of Rooms
(702) 385-7111	(702) 386-8362	(800) 634-3454	AAA	1,907
(702) 798-1111	(702) 798-7138	(800) 300-7389	Senior, AAA, government	150
(702) 734-0711	(702) 734-2954	(800) 633-1777		201
(702) 617-7777	(702) 617-7778	(866) 782-9487		247
(702) 948-8100	(702) 948-8101	(800) 426-7866	AAA, corporate	320
(702) 693-5000	(702) 693-5010	(800) 413-1638		667
(702) 369-5000	(702) 369-5008	(800) HARRAHS		2,700
(702) 736-0098	(702) 736-0084	(800) 732-7899	AAA, AARP, government	177
(702) 382-1600	(702) 384-1574	(800) 937-6537		354
(702) 798-2777	(702) 736-8295	(800) 634-6439	Senior, AAA, government	325
(702) 567-1234	(702) 567-6067	(800) 55-HYATT	Senior, AAA, government	496
(702) 731-3311	(702) 735-8578	(800) 634-6441		2,700
(702) 869-7515	(702) 869-7771	(877) 869-8777		541
(702) 733-7777	(702) 369-6911	(800) 634-6617	Senior	300
(702) 796-9000	(702) 796-3537	(800) NU-ROOMS	Senior	251
(702) 798-7736	(702) 798-5951	(800) 531-5900	AAA	59
(702) 477-3000	(702) 477-3002	(800) LADY-LUCK		792
(702) 385-1664	(702) 387-6071	(800) 634-6532		410
(702) 732-5111	(702) 794-3611	(800) 732-7117	Senior, military, government	3,174
(702) 650-2000	(702) 650-9466	(800) 244-3364	Senior, AAA	278
(702) 262-4000	(702) 262-4452	(800) 288-1000		4,407

Hotel	Check Out Time	Non-Smoking	Rack Rate	Room Quality	Room Value
Golden Nugget	Noon	Floors	$$-	83	58
Golden Palm Hotel	11	Floors	$-	50	28
Greek Isles	Noon	✓	$$-	73	39
Green Valley Ranch	Noon	✓	$$$$+	84	21
Hampton Inn Tropicana	Noon	✓	$+	73	36
Hard Rock Hotel	Noon	Floors	$$$$$$-	86	17
Harrah's	Noon	Floors/ Part of casino	$+	82	53
Holiday Inn Express Las Vegas	Noon	✓	$$$-	74	24
Horseshoe	Noon		$-/ $-	64/ 53	77/ 47
Howard Johnson Airport	Noon	✓	$-	52	30
Hyatt Regency at Lake Las Vegas	11	✓	$$$$-	88	26
Imperial Palace	Noon	Floors	$-	65	55
JW Marriott Las Vegas	Noon	✓	$$$$$-	95	24
Key Largo Casino and Quality Inn	Noon	✓	$-	64	74
La Quinta	Noon	✓	$$+	69	23
La Quinta Tropicana	Noon	✓	$+	58	29
Lady Luck	Noon	✓	$+/ $+	65/ 59	45/ 34
Las Vegas Club	Noon	✓	$-/ $-	73/ 58	90/ 59
Las Vegas Hilton	Noon	✓	$-	87	99
Las Vegas Marriott Suites	Noon	✓	$$$+	84	28
Luxor	11	✓	$$	82	40

Concierge	Convention Facilities	Meeting Rooms	Valet Parking	RV Park	Room Service	Free Breakfast
✓	✓	✓	✓			✓
	✓		✓		✓	Coffee
		✓	✓			✓
✓	✓	✓	✓			✓
	✓	✓	✓			✓
✓	✓	✓	✓			✓
	✓	✓	✓			✓
		✓				✓
			✓			✓
		✓				
✓	✓	✓	✓			✓
	✓	✓	✓			✓
✓	✓	✓	✓		✓	✓
		✓				
		✓				✓
		✓				
			✓			✓
	✓	✓	✓			✓
	✓	✓	✓			✓
✓	✓	✓				✓
✓	✓	✓	✓			✓

Hotel	Fine Dining/ Type of Food	Coffee Shop	24-hr. Café	Buffet	Casino
Golden Nugget	Italian, Chinese, Continental	✓	✓	✓	✓
Golden Palm Hotel		✓	✓		✓
Greek Isles	Greek, American	✓			Slots
Green Valley Ranch	Irish, Italian, Steak, Seafood, American, Chinese	✓		✓	✓
Hampton Inn Tropicana		No (In-room coffee service)			Gaming machines
Hard Rock Hotel	Italian, Steak, Japanese, Continental, Mexican	✓	✓		✓
Harrah's	Steak/Seafood, Italian, Asian	✓	✓	✓	✓
Holiday Inn Express Las Vegas					
Horseshoe	Steak, Chinese	✓	✓	✓	✓
Howard Johnson Airport					✓
Hyatt Regency at Lake Las Vegas	American, Pacific	✓			✓
Imperial Palace	Steak, Seafood, Chinese, Ribs, Pizza	✓	✓	✓	✓
JW Marriott Las Vegas	Buffet, Health Food	✓	✓	✓	✓
Key Largo Casino and Quality Inn	American	✓	✓		✓
La Quinta					
La Quinta Tropicana					
Lady Luck	Steak/Seafood, Italian	✓	✓	✓	✓
Las Vegas Club	Steak/Seafood	✓	✓		✓
Las Vegas Hilton	French, Asian, Seafood Mexican, Italian, Japanese	✓	✓	✓	✓
Las Vegas Marriott Suites	American/ Southwestern				
Luxor	American, Seafood, Steak	✓	✓	✓	✓

Lounge	Showroom Entertainment	Gift Shop Drugs/News	Pool	Exercise Rooms	Tennis & Racquet Games
✓	Production show, headliners	✓	✓ Heated		
✓	Variety, changes nightly		✓		
✓	Magic, headliners		Under construction		Nearby
✓	Headliners	✓	✓	✓	Nearby
✓		✓	✓	✓	
✓	Live music	✓	✓ Heated	Health spa	
✓	Production show, comedy show	✓	✓	✓	✓
			✓		
✓		✓	✓		
			✓		
✓		✓	✓	✓	✓
✓	Impersonator show	✓	✓	✓	
✓	Entertainment in casino and restaurants	✓	✓ Heated	✓	✓
✓	Live music	✓	✓ Heated		
			✓ Heated	✓	
			✓		
	Production show, magic, impersonator show	✓	✓		
✓			✓	Privileges	
✓	Production show	✓	✓ Heated	✓	
✓		✓	✓ Heated	✓	
✓	Live entertainment changes nightly	✓	✓ Heated	✓	

Hotel	Star Rating	Zone	Street Address
Main Street Station	★★★½	2	200 North Main Street Las Vegas, 89101
Mandalay Bay	★★★★½	1	3950 Las Vegas Boulevard South Las Vegas, 89193
Manor Suites	★★★½	3	7230 Las Vegas Boulevard South Las Vegas, 89119
Marriott Suites, Las Vegas	★★★★	1	325 Convention Center Drive Las Vegas, 89109
MGM Grand	★★★★	1	3799 Las Vegas Boulevard South Las Vegas, 89109
Mirage	★★★★½	1	3400 Las Vegas Boulevard South Las Vegas, 89109
Monte Carlo	★★★½	1	3770 Las Vegas Boulevard South Las Vegas, 89109
Montelago Village Resort	★★★★	5	30 Strada di Villaggio Henderson, 89118
Motel 6 Tropicana	★★	1	195 East Tropicana Las Vegas, 89109
Nevada Palace	★★½	5	5255 Boulder Highway Las Vegas, 89122
New Frontier	★★★/ ★★★½	1	3120 Las Vegas Boulevard South Las Vegas, 89109
New York–New York	★★★	1	3790 Las Vegas Boulevard South Las Vegas, 89109
Orleans	★★★½/ ★★★	3	4500 West Tropicana Avenue Las Vegas, 89103
Palace Station	★★★½/ ★★★	1	2411 West Sahara Avenue Las Vegas, 89102
Palms	★★★★	1	4321 West. Flamingo Road Las Vegas, 89103
Paris	★★★★½	1	3655 Las Vegas Boulevard South Las Vegas, 89109
Plaza	★★½	2	One Main Street Las Vegas, 89101
Residence Inn Las Vegas South	★★★★	1	5875 Industrial Road Las Vegas, 89118
Residence Inn by Marriott	★★★★	1	3225 Paradise Road Las Vegas, 89109
Rio	★★★★	1	3700 West Flamingo Road Las Vegas, 89103
Ritz-Carlton Lake Las Vegas	★★★★★	5	1610 Lake Las Vegas Parkway Henderson, 89011

Local Phone	Fax	Toll-Free Reservations	Discount Available	Number of Rooms
(702) 387-1896	(702) 386-4421	(800) 465-0711		406
(702) 632-7777	(702) 632-7190	(877) 632-7000		3,276
(702) 939-9000	(702) 939-9014	(800) 691-7169		258
(702) 650-2000	(702) 650-9466	(800) 244-3364	Senior, AAA	278
(702) 891-1111	(702) 891-3036	(800) 929-1111		5,005
(702) 791-7111	(702) 791-7446	(800) 627-6667		3,049
(702) 730-7777	(702) 730-7200	(800) 311-8999		3,002
(702) 564-4700	(702) 564-4777	(866) 564-4799		177
(702) 798-0728	(702) 798-5657	(800) 4-MOTEL-6		608
(702) 458-8810	(702) 458-3361	(800) 634-6283		209
(702) 794-8200	(702) 794-8410	(800) 634-6966		986
(702) 740-6969	(702) 891-5285	(800) NY-FOR-ME		2,035
(702) 365-7111	(702) 365-7500	(800) ORLEANS		840
(702) 367-2411	(702) 221-6510	(800) 634-3101		1,028
(702) 942-7777	(702) 942-7001	(866) 942-7777	AAA, government	447
(702) 946-7000	(702) 967-3830	(888) 266-5687	Senior, AAA	2,917
(702) 386-2110	(702) 382-8281	(800) 634-6575		1,052
(702) 795-7373	(702) 7953288	(800) 331-3131	Government, corporate	160
(702) 796-9300	(702) 796-6571	(800) 331-3131	Senior, military, AAA	192
(702) 252-7777	(702) 253-6090	(800) PLAYRIO		2,563
(702) 567-4700	(702) 567-477	(800) 241-3333		349

Hotel	Check Out Time	Non-Smoking	Rack Rate	Room Quality	Room Value
Main Street Station	11	Floors	$+	75	61
Mandalay Bay	11	Floors	$$$$$-	92	23
Manor Suites	11	✓	$$-	79	43
??Marriott Suites, Las Vegas	Noon	✓	$$$-	84	28
MGM Grand	11	Floors	$$	87	48
Mirage	Noon	Floors	$$$-	90	41
Monte Carlo	11	Floors	$$	81	39
Montelago Village Resort	Noon	✓	$$$$-	90	25
Motel 6 Tropicana	11	✓	$-	52	31
Nevada Palace	Noon	✓	$+	59	32
New Frontier	Noon	Floors	$-/ $	82/ 75	85/ 73
New York–New York	11	Floors	$$-	75	35
Orleans	Noon	Floors	$+/ $+	75/ 67	61/ 47
Palace Station	Noon	Floors	$$$+/ $$$+	81/ 74	22/ 17
Palms	Noon	✓	$$+	84	44
Paris	11	Floors	$$+	91	52
Plaza	Noon	✓	$-	60	43
Residence Inn Las Vegas South	Noon	✓	$$$-	N/A	N/A
Residence Inn by Marriott	Noon	✓	$$$-	83	33
Rio	Noon	Floors	$$	85	47
Ritz-Carlton Lake Las Vegas	Noon	✓	$$$$	97	34

Concierge	Convention Facilities	Meeting Rooms	Valet Parking	RV Park	Room Service	Free Breakfast
			✓		Privileges	
✓	✓	✓	✓			✓
✓	✓	✓				✓
✓	✓	✓	✓			✓ ✓
✓	✓	✓	✓			✓
✓	✓	✓	✓			✓
✓		✓	✓ Complementary			
	✓	✓			✓	
		✓	✓			✓
✓	✓	✓	✓			✓
		✓	✓			✓
✓	✓	✓	✓			✓
✓	✓	✓	✓			✓
✓	✓	✓	✓			✓
		✓	✓			✓
		✓	✓ Complementary		✓ (Dinner only from local rest.)	✓
		✓			✓	✓
✓	✓	✓	✓		✓	Coffee
✓	✓	✓	✓			✓

Hotel	Fine Dining/ Type of Food	Coffee Shop	24-hr. Café	Buffet	Casino
Main Street Station	Steak, Brewery	✓	✓	✓	✓
Mandalay Bay	American, Chinese, Fusion Southern, Italian, Mexican,	✓	✓	✓	✓
Manor Suites					
Marriott Suites, Las Vegas	American/ Southwestern				
MGM Grand	Steak, Italian, Chinese Seafood, American, Mexican	✓	✓	✓	✓
Mirage	French, Japanese, Steak/ Seafood, Italian, Chinese	✓	✓	✓	✓
Monte Carlo	Steak, Chinese, Italian, French	✓	✓	✓	✓
Montelago Village Resort	Steak, Seafood, Italian	✓	✓		✓
Motel 6 Tropicana	American		✓		
Nevada Palace	Italian, Steak, Seafood	✓	✓	✓	✓
New Frontier	Steak, Mexican	✓	✓	✓	✓
New York–New York	Steak, Chinese, Italian	✓	✓	✓	✓
Orleans	Italian, Steak	✓	✓		✓
Palace Station	Seafood, Chinese, Mexican, Italian	✓	✓	✓	✓
Palms	Asian, French, Steak, Mexican	✓	✓	✓	✓
Paris	French, American	✓	✓	✓	✓
Plaza	American, Continental	✓	✓	✓	✓
Residence Inn Las Vegas South				✓ (Free breakfast)	
Residence Inn by Marriott					
Rio	Italian, Oysters, Cajun, Chinese, Southwestern	✓	✓	✓	✓
Ritz-Carlton Lake Las Vegas	Italian, Spa fare	✓			✓

Lounge	Showroom Entertainment	Gift Shop Drugs/News	Pool	Exercise Rooms	Tennis & Racquet Games
		✓	Privileges		
✓	Headliners, live music, sports	✓	✓		
			✓		
✓		✓	✓ Heated	✓	
✓	Production show, celebrity headliner	✓	✓ Heated	✓	✓
✓	Production show, celebrity headliner	✓	✓ Heated	Health spa	
✓	Magic show	✓	✓ Heated	Health spa	
✓		✓	✓	✓	
			✓		
		✓	✓		
	Country-Western nightly	✓	✓ Heated		
✓	Production show	✓	✓	Health spa	
✓	Celebrity headliners on weekends	✓	✓ Heated		
✓	Live music	✓	✓		
✓	Headliners, DJs		✓	✓	Nearby
✓	Hunchback of Notre Dame in English	✓	✓ Rooftop		
✓	Production show, varies	✓	✓ Heated		Tennis
		✓	✓	✓	
			✓ Heated	Privileges	
✓	Live entertainment	✓	✓ Heated		
✓				✓	✓

Hotel	Star Rating	Zone	Street Address
Riviera	★★★/ ★★★	1	2901 Las Vegas Boulevard South Las Vegas, 89109
Royal Resort	★★½	1	99 Convention Center Drive Las Vegas, 89109
Sahara	★★★	1	2535 Las Vegas Boulevard South Las Vegas, 89109
Sam's Town	★★★½	5	5111 Boulder Highway Las Vegas, 89122
San Remo	★★★	1	115 East Tropicana Avenue Las Vegas, 89109
Santa Fe Station	★★★	4	4949 North Rancho Drive Las Vegas, 89130
Silverton	★★★½/ ★★★	3	3333 Blue Diamond Road Las Vegas, 89139
St. Tropez	★★★★	1	455 East Harmon Avenue Las Vegas, 89109
Stardust	★★★½	1	3000 Las Vegas Boulevard South Las Vegas, 89109
Stratosphere	★★★½	1	2000 Las Vegas Boulevard South Las Vegas, 89104
Suncoast	★★★½	4	9090 Alta Drive Las Vegas, 89145
Sunset Station	★★★½	5	1301 Sunset Road Las Vegas, 89014
Super 8	★★	1	4250 Koval Lane Las Vegas, 89109
Terrible's	★★½	1	4100 South Paradise Road Las Vegas, 89109
Texas Station	★★★	3	2101 Texas Star Lane Las Vegas, 89030
THEhotel at Mandalay Bay (all suites)	★★★★½	3	3950 Las Vegas Boulevard South Las Vegas, 89118
Travelodge Sahara Westwood Inn	★★	1	1501 West Sahara Las Vegas, 89102
Treasure Island	★★★★	1	3300 Las Vegas Boulevard South Las Vegas, 89109
Tropicana	★★★	1	3801 Las Vegas Boulevard South Las Vegas, 89109
Tuscany	★★★★	1	255 East Flamingo Road Las Vegas, 89109
The Venetian	★★★★½	1	3355 Las Vegas Boulevard South Las Vegas, 89109

Local Phone	Fax	Toll-Free Reservations	Discount Available	Number of Rooms
(702) 734-5110	(702) 794-9451	(800) 634-6753		2,075
(702) 735-6117	(702) 735-2546	(800) 634-6118		236
(702) 737-2111	(702) 791-2027	(888) 696-2121	Senior, military, government	1,758
(702) 456-7777	(702) 454-8014	(800) 634-6371		650
(702) 739-9000	(702) 736-1120	(800) 522-7366		711
(702) 658-4900	(702) 658-4919	(800) 872-6823	Military, government, corporate	200
(702) 263-7777	(702) 896-5635	(800) 588-7711		300
(702) 369-5400	(702) 369-1150	(800) 666-5400	Senior, military, AAA	149
(702) 732-6111	(702) 732-6257	(800) 824-6033		2,431
(702) 380-7777	(702) 383-5334	(800) 99-TOWER	Senior, AAA	1,500
(702) 636-7111	(702) 636-7288	(877) 677-7111		432
(702) 547-7777	(702) 432-7730	(888) SUNSET 9		457
(702) 794-0888	(702) 794-3504	(800) 888-8000		290
(702) 733-7000	(702) 691-2423	(800) 640-9777		400
(702) 631-1000	(702) 631-8120	(800) 654-8888	AAA	200
(702) 632-7777	(702) 632-7190	(800) 632-7800	Senior	1,120
(702) 733-0001	(702) 733-1571	(800) 578-7878	Senior, military, AAA	223
(702) 894-7111	(702) 894-7446	(800) 944-7444		2,900
(702) 739-2222	(702) 739-2469	(800) 634-4000		1,874
(702) 893-8933	(702) 947-5994	(877) TUSCAN-1		716
(702) 733-5000	(702) 414-4805	(888) 2VENICE		3,000

Hotel	Check Out Time	Non-Smoking	Rack Rate	Room Quality	Room Value
Riviera	11	✓	$+/ $+	75/ 73	42/ 41
Royal Resort	Noon	Floors	$$-	76	30
Sahara	Noon	Floors	$+	69	48
Sam's Town	Noon	✓	$+	78	58
San Remo	Noon	Floors	$-	69	64
Santa Fe Station	Noon	✓	$$-	73	34
Silverton	Noon	Floors	$-/ $+	82/ 73	89/ 41
St. Tropez	Noon	✓	$$	88	49
Stardust	Noon	Floors	$+	76	64
Stratosphere	11	Floors	$+	79	55
Suncoast	Noon	✓	$$-	82	50
Sunset Station	Noon	Floors	$+	82	57
Super 8	Noon		$+	52	26
Terrible's	Noon		$-	63	64
Texas Station	Noon	Floors	$$-	70	36
THEhotel at Mandalay Bay (all suites)	11	✓	$$$$$+	96	22
Travelodge Sahara Westwood Inn	Noon	✓	$-	50	40
Treasure Island	Noon	Floors	$$-	84	52
Tropicana	Noon	Floors	$+	73	51
Tuscany	11	✓	$$-	84	52
The Venetian	11	Floors	$$$+	94	33

Concierge	Convention Facilities	Meeting Rooms	Valet Parking	RV Park	Room Service	Free Breakfast
✓	✓	✓	✓			✓
						Breakfast & lunch
		✓	✓			✓
						None
	✓	✓	✓			✓
	✓	✓	✓			
	✓	✓	✓		✓	✓
✓		✓				✓
	✓	✓	✓			✓
✓		✓	✓			✓
	✓	✓	✓			✓
✓	✓	✓	✓			✓
			✓			
						✓
✓			✓			✓
✓	✓	✓	✓ Complementary		✓ (Dinner from local rest.)	✓
		✓	✓			✓
✓	✓	✓	✓			✓
✓	✓	✓	✓			✓
✓		✓	✓			✓
✓	✓	✓	✓			✓

Hotel	Fine Dining/ Type of Food	Coffee Shop	24-hr. Café	Buffet	Casino
Riviera	Steak/Seafood, Chinese, Italian	✓	✓	✓	✓
Royal Resort			✓		
Sahara	Steak, Mexican	✓	✓	✓	✓
Sam's Town	Steak, Italian, American	✓	✓	✓	✓
San Remo	Italian, Japanese, Steak/Seafood	✓	✓	✓	✓
Santa Fe Station	Mexican, Steak French, Italian	✓	✓	✓	✓
Silverton		✓	✓	✓	✓
St. Tropez	Adjacent				
Stardust	Rib, Steak/Lobster, Mexican, Sushi	✓	✓	✓	✓
Stratosphere	Continental, Steak, Italian, American	✓	✓	✓	✓
Suncoast	Italian, American, English, Mexican	✓	✓	✓	✓
Sunset Station	American, Italian, Steak/Seafood, Mexican	✓	✓	✓	
Super 8					
Terrible's	American		✓	✓	
Texas Station	Seafood, Italian, Mexican, Steak, Chinese	✓	✓	✓	✓
THEhotel at Mandalay Bay	The Mix restaurant opens end of 2004	✓	✓	✓	✓
Travelodge Sahara Westwood Inn					
Treasure Island	Seafood/Steak, American, Chinese, Italian	✓	✓	✓	✓
Tropicana	Steak, Chinese, Japanese, Italian	✓	✓	✓	✓
Tuscany	Italian, European	✓	✓	✓	✓
The Venetian	Italian, Gourmet	✓	✓		✓

Lounge	Showroom Entertainment	Gift Shop Drugs/News	Pool	Exercise Rooms	Tennis & Racquet Games
✓	Production show, female impersonators, comedy club	✓	✓ Heated	✓	Tennis
✓			✓	✓	
✓	Production shows, variety	✓	✓		
✓	Western dance hall/ production show	✓	✓		
✓	Production show	✓	✓ Heated		
✓		✓	✓		
✓	Live music	✓	✓ Heated		
			✓ Heated	✓	
✓	Production show	✓	✓ Heated	✓	
✓	Production show	✓	✓ Heated		
✓	Headliner	✓	✓	✓	Nearby
	Live entertainment, concerts		✓	✓	
✓			✓	✓	
✓		✓	✓		
✓	Live entertainment nightly	✓	✓		
✓	✓	✓	✓	✓	
		✓	✓		
✓	Production show	✓	✓ Heated	✓	
✓	Production show, comedy club, magic	✓	✓ Heated	✓	
✓	Special events	✓	✓	✓	
✓	Headliners, live music	✓	✓	✓	✓

Hotel	Star Rating	Zone	Street Address
Westin Casuarina Hotel and Spa	★★★★	I	160 East Flamingo Road Las Vegas, 89109
Westward Ho	★★½	I	2900 Las Vegas Boulevard South Las Vegas, 89109
Wild Wild West	★★	I	3330 West Tropicana Avenue Las Vegas, 89103

Hotel	Check Out Time	Non-Smoking	Rack Rate	Room Quality	Room Value
Westin Casuarina Hotel and Spa	Noon	✓	$$$$$$$-	85	14
Westward Ho	11		$	55	38
Wild Wild West	Noon	✓	$-	51	47

Hotel	Fine Dining/ Type of Food	Coffee Shop	24-hr. Café	Buffet	Casino
Westin Casuarina Hotel and Spa	California cuisine	✓	✓		✓
Westward Ho		✓	✓		
Wild Wild West		✓	✓		✓

Local Phone	Fax	Toll-Free Reservations	Discount Available	Number of Rooms
(702) 836-9775	(702) 836-9776	(888) 625-5144		826
(702) 731-2900	(702) 731-3544	(800) 638-6803		777
(702) 740-0000	(702) 736-7106	(800) 634-3488	Senior, AAA	300

Concierge	Convention Facilities	Meeting Rooms	Valet Parking	RV Park	Room Service	Free Breakfast
✓	✓	✓	✓		✓	
						✓

Lounge	Showroom Entertainment	Gift Shop Drugs/News	Pool	Exercise Rooms	Tennis & Racquet Games
✓	✓		✓	✓	
		✓	✓		
✓		✓	✓		

Part Two

Entertainment and Nightlife

Las Vegas Shows and Entertainment

Las Vegas calls itself the "Entertainment Capital of the World." This is arguably true, particularly in terms of the sheer number of live entertainment productions staged daily. On any given day in Las Vegas, a visitor can select from dozens of presentations, ranging from major production spectaculars to celebrity headliners, from comedy clubs to live music in lounges. The standard of professionalism and value for your entertainment dollar is very high. There is no other place where you can buy so much top-quality entertainment for so little money.

But here's the bad news: The average price of a ticket to one of the major production shows topped $58 in 2004, a whopping 100% increase since 1994. To balance the picture, however, the standard of quality for shows has likewise soared. And variety, well, there's now literally something for everyone, from traditional Las Vegas feathers and butts to real Broadway musicals. And believe it or not, the value is still there. Maybe not in the grand showrooms and incessantly hyped productions, but in the smaller showrooms and lounges and in the main theaters of off-Strip hotels. There's more of everything now, including both overpriced shows and bargains. Regarding the former, you'll be numbed and blinded by their billboards all over town. As concerns the latter, you'll have to scout around, but you'll be rewarded with some great shows at dynamite prices. Want to see the Doobie Brothers or Crystal Gayle? They're a mile from the Strip at the Orleans. Meanwhile, catch Confederate Railroad or José Feliciano at Boulder Station's Railhead Saloon. *Second City*, a comedy act at the Flamingo, is one of the best buys in town, at about $30 plus tax, and there are always discount coupons floating around for productions at the downtown showrooms.

Choices, Choices, Choices

Most Las Vegas live entertainment offerings can be lumped into one of several broad categories:

- Celebrity Headliners
- Long-Term Engagements
- Production Shows
- Impersonator Shows
- Comedy Clubs
- Lounge Entertainment

Celebrity Headliners   As the name implies, these are concerts or shows featuring big-name entertainers on a limited-engagement basis, usually one to four weeks, but sometimes for a one-night stand. Headliners are usually backed up by a medium-sized orchestra, and the stage sets and special production effects are kept simple. Performers such as Kenny Rogers, Wynonna, David Copperfield, and Tom Jones play Las Vegas regularly. Some even work on a rotation with other performers, returning to the same showroom for several engagements each year. Other stars, such as Barbra Streisand and Paul McCartney, play Las Vegas only rarely, transforming each rare appearance into a truly special event. While there are exceptions, the superstars are regularly found at the MGM Grand, Mandalay Bay, Aladdin, Las Vegas Hilton, and Bally's; sometimes at the Mirage and the Riviera; and occasionally at the Hard Rock. Big-name performers in the city's top showrooms command premium admission prices. Headliners of slightly lesser stature play at various other showrooms. Many of the newer hotels, including the Venetian, Mandalay Bay, Aladdin, Sam's Town, Suncoast, Sunset Station, Texas Station, Orleans, Hard Rock, and MGM Grand, have concert and special-event venues where artists ranging from John Lee Hooker to Sheryl Crow to the Rolling Stones perform, with World Championship Wrestling and Champions on Ice thrown in for balance.

Long-Term Engagements   These are shows by the famous and once-famous who have come to Las Vegas to stay. Wayne Newton, for example, has signed an exclusive ten-year contract for $25 million per year with the Stardust—he'll perform for 40 weeks and have 12 weeks off each year. Similarly, Clint Holmes has found a long-term home at Harrah's, and comic Rita Rudner has been making a go of it at New York–New York. Gladys Knight holds court at the Flamingo. None of the long-run headliners have made a bigger splash than diva Celine Dion, who opened in March 2003 at the Coliseum (theater) at Caesars Palace. The show features Dion's hit songs elaborately integrated into a technologically groundbreaking spectacle created by *Cirque du Soleil* visionary Franco Dragone. The combination of Dion's music and Dragone's sets, effects, and choreography will knock you out. So will the prices, the highest in Las Vegas entertainment history for a long-running show.

Production Shows   These are continuously running, Broadway-style theatrical and musical productions. Cast sizes run from a dozen performers to well over a hundred, with costumes, sets, and special effects spanning a comparable range. Costing hundreds of thousands, if not millions, to produce, the shows feature elaborate choreography and great spectacle. Sometimes playing twice a night, six or seven days a week, production shows often run for years.

Production shows generally have a central theme to which a more or less standard mix of choreography and variety acts (also called specialty acts) are added. Favorite central themes are magic/illusion—six such shows are currently running—and a "best of Broadway" theme, which figures prominently in four current shows. Defying categorization, *Cirque du Soleil* now offers three shows.

In one common format, the show will open with an elaborate production number featuring dancers and, often, topless showgirls. As the presentation continues, variety acts alternate with either magic or musical numbers, depending on the theme. Variety acts frequently integrated into production shows include stand-up comics, jugglers, acrobats, balancing artists, ventriloquists, martial arts specialists, bola-swinging gauchos, and even archers. If magic is not the central theme of the show, a magician or illusionist is usually included among the variety acts. As a rule, the show closes with a spectacular finale showcasing the entire cast in some unimaginably colossal set, augmented by an impressive array of costuming, lighting, and special effects. Special effects figure prominently in Las Vegas production shows, and even more prominently in advertisements for Las Vegas production shows. Special effects are defined as "better than regular effects." Nobody knows what regular effects are.

Las Vegas puts its own distinctive imprint on all this entertainment, imparting a great deal of homogeneity and redundancy to the mix of productions. The quality of Las Vegas entertainment is quite high, even excellent, but most production shows seem to operate according to a formula that fosters a numbing sameness. Particularly pronounced in the magic/illusion shows and the Broadway-style musical productions, this sameness discourages sampling more than one show from each genre. While it is not totally accurate to say that "if you've seen one Las Vegas production or magic show, you've seen them all," the statement comes closer to the truth than one would hope.

In the magic/illusion shows, the decade-long rage is to put unlikely creatures or objects into boxes and make them disappear. Some featured magicians repeat this sort of tiresome illusion more than a dozen times in a single performance, with nothing really changing except the size of the box and the object placed into it. Into these boxes go doves, ducks, turkeys, parrots, dwarfs, showgirls, lions, tigers, sheep dogs, jaguars, panthers, motorcycles (with riders), TV cameras (with cameramen), and even elephants. Sometimes the illusionist himself gets into a box and disappears, reappearing moments later in the audience. Generally the elephants and other animals don't reappear until the next performance. These box illusions are amazing the first time or two, but become less compelling after that. After they had seen all of the illusion shows in Las Vegas, our reviewers commented that they had witnessed the disappearance in a box of everything except Jerry Falwell. Food for thought.

The Broadway-style musical productions likewise lack differentiation, tending to merge after more than one sample into a great blur of bouncing bare breasts and fanciful, feathery costumes. It should be reiterated, however, that like the magic productions, most of the musicals are well done and extremely worthwhile. But like the magic productions, the musicals offer only slight variations of the same theme.

While they share a common format, production shows, regardless of theme, can be differentiated by the size of the cast and by the elaborateness of the production. Other discriminating factors include the creativity of the choreography, the attractiveness of the performers, the pace and continuity of the presentation, and its ability to build to a crescendo. Strength in these last-mentioned areas sometimes allows a relatively simple, lower-budget show to provide a more satisfying evening of entertainment than a lavish, long-running spectacular.

Breaking new ground in the production-show category are the magnificent, aquatic *Cirque du Soleil* production *"O"* at the Bellagio, impressionist *Danny Gans* at the Mirage, percussionist *Blue Man Group* at the Luxor, *Tony 'n' Tina's Wedding,* a quirky interactive dinner-theater presentation at the Rio, and in a genre where you wouldn't expect much creativity, the steamy striptease production, *La Femme,* imported from Paris and playing at the MGM Grand. Though some might quibble about lumping a celebrity headliner in the production show category, *Celine Dion's A New Day* at Caesars Palace, is one of the most compelling, elaborate, and technologically advanced shows in town.

Impersonator Shows   These are usually long-running production shows, complete with dancers, that feature the impersonation of celebrities both living (Joan Rivers, Cher, Neil Diamond, Tina Turner, Madonna) and deceased (Marilyn Monroe, Elvis, Liberace, the Blues Brothers). In shows such as the Imperial Palace's *Legends in Concert,* and the Stratosphere's *American Superstars,* the emphasis is on the detail and exactness of the impersonation. In general, men impersonate male stars and women impersonate female stars (as you might expect). *La Cage* at the Riviera, however, features males impersonating female celebrities. No one, dead or alive, male or female, is impersonated as frequently as Elvis. According to the Las Vegas Convention and Visitors Authority, there are at least 260 Elvis impersonators in Las Vegas. We'd love to see them all in the same show. Wouldn't that be a "hunka, hunk of burning love?"

Comedy Clubs Stand-up comedy has long been a tradition in Las Vegas entertainment. With the success of comedy clubs around the country and the comedy-club format on network and cable television, stand-up comedy in Las Vegas was elevated from lounges and production shows to its own specialized venue. Las Vegas comedy clubs are small- to medium-sized showrooms featuring anywhere from two to five comedians per show. As a rule, the shows change completely each week, with a new group of comics rotating in. Each showroom has its own source of talent, so there is no swapping of comics from club to club. Comedy clubs are one of the few Las Vegas entertainments that draw equally from both the tourist and local populations. While most production shows and many celebrity headliner shows are packaged for the over-40 market, comedy clubs represent a concession to youth. Most of the comics are young, and the humor is often raw and scatological, and almost always irreverent.

Lounge Entertainment Many casinos offer exceptional entertainment at all hours of the day and night in their lounges. For the most part, the lounges feature musical groups. On a given day almost any type of music, from oldies rock to country to jazz to folk, can be found in Las Vegas lounges. Unlike the production and headliner showrooms and comedy clubs, no reservations are required to take advantage of most lounge entertainment. If you like what you hear, just walk in. Sometimes there is a two-drink minimum for sitting in the lounge during a show, but just as often there are no restrictions at all. You may or may not be familiar with the lounge entertainers by name, but you can trust that they will be highly talented and very enjoyable. To find the type of music you prefer, consult one of the local visitor guides available free from the front desk or concierge at your hotel.

Lounge entertainment is a great barometer of a particular casino's marketing program; bands are specifically chosen to attract a certain type of customer. In general, if you find a casino with lounge entertainment that suits your tastes, you will probably be comfortable lodging, dining, and gambling there also.

As an alternative to high ticket prices in Las Vegas showrooms (a dozen shows now cost upwards of $70), several casinos have turned their nightclubs and lounges into alternative show venues with ticket prices in the $20–$35 range. **Ra** at the Luxor, **The Nightclub** at the Las Vegas Hilton, and the **Lizard Lounge** at Santa Fe Station all operate several nights each week as mini-showrooms. We've seen a number of marginal or unsuccessful clubs turned into showrooms over the years, but this is the first time we've observed highly successful nightspots converted. In the main, we don't care for this trend. True, it offers some low-price shows, but at the cost of sacrificing some of the city's best lounges and nightclubs.

They Come and They Go

Las Vegas shows come and go all the time. Sometimes a particular production will close in one Las Vegas showroom and open weeks later in another. Some shows actually pack up and take their presentations to other cities, usually Reno/Lake Tahoe or Atlantic City. Other shows, of course, close permanently. During the past years, we have seen the following productions disappear from the Las Vegas scene:

Abracadabra (Aladdin)	Lido de Paris (Stardust)
Alakazaam (Aladdin)	Luck Is a Lady (Lady Luck)
At the Copa with David Cassidy (Rio)	MADhattan (New York–New York)
Bare Essence (Sands)	Marty Allen & Steve Rossi
Brazilia (Rio)	(Vegas World)
Cabaret Circus (Lady Luck)	Melinda: First Lady of Magic
Caesar's Magical Empire	(Venetian)
(Caesars Palace)	Men Are from Mars (Flamingo)
Chicago (Mandalay Bay)	Naked Angels (Plaza)
City Lites (Flamingo)	Nashville USA (Boomtown)
Comedy Cabaret (Maxim)	Notre Dame de Paris (Paris)
Copacabana (Rio)	Nudes on Ice (Plaza)
Country Fever (Golden Nugget)	Outrageous (San Remo)
Country Tonite (Aladdin)	Playboy's Girls of Rock & Roll
De la Guarda (Rio)	(Maxim)
EFX! (MGM Grand)	Rodney's Place (El Rancho)
Enter the Night (Stardust)	Showstopper (Desert Inn)
Fire & Ice (Hacienda)	Spellbound (Harrah's)
Forbidden Vegas (Plaza)	Starlight Express (Las Vegas Hilton)
Great Radio Music Hall Spectacular	Storm (Mandalay Bay)
(Flamingo)	Swing, Swing, Swing (Sands)
Hanky Panky (San Remo)	Thriller (Aladdin)
Hell on Heels (Maxim)	Tropical Heat (Rio)
Hot Stuff (Sands)	Wild Things (Dunes)
Imagine (Luxor)	Winds of the Gods (Luxor)
Keep Smilin' America (Holiday)	

The bottom line: it's hard to keep up with all this coming and going. Do not be surprised if some of the shows reviewed in this guide have bitten the dust before you arrive. Also do not be surprised if the enduring shows have changed or moved to another casino.

Learn Who Is Playing before You Leave Home

On the Internet, check out **www.vegas.com/shows.** The site also provides information and reviews on long-run headliners and production shows. The Las Vegas Convention and Visitors Authority publishes an entertainment calendar for all showrooms and many lounges. The brochure *Showguide,* organized alphabetically according to host hotel, tells who is playing, provides appearance dates, and lists information and reservation numbers.

The *Showguide* can be obtained without charge by writing or calling:

Las Vegas Convention and Visitors Authority
Visitor Information Center
3150 Paradise Road
Las Vegas, NV 89109-9096   (702) 892-7576 or (702) 892-0711

Show Prices and Taxes

Admission prices for Las Vegas shows range from around $15 all the way up to $200 per person. Usually show prices are quoted exclusive of entertainment and sales taxes. Also not included are server gratuities.

As recently as 1990, there was no such thing as a reserved seat at a Las Vegas show. If you wanted to see a show, you would make a reservation (usually by phone) and then arrive well in advance to be assigned a seat by the showroom maître d'. Slipping the maître d' a nice tip ensured a better seat. Typically, the price of the show included two drinks, or there would be waitstaff service and you would pay at your table after you were served. While this arrangement is still practiced in a few showrooms, the prevailing trend is toward reserved seating. With reserved seating, you purchase your tickets at the casino box office (or by phone in advance with your credit card). As at a concert or a Broadway play, your seats are designated and preassigned at the time of purchase, and your section, aisle, and seat number will be printed on your ticket. When you arrive at the showroom, an usher will guide you to your assigned seat. Reserved seating, also known as "hard" or "box office" seating, sometimes includes drinks but usually does not.

A common package (once *the* most common package) is the cocktail show, where your admission usually includes the show and one or two drinks. If the quoted admission price for the cocktail show is $40 per person, your actual cost will be approximately as follows:

Cocktail-show admission	$40.00
Entertainment and sales tax (17%)	$6.80
Total (before gratuities)	$46.80

If there are two performances per night, the early show is often (but not always) more expensive than the late show. In addition, some shows add a "surcharge" on Saturdays and holidays. If you tip your server a couple of bucks and slip the maître d' or captain some currency for a good seat (in a showroom without reserved seating), you can easily end up paying $27 or more for a $20 list-price show and $63 or more for a $50 list-price show.

How to Save Big Bucks on Show Tickets

The easiest way to save is to see *Dr. Naughty X-Rated Hypnosis* instead of *Celine Dion*. OK, OK, just kidding. Here are some more practical tips:

1. Most of the high-price shows are in new, state-of-the art theaters, which often have several classification of seats. You can see *Celine Dion* at Caesars Palace, for example, for $88 from a mezzanine seat. A front orchestra seat at the same show sells for $200.

2. There is a half-price-ticket outlet in the Showcase Mall just north of the MGM Grand called **Tickets2Nite.** The discounter sells tickets for same-day shows for half price plus a $3 service fee. Open noon–9 p.m., sales are first come, first serve. Generally speaking, you won't find tickets available for top tier productions like the *Cirque du Soleil* shows, *Danny Gans,* and *Celine,* because, among other reasons, they sell out every night. Many, if not most of the other shows, turn up at Tickets2Nite, some routinely, some periodically. Tickets2Nite has a Web site, **www.tickets2nite.com,** but doesn't list what shows are available on a particular day. According to Tickets2Nite, "agreements with the shows restrict us from disclosing that information except on our menu boards after 11:30 a.m. daily." So yes, that means you have to troop over to the Tickets2Nite box office in person to see what's available. A second half-price outlet is Tix4Tonight, located next door to the Harley Davidson Café on the Strip. Tix4Tonight operates in pretty much the same way as Tickets2Nite, but often offers more shows than Ticket2Nite, and charges a lower handling fee. Tix4Tonight and Tickets2Nite sell largely the same shows, but each handles a number of shows the other doesn't sell. The two discounters are located so close together that it's easy and convenient to comparison shop. Shopping the two outlets is easy enough if you're on foot but an incredible hassle if you're driving—the traffic is horrendous and parking is problematic. Showcase Mall has a $3 pay lot. You can park at the MGM Grand, New York–New York, or the Tropicana, but these are not very convenient. You can also park at the small free deck behind the Harley Davidson Café at the corner of the Strip and Harmon Avenue; it's mostly empty during the afternoon, which is the best time to hit the discount ticket outlets.

3. Showrooms, like other Las Vegas hotel and casino operations, sometimes offer special deals. Sometimes free or discounted shows are offered with lodging packages. Likewise, coupons from complementary local tourist magazines or casino funbooks (see page 19) provide discounts or "two-for-one" options. Since these specials come and go, your best bet is to inquire about currently operating deals and discounts when you call for show reservations. If you plan to lodge at a hotel-casino where there is a show you want to see, ask about room/show combination specials when you make your room reservations. When you arrive in Las Vegas, pick up copies of the many visitor magazines distributed in rental-car agencies and at hotels. Scour the show ads for discount coupons.

How to Make Reservations for Las Vegas Shows

Almost all showrooms take phone reservations. The process is simple and straightforward. Either call, using the reservation numbers listed in this book, or have your hotel concierge call. Most shows will accept reservations at least one day, and often several days in advance. Many will accept reservations weeks in advance.

Some shows, when you call for reservations, will take only your name and the number of people in your party. Under this arrangement, you will either pay at the box office on the day of the show or, alternatively, pay in the showroom after you are seated.

Most shows will allow you to prepurchase your admission on the phone using a credit card. If you prepay, usually you will have to pick up your tickets at the box office before the show. Also, many tickets are now available from Ticketmaster at (702) 474-4000, or online at **www.ticket master.com.**

Hotel Lobby Ticket Sales

For some reason many people do not trust the phone reservation system, though it works perfectly well. These folks often purchase show tickets at booths operated by independent tour brokers in the hotel lobbies, paying substantial booking and gratuity surcharges for the privilege of having a ticket. Upon arriving at the showroom they discover that the ticket does not guarantee a reserved seat. In fact, they learn that it offers nothing except a mechanism for prepayment (sometimes at an inflated price). Further, at several showrooms, the ticket purchased earlier must be exchanged for one of the showroom's own tickets, thus necessitating another wait in line. Finally, not all shows are available through the brokers.

In some casinos there are both independent operators selling tickets to shows all over town and (in another location in the same casino) a reservations and ticket booth for the shows that are playing at that specific casino. The official reservations/ticket booth will usually sell tickets or make reservations only for the casino's own shows and, unlike the independent operator, will not tack on any extra charges. When you pay your admission before entering the showroom, be sure to ask whether drinks, gratuities, and tax are included.

Trying to See a Show without a Reservation or Ticket

On Sunday through Thursday, you have a fair shot at getting into most Las Vegas shows just by asking the maître d' to seat you or by purchasing a ticket at the box office if reserved seats are sold.

On most Fridays and Saturdays, however, it is a different story. If you decide on the spur of the moment that you would like to see the show at the casino where you have been dining or gambling, do not wait in line at the entrance to the showroom to make your inquiry. Instead, go directly to the box office, maître d', or to one of the other show personnel at the entrance and ask if they have room for your party. In some instances, you may be asked to join the end of the guest line or stand by while they check for no-shows or cancellations. You will, of course, be charged the regular admission price, but an amazing percentage of the time you will be admitted. Superstar celebrity headliner shows like Celine Dion and performances of *Cirque du Soleil's Mystère* and *"O," Blue Man Group, Danny Gans, Legends in Concert,* and *Tournament of Kings* are generally the most difficult shows to see on an impromptu basis.

Dinner Shows

Some dinner shows represent good deals, others less so. Be aware, however, that with all dinner shows, your drinks (if you have any) will be extra, and invariably expensive. Food quality at dinner shows varies. In general, it can be characterized as acceptable, but certainly not exceptional. What you are buying is limited-menu banquet service for 300–500 people. Whenever a hotel kitchen tries to feed that many people at once, it is at some cost in terms of the quality of the meal and the service.

Tournament of Kings at the Excalibur does not provide the cocktail option. At *Tournament of Kings,* all shows automatically include dinner of Cornish hen with soup, potatoes, vegetable, dessert, and choice of nonalcoholic beverage for about $45 per person, taxes and gratuities included. *Tournament of Kings* is described in detail later in the chapter. There are two dinner shows, *Tony 'n' Tina's Wedding* at the Rio and *Ba-Da-Bing* at Desert Passage in the Aladdin, that integrate the meal into the unfolding storyline of the show. At *Tony 'n' Tina's,* you're a wedding guest and similarly, at *Ba-Da-Bing,* you're a guest at the mafia godfather's birthday party. In both cases, you're sucked into the story and expected to role play as the show demands.

Several casinos offer show-and-dinner combos where you get dinner and a show for a special price, but dinner is served in one of the casinos' restaurants instead of in the showrooms. Many restaurants provide only coffee-shop ambience, but the food is palatable and a good deal for the money. At each casino, you can eat either before or after the early show.

Early vs. Late Shows

If you attend a late show, you will have time for a leisurely dinner prior to the performance. For those who prefer to eat late, the early show followed by dinner works best. Both shows are identical except that for some productions the early show is covered and the late show is topless.

On weekdays, late shows are usually more lightly attended. On weekends, particularly at the most popular shows, the opposite is often the case.

Practical Matters

What to Wear to the Show

While it is by no means required, guests tend to dress up a bit when they go to a show. For a performance in the main showrooms at Bally's, Bellagio, Caesars Palace, Mandalay Bay, or the Mirage, gentlemen will feel more comfortable in sport coats, with or without neckties. Women generally wear suits, dresses, skirt and blouse/sweater combinations, and even semiformal attire. That having been said, however, you'll find a third to a half of the audience at any of these casinos dressed more casually than described.

Showrooms at the Luxor, the Stratosphere, Monte Carlo, New York–New York, Treasure Island (T. I.), the MGM Grand, Harrah's, the Rio, the Flamingo, Las Vegas Hilton, Paris Las Vegas, Tropicana, Aladdin, the Riviera, the Sahara, and the Stardust are a bit less dressy (sport coats are fine, but slacks and sweaters or sport shirts are equally acceptable for men), while showrooms at the Excalibur, the Imperial Palace, the Orleans, Sam's Town, Suncoast, Sunset Station, Texas Station, the House of Blues at Mandalay Bay, the Golden Nugget, and the Hard Rock are the least formal of all (come as you are). All of the comedy clubs are informal, though you would not feel out of place in a sport coat or, for women, a dress.

Getting to and from the Show

When you make your reservations, always ask what time you need to arrive for seating, and whether you should proceed directly to the showroom or stop first at the box office. You are normally asked to arrive one hour before the curtain rises, though a half-hour will do if you already have your reserve-seat tickets (ticket will show a designated row and seat number). If you are driving to another hotel for a show and do not wish to avail yourself of valet parking, be forewarned that many casinos' self-parking lots are quite distant from the showroom. Give yourself an extra 15 minutes or more to park, walk to the casino, and find the showroom. If you decide to use valet parking, be advised that the valet service may be swamped immediately following the show.

A show with a large seating capacity in one of the major casinos can make for some no-win situations when it comes to parking. At all of the megahotels, self-parking is either way off in the boonies or in a dizzying multistory garage, so your inclination may be to use valet parking. After the show, however, 1,000–1,650 patrons head for home, inundating the valets, particularly after a late show. If you encounter this situation, your best bet is to use self-parking and give yourself some extra time, or use valet parking and plan to stick around the casino for a while after the show.

Invited Guests and Line Passes

Having arrived at the casino and found the showroom, you will normally join other show-goers waiting to be seated. If the showroom assigns reserved seats, the process is simple: Just show your tickets to an usher and you will be directed to your seats. At showrooms without reserved seating, you will normally encounter two lines. One line, usually quite long, is where you will queue up unless you are an "Invited Guest." There is a separate line for these privileged folks that allows them to be seated without waiting in line or coming an hour early. Most invited guests are gamblers who are staying at the host casino. Some have been provided with "comps" (complementary admission) to the show. These are usually regular casino customers or high rollers. If you are giving the casino a lot of action, do not be shy about requesting a comp to the show.

Gamblers or casino hotel guests of more modest means are frequently given line passes. These guests pay the same price as anyone else for the show but are admitted without waiting via the Invited Guest line. To obtain a line pass, approach a floorman or pit boss (casino supervisory personnel are usually distinguished from dealers by their suits and ties) and explain that you have been doing a fair amount of gambling in their casino. Tell him or her that you have reservations for that evening's show and ask if you can have a line pass. Particularly if you ask on Sunday through Thursday, your chances of being accommodated are good.

If you are an invited guest under any circumstances, always arrive to be seated at least 30 minutes early.

Reservations, Tickets, and Maître d' Seating

If, like most guests, you do not have a line pass, you will have to go through the process of entering the showroom and being seated. A dwindling number of showrooms practice what is known as maître d' seating. This means that, except in the case of certain invited guests, no seats are reserved. If you called previously and made a reservation, that will have been duly noted and the showroom will have your party listed on the reservations roster, but you will not actually be assigned a seat until you appear before the maître d'. At some showrooms with maître d' seating, you are asked to pay your waiter for everything (show, taxes, drinks, etc.) once you have been seated and served.

At the comedy clubs and an increasing number of major showrooms, you will be directed to a booth variously labeled "Tickets," "Reservations," "Box Office," or "Guest Services." The attendant will verify your reservation and ask you to go ahead and pay. Once paid, you will receive a ticket to show the maître d' on entering the showroom. This arrangement eliminates any requirement for paying the tab at your table (unless drinks are not included), thus simplifying service once you are seated.

The ticket does not reserve you any specific seat; you still need to see the maître d' about that. Also, the ticket does not include gratuities for your server in the showroom unless specifically stated.

As discussed earlier, most showrooms have discarded maître d' seating in favor of "box office" or "hard" seating. At the Mirage, Bellagio, Orleans, the MGM Grand, the Luxor, T. I., Monte Carlo, the Excalibur, the Stardust, Bally's, the Las Vegas Hilton, Mandalay Bay, Aladdin, New York–New York, Venetian, Paris, and Caesars Palace, among others, specific reserved-seat assignments are printed on each ticket sold, as at a football game or on Broadway.

Most showrooms that issue hard (reserved-seat) tickets will allow you to charge your tickets over the phone using your credit card. If you charge your tickets over the phone, however, the quality of your seat assignments is at the mercy of the box office. On the other hand, if you take the trouble to buy your tickets in person at the hotel box office, you can review the seating chart and pick your seats from all seats available.

Where to Sit

When it comes to show seating, there are two primary considerations: visibility and comfort. The newer main showrooms at Caesars Palace, Mandalay Bay, Bellagio, the Mirage, T. I., MGM Grand, Paris, Luxor, Aladdin, Monte Carlo, New York–New York, Stratosphere, and the Las Vegas Hilton provide plush theater seats, many with drink holders in the arms. The best accommodations in older showrooms are roomy booths, which provide an unencumbered view of the show. The vast majority of seats in these showrooms, however, and all in some, will be at banquet tables—a euphemism for very long, narrow tables where a dozen or more guests are squeezed together so tightly they can hardly move. When the show starts, guests seated at the banquet tables must turn their chairs around in order to see. This requires no small degree of timing and cooperation, since every person on the same side of the table must move in unison.

Showrooms generally will have banquet table seating right in front of the stage. Next, on a tier that rises a step or two, will be a row of plush booths. These booths are often reserved for the casino's best customers (and sometimes for big tippers). Many maître d's would rather see these booths go unoccupied than have high rollers come to the door at the last minute and not be able to give them good seats. Behind the booths but on the same level will be more banquet tables. Moving away from the stage and up additional levels, the configuration of booths and banquet tables is repeated on each tier.

For a big production show on a wide stage like *Jubilee!, Lord of the Dance, Cirque du Soleil,* the *Folies Bergere,* or *Celine Dion,* you want to sit in the middle and back a little. Being too close makes it difficult to see everything without wagging your head back and forth as if you were at a tennis match.

Likewise, at a concert by a band or musical celebrity headliner (Tom Jones, Al Jarreau, B. B. King, etc.), partway back and in the center is best. This positioning provides good visibility and removes you from the direct line of fire of amplifiers and lights. This advice, of course, does not apply to avid fans who want to fling their underwear or room keys at the star.

For smaller production shows on medium-sized stages (*Lance Burton, Legends in Concert,* etc.), right up front is great. This is also true for headliners like Bill Cosby, Rita Rudner, and David Copperfield. For female impersonators (*La Cage*), the illusion is more effective if you are back a little bit.

At comedy clubs and smaller shows, there are really no bad seats, though the *Comedy Stop* at the Tropicana has some columns in the showroom you want to avoid. Finally, be aware that comedians often single out unwary guests sitting down front for harassment, or worse, incorporate them into the act.

Getting a Good Seat at Showrooms with Maître d' Seating

1. Arrive early   No maître d' can assign you a seat that's already taken. This is particularly important for Friday and Saturday shows. We have seen comped invited guests (the casino's better customers) get lousy seats because they waited until the last minute to show up.

2. Try to go on an off night, i.e., Sunday through Thursday   Your chances of getting a good seat are always better on weeknights, when there is less demand. If a citywide convention is in town, weekdays may also be crowded.

3. Try to know where (as precisely as possible) you would like to sit   In showrooms with maître d' seating, it is always to your advantage to specifically state your seating preferences.

4. Understand your tipping alternatives   Basically, you have three options:

- Don't tip
- Tip the maître d'
- Tip the captain (instead of the maître d')

Don't tip   Politely request a good seat instead of tipping. This option actually works better than you would imagine in all but a few showrooms, particularly Sunday–Thursday. If the showroom is not sold out and you arrive early, simply request a seat in a certain area. Tell the maître d', "We would like something down front in the center." Then allow the captain (the showroom staff person who actually takes you to your seat) to show you the seats the maître d' has assigned. If the assigned seat is not to your liking, ask to be seated somewhere else of your choosing. The captain almost always has the authority to make the seat assignment change without consulting the maître d'.

On slower nights, the maître d' will often "dress the showroom." This means that the maître d', not expecting a full house, will distribute patrons pretty equally throughout the showroom, especially nearer the stage. This procedure, which makes the audience look larger than it really is, is done for the morale of the performers and for various practical reasons, such as ensuring a near-equal number of guests at each server station. On these nights, you have a pretty good shot at getting the seats you want simply by asking.

Tip the maître d' When you tip the maître d', it is helpful to know with whom you are dealing. First, the maître d' is the man or woman in charge of the showroom. The showrooms are their domain, and they rule as surely as battalion commanders. Maître d's in the better showrooms are powerful and wealthy people, with some maître d's taking in as much as $1,650 a night. Even though these tips are pooled and shared in some proportion with the captains, it's still a lot of money.

When you tip a maître d', especially in the better showrooms, you can assume it will take a fairly hefty tip to impress him, especially on a busy night. The bottom line, however, is that you are not out to impress anyone; you just want a good seat. Somebody has to sit in the good seats, and those who do not tip, or tip small, have to be seated regardless. So, if you arrive early and tip $15–$20 (for a couple) in the major showrooms, and $5–$10 in the smaller rooms, you should get decent seats. If it is a weekend or you know the show is extremely popular or sold out, bump the tip up a little. If you arrive late on a busy night, ask the maître d' if there are any good seats left before you proffer the tip.

Have your tip in hand when you reach the maître d'. Don't fool around with your wallet or purse as if you are buying hot dogs and beer at the ball park. Fold the money and hold it in the palm of your hand, arranged so that the maître d' can see exactly how big the tip is without unfolding and counting the bills. State your preference for seating at the same time you inconspicuously place the bills in the palm of his hand. If you think all this protocol is pretty ridiculous, I agree. But style counts, and observing the local customs may help get you a better seat.

A variation is to tip with some appropriate denomination of the casino's own chips. Chips are as good as currency to the maître d' and implicitly suggest that you have been gambling with that denomination of chips in his casino. This single gesture, which costs you nothing more than your cash tip, makes you an insider and a more valued customer in the eyes of the maître d'.

Many maître d's are warm and friendly and treat you in a way that shows they appreciate your business. These maître d's are approachable and reasonable and will go out of their way to make you comfortable. There are also a number of maître d's and captains, unfortunately, who are extremely cold, formal, and arrogant. Mostly older men dressed in tuxedos, they usually have gray hair and a military bearing and can seem rather imposing or hostile. Do not be awed or intimidated. Be forthright and, if necessary, assertive; you will usually be accommodated.

Tip the captain   Using this strategy, tell the maître d' where you would like to sit but do not offer a tip. Then follow the captain to your assigned seats. If your seats are good, you have not spent an extra nickel. If the assigned seats are less than satisfactory, slip the captain a tip and ask if there might be something better. If you see seats you would like to have that are unoccupied, point them out to the captain. Remember, however, that the first row of booths is usually held in reserve.

Before the Show Begins

For years, admission price to cocktail shows has included two drinks. For several years, however, this policy has been subject to experimentation, resulting in a confusing and constantly changing variety of drink inclusions and exclusions. While many showrooms continue to offer two drinks with admission, others have gone to either one or none.

The inclusion of drinks is not what makes Las Vegas shows a good entertainment value, but the absence of any standard practice in this regard certainly creates enough ill will and confusion to bias the customer's perception of value. From a consumer perspective, a package that includes drinks is straightforward, understandable, and a lot easier to administer in the showroom.

Some of the variations you will encounter are as follows: There will be a cash bar and no table service; if you want a drink before the show, you walk to the bar and buy it. At some showrooms, drinks are included but there is no table service. You take a receipt stub to the bar and exchange it for drinks.

In most other showrooms there is table service where you can obtain drinks from a server. If drinks are included, some slip of paper, a receipt stub, or other type of documentation will be deposited at your place by the captain when you are seated. This scrap of paper will alert your server that you have some drinks coming. When the server takes your order or, alternatively, when the drinks are delivered, he or she will remove the paper. If drinks are not included, there will usually be a small table sign or drink menu with prices listed.

In showrooms where there is table service, the servers run around like crazy trying to get everybody served before the show. Since all of the people at a given table are not necessarily seated at the same time, the server responsible for that table may make five or more passes before everyone is taken care of. If your party is one of the last to be seated at a table, stay cool. You *will* be noticed and you *will* be served.

Servers in showrooms are generally well organized and have their own way of getting things done. You can depend on your waiter or waitress to advise you when it is time to settle your tab. Until then, just relax. Do not try to offer the server a gratuity until the final bill is brought. Normally your server will collect for any drinks not included (and for your show admission in some showrooms with maître d' seating) just before the performance begins. On busy nights in large showrooms, the tab might not be presented until after the curtain has gone up. Most showrooms accept major credit cards and traveler's checks in addition to cash.

If you have prepaid for admission and drinks, your gratuity may have been included in your prepayment. If drinks and admission are prepaid, but not the gratuity, you should tip the server when your drinks are delivered (a dollar or two per person served is about right). If you are not sure whether drinks, gratuities, or anything else is included, ask.

Bladder Matters Be forewarned that in most showrooms there is no rest room, and that the nearest rest room is invariably a long way off, reachable only via a convoluted trail through the casino. Since the majority of show-goers arrive early and consume drinks, it is not uncommon to start feeling a little pressure on the bladder minutes before show time. If you assume that you can slip out to the rest room and come right back, think again. If you are at the Las Vegas Hilton, Caesars, or the Tropicana, give yourself more than ten minutes for the round trip, and prepare for a quest. If you get to the can and back without getting lost, consider yourself lucky.

At most other showrooms, rest rooms are somewhat closer but certainly not convenient. The Riviera, the Imperial Palace, Luxor, Harrah's, New York–New York, the MGM Grand, Stratosphere, Venetian, and the Mirage, however, seem to have considered that show guests may not wish to combine emptying their bladders with a five-mile hike. Showrooms in these casinos are situated in close and much-appreciated proximity to the rest rooms.

Selecting a Show

Selecting a Las Vegas show is a matter of timing, budget, taste, and schedule. Celebrity headliners are booked long in advance but may play only for a couple of days or weeks. If seeing Elton John, Bob Dylan, or Jerry Seinfeld in concert is a big priority for your Las Vegas trip, you will have to schedule your visit to coincide with their appearances. If the timing of your visit is not flexible, as in the case of conventioneers, you will be relegated to picking from those stars playing when you are in town. To find out which shows and headliners are playing before you leave home, call the Las Vegas Convention and Visitors Authority at (702) 892-7576 and ask them to mail you a Las Vegas *Showguide*. On the Internet, log on to **www.vegas.com/shows.**

Older visitors are often more affluent than younger visitors. It is no accident that most celebrity headliners are chosen, and most production shows created, to appeal to the 40-and-over crowd. If we say a Las Vegas production show is designed for a mature audience, we mean that the theme, music, variety acts, and humor appeal primarily to older guests. Most Las Vegas production shows target patrons 40–50 years old and up, while a few appeal to audiences 55 years of age and older.

As the post–World War II baby boomers have moved into middle age and comparative affluence, they have become a primary market for Las Vegas. Stars from the "golden days" of rock and roll, as well as folk singers from the 1960s, are turning up in the main showrooms of the Hard Rock and Bally's with great regularity. On one occasion, Paul Revere and the Raiders, the Four Seasons, the Mamas and the Papas, the Temptations, the Four Tops, B. J. Thomas, and Arlo Guthrie were playing in different showrooms on the same night.

The most hip, avant-garde show in town is *Blue Man Group* (Luxor), which targets younger audiences with a show that is wild, loud, and conceptually quite different from anything else in town.

If you are younger than 35 you will also enjoy the Las Vegas production shows, though for you their cultural orientation (and usually their music) will seem a generation or two removed. Several production shows, however, have broken the mold, in the process achieving a more youthful presentation while maintaining the loyalty of older patrons. *Splash* (Riviera) is a youthful, high-energy show—intensity, action, and volume personified. *Cirque du Soleil's Mystère* (T. I.) is an uproarious yet poignant odyssey in the European tradition, brimming over with unforgettable characters. Ditto for *Cirque's "O"* at the Bellagio. *Lance Burton* (Monte Carlo) is a smaller production but is extremely creative and works well for all ages. And, again, the comedy clubs have a more youthful orientation.

Las Vegas Shows for the Under-21 Crowd

An ever-increasing number of showrooms offer productions appropriate for younger viewers. Circus Circus provides complimentary, high-quality circus acts about once every half an hour, and *Tournament of Kings* at the Excalibur is a family dinner show featuring jousting and other benign medieval entertainments. Other family candidates include *Legends in Concert,* a celebrity impersonation show at the Imperial Palace; *Lance Burton* at the Monte Carlo; *Cirque du Soleil's Mystère* at T. I. and *"O"* at Bellagio.

Many of the celebrity headliner shows, including Celine Dion, are fine for children, and a few of the production shows offer a covered early show to accommodate families. Of the topless production shows, some operate on the basis of parental discretion while others do not admit anyone under age 21. Comedy clubs and comedy theater usually will admit teenage children accompanied by an adult. All continuously running shows are profiled later in this section. The profile will tell you whether the show is topless or particularly racy. If you have a question about a given showroom's policy for those under age 21, call the showroom's reservation and information number listed in the profile.

Celebrity Headliner Rooms

Choosing which celebrity headliner to see is a matter of personal taste, though stars like Wayne Newton and Engelbert Humperdinck seem to have the ability to rev up any audience. We talked to people who, under duress, were essentially dragged along by a friend or family member to see Wayne Newton. Many of these folks walked into the showroom prepared to hate Wayne Newton. Yet despite their negative attitude, Newton delighted and amazed them.

My point is not to hype Wayne Newton but to suggest that the talent, presence, drive, and showmanship of many Las Vegas headliners often exceed all expectations, and that adhering to the limitations of your preferences may prevent you from seeing many truly extraordinary performers. Las Vegas is about gambling, after all. Do not be reluctant to take a chance on a headliner who is not readily familiar to you.

Most of the major headliners play at a relatively small number of showrooms. Profiles of the major celebrity showrooms and their regular headliners follow. The list is not intended to be all-inclusive but rather to give you an idea of where to call if you are interested in a certain headliner. Long-running (i.e., a year or more) celebrity headliner shows including *Celine Dion, Rita Rudner, Wayne Newton, Gladys Knight, Clint Holmes, Danny Gans,* etc., are reviewed in depth in our coverage of continuously running production shows later in this chapter.

Hard Rock Hotel—The Joint

Reservations and Information (702) 693-5066 or (702) 226-4650
Frequent Headliners Top current and oldies rock, pop, blues, folk, and world music stars
Usual Show Times 8 p.m.
Approximate Admission Price $15–$180
Drinks Included None
Showroom Size 1,800 persons

Description and Comments Have you ever been to a major rock concert in a facility so large that you needed binoculars to see the band? And did you wish that just once you could enjoy that band in a smaller, more intimate setting? Hard Rock Hotel's The Joint is that setting, a medium-sized two-level venue for rock-and-roll concerts, hosting the likes of Bob Dylan, the Black Crowes, Melissa Etheridge, the Eagles, and Seal. True, seeing Bob Dylan in a 1,400-person showroom is not as cozy as having him in your living room, but it sure beats Yankee Stadium. Because most performers playing The Joint are booked for short, limited engagements, each show is a special event.

On the floor, the tightly packed audience sits on folding chairs and barstools around small tables; there are 1,000 of these reserved seats. The stage is high and the floor is on an incline, so visibility is good. Acoustics are excellent, especially in the middle of the floor and in front of the balcony.

Consumer Tips   When the reserved seats are sold out (or if someone *wants* to stand), 400 or so "standing-room" tickets are sold. These entitle patrons to a spot toward the back of the floor (by the bar), the back of the balcony, or in "the pit." Visibility from a standing-room position on the balcony is limited (except from the first few rows, which are reserved). And stageside at The Joint, be prepared for ear-splitting, head-pounding acoustics, not to mention being hemmed in by the crowd. If you don't want to be put in balcony Siberia where you can hear well enough but see nothing, or pinned against the stage for the whole show by a crush of sweaty rowdies, don't buy standing-room tickets. Book early for reserved seating—or shrug and say, "Oh well."

The Hard Rock Hotel box office sells reserved seats to shows at The Joint. You can purchase tickets via phone using your credit card or in person at the box office. Shows at The Joint are hot tickets in Las Vegas and sell out quickly, so buy your tickets as far in advance as possible.

Las Vegas Hilton—Hilton Theater

Reservations and Information   (702) 732-5111 or (800) 222-5361
Frequent Headliners   Trisha Yearwood, Johnny Mathis, Engelbert Humperdinck, Dwight Yoakam, Wynonna, Tim Conway
Usual Show Times   Varies   **Dark**   Varies
Approximate Admission Price $30–$85
Drinks Included   None
Showroom Size   1,650 seats

Description and Comments   The Hilton Theater has been home to some of the biggest names to play Las Vegas, from Elvis to Wayne Newton, with Bill Cosby along the way. Offerings run the gamut, including rock and country stars as well as top pop singers and comedians. Engagements run from a couple of days to two weeks.

Consumer Tips   Because of the Las Vegas Hilton's enormous size and booming convention business, the showroom is almost as likely to sell out on a weekday as on a weekend. Reserved seat tickets can be purchased up to four weeks in advance over the phone with a credit card, or at the box office. While the Hilton will not guarantee the location of seats purchased over the phone, persons who come in person to the box office can choose from the available seating as shown on the showroom diagram. If you use the Hilton's self-parking, give yourself at least ten minutes for the long walk to the showroom.

Mandalay Bay—House of Blues

Reservations and Information   (702) 632-7600 or (877) 632-7400;
www.hob.com
Frequent Headliners   Current and former pop, rock, R&B, reggae, folk, and country stars
Usual Show Times   8 p.m.
Approximate Admission Price $13–$85
Drinks Included   None
Showroom Size   1,800 seats

Description and Comments   House of Blues is a newer Las Vegas concert hall, very different from The Joint at the Hard Rock with which it competes head-on for performers and concert-goers. The House of Blues is more like an opera house (than the high school–gym Joint): low ceilinged, multitiered, and split-leveled, which gets the audience as close to the act as possible. To that end, the acoustics are much better than the Joint's, but the House of Blues can get claustrophobic; the more crowded, the less comfortable it is. Also, the sight-lines are highly variable, even bizarre, especially for a new room—it's almost as if the designers were modifying an old theater rather than opening a new one. And it doesn't seem to have much to do with how much you pay for a seat: some bad seats (in the nosebleed section and on the sides of the stage) don't cost much less than the best seats or much more than the cheapest tickets.

Live music is presented almost every night of the year. Major headliners, with tickets going for $30–$100, appear once or twice a week at 8 p.m.; for these shows you must be 21 to attend. Recent performers have included B. B. King, the Go-Go's, Peter Frampton, Chris Isaak, Ziggy Marley, and De la Soul. Filling in the booking gaps are minor shows, with tickets in the $12–$30 range; check the hotline and Web site; you must be 18 or over for most of them (the few others are designated "all ages"). One recent line-up of minor artists consisted of the Low-Fidelity All-Stars, God Among Men, Orbital, and Angry Salad.

Consumer Tips House of Blues ticket agents are very difficult to get by telephone; to save yourself an exorbitant phone bill, use the toll-free number listed above (and press 4). The box office is open 8 a.m.–midnight; the best time to call is right at 8 a.m. Once you have the operator (there's probably only one!) on the line, you'll often hear more bad news. The headliner shows sell out extremely fast, though you can usually pick up standing-room only tickets, where you'll be sardined in front of the stage (watch your wallet). If money is no object, try to get a VIP seat front and center in the balcony (the first ten rows are prime). If you can't, you might as well just opt for the cheap standing room, as the upper balcony and many of the loge seats aren't worth the extra money. Indeed, many people give up their bad reserved seats to move down to the floor where they can see the whole stage!

Mandalay Bay—Mandalay Bay Theater

Reservations and Information (702) 632-7580
Frequent Headliners Broadway Musicals
Usual Show Times 7:30 p.m. (varies) **Dark** Varies
Approximate Admission Price $45–$100
Drinks Included None
Showroom Size 1,700 seats

Description and Comments The Mandalay Bay Theater opened with the hit musical *Chicago* for an engagement of over a year. More recently, the theater has hosted a number of traveling Broadway productions—including *Annie*. Occasionally the theater is used as a dance or concert venue. For two years, the theater has been home to the musical comedy, *Mamma Mia!*

Consumer Tips The theater is new, gorgeous, and a little too big. With 1,700 seats, it's one-third larger than almost all Broadway houses. The floor and lower mezzanine seats are all good, but the upper mezzanine is pretty far away, especially for the price. If you go, spring for the extra $10 or $20 for the better seats.

Tickets can be ordered as far in advance as you want through the Mandalay Bay box office or Ticketmaster (phone (702) 474-4000). The cancellation policy is that there is none, so if you buy 'em you own 'em. You're given a confirmation number, which you're required to show when you pick up your tickets, along with a photo ID—that's for your own protection, they told us. Just in case someone overhears you making the reservations, cribs your confirmation number, picks your pocket, and shows up with your credit card for the tickets.

You can buy drinks at the bar in the theater lobby and carry them in; all the seats have cup holders. Beer starts at $4, mixed drinks at $6.50.

The intermission situation is interesting. Within 30 seconds of the curtain coming down, there's a long line at the rest room. It's best to pick up a re-entry pass and head into the casino; there's a bigger rest room just outside the theater.

MGM Grand—Garden Arena

Reservations and Information (702) 891-7777 or (800) 646-7787; www.mgmgrand.com

Frequent Headliners National acts, superstars, televised boxing, wrestling, and other sporting events

Usual Show Times Varies **Dark** Varies

Approximate Admission Price $20–$800

Drinks Included None

Showroom Size 17,157 seats

Description and Comments This 275,000-square-foot special-events center is designed to accommodate everything from sporting events and concerts to major trade exhibitions. The venue also offers auxiliary meeting rooms and ballrooms adjacent to the entertainment center. Barbra Streisand christened this venue with her first concert in more than 20 years on New Year's Eve 1993. Championship boxing events are favorite attractions at the Grand Garden Arena, as are the many big-name musical concerts.

Consumer Tips Reserved-seat tickets can be purchased one to two months in advance with your credit card by calling the MGM Grand main reservations number or Ticketmaster outlets, for most but not all shows (phone (702) 474-4000). If you are not staying at the MGM Grand, either arrive by cab or give yourself plenty of extra time to park and make your way to the arena.

MGM Grand—Hollywood Theater

Reservations and Information (800) 646-7787

Frequent Headliners Liza Minnelli, Sheena Easton, Carrot Top, Don Rickles, George Carlin, Engelbert Humperdinck

Usual Show Times Varies **Dark** Varies

Approximate Admission Price $40–$100

Drinks Included None

Showroom Size 650 seats

Description and Comments A very modern and comfortable showroom, with all front-facing seats, the Hollywood Theater hosts a wide range of musical and celebrity headliner productions for one- to three-week engagements.

Consumer Tips Reserved-seat show tickets can be purchased one to two months in advance with your credit card by calling the MGM Grand's main reservations number. Children are allowed at most presentations; check first to make sure. If you are not staying at the MGM Grand, either arrive by cab or give yourself plenty of extra time to park and make your way to the showroom.

Orleans—Orleans Showroom

Reservations and Information (702) 365-7075

Frequent Headliners Neil Sedaka, Frankie Valli and the Four Seasons, and Engelbert Humperdinck

Usual Show Times Varies   **Dark** Varies
Approximate Admission Price $35–$40
Drinks Included None
Showroom Size 800 seats

Description and Comments This small but comfortable showroom offers tiered theater seats arranged in a crescent around the stage. Designed for solo performers and bands, the Orleans Showroom is an intimate venue for concerts with good visibility from anywhere in the house. The star lineup runs the gamut with a concentration in country-and-western singer celebrities.

Consumer Tips This showroom features some great talent at bargain prices. All seats are reserved. Tickets can be purchased at the box office to the left of the showroom or over the phone using your credit card.

Production Shows

Las Vegas Premier Production Shows: Comparing Apples and Oranges

While we acknowledge that Las Vegas production shows are difficult to compare and that audiences of differing tastes and ages have different preferences, we have nevertheless ranked the continuously running shows to give you an idea of our favorites. This is definitely an apples-and-oranges comparison (how can you compare *Zumanity* to *Blue Man Group?*), but one based on each show's impact, vitality, originality, pace, continuity, crescendo, and ability to entertain.

We would hasten to add that even the continuously running shows change acts and revise their focus periodically. Expect our list, therefore, to change from year to year. Also, be comforted by the knowledge that while some shows are better than others, there are only one or two real dogs. The quality of entertainment among the continuously running production shows is exceptional. By way of analogy, we could rank baseball players according to their performance in a given All-Star game, but the entire list, from top to bottom, would still be All-Stars. You get the idea.

A Word about Small Showrooms

During the past couple of years, we have seen a number of casinos convert their lounge into a small showroom. Though the stage in these showrooms is routinely about the size of a beach towel, productions are mounted that include complex choreography, animal acts, and, in one notable case, an illusionist catching bullets in his teeth. In the case of musical revues, as many as four very thin or three average-sized hula dancers can fit comfortably on the stage at one time.

A real problem with some smaller shows is that they often cost as much as productions in Las Vegas's major showrooms. We once reviewed *Hell on Heels* at the now defunct Maxim, for instance, and paid about

$21, including tax and tip. Though *Hell on Heels* was a decent show and professionally performed, it could not compare in scope, talent, and spectacle to the lavish *Folies Bergere* at the Tropicana, available for only a few extra dollars.

Another problem is that small shows often play to even smaller crowds. We saw a performance of *That's Magic* at O'Shea's where the cast outnumbered the audience. Though the show featured talented illusionists, a good ventriloquist, and some dancers, the small facility made the production seem amateurish. It was heartrending to see professional entertainers work so hard for such a tiny audience. We felt self-conscious and uncomfortable ourselves, as well as embarrassed for the performers.

When it comes to smaller showrooms, simpler is better. That's why *Second City* and *Crazy Girls* work so well: Both shows take a minimalist approach. Additionally, both shows play in casinos large enough to draw an audience. Little showrooms in smaller casinos that attempt to mount big productions create only parody and end up looking foolish. Better that they revert to offering lounge shows.

We have abandoned trying to cover the productions that play in these small showrooms, mostly because the shows are very short-lived. If a small showroom production is exceptionally good and demonstrates staying power, however, we sometimes review it right along with the full-scale shows. In this edition, for example, we provide full reviews of seven small-room productions. This discussion, by the way, does not apply to comedy clubs, which work best in small rooms.

Production Show Hit Parade

Simply based on excellence, here's how we rank the Las Vegas production shows. Excluded from the list are short-run engagements (i.e., comedy clubs (see page 249), comedy theater, and short-engagement celebrity headliners) and afternoon-only shows (see page 245).

Show prices increased again during 2004, resulting in fewer bargains than in previous years. Prices in the last decade escalated by more than 100%, with most of the increase in the last four years.

PRODUCTION SHOW HIT PARADE	
Rank and Show	**Location**
1. *Cirque du Soleil's Mystère*	T. I.
2. *Cirque du Soleil's "O"*	Bellagio
3. *Celine Dion—A New Day*	Caesars Palace
4. *Blue Man Group*	Luxor
5. *Zumanity*	New York–New York
6. *Legends in Concert*	Imperial Palace
7. *Gladys Knight*	Flamingo

PRODUCTION SHOW HIT PARADE *(continued)*

Rank and Show	Location
8. *Danny Gans*	Mirage
9. *Mamma Mia!*	Mandalay Bay
10. *Lance Burton: Master Magician*	Monte Carlo
11. *The Amazing Jonathan*	Riviera
12. *Wayne Newton*	Stardust
13. *Jubilee*	Bally's
14. *Clint Holmes: Takin' It Uptown*	Harrah's
15. *La Femme*	MGM Grand
16. *Chippendales*	Rio
17. *V: The Ultimate Variety Show*	Desert Passage
18. *The World's Greatest Magic Show*	Greek Isles
19. *X: An Erotic Adventure*	Aladdin
20. *Tony 'n' Tina's Wedding*	Rio
21. *Second City*	Flamingo
22. *Rita Rudner*	New York–New York
23. *Folies Bergere*	Tropicana
24. *Splash*	Riviera
25. *American Superstars*	Stratosphere
26. *Tournament of Kings*	Excalibur
27. *Tribute to Frank, Sammy, Joey, and Dean*	Greek Isles
28. *The Platters, Coasters, & Drifters*	Sahara
29. *Crazy Girls*	Riviera
30. *Thunder from Down Under*	Excalibur
31. *Steve Wyrick, Mind-Blowing Magic*	Aladdin
32. *Showgirls*	Rio
33. *Scintas*	Rio
34. *Dirk Arthur's New Art of Magic*	Plaza
35. *An Evening at La Cage*	Riviera
36. *Spirit of the Dance*	Golden Nugget
37. *David Brenner*	Westin Casuarina
38. *Showgirls of Magic*	San Remo
39. *America's Tribute to Neil Diamond*	Riviera
40. *Skintight*	Harrah's
41. *Ba-Da-Bing*	Desert Passage
42. *Midnight Fantasy*	Luxor
43. *Hip-Nosis*	O'Shea's
44. *Hypnosis Zone*	Riviera
45. *Exotic Hypnotics*	Riviera
We Will Rock You (Not open at press time)	Paris

PRODUCTION SHOWS BY VALUE RATING†

Rank and Show		Value Rating
1.	Legends in Concert	★★★★★
2.	Honky Tonk Angels	★★★★★
3.	Second City	★★★★★
4.	The Amazing Jonathon	★★★★
5.	Gladys Knight	★★★★
6.	Dirk Arthur's New Art of Magic	★★★★
7.	Blue Man Group	★★★★
8.	Lance Burton: Master Magician	★★★★
9.	Tournament of Kings	★★★★
10.	Wayne Newton	★★★★
11.	Cirque du Soleil Mystère	★★★½
12.	Zumanity	★★★½
13.	Chippendales	★★★½
14.	X: An Erotic Adventure	★★★
15.	World's Great Magic Show	★★★
16.	Mamma Mia!	★★★
17.	V: The Ultimate Variety Show	★★★
18.	Clint Holmes: Takin' It Uptown	★★★
19.	American Superstars	★★★
20.	Cirque du Soleil "O"	★★★
21.	Crazy Girls	★★★
22.	Thunder From Down Under	★★★
23.	La Femme	★★★
24.	Celine Dion A New Day	★★★
25.	The Platters, Coasters, & Drifters	★★★
26.	Rita Rudner	★★★
27.	Danny Gans	★★★
28.	Jubilee	★★★
29.	Tony 'n' Tina's Wedding	★★½
30.	Folies Bergere (The Best of)	★★½
31.	An Evening at Le Cage	★★½
32.	Steve Wyrick, Mind-Blowing Magic	★★½
33.	Showgirls	★★
34.	Showgirls of Magic	★★
35.	Splash	★★
36.	Spirit of The Dance	★★
37.	David Brenner	★★
38.	America's Tribute to Neil Diamond	★½
39.	Scintas	★½

PRODUCTION SHOWS BY VALUE RATING† (continued)	
Rank and Show	**Value Rating**
40. *Skintight*	★½
41. *Midnight Fantasy*	★½
42. *Ba-Da-Bing*	★½
43. *Hip-Nosis*	★
44. *Exotic Hypnotics*	★
45. *Hypnosis Zone*	★

★★★★★	Exceptional value, a real bargain	★★	Somewhat overpriced
★★★★	Good value	★	Significantly overpriced
★★★	Absolutely fair, you get exactly what you pay for		

† **Note:** *A high value rating does not indicate show quality, only that your dollar is working harder there than at a show rated at a lower value. See the* **Production Show Hit Parade** *on pages 205–206 for a ranking of shows by overall excellence.*

Production Show Profiles

Following is a profile of each of the continuously running production shows, listed alphabetically by the name of the show. If you are not sure of the name of a show, consult the previous section. Comedy clubs, afternoon shows, and limited-engagement celebrity-headliner showrooms are profiled in separate sections. Prices are approximate and fluctuate about as often as you brush your teeth.

The Amazing Jonathan

Type of Show Comedy
Host Casino and Showroom Riviera—La Cage Theatre
Reservations and Information (702) 992-7970
Admission Cost with Taxes $48 and $59
Cast Size 2
Nights of Lowest Attendance Tuesday
Usual Show Times Friday–Wednesday, 10 p.m. **Dark** Thursday
Special Comments No children under age 14 admitted, under 18 with adult only
Topless No
Author's Rating ★★★★
Overall Appeal by Age Group

Under 21 —	21–37 ★★★★	38–50 ★★★★	51 and older ★★★½

Duration of Presentation 1 hour and 30 minutes

Description and Comments The Amazing Jonathan is very blue, a sort of George Carlin of inept magicians. He's also incredibly funny. Playing to a sold-out house every night, Jonathan went from a trial balloon production to a fixture at the Golden Nugget in less than half a year before moving to the Flamingo and then to the Riviera.

As a character, Jonathan is eerily appealing and totally frightening (if you're con-scripted from the audience to help out on stage you'll know what we mean). Naturally, he's supposed to do some tricks, but most are never completed, and in any case the magic merely serves as the glue that binds the gags. Jonathan has an assistant, a lovable ditzy blond, who almost steals the show. The two of them in combination are a comedic tour de force unparalleled in our view by any two comics that we've seen in Las Vegas for 15 years. If you can stand some rough language and blue humor (or if you can suspend your moral rectitude and political correctness for just 90 minutes), this show is a must-see.

Consumer Tips If you're looking for magic and illusion, forget Jonathan. If you want a PG version of Jonathan, the closest thing is Mac King at Harrah's. If you decide to go, buy your admission in advance: tickets to Jonathan are among the hottest in town. To avoid being part of the show, ask for seats a row or two back.

American Superstars

Type of Show Celebrity impersonator production show
Host Casino and Showroom Stratosphere—Star Showroom
Reservations and Information (702) 382-4446 (reservations necessary)
Admission Cost with Taxes $29 (ages 5–12); $40 (adults)
Cast Size Approximately 24
Nights of Lowest Attendance Sunday, Monday
Usual Show Times Sunday–Tuesday, 7 p.m.; Wednesday, Friday, and Saturday, 6:30 and 8:30 p.m. **Dark** Thursday
Special Comments Much enhanced on the larger stage
Topless No
Author's Rating ★★★½
Overall Appeal by Age Group

Under 21 ★★★	21–37 ★★★½	38–50 ★★★★	51 and older ★★★½

Duration of Presentation 1 hour and 30 minutes

Description and Comments *American Superstars* is a celebrity-impersonator show similar to *Legends in Concert* (Imperial Palace). Impersonated stars, which change from time to time, include Madonna, Michael Jackson, Gloria Estefan, the Spice Girls, and the ever-present Elvis. The impersonators, who do their own singing, are sup-ported by a live band and (frequently upstaged) by an energetic troupe of dancers.

American Superstars is a fun, upbeat show. While the impersonations are, in general, not as crisp or realistic as those of *Legends in Concert,* the show exhibits a lot of drive and is a great night's entertainment.

Consumer Tips The Stratosphere's main showroom has allowed the production to improve and become truly competitive with *Legends in Concert.* Though tickets must be purchased in advance, seat assignment is at the discretion of the maître d'. Drinks are not included, but can be purchased at a bar outside the showroom. The showroom is situated at the end of the shopping arcade near the elevator bank for the Stratosphere Tower. *Note:* A $42 package is available, including the show, drinks, buffet dinner, and tickets to the Tower.

America's Tribute to Neil Diamond

Type of Show Impersonator and band cover Neil Diamond's many hits
Host Casino and Showroom Riviera—Le Bistro Theatre
Reservations and Information (877) 892-7469

Admission Cost with Taxes $48 and $59
Cast Size 6
Night of Lowest Attendance Tuesday
Usual Show Times Sunday–Thursday, 7 p.m.   **Dark** Friday and Saturday
Topless No
Author's Rating ★★
Overall Appeal by Age Group

Under 21 ★ | 21–37 ★½ | 38–50 ★★★ | 51 and older ★★½

Duration of Presentation 1 hour

Description and Comments   Despite their idol's long career and army of hit singles, Neil Diamond impersonators aren't nearly as common as those who imitate Elvis, the Rat Pack, the Beatles, or other such worthies. It may be the cheese factor, as Diamond's overwrought balladeering hasn't aged as well as some. Still, Jay White is far and away the best Neil Diamond impersonator in Vegas, with a pretty close physical resemblance and dead-on vocals. This is definitely a niche show, but those who love Neil will go nuts. White's band is tight and professional, and though the onstage patter is on the lame side, who cares? Neilophiles in our audience leaped from their seats and danced in the aisles.

Consumer Tips   The Le Bistro Theatre's small stage is ringed by lounge tables and chairs, with circular booths making up the outside border. However, since the showroom is actually just a curtained alcove off the main gambling floor, casino noise inevitably filters in to the booths. Even so, the room is small enough that there are no bad sightlines.

Avenue Q

Type of Show Tony Award–winning Broadway musical
Host Casino and Showroom Wynn Las Vegas

Description and Comments   *Avenue Q* will set up shop at Wynn Las Vegas, Steve Wynn's new mega-casino, soon after the property opens in 2005. Playing in a custom-built showroom, *Avenue Q* will become the first Broadway production to play Las Vegas on an exclusive long-term contract. In other words, if you want to see *Avenue Q* you've got two choices: Broadway and Las Vegas. *Avenue Q* is a sassy, musical comedy about a down-on-its-heels, New York outer-borough neighborhood where the residents, both puppet and human, face the challenges of working, loving, and defining their lives. Warm, witty, irreverent, and sometimes blue, *Avenue Q's* characters are familiar and lovable and sometimes blue. The music is funny and memorable, and the whole production is ultra hip.

Consumer Tips   As of press time, no ticket prices or performance times had been released.

Ba-Da-Bing

Type of Show Interactive comedy dinner theater
Host Casino and Showroom Desert Passage—Aladdin
Reservations and Information (702) 992-7970; www.badabingshow.com
Admission Cost with Taxes $35, general; $80, VIP includes 3-course dinner
Cast Size 8–12
Nights of Lowest Attendance Monday
Usual Show Times Daily, 7:30 p.m.

Special Comments Moving to the Stardust before the end of 2004
Topless No
Author's Rating ★★
Overall Appeal by Age Group

Under 21 ★★ | 21–37 ★★★½ | 38–50 ★★★ | 51 and older ★★½

Duration of Presentation 1 hour and 45 minutes
Description and Comments Building on the success of interactive dinner shows like *Tony 'n' Tina's Wedding*, *Ba-Da-Bing* is a dem-dese-dose gangster comedy. Much enhanced on the larger stage, the plot concerns a disgraced hood's scheme to regain favor with his boss, Mr. Big, by throwing a surprise birthday party for the head honcho. However, a possible plot to kill the boss is uncovered, and the audience is enlisted to make sure the party succeeds without the big man getting whacked. There are a few romantic subplots and musical numbers, and audience members are dragooned into various games and contests. Wandering cast members accost any diners who might have escaped the more organized tomfoolery. The laughs are very basic: The gangsters are dummies, the women are ditzes, and everything works out in the end.

Consumer Tips As with *Tony 'n' Tina's Wedding*, your enjoyment of *Ba-Da-Bing* will depend on your interest in interacting with the players. If that's not your bag, the show is largely forgettable, with the handful of central characters far exceeding the supporting cast in both acting and singing ability. However, if you are in the mood for interaction but not for the higher ticket price of *Tony 'n' Tina*, this is an acceptable alternative. The venue is a private dining room off the main Sazio restaurant, and though small, the clusters of tables and diners can obstruct views of wandering actors. Some tables along the back wall are reserved for those who don't wish to interact with the cast at all. The dinner itself is fair to good, with choice of ribeye, chicken, or salmon (we recommend the salmon), plus salad, dessert, a (nonalcoholic) beverage, and a glass of champagne.

Blue Man Group

Type of Show Performance art production show
Host Casino and Showroom Luxor—Luxor Theatre
Reservations and Information (702) 262-4400 or (800) 557-7428
Admission Cost with Taxes $93.50 for floor seats and balcony seats
Cast Size 3 plus a 15-piece band
Nights of Lowest Attendance Sunday and Monday
Usual Show Times Tuesday and Thursday, 7 p.m.; Monday, Wednesday, and Friday, 7 and 10 p.m.; Saturday 4, 7, and 10 p.m.; Sunday, 7 p.m.
Topless No
Special Comments Teenagers will really like this show, but the blue guys, loud music, and dark colors could scare small children (5 years minimum age).
Author's Rating ★★★★
Overall Appeal by Age Group

Under 21 ★★★★ | 21–37 ★★★★½ | 38–50 ★★★★ | 51 and older ★★★½

Duration of Presentation 1 hour and 45 minutes
Description and Comments *Blue Man Group* gives Las Vegas its first large-scale introduction to that nebulous genre called "performance art." If you're from Mars and the designation "performance art" confuses you, relax—it won't hurt a bit. The *Blue Man Group* gives a stunning performance that can be appreciated by all kinds of folks.

The three blue men are just that—blue—and bald and mute. Their fast-paced show uses music and multimedia effects to make light of contemporary art and life in the information age.

Funny, sometimes poignant, and always compelling, *Blue Man Group* pounds on complex instruments (made of PVC pipes) that could pass for industrial intestines. At times the mostly percussive music is overcome by eerie melodies, and the drumming blends with a seemingly spontaneous eruption of visual art rendered in mediums as diverse as marshmallows and a mysterious goo. *Blue Man Group* challenges the audience to keep up with them, sometimes forcing you to choose between three different areas of activity. This is effective, albeit frenetic, and not a little exhausting.

Staged in the 1,200-seat Luxor Theatre, the sound and lighting are technically awesome. The stage is set with large industrial shapes and lit with deep electric blues, blacks, and purples. Against these dark colors, the blue men wield props, paints, and instruments, all in fluorescent whites, pinks, yellows, and blues. There are also a host of other costly and ultra high-tech special effects, most notably an animated sculpture that dances with the help of strobe lights.

A 15-piece percussion band backs the *Blue Man Group* with a relentless and totally engrossing industrial dance riff. The band resides in long dark alcoves above the stage. At just the right moments, their lofts are lit to reveal a group of neon-colored pulsating skeletons.

The blue men themselves play a group of instruments of their own creation, most of which are pipes of varying diameters and configurations with names like *tubulum* and *gyro shot*. Some resemble tubas, xylophones, or pipe organs. All are as stimulating visually as they are aurally.

Audience participation completes the *Blue Man* experience. The blue men often move into the audience and twice bring audience members on stage. One poor soul is offered a meal of industrial slime and becomes instrumental in the creation of a piece of art or an unfortunate stew—depending on your perspective. At the end of the show, the entire audience is involved in an effort to move a sea of paper across the theater. And a lot of folks can't help standing up to dance—and laugh.

Consumer Tips This show is decidedly different and requires an open mind to be appreciated. It also helps to be a little loose, because, like it or not, everybody gets sucked into the production. If you're uptight or believe that audiences should be passive rather than demonstrative, *Blue Man Group* will make you feel uncomfortable.

The Luxor Theater will knock you out. It's simply one of the best show venues in Las Vegas. All seats are reserved. If you don't want to get slimed by the blue men, ask to be seated five or six rows from the front of the stage. Tickets can be purchased at the box office, over the phone using your credit card, and through Ticketmaster. No drinks are included, but there is a cash bar outside the showroom.

Celine Dion—A New Day . . .

Type of Show Celebrity headliner
Host Casino and Showroom Caesars Palace—Coliseum
Reservations and Information (702) 731-7333 or (877) 4-CELINE
Admission Cost with Taxes $88–$225 depending on location of seat
Cast Size 74, including musicians and dancers
Nights of Lowest Attendance Thursday
Usual Show Times Wednesday–Sunday, 8 p.m.   **Dark** Monday and Tuesday

Special Comments No age restrictions
Topless No
Author's Rating ★★★★½
Overall Appeal by Age Group

Under 21 ★★★★½ | 21–37 ★★★★½ | 38–50 ★★★★ | 51 and older ★★★★½

Duration of Presentation   1 hour and 40 minutes

Description and Comments   The name of the show is *A New Day*, but it could just as easily be *Road Weary Diva Joins Circus*. Er, make that joins *Cirque du Soleil*. Celine Dion's Las Vegas tour de force was created by *Cirque du Soleil* visionary Franco Dragone. In it he masterfully blends a whopping 22 of Dion's songs with the surreal characters, imagery, and athletic (often acrobatic) choreography that distinguishes *Cirque du Soleil*. *A New Day* is more superficial than *Cirque's Mystère* or *"O,"* but in its best moments it approximates their power and depth. Dragone augments *A New Day's* amazing costumes and sets with an enormous LED screen, the largest in the world, that wraps around the entire rear of the stage in a sweeping half circle. Displayed on it are razor-sharp moving images, both powerful and hypnotic, that add haunting texture and context to what is happening on stage. The cast alone could carry *A New Day*, but the incorporation of this technological marvel exponentially leverages their considerable talent, wowing audiences in the same way that the introduction of sound or color once amazed moviegoers. *A New Day* is not just another Las Vegas spectacle, though as a production show it's truly groundbreaking in its special effects and choreography. What makes it transcendent is a diva who has the chutzpah to share the stage with such technology and talent. There are times, literally, when the dancing and LED images (everything from Times Square to a passing storm) are so compelling that you momentarily forget Celine Dion is singing. But when you refocus your attention on her, you begin to understand the seamless way the elements of this production are integrated.

The show has two weaknesses. First, the stage and showroom are so large that it's impossible to establish the intimacy that drives the better headliner shows. The second weakness (perhaps an attempt to mitigate the first) is the seemingly inevitable compunction of all headliners, including Celine Dion, to speak personally to the audience. Celine emotes about her husband, child, world peace (or lack thereof), and myriad other topics of interest to her but not necessarily to the audience. Of course Celine's fans (who are legion) eat this up. For the rest, these syrupy interludes are somewhat uncomfortable (in addition to disrupting the flow of the production). To compound matters, all this "sharing" is punctuated by individual fans hollering, "We love you, Celine!" from every corner of the theater. Lest we overstate the case, however, there's not all that much time for "getting to know each other" (read "getting to know me") when you've got almost two dozen songs to belt out before the curtain comes down.

Consumer Tips   The big question hanging over Celine Dion's show is whether it's worth the not-inconsiderable price. Although it's a great show by any standard, the cost is infinitely easier to swallow if you're a Celine fan. If you're neutral, or just don't know much about Celine, the question is iffier, and the answer really comes down to what you're comfortable spending.

A New Day is a hot ticket. Even at record-breaking prices for a continuously running show, it's advisable to purchase tickets as far in advance as possible. Concerning seat selection, there are good sight lines from every seat in the new, well designed Coliseum theater. Plus, the enormity of the stage and the scope of the production make sitting close to the stage less than desirable unless you desire to consult with Celine on international monetary policy or some such. If you drive to Caesars, use the valet parking at the adjoining Forum Shops rather than the hotel/casino valet service at the Caesars' main entrance. There is also valet parking and self-parking at the garages to the rear of the hotel, with an entrance that is convenient to the theater. Give yourself lots of extra time to process through the metal detectors and bag/purse search at the entrance to the theater.

Chippendales

Type of Show Male revue
Host Casino and Showroom Rio—Scintas Showroom
Reservations and Information (702) 777-7776 or (888) 746-7784
Admission Cost with Taxes $38.45 general admission; $49.45 VIP/floor seating
Cast Size 12
Nights of Lowest Attendance Wednesday
Usual Show Times Wednesday and Friday–Monday, 10 p.m.; Thursday, 8 p.m.
Dark Tuesday
Topless Yes (male)
Author's Rating ★★★★
Overall Appeal by Age Group

Under 21 ★★★★ | 21–37 ★★★★ | 38–50 ★★★★ | 51 and older ★★★½

Duration of Presentation 1 hour and 15 minutes

Description and Comments *Chippendales* strives to be the ultimate ladies night out and succeeds. The show, which originated in Los Angeles and celebrated its 25th anniversary in 2003, is a mesmerizing erotic exploration of female fantasies. Performed by a cast of one dozen flawless model types, the men of *Chippendales* exude sex appeal while acting out a sequence of eleven vignettes. Most of the tightly synchronized dance routines are performed to contemporary R&B slow jams, creating a seductive and sensual atmosphere. Unlike the comparatively tame *Thunder From Down Under,* the *Chippendales* dancers feign sex acts and remove their G-strings entirely at several times during the show (albeit only when the guys have their backs turned to the audience). Large video screens surround the 600 or more person showroom, offering a close-up view of the dancers, who can be difficult to see at times from the general-admission seating. The dancers also venture out into the audience at various points throughout the performance, although not as much as the *Thunder* cast. After the show, the men of *Chippendales* host a meet-and-greet session for an extended close-up look.

Consumer Tips No smoking is allowed during the show. On weekends, tables are removed from the VIP/floor section to provide more seating, requiring guests to hold their drinks (which can be pricey, so be careful not to spill). Drink prices and types vary greatly, from $2.50 for soda to $335 for a bottle of Louis Roederer Cristal Champagne. Other choices include: beer, $4.50–$5.50; wine by the glass, $6; frozen drinks, $7; and mixed drinks, $6–$9.50. The bathroom is located next to the Masquerade Bar, diagonally across the casino. Paying the extra for floor seats is well worth it for ladies seeking the best view. Hold onto your ticket stub, which includes a free entry to Club Rio Thursday–Saturday (up to a $20 value for men on Friday and Saturday nights).

Cirque du Soleil's Mystère

Type of Show Circus as theater
Host Casino and Showroom T.I.—*Cirque du Soleil* Showroom
Reservations and Information (702) 894-7722 or (800) 392-1999

Admission Cost with Taxes $95/ $60, limited seats

Cast Size 75

Nights of Lowest Attendance Thursday

Usual Show Times Wednesday–Saturday, 7:30 and 10:30 p.m.; Sunday, 4:30 and 7:30 p.m. **Dark** Monday and Tuesday

Special Comments No table service (no tables!)

Topless No

Author's Rating ★★★★★

Overall Appeal by Age Group

Under 21 ★★★★ | 21–37 ★★★★★ | 38–50 ★★★★★ | 51 and older ★★★★½

Duration of Presentation 1 hour and 30 minutes

Description and Comments *Mystère* is a far cry from a traditional circus but retains all of the fun and excitement. It is whimsical, mystical, and sophisticated, yet pleasing to all ages. The action takes place on an elaborate stage that incorporates almost every part of the theater. The original musical score is exotic, like the show.

Note: In the following paragraph, we get into how the show *feels* and why it's special. If you don't care how it feels, or if you are not up to slogging through a boxcar of adjectives, the bottom line is simple: *Mystère* is great. See it.

Mystère is the most difficult show in Las Vegas to describe. To categorize it as a circus does not begin to cover its depth, though its performers could perform with distinction in any circus on earth. *Cirque du Soleil* is more, much more, than a circus. It combines elements of classic Greek theater, mime, the English morality play, Dali surrealism, Fellini characterization, and Chaplin comedy. *Mystère* is at once an odyssey, a symphony, and an exploration of human emotions. The show pivots on its humor, which is sometimes black, and engages the audience with its unforgettable characters. Though light and uplifting, it is also poignant and dark. Simple in its presentation, it is at the same time extraordinarily intricate, always operating on multiple levels of meaning. As you laugh and watch the amazingly talented cast, you become aware that your mind has entered a dimension seldom encountered in a waking state. The presentation begins to register in your consciousness more as a seamless dream than as a stage production. You are moved, lulled, and soothed as well as excited and entertained. The sensitive, the imaginative, the literate, and those who love good theater and art will find no show in Las Vegas that compares with *Mystère* except *Cirque's* sister productions *"O"* at the Bellagio and *Zumanity* at New York–New York.

Consumer Tips Be forewarned that the audience is an integral part of *Mystère* and that at almost any time you might be plucked from your seat to participate. Our advice is to loosen up and roll with it. If you are too rigid, repressed, hungover, or whatever to get involved, politely but firmly decline to be conscripted.

Because *Mystère* is presented in its own customized showroom, there are no tables and, consequently, no drink service. In keeping with the show's circus theme, however, spectators can purchase refreshments at nearby concession stands. Tickets for reserved seats can be purchased 7 days in advance at the *Cirque's* box office or over the phone, using your credit card. For a comparison of *Mystère* and *Cirque du Soleil's "O"* at the Bellagio, see Description and Comments and Consumer Tips for *"O"* following this profile.

Cirque du Soleil's "O"

Type of Show Circus and aquatic ballet as theater
Host Casino and Showroom Bellagio—Bellagio Theater
Reservations and Information (702) 693-7722
Admission Cost with Taxes $150 main floor; $125 balcony ($99, limited view)
Cast Size 74
Nights of Lowest Attendance Sunday and Monday
Usual Show Times Wednesday–Sunday, 7:30 and 10:30 p.m.;
Dark Monday and Tuesday
Topless No
Author's Rating ★★★★
Overall Appeal by Age Group

Under 21 ★★★★ | 21–37 ★★★★★ | 38–50 ★★★★★ | 51 and older ★★★★½

Duration of Presentation 1 hour and 30 minutes

Description and Comments   We read an article a while back, where *Cirque du Soleil* was described as "a circus without animals," a description so woefully inadequate that it really ticked me off. Truly, the writer who penned those words has the sensitivity of a slug. *Cirque* is not the sum of various tricks and stunts, rather it is an artistic theatrical collage replete with life and all of its meaning, emotion, and color. If a performer swings from rope or juggles a hoop it is as incidental, yet as integral, as a single dollop of paint on a Rembrandt canvas. It's not the single trick that matters, it's the context.

The title *"O"* is a play on words derived from the concept of infinity, with 0 (zero) as its purest expression, and from the phonetic pronunciation of *eau,* the French word for water. Both symbols are appropriate, for the production (like all *Cirque* shows) creates a timeless dream state and (for the first time in a *Cirque* show) also incorporates an aquatic dimension that figuratively and literally evokes all of the meanings, from baptism to boat passage, that water holds for us. The foundation for the spectacle that is *"O"* resides in a set (more properly an aquatic theater) that is no less than a technological triumph. Before your eyes, in mere seconds, the hard, varnished surface of the stage transforms seamlessly into anything from a fountain to a puddle to a vast pool. Where only moments ago acrobats tumbled, now graceful water ballerinas surface and make way for divers somersaulting down from above. The combined effect of artists and environment is so complete and yet so transforming that it's almost impossible to focus on specific characters, details, or movements. Rather there is a global impact that envelops you and holds you suspended. In the end you have a definite sense that you *felt* what transpired rather than having merely seen it.

Though *"O"* is brilliant by any standard and pregnant with beauty and expression, it lacks just a bit of the humor, accessibility, and poignancy of *Cirque's Mystère* at sister casino T. I. Where *"O"* crashes over you like a breaking wave, *Mystère* is more personal, like a lover's arrow to the heart. If you enjoyed *Mystère,* however, you will also like *"O,"* and vice versa. What's more, the productions, while sharing stylistic similarities, are quite different. Though you might not want (or be able to afford) to see them both on the same Las Vegas visit, you wouldn't feel like you saw the same show twice if you did.

Consumer Tips   If you've never seen any of the Las Vegas *Cirque du Soleil* productions, we recommend catching *Mystère* first. For starters, it's $55 per person less expensive and, in our opinion, just as good (if not a smidge better). Plus, *Mystère* is more representative of *Cirque du Soleil's* hallmark presentation and tradition.

Unless you just went public with an Internet company, you're probably wondering if either of the *Cirque* productions are worth the hefty tariff. Truth be told, we've wagged on that question ourselves—$95–$150 is a lot of money. In the final analysis, however, *Mystère* is so special that we think it's a fair value at $95. And although we understand why *"O"* is more expensive (technology, physical plant, etc.), we also believe that $150 ($125 for balcony seats) is pushing the envelope a little too hard. *"O"* is a great show and the Bellagio is a classy joint, but a hundred-bucks-plus? I dunno. *Zumanity* of New York–New York is less expensive than *"O,"* but is a much simpler production.

In any event, both shows are very popular. If you want to go, buy tickets via credit card over the phone before you leave home. If you decide to see *"O"* at the spur of the moment, try the box office about 30 minutes before show time. Sometimes seats reserved for comped gamblers will be released for sale.

Cirque du Soleil's Zumanity

Type of Show A risqué *Cirque du Soleil*
Host Casino and Showroom New York–New York
Reservations and Information (702) 740-6815 and at www.zumanity.com
Admission Cost with Taxes $65–$105 depending on choice of seat
Cast Size 50
Nights of Lowest Attendance Wednesday
Usual Show Times Tuesday–Friday, 7 and 10 p.m
Dark Wednesday and Thursday
Topless Yes
Author's Rating ★★★★
Overall Appeal by Age Group

Under 21—	21–37 ★★★★	38–50 ★★★★	51 and older ★★★½

Duration of Presentation 1 hour and 30 minutes

Description and Comments *Zumanity* is about love, emotional and physical, in all its unrequited, sated, comedic, tender, and lunatic dimensions. It is also the first *Cirque* production to chart a decidedly adult course. *Cirque* spokesmen tell us that "flirtatious performers and musicians reach out to take the audience on a 90-minute encounter, awakening the most primal urges to a new form of eroticism blending movement, style, acrobatics, uninhibited costumes and beautiful bodies with the sensual caress of the human voice and the insistent pulse of exotic rhythms. This production is an intense visit to a world where human inhibitions are both unveiled and discarded, where style and intense sensual passion share an uncommon stage." Gulp. As it turns out, *Cirque* does love and sex as well as it does everything else, and *Zumanity* is a hell of a ride.

Zumanity is zany, raucous, and decidedly outrageous. It is lovable in its humor and insightful in its understanding of sex. The visually rich production blends its challenging theme with *Cirque du Soleil's* signature music, color, acrobatics, and dance. *Zumanity* is sometimes very tender but at other moments hard-edged. It urges us to look at how we define human beauty and makes a plea for the acceptance of differences, *Zumanity* delivers a powerful message.

Like all *Cirque* productions *Zumanity* is hauntingly dreamlike. But where other *Cirque* shows operate on multiple levels of meaning and interpretation, *Zumanity* tells us in unambiguous terms that sex is amazing, infinitely varied, and wonderful. As the production unfolds, you witness an artful sequence of sexual vignettes celebrating heterosexual sex, gay sex, masturbation, sex between obese lovers, sex with midgets, group sex, sadomasochistic sex, and sex enjoyed by the very old. As the name *Zumanity* implies, sex and the varied emotions we bring to it is a defining element of our humanity. Sex is happy, sex is sad, sex is of the moment, sex is transcendent, sex is funny, sex is bewildering. And as *Zumanity* so ably demonstrates, sex is a window into our essential being.

Now, after digesting the above, you might be thinking that's one window you're uncomfortable peering into, that you really don't need to know all that much about our essential being. But there's also this nagging impulse to take a little peek. You might even want to take a big peek, but aren't sure it's a good idea with your wife, mother, or father-in-law sitting beside you. That's the genius of *Zumanity*: it forces you to confront your own sexuality, including your hangups—all in the presence of your friends, family, and possibly your own lover (plus of course, 2,000 strangers). For some it's very disquieting, even frightening. Tension is palpable. Some shift continuously in their seats. They laugh a bit too loud at the jokes, try to appear unaffected by the orgasmic groaning, pretend they're quite accustomed to leather and whips, and attempt to will themselves not to be aroused. Most people, however, will find *Zumanity* to be exhilarating, and more than a few find it absolutely liberating.

Consumer Tips   *Zumanity* is brilliant, but clearly not for everyone. Certainly, it's not for prudes, the sexually repressed (probably half of America), the sexually phobic, or for the self-righteous who seek to impose their sexual mores on the rest of us. Equally, it's not for the "gentlemen's club" set. *Zumanity* is altogether too complex, cerebral, and theatrical for their taste.

Zumanity is staged in a 1,256-custom-seat, custom-designed showroom that facilitates a performer and audience intimacy remarkable for a theater so large and for a production of *Zumanity's* scope. With the exception of some first-floor seats (under the balcony outcropping) that make viewing aerial acts impossible, sight lines are excellent. The best seats are on the lower-floor center and about 12 rows or more back. As with all *Cirque du Soleil* shows, audience members are at risk of being hauled into the performance.

Clint Holmes: Takin' It Uptown

Type of Show   Live concert by Clint Holmes
Host Casino and Showroom   Harrah's—Harrah's Main Showroom
Reservations and Information   (702) 369-5111 or (800) 392-9002
Admission Cost with Taxes $71
Cast Size   14
Nights of Lowest Attendance   Monday, Tuesday
Usual Show Times   Monday–Saturday, 7:30 p.m.   **Dark**   Sunday
Topless   No
Author's Rating   ★★★½
Overall Appeal by Age Group

Under 21 ★★½ | 21–37 ★★★½ | 38–50 ★★★★ | 51 and older ★★★½

Duration of Presentation   1 hour and 30 minutes

Description and Comments   *Clint Holmes: Takin' It Uptown* feels like an intimate concert performed by a seasoned jazz ensemble. There are no specialty acts, magicians, or contortionists, just a group of musicians giving it their all. Seating less than 600 people, Harrah's showroom is the perfect venue for the warm vocals of Clint

Holmes. The locals seem to have embraced Holmes—he was recently voted "Best Singer in Las Vegas" according to the *Las Vegas Review-Journal,* the city's largest newspaper. Locals and tourists alike will appreciate this show, which offers family-friendly entertainment on the Strip. Though younger patrons are welcome, the sophisticated set-list will be most appreciated by those in their 40s and 50s.

You'll hear well-known jazz and blues standards, as well as pop favorites by Elton John, Jackson Browne, and others. The eclectic musical selection even includes a little samba. Holmes is complemented by an accomplished female vocalist, and the band, led by Bill Fayne, is at times fantastic, especially when the five-piece horn section struts its stuff.

Weaving heartfelt autobiographical storytelling into his show, Holmes graciously connects with the audience. His mother was a British opera singer and his father was an African American jazz musician. Holmes shares some thoughts on the challenge of his biracial identity and the blessing of growing up with music in his home. Pretty deep stuff for a Las Vegas production show.

Consumer Tips Harrah's Main Showroom has some booths and some free-standing chairs. The chairs are horribly uncomfortable, so ask for a booth. Drinks are available at a bar inside the showroom, and the rest rooms are easy to access.

Crazy Girls

Type of Show Erotic dance and adult comedy
Host Casino and Showroom Riviera—Mardi Gras Showrooms, second floor
Reservations and Information (702) 794-9301 or (800) 634-3420
Admission Cost with Taxes $42
Cast Size 8
Nights of Lowest Attendance Wednesday, Monday
Usual Show Times Nightly, 8:30 and 9:30 p.m.
Dark Tuesday
Topless Yes
Author's Rating ★★★½
Overall Appeal by Age Group

Under 21 — | 21–37 ★★★½ | 38–50 ★★★½ | 51 and older ★★★½

Duration of Presentation 1 hour

Description and Comments *Crazy Girls* gets right to the point. This is a no-nonsense show for men who do not want to sit through jugglers, magicians, and half the score from *Oklahoma!* before they see naked women. The focus is on eight engaging, talented, and athletically built young ladies who bump and grind through an hour of exotic dance and comedy. The choreography (for anyone who cares) is pretty creative, and the whole performance is highly charged and quickly paced, though most vocals are lip-synced. The dancers are supported by a zany comedienne who doesn't shy away from X-rated humor. Solo routines (which may be dances or just sexy writhing) are shown in close-up on large video screens, but the videos are from previous performances, creating an odd disconnect when the video and onstage performer get out of sync.

Consumer Tips The show is not really as risqué as the Riviera would lead you to believe, and the nudity does not go beyond topless and G-strings (how could it?). While designed for men, there is not much of anything in the show that would make women or couples uncomfortable. Men looking for total nudity should try the Palomino Club in North Las Vegas.

Ticket and box office information is the same as for *La Cage* (see Consumer Tips under *An Evening at La Cage,* page 222). VIP, up-close seating is available for old poots who forgot their glasses, and includes a line pass. There are a few columns in the middle section that can obstruct views from back-center seats.

Danny Gans: Entertainer of the Year

Type of Show Impressions and variety
Host Casino and Showroom Mirage—Danny Gans Theater
Reservations and Information (702) 791-7111 or (800) 963-9634
Admission Cost with Taxes $100
Cast Size Approximately 7
Nights of Lowest Attendance Wednesday
Usual Show Times 8 p.m., Tuesday–Thursday, Saturday and Sunday **Dark** Monday and Friday
Topless No
Author's Rating ★★★★
Overall Appeal by Age Group

Under 21 ★★★ | 21–37 ★★★½ | 38–50 ★★★★ | 51 and older ★★★★

Duration of Presentation 1 hour and 10 minutes

Description and Comments Danny Gans was well on his way to a promising career in major league baseball when he suffered a career-ending injury. Baseball's loss is Las Vegas entertainment's gain. This "man of many voices" is a monster talent. He does upwards of 100 impressions during the show: Michael Jackson; Willie Nelson; James Stewart; Kermit the Frog; Pee Wee Herman; John Travolta; Peter Falk; Garth Brooks; Sammy, Frank, and Dino; Walter Cronkite with Presidents Clinton, Bush, Reagan, Carter, and Ford; Billy Joel; Bruce Springsteen; Stevie Wonder; Ray Charles; Sylvester Stallone; Homer and Marge Simpson talking to Dr. Ruth's answering machine; Henry Fonda and Katharine Hepburn doing *On Golden Pond;* Paul Lynde; Wayne Newton; Neil Diamond; Sammy Davis Jr.; Natalie and Nat King Cole; Sarah Vaughan; Prince; Bill Cosby; and, of course, Elvis. And that's a *short* list. At the end, he even does Danny Gans—typically a selection from his Christian pop album.

Gans not only does impressions, but also expressions. He captures his characters' faces, postures, and moves; he gets maximum effect from minimal props; he even plays a mean trumpet (for the Louis Armstrong bit). But that's not all. This is perhaps the tightest show in Las Vegas. Gans, his band, and the lighting are in perfect sync every note of the night. *Danny Gans* is great for Las Vegas. Tough luck for baseball.

In case you're wondering, Danny Gans is the best of the solo impressionists working Las Vegas showrooms. We rank Andre-Phillipe Gagnon (limited engagements at Paris) second, and Bill Acosta third.

Consumer Tips *Danny Gans* is outstanding and a reasonable buy for the $100 seats. In any event, the show is more of an auditory than a visual experience. The Mirage is a bustling place in the evenings so allow yourself an extra 15 minutes to park and get to the showroom.

David Brenner

Type of Show Celebrity headliner
Host Casino and Showroom Westin Casuarina Hotel and Casino—David Brenner Theater
Reservations and Information (702) 836-9775
Admission Cost with Taxes $57

Cast Size 1
Nights of Lowest Attendance Sunday, Monday
Usual Show Times Wednesday–Monday, 7:30 p.m.   **Dark** Tuesday
Topless No
Author's Rating ★★★★
Overall Appeal by Age Group
Under 21 ★★ | 21–37 ★★★★ | 38–50 ★★★ | 51 and older ★★★

Duration of Presentation 1 hour

Description and Comments David Brenner works hard to keep his head above water, and even though he resorts to the use of note cards on stage he's still funny. A big fan of the old Vegas days when a handshake really meant "kid, you've got a deal," Brenner enjoys dissecting the New World Order with his sanguine wit. A stay-informed kind of guy, Brenner comes across as a well-read insider who knows exactly where the hem of society is beginning to tear. Using snippets from popular newsmagazines, Brenner steadily pulls at loose threads, making a comedic case for what really must have been the good old days. But don't worry about being lectured or being short-changed on potty humor. Brenner is a master at working a main theme, while simultaneously diverging off onto irreverent personal tangents. A big name dropper, Brenner probably has earned the right. He's appeared on the *Tonight Show* over 150 times, whatever that's worth, and has been playfully kicking up dirt in Las Vegas for three decades.

Consumer Tips The eponymous David Brenner Theater is about as plain as the Westin's small casino, but the fare that Brenner serves up is much better than the on-site Silver Peak Grill. For a bite to eat before the show, head to Starbucks, which is just across from the theater inside the casino.

Dirk Arthur's New Art of Magic

Type of Show Magic and Illusion
Host Casino and Showroom Plaza—Plaza Showroom
Reservations and Information (702) 386-2444
Admission Cost with Taxes Show only, $35–$46; show and buffet, $41
Cast Size 5
Nights of Lowest Attendance Thursday
Usual Show Times Wednesday–Saturday, 7 p.m.; Sunday, 3 and 7 p.m.
Dark Monday and Tuesday
Topless No
Author's Rating ★★★
Overall Appeal by Age Group
Under 21 ★★★½ | 21–37 ★★★ | 38–50 ★★★ | 51 and older ★★★

Duration of Presentation 1 hour and 20 minutes

Description and Comments Dirk Arthur is an excellent illusionist specializing (like rival Steve Wyrick) in making big things disappear and appear (cars, tigers, helicopters, etc.). There's nothing cutting edge here, and there's a redundant dependence on gimmicks, devices, and technology, but it's a good show and a bargain if you're up for a little magic.

Consumer Tips Dirk Arthur, along with *Steve Wyrick* at the Aladdin, and *Lance Burton* at Monte Carlo, is an excellent illusionist. *Wyrick* is good but overpriced, especially when you can see *Lance Burton* for about $10 less. Dirk Arthur's show doesn't have the ensemble that augments Lance Burton's show (and to a lesser extent, Wyrick's), but is a great value if you're primarily interested in magic and illusion.

An Evening at La Cage

Type of Show Female-impersonator revue
Host Casino and Showroom Riviera—Mardi Gras Showrooms, third floor
Reservations and Information (702) 794-9433 or (800) 634-3420
Admission Cost with Taxes $40
Cast Size Approximately 20
Nights of Lowest Attendance Sunday and Monday
Usual Show Times Nightly, 7:30 p.m.   **Dark** Tuesday
Topless No
Author's Rating ★★★
Overall Appeal by Age Group

Under 21 — | 21–37 ★★★½ | 38–50 ★★★ | 51 and older ★★★

Duration of Presentation 1 hour and 15 minutes

Description and Comments   *La Cage* re-creates the female-impersonator revue made famous by productions of the same name in New York and Los Angeles. A high-tempo show with a great sense of humor, *La Cage* is at once outrageous, lusty, weird, and sensitive. All of the performers, of course, are men. Celebrities impersonated include Joan Rivers, Tina Turner, Cher, Carol Channing, Shirley MacLaine, Bette Midler, and Madonna. A crew of dancers (also men impersonating women) give the presentation the feel of a quirky production show.

Some of the impersonators are convincing and pretty enough to fool just about anyone. Their costumes reveal slender, feminine arms and legs and hourglass figures. Others, however, look just like what they are—men in drag. The cast performs with great self-effacement and gives the impression that nobody is expected to take things too seriously. As one impersonator quipped, "This is a hell of a way for a 40-year-old man to be earning a living."

La Cage is kinky yet solid entertainment. It is also very popular and plays to appreciative heterosexual audiences. If you are curious, broad-minded, and looking for something different, give it a try. If the idea of a bunch of guys traipsing around in fishnet stockings and feather boas gives you the willies, opt for something more conventional.

Consumer Tips   In addition to *La Cage*, you can see the production show *Splash*, which plays off the main casino (see page 238). Shows can be purchased in conjunction with a meal, usually the buffet. The food on the show-dinner combos won't knock you out, but is a pretty good deal for the money. Also, it's quick and convenient. There is usually plenty of time to eat between shows.

Tickets for *La Cage* and the other Mardi Gras shows may be reserved up to 21 days in advance at the Riviera box office, or over the phone using your credit card up to ten days in advance. Seating is by the maître d'. Once seated, you can fetch your own drinks from the bar.

The Exotic Hypnotics

Type of Show Hypnosis comedy
Host Casino and Showroom Riviera—Le Bistro Theatre

Reservations and Information (877) 892-7469
Admission Cost with Taxes $28–$34
Cast Size 2, plus 10–15 audience volunteers
Nights of Lowest Attendance Thursday
Usual Show Times 11:30 p.m   **Dark** Monday
Topless No
Author's Rating ★
Overall Appeal by Age Group

Under 21 ★ | 21–37 ★½ | 38–50 ★★ | 51 and older ★

Duration of Presentation 1 hour and 15 minutes

Description and Comments   Replacing the late and definitely unlamented Dr. Naughty as Las Vegas's most excruciating hypnosis show are Genie and Richard, the "World's First Comedy Hypnosis Team." Genie and Richard mean well, they really do. But their performance and stage patter fairly reek of desperation, and their inability to convince people to volunteer—pretty essential for a hypnosis show—leads to some painfully awkward moments. When we visited, the duo resorted to giving out free drinks in an attempt to draw a crowd, though they weren't above trying to make the audience feel guilty about drinking on their tab. Some volunteers go through the motions of being hypnotized, but it's even less credible than usual for this type of production. Genie and Richard attempt to go a little blue in terms of humor, but in Genie's case in particular, the sexual innuendo just comes across as creepy.

Consumer Tips   If you must go, and you wish to be hypnotized, sit near the front (though Genie or Richard will no doubt swoop down on you wherever you are). This show is often heavily discounted and comped, so look and ask around for coupons or freebies before shelling out full price.

Folies Bergere (The Best of)

Type of Show   Music, dance, and variety production show
Host Casino and Showroom   Tropicana—Tiffany Showroom
Reservations and Information   (702) 739-2411 or (800) 634-4000
Admission Cost with Taxes $57, general; $63, VIP
Cast Size   Approximately 90
Nights of Lowest Attendance   Monday, Tuesday, and Sunday
Usual Show Times   Tuesday and Friday, 8:30 p.m.; Monday, Wednesday, Thursday, and Saturday, 7 and 10 p.m.   **Dark** Sunday
Topless   8:30 and 10 p.m. shows only
Author's Rating ★★★
Overall Appeal by Age Group

Under 21 ★★ | 21–37 ★★★ | 38–50 ★★★ | 51 and older ★★★★

Duration of Presentation 1 hour and 30 minutes

Description and Comments   The *Folies Bergere,* a Las Vegas tradition modeled on the bawdy Parisian revue of the same name, has been playing at the Tropicana on and off since 1959. The show, which changes almost every year, is a classy dance and musical variety production with a large cast.

The *Folies Bergere* is pretty much what you would expect: exotically clad (or unclad) showgirls and cancan dancers, chorus lines, singers, and music with a fin-de-sieclé French cabaret feel. The show runs through about 14 different scenes, celebrating the music and dance traditions of Paris, Hollywood, and Las Vegas from the 1860s to the 1960s. The *Folies Bergere* is elaborate and colorful but not particularly compelling. The singing and dancing are competent and professional but, with one or two exceptions, not creative or exciting. The *Folies* has been successful for over 45 years, so it is understandable that the producers would be reluctant to tamper with the formula. The ante for competing in the big leagues, however, has gone up. The production innovations of *Siegfried & Roy* and the energy of *Cirque du Soleil* established new standards for action, tempo, and creativity in Las Vegas production shows. The *Folies Bergere* has failed to keep pace.

In fairness, the *Folies* change and update various elements of the show every year. Recent changes make the show more appealing to the baby-boomer generation who cut their teeth on rock (music, that is). Updated or not, however, the *Folies* has become a sort of treasured relic, a nostalgic symbol of Las Vegas in those heady early days of the Strip.

Given the music and style of the *Folies*, you will be more likely to appreciate the production if you are over age 50. Younger patrons will fail to identify with the nostalgic music and dance of *la belle epoque,* or find much spontaneity in the overall *Folies* theme; the *Lion King* finale, for example, is strange and overwrought. But imaginative sets and costumes, elaborate staging, a diverse soundtrack, and the contemporary choreography that revs up near the end give this show some pop.

Consumer Tips The *Folies* is presented on a wide stage in the nicely designed Tiffany Showroom. There is a lot more booth seating than in most showrooms and a good view from practically every seat in the house. Dinner is no longer offered in the showroom, though there's a buffet show package for a few dollars extra. No drinks come with the price of the show. If you need to use the distant rest room before the show, allow yourself plenty of time.

Reservations can be made up to a month in advance, and all seats are reserved, so you can show up five minutes prior to show time and your seats will be waiting.

Gladys Knight

Type of Show Celebrity headliner
Host Casino and Showroom Flamingo—Flamingo Showroom
Reservations and Information (702) 733-3333
Admission Cost with Taxes $80 main level, $69 balcony
Cast Size 10 (includes band)
Usual Show Times Tuesday–Saturday, 7:30 p.m.
Dark Sunday and Monday
Nights of Lowest Attendance Wednesday
Topless No
Author rating ★★★★
Overall Appeal by Age Group

Under 21 ★★★★ | 21–37 ★★★★ | 38–50 ★★★★ | 51 and older ★★★★

Duration of Presentation 1 hour and 30 minutes

Description and Comments Gladys Knight works "Pip-less" in this sentimental retrospective of her career. Connecting with the audience immediately, Knight punctuates her singing with remembrances of the Pips, her challenges, and her beliefs.

Although this kind of presentation often falls flat, Knight pulls it off with great grace and humor. Songs cover a surprising range, including gospel, soul, pop, and country in addition to Knight's trademark Motown standards. She's accompanied by a dynamite seven-piece band, backup singers, and her brother Bubba, an original Pip. The music's great, and the overall experience very happy and upbeat. If you're looking for something to lift your spirits, Gladys Knight is your ticket.

Consumer Tips Gladys Knight, both in terms of music and style, is so hip that she appeals to every age group. The Flamingo Showroom is a perfect size for her show and there is a good line of sight from almost every seat. Dinner/show combos are available with preset menu at the Flamingo Room restaurant.

Hip-Nosis

Type of Show Rambunctious hypnosis exhibition
Host Casino and Showroom O'Shea's—O'Shea's Comedy Theatre
Reservations and Information (702) 737-1343
Admission Cost with Taxes $39
Cast Size 1
Night of Lowest Attendance Wednesday
Usual Show Times Monday–Friday, 9 p.m.; Saturday, 8 and 11 p.m. **Dark** Sunday
Special Comments Skeptics should look elsewhere
Topless No
Author's Rating We just don't buy it; ★½
Overall Appeal by Age Group

Under 21 ★★★ | 21–37 ★★★ | 38–50 ★★★ | 51 and older ★½

Duration of Presentation 1 hour and 15 minutes

Description and Comments Part hypnotherapist and part drill sergeant, the frenetic Justin Tranz psychologically bludgeons people into a hypnotic state. Given its participatory nature, the willingness of the audience and volunteers to play along contribute directly to how much everyone enjoys the show. Such positive contributions also help maintain the mental stability of host Tranz, who tends to get accusingly petulant and even enraged when his volunteers don't explore their subconscious quickly enough to suit him. Any and all volunteers are encouraged to take the stage, where Tranz sorts them out by suitability. Yelling, screaming, and even slapping his volunteers around occasionally, Tranz is a spectacle unto himself even if the hypnosis routines don't grab you. He definitely works up crowd enthusiasm better than the various hypnosis showcase acts over at the Riviera. The hypnotized are then commanded to dance around, psychologically regress to childlike states, or perform other acts of amusing humiliation.

Consumer Tips Groups enjoy these shows the most. A healthy suspension of disbelief also helps. The smallish showroom has movie theater–style seats, all of which have good views of the action.

Honky Tonk Angels

Type of Show Country/Western music impersonator show
Host Casino and Showroom Gold Coast
Reservations and Information (888) 402-6278 or (702) 251-3574
Admission Cost with Taxes Locals, $22; visitors, $28

Cast Size 3–8
Nights of Lowest Attendance Wednesday
Usual Show Times Wednesday–Sunday, 8 p.m.   **Dark** Monday and Tuesday
Topless No
Author's Rating ★★★½
Overall Appeal by Age Group

Under 21 ★★½ | 21–37 ★★★ | 38–50 ★★★★ | 51 and older ★★★★

Duration of Presentation 1 hour and 30 minutes

Description and Comments *Honky Tonk Angels* may be the best-kept secret, as well as the biggest entertainment bargain, in Las Vegas. The performers who sing the songs of Reba McEntire, Dolly Parton, Patsy Cline, Bonnie Raitt, Garth Brooks, and (curiously) the Andrews Sisters are far from physical clones, but they are certainly kindred spirits. The vocals are right on, no exceptions. And surprisingly for such an affordable show, a real band backs the vocalists. It helps if you like country music, of course, but even if it's not your regular diet, this show will have you drumming on the cocktail table and stomping (better than tapping) you foot within five minutes.

Consumer Tips The showroom is intimate, but the tables are spread far enough apart that there's lots of elbowroom. Lines of sight are good from anywhere in the room. The Gold Coast showroom, specializing in country/western music, fields other similar, impersonators shows during the year. Recently, for example, the Gold Coast offered a production called *Outlaws, Cowboys, and Men in Black* featuring the music of Willie Nelson, Waylon Jennings, and Johnny Cash.

Hypnosis Zone

Type of Show Hypnosis comedy

Host Casino and Showroom Riviera–Le Bistro Theatre
Reservations and Information (877) 892-7469
Admission Cost with Taxes $28–$34
Cast Size Varies, usually 2 with 10–11 audience volunteers
Nights of Lowest Attendance Wednesday
Usual Show Times 10 p.m.   **Dark** Monday, Thursday, Friday
Topless No
Author's Rating ★½
Overall Appeal by Age Group

Under 21 ★ | 21–37 ★★ | 38–50 ★★½ | 51 and older ★½

Duration of Presentation 1 hour and 15 minutes

Description and Comments The *Hypnosis Zone* is a round-robin hypnotism show, with a revolving cast of hypnotists showing up for duty. There's no telling who will be on deck for a particular night, and since the success or failure of a hypnosis show rests squarely on the shoulders of the hypnotist in charge, this is a real crap-shoot. Regardless of who's doing the hypnotizing, though, this production faithfully relies on the chestnuts of the genre. There will be some nutty off-color jokes, volunteers will be cajoled or shoved forward by friends, and hypnotize-ees will get arranged in embarrassing tableaux. You will have the most fun here if you convince a friend to go up on stage and be humiliated for the crowd's amusement.

Consumer Tips Since the onstage talent is random, our advice is to check out the crowd before you go in. If there's a rowdy bunch of mixed age and type, it might be worth a few laughs. But if the lounge is one-third full of a few senior couples eyeing each other warily, you're better off elsewhere. For what it's worth, both performers and crowd can be counted on to be more entertaining than at *The Exotic Hypnotics,* which follows at 11:30 p.m. in the same showroom. As with most Le Bistro Theatre shows, this one is heavily discounted, couponed, and comped at the ticket outlets and in local mags.

Jubilee!

Type of Show Grand-scale musical and variety production show

Host Casino and Showroom Bally's—The Jubilee Theater

Reservations and Information (702) 967-4567 or (800) 237-SHOW

Admission Cost with Taxes $55–$74 ($6 extra on credit card purchase)

Cast Size 100

Nights of Lowest Attendance Sunday, Thursday

Usual Show Times Daily, 7:30 and 10:30 p.m.   **Dark** Friday

Topless Yes

Author's Rating ★★★★

Overall Appeal by Age Group

Under 21 — | 21–37 ★★★ | 38–50 ★★★½ | 51 and older ★★★★

Duration of Presentation 1 hour and 30 minutes

Description and Comments *Jubilee!* is the quintessential, traditional Las Vegas production show. Faithfully following a successful decades-old formula, *Jubilee!* has elaborate musical production numbers, extravagant sets, beautiful topless showgirls, and quality variety acts. In *Jubilee!* you get what you expect—and then some.

With a cast of 100, an enormous stage, and some of the most colossal and extraordinary sets found in theater anywhere, *Jubilee!* is much larger than life. Running an hour and 30 minutes each performance, the show is lavish, sexy, and well performed, but redundant to the point of numbing.

Two multiscene production extravaganzas top the list of *Jubilee!* highlights. The first is the sultry saga of Samson and Delilah, climaxing with Samson's destruction of the temple. Not exactly biblical, but certainly awe-inspiring. The second superdrama is the story of the *Titanic,* from launch to sinking. Once again, sets and special effects on a grand scale combine with nicely integrated music and choreography to provide an incredible spectacle.

Jubilee!'s opening act kicks things off in a big way. Based on a popular song by Jerry Herman, *Hundreds of Girls,* it showcases 75 singers, dancers, and showgirls multiplied by gargantuan mirrors. The opening is said to have cost $3 million to produce. The above-average specialty acts include an illusionist executing big-stage tricks, a juggler-acrobat couple whose main prop is a giant aluminum cube, and a strongman who performs mostly upside-down. The production concludes with "The Jubilee Walk," a parade of elaborately costumed showgirls patterned after the grand finale of the *Ziegfeld Follies.*

Consumer Tips The 1,035-seat Jubilee Theater, with its high, wide stage and multitiered auditorium, is one of the best-designed showrooms in town. It underwent a complete $2.5 million renovation in the late 1990s. It now consists of seating at banquet tables at the foot of the stage (too close and cramped); a row of booths above the tables (more expensive but worth it); and 789 theater-style seats. The table and booth seats come with cocktail service; the theater-seat audience has to carry in their own drinks.

Reserved seats for *Jubilee!* can be purchased over the phone with a credit card up to six weeks in advance. Tickets can also be purchased in person at the Bally's box office. The price of a ticket covers admission and taxes.

La Femme

Type of Show Artsy topless dance performance from France
Host Casino and Showroom MGM Grand—*La Femme* Theatre
Reservations and Information (702) 699-9196
Admission Cost with Taxes $59
Cast Size 12
Night of Lowest Attendance Sunday
Usual Show Times Wednesday–Monday, 8:30 and 10:30 p.m.   **Dark** Tuesday
Topless Yes
Author's Rating ★★★★
Overall Appeal by Age Group

Under 21 — | 21–37 ★★★★ | 38–50 ★★★½ | 51 and older ★★★

Duration of Presentation 1 hour and 15 minutes
Description and Comments Imported from the legendary Crazy Horse club in Paris, *La Femme* is something of an oddity. The new showroom is quite beautiful, done up in plush reds that call to mind an upscale bordello. All the dancers are Parisian imports as well, and they must not only be in excellent physical condition—they also are not allowed surgical enhancements. So what you see is *au naturel.* There's a wide variety of musical and dance numbers, and these are mixed with the odd comedy interlude or a bit of historical footage from the Crazy Horse. The show's erotic routines are decidedly European, relying on arty lighting, sensuous music, and a lot of writhing. There's not anything else like it in Vegas (certainly not the *Folies Bergere,* also originally a French show). On the whole, *La Femme* is diverting, cool, and sexy.
Consumer Tips The stage for *La Femme* is very small for such a large room, so seats in the rear may result in eyestrain. The show is general admission with usher seating, so arrive as early as possible in order to get the best spot.

Lance Burton: Master Magician

Type of Show Magical illusion with dancing and specialty acts
Host Casino and Showroom Monte Carlo—Lance Burton Theatre
Reservations and Information (702) 730-7000 or (800) 311-8999
Admission Cost with Taxes $73 balcony seating; $67 main-floor seating
Cast Size 14
Nights of Lowest Attendance Thursday, Friday
Usual Show Times Tuesday and Saturday, 7 and 10 p.m.; Wednesday, Thursday, and Friday, 7 p.m.   **Dark** Sunday and Monday
Special Comments No drinks included
Topless No
Author's Rating ★★★★
Overall Appeal by Age Group

Under 21 ★★★★ | 21–37 ★★★★ | 38–50 ★★★★ | 51 and older ★★★★

Duration of Presentation 1 hour and 30 minutes

Description and Comments In a showroom designed especially for him, Lance Burton stars in an innovative and iconoclastic magic show, one of only two magic production shows in town to escape the curse of redundancy. Performing in tight-fitting clothing with rolled-up sleeves (nothing can be concealed), Burton displays some extraordinary sleight of hand in a repertoire of illusions that cannot be seen in other showrooms. Augmented by comely assistants, a comedic juggler, and a talented dance troupe, *Lance Burton* delivers quality entertainment.

Consumer Tips The Lance Burton Theatre is an opulent imitation of a Parisian opera house and is both beautiful and comfortable. Theater seats ensure that no one gets wedged sideways at cramped banquet tables. On the down side, the venue is so large that it's hard to appreciate Burton's exquisite and subtle sleight of hand if you are seated in the boonies. Also, some illusions are difficult to see from the balcony seats. Try to get seats on the main floor close to the stage. *Lance Burton* tickets can be purchased over the phone or at the Monte Carlo box office up to two months in advance.

Legends in Concert

Type of Show Celebrity-impersonator and musical production show

Host Casino and Showroom Imperial Palace—Imperial Theatre

Reservations and Information (702) 794-3261

Admission Cost with Taxes $40 adults (includes tax, 2 drinks, and tip); $25 children (ages 12 and under); dinner show package, $45

Cast Size Approximately 20

Nights of Lowest Attendance Wednesday, Thursday

Usual Show Times Monday–Saturday, 7 and 10 p.m.   **Dark** Sunday

Topless No

Author's Rating ★★★★

Overall Appeal by Age Group

Under 21 ★★★★	21–37 ★★★★	38–50 ★★★★	51 and older ★★★★

Duration of Presentation 1 hour and 30 minutes

Description and Comments *Legends in Concert* is a musical production show featuring a highly talented cast of impersonators who re-create the stage performances of such celebrities as Elvis, Richie Valens, Prince, Cher, Rod Stewart, the Four Tops, and Gloria Estefan. Impersonators actually sing and/or play their own instruments, so there's no lip-syncing or faking. In addition to the Las Vegas production, *Legends in Concert* also fields a road show. The second show makes possible a continuing exchange of performers between the productions, so that the shows are always changing. In addition to the impersonators, *Legends* features an unusually hot and creative company of dancers, much in the style of TV's *Solid Gold* dancers of old. There are no variety acts.

The show is a barn-burner and possibly, minute-for-minute, the fastest-moving show in town. The impersonations are extremely effective, replicating the physical appearances, costumes, mannerisms, and voices of the celebrities with remarkable likeness. While each show features the work of about eight stars, with a roster that ensures something for patrons of every age, certain celebrities (most notably Elvis) are always included. Regardless of the stars impersonated, *Legends in Concert* is fun, happy, and upbeat. It's a show that establishes rapport with the audience—a show that makes you feel good.

Consumer Tips Admission includes two drinks. Payment must be made at the box office any time prior to the show. Arrive 40 minutes before show time for seating by the maître d'. If you drive to the Imperial Palace and intend to use the self-parking, give yourself a little extra time. Since *Legends* is very popular and almost always plays to a full house on weekends, be sure to make your reservations early.

Mamma Mia!

Type of Show Musical comedy
Host Casino and Showroom Mandalay Bay—Mandalay Bay Theatre
Reservations and Information (702) 632–7580
Admission Cost with Taxes $45–$100 depending on choice of seats
Cast Size 36, including musicians
Night of Lowest Attendance Thursday
Usual Show Times Monday–Thursday, 7 p.m.; Saturday and Sunday, 5 and 9 p.m.;
Dark Friday
Topless No
Author's Rating ★★★★
Overall Appeal by Age Group

Under 21 ★★★½ | 21–37 ★★★★ | 38–50 ★★★★ | 51 and older ★★★★

Duration of Presentation 2 hours and 30 minutes (with intermission)

Description and Comments   *Mamma Mia!* is a musical comedy featuring the music of the Swedish pop group ABBA. Active between 1974 to 1982, ABBA was once the world's best-selling band, scoring ten Top-20 hits worldwide. With over 350 million records sold to date, ABBA's music continues to attract new fans.

 Mamma Mia! was launched in London in 1999 and became a huge hit there before being exported to the United States. The story takes place on a Greek isle where three fellows wooed and slept with, in short order, the same woman. The woman became pregnant and had a little girl, Sophie, whom she raised without ever establishing the identity of the father. Now engaged to be married, Sophie contrives to use the occasion of her wedding to find her unknown father. After discovering three possible candidates in her mother's diary, she invites them to her wedding without, of course, telling mom. You get the idea.

 In the creation of most musicals, the script is written first and then the music developed to support the storyline. *Mamma Mia!* is an anomaly in that the script was developed to fit ABBA's music. Amazingly, this "square-peg-in-a-round-hole" approach produced a plot/music relationship as congruent as that of most musicals produced in the traditional way. There are a couple of the whopping 22 ABBA songs included that are a pretty loose fit, but in general the music integrates very nicely. Even at two-and-a-half hours (with a 20-minute intermission), *Mamma Mia!* is fast paced, with a clever script and engaging characters. What's really refreshing, however, is *Mamma Mia!'s* essential lightness and simplicity. It's sweet, upbeat, humorous, and just for fun.

Consumer Tips   Though there are really no bad seats in the Mandalay Bay Theatre, it's probably worth the money to spring for closer, more expensive seats. Self-parking at Mandalay Bay is relatively convenient to the showroom. From the entrance to the casino, bear left past several restaurants and then continue left, passing the sports book en route. Although there are rest rooms just outside the theatre and a bar in the theatre lobby, you'll save time, especially during intermission, by using rest room and bar facilities in the main casino. Hold on to your ticket stub—you'll need it to get back in the showroom.

Michael Flatley's Lord of the Dance

Type of Show Celtic music and dance production
Host Casino and Showroom At press time, *Lord of the Dance* was negotiating a contract for a new showroom.
Cast Size 44
Special Comments Michael Flatley does not dance
Topless No
Author's Rating Rollicking fun; ★★★★
Overall Appeal by Age Group

Under 21 ★★★★ | 21–37 ★★★★ | 38–50 ★★★★ | 51 and older ★★★★

Duration of Presentation 1 hour and 30 minutes

Description and Comments *Lord of the Dance* is a clone of *Riverdance,* the Celtic stepdance production that burst onto the world entertainment scene, astounding audiences with its energy and unerring footwork. Michael Flatley, once the male star of *Riverdance,* left the company and opened *Lord of the Dance* in Dublin in 1996. Since that time the two productions have been fierce competitors.

With its jubilant score, relentless pace, and exacting precision, *Lord of the Dance* is decidedly an upper—an evening's entertainment that leaves you curiously both energized and drained. Though the production operates within a story of good versus evil, and while there's great subtlety and delicacy at various points along the journey, it is when the entire cast of dancers is on stage at once with 80 feet thundering in flawless unison that *Lord of the Dance* realizes its potential. As the tempo builds and the pounding rhythm of shoes on hardwood echoes in your chest, you are drawn into such a spiraling, driving crescendo of energy that it's almost impossible to stay seated.

We like *Lord of the Dance* and think you will, too. You don't have to be a ballet, or even a dance, fan to get excited about this production. On the other hand, it's not the typical Las Vegas show: There are no feathered showgirls, magicians, or jugglers. What you get is a mainline dose of Celtic music and dance. Believe us, that's enough.

Consumer Tips If you've seen a live performance of *Riverdance, Lord of the Dance* is essentially more of the same. If you've seen *Riverdance* only on video and liked it, we heartily recommend *Lord of the Dance.* The live production (of either show) has an impact and presence that can only be imagined by watching a video.

Midnight Fantasy

Type of Show Topless dance and comedy revue
Host Casino and Showroom Luxor—Pharoah's Theater
Reservations and Information (702) 262-4400
Admission Cost with Taxes $39
Cast Size Approximately 8
Nights of Lowest Attendance Wednesday and Thursday
Usual Show Times Tuesday, Thursday, Saturday, and Sunday, 8:30 p.m.; Tuesday–Saturday, 10:30 p.m.   **Dark** Monday
Topless Yes
Author's Rating ★★½

Overall Appeal by Age Group

Under 21 — | 21–37 ★★★ | 38–50 ★★½ | 51 and older ★★

Duration of Presentation I hour and I5 minutes

Description and Comments A breathy female voiceover starts things up, describing for the audience a sultry "midnight fantasy" of luxurious life in ancient Egypt (the Luxor's theme). So begins this largely incoherent show, which bounces from olden times to a cowgirl hoedown to a male Tina Turner impersonator. After the voiceover relates a particular scenario, dancers and singers come forth to sashay about in costumes appropriate for the scene. There's some half-naked cavorting, of course, but not as much as one might think from the suggestive nature of the show. And despite the panting over the loudspeakers, the dancing is not particularly erotic—it's almost like you're watching a normal, G-rated dance number where some of the performers just forgot their tops. The whole thing has a sort of dorky appeal, and it's pretty fun to watch as long as you're not dead-set on maximum nudity. Interludes between dance routines are filled by a DJ/MC/impressionist guy (who dragoons an audience member for a forced Elvis impression) and a standard-Vegas-issue foulmouthed comic.

Consumer Tips Tickets for *Midnight Fantasy* must be purchased or picked up at the box office on the second floor of the Luxor, not at the one off the main casino floor. The large size of the stadium-style theater means there are lots of seats, but the higher rows can make good views of the distant stage problematic. The show is general admission, so just arrive a little early to ensure a good seat.

The Platters, Cornell Gunter's Coasters, and Beary Hobb's Drifters

Type of Show 1950s and 60s oldies

Host Casino and Showroom Sahara—Sahara Theater

Reservations and Information (702) 737-2515

Admission Cost with Taxes $45 and $51

Cast Size 13 singers plus backup band

Nights of Lowest Attendance Tuesday and Wednesday

Usual Show Times Nightly, 8 p.m.

Topless No

Author's Rating ★★★½

Overall Appeal by Age Group

Under 21 ★★★½ | 21–37 ★★★½ | 38–50 ★★★ | 51 and older ★★★½

Duration of Presentation I hour and 20 minutes

Description and Comments This show is inspired by the music of legendary vocal groups: the Platters, the Coasters, and the Drifters. I say inspired because there's not one original member of any of the groups in the production. Cornell Gunter was a bona fide Coaster and Beary Hobbs an original Drifter, but they just lend their names to the acts. Does it really matter? Not if you're there just for the music. Sure, it's always fun to see the original groups still rockin' 'n' rollin', but most of all you want the music to be right. In this show you can close your eyes and believe you're listening to the original groups. It's that perfect. And with your eyes open, well, about half the performers are old enough to have been originals, so they look right. Regardless of age, they've got the moves and the choreography nailed. The only shortcoming is that Dave Backers' band, providing the instrumental accompaniment, doesn't have a sax. Anyone who knows their oldies will tell you that covering the Coasters without a sax is like covering Jerry Lee Lewis without a piano.

Consumer Tips The Sahara Theater is an old-fashioned, maître d' seating show-room, plenty big enough for 20 performers to be on stage at once (as in the finale of this show), but small enough to provide a very intimate concert experience. There's a cash bar outside the showroom. If you use the self-parking facility or the valet parking off Paradise, be forewarned that it's an eight- to ten-minute hike to the showroom.

Rita Rudner

Type of Show Stand-up comedy
Host Casino and Showroom New York–New York (Cabaret Theater)
Reservations and Information (702) 740-6815
Admission Cost with Taxes $57 and $74
Cast Size 1
Nights of Lowest Attendance Wednesday
Usual Show Times Sunday–Thursday, 8 p.m.; Friday and Saturday, 9 p.m.
Topless No
Author's Rating ★★★½
Overall Appeal by Age Group

Under 21 ★★ | 21–37 ★★★★ | 38–50 ★★★★ | 51 and older ★★★★

Duration of Presentation 1 hour and 30 minutes

Description and Comments Rita Rudner walks onto the stage and holds forth for almost 90 minutes. No band, no singers or dancers, just Rita. And even if you've never heard of Rita Rudner, those 90 minutes will seem like ten. Her topics, male–female relationships, shopping, Las Vegas, are worn, but her perspective is fresh and her humor is sharp, very sharp. Like a good elementary-school teacher, she monitors her room, stopping to connect personally with a look, a smile, or even a question. In the end, we're all Miss Rudner's students and we find ourselves trying to file away some of her stories and zippy one-liners to repeat later to friends. But they come too fast, so finally we just go with it and enjoy.

Consumer Tips Rita Rudner has to be the cleanest stand-up comic working in Las Vegas. You forget that it's possible to be uproarious in PG mode. The only drawback to this show is the cramped seating.

Scintas

Type of Show Musical and comedy review
Host Casino and Showroom Rio—Copacabana Showroom
Reservations and Information (702) 252-7776 or (800) PLAY-RIO
Admission Cost with Taxes $66
Cast Size 4
Nights of Lowest Attendance Monday, Tuesday
Usual Show Times Friday–Wednesday, 7:30 p.m.
Dark Thursday
Topless No
Author's Rating ★★★
Overall Appeal by Age Group

Under 21 ★★ | 21–37 ★★★ | 38–50 ★★★½ | 51 and older ★★★½

Duration of Presentation 1 hour and 30 minutes

Description and Comments Though the Scintas are also billed as a comedy troupe, they shine most when playing music. With a heavy emphasis on God and patriotism, this show would be more at home in Branson, Missouri.

The cast of *Scintas* includes siblings Frankie, Joe, and Chrissi Scinta. Frankie Scinta provides much of the comedy and plays a variety of instruments, including keyboards. But his passion is the banjo. Joe Scinta is a stereotypically dry bass player and sometime comedian. Baby-sister Chrissi sings a few numbers throughout the show, but isn't a constant stage presence. Italian pride notwithstanding, the group's drummer is handsome Irishman Peter O'Donnell.

The Scintas enjoy performing comedy, but the comedy can be trite; comedy routines include Frankie Scinta covering Tom Jones songs with socks stuffed down his pants. Some of the comedy is mildly racist and sexist—undertones which might have played well 20 years ago, but now seem unnecessary, not to mention odd juxtaposed with all of the God and Country stuff.

On the other hand, music is delivered with a great deal of warmth and skill. The set list includes typical Las Vegas fare such as Dean Martin and Elvis covers. But the Scintas also cover Billy Joel and Joe Cocker. Many songs are performed as parts of seamless medleys. With a versatile and pleasant voice, Frankie Scinta does most of the singing. Sister Chrissi sings louder and longer than her brothers, delivering a patriotic medley as well as an emotional *I Will Always Love You* (penned by Dolly Parton and made famous by Whitney Houston).

Consumer Tips The Copacabana Showroom is one of the best designed and most comfortable showrooms in Las Vegas. Though some seats are a bit distant, the line of site is uniformly excellent and the sound system is awesome. A cocktail waitress will visit your booth or table, and there is a small snack kiosk near the entrance to the showroom. Less than $40, Scintas tickets are reasonably priced even though they don't include drinks or tips.

Second City

Type of Show Sketch comedy
Host Casino and Showroom Flamingo—Bugsy's Celebrity Theatre
Reservations and Information (702) 733-3333
Admission Cost with Taxes $30
Cast Size 5
Nights of Lowest Attendance Tuesday
Usual Show Times Thursday–Tuesday, 8 p.m.; Thursday–Saturday and Monday, 10:30 p.m. **Dark** Wednesday
Topless No
Author's Rating ★★★★
Overall Appeal by Age Group

Under 21 ★★★½ | 21–37 ★★★★ | 38–50 ★★★★ | 51 and older ★★★★

Duration of Presentation 1 hour and 15 minutes

Description and Comments *Second City* is a team of improvisational comedians, one of several franchised groups of comics playing around the country under the same name. The difference between an improvisational group and the stand-up comedians that work the Las Vegas comedy clubs is that the improv groups specialize in skits and songs as opposed to monologues. *Second City* is an amazingly talented lot individually and complement and balance each other well as a team. They do a crack job on the improvisational stuff, taking their cues from audience suggestions, but it's their set pieces that really demonstrate their genius.

Consumer Tips   Bugsy's Celebrity Theater is really an enclosed lounge, small and intimate, perfect for acts like *Second City*. Seating is by the maître d'. Because there really aren't any bad seats, tipping the maître d' is a waste of money unless you want to be right next to the stage. Sitting next to the stage at a comedy venue, however, is always risky because you might suddenly find yourself part of the show.

Showgirls

Type of Show   Tribute to risqué dance numbers through the ages
Host Casino and Showroom   Rio—Samba Theater
Reservations and Information   (888) 746-7784
Admission Cost with Taxes $56
Cast Size   12
Usual Show Times   11 p.m.   **Dark**   Tuesday
Nights of Lowest Attendance   Monday and Wednesday
Topless   Yes
Author rating   ★★½
Overall Appeal by Age Group

Under 21 ★★*	21–37 ★★½	38–50 ★★★	51 and older ★★½

*Under 18 not admitted.
Duration of Presentation   1 hour and 15 minutes

Description and Comments   There is vintage choreography, but not vintage attire in this all-topless revue. *Showgirls'* nine dancers take the stage in flamingo-esque headgear and "bikinis" that bear their breasts, but eschew the erotic writhing of Vegas's new-generation topless acts for classic burlesque choreography (which by contemporary standards amounts to striking a succession of poses at a relaxed pace). The dance routines each evoke performances by famous troupes to tell the "history of showgirls." A narrated video documentary provides actual, if scant, historic detail about the Ziegfeld Follies, Havana's 1950s heyday as a proto-Vegas, Busby Berkeley's choreography, and the like, with footage sometimes supplementing the dancing onstage.   As it turns out, a showgirls-through-the-ages theme doesn't provide as much material as one might expect, so *Showgirls'* dance numbers are interspersed with songs by a female trio dubbed Stars. When not engaged in corny comic banter, the trio relies heavily on Motown material, including a Supremes tribute in a single, shared dress. As the program progresses, its theme grows tenuous, descending from Vegas's rebirth in the 1980s to music video dancers to strippers. The dancing reaches a suggestive zenith when an audience member is pulled onstage for a "lap dance," a crowd favorite provided the nervous recipient perennially eyes his still-seated wife.

Consumer Tips   As the nostalgic theme and soundtrack would suggest, *Showgirls* draws an older audience with more females than its more overtly erotic counterparts. In an effort to fill seats, *Showgirls* frequently offers two-for-one deals. On nights of light attendance, the ushers may offer you better seats than your ticket designates.

Showgirls of Magic

Type of Show   Cabaret with magic and strippers
Host Casino and Showroom   San Remo—Showgirls of Magic Showroom
Reservations and Information   (702) 597-6028
Admission Cost with Taxes $39, includes 2 drinks and photo with the Showgirls

Cast Size 7
Usual Show Times Tuesday–Sunday, 8 p.m.   **Dark** Monday
Nights of Lowest Attendance Sunday
Topless Yes
Author rating ★★★
Overall Appeal by Age Group

Under 21 — | 21–37 ★★★ | 38–50 ★★★ | 51 and older ★★★

Duration of Presentation 1 hour

Description and Comments Lots of purple fabric, pink lights, black curtains, white theatrical smoke, and tanned bare breasts make this onstage magic revue actually seem incredible. Set in a small, intimate theater, five luridly dressed cabaret vixens perform fast-paced tricks to a variety of modern and classic showroom tunes. How does Katie survive being sliced and pierced inside her wooden box? After the second free drink, who cares? She looks really good being dissected by her partners in topless crime. To keep adrenalin nonstop, the show breaks open at three points in the set. First, veteran guest comedian Russ Merlin storms the stage concocting a semi-funny hypnotize-audience-members routine. What does make it amusing are the goofy rubber masks that the victims are forced to wear. Of course, Russ is a chatterbox and occasionally lets slip a memorable line or two. The second moment of rapture occurs to only one lucky male in the audience. The Showgirls lustily strap him to an inclined board and manage to slither and slide over his trapped personage while music blares, more smoke belches, and a strategically placed silk scarf rises to the occasion. If that won't do you, then the human cartoon, Joe Trammel, will whip you into shape with his dizzying rendition of "I will impersonate 10,000 people in ten minutes." It's a sight to see, but rightly sandwiched between the energetic undoings of the lovely *Showgirls of Magic*.

Consumer Tips Simple rows of chairs make up the bulk of theater seating. There are a few small tables up front. Being early does not guarantee you a seat up front, but the theater is so intimate, that any seat in the house will do.

Siegfried & Roy

The production that revolutionized showroom entertainment in Las Vegas closed abruptly on October 3, 2003, after star illusionist Roy Horn was attacked by one of his signature white tigers. The incident occurred during a performance when the tiger, a veteran of hundreds of shows, evidently thought Horn was falling. Lunging, according to co-star Siegfried Fischbacher, to break Horn's fall, the tiger gripped Horn's head and neck in its mouth and carried him off-stage where he was immediately released. Though Horn lost a great deal of blood, the most severe damage was the result of a stroke suffered following the incident. The performance was terminated on the spot and the show shut down permanently. Though it is not thought that Horn will be able to return to the stage, he has, through six hours of rehabilitation therapy each day, already far surpassed even the most optimistic predictions of his physicians. The mauling ended 36 consecutive years of Siegfried and Roy performing together.

Skintight

Type of Show Topless dance show
Host Casino and Showroom Harrah's—Harrah's Showroom
Reservations and Information (702) 369-5111
Admission Cost with Taxes $56

Cast Size Approximately 16

Nights of Lowest Attendance Sunday, Tuesday

Usual Show Times Saturday–Wednesday, 10:30 p.m.; Friday, 10 p.m. and midnight; Sunday, 7:30 p.m. **Dark** Thursday

Special Comments This topless show permits ages 18 and up, as opposed to ages 21 and up.

Topless Yes

Author's Rating ★★★½

Overall Appeal by Age Group

Under 21 ★★★★ | 21–37 ★★★½ | 38–50 ★★★ | 51 and older ★★

Duration of Presentation 1 hour and 30 minutes

Description and Comments An elaborately staged and choreographed production, *Skintight* gives the Riviera's *Crazy Girls* a run for its money as the best casino-based girlie show in Las Vegas. Still, unlike the unselfconscious *Crazy Girls*, *Skintight* has aspirations to putting on a bitchin' dance party. To that end, there's lots of pounding rock-and-pop dance numbers which are probably the aged producers' idea of what the kids on MTV are up to these days. Skin is frequently visible and widespread among the buff female and male cast, though it's still something of an afterthought even amid all the crotch-grabbing and pelvic grinds. The dancing and singing are nonetheless quite accomplished, helmed as they are by a talented vocalist and a lithe choreographer. In addition, extremely pneumatic former Playboy Playmate Cynthia Brimhall makes occasional appearances to sing a little or heckle the crowd. The most genuinely erotic and sensual moments, however, involve members of audience—the lucky goggle-eyed few dragged onstage for lap dances or an intimate bit of crooning from Brimhall herself.

Consumer Tips Sitting near the center aisle seems to increase one's chances of being selected for onstage antics. Discount coupons are available in the Harrah's casino and in visitor magazines.

Spirit of the Dance

Type of Show Irish dancing with variety numbers thrown in

Host Casino and Showroom Golden Nugget—Golden Nugget Theatre Ballroom

Reservations and Information (866) 946-5336 or (702) 386-8100

Admission Cost with Taxes Adults, $45; children, $35

Cast Size 16

Nights of Lowest Attendance Sunday and Monday

Usual Show Times 7:30 p.m.

Topless No

Author's Rating ★★½

Overall Appeal by Age Group

Under 21 ★★ | 21–37 ★★½ | 38–50 ★★★ | 51 and older ★★

Duration of Presentation 1 hour

Description and Comments Yet another digression, tribute, or rip-off (depending on your point of view) of the Irish folk-dancing trend popularized by *Riverdance*, *Spirit of the Dance* offers variations on the theme of Irish stepping. After a hokey intro, the dancers put a few more modern spins on the traditional line and step dances. The finale is by far the most entertaining part of the show, even though it has nothing Irish about it, nor is it a dance—we can only describe it as "Super Pattycake." One sad piece of chicanery: though we're not 100 percent certain, it appeared at several times during the show that the sounds of the dancers' shoes hitting the stage were supplemented (or drowned out) by canned cadence supplied by the sound system.

Consumer Tips　The small house and small, close stage mean there are really no bad seats in this venue. Row seating dominates the front, left, and right, with tiered table seating starting in the center and rising to the back of the room.

Splash

Type of Show　Musical variety aquacade show
Host Casino and Showroom　Riviera—Splash Theater
Reservations and Information　(702) 794-9301 or (800) 634-3420
Admission Cost with Taxes　Adults $67–$82
Cast Size　Approximately 50
Nights of Lowest Attendance　Sunday, Tuesday, Wednesday
Usual Show Times　Tuesday–Thursday and Saturday, 8 and 10:30 p.m.; Sunday and Monday, 8 p.m.　**Dark**　Friday
Special Comments　No drinks included
Topless　Late show only
Author's Rating　★★★
Overall Appeal by Age Group

Under 21 ★★★ | 21–37 ★★★½ | 38–50 ★★★½ | 51 and older ★★★

Duration of Presentation　1 hour and 30 minutes

Description and Comments　When *Splash* first rolled into Las Vegas in 1985, it was like a peppy, young, jet-ski revue buzzing among ponderous cruise-ship extravaganzas. Though the ride was a bit bumpy—the show alternated frenetic production numbers with bizarre variety acts and you walked away with a mild case of whiplash—*Splash* managed to stay afloat for nearly ten years on rock and roll, great dancing, and pure exuberance. Ultimately, however, a new wave of contemporary entertainment churned into town and left *Splash* bobbing in the wake.

Outclassed in the water-ballet and diving department by *Cirque du Soleil's "O," Splash* traded in its trademark Sea World–sized fishbowl for a tiny ice rink. Not changed was the name of the production, even though there's nothing left to splash. Also not changed was the chaotic, frenzied, incongruous mix of singing, dancing, and various specialty acts. In *Splash* you will see: topless showgirls (lots), ice skaters (two), motorcyclists (too many), contortionists (one, we think—it's hard to tell with all the parts in the wrong places), singers (LOUD), jugglers (furious), and dancers.

The show features top-notch ice skating performed remarkably on a birdbath-sized (35-foot by 15-foot) rink. The other anchor act is the "Globe of Death" in which four motorcyclists blaze around inside a 14-foot-diameter mesh dome. In between are bola-swinging gauchos, jugglers, dancers, and showgirls, and some good choreographed impersonations of Madonna, Cher, and Janet Jackson in scenes re-created from their MTV videos.

When it's all over, a few in the audience look a little disoriented, like they somehow missed the boat, and others seem to be suffering from culture shock, like they'll never use that travel agent again. But for most people, this is exactly the kind of entertainment they expect out of a Las Vegas extravaganza.

Consumer Tips　All seats are reserved and assigned in the order in which the reservations are received; the earlier you buy, the better your seats will be. Tickets may be purchased up to three weeks in advance over the phone or in person at the box office. Tickets may be picked up at the box office prior to the show. The Versailles Theater has been remodeled, and though it's still big and the back seats are as far away as ever, the VIP section has replaced the dreaded banquet tables (except for one row of four-seaters directly behind the VIPs)—in short, everyone in the audience has an unobstructed view.

Splash is four-walled (meaning the producer gets the "gate" or proceeds from the ticket sales, and leases the showroom from the hotel), and it seems the producer and the hotel weren't able to get together over the drink situation. Glassware is not allowed in the showroom. You must carry in your own fluid refreshments in plastic cups. There's a bar just outside the theater entrance that will provide you with the complementary drink. Meal deals at the Riviera's Mardi Gras Food Court are often bundled with the show. See local visitor magazines for money-saving coupons.

Steve Wyrick, Mind-Blowing Magic

Type of Show Magic tricks, special effects, stunt magic
Host Casino and Showroom Aladdin—Steve Wyrick Theatre
Reservations and Information (702) 735-5000
Admission Cost with Taxes $70–$90
Cast Size 16
Nights of Lowest Attendance Thursday
Usual Show Times 7 and 10 p.m.   **Dark** Tuesday
Topless No
Author's Rating ★★★
Overall Appeal by Age Group

| Under 21 ★★★½ | 21–37 ★★★½ | 38–50 ★★★ | 51 and older ★★★ |

Duration of Presentation 1 hour and 30 minutes

Description and Comments *Steve Wyrick, Mind-Blowing Magic* is the Las Vegas show scene's version of "we try harder." With four or five magic-themed production shows playing in town at any given time, it takes a fair amount of creativity to be different. Steve Wyrick digs deep and delivers some great illusion and sleight of hand that you won't see in other showrooms. While his style and presentation, particularly his ability to connect with his audience, are reminiscent of *Lance Burton*, each illusion has a special twist that makes it unique. If you go for the magic you won't be disappointed. Expect lots of flash and thunder—pyrotechnics, roaring engines, and a pounding soundtrack.

Recently moved from the large Sahara showroom to the more "intimate" (and now renamed) Steve Wyrick Theatre at the Aladdin, some of Wyrick's illusions had to be downsized to fit the smaller space. One new illusion—the somewhat ludicrous "Death Crane"—appears to have been created for the smaller stage, though it borders on being a dud. On our visit, Wyrick also muffed a number of the sleight-of-hand tricks which are his signature, and which he usually performs flawlessly. Hopefully, he's just getting used to his new home.

Consumer Tips The smaller room hasn't stopped *Wyrick's* price from going up—his tickets are now just as expensive (or more) than longtime magician rival *Lance Burton*'s. Though Wyrick's illusions can be flashier, Burton remains the more classic and practiced act. With the former's jacked-up ticket prices, the latter becomes the obvious better value.

Thunder From Down Under

Type of Show Male revue
Host Casino and Showroom Excalibur—Merlin's Theater
Reservations and Information (702) 597-7600 or (800) 933-1334
Admission Cost with Taxes $44
Cast Size 8
Nights of Lowest Attendance Monday
Usual Show Times Friday–Wednesday, 8:30 and 10:30 p.m.   **Dark** Thursday
Topless Yes (male)
Author's Rating ★★★
Overall Appeal by Age Group

Under 21 ★★★ | 21–37 ★★★ | 38–50 ★★★ | 51 and older ★★★

Duration of Presentation 1 hour and 15 minutes

Description and Comments *Thunder From Down Under* offers a naughty night of ladies' fun for the bachelorette, recently divorced, and 21st-birthday crowd—a girls' night out that won't cause complete embarrassment for the conservative set. These Aussies are the guys next door—friendly and cute, but not the Chippendales. Thunder is suggestive, but not explicit, and is much tamer than its American-based competitor. *Thunder's* scantily clad cast performs upbeat dance, acrobatics, and martial arts routines, with a few comedy sketches tossed in (including one done in drag). Acts are performed to a varied soundtrack, resulting in a fast-paced, high-energy—but not always sexy—show.

There's lots of audience interaction as the Thundermen constantly pull girls out of the crowd and onto the stage. If you're shy and want to remain inconspicuous, try sitting in the back, where the lighting is also softer (our reviewer experienced light-blindness a few times from harsh overheads above her front-center seat in the 400-person showroom). After the show, cast members stick around to mingle with guests and offer photo opportunities.

Although there's lots of teasing and suggestion, the Thundermen never fully remove their G-strings (unlike Chippendales). *Thunder* seemingly presumes that women can't appreciate blatantly risqué entertainment. Our female reviewer also got the distinct impression that the guys of *Thunder* would be more interested in each other than any of the hundreds of girls in the audience, which for some may take away from the show's sex appeal.

Consumer Tips No smoking is allowed in Merlin's Theater, located on the "Medieval" level, above the casino. Conveniently, there's a bathroom within the showroom. Drinks must be purchased directly from the bar (no at-the-table cocktail service) and range from $4.50 for soda, bottled water, or juice to $10.95 for frozen or mixed drinks in a 22-ounce souvenir glass. Bottled beer ranges from $4.75 to $5.50 and house wine is $4.50 per glass.

Tony 'n' Tina's Wedding

Type of Show Interactive dinner theater
Host Casino and Showroom Rio—Calypso Room
Reservations and Information (888) 746-7784 or (702) 777-7776
Admission Cost with Taxes $87
Cast Size 20

Nights of Lowest Attendance Monday
Usual Show Times Nightly, 7 p.m.
Topless No
Author's Rating ★★★½
Overall Appeal by Age Group

Under 21 ★ | 21–37 ★★★½ | 38–50 ★★★½ | 51 and older ★★★

Duration of Presentation 2 and 30 minutes

Description and Comments Have you ever been to a wedding or wedding reception where you really didn't know anyone? Well, that's the premise for *Tony 'n' Tina's Wedding.* You're a wedding guest, welcomed into a large banquet hall and seated at a dinner table with total strangers. There you sit befuddled and somewhat uncomfortable as members of the bride's family (actors) stop to say hello and reminisce about Tony and Tina. And this is just the beginning. If you thought you could sit passively and watch a show, you're quite mistaken. During the course of a panicky few minutes, you become acutely aware that you are being sucked into the cast of this strange piece of theater, or if you can suspend your disbelief, this wedding. First there's the ceremony, then obligatory toasts, then dancing, then dinner followed by more toasts, and the tossing of the bouquet and the garter. As it unfolds, you are taken back to all those weddings in your life where one of the bridesmaids gets drunk, where an uninvited guests makes a five-minute toast, and where the best man wants to sing with the band. Inevitably it's you that the inebriated bridesmaid wants to spin around the dance floor, you who are pushed into the conga line, and you who are pulled into the throng to vie for the bouquet or garter.

There's a storyline, of course, plus enough subplots to give Robert Ludlum a run for his money. The families don't get along well, and each in its own way tries to monopolize the reception. The strain is almost too much for the happy couple and for a while their minutes-old marriage hangs in the balance.

Consumer Tips Is this fun? At the show we attended we observed a pretty diverse range of audience reaction (if you can call it that). Some really got into it, danced to every tune, and role played right along with cast. Others kept as much as possible to themselves, refusing to the extent possible to be drawn in. With some difficulty, we warmed to the proceedings, but nonetheless kept a wary lookout for the sloshed bridesmaid. It was impossible not to admire how exactly the production nailed every wedding cliché, and how, if you weren't familiar with the family members as individuals, you had met their characters at similar events dozens of times in real life. If it helps you make up your mind, we'll tell you that the dinner was passable, sort of a pasta buffet, and that you had one chance to go through the line and load up your plate. The only alcohol served was a splash of Champagne for one of the toasts, though there was a cash bar (where we spent a goodly sum trying to improve our attitude).

Tournament of Kings

Type of Show Jousting and medieval pageant
Host Casino and Showroom Excalibur—King Arthur's Arena
Reservations and Information (702) 597-7600
Admission Cost with Taxes $56, includes dinner
Cast Size 35 (with 38 horses)
Nights of Lowest Attendance Monday and Tuesday
Usual Show Times 6 and 8:30 p.m. nightly
Topless No

Author's Rating ★★★
Overall Appeal by Age Group

Under 21 ★★★★ | 21–37 ★★★★ | 38–50 ★★★★ | 51 and older ★★★★

Duration of Presentation 1 hour and 30 minutes

Description and Comments *Tournament of Kings* is a retooled version of *King Arthur's Tournament,* which logged 6,000 performances (from Excalibur's opening night in June 1990 till late 1998). It's basically the same show, with a slightly different plot twist. If you saw one, the other will come as no surprise.

The idea is that Arthur summons the kings of eight European countries to a sporting competition in honor of his son Christopher. Guests view the arena from dinner tables divided into sections; a king is designated to represent each section in the competition. Ladies-in-waiting and various court attendants double as cheerleaders, doing their best to whip the audience into a frenzy of cheering for their section's king. The audience, which doesn't require much encouragement, responds by hooting, "huzzarring," and pounding on the dinner tables. Watch your drinks—all the pounding can knock them over.

Soup is served to the strains of the opening march. The kings enter on horseback. Precisely when the King of Hungary is introduced, dinner arrives (big Cornish hen, small twice-baked potato, bush of broccoli, dinner roll, and dessert turnover). The kings engage in contests with flags, dummy heads, javelins, swords, and maces and shields and joust a while, too. The horse work, fighting, and especially the jousting are exciting, and the music (by a three-man band) and sound effects are well executed.

Right on cue, Mordred the Evil One crashes the party, accompanied by his Dragon Enforcers. Arthur is mortally slain and all the kings are knocked out, leaving Christopher to battle the forces of evil and emerge—surprise!—victorious in the end.

Except that . . . it's not over. The coronation is the culmination, after some acrobatics and human-tower stunts from a specialty act. Finally, the handsome new king goes out in a (literal) blaze of glory. It's a bit anticlimactic and bogged down, which helps hurry you out so the crew can quickly set up for the second show or clean up and go home.

Consumer Tips One of the few Las Vegas shows suitable for the whole family, and one of the fewer dinner shows, *Tournament of Kings* enjoys great popularity and often plays to a full house. Reserved seats can be purchased with a credit card up to five days in advance by calling the number listed above (there's an extra $2 charge if you order by phone). Or you can show up at the Excalibur box office, which opens at 8 a.m., up to five days ahead.

No matter where you sit, you're close to the action—and the dust and stage smoke. The air-conditioning system is steroidal, so you might consider bringing a wrap. Seating is reserved, so you can walk in at the last minute and don't have to tip any greeters or seaters.

Dinner is served without utensils and eaten with the hands, so you might want to wash up beforehand. Eating a big meal is a bit awkward with the show going on and all the cheering duties, so you might consider bringing some aluminum foil and a bag to take out the leftover bird. Beverage is limited to soda with dinner, but the food server will bring you water, and a cocktail waitress will bring you anything else. Service is adequate; no one tips, so you'll be a hero if you do.

Tribute to Frank, Sammy, Joey, and Dean

Type of Show Celebrity impersonation
Host Casino and Showroom   Greek Isles—Star Theatre
Reservations and Information   (702) 727-5540
Admission Cost with Taxes $45, show only; $55, dinner show; $60, VIP
Cast Size   17, including 12-piece band
Night of Lowest Attendance   Wednesday
Usual Show Time   Daily, 7 p.m., 5:30 p.m. seating for dinner   **Dark** Friday
Topless   No
Author's Rating   ★★★½
Overall Appeal by Age Group

Under 21 — | 21–37 ★★★ | 38–50 ★★★½ | 51 and older ★★★½

Duration of Presentation   1 hour and 15 minutes
Description and Comments   The heart and soul of the original Rat Pack were crooners Frank Sinatra, Dean Martin, and Sammy Davis Jr., and comedian Joey Bishop. They all worked the Las Vegas showrooms of the 1960s, sometimes dropping in on each others shows and sometimes working together. Their late night antics at the old Sands, particularly, are among the richest of Las Vegas showroom legends.

Tribute to Frank, Sammy, Joey, and Dean recreates a night when the acerbic Bishop and hard-drinking Martin team up with Davis and Sinatra. Backed by piano, bass, drums, along with, get this, a nine-piece horn section, four talented impersonators take you back to a night at the Sands Copa Room in 1963. The impersonations are excellent. Each impersonator captures his character's voice, singing style, and body language. The impersonators playing Bishop and Davis bear a strong physical resemblance to the originals, and the Sinatra impersonator squeaks by, but the Martin character looks more like an Elvis impersonator. A Marilyn Monroe look-alike plays a supporting role quite effectively.

The casual interplay among the four effectively transports you back to the 1960s, and what you see is pretty much how it was. The humor was racist, sexist, and politically incorrect, the showroom was packed and smoky, and the music, well…drop-dead brilliant.
Consumer Tips   The showroom, designed by Debbie Reynolds and modeled on the Crystal Room at the Desert Inn, is perfect for this production. Banquet-table seating, however, is pretty cramped, especially if you get the dinner-show package. Speaking of which, the food is pretty good and at only $10 more than the show alone, represents a good value. Self-parking is a breeze and the casino so small that it takes barely three minutes to walk from your car to the showroom. There are usually discount coupons for *Tribute to Frank, Sammy, Joey, and Dean* in the local tourists mags.

Wayne Newton

Type of Show   Celebrity headliner
Host Casino and Showroom   Stardust—Wayne Newton Theater
Reservations and Information   (702) 732-6325
Admission Cost with Taxes $67, includes 1 drink
Cast Size   21, includes band

Nights of Lowest Attendance Monday
Usual Show Times Saturday–Thursday, 9 p.m.　**Dark** Friday
Topless No
Author's Rating ★★★★
Overall Appeal by Age Group

Under 21 ★★★ | 21–37 ★★★ | 38–50 ★★★½ | 51 and older ★★★★

Duration of Presentation 2 hours

Description and Comments Folks who only recently discovered Las Vegas remember Wayne Newton as that little, scrub-faced fat kid with the high voice on TV (that is, if they're old enough to remember him at all). Wrong. Wayne Newton reinvented himself in Las Vegas many years ago, transforming from the pudgy little kid singing "Danke Schoen" to a 6-foot, 4-inch crooning linebacker. Always a chick magnet (now a hen magnet), Newton's core fans are women over 50. That's too bad, because he'll make a believer out of anyone who sees his show. With a 16-piece band and four backup singers, Newton sings pop and standards, plays banjo, fiddle, bass, and piano (he plays more than a dozen instruments), and demonstrates an under-reported skill as a stand-up comic. He still sings "Danke Schoen" and "MacArthur Park," and he still mingles with the audience in the best Las Vegas showroom tradition. Beyond those passing acknowledgements of his roots, there's nothing dated about this driving two-hour performance.

Consumer Tips The theater was designed for full-fledged, topless production shows, which means that some of the seating is a little distant for a celebrity-headliner show. The best seats are those in the middle, right, about halfway back.

V: The Ultimate Variety Show

Type of Show A hodgepodge of variety acts
Host Casino and Showroom Desert Passage—V Theatre
Reservations and Information (888) 283-6423
Admission Cost with Taxes $69 VIP, $59 general
Cast Size About 12 (varies)
Nights of Lowest Attendance Monday, Wednesday
Usual Show Times Nightly, 7 and 9 p.m.
Special Comments Some of Las Vegas's quirkiest acts; great fun
Topless No
Author's Rating ★★★★
Overall Appeal by Age Group

Under 21 ★★★½ | 21–37 ★★★ | 38–50 ★★★ | 51 and older ★★½

Duration of Presentation 1 hour and 15 minutes

Description and Comments In quite a few headlining Las Vegas shows, old and new, intermissions are handled by variety acts—comics, jugglers, acrobats, magicians, ventriloquists, and more. And in several of these cases (particularly the older ones), these variety acts become more entertaining than the headliners. The advantage of V is that the cast consists of a rotating stable of variety acts culled from Vegas and elsewhere. This means that no act lasts longer than a few minutes; it's the show for the short-attention-span set. Most of the acts are quite good. The MC is a hilariously queeny and aggressive comic/magician, and when we visited, there was also an amusingly abusive juggler, a few species of acrobats, and a bizarre ventriloquist who uses audience volunteers as his "dummies," among others. Some of the acts are admittedly hit or miss, but as we said, nobody's on stage for long.

Consumer Tips The V Theatre is located in the Desert Passage shopping venue at the Aladdin. Self-parking at the Aladdin is complicated, so we recommend you use the valet service. Likewise, the Desert Passage is a convoluted affair, so give yourself extra time to find the showroom. Because there are only a couple of windows at the box office, it's advisable to arrive 40 minutes or more before showtime if you are buying or picking up tickets, or redeeming ticket vouchers. The split-level showroom has a bar on a mezzanine floor and most seating on ground level. Because the V Theatre is a multifunctional facility there's no vertical rise from front to back for the seating. If you sit behind someone tall, in other words, your line of sight will be majorly obstructed. Also be aware that the available rest rooms are totally inadequate for the size of the audience.

We Will Rock You

Type of Show   Musical based on the songs of the rock band Queen
Host Casino and Showroom   Paris–Paris Theatre des Arts
Reservations and Information   (702) 946-4567
Admission Cost with Taxes $81, $97, and $114
Cast Size   45
Nights of Lowest Attendance   Tuesday
Usual Show Times   Monday and Friday, 9 p.m.; Tuesday, Wednesday, and Saturday, 7 and 10:30 p.m.; Sunday, 5 and 9 p.m.   **Dark:** Thursday
Topless   No
Author's Rating   Not open at press time
Duration of Presentation   90 minutes

Description and Comments   Originating in London's West End and skipping Broadway to make its American debut in Las Vegas, We Will Rock You weaves 25 of rock band Queen's greatest hits around an improbable dystopian plot. The action takes place in a futuristic world where musical instruments are banned and conformity rules. Predictably, a group of rebels rise against the system brandishing the music of Queen as their primary weapon. It's a bit of a stretch, but the music (not the plot) is the big burrito of We Will Rock You. Consistent with the best Las Vegas tradition of excess, the production is augmented by extremely cool laser lights and special effects broadcast on six enormous plasma screens.

Consumer Tips   The London version of We Will Rock You plays to sell-out crowds much of the time, so we expect high demand for the Las Vegas show as well. For the presentation's first year, buying your tickets well in advance is probably a good idea.

The World's Greatest Magic Show

Type of Show   Magic variety show with assortment of performers
Host Casino and Showroom   Greek Isles—Star Theatre
Reservations and Information   (800) 634-6787, (702) 597-5970
Admission Cost with Taxes $72–$84
Cast Size   About 20
Nights of Lowest Attendance   Tuesday and Wednesday
Usual Show Times   9 p.m.
Topless   No
Author's Rating   ★★★½
Overall Appeal by Age Group

Under 21 ★★★★ | 21–37 ★★★½ | 38–50 ★★★½ | 51 and older ★★★

Duration of Presentation 1 hour and 30 minutes

Description and Comments   Merging a magic show with the variety show revival, the creators of *The World's Greatest Magic Show* have hit on a winner. Like the successful incarnations of other variety shows, the best thing here is that if one act bores you, there's always something else coming up in a few minutes. But what's surprising is the high standard of talent, plus, there truly is a considerable variety in class and style. When we attended, the show was hosted by a rowdy MC who specialized in both sleight-of-hand and big-boom illusions, and the gallery of magicians included (but was not limited to) a wonderfully strange prop magician, a suave European classical illusionist, a bizarre younger fellow with an inclination for amputation, and a leatherclad Valkyrie who whipped the gentlemen into a frenzy. That last entry notwithstanding, this show was also a standout for being pointedly family friendly, with children invited to participate in several of the acts.

Consumer Tips   As we were going to press, *The World's Greatest Magic Show* moved from the Sahara to the Greek Isles. It appears that their rotating lineup of magicians also went through a reshuffling, so buyer beware. The price is relatively similar to big-name solo magic acts like *Lance Burton* and *Steve Wyrick*, so be sure you're into the variety aspect rather than a single marquee performer.

Afternoon Shows

Afternoon shows have become an affordable alternative to the high-priced productions playing in the major showrooms at night. Most cost under $20 (sometimes including a drink) and many can be enjoyed for even less by taking advantage of coupons and special offers found in the local freebie visitor magazines. Here is a list of the profiled afternoon shows, ranked in terms of overall excellence.

AFTERNOON SHOWS	
Rank and Show	**Location**
1. *Mac King Comedy Magic Show*	Harrah's
2. *Illusionary Magic of Rick Thomas*	Tropicana
3. *Ronn Lucas*	Rio
4. *Viva Las Vegas*	Stratosphere
5. *San Remo Impersonator Shows*	San Remo
Bottoms Up	Flamingo
(Not ranked because it's already rank enough.)	

There's been a numbing proliferation of afternoon shows recently, and as you might expect, the shows vary immensely in quality. Finding the good ones and avoiding the bad ones is not unlike threading your way through a minefield. The good ones are better than a lot of the high-ticket productions holding down stages around town at night. But the bad ones, oh, the bad ones: Heaven help us. From fat ladies making whoopee cushion noises with their armpits, to magicians sucking raw eggs out of the shell with their nose, to Elvis impersonators who sweat like Elvis but sing like Alvin the chipmunk, there is a dismal parade of frustrated humanity intent on torturing us.

Unfortunately, because afternoon shows erupt like wildflowers (or weeds) and disappear just as fast, we can't cover all of them in the *Unofficial Guide*. What we can do, however, is to provide a short profile of those afternoon shows that have demonstrated staying power. Show times for specific afternoon productions are usually in the 2–4:30 p.m. range, but change almost on a weekly basis. Call the information and reservations number provided for performance times during your visit. The following profiles are arranged alphabetically.

Bottoms Up

Type of Show Topless Las Vegas production show
Host Casino and Showroom Flamingo—Flamingo Showroom
Reservations and Information (702) 733-3333
Admission Cost $16
Cast Size 10
Author's Rating ½
Appropriate for Children No
Length of Presentation Seemingly endless

Description and Comments *Bottoms Up* has been staged in a variety of forms for decades, in Las Vegas and elsewhere. In its current incarnation, it's quite likely the worst show in town. Imagine an offensive, ultra-corny series of excruciatingly stale comedy sketches, periodically interrupted by smarmy stand-up or awful show tunes rendered by wizened core performers. In a town where anything goes, this production manages to find something to offend virtually everyone—when was the last time you chuckled at an unwed mother joke? Despite the show's relative brevity, you'll still get the feeling of being trapped in the showroom for a prolonged episode of torture. We can only hope that the abject humiliation of participating in this disaster will ultimately lead to better things for the younger performers (i.e., the lovely, topless showgirls).

Consumer Tips If it's imperative that you see a topless show in the afternoon, at least this one is very cheap. Otherwise, avoid *Bottoms Up* at all costs. As one dissatisfied customer complained, "I wish I'd spent my money on the slot machines" (and he got in for $5 with a coupon!). Consider yourself warned that the price of seeing this show is not strictly monetary.

The Illusionary Magic of Rick Thomas

Type of Show Magic and illusion
Host Casino and Showroom Tropicana—Tiffany Showroom
Reservations and Information (702) 739-2411
Admission Cost $21 and $27, depending on choice of seats
Cast Size 4
Usual Show Times Monday–Saturday, 2 and 4 p.m. **Dark** Sunday
Author's Rating ★★★½
Appropriate for Children Yes
Length of Presentation 50 minutes

Description and Comments Rick Thomas is as good as the big show magicians but prefers to work days. You'll see excellent close work coupled with cutting-edge big-stage illusion. Like Mac King, Thomas easily connects with his audience.

Consumer Tips   Coupons and discounts are sometimes available. Be aware that the Tiffany Showroom has its own box office adjacent to the showroom. Many folks spend a long time in line at the Tropicana's main box office by mistake.

The Mac King Comedy Magic Show

Type of Show Mostly comedy with some magic thrown in
Host Casino and Showroom Harrah's—Comedy Cabaret
Reservations and Information (702) 369-5111
Admission Cost $19
Cast Size 1
Author's Rating ★★★★
Appropriate for Children Yes
Length of Presentation 1 hour and 10 minutes

Description and Comments   Our pick for the best afternoon show in town, *Mac King* uses magic and illusion as a platform for his unique brand of comedy. His humor pokes fun at Las Vegas, other Vegas magicians, and at himself. The presentation is fresh and imaginative, and the illusions are good. But it's King's ability to work an audience, coupled with his sheer insanity, that keeps audiences rolling. If it's really magic you crave (as opposed to comedy), then *Rick Thomas,* also described in this section, is a better choice.

Consumer Tips   Harrah's runs two-fer and discount specials on *Mac King,* but they come and go. Unique among afternoon shows, *Mac King* frequently sells out. So purchase tickets in advance if possible.

Ronn Lucas

Type of Show Ventriloquist—comedy
Host Casino and Showroom Rio—Copacobana Showroom
Reservations and Information (702) 777-7776
Admission Cost $28
Cast Size 1
Author's Rating ★★★½
Appropriate for Children Yes
Length of Presentation 1 hour and 30 minutes

Description and Comments   Lucas is a world-class ventriloquist whose ability to "throw" his voice is really quite astounding. His act includes stories about how his singular talent and mischievous mind have landed him in hot water with everyone from his parents to the Secret Service. Warm, funny, and in constant touch with his audience, Lucas is a performer who, like Mac King and Rick Thomas, could be a hit in any showroom.

Consumer Tips   Lucas performs in such a large theater that it rarely fills. Thus, good seats up close are almost always available.

Viva Las Vegas

Type of Show Variety comedy and musical show
Host Casino and Showroom Stratosphere—Star Showroom
Reservations and Information (800) 998-6937
Admission Cost with Taxes $17
Usual Show Times Monday–Saturday, 2 and 4 p.m.   **Dark** Sunday

Cast Size 12

Author's Rating ★★½

Appropriate for Children Yes

Duration of Presentation 1 hour and 30 minutes

Description and Comments   Probably the most upmarket of the inexpensive afternoon shows, *Viva Las Vegas* provides contemporary stand-up comedy as well as traditional Vegas musical numbers (complete with feathered dancing girls). The comics include an irate cowboy fella and a magician/animal trainer/pyrotechnician among others, and all are pretty amusing. The stand-up alternates with the songs—crooned by accomplished female vocalists backed up by the dancers—giving the audience a sampler of Vegas-style production show acts.

Consumer Tips   Though ticket counters are located above the Stratosphere's main casino floor, the Star Showroom is a long hike through the shopping plaza. Once you arrive, the showroom itself is nicely appointed and spacious. However, tables at the back top tier are pretty distant from the stage and views in the rear center and to the immediate left and right of the stage are somewhat obstructed by video and audio equipment. Sitting closer to the stage increases the chance of getting harassed by the comics, as per usual. Coupons for the show are widely available.

Comedy Clubs

There is a lot of stand-up comedy in Las Vegas, and several of the large production shows feature comedians as specialty acts. In addition, there is usually at least one comedy headliner playing in town. Big names who regularly play Las Vegas include Bill Cosby, Jerry Seinfeld, Rita Rudner, Tim Conway, the Smothers Brothers, Joan Rivers, Andrew Dice Clay, George Carlin, Yakov Smirnoff, Don Rickles, and Rich Little. Finally, there are the comedy clubs.

A comedy club is usually a smaller showroom with a simple stage and two to five stand-up comics. In most Las Vegas comedy showrooms, a new show with different comedians rotates in each week. There are six bona fide Las Vegas comedy clubs:

Greek Isles	Sandy Hackett's Comedy Club
Harrah's	An Evening at the Improv
Palace Station	Gabe Kaplan's Laugh Trax
Riviera	Comedy Club
Tropicana	Comedy Stop

The comedy clubs, unlike the production showrooms, are almost never dark. There are usually two shows each night, seven days a week. The humor at the comedy clubs, as well as the audience, tends to be young and irreverent. A favorite and affordable entertainment for locals as well as for tourists, comedy clubs enjoy great popularity in Las Vegas.

The comedy-club format is simple and straightforward. Comedians perform sequentially, and what you get depends on who is performing. The range of humor runs from slapstick to obscene to ethnic to topical to just about anything. Some comics are better than others, but all of the talent is solid and professional. There is no way to predict which club will have the best show in a given week. In fact, there may not be a "best" show, since response to comedy is a matter of individual sense of humor.

Comedy Club

Type of Show Stand-up comedy
Host Casino and Showroom Riviera—Mardi Gras Showrooms, second floor
Reservations and Information (702) 794-9433
Admission Cost with Taxes $27 general admission; $38 VIP (includes tax, tip, and 2 drinks); weekend late-night shows of more risqué "Extreme Comedy" are $19
Cast Size Approximately 4
Nights of Lowest Attendance Sunday–Wednesday
Usual Show Times Nightly, 10:30 p.m.
Duration of Presentation 1 hour and 15 minutes

Description and Comments Three shows—*Riviera Comedy Club, Crazy Girls,* and *La Cage*—are staged on the second and third floors above the Riviera casino in what are called the Mardi Gras Showrooms. In addition, the production show *Splash* plays off of the main casino in the Splash Theater. It is not possible to schedule different shows back to back unless there is a minimum of an hour and 30 minutes between performances. Show tickets can also be purchased as a package with the Riviera's buffet. The food with the show-dinner combo is a good deal for the money but is not exactly a culinary breakthrough. The buffet is fast and convenient, however, and there is usually plenty of time to eat between shows.

Tickets for the *Comedy Club* may be purchased 21 days in advance at the Riviera box office located in the front center of the casino or by phone with a credit card. Seating is by the maître d'. There is no table service. After you are seated, proceed to the bar and turn in your ticket stub for drinks. Drinks are included even with the dinner combos.

Comedy Stop

Type of Show Stand-up comedy
Host Casino and Showroom Tropicana—Comedy Stop Showroom
Reservations and Information (702) 739-2714
Admission Cost with Taxes $17.50, includes 2 drinks and gratuity
Cast Size Usually 3 comedians
Nights of Lowest Attendance Monday–Wednesday
Usual Show Times 8 p.m. (nonsmoking) and 10:30 p.m. (smoking)
Special Comments Admission includes 2 drinks
Duration of Presentation 1 hour and 30 minutes

Description and Comments To reach the Comedy Stop Showroom, take the elevator (between the main casino and the shopping arcade) up one floor. The 400-person showroom is rectangular, with the stage on the long side. All seating is at banquet tables. Tickets may be purchased up to two weeks in advance by phone with a credit card, or admission can be prepaid at the Comedy Stop guest desk near the showroom entrance. After being seated, patrons trade their ticket stubs at a self-service bar for two drinks. If you use the Trop's self-parking lot, allow an extra ten minutes to get to the showroom.

An Evening at the Improv

Type of Show Stand-up comedy

Host Casino and Showroom Harrah's—The Improv
Reservations and Information (702) 369-5111
Admission Cost with Taxes $28; dinner show $60
Cast Size 3–4 comedians
Nights of Lowest Attendance Wednesday, Thursday
Usual Show Times 8:30 and 10:30 p.m.   **Dark** Monday
Duration of Presentation 1 hour and 10 minutes

Description and Comments Drinks are not included, but there is a cash bar. The showroom is on the second floor at the top of the escalator from the main casino. Reserved seats may be purchased by phone or in person up to 30 days in advance.

Gabe Kaplan's Laugh Trax

Type of Show Celebrity headliner, stand-up comedy
Host Casino Palace Station
Reservations and Information (702) 367-2411
Admission Cost with Taxes $14
Cast Size 2 or 3
Nights of Lowest Attendance Wednesday
Usual Show Times Tuesday–Thursday, 7:30 p.m.; Friday and Saturday, 7:30 and 10 p.m.
Dark Sunday and Monday
Duration of Presentation 1 hour and 15 minutes

Description and Comments This venue is a cross between a garden-variety comedy club and a celebrity headliner showroom. Kaplan entertains following a warm-up comic when he's in town. When's he not, worthy subs ensure the quality of the show. Admission is a bargain, but you're obliged to buy a minimum of one drink at $4 and up.

Sandy Hackett's Comedy Club

Type of Show Stand-up comedy
Host Casino Greek Isles
Reservations and Information (702) 228-7591
Admission Cost with Taxes $18; dinner included, $19
Cast Size 2–4
Usual Show Times Nightly, 9 p.m.
Nights of Lowest Attendance Tuesday
Duration of Presentation About 1 hour and 10 minutes

Description and Comments The Greek Isles is a small casino that experiments constantly with its entertainment mix. In the past, there have been four or more shows of various (and dubious) ilk running there concurrently. Comic Sandy Hackett hosts one or more visiting comedians nightly. For an extra couple of bucks, a show-and-dinner combo is available.

Las Vegas Nightlife

When it comes to nightspots, visitors and locals tend to go in different directions. With the exception of patronizing the comedy clubs, locals stay away from the Strip; visitors, conversely, almost never leave it. Both groups are missing out on some great nightlife.

Several of the Strip casinos have added small bars or lounges just off their main gambling floors. These are typically stylish, no-cover rooms that catch the overflow from the casino or the crowds who don't want to shell out major bucks to enter the premier nightspots. Examples include **Shadow Bar** at Caesars Palace, **Mist** at T. I., **Zuri** at MGM Grand.

We don't profile such lounges and restaurant bars individually because they don't merit a specific visit. However, they can be a nice escape if you just want to relax—unless they have a DJ blasting everyone in the tiny room into submission. We recommend you check them out during the day or early evening if you want a break, as they become just as packed as their upscale cousins on weekend nights.

Another category of club that appeared a couple of years ago (invented by promoters, as far as we can tell) is the "ultralounge"—luxurious nightspots that attempt to ride the bleeding edge of Vegas nightlife. The only places using this appellation so far are Paris's **Risque,** the MGM Grand's **Tabu,** and the newest of the ultras, **Ice** (see profiles). While all are chic and loud, we can't figure out exactly what makes them "ultra." If you're dead set on visiting these or other hype-worthy hotspots, consider going early on weeknights. You can often get in without even paying a cover, and you may get to lounge at a VIP table for awhile (until the actually VIPs start arriving). And while on the subject of cover charges, serious club hoppers should consider the front-of-the-line passes offered by **www.vegas.com,** which start at $10. Not all clubs are included, but some major draws are (including Studio 54, Rain in the Desert, Coyote Ugly, and Sevilla—all profiled), and on a weekend, skipping a few lines could save you hours.

Happily, lounges and clubs all over town are friendly and open, welcoming anyone who walks through the door. Visitors can feel comfortable in places primarily frequented by locals, and vice versa. This kind of acceptance allows for a wide range of choices when it comes to nightlife.

Since you don't have to worry about feeling unwanted or out of place, you can select your nighttime entertainment on the basis of personal taste. Listed alphabetically below are profiles of the better nightspots in town. Celebrity headliner shows, production shows, and comedy clubs are detailed in the preceding section. Striptease shows (for men and women) are described in the following section, "Las Vegas below the Belt." Microbreweries also offer a fine choice for an evening of entertainment. Check out "The Best Brewpubs" section in Part Four, "Dining and Restaurants" (page 347).

	NIGHTCLUBS BY ZONE	
Club	**Type of Club**	**Zone**
The Bar at Times Square	Top 40, show tunes, sing-along	1
The Beach	Dance music of the 1970s, 1980s, and 1990s	1
C2K*	Dance club in search of a crowd	1
Club Rio	Top 40 music	1
Coyote Ugly	Drink-slinging barmaids stomp and holler above the crowd	1
Curve	Luxe dance club and lounge	1
Ghost Bar	Otherworldly lounge high above the Strip	1
Gilley's Saloon	Live country and rock-and-roll	1
House of Blues	Blues, R&B	1
Light	New York club chic, Vegas style	1
The Nightclub	Top 40/show combination	1
Nine Fine Irishmen	Live Celtic music pub	1
RA	Top 40, techno, and dance	1
Rain in the Desert	Mondo dance orgy with fire-spewing lighting rig	1
Risque	Euro-style club and meat market	1
rumjungle	Dance, techno, industrial, rap music	1
Seven	Dance, techno, rap, jazz	1
Sevilla	Spanish/Latin themed dance venue	1
Studio 54	Dance, top 40	1
Tabu	Über-lounge	1
Tommy Rocker's Cantina and Grill	Top 40 and Jimmy Buffett–style music	1
VooDoo Lounge	Live music with best view of the Strip	1
Sand Dollar Blues Lounge	Rhythm and blues	3
Dylan's Saloon & Dance Hall	Recorded country music	5

*Closed until January 2005

Nightclub Profiles

The Bar at Times Square

TOP 40, SHOW TUNES, SING-ALONG

Who Goes There 21–45; college students, tourists

3790 Las Vegas Boulevard South (New York–New York); (702) 740-6969; www.nynyhotelcasino.com/pages/ent_tsquare.asp   Strip Zone 1

Cover Friday and Saturday, $10 (kicks in at 8 p.m. when music starts) **Minimum** None **Mixed drinks** $4.75–$6.50 **Wine** $5–$8 **Beer** $4.25–$6 **Dress** Anything goes **Specials** None **Food available** In casino

Hours Daily, 5 a.m.–4 a.m.; shows 8 p.m.–2 a.m.

What goes on The Bar at Times Square is to karaoke night at the corner pub what the Boston Pops on July 4th is to a kiddie chorus at the corner kindergarten. This joint, in other words, has muscle. Two pianos face each other in the middle of room, at which dueling piano players (often a guy and a girl) pound out Top-40 tunes ("Walk This Way," "Why Do You Build Me Up, Buttercup?," "Me and Bobby McGee," etc.) or show tunes, and engage in witty repartee with each other and the crowd. Most people get into it and sing along (though it gets so loud that the bartenders wear cotton in both ears); many patrons walk up to the pianos and write down requests on yellow sheets of paper.

Setting & atmosphere The room is plainly decorated like an old New York City licensed premises, with polished-wood floors and historical photos of the Big Apple on the walls. The pianos divide the room in half. At the end is the bar, in front of which the often standing-room-only crowd hangs around with drinks in their hands, singing their heads off in each others' ears. On the other side are a couple dozen tables; it's a bit less raucous over here, though no less crowded—you have to arrive early to get a seat.

If you go If you have a headache, you won't care for this scene. But if you're in the mood to exercise your lungs and lend your voice to a rowdy chorus, you'll have a good time. A couple of drinks help the cause, and luckily, they're reasonably priced. But if you just want to see what goes on, or listen to the music, join the small crowd milling around outside the front doors, avoiding the cover charge and the subway-at-rush-hour claustrophobia.

The Beach

DANCE MUSIC OF THE 1970s, 1980s, AND 1990s

Who Goes There 21–40+; locals, visitors, conventioneers (cosmopolitan mix)

365 Convention Center (corner of Paradise and Convention Center, across from the Convention Center); (702) 731-1925; www.beachlv.com Strip Zone 1

Cover Local males free before midnight; ladies free except for special events; Sunday–Thursday, $10 (after midnight, $5); Friday and Saturday, $15 (after midnight, $10); **Minimum** None **Mixed drinks** $4.50 and up **Beer** $4 and up **Dress** Very specific and strict (call for restrictions) **Specials** Friday is Hurricane Beach party; Thursday is Aquadance; call for concert information; ladies night Sunday, Monday, and Wednesday **Food available** Lunch only

Hours Varies according to entertainment. Sports bar, open 24 hours; dance bar open 10 p.m.–4 a.m., Sunday–Thursday and until 6 a.m. Friday and Saturday

What goes on These beach lovers don't miss the sand or the surf, because all the action is indoors. On the main floor, singles, couples, and new friends alike dance, drink, eat, and laugh the night away in this "local's favorite" party club. The fun is so contagious that even the bartenders and cocktail waitresses join in the dancing. From the second-floor sports bar, patrons watch games on over 60 TVs (including five big screens); play slots, video poker, or pool; and view the action on the main floor. The Beach is an unpretentious and fun-loving spot that radiates positive energy and vibes.

Setting & atmosphere Neon beer lights, palms, coconuts, surfboards, and brightly painted murals give the club a beach flavor without adding salt or sand. The wood walls offer excellent acoustics for live performances and the DJ's music. The main floor has five bars, high-table seating, and a dance area. Adjacent to the upstairs sports bar is a room available for private parties or extra party space. ATM machines are on each floor.

If you go Long lines begin at 9 p.m. and continue well past 2 a.m. on weekends. Also, please note that the four-story garage is reserved for valet on weekends, so use the Convention Center parking lot across the street. Plan to arrive very early or take a cab. Smoke can be heavy in some corners of the club. Women on their own can expect to find company. Call ahead for special-events information.

C2K

DANCE CLUB IN SEARCH OF A CROWD

Who Goes There 21–40; casino drifters and club kids on the Vegas dance circuit

3355 Las Vegas Boulevard South (Venetian Hotel); (702) 414-1133; www.clubc2k.com Strip Zone 1

Cover $15 men, $10 women, free for local women on Friday and Saturday **Minimum** None **Mixed drinks** $5 and up **Wine** $4.50 and up **Beer** $3.75 and up **Dress** Semi-formal; stylish clubwear encouraged **Specials** Theme nights, plus ever-changing menu of shooters and vodka specialties **Food available** None

Hours Closed until January 2005, check hours before show; at press time, Wednesday–Sunday, 10:30 p.m. until

What goes on Appearing on the tail end of the Vegas trend for glitzy new dance clubs, C2K is still trying to figure out what to do with itself. On the one hand, it's a huge, versatile space with plenty of room. However, it's also somewhat hard to find inside the already labyrinthine Venetian, it has no easy way to get in from outside, and it has no recognizable theme like most of the other flashy casino clubs. All that aside, both cover charges and drink prices are cheaper than at comparable places elsewhere, so you can get your groove on without as much financial pain.

Setting & atmosphere The high room is a converted showroom (it still serves as a production space occasionally). The tiered showroom setup allows for good views of the large dance floor, and the bars are easy to access. Lighting and sound are both first-rate, and C2K is gradually gaining street cred as a favorite among local DJs.

If you go Call for hours before show; at press time, C2K was closed until January 2005. Go late, and go on a weekend night. Anything but a large crowd will get lost in this cavernous room, and it's only fun when the dance floor is really packed and jumping.

Club Rio

NIGHTCLUB—TOP 40 MUSIC

Who Goes There 25–35 professionals; locals and visitors

3700 West Flamingo Road (Rio Hotel); (702) 252-7777; www.harrahs.com/our_casinos/rlv/amenities/club_rio.html Strip Zone 1

Cover Local ladies, free; men, $20; out-of-state ladies, $10 **Minimum** None **Mixed drinks** $5 and up **Wine** $4.25 and up **Beer** $3.75 and up **Dress** Collared shirts for men; no jeans, shorts, tennis shoes, or sandals **Specials** Wednesday, Fantasmic Universe night; Thursday, Latin Libido night; Friday and Saturday, DJ music **Food available** Restaurants on property

Hours Thursday, Friday, and Saturday, 11 p.m.–4 a.m.

What goes on Sexy and stylish, Club Rio is the hottest nightclub for successful singles and the chic well-to-do. Dancers fill the spacious dance floor. Couples snuggle in the showroom's comfy booths, while others search for and mingle with potential partners. Although the music is loud and pulsating, there's little trouble conversing with new friends or ordering drinks from the attractive cocktail waitresses.

Setting & atmosphere After the last show, the Copacabana showroom is transformed into a cosmopolitan nightclub with table lamps, mosaic laser lights, and giant video panels. Selected sections of booth seating are reserved for casino players. The sound system is clean, clear, and loud, but not too loud.

If you go Arrive early to avoid the long lines after 11 p.m. The dress code encourages stylish attire (jackets for the men and dresses for the women). Watch your step along the showroom's terraced levels as you make your way to and from the dance floor. The club is located off the new Masquerade Village.

Coyote Ugly

DRINK-SLINGING BARMAIDS STOMP AND HOLLER ABOVE THE CROWD

Who Goes There 21–35; curious passersby and booze-crazed barflies

3790 Las Vegas Boulevard South (New York–New York); (702) 740-6969; www.coyoteuglysaloon.com/lasvegas.html   Strip Zone 1

Cover $10 (after 8 p.m.) **Minimum** None **Mixed drinks** $5 and up **Wine** $5 and up **Beer** $4 and up **Dress** Casual **Specials** Too many to list, some of which will be poured directly into your mouth **Food available** None

Hours Daily, 6 p.m.–4 a.m.

What goes on An imported concept from New York City (and made famous by the eponymous movie), Coyote Ugly is a rootin'-tootin' saloon whose main attractions are the slinky female bartenders who leap atop the bars and stomp, clog, sing, dance, and generally whip the crowd into a drunken frenzy (sometimes literally pouring shots into the mouths of the howling masses). The crowd is an almost immobile press, broken only by the occasional scuffle as the security thugs eject a too-rowdy patron. A small back room offers some relief, but you have to force your way through the mob in order to get there.

Setting & atmosphere Vaguely reminiscent of a wood-floored honky-tonk, the surprisingly small room has two bars on opposite walls. That's where you'll find the strutting barmaids doing their stuff. If you can make it through the packed gawkers, an even smaller room in back is only slightly more subdued.

If you go Forget having a conversation and get ready for some serious, protracted yee-haws. If ogling the barmaids and standing in a crowd are not your bag, you should probably go elsewhere for the evening.

Curve

LUXE DANCE CLUB AND LOUNGE

Who Goes There 21–35; hipsters and club-hoppers

3667 Las Vegas Boulevard South (Aladdin); (702) 785-5525   Strip Zone 1

Cover Nonresidents, $20; local men, $10; local women, free **Minimum** None **Mixed drinks** $7 and up **Wine** $6 and up **Beer** $6 and up **Dress** Upscale dressy-cool and fashionable **Specials** None **Food available** None

Hours Friday and Saturday, 10:30 p.m.–5 a.m.

What goes on Curve's layout of several interconnected rooms makes it easy to find the vibe you want. Loungers lounge in quieter rooms and couch-filled nooks, while rump-shakers throw down on the dance floors. The crowd is young and energetic, but the ample space keeps it relatively uncongested. The fact that Curve is set in a secluded part of the somewhat secluded Aladdin also seems to keep crowds down.

Setting & atmosphere Curve was carved out of space reserved for the London Club, which is Aladdin's high-roller area. You must actually walk among the remaining high-stakes tables to get to the nightclub. That's rare for Vegas, and we imagine it dims the aura of exclusivity normally reserved for the high rollers. When we visited, a little person in a Roaring Twenties gangster zoot suit was dancing on a pedestal next to the nightclub's admission queue—why, we don't know. Inside, Curve is subdivided into several rooms, some with dance floors, some designed for relaxing among overstuffed chairs, couches, divans, and the like. There are four bars to serve your thirst, and a balcony that's often packed with social smokers.

If you go This is one of the few upscale Vegas clubs that allows people with different tastes to enjoy the same venue. Dancing fools can go nuts in their rooms, and lounge lizards can chill in theirs. Note, though, that even the "quiet" rooms have a DJ nearby to supply the evening's soundtrack.

Dylan's Saloon & Dance Hall

RECORDED COUNTRY MUSIC

Who Goes There 25–50; urban and rodeo cowboys

4660 South Boulder Highway; (702) 451-4006   Southeast Zone 5

Cover None **Minimum** None **Mixed drinks** $4 and up **Wine** $5 and up **Beer** $3.50 and up **Dress** Jeans and cowboy hats **Specials** Line-dance lessons, Friday and Saturday, 7:30–9 p.m. **Food available** Typical bar fare

Hours Friday–Saturday, 7 p.m. till dawn

What goes on Whether it's doing the two-step, shooting a game of pool, or enjoying a warm summer evening under the star-filled sky, the young and lively crowd whoops it up on the weekends. From ballads to rockabilly and honky-tonk, the DJ mixes the music to the crowd's delight. Seating around the dance floor is at a premium as singles look to meet new partners.

Setting & atmosphere This dance hall has a spacious, 2,400-square-foot, silky smooth dance floor, two bars, friendly folks, and the usual rodeo decor. The party flows onto the patio and, on busy nights, the chain-linked, flood-lit, dirt area adjacent to the parking lot. As the night parties on, the odors of beer and cigarette smoke get thicker.

If you go The attitude is looser and hipper than at Sam's Town Dance Hall. Arrive early for good seating. Because the parking lot is quite dark in areas, women on their own are advised to ask for an escort to their car.

Ghost Bar

OTHERWORLDLY LOUNGE HIGH ABOVE THE STRIP

Who Goes There 21–40; the superglitzy and clubgoing elite

*4321 West Flamingo Road (Palms Hotel); (702) 942-7777; www.n9negroup.com
Strip Zone 1*

Cover $10–$20 **Minimum** None **Mixed drinks** $8 and up **Wine** $6 and up **Beer**

$5 and up **Dress** "Stylish nightlife attire"; no jeans or tennis shoes **Specials** None **Food available** Light pub fare

Hours Nightly, 7 p.m. until

What goes on All cool lines and chilly shades of white and blue, Ghost Bar is a scenester's dream. Models of both sexes float about the main lounge space, occasionally alighting on a puffy chair or delicately sipping a translucent drink. Perched on the Palms' 55th floor, Ghost Bar is like a butterfly preserve for the beautiful people. Patrons waft out onto the patio, then waft back in for another circuit of the lounge. The place doesn't vibe meat market—rather, it's a spot to clinically evaluate who's hot, what they're wearing, and if they'll come with you to someplace a bit more rowdy.

Setting & atmosphere The beautiful main room is chic to the max, though the icy lighting and color schemes make the place feel like a giant display case (appropriately enough). The room is sparsely populated with a few chairs, benches, and cocktail tables. The outdoor patio has great views of the Strip, not to mention a large square of glass in the floor that's great for evaluating your fear of heights.

If you go Consider the perambulations of the salon-tanned and surgically enhanced, and definitely walk a few steps on the scary glass square. If you'd rather be dancing, check out the always-frenetic Rain on the ground floor of the Palms.

Gilley's Saloon, Dance Hall, and Barbecue

LIVE COUNTRY AND ROCK-AND-ROLL

Who Goes There 21–55; real and urban cowboys, locals and tourists

3120 Las Vegas Boulevard South (New Frontier); (702) 794-8200; www.frontierhotel-casino.com/gilleyswork.htm   Strip Zone 1

Cover Wednesday–Saturday after 10 p.m., $10; valid NV ID-holders, free **Minimum** None **Mixed drinks** $5.75 and up **Beer and Wine** $4 and up **Dress** Come as you are; in jeans, boots, and a big hat you'll feel right at home **Specials** Free line, swing, and two-step dance lessons, Sunday at 7:30 p.m. **Food available** Full menu of chuckwagon fare, 4–10 p.m. Nightly, Angus steak with fixin's, $10.

Hours Daily, 4 p.m. until; dinner 4–10 p.m.

What goes on Gilley's house band starts at 4 p.m. Tuesday–Saturday; a DJ spins the tunes on Wednesday, Friday, and Saturday. The band plays two-minute country tunes, complete with pedal-steel guitar and fiddle, during the late dinner sets, then cranks up the tempo later in the evening. The big dance floor gets crowded with two-steppers and line-dancers. Watchers sit at bar tables munching free peanuts from galvanized buckets. If the beer skews up your courage, you can attempt to ride Gilley's signature mechanical bull. Good luck.

Setting & atmosphere The smell of beer-battered onion rings, rotisserie chicken, and hickory-smoked pork permeates the place from the kitchen on one end. On the other end are the two bars. In between are the dance floor, eating areas, and mechanical bronc. Bales of hay, a Mickey Gilley logo counter, and peanut shells on the floor complete the scene. The atmosphere is as heavily country as anywhere else in town—the heaviest on the Strip.

If you go As long as it stands, the price is right no matter what mood you're in, but it helps to either be in, or ready for, cowboy hats, silver buckles, and fringed blouses. The joint is sedate till late, when everyone's finished eating, but then gets rocking and fun.

Round about 11 p.m. (except on Mondays, when it closes at midnight) Gilley's loses its barbecue feel and lives up to the rest of its handle: saloon and dance hall.

House of Blues

RHYTHM AND BLUES

Who Goes There 21–60; locals, tourists, music lovers

3950 Las Vegas Boulevard South (Mandalay Bay); (702) 632-7000; www.hob.com/venues/clubvenues/lasvegas/ Strip Zone 1

Cover Varies per venue **Minimum** None **Mixed drinks** $5.25–$6.75 **Wine** $6.25–$8 **Beer** $4.50–$6 **Dress** Clothes **Specials** None **Food available** Daily lunch and dinner, and Sunday Gospel Brunch; Creole/Cajun and Southern favorites (fried catfish, ribs); entrées $10–$17

Hours Sunday–Thursday, 8 a.m.–midnight, Friday and Saturday, 8 a.m.–1 a.m. (event nights till 2 a.m.)

What goes on First things first. House of Blues sports two venues: the 1,800-seat concert auditorium downstairs and the restaurant-bar upstairs (casino level). In this review, we're talking about the live music that takes place in the restaurant Thursday–Saturday 10:30 p.m.–1 a.m, when blues and R&B performers take the stage under lights that spell out "Have Mercy, Las Vegas." Three- and four-piece bands serenade the restaurant-bar patrons—some people eating, some people drinking, some people dancing, with waiters and waitresses weaving among them. It's a cool, casual, and not-too-cacophonous scene, with an eclectic audience mix all grooving to some hot licks.

Setting & atmosphere The House of Blues is one of the more evocative dining rooms in town, set to resemble an outdoor courtyard in the middle of a small Bayou village, with a huge tree in the middle and tables on a stone floor under and around it, as well as up on patio-type wooden decks. Wrought-iron railings, stone walls, etched and stained glass, and the facades of swamp shacks extend the theme, all under dim lighting. (They also account for the good acoustics.) The bar itself is decorated with Catholic iconography, mostly crosses made from bottle caps; Voodoo folk art and symbology round out the decor. The only incongruity is the collection of TV monitors on various walls throughout.

If you go Anything seems to go here during the music: big tables of beer-drinking college kids; couples (and singles) dancing all around the room; unreconstructed barefoot hippies in peasant blouses and patchouli perfume praising the Lord; lead singers or guitarists roaming the room wireless and interacting directly with the audience. It's best on Thursday nights when there's no concert downstairs and only those in the know are upstairs, enjoying some of the best bargain (free) entertainment in town.

Ice

METACLUB—BOOM, BOOM, BOOM

Who Goes There 21–35 professionals; locals and visitors

200 East Harmon Avenue; (702) 699-5528 for VIP reservations, (702) 699-9888 for information; www.icelasvegas.com Strip Zone 1

Cover $20, local ladies free (unless special even occurring) **Minimum** None **Mixed drinks** $7 and up **Wine** $5 and up **Beer** $5 and up **Dress** Officially it's business/casual, but if you're really hot, wear what you want; tight, revealing jeans okay for ladies only **Specials** DJ battles on Thursday, ladies drink free 11 p.m.–1 a.m. Service Industry Night on Sunday **Food available** Olives

Hours Tuesday, Thursday, Saturday, 11 p.m.–5 a.m.; Friday and Saturday 10:30 p.m.–5 a.m.

What goes on Amid the techno thunder of 100,000 watts of nail pounding beats, sassy and classy men and ladies in their prime stand around, gyrate, and occasionally sit down, while being buffeted by 100 mph sound blasts. The club keeps a jumping calendar, which can be viewed at their Web site.

Setting & atmosphere Featuring six micro-environments spread across 17,000 square feet of club space, walking around inside Ice is like walking around a stranger's fabulous house. Unless you're a regular, the curiosity to take the tour and continue wandering about is more urgent than to stay put and dance. Our favorite retreat is the cozy upstairs lounge, replete with cushy couches and fat pillows. From the railing you can watch the crowd, and the DJs feed off one another.

If you go Valet parking is de rigueur here unless you head down the street and park behind the shiny, silver club. It's residential back there, but it's free. If you're alone, you probably want the valet option.

Light

NEW YORK CLUB CHIC, VEGAS STYLE

Who Goes There 25–45; the well-to-do and sedentary

3600 Las Vegas Boulevard South (Bellagio Hotel); (702) 693-8300; www.lightlv.com Strip Zone 1

Cover $25 **Minimum** None **Mixed drinks** $7 and up **Wine** $6 and up **Beer** $4.50 and up **Dress** Stylish and formal; no sneakers or sandals, jeans discouraged **Specials** None **Food available** None

Hours Lounge, 5 p.m.–4 a.m; Thursday–Sunday, nightclub, 10:30 p.m.–4 a.m.

What goes on Light caters to those who can spring for a bottle of wine, which is what gets you a "reservation" at one of the tables. The prices for this bottle service are all on the high side—$200 or more—though they vary by vintage and the number of people in your party. The vibe is one of privileged membership in the elite set, and the emphasis is on relaxation rather than partying hearty. It's definitely a laid-back, low-energy place.

Setting & atmosphere Light is reached via escalator from the casino floor, so you get your first taste of ascending to Shangri-La before you even cross the threshold. The windowless room is red, plush, and dark, though not particularly distinctive. The rarely-full dance floor is bordered by reservation-only tables. Stools face the dance floor from the outside and also run the length of the bar, making up the only free seats in the house. Another tier of reservable tables cluster near the entrance.

If you go Given how limited non-reservation seating is at Light, those not interested in shelling out for the reserved spaces should probably go elsewhere. Tables fill up on weekends, so a bottle service reservation in advance is recommended.

The Nightclub

TOP 40/SHOW COMBINATION

Who Goes There 30–50; visitors, locals, convention-goers/businesspeople

3000 Paradise Road, (Las Vegas Hilton); (702) 732-5755 or (702) 732-5422; www.lv-hilton.com Strip Zone 1

Cover None **Minimum** None **Mixed drinks** $5–$6.75 **Wine** $4.50 and up **Beer** $3.50 and up **Dress** Upscale casual **Specials** Live entertainment starts at 8 p.m. (changes regularly) **Food available** In casino

Hours Sunday, Wednesday, and Thursday, 10 p.m.–2 a.m.; Friday and Saturday, 11–4 a.m.

What goes on Couples and friends boogie to good live renditions of pop music on the small, curvy dance floor. Others are content to watch the leather-clad dancers on stage cavorting with the musicians. Meanwhile, onlookers admire the whole scene. Singles can either sit back and enjoy the show or meet new friends.

Setting & atmosphere A combination of a Las Vegas showroom and a New York dance club, The Nightclub is a trendy art deco hot spot. The bar, situated in the rear of the 450-seat lounge, serves up libations and hosts more intimate conversation. On the wall to the left of the stage is a mutely painted mural of an art deco cityscape. The second floor provides a bird's-eye view of the band and offers a bit more seating space. On some nights a reserved ticket show is performed in the venue. At the conclusion of the show, the dance club cranks up.

If you go Arrive early for choice seating. Cocktail service tends to be relaxed in this no-pressure environment. Because of the long hike from the public parking areas, take a cab or use valet for convenience. Dress is upscale yet casual.

Nine Fine Irishmen

IRISH PUB AND RESTAURANT WITH LIVE CELTIC MUSIC

Who Goes There Visitors and locals of all ages

3790 Las Vegas Boulevard South (New York–New York); (702) 740-6463; www.nine fineirishmen.com; Strip Zone 1

Cover Friday and Saturday, $10; Wednesday and Thursday, $5 **Minimum** None **Mixed drinks** $6 and up **Wine** $6–$7.50 **Beer** $6–$6.50 (English pint) **Dress** Anything goes **Specials** Guinness Stout and Irish whiskeys **Food available** Traditional Irish fare

Hours Sunday–Thursday, 11 a.m.–2:30 a.m.; Friday–Saturday, 11 a.m.–3:30 a.m.

What goes on Located on the casino level of New York–New York, Nine Fine Irishmen offers nightly live Celtic music and dancing, a large selection of draft beers, and a totally upbeat experience that appeals to all age groups.

Setting & atmosphere Built in Ireland and shipped to America, it's wood paneled throughout, it's two-story with bars on both levels. A bandstand on the lower level is home to talented Celtic singers, dancers, and bands. The bandstand is visible from the stairway and the upper level. No hidden agendas here, Nine Fine Irishmen is just for fun.

OPM

MULTIROOM DANCE CLUB ABOVE THE FORUM SHOPS

Who Goes There 21–35; early clubbers

3500 Las Vegas Boulevard South (Caesars Palace); (702) 387-3840; www.o-pm.com/lv; Strip Zone 1

Cover $20 **Minimum** None **Mixed drinks** $8 and up **Wine** $8–$12 **Beer** $4–$6

Dress Hip, trendy, sexy; no jeans or sneakers **Specials** None **Food available** Limited from downstairs restaurant

Hours Thursday–Sunday, 10 p.m.–dawn

What goes on Tucked away deep in Forum Shops above Chinois restaurant, OPM seems to attract early clubgoers who start out their evening here and move on. Crowds arrive early but don't get too pressing, and there's a lot of turnover. The meandering layout, plentiful bar space, and long gallery of cocktail tables make this an easy place to find your own vibe.

Setting & atmosphere The main room has two bars, a large dance floor, impressive lighting and sound, and the de rigueur stacks of video monitors projecting trippy light shows. Music tends toward pounding dance-pop mixes. The adjacent chill-out room has big poofy chairs and couches that can swallow you whole; it has its own bar, and a separate DJ plays more downbeat light trance or house mixes. A slim gallery wanders out and over the Forum Shops, with small tables lining the walls and a final small bar at the tail end.

If you go Dress well, as the no-jeans rule is strictly enforced. A lot of clubgoers tend to filter in and out despite the high cover, so patience will let you scam a table if you prefer to sit out the dance party. Waitstaff in the chill-out lounge are tolerant of customers sitting at reservation-only tables until paying clients arrive.

RA

TOP 40, TECHNO, AND DANCE

Who Goes There 21–35; locals and tourists, college students to professionals

3900 Las Vegas Boulevard South (Luxor); (702) 262-4000; www.luxor.com/entertainment *Strip Zone 1*

Cover Ladies, $10; men, $20 (prices vary with special events) **Minimum** None **Mixed drinks** $5 and up **Wine** $4.75–$6 **Beer** $4 **Dress** Club attire (no athletic shoes or work boots; no hats; no baggy, ripped, or torn jeans) **Specials** None **Food available** Hamada of Japan sushi bar is next to nightclub; restaurants in casino

Hours Wednesday–Saturday, 10 p.m.–5 a.m.

What goes on Ever wonder what the Egyptian sun god does after a hard day's work? He parties with the night-worshipping crowd until the wee hours of the morning. Singles line up at the railing for the best view of the dance floor. Couples and friends enjoy themselves at the booths and the two huge bars. On each end of the stage, go-go dancers lead the dancing throngs to the rhythmic music. Cigar aficionados can enjoy their evening in one of two lounges.

Setting & atmosphere Journey through the misty temple entrance, pay homage (admission) at the gate, then enter the futuristic Egyptian-themed nightclub. Huge Ra statues adorn the two bars at each end of the room. All seating focuses on the dance floor and center stage during live performances. State-of-the-art lighting and sound systems complete the ambience.

If you go RA is located off the main entrance, so use valet parking. Lines are long by midnight, so arrive early or be prepared to wait (hotel guests can use the VIP line). Call ahead for special events such as cage dancing contests and 1980s nights.

Rain in the Desert

MONDO DANCE ORGY WITH FIRE-SPEWING LIGHTING RIG

Who Goes There 21–35; dancing fiends and VIP wannabes

*4321 West Flamingo Road (Palms Hotel); (702) 942-7777; www.n9negroup.com
Strip Zone 1*

Cover $20; local ladies free **Minimum** None **Mixed drinks** $8 and up **Wine** $6 and up **Beer** $5 and up **Dress** Stylish and sexy; jeans and sneakers discouraged, but forgivable if you're a hottie; no sandals on men **Specials** None **Food available** In VIP areas

Hours Thursday, 11 p.m.–5 a.m.; Friday and Saturday, 10 p.m.–5 a.m.

What goes on A truly assaultive spectacle of a dance club, Rain (nobody really uses "in the Desert") is a marvel of gleeful excess. There's booming dance music on tap at all times, the only exception being when Rain hosts headlining rock and hip-hop acts. The crowds fling themselves into the beat, barely restained by armies of security thugs. Three hierarchic levels of 19 VIP areas create a complicated class system (militantly enforced by said thugs). Patrons are dressed to dance and seduce, with sexy, clingy, and revealing being the watchwords.

Setting & atmosphere The large, tiered room focuses on an elevated dance floor, which is also the focus of numerous fountains, fog machines, and a huge, spidery lighting rig that periodically shoots jets of flame. Nondancers can enjoy primo people-watching, and can even climb to the upper tiers for a good vantage, but the best roosting spots are cordoned off by the dreaded velvet ropes.

If you go Hurl yourself into the mob with abandon. Just be prepared to navigate a serious crush at the bars whenever you need to rehydrate. If you're really in the mood to splurge, you can reserve a VIP area to serve as home base—anything from a booth with water-filled leather banquettes ($300) to your own private skybox ($1000).

Risque

EURO-STYLE COOL

Who Goes There 21–30; club kids, beautiful babies

3655 Las Vegas Boulevard South (Paris); (702) 967-4729   Strip Zone 1

Cover Men, $20; ladies, $10; local ladies, free **Minimum** None **Mixed drinks** $8 and up **Wine** $7 and up **Beer** $5 and up **Dress** Classy, cool, and hip **Specials** None **Food available** Dessert case stocked by downstairs Ah Sin restaurant

Hours Wednesday–Sunday, 10 p.m.–4 a.m.

What goes on Set upstairs near the front of the Paris casino, Risque's main advantage is its row of little balconies overlooking the Strip. If you can get there soon enough to claim this prime real estate, you'd be well advised to keep it all night (send deputies to retrieve drinks). Otherwise, crowds groove on the dance floor in the main room or hover at the perimeter, eyeballing the mating games in full swing.

Setting & atmosphere Risque has a smallish dance floor and main lounge area with a long bar. There's also a nearby chill-out room with its own bar and a DJ playing more downbeat tracks; when we visited, a large plasma-screen TV displayed a continuous loop of NASA space footage. The high-ceilinged rooms are sparsely decorated with that breed of European furnishings that somehow manages to look eclectic and generic at the same time.

If you go Hit the place early and grab a balcony spot. Though nice, the rest of Risque is not enough to warrant hanging around for long, despite its "ultralounge" billing.

rumjungle

DANCE, TECHNO, INDUSTRIAL, RAP MUSIC

Who Goes There 21–35; locals, tourists, scene-makers

3950 Las Vegas Boulevard South (Mandalay Bay); (702) 632-7408   Strip Zone 1

Cover $10–$20; local ladies free **Minimum** None **Mixed drinks** $6.50–$11.50 **Wine** $7–$12 **Beer** $5–$10 **Dress** Club attire is strictly enforced: no tennis shoes or work boots; no ripped, oversized, or baggy jeans; no hats, tank tops, or sports attire; collared shirts. **Specials** None **Food available** Dinner served (5–11:30 p.m.) Rodizio-style with meat and fish on skewers. Dinner prices $18–$36

Hours Sunday–Wednesday, 10:30 p.m.–2 a.m.; Thursday–Saturday, 10:30 p.m.–4 a.m.

What goes on White-bikinied go-go dancers writhe and squirm under black lights on platforms above the bar, in cages above the tables, and along the catwalk above the spacious concrete dance floor at the rear of the club and up a flight of stairs. The dancing is presided over by dueling percussionists riffing off of the deafening and mind-numbing recorded rap and disco music, which gets the young bodies bumping and grinding against each other—the only practical form of communication in a place where the audio volume long ago blew out the decibel meter.

Setting & atmosphere A "wall of fire" greets you outside rumjungle, then you walk in (after paying a masochistic $15) where water falls down eight big vertical sheets of glass, enhancing the jungle setting. The central bar is huge and elongated, with a colorfully backlit bartop and a dozen shelves containing more than 100 bottles of rum rising almost to the high ceiling. Oh-so aloof bartenders pour rum drinks ($6.50–$32; try the Painkiller #4), while grim-faced bouncers circulate continually, hoping for trouble. Of course, rumjungle is so dark that trouble would be hard to see even if it did start.

If you go If you're not young enough not to care about your hearing, or you're not a lady who gets in for free, or you're not with a group of friends to party with, you might consider forsaking rumjungle in favor of Mandalay Bay's Island Lounge (rock), Orchid Lounge (jazz), Coral Reef Lounge (disco), or House of Blues (R&B), all of which are lighter, quieter, more conducive to conversation, and free.

Sand Dollar Blues Lounge

RHYTHM AND BLUES

Who Goes There Bikers to yuppies

3355 Spring Mountain Road (at Polaris); (702) 871-6651   Southwest Zone 3

Cover $3, Tuesday–Thursday; $5, Friday and Saturday; free, Monday **Minimum** None **Mixed drinks** $4 and up **Wine** $3.50 and up **Beer** $3 and up **Dress** Casual **Specials** Drink specials and prices depend on the event **Food available** Packaged snack food—no kitchen

Hours Open 24 hours; music starts at 10 p.m. nightly

What goes on Everyone from attorneys to bikers sits back for an evening full of moody and marvelous blues by popular Las Vegas or out-of-town bands. It's standing-room only on Friday, Saturday, and special-event nights. Strip musicians gather for various jam sessions. In the back, pool players croon to the blues.

Setting & atmosphere The exterior is nondescript. Both the interior and the patrons are earthy and full of character. The low ceiling keeps the lounge quite smoky. The U-shaped bar separates the dance floor from the pool tables. Nautical rope, worn wood pilings, small fishing nets, and sand dollars add to the bar's salty character. Neon beer signs and handwritten flyers dot the walls.

If you go The club's unshaven appearance may deter some solo ladies from experiencing a night of great blues. The regulars make sure everything stays cool. The Sand Dollar is hard to spot at night, so arrive early or come by cab.

Seven

DANCE, TECHNO, RAP, JAZZ

Who Goes There 21–35; LOCALS, TOURISTS, PASSERS-BY

3724 Las Vegas Boulevard South; (702) 739-7744   Strip Zone 1

Cover $20, locals $10 **Minimum** None **Mixed drinks** $7–$9 **Wine** $6–$15 **Beer** $5–$10 **Dress** Casual **Specials** 2-for-1 sushi Fridays, 10:30–closing **Food available** Sushi bar, $4.50–$5; late-night appetizer menu, $10–$13

Hours Monday–Wednesday, 11 p.m.–2 a.m.; Thursday–Saturday, 11 p.m.–5 a.m.

What goes on Seven started life as a big stand-alone theme restaurant (Country Star) that went out of business and was converted into a nightclub. It takes advantage of an excellent location on the corner of Harmon and the Strip, with loud recorded rap, disco, or jazz blaring onto an outside deck under an awning, right on the Strip. There's no cover charge, so you can simply wander in and make the scene—as long as you're not a square peg trying to fit into a hip hole. The young crowd exhibits more bare flesh on legs, arms, and, especially, midriffs than is covered with cloth.

Setting & atmosphere There are three different sections to Seven: the outside deck and bar; the big dance floor, with lasers, strobes, smoke, and dueling percussionists raising a racket over the recorded techno music; and the VIP room in the back (make reservations to get in). One appropriate touch: TV monitors throughout display psychedelic video patterns that mesh quite nicely with the trance music. You can also sit at the somewhat out-of-place sushi bar, which separates the deck from the main dance floor.

If you go There's no cover charge, so if you're at all interested in this scene, you might as well stop in on your way between Bellagio and New York–New York. Of course, the free admission might work against you; this place can get crowded and crazy. Some smooth dancers seem to make Seven a second home, so if you like to watch, you can often catch a pretty good impromptu show.

Sevilla

IBERIAN AND LATIN RESTAURANT BY DAY, ATRIUM-CENTERED DANCECLUB BY NIGHT

Who Goes There 21–30; college students, aspirant eurotrash

3663 South Las Vegas Boulevard (Desert Passage at the Aladdin); (702) 992-7970 Strip Zone 1

Cover $20 **Minimum** None **Mixed drinks** $7 and up **Wine** $7 and up **Beer** $5 and up **Dress** Trendy trumps formal here **Specials** None **Food available** Tapas ($5–$8), pizza ($8–$12), paella ($7–$27), and steak ($25 and up), but only in the restaurant. On nights the club is open, the terrace steakhouse closes at 11 p.m. And the patio tapas menu is available until 3 a.m., except on Sundays, when the patio stops serving at 9 p.m.

Hours Friday–Sunday, 10:30 p.m.–4 a.m. (the restaurant opens at 11 a.m.)

What goes on As a restaurant, Sevilla has a Latin American "rodizio" serving Brazilian barbeque, tapas, sandwiches, pizza, etc. And a nicer Spanish steakhouse upstairs, which offers some tapas and paella. At night, the upper tiers give way to VIP rooms overlooking an expansive dancefloor. DJs in a central booth blend Latin-tinted dance tracks into a trancy stew while revelers pretend its Spring Break (unless it really is) under the multicolor strobe lights in the haze of smoke machines. Expect a Miami-style mix, heavier on the house and garage than Afro-Cuban rhythms.

Setting & atmosphere With stucco walls, red-bulbed wrought-iron chandeliers, velvet-curtained interior balconies, and a fountain below, the atrium mimics the court-yard of a Spanish or Spanish Colonial villa. Indeed, Sevilla is a Spanish/Latin hybrid; the decor, menu, and soundtrack borrow from both continents. (Split the difference between Rio and Ibiza and you get South Beach.) Sevilla's elaborate theme decor is right at home in the Aladdin's fantasy-Moorish Desert Passage.

If you go Spring for bottle-service on a private balcony, one of which has a queen bed, overlooking the dancing hordes below ($300–$500). Or, if the odds beat you in the casino, come ready to dance your cares away in the undulating sea of flesh.

Studio 54

DANCE, TOP 40

Who Goes There 25–40; locals, tourists, and trendy people

3799 Las Vegas Boulevard South (MGM Grand); (702) 891-7254; www.mgmgrand.com/lv/pages/ent_studio54.asp   Strip Zone 1

Cover Ladies, free; men, $10–$20 **Minimum** None **Mixed drinks** $5–$8 **Wine** $5 and up **Beer** $4–$5.50 **Dress** Club attire is enforced; collared shirt or sports coat for men; no baggy jeans, flannel shirts, T-shirts, sandals, or sneakers **Food available** In casino

Hours Tuesday–Saturday, 10 p.m.–5 a.m.

What goes on The New York club that set the standard during disco's heyday in the 1970s comes to Las Vegas. Stylish, beautiful people gather for a night of high energy, music, dance, and socializing.

Setting & atmosphere It's three stories tall with dance floors, bars, and conversation areas on each level. The black-girder-and-steel-grate flooring and exposed elevator lifts give the club an industrial, high-tech feel. Black-and-white photographs of celebrities and trendsetters visiting the New York Studio 54 line the walls on the second floor.

If you go If you love a club with an attitude, then Studio 54 is for you. If you prefer a bit more fun and friendliness, try RA or Club Rio. Studio 54 is located at the Trop-icana and Las Vegas Boulevard entrance—it's a long walk from both valet and the parking garages.

Tabu

SUPER-COOL LOUNGE WHERE THE LOADED GET LOADED

Who Goes There 21–40; high rollers and young hotties of all persuasions

3799 Las Vegas Boulevard South (MGM Grand); (702) 891-7183   Strip Zone 1

Cover $20 **Minimum** None **Mixed drinks** $7 and up **Wine** $7 and up **Beer** $5 and up **Dress** Sexy chic **Specials** None **Food available** None

Hours Tuesday–Sunday, 10 p.m. until

What goes on Hyped as an "ultralounge," Tabu may come close to whatever that means. If you can get past the crush at the door, you'll be rewarded with some excel-lent eye candy via both the space and its inhabitants. The staff are dressed to kill and seem to be cloned from a diverse assortment of supermodels and porn stars; the patrons do their best to rise to that standard. If you've had a great day in the casino and want to really test your meat-market mettle, this is the place.

Setting & atmosphere The main room is plushly decorated with frosted glass and subtle lighting, and there are plenty of tables and chairs for the daring (since all are reservable, you'll be sitting on borrowed time unless you ante up). Two tables in the main room project images on their surface that ripple or change color in reaction to your presence or body heat. There's a second, smaller room off to the side that's a little more intimate, and it has its own bar as well. Last is the egg-shaped "Tundra" room (usually called the Egg), done up in appropriate whites, carpets, and cushions.

If you go There was no organized line to get in when we first visited; rather, would-be patrons formed a mob around the bouncers, and a Darwinian process dictated who fought their way inside. When we came back early on another night, we walked in without even paying a cover. In addition, early birds can often sit at reserved VIP tables until kicked out by those who have paid for the space (check with waitstaff or the VIP hostess about which tables to avoid).

Tommy Rocker's Cantina and Grill

TOP 40 AND JIMMY BUFFETT—STYLE MUSIC

Who Goes There 25–30; professionals and career starters

4275 South Industrial Boulevard; (702) 261-6688; www.tommyrocker.com Strip Zone 1

Cover None **Minimum** None **Mixed drinks** $3–$4; wide selection of tequilas and rums **Wine** $2.75 and up **Beer** $3–$5; many microbrew draft selections **Dress** Casual to sporty **Specials** $1.99 breakfast special; happy hour 5–7 p.m. With $1 off all drinks and appetizers, 50¢ off imports and domestic drafts; they are also the official Jimmy Buffett fan club location—call for special event information **Food available** Sports bar–type food

Hours Open 24 hours

What goes on Singles and couples gather to check out the music and gregarious repartee of Tommy Rocker, the club's owner and professional musician, when he's in town. Otherwise, they enjoy meeting new friends, singing Jimmy Buffett songs, shooting a friendly game of pool, cheering their favorite team on the big-screen TV, and indulging in the tasty libations and food fare.

Setting & atmosphere An eclectic mix of Indian petroglyph images, palm trees, parrots, and neon gives Tommy Rocker's Cantina and Grill a refreshing twist to the beach-style bar scene. In addition to the big-screen TV and two pool tables, the club offers a small dance floor, and a standard center bar.

If you go Voted best live music club in a local survey, Tommy Rocker's offers plenty of parking, friendly yet professional security, and a great attitude. The music is loud but not deafening, allowing for conversation. Come early for best seating.

VooDoo Lounge

LIVE MUSIC WITH BEST VIEW OF THE STRIP

Who Goes There 21–35; visitors and chic clubgoers

3700 West Flamingo Road (Rio Hotel); (702) 247-7923; www.harrahs.com/our_casinos/rlv/amenities/voodoo_cafe.html   Strip Zone 1

Cover $10 after 8 p.m. **Minimum** None **Mixed drinks** $6 and up **Wine** $5 and up **Beer** $4.25 and up **Dress** Business casual; no torn jeans, tennis shoes, sandals, or T-shirts **Specials** None **Food available** Downstairs in VooDoo Café

Hours Nightly, 5 p.m.–3 a.m.

What goes on The cozy darkness of the VooDoo Lounge is only broken by the doors to the outside patio, which floats on the 51st floor of the Rio and offers great views of the Strip. Dextrous bartenders flip bottles and glasses around while the lady customers swoon, and live bands play cool-cat jazz and R&B most nights. There's a small dance floor, but patrons are mostly content to chill out in the ample multilevel seating.

Setting & atmosphere The room is dim, but there's plenty to see. Comfy chairs and sofas cluster around intimate cocktail tables, providing views of the stage, bar, and the tinted windows on two walls. The patio has some tables of its own, but the gorgeous view and cool night air make these premium real estate…grab one if you can. The vibe is hip and relaxed.

If you go Enjoy the band if the night's music is to your liking, but you must spend at least some time on the patio. It would be a crime to miss this literally stellar view. If you want a different take on the same concept (and don't mind shelling out another cover charge), stop by Ghost Bar at the nearby Palms.

Las Vegas below the Belt

Don't Worry, Be Happy

In many ways, Las Vegas is a bastion of hedonism. Just being there contributes to a loosening of inhibitions and a partial discarding of the rules that apply at home. Las Vegas exults in its permissiveness and makes every effort to live up to its image and to bestow upon its visitors the freedom to have fun. Las Vegas has a steaminess, a sophisticated cosmopolitan excitement born of superabundance, an aura of risk and reward, a sense of libertine excess. The rules are different here; it's all right to let go.

Behind the illusion, however, is a community, and more particularly, a police department that puts a lot of effort into making it safe for visitors to experience the liberation of Las Vegas. It is hard to imagine another city where travelers can carry such large sums of money so safely. A tourist can get robbed or worked over in Las Vegas, but it is comparatively rare, and more often than not is due to the visitor's own carelessness or naivete. The Strip and downtown, especially, are well patrolled, and most hotels have very professional in-house security forces.

In general, a tourist who stays either on the Strip or downtown will be very safe. Police patrol in cars, on foot, and, interestingly, on mountain bikes. The bikes allow the police to quickly catch pickpockets or purse snatchers attempting to make their escape down sidewalks or through parking lots. Cross-streets that connect the Strip with Paradise Road and the Las Vegas Convention Center are also lighted and safe. When tourists get robbed, they are commonly far from downtown or the Strip and often in pursuit of drugs or sex.

Organized Crime and Cheating

Very few visitors walk through a casino without wondering if the games are rigged or if the place is owned by the mafia. During the early days of legalized gambling, few people outside of organized crime had any real experience in managing gaming operations. Hence a fair number of characters fresh from Eastern gangs and crime families came to work in Nevada. Since they constituted the resource pool for experienced gambling operators, the state suffered their presence as a necessary evil. In 1950, Tennessee senator Estes Kefauver initiated an attack on organized crime that led (indirectly) to the formation of the Nevada Gaming Commission and the State Gaming Control Board. These agencies, in conjunction with federal efforts, were ultimately able to purge organized crime from Las Vegas. This ouster, coupled with the Nevada Corporate Gaming Acts of 1967 and 1969 (allowing publicly held corporations such as Hilton, Holiday Inn, Bally, and MGM to own casinos), at last brought a mantle of respectability to Las Vegas gambling.

Today the Gaming Control Board oversees the activities of all Nevada gaming establishments, maintaining tight control through frequent unannounced inspections of gambling personnel and equipment. If you ever have reason to doubt the activity or clout of the Gaming Control Board, try walking around the Strip or downtown in a dark business suit and plain black shoes. You will attract more attention from the casino management than if you entered with a parrot on your head.

Ostensibly, cheating exists in Las Vegas gambling to a limited degree. But a case of a Nevada casino cheating customers hasn't been publicized for decades. In fact, "gaffing" the games is seldom perpetrated by the house itself. In fact, most cheating is done at the expense of the house, though honest players at the cheater's table may also get burned. Sometimes a dealer, working alone or with an accomplice (posing as a player), will cheat, and there are always con artists, grab-and-run rip-off artists, and rail thieves ready to take advantage of the house and legitimate players.

Skin Games—Sex in Las Vegas Though nudity, prostitution, and pornography are regulated more tightly in Las Vegas than in many Bible Belt cities, the town exudes an air of sexual freedom and promiscuity. Las Vegas offers a near-perfect environment for marketing sex. Over 50 percent of all visitors are men, most between the ages of 21 and 59. Some come to party, and many, particularly convention-goers, are alone and ready for action. Almost all have time and money on their hands.

Las Vegas evolved as a gambler's city, proudly projecting the image of a trail town where a man could be comfortable and just about anything could be had for a price. It was not until strong competition developed for the gambling dollar that hotels sought to enlarge their market by targeting women and families. Today, though there is something for everyone in Las Vegas, its male orientation remains unusually strong.

Las Vegas, perhaps more than any other American city, has objectified women. A number of Las Vegas production shows continue to feature topless showgirls and erotic dance, even though audiences are mostly couples. Lounge servers and keno runners are almost exclusively women, invariably attired in revealing outfits. Video marquees, highway billboards, taxi banners, magazine ads, and tabloids in curbside newspaper vending machines all tout naked women to some degree. Showroom comedians, after 30 years, persist in describing Las Vegas as an adult Disneyland.

Stripping on the Strip   Compared to the live adult entertainment in many cities, "girlie" (and "boy") shows in Las Vegas, both downtown and on the Las Vegas Strip, are fairly tame. In some of the larger showrooms, this is an accommodation to the ever-growing percentage of women in the audience. More often, however, it is a matter of economics rather than taste, the result of a curious City of Las Vegas law that stipulates that you can offer totally nude entertainment or you can serve alcoholic beverages, but not both.

Up until only a few years ago, topless showgirls were a mere embellishment to a production that featured song, dance, and variety acts. For the most part, the partial nudity was incidental and unimportant. Of course, a half-dozen veteran large-production shows included one or more steamy, highly erotic dance numbers, which allowed the publicists— and hotel photographers—to play up the naughtiness of the entertainment scene. But over the last few years, sex has exploded in Las Vegas showrooms, with such cross-over shows as *La Femme, Skintight,* a dirtied-up *Crazy Girls,* and *X: An Erotic Adventure,* and several others that now emphasize naked women, instead of using them merely to dress up a show.

If you want to see stunning topless showgirls and dancers, the most erotic of the continuously running productions are *La Femme* at MGM Grand, *Skintight* at Harrah's, *Zumanity* at New York–New York, and *Crazy Girls* at the Riviera followed by *Jubilee!* at Bally's. *La Femme* is as risqué as a Las Vegas production show is allowed to be (direct from Paris). *Skin Tight* features Miss Nude World. *Crazy Girls* is a steamy topless, all-girl revue. *Jubilee!* is a production spectacular that has prettier-than-average showgirls and sultrier-than-average dance numbers. *Zumanity* is a *Cirque du Soleil* production celebrating sex.

Skintight at Harrah's is the only midlevel topless show worth the price of entry, but it's still a midlevel show; the more upmarket *Crazy Girls* and *La Femme* are far superior.

Male Strippers   Economics and the market have begun to redress (or undress) the inequality of women's erotic entertainment in Las Vegas. Spearheaded by the Rio, which features (*Chippendales*) male strippers for lengthy engagements, and empowered by the ever-growing number of professional women visiting Las Vegas for trade shows and conventions, the rules for sexual objectification are being rewritten. Today in Las Vegas, if watching a young stud flex his buns is a woman's idea of a good time, that experience is usually available. In addition to the Rio, male strippers perform at the Olympic Gardens nightclub, and *Thunder from Down Under,* the Australian male review, plays at the Excalibur.

Expensive Voyeurism   Just off the Strip are a number of adult nightspots that feature total nudity. One bills itself as the "only totally nude show in Las Vegas" and promises to "leave nothing to your imagination." Its claim is justified when it comes to the girls; they are indeed beautiful, young, and plentiful. What is left to the imagination, however, is the alcohol in your drink—there isn't any! And beyond your imagination is the price tag on these nonalcoholic concoctions. Never again will you have the opportunity to pay so much for fruit punch.

As expensive as the fruit punch is, there are other Las Vegas nude nightspots that can be far more expensive, not to mention embarrassing. Most of the clientele is funneled to these places by cab drivers who get a kickback for every customer delivered. Usually, as the scenario goes, a lonely tourist or businessman asks the cabbie about places where he can pick up a girl, or, more explicitly, find a prostitute. For a hefty tip the naive fellow is delivered to a sex-tease nightclub, which the cabbie describes as a "swinger's club: the hottest place in town—just what you are looking for." Inside, the lights are low and there are a number of alluring young women, some nude, and some clad in negligees or other scanty attire. On the walls, barely readable in the dim light, are signs that state, "Prostitution Is Illegal in Las Vegas," and "No Alcoholic Beverages Shall Be Served or Consumed on These Premises."

There is no entertainment other than taped music or perhaps a jukebox; no dancers, no performers, no show. After paying a cover charge of up to $50 and being seated, the customer is invariably joined by a woman who gives every impression that she is prepared to have sex with him. In getting acquainted, she encourages him to buy her a drink, once again some astronomically priced nonalcoholic potion. If the fellow consents, she strings him along, ordering more drinks and promising great things to come. Later, she suggests that he buy a bottle of champagne (nonalcoholic), and they retire to a private back room.

In the back room she continues to come on to him and play him for additional bottles of champagne. This continues as long as he is willing to keep buying. Should he become impatient and demanding, insist on sex, or refuse to buy more champagne, she will excuse herself on the pretext of using the rest room. Moments later, one or more bouncers enter the private room and forcibly eject the fellow from the club. Because of his complicity in soliciting the services of a prostitute, the customer has no legal recourse without incriminating or at least embarrassing himself.

The Palomino Club   In North Las Vegas, a separate jurisdiction, there is no prohibition against nude entertainment and alcoholic beverages under the same roof. At the **Palomino Club,** ten minutes from downtown, the customer can have it all.

The Palomino Club is not inexpensive, but at least they're upfront about what they're selling. There is a $30 cover charge without a Nevada ID, and a $15 cover charge with a Nevada ID and a one-drink minimum. To get one of the better seats, you should arrive before 10 p.m. and tip the maître d'. Once you have purchased your drink, you can stay as long as you can stand it—all night if you wish.

An average of seven professionals dance every night, performing in rotation and stripping nude. The pros are supplemented by four or more alleged amateurs who compete for prize money and tips in a strip contest held nightly at 11 p.m. All of the women, both pro and amateur, are attractive, well-built, and athletic. A stand-up comic rounds out the entertainment. The Palomino is without pretense. It delivers some of the best erotic dancing in town for about the same cost as a production show on the Strip. Conventioneers, tourists, and locals are the usual clientele.

Topless Bars   The main difference between a topless bar and a totally nude nightclub (aside from the alcohol regulations) is a G-string. Unless you're a gynecology intern, you might be satisfied with a topless bar. If you have more than a few drinks, the topless bars aren't less expensive than the Palomino but are often more conveniently located. Downtown, on Fremont Street, is the **Girls of Glitter Gulch.** There's no cover charge, but drinks average a stiff (no pun intended) $6.75 each, with a two-drink minimum. A U-shaped stage/runway ensures a good view from most seats.

A very upscale and elegant topless bar is **Club Paradise** at 4416 Paradise Road, not far from the Strip. Catering to a professional clientele, high rollers, and conventioneers, Club Paradise is the Rolls Royce of topless bars. The cover charge is $20 and there is a two-drink minimum, unless you elect to sit in the VIP section, where you are obligated to consume at least $80 worth of drinks. Fortunately, because drinks go for $4.75 and up, this is not difficult.

The **Sapphire Club** which claims 6,000 women on its lineup of strippers (insiders say it's closer to 2,000, which is still plenty). By observation, the later you arrive in the evening, the better-looking the dancers. Though the club is the largest of its kind in the world, much of the space is allocated to private rooms, VIP areas, etc. For the average patron, Sapphire is new and upscale, but doesn't seem all that big. Sapphire is owned by the same group that runs Olympic Garden, which is less expensive, more intimate, and has foxier entertainers.

Another plush topless bar is **Cheetah's,** at 2112 Western Avenue; (702) 384-0074. Cover is $20 after 6 p.m.; $10 for locals with a two-drink minimum, and drink prices start at about $4. An equally upscale venue is the **Olympic Garden** at 1531 South Las Vegas Boulevard. Considered by locals and connoisseurs to be the best topless club in town, the Olympic Garden is the only club that also features male strippers for its female customers (in a separate showroom). The cover for Cheetah's is $10 with a two-drink minimum. Olympic Garden charges a $20 cover but the price includes two drinks.

Prostitution: Now You See It, Now You Don't

The people of Nevada have always maintained a practical and essentially laissez-faire attitude toward prostitution. For years prostitution was allowed to flourish and was accorded an implicit legal status by a body of some 50 statutes enacted to regulate it. The circumstances were similar to an equally confusing situation on Mississippi's Gulf Coast 35 years ago.

Mississippi was a dry state, but along the coast there were bars everywhere, recognized as a necessary adjunct to the developing tourist industry. It was laughable to watch the local police attempt to structure and regulate an illegal industry. How do you make rules for something that is against the law?

The history of prostitution in Nevada is essentially the same story. Prostitution was against the law, yet was administered as conscientiously as tax collection. Nevadans, while of conservative, principled, pioneer origins, always accepted prostitution as a practical reality, something as predictable and inevitable as cactus in the desert. Prostitution both filled a need and, by way of payoffs, augmented the meager income of law enforcement officials, county commissioners, and others. Prostitution was making great strides as a growth industry in Nevada, moving rapidly in the direction of total legalization, until it had a head-on collision with another growth industry—gambling.

At first glance, prostitution and gambling looked like a perfect team. The legalization of gambling perpetuated the Wild West, mining-town atmosphere of Nevada cities. There had always been women to take care of the prospectors, the speculators, the railroad workers, and later the dam builders and soldiers. It seemed the most natural thing in the world, completely in keeping with the state's robust, pragmatic Western image, for gambling and prostitution to work hand in glove to stimulate the burgeoning tourism industry.

The gaming czars, however, saw it differently. They were trying to get gambling out of the back room and install it as a respectable form of recreation (like bowling or shuffleboard, only more lucrative). Elderly ladies, married couples, and even Episcopal priests could enjoy a little innocent gambling, but prostitution was a different story. There was no way to make prostitution innocent, no way to separate it from infidelity, syphilis, and gonorrhea.

On the practical side, casino owners recognized that legal or illegal, prostitution was a fact of life (if not an out-and-out necessity) in every major convention and tourist city in the United States. The owners also realized that the wild, "anything goes" Western tradition (the thematic foundation of all Nevada tourism) demanded that sex be a part of the gambling-town product mix. The real question, as the gaming industry perceived it, was, how do you impart a little sexual sauciness to your operation without actually providing for the satisfaction of appetites aroused? In other words, what were you going to do with 5,000 conventioneers who had been fed a steady diet of topless showgirls and provocatively clad lounge waitresses and keno runners? Gambling and sex were like Siamese twins, an unfortunate pairing that defied separation. Reid and Demaris did not mince words in their classic *Green Felt Jungle* when they wrote, "Money mysteriously breeds prostitutes the way decaying flesh breeds maggots. Where there's easy money there's whores; it's that basic. And where there's gambling, there's easy money."

The uneasy conclusion was that prostitution had to be illegal, yet available. Gambling, with its newfound respectability, had to distance itself from prostitution without precipitating its demise. Las Vegas, in particular, had to have the best, most efficient prostitution system in the world while appearing as wholesome as Disneyland. When it came to sex, part of the market needed to be assured that Las Vegas was not pure form with no underlying substance. Another part of the market needed to believe that Vegas was a clean resort town, that gambling was a legitimate form of recreation, and that the tourism industry and the police were doing their best to stamp out prostitution.

This paradox was reconciled, incredibly, through a curious combination of legislation and role-playing. The casinos and the convention authority came down on prostitution with the righteous wrath of the Moral Majority. Joined by conservative locals, largely Mormon, they used their combined clout to have prostitution outlawed in counties with a census of over 250,000 residents. In addition, the gaming commission was persuaded to further accentuate the difference between wholesome recreational gambling and the carnality of whoring by denying gambling licenses to hotels or other properties that engaged in or supported prostitution. Later, with the election of John Moran as Clark County sheriff in the early 1980s, the streetwalkers were effectively run off the Strip.

As intended, prostitution remained alive and healthy. So-called legal prostitution, symbolized by the large brothels, was just chased over the county line into Nye County where it was allowed to operate under stringent state regulation, but basically without interference. In Las Vegas and Clark County (where prostitution was declared illegal), the world's oldest profession simply switched to an entrepreneurial base. Where hotels and casinos previously had a virtual oligopoly in procuring women, they now stepped aside to permit a broad freelance trade to develop. A quintessential case of having your cake and eating it too, prostitution had been removed from sight without otherwise being harmed.

The flaw in the plan, predictably, was that the ever-increasing corps of sexual entrepreneurs could not be controlled. Part of the original procurement business devolved from hotel top management to any number of bellmen, pitmen, and other small operatives who kept male guests as happy as ever but did it quietly and discreetly, with nothing required of the host property. It was the other players, the small prostitution rings, the freelancers, and the "weekend warriors," who managed to unsettle the status quo.

Unlike the bellmen and other hotel personnel, who worked without fanfare from a private list of known and highly recommended professional courtesans, the freelancers were as visible as a K-mart grand opening, taking out ads in the Las Vegas Yellow Pages and distributing free "adult entertainment" magazines up and down the Strip. Las Vegas was again becoming a Sodom and Gomorrah, with gambling looking less all-American as a function of guilt by association.

What's in a Name?

Since it is against the law to promote and advertise prostitution in Las Vegas, the inventive carnal entrepreneurs started off by listing themselves as massage parlors. This, of course, outraged legitimate professional masseurs ("We don't do genitals"), who forced the state to pass standards and licensing legislation. Unable to meet the standards, the freelancers reappeared as escort or dating services. Once again, stringent licensing standards were applied, and the freelancers disappeared temporarily from sight. When they next surfaced, they were private dancers, entertainers, or party services. This most recent, and highly visible, reincarnation continues to this day. The Las Vegas Yellow Pages are chock-full of lurid ads.

NUDE STRIPPERS DIRECT TO YOUR ROOM

LET US EXPLORE YOUR FANTASIES . . .

24 HOURS—MOST MAJOR CREDIT CARDS ACCEPTED

For tourists who do not sit around reading the Yellow Pages, adult entertainment newsprint tabloids, with the same ads, are distributed gratis up and down the Strip.

A couple of visiting businessmen, slightly inebriated and in high spirits, decided to call a number from one of the ads and have a stripper sent over. Both men, being married and absolutely terrified of sexually transmitted disease, had no intention of having intercourse. They simply wanted, as the ad promised, "sizzling hot erotic dancing, direct to your room." What they expected was a naughtier-than-average version of the wholesome young ladies, available in every city, who perform tasteful striptease at yuppie birthday parties. What they got was a sullen prostitute who made it abundantly clear (the ad notwithstanding) that if they wanted to see dancing, they could "march right over and buy a ticket to the *Folies Bergere*."

In a similar situation, three unsophisticated conventioneers from Little Rock phoned a private dancer service and requested information and prices. What the callers understood was that they could buy an hour of private dancing for $125, payable in advance with cash or credit card. What they were told, however, quite deliberately, was that the fee was $125 for "up to an hour" of private dancing. When the prostitute arrived and discovered, to her amazement, that these guys really wanted dancing, she obligingly took their money and launched into a perfunctory disrobing, without music or other artistic embellishment. In five minutes she was gone with the $125.

The most recent variation on the theme, taking advantage of growing consumer outrage, is "adult entertainment information services." These operations, ostensibly consultation services that "assist you in getting what you want without being ripped off," are nothing more than referral services, owned and operated by the prostitution agencies. It's only a matter of time, of course, before the authorities force prostitution into yet another metamorphosis. *Unofficial Guide* contributor Deke Castleman speculates that in future phone books, we may find prostitutes variously listed as "Bedroom Accessories," or "Temporary Services," or even "All-Purpose Rentals." The possibilities are endless.

Who's on First?

The cast of players in the Las Vegas prostitution game is a little confusing. At the top of the caste are select call girls with a small, but extremely lucrative, regular clientele. Another population of respected, highly recommended professionals work quietly on an on-call basis at the request of bell captains, pit bosses, and maître d's. Next come a cadre of seasoned and novice, but less exclusive, prostitutes whose services are marketed by cab drivers, bartenders, and even convenience-store clerks. Tied with these are the entertainers, the contingent that forms the stable of the private dancers and other operations that deal directly with customers. At the bottom of the heap are the streetwalkers, often past their prime, diseased, or drug-addicted. Driven off the streets by the law, streetwalkers work out of lounges, lobbies, transportation terminals, and hotel shopping arcades, but only rarely on the street.

A final category that defies any ranking is that of the weekend warriors. These are working girls and professional women (teachers, nurses, sales clerks) from Utah, Southern California, and Arizona who augment their income by turning tricks in Las Vegas on weekends. While some of these women develop connections with specific procurers, most work alone and freelance out of casino lounges and singles bars. Nicely dressed and usually intelligent, they have a style more like that of a single woman cruising than that of a prostitute soliciting business. When it comes to striking a deal, however, they play hardball as well as their full-time sisters. There are no free samples.

Pay Now, Pay Again Later

All prostitutes plying their trade in Las Vegas and Clark County operate illegally. Regardless of their exclusivity or clientele, these women are not regulated by the standards applied to prostitutes working for the legal brothels in less-populated counties. Women of this latter group are checked weekly by a physician for communicable disease and work under very strict guidelines on the premises of their employer.

In Las Vegas, sexually transmitted diseases, including syphilis, gonorrhea, genital herpes, and AIDS, are routinely passed from prostitute to client; customers of streetwalkers are most at risk. Las Vegas police work incessantly to identify disease-carrying prostitutes and get them off the street, but it's like excavating a bottomless pit.

Be forewarned that it is just as illegal in Las Vegas for you to solicit the services of a prostitute as it is for them to solicit you, and that sometimes policewomen work undercover. If you are determined to have a sexual adventure, you had better drive to the lawful Nye County brothels.

Deadly Games People Play

Not all of the sex games played in Las Vegas involve prostitution. In Las Vegas, as in any resort town, many men and women keep their eyes open for a little romance. Frequently lonely and vulnerable, these tourists fall prey to any number of deceptions.

Women who allow themselves to come under the influence of an unknown male risk the possibility of being robbed and/or raped. Sometimes the crime is premeditated, but more often it is a variation of date rape, where the man, rejected, refuses to take no for an answer. To many men, tourists and locals alike, the Las Vegas female stereotype is a bimbo showgirl, good only for sex and decoration. If a woman looking for companionship hooks up with a guy who subscribes to this myth, she might well be in for a rough time.

Interestingly, middle-aged men are the most common victims of sex scams in Las Vegas. In a common scenario, a comely, well-dressed woman will make eye contact with a middle-aged man at the gaming tables. Always subtle, she may favor him with a smile when he wins or an expression of consolation when he loses. Working slowly and deliberately, sharing the moment and perhaps exchanging a few innocent words, she becomes an unintroduced friend. She does not push or direct, but instead allows the man to take the initiative. He likes her, invites her to grab a bite to eat or have a drink. They talk about their jobs, music, food, and all the other things people discuss when getting acquainted. If things proceed as she hopes, he finally asks her to his room for a drink. Making all the pro forma protestations, she ultimately pretends to be persuaded. Once in the room, he makes drinks. Talking and passing the time, she waits until he uses the rest room, then takes advantage of his absence to slip a powerful, quick-acting drug into his drink. A half hour later he is in dreamland. Usually with a male accomplice, the woman searches the room as the victim slumbers. Everything of value is stolen. The victim of this drug-induced trick roll commonly sleeps anywhere from 8 to 20 hours. Occasionally, if the victim is hypersensitive to the drug or has a medical condition, he dies.

How the Bad Guys Choose Their Victims Felons choose their marks by observing a potential victim's attire and behavior. Wearing lots of jewelry and flaunting big bills is a sure way to attract attention. Stupid bets suggest inexperience, and excessive drinking lowers inhibitions and defenses. Playing without friends suggests that you are a solitary business traveler or on vacation and perhaps hungry for companionship.

If you meet somebody interesting, resist the urge to rush the relationship. In Las Vegas, as in any city, you should exercise caution. Proceed slowly with your new friendship. No matter what, keep the drinking under control and do not go anywhere to be alone. If you have a nice evening in the casino or over drinks or dinner, you can arrange to meet again tomorrow.

In the behavior department, learn the table games before you play, and make sensible bets. Go light on glitzy jewelry and refrain from flaunting your bankroll. Limit your alcohol intake and do not drink on an empty stomach. Beware of loners of either sex. Do not divulge your room number. Do not extend an invitation to come to your room or accept an invitation to go to the other party's room. If you are traveling alone, keep that to yourself.

Here's a surefire way to tell if you're in danger of being trick-rolled—in the inimitable words of Max Rubin, author of *Comp City: A Guide to Free Casino Vacations.* "If she's cute and she thinks you're slick, then something's wrong!"

Part Three

Gambling

The Way It Is

Gambling is the reason Las Vegas (in its modern metamorphosis) exists. It is the industry that fuels the local economy, paves the roads, and gives the city its identity. To visitors and tourists, gambling may be a game. To those who derive their livelihood from gambling, however, it is serious business.

There is an extraordinary and interesting dichotomy in the ways gambling is perceived. To the tourist and the gambler, gambling is all about luck. To those in the business, gambling is about mathematics. To the visitor, gambling is a few hours a day, while to the casinos, gambling is 24 hours a day, all day, every day. The gambler *hopes* to walk away with a fortune, but the casinos *know* that in the long run that fortune will belong to the house. To visitors, gambling is recreation combined with risk and chance. To the casinos, gambling is business combined with near certainty.

The casino takes no risk in the games themselves. In the long run the house will always win. The games, the odds, and the payoffs are all carefully designed to ensure this outcome. Yet the casino does take a chance and is at risk. The casino's bet is this: that it can entice enough people to play.

Imagine a casino costing millions of dollars, with a staff numbering in the hundreds. Before a nickel of profit can be set aside, all the bills must be paid, and the payroll must be met. Regardless of the house's overwhelming advantage at the tables, it cannot stay in business unless a lot of people come to play. The larger the casino, the more gamblers are required. If the casino can fill the tables with players, the operation will succeed and be profitable, perhaps incredibly so. On the other hand, if the tables go empty, the casino will fail.

The casino business is competition personified. Every owner knows how absolutely critical it is to get customers (gamblers) through the door. It is literally the sine qua non: no players, no profit. The casinos are aggressive and creative when it comes to luring customers, offering low-cost buffets, dollar shrimp cocktails, stage shows, lounge entertainment, free drinks, gambling tournaments, and slot clubs.

The most common tactic for getting customers through the door is to package the casino as a tourist attraction in its own right. Take the Mirage, for example. There are exploding volcanoes in the front yard, white tigers in the entrance hall, palm trees in the living room, and live sharks in the parlor. Who, after all, wants to sip their free drink in a dingy, red-Naugahyde-upholstered catacomb when they could be luxuriating in such a resplendent tropical atrium?

The Short Run

If you ask a mathematician or a casino owner if you can win gambling in a casino, the truthful answer is yes, but only in the short run. The longer you play, the more certain it is that you will lose.

I learned about the short run (and the long run) on a road trip when I was in the fifth grade. My family lived in Kentucky, and every year we were fortunate enough to take a vacation to Florida. This particular year I was permitted to invite a schoolmate to come along.

As the long drive progressed, we became fidgety and bored. To pass the time, we began counting cars traveling in the opposite direction. Before many miles had passed, our counting evolved into a betting game. We each selected a color and counted the cars of that color. Whoever counted the most cars of his chosen color would win.

My friend chose blue as his color. I was considering red (my favorite), when I recalled a conversation between my mother and a car salesman. The salesman told my mother that white was by far the most popular color "these days." If this were true, I reasoned, there should be more white cars on the road than blue cars. I chose white.

As we rumbled through the hilly Kentucky countryside between Bowling Green and Elizabethtown my friend edged ahead. This puzzled me and I began to doubt the word of the car salesman. By the time we made Bowling Green, my friend Glenn was ahead by seven cars. Because I was losing, I offered to call it quits and pay up (a nickel for each car he was ahead). Glenn, not unexpectedly, was having a high time and insisted we continue playing.

By the time we crossed the Tennessee line I had pulled even. Once again I suggested we quit. Glenn would have none of it. Gloating enormously, he regained a three-car lead halfway to Nashville. Slowly, however, I overtook him, and by Nashville I was ahead by four cars. Tired of the game, I tried once more to end it. Since he was behind, Glenn adamantly demanded that we play all the way to Atlanta. We did, and by the time we got there Glenn owed me almost $4.

After a night in Atlanta and a great deal of sulking on Glenn's part, we resumed our travels. To my amazement, Glenn insisted—demanded, in fact—the opportunity to win back his previous day's losses. There would be one great "do-or-die battle, blues against whites," he said, all the way to our destination (St. Augustine, Florida). As we drove south, I went ahead by a couple of cars, and then Glenn regained the lead by a small margin. By the time we made St. Augustine, however, Glenn owed me another $5.40.

Outraged (and broke), Glenn exercised the only option remaining— he complained to my parents. Shaking his head, my father said, "Give Glenn his money back. Everybody knows that there are more white cars than blue cars." Not so. Glenn didn't.

While Glenn's behavior is not particularly unusual for a preadolescent, you would assume that adults have better sense. Everybody knows there are more white cars than blue cars, remember? In Las Vegas, however, the casinos are full of Glenns, all over age 21, and all betting on blue cars.

I nailed Glenn on the cars because I knew something that he didn't. In casino games, patrons either do not understand what they are up against, or alternatively (and more intelligently), they do understand, but chalk up their losses as a fair price to pay for an evening's entertainment. Besides, in the short run, there's a chance they might actually win.

Glenn's actions on our trip mirrored almost exactly the behavior of many unfortunate casino gamblers:

1. He did not understand that the game was biased against him.
2. He did not take his winnings and quit when he was ahead in the short run.
3. On losing, he continued playing and redoubled his efforts to pull even or win, ultimately (in the long run) compounding his losses.

Eagles and Robins

If on our drive I had said, "Let's count birds. You take eagles and I'll take robins," Glenn would have laughed in my face, instantly recognizing that the likelihood of spotting an eagle was insanely remote. While the casinos will not offer a fair game (like betting even money on the flip of a coin), they do offer something a bit more equitable than eagles and robins.

I had another friend growing up who was big for his age. Whenever I went to his house to play, he would beat me up. I was not a masochist, so I finally stopped going to his house. After a few days, however, he asked me to come back, offering me ice cream and other incentives. After righteously spurning his overtures for a time, I gave in and resumed playing at his house. True to his word, he gave me ice cream and generously shared his best toys, and from that time forward he beat me up only once a week.

This is exactly how the casinos operate, and why they give you a better deal than eagles vs. robins. The casinos know that if they hammer you every time you come to play, sooner or later you will quit coming. Better to offer you little incentives and let you win every once in a while. Like with my big friend, they still get to beat you up, but not as often.

The Battle and the War

In casino gambling, the short run is like a battle, and either player or casino can win. However, the casino always wins the war. The American Indians never had a chance against the continuing encroachment of white settlers. There were just too many settlers and too few Indians for the outcome ever to be in doubt. Losing the war, however, did not keep the Indians from winning a few big battles. So it goes in casino gambling. The player struggles in the face of overwhelming odds. If he keeps slugging it out, he is certain to lose. If, on the other hand, he hits and runs, he may come away a winner. It's like a commando raid: the gambler must get in, do some damage, and get out. Hanging around too long in the presence of superior force can be fatal.

To say that this takes discipline is an understatement. It's hard to withdraw when you are winning, and maybe even harder to call it quits when you are losing. Glenn couldn't do either, and a lot of gamblers are just like Glenn.

The House Advantage

If casinos did engage in fair bets, they would win about half the bets and lose about half the bets. In other words, the casino (and you), on average, would break even, or at least come close to breaking even. While this arrangement would be more equitable, it would not, as a rule, generate enough money for the casino to pay its mortgage, much less foot the bill for the white tigers, pirate battles, lounge shows, $2 steaks, and free drinks.

To ensure sufficient income to meet their obligations and show a profit, casinos establish rules and payoffs for each game to give the house an advantage. While the house advantage is not strictly fair, it is what makes bargain rates on guest rooms, meals, and entertainment possible.

There are three basic ways in which the house establishes its advantage:

1. The rules of the game are tailored to the house's advantage   In blackjack, for instance, the dealer by rule always plays his own hand last. If any player busts (attains a point total over 21), the dealer wins by default without having to play out his hand.

2. The house pays off at less than the actual odds   Imagine a carnival wheel with ten numbers. When the wheel is spun, each number has an equal chance of coming up. If you bet a dollar on number six, there is a one in ten chance that you will win and a nine in ten chance that you will lose. Gamblers express odds by comparing the likelihood of losing to the likelihood of winning. In this case, nine chances to lose and one to win, or nine to one. If the game paid off at the correct odds, you would get $9 every time you won (plus the dollar you bet). Each time you lost you would lose a dollar.

Let's say you start with $10 and do not win until your tenth try, betting your last dollar. If the game paid off at the correct odds, you would break even. Starting with $10, you would lose a dollar on each of your first nine attempts. In other words, you would be down $9. Betting your one remaining dollar, you win. At nine to one, you would receive $9 and get to keep the dollar you bet. You would have exactly the $10 you started with.

As we have seen, there is no way for a casino to play you even-up and still pay the bills. If, therefore, a casino owner decided to install a wheel with ten numbers, he would decrease the payoff. Instead of paying at the correct odds (nine to one), he might pay at eight to one. If you won on your last bet and got paid at eight to one (instead of nine to one), you would have lost $1 overall. Starting with $10, you lose your first nine bets (so you are out $9) and on your last winning bet you receive $8 and get to keep the dollar you bet. Having played ten times at the eight-to-one payoff, you have $9 left, for a total loss of $1. Thus the house's advantage in this game is 10% (one-tenth).

The house advantage for actual casino games ranges from less than 1% for certain betting situations in blackjack to in excess of 27% on keno and some slots. Although 1% doesn't sound like much of an advantage, it will get you if you play long enough. Plus, for the house it adds up.

Because of variations in game rules, the house advantage for a particular game in one casino may be greater than house advantage for the same game in another casino. In most Las Vegas casinos, for instance, the house has a 5.26% advantage in roulette. At Sam's Town, however, because of the elimination of 00 (double zero) on certain roulette wheels, the house advantage is pared down to about 2.7%.

Rule variations in blackjack swing the house advantage from almost zero in single-deck games (surrender, doubling on any number of cards, dealer stands on soft 17, etc.), to more than 6% in multiple-deck games with draconian rules. Quite a few mathematicians have taken a crack at computing the house's advantage in blackjack. Some suggest that the player can actually gain an advantage over the house in single-deck games by keeping track of cards played. Others claim that without counting cards, a player utilizing a decision guide known as "basic strategy" can play the house nearly even. The reality for 95% of all blackjack players, however, is a house advantage of between 0.5% and 5.9%, depending on rule variations and the number of decks used.

Getting to the meat of the matter: blackjack played competently, baccarat, and certain bets in craps minimize the house advantage and give the player the best opportunity to win. Keno and wheel of fortune are outright sucker games. Slots, most video poker, and roulette are only marginally better.

How the house advantage works in practice causes much misunderstanding. In most roulette bets, for example, the house holds a 5.26%

advantage. If you place a dollar on black each time the wheel is spun, the house advantage predicts that, on average, you will lose 5.26 cents per dollar bet. Now, in actual play you will either lose one whole dollar or win one whole dollar, so it's not like somebody is making small change or keeping track of fractional losses. The longer you play, however, the greater the likelihood that the percentage of your losses will approximate the house advantage. If you played for a couple of hours and bet $1,000, your expected loss would be about $53.

HOUSE ADVANTAGES

Baccarat	1.17% on bank bets, 1.36% on player bets
Blackjack	0.5% to 5.9% for most games
Craps	1.4% to almost 17%, depending on the bet
Keno	20% to 35%
Roulette	5.26% to 7.89%, depending on the bet
Slots	2% to 25% (average 4% to 14%)
Video poker	1% to 12% (average 4% to 8%)
Wheel of fortune	11% to 24%

All right, you think, that doesn't sound too bad. Plus, you're thinking: I would never bet as much as $1,000. Oh, yeah? If you approach the table with $200 and make 20 consecutive $10 bets, it is not very likely that you will lose every bet. When you take money from your winning bets and wager it, you are adding to your original stake. This is known as "action" in gambling parlance, and it is very different from bankroll. Money that you win is just as much yours as the stake with which you began. When you choose to risk your winnings in additional betting, you are giving the house a crack at a much larger amount than your original $200. If you start with $200, win some and lose some, and keep playing your winnings in addition to your original stake until you have lost everything, you will have given the house (on average) about $3,800 worth of action. You may want to believe you only lost $200, but every penny of that $3,800 was yours.

3. The house takes a commission   In all casino poker games and in certain betting situations in table games, the house will collect a commission on a player's winnings.

Sometimes the house combines its various advantages. In baccarat, for instance, rules favor the house; payoffs are less than the true odds; and in certain betting situations, the house collects a commission on the player's winnings.

Games of Chance and the Law of Averages

People get funny ideas about the way gambling works. In casinos there are games of chance (roulette, craps, keno, bingo, wheel of fortune, slots, baccarat) and games of chance *and* skill (poker and blackjack).

A game of chance is like flipping a coin or spinning a wheel with ten numbers. What happens is what happens. A player can guess what the outcome will be but cannot influence it. Games of chance operate according to the law of averages. If you have a fair coin and flip it ten times, the law of averages leads you to expect that approximately half of the tosses will come up heads and the other half tails. If a roulette wheel has 38 slots, the law of averages suggests that the ball will fall into a particular slot one time in 38 spins.

The coin, the roulette ball, and the dice, however, have no memory. They just keep doing their thing. If I toss a coin and come up with heads nine times in a row, what are my chances of getting heads on the tenth toss? The answer is 50%, the same chance as getting heads on any toss. Each toss is completely independent of any other toss. When the coin goes up in the air that tenth time, it doesn't know that tails has not come up for a while, and certainly has no obligation to try to get the law of averages back into whack.

Though most gamblers are familiar with the law of averages, not all of them understand how it works. The operative word, as it turns out, is "averages," not "law." If you flip a coin a million times, there is nothing that says you will get 500,000 heads and 500,000 tails, no more than there is any assurance you will get five heads and five tails if you flip a coin ten times. What the law of averages *does* say is that, *in percentage terms,* the more times you toss the coin, the closer you will come to approximating the predicted average.

If you tossed a coin ten times, for example, you would not be surprised to get six tails and four heads. Six tails is only one flip off the five tails and five heads that the law of averages tells you is the probable outcome. By percentage, however, tails came up 60% (six of ten) of the time, while heads only came up 40% (four of ten) of the time. If you continued flipping the coin for a million tries, would you be surprised to get 503,750 tails and only 496,250 heads, a difference of 7,500 more tails than heads? The law of averages stipulates that the more we toss (and a million tosses are certainly a lot more than ten tosses) the closer we should come to approximating the average, but here we are with a huge difference of 7,500 more tails. What went wrong?

Nothing went wrong. True, after ten flips, we had only two more tails than heads, while after a million flips we had 7,500 more tails than heads. But in terms of percentage, 503,750 tails is 50.375% of one million, only about one-third of a measly percent from what the law of averages predicts. The law of averages is about percentages. Gambling is about dollars out of your pocket. If you had bet a dollar on heads each toss, you would have lost $2 after ten flips. After a million flips you would have lost $7,500. The law of averages behaved just as mathematical theory predicted, but that's probably not much consolation for going home broke.

Games of Chance and Skill

Blackjack and poker are games of chance and skill, meaning that the knowledge, experience, and skill of the player can have some influence on the outcome. All avid poker players or bridge players can recall nights when they played for hours without being dealt a good hand. That's the chance part. In order to win (especially in blackjack, where there is no bluffing), you need good cards. There is usually not much you can do if you are dealt a bad hand. As the Nevada mule drivers say, "You can't polish a turd."

If you are dealt something to work with, however, you can bring your skill into play and try to make your good hand even better. In casino poker, players compete against each other in the same way they do at Uncle Bert's house back home. The only difference is that, in the casino, the house takes a small percentage of each winning pot as compensation for hosting the game (are you listening, Uncle Bert?). Although not every casino poker player is an expert, your chances of coming up against an expert in a particular game are good. Our advice on casino poker: if you are not a tough fish, better not try to swim with the sharks.

Blackjack likewise combines chance and skill. In blackjack, however, players compete against the house (the dealer). Players have certain choices and options in blackjack, but the dealer's play is completely bound by rules. Much has been written about winning at blackjack. It's been said that by keeping track of cards played (and thereby knowing which cards remain undealt in the deck), a player can raise his or her bets when the deck contains a higher-than-usual percentage of aces, tens, and picture cards. In practice, however, the casino confounds efforts to count cards by combining several decks together, "burning" cards (removing undisclosed cards from play), and keeping the game moving at a fast pace. If an experienced gambler with extraordinary memory and power of concentration is able to overcome these obstacles, the casino will simply throw this person out.

In blackjack, as in every other casino game, it is ludicrous to suggest that the house is going to surrender its advantage. Incidentally, a super-gambler playing flawlessly in a single-deck game and keeping track of every card will gain only a nominal and temporary advantage over the house. On top of playing perfectly and being dealt good cards, the super-gambler must also disguise his play and camouflage his betting so the house won't know what he's up to. If you really want to make money on blackjack, write a book about it.

THE INTELLIGENCE TEST

If you have been paying attention, here is what you should understand by now:

1. That all gambling games are designed to favor the house, and that in the long run the house will always win.

2. That it costs a lot to build, staff, and operate a casino, and that a casino must attract many players in order to pay the bills and still make a profit.

3. That casinos compete fiercely for available customers and offer incentives ranging from 50-cent hot dogs to free guest rooms to get the right customers to their gaming tables.

Question: Given the above, what kind of customer gets the best deal?

Answer: The person who takes advantage of all the incentives without gambling.

Question: What kind of customer gets the next best deal?

Answer: The customer who sees gambling as recreation, gambles knowledgeably, makes sensible bets, sets limits on the amount he or she is prepared to wager, and enjoys all of the perks and amenities, but stays in control.

Question: What kind of customer gets the worst deal?

Answer: The person who thinks he or she can win. This person will foot the bill for everyone else.

Playing It Smart

Experienced, noncompulsive, recreational gamblers typically play in a very disciplined and structured manner. Here's what they recommend:

1. **Never gamble when you are tired, depressed, or sick.** Also, watch the drinking. Alcohol impairs judgment and lowers inhibitions.

2. **Set a limit before you leave home on the total amount you are willing to lose gambling.** No matter what happens, do not exceed this limit.

3. **Decide which game(s) interest you and get the rules down before you play.** If you are a first-timer at craps or baccarat, take lessons (offered free at the casinos most days). If you are a virgin blackjack player, buy a good book and learn basic strategy. For all three games, spend an hour or two observing games in progress before buying in. Stay away from games like keno and wheel of fortune, in which the house advantage is overwhelming.

4. **Decide how long you want to play and work out a gambling itinerary consistent with the funds you set aside for wagering.** Let's say you plan to be in Las Vegas for two days and want to play about five hours each day. If you have $500 gambling money available for the trip, that's $250 a day. Dividing the $250 a day by five hours, you come up with $50 an hour.

    Now, forget time. Think of your gambling in terms of playing individual sessions instead of hours. You are going to play five sessions a day with $50 available to wager at each session.

5. **Observe a strategy for winning and losing.** On buying in, place your session allocation by your left hand. Play your allotted session money only once during a given session. Anytime you win, return your original bet to the session-allocation

stack (left hand), and place your winnings in a stack by your right hand. Never play any chips or coins you have won. When you have gone through your original allocation once, pick up the chips or coins in your winning stack (right hand) and quit. The difference between your original allocation and what you walk away with is your net win or loss for the session.

During the session, bet consistently. If you have been making $1 bets and have lost $10, do not chase your losses by upping your bets to $10 in an effort to get even in a hurry.

If you were fortunate and doubled your allocated stake during the session (in this case, walked away with $100 or more), take everything in excess of $100 and put it aside as winnings, not to be touched for the remainder of your trip. If you won, but did not double your money, or if you had a net loss (quit with less than $50 in your win stack), use this money in your next playing session.

6. **Take a break between sessions.** Relax for a while after each session. Grab a bite to eat, enjoy a nap, or go for a swim.

7. **When you complete the number of sessions scheduled for the day, stop gambling.** Period.

Indecent Expectations

Each month the *Las Vegas Advisor* (a newsletter published by Huntington Press; (702) 252-0655) runs a feature on gambling. The following article from a past issue will give you an idea what gamblers talk about at cocktail parties.

"The Odds against Woody Harrelson and Demi Moore"

Folks still talk about the plot of the hit 1990s movie *Indecent Proposal*. A young couple (Woody Harrelson and Demi Moore) find themselves desperate for money, and head to Las Vegas. There, they meet up with a "billionaire" gambler played by Robert Redford. Redford offers Moore a million dollars, and all she has to do is spend the night with him. Moore and Harrelson decide to accept the offer. The talk-show circuit went wild with discussions about morality and relationships, but we were more intrigued by an interesting and pertinent gambling question buried within the plotline. Namely: What are the chances of turning a little money into a lot by gambling?

In the movie, the couple takes a $5,000 stake to Las Vegas in an attempt to turn it into $50,000. What were the odds against achieving their goal? By applying an optimal strategy of "bold" play at craps (line bets) or baccarat, the odds would have been about 9.5 to 1 against them. Bold play requires betting the entire $5,000 on a single coup, then rebetting the original wager, plus winnings, until either reaching the $50,000 goal or going broke (see chart). Any departure from this strategy raises the odds against success. Unfortunately for our heroes, they departed dramatically. Though it cannot be determined from the movie what the exact wagers were, it appears that the couple split their stake and made multiple wagers of $300 to $400 per coup, a decision that doomed their chances. Given this method, the odds against their winning the $50,000 were greater than *one million to one!*

The analysis above deals with a concept known as "gambler's ruin" and has implications for virtually all recreational gamblers, who find that they must choose between (1) optimizing their chances of winning and (2) getting in playing time at their game of choice.

There's a clearly defined trade-off. Assuming you want to win a specific amount of money, your best strategy is to bet as much as you can on as few wagers as possible until you reach your goal. You'll either go broke or reach your win figure—quickly. The first outcome is obviously undesirable. But so is the second (for most), since this strategy dictates that you now refrain from gambling any more.

BOLD-PLAY STRATEGY

Bet entire $5,000.

If lose, go home; if win, bet $10,000.

If lose, go home; if win, bet $20,000.

If lose, go home; if win, bet $10,000 (of $40,000 total).

If win, succeed; if lose, bet $20,000 (of $30,000 total).

If win, succeed; if lose, begin again betting entire $10,000.

If you divide your stake and make smaller bets, you are assured of gambling longer, but your chances of winning are diminished. Faced with this dilemma, most turn to the mystical idea of money management. Unfortunately, no system of money management can earn a profit (long-term) in a negative expectation game. In fact, most money-management systems require that you divide your stake into many units, and we've already seen that this leads to ultimate doom.

So, you have two choices:

1. Play only positive expectation games—certain blackjack (for expert card counters) and video poker games, promotions, coupons, the things we tell you about in the LVA. Dividing your stake is desirable when you have the advantage.

2. Accept the fact that you gamble for entertainment value and are destined to pay a fee (your losses) for "admission," just as surely as you must pay to see a concert or a sporting event.

In a sidebar to the *Las Vegas Advisor* article, mathematician and gambling author Peter Griffin had this to add:

The best the couple [Woody and Demi] could have done is apply a complicated combination of bold play and a betting method that utilizes 10 x odds [at a craps table]. This betting method is "99 and 44/100% pure," i.e., it gives .09944 chance of success (only about 9 to 1 against, which are the lowest odds achievable given Las Vegas's negative expectation gambling options).

What about blackjack at a casino like the New Frontier where favorable rules afford a basic strategy player [with perfect play] a slight edge?

The couple needed $50,000 quickly, else they might have gone to work and saved (probably ruled out by the Hollywood media elite since they don't want to encourage such values). This also rules out playing blackjack. Playing $1 per hand (perfect basic strategy), they would be virtually assured of turning their $5,000 into $50,000. However, it would take about 30 million hands. At 1,000 hands per day, both playing, that's about 40 years. At $5 per hand, they would reach their goal about 97% of the time, and it would take about six million hands or about eight years. Plus, they'd win New Frontier free-room tokens redeemable for nearly 30,000 nights.

Gaming Instruction and Resources

Most casino games are actually fairly simple once you know what's going on. A great way to replace inexperience and awkwardness with knowledge and confidence is to take advantage of the free gaming lessons offered by the casinos. Friendly, upbeat, and fun, the lessons introduce you not only to the rules, but also to the customs and etiquette of the respective games. Going slow and easy, the instructors take you step by step through the play and the betting without your actually wagering any money. Many casinos feature low-minimum-bet "live games" following the instruction. We also recommend the lessons to nonplaying companions of gamblers. For folks who usually spend a fair amount of time as spectators, casino games, like all other games, are more interesting if you know what is going on.

No matter how many books you have read, take a lesson in craps before you try to play in a casino. You don't need to know much to play baccarat, but *understanding* it is a different story. Once again, we strongly recommend lessons. Though you can learn to play blackjack by reading a book and practicing at home, lessons will make you feel more comfortable.

When "new games" are added to the traditional selection, casinos often offer instruction for a limited time. The latest rages are poker, Let It Ride, Caribbean Stud, and, owing to the increasing number of Asian gamblers, Pai Gow and Pai Gow poker. Lessons are also available in traditional poker. The San Remo offers regularly scheduled gaming lessons in Japanese. For information on gaming lessons, inquire at your hotel or check the gaming section of one of the local visitor freebie magazines like *What's On.*

Written References and the Gambler's Book Club   Most libraries and bookstores offer basic reference works on casino gambling. If you cannot find what you need at home, call the Gambler's Book Club at (800) 634-6243 for a free catalog. If you would like to stop in and browse while you are in Las Vegas, the club's store is located at 630 South 11th Street, just off East Charleston Boulevard. The local phone is (702) 382-7555.

Before you buy, check our list of recommended reading on page 461. Gambler's Book Club, incidentally, sells single issues of the *Las Vegas Advisor,* quoted above.

Casino games, not unexpectedly, are entrenched in jargon. Most of the terminology you can figure out intuitively, and much of the rest is useless in any event. The terms below, however, keep popping up in ads, in coupons, and on marquees, and manage to confuse a lot of people.

Crapless Craps In crapless craps, dice totals of 2, 3, 11, and 12 count as point numbers. For information on the rules of craps, see pages 313–318.

Double Exposure 21 A version of blackjack in which both of the dealer's cards are dealt face up.

Double Odds The option in craps of making an odds bet twice the size of your line bet. See "Craps," pages 313–318.

Funbooks Little booklets of coupons available without charge from certain casinos. The coupons in funbooks vary widely from casino to casino but usually include coupons for souvenir gifts, discount show tickets, discount meals, two-for-one or free drinks, and matchplay (see below). Some funbooks offer exceptional value, while others are nothing more than a hustle. Coupons for keno and slots, for example, are practically worthless, while matchplay coupons for table games can be valuable. On balance, coupon books are worth checking out.

Loose Slots Slot machines that are programmed to pay off more frequently. The term is usually applied to machines with a return rate of 94% or higher, meaning that the house advantage is 6% or less.

Matchplay Coupons Coupons from funbooks or print ads that can be redeemed for matchplay chips. The matchplay chips must be combined with an equal amount of your own money on certain table game bets. If you win, you are paid off for the entire bet in real money. If you bet $5 in matchplay chips and $5 of your bankroll on the color black in roulette, you will win $10 of real money if the ball lands in a black slot. When you are paid off, the dealer collects your matchplay chips, which can only be used once, but you keep the $5 in real money you bet. If you lose, of course, the dealer will take both the real money and the matchplay chips.

Megabucks Slots A statewide progressive slot machine network with grand jackpots in excess of $5 million. For additional information on progressive slot systems, see page 296.

Single-Deck Blackjack Blackjack dealt from a single deck as opposed to two or more decks shuffled together.

Triple Odds The option in craps of making an odds bet three times the size of your line bet. See "Craps," pages 313–318.

Where to Play

We receive a lot of mail from readers asking which casino has the loosest slots, the most favorable rules for blackjack, and the best odds on craps. We directed the questions to veteran gambler and tournament player Anthony Curtis, publisher of the *Las Vegas Advisor.* Here's Anthony's reply:

Where's the best casino in Las Vegas to play blackjack, video poker, and the rest of the gambling games? It could be almost anyplace on any given day due to spot promotions and changing management philos-ophies. A few casinos, however, have established reliable track records in specific areas. Absent a special promotion or change in policy, I recommend the following casinos as the best places to play each of the games listed:

ANTHONY'S RECOMMENDED BEST PLACES TO PLAY

Blackjack *Binion's Horseshoe*	Still plenty of single-deck games with a skinny 0.15% casino edge versus basic strategy. Where many single decks are going to the bad 6-5 payout for a natural, Binion's holds the line with the traditional 3-2.
Quarter Slots *Palms*	The Palms has kept its returns loose at all levels to compete in the tough locals market. The casino runs lots of promotions.
Dollar Slots *Las Vegas Hilton*	Highest rate of slot cashback, plus free tournaments and juicy offers for slot club members.
Craps *Casino Royale*	Only casino in Las Vegas that still offers 100X odds. Also low limits on the line and the propositions. There's also an excellent funbook for new slot club members.
Quarter Video Poker *Fiesta Ranchero*	This is Las Vegas's new video poker paradise, with "full-pay" (best schedules for a given game) machines all over the casino. Many return greater than 100% with perfect play.
Dollar Video Poker *Las Vegas Hilton*	The Hilton also pays the highest cashback rate on video poker, and offers lots of Pick 'Em Poker games. Pick 'Em is an intuitively easy-to-play video poker variation that returns 99.95% with perfect play.
Roulette *Nevada Palace*	Deals a single-zero game 24 hours a day, with a 10¢ minimum bet on the inside numbers ($1 aggregate required).
Baccarat *Palace Station*	Action around the clock at oversized mini baccarat tables. Minimums as low as $5.
Keno *Silverton*	A comparison of keno return percentages shows casinos that target locals offer the best chance of winning.

ANTHONY'S RECOMMENDED BEST PLACES TO PLAY *(continued)*	
Bingo **Palms**	The Palms is working for bingo patronage. Lots of specials in the room, including free slot play and acceptance of other casinos' bingo coupons.
Poker **Stardust**	Bellagio has most of the action, but Stardust is better for lower stakes. Reasonable action and good promotions.
Race and Sports Betting **Imperial Palace**	Famous for its wild proposition bets on big events. You can bet on more things here than anywhere else in town. Also a drive-through ticket window.
Let It Ride **Boardwalk**	Not much separates one Let It Ride game from another, but Boardwalk continues to deal a $3 minimum, compared to $5 and $10 minimums at most other casinos.
Caribbean Stud **Golden Nugget**	Usually a couple of tables in operation with fast meters on the progressive, which means the bonus jackpot has a better chance to move into positive-return territory.
Pai Gow Poker **Gold Coast**	Lots of action around the clock, and low minimums.

Changes in Attitude, Changes in Latitude

Most people who love to gamble are not motivated by greed. Usually it is the tension, excitement, and anticipation of the game that they enjoy. Misunderstanding this reality has led many naive and innocent people into the nightmare of addictive gambling.

Ed was attending a convention on his first visit to Las Vegas. One evening, he decided to try his luck at roulette. Approaching the table, Ed expected to lose ("I'm not stupid, after all"). His intentions were typical. He wanted to "try" gambling while in Nevada, and he was looking for an adventure, a new experience. What Ed never anticipated was the emotional impact gambling would have on him. It transcended winning and losing. In fact, it wasn't about winning or losing at all. It was the *playing* that mattered. The "action" made him feel alive, involved, and terribly sophisticated. It also made him crazy.

The "high" described by the compulsive gambler closely parallels the experience of drug and alcohol abusers. In fact, there is a tendency for chemical addiction and gambling compulsion to overlap. The compulsive gambler attempts to use "the action" as a cure for a variety of ills, in much the same way that people use alcohol and drugs to lift them out of depression, stem anxiety or boredom, and make them feel more "in control."

Some people cannot handle gambling, just as some people cannot handle alcohol. The problem, unfortunately, is compounded by the attitude of our society. As we profess to admire the drinker who can "hold his liquor," we reinforce the gambler who beats the odds in Las Vegas. By glamorizing these behaviors we enable afflicted individuals to remain in denial about the destructive nature of their problem. The compulsive gambler blames circumstances and other people for the suffering occasioned by his or her affliction. One may hear excuses like: "I didn't get enough sleep; I couldn't concentrate with all the noise; I lost track of the time; I'm jinxed at this casino."

If this sounds like you or someone you love, get help. In Las Vegas there is a meeting of Gamblers Anonymous almost every night. Call (702) 385-7732. If, like Ed, you catch something in Las Vegas and take it home with you, Gamblers Anonymous is listed in your local *White Pages*.

Rules of the Games

Slot Machines

Slot machines, including video poker, have eclipsed the table games in patron popularity. There are few casinos remaining that have not allocated more than half of their available floor space to various types of slot machines.

The popularity of slots is not difficult to understand. First, slots allow a person to enjoy casino gambling at low or high stakes. In downtown Las Vegas at the Nevada and the Gold Spike, for instance, you can play the slots for a penny a pop. Nickel slots, meanwhile, can be found in virtually every casino in town. Quarter slots are the most popular and the most common. Higher-stakes players can find machines that accept bets of $1 to $500 (high-stakes slots use special tokens instead of coins).

Second, many people like the slots because no human interaction is required. Absent in slot play is the adversarial atmosphere of the table games. Machines are less intimidating—at least more neutral—than dealers and pit bosses. A patron can sit at a machine for as long as his stamina and money last and never be bothered by a soul.

Finally, slot machines are simple, or at least ostensibly so. Although there are a number of things you should know before you play the slots, the only thing you have to know is how to put money into the machine (sometimes coins, but more often bills) and press the spin button (most slot machines no longer have handles).

What You Need to Know before You Play Slot Machines

For the moment we will confine our discussion to traditional slot machines, the so-called one-armed bandits. Later we will take a look at video poker.

An old-style reel slot machine that still accepts coins and has a handle.
(Courtesy of Las Vegas News Bureau)

Starting at the beginning: All slot machines have a slot for inserting coins (or a sort of account card that defines your stake and debits or credits the card depending on whether you win or lose), a button to push (most machines no longer have handles) to activate the machine, a visual display where you can see the reels spin and stop on each play, and a coin tray that you hope some winnings will drop into. Today, almost all slot machines are essentially computers attached to a monitor. Gone are the mechanical reels, replaced by an electronic depiction of reels illustrated on the monitor.

While slot machines used to have 3 mechanical reels, most today have been replaced by video screens with up to 12 depictions of reels. Each video illustrated reel has some number of "stops," positions where the reel can come to rest. Reels with 20, 25, or 32 stops are the most common. On each reel at each stop (or resting position) is a single slot symbol (a cherry, orange, bar, plum, etc.). What you hope will happen (when the video reels stop spinning) is that three or more of the same symbol will line up on the pay line. If this happens, you win some number of coins or credits based on the particular symbols. With the old slot machines things were pretty simple. There was one coin slot, one handle to pull, and a display with one pay line. Symbols either lined up on that line or they didn't. The newer machines are much more complex. Almost all modern machines accept more than one coin per play (usually three to five). No matter how many coins the machine will take, it only requires one to play.

If you put in additional coins (bet more), you will buy one of the following benefits:

1. **Payoff schedules**   On a certain type of machine, two, three, four, or five different payoff schedules are posted on the front of the machine above the reel display. If you study these schedules you will notice that by playing extra coins you can increase your payoff should you win the grand jackpot. Usually there is a straightforward increase. If you play two coins, you will win twice as much as if you play one coin. If you play three coins, you will win three times as much as if you play one coin, and so on. Some machines, however, have a grand jackpot that will pay off only if you have played the maximum number of coins. If you line up the symbols for the grand jackpot but have not played the maximum number of coins, you will not win the maximum amount possible. Always read the payoff schedule for a machine before you play and make sure you understand it. If you do not, ask an attendant or find a simpler machine.

    Though most casino slot machines are kept in good working order, watch to make sure a section of the payoff schedule lights up for every coin you play. If you are playing a machine with four payoff schedules, the schedules should light up, one at a time, as you put in your coins. On machines where the payoff schedules do not illuminate, there will ordinarily be a light (or lights) above or below the reel display that will verify that the machine has accepted your coins. If you put in multiple coins without the appropriate lights coming on, do not play until you check things out with an attendant.

2. **Multiple pay lines**   When you play your first coin, you buy the usual pay line, right in the center of the display. By playing more coins, you can buy additional pay lines.

    Each pay line you purchase gives you another way of winning. Instead of being limited to the center line, the machine will pay off on the top, center, or bottom lines, and five-coin machines will pay winners on diagonal lines. If you play machines with multiple pay lines, make sure that each pay line you buy is acknowledged by a light before you push the button.

    An irritating feature of many multiple-line machines are "blanks" or "ghosts." A blank is nothing more than an empty stop on the reel—a place where you would expect a symbol to be but where there is nothing. As you have probably surmised, you cannot hit a winner by lining up blanks.

Nonprogressive versus Progressive Slot Machines   Nonprogressive slot machines have fixed payoffs. You can read the payoff schedules posted on the machine and determine exactly how much you will get for each winning combination for any number of coins played.

A second type of machine, known as a progressive, has a grand jackpot that grows and grows until somebody hits it. After the grand jackpot has been won, a new jackpot is established and starts to grow. While individual machines can offer modest progressive grand jackpots, the really big jackpots (several thousand to several million dollars) are possible only on machines linked in a system to other machines. Sometimes an "island," "carousel," or "bank" of machines in a given casino is hooked up to create a progressive system. The more these machines are played, the faster the progressive grand jackpot grows. The largest progressive jackpots, however, come from huge multicasino systems that sometimes cover the entire state. Players have won up to $27.5 million by hitting these jackpots.

While nothing is certain in slot play, it is generally accepted that nonprogressives will pay more small jackpots. Progressives, on the other hand, offer an opportunity to really strike it rich, but they give up fewer interim wins. Each type of machine targets a certain player. The nonprogressive machine appeals to the player who likes plenty of action, who gets bored when coins aren't clanking into the tray every four or five pulls. The progressive machine is for the player who is willing to forego frequent small payouts for the chance of hitting a really big one.

How Slot Machines Work

Almost all slot machines used in casinos today are controlled by microprocessors. This means the machines can be programmed and are more like computers than mechanical boxes composed of gears and wheels. During the evolution of the modern slot machine, manufacturers eliminated the traditional spinning reels in favor of a video display, and replaced the pull handle with a button. Inside the newer machines, there is a device that computer people call a "random number generator" and that we refer to as a "black box." What the black box does is spit out hundreds of numbers each second, selected randomly (i.e., in no predetermined sequence). The black box has about four billion different numbers to choose from, so it's very unusual (but not impossible) for the same number to come up twice in a short time.

The numbers the black box selects are programmed to trigger a certain set of symbols on the display, determining where the reels stop. What most players don't realize, however, is that the black box pumps out numbers continuously, regardless of whether the machine is being played or not. If you are playing a machine, the black box will call up hundreds or thousands of numbers in the few seconds between plays while you sip your drink, put some money in the slot, and push the button.

Why is this important? Try this scenario: Mary has played the same quarter machine for two hours, pumping an untold amount of money into it. While she turns for a moment to buy gum from a cigarette girl, a man walks up to Mary's machine and wins the grand jackpot. Mary is livid. "That's my jackpot," she screams. Not so. While Mary bought her gum, thousands of numbers and possible symbol combinations were

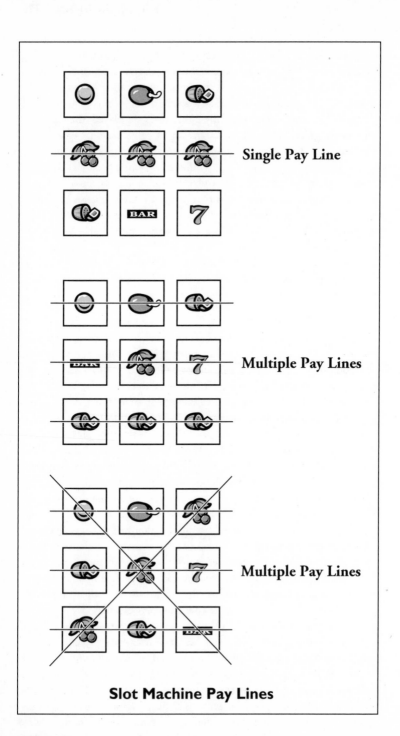

Single Pay Line

Multiple Pay Lines

Multiple Pay Lines

Slot Machine Pay Lines

generated by the black box. The only way Mary could have won the grand jackpot (even if the man had not come along) would have been to activate the machine at that same exact moment in time, right down to a fraction of a millisecond.

There is no such thing as a machine that is "overdue to hit." Each spin of the reels on a slot machine is an independent event, just like flipping a coin. The only way to hit a jackpot is to activate the machine at the exact moment that the black box randomly coughs up a winning number. If you play a slot machine as fast as you can, jamming in coins and pushing the button like a maniac, the black box will still spew out more numbers (and possible jackpots) between each try than you will have pulls in a whole day of playing.

Cherry, Cherry, Orange   The house advantage is known for every casino game except slots. With slot machines, the house advantage is whatever the casino programs it to be. In Atlantic City the maximum legal house advantage is 17%. Nevada's limit for slot machines is a hold of 75%. This means that Nevada slot machines can have a house advantage of up to 25%. In theory, a casino could program a machine to keep 50% of all the coins played. Interviews with ex–casino employees suggest, however, that the house advantage on casino slots in Las Vegas ranges from about 2.5% to 25%, with most machines giving the house an edge of between 4% and 14%.

Casinos advertise their slots in terms of payout or return rate. If a casino states that its slots return up to 97%, that's another way of saying that the house has a 3% advantage. Some casinos advertise machines that pay up to 98%, and one casino even claims to offer slots paying 101%!

Slot Quest   A slot machine that withholds only a small percentage of the money played is referred to as "loose," while a machine that retains most of the coins it takes in is called "tight." "Loose" and "tight" are figurative descriptions and have nothing to do with the condition of the machine. Because return rates vary from casino to casino, and because machines in a given casino are programmed to withhold vastly differing percentages of the coins played, slot players devote much time and energy to finding the best casinos and the loosest machines. Exactly how to go about this is the subject of much discussion.

In terms of choosing a casino, there are several theories which have at least a marginal ring of truth. Competition among casinos is often a general indicator for finding loose slots. Some say that smaller casinos, which compete against large neighbors, must program their slots to provide a higher return. Alternatively, some folks will play slots only in casinos patronized predominantly by locals (Gold Coast, Palace Station, Boulder Station, Fiesta, Suncoast, Orleans, Texas Station, El Cortez, Gold Spike,

Castaways, Sam's Town, Arizona Charlie's, and Santa Fe Station, among others). The reasoning here is that these casinos vie for regular customers on a continuing basis and must therefore offer extremely competitive win rates. Downtown Las Vegas is likewise cast in the "we try harder" role because smaller downtown casinos must go head to head with the Strip to attract patrons.

Extending the logic, machines located in supermarkets, restaurants, convenience stores, airports, and lounges are purported to be very tight. In these places, some argue, there is little incentive for management to provide good returns because the patrons will play regardless (out of boredom or simply because the machine is there).

Veteran slot players have many theories when it comes to finding the loose machines in a particular casino. Some will tell you to play the machines by the door or in the waiting area outside the showroom. By placing the loose machines in these locations, the theory goes, the casino can demonstrate to passersby and show patrons that the house has loose slots. A more labor-intensive suggestion for sniffing out the loose machines is to hang around the casino during the wee hours of the morning when the machines are being emptied. Supposedly machines with the least number of coins in the hopper have been paying off more frequently. Or maybe these machines have just been played less often.

Of the theories for finding the loose machines in a specific casino, the suggestion that makes the most sense is to select a casino and play there long enough to develop a relationship with the slot attendants. Not as difficult as it sounds, this means being friendly and engaging the attendants in pleasant conversation. If the casino has a slot club, join up and use the club card so the slot personnel will regard you as a regular. If the attendants are responsive and kind, and particularly if you win, give them a tip. After a couple of hours, the attendants will begin to take an interest in you. Ask them candidly and forthrightly to point out a good (i.e., loose) machine. Tip them for the information and tip again if you do well on the machine. If the machine is not hitting for you, don't blame the attendant. Continue to be positive and build the relationship. In the long run, it is in your best interest, as well as in the best interest of the attendant and of the house, for the relationship to prosper. If the attendant turns you on to the loosest machine in Las Vegas, the house is still going to make money in the long run. If the force is with you, however, you might rack up a nice short-term win or at least get more play for your money.

I have had a slot manager admit to me that his nickel machines are tighter than his quarter machines and that his dollar and five-dollar machines are the loosest of all. Tight or loose, however, all slots are programmed to give the casino a certain profit over the long run. It is very unlikely, in any event, that you will play a machine long enough to experience the theoretical payoff rate. What you are concerned about is the short run. In the short run anything can happen, including winning.

Maximizing Your Chances of Winning on the Slots   If you play less than the maximum number of coins on a progressive, you are simply contributing to a jackpot that you have no chance of winning. If you don't want to place a maximum bet, play a nonprogressive machine.

Slot Machine Etiquette and Common Sense

Regardless of whether you are playing a one-armed bandit, a video-poker machine, or any other type of coin-operated slot machine, there are some things you need to know:

1. Realize that avid slot players sometimes play more than one machine at a time. Do not assume that a machine is not in use simply because nobody is standing or sitting in front of it. Slot players can be fanatically territorial.

2. Before you start to play, check out the people around you. Do you feel safe and comfortable among them?

3. Read and understand the payout schedule of any machine you play.

4. Check to see if the machine automatically pays coins into the tray or whether your winnings are registered on a credit meter. If your machine has a credit meter, be sure to cash out your credits before you abandon the machine.

5. If the casino has a slot club, join (this usually takes less than five minutes on-site, but can be accomplished through the mail prior to your trip). Use the club card whenever you play. When you quit, don't forget to take your club card with you.

6. Never play more machines than you can watch carefully. Be particularly vigilant when playing machines near exits and corridors. If you are asleep at the switch, a thief can dip into your coin tray or bucket and be out the door in seconds.

7. Keep your purse and your money in sight at all times. Never put your purse on the floor behind you or to the side.

8. If you line up a winner and nothing happens, don't leave the machine. Sometimes large jackpots exceed the coin capacity of the machine and must be paid directly by the casino cashier. Call immediately for an attendant but do not wander off looking for one. While you wait, refrain from further play on the machine in question. When the attendant arrives, check his casino employee identification.

9. If the appropriate payout sections or pay lines fail to illuminate when playing multiple coins, do not leave or activate the machine (push the button) until you have consulted an attendant.

Slot Clubs and Frequent-Player Clubs

Most Las Vegas casinos now have slot or frequent-player clubs. The purpose of these clubs is to foster increased customer loyalty among gambling patrons by providing incentives.

You can join a club by signing up at the casino or (at some casinos) by applying through the mail. There is neither a direct cost associated with joining nor any dues. You are given a plastic membership card that very much resembles a credit card. This card can be inserted into a receptacle on certain quarter and dollar slots (including video-poker machines). As long as your card is in the receptacle, you are credited for the amount of action you give that machine. Programs at different casinos vary, but in general, you are awarded "points" based on how long you play and how much you wager. Some clubs award points for both slot and table play, while other clubs confine their program to slots. As in an airline frequent-flyer program, accumulated points can ultimately be redeemed for awards. Awards range from casino logo apparel to discounts (or comps) on meals, shows, and rooms.

The good thing about slot clubs is that they provide a mechanism for slot players to obtain some of the comps, perks, and extras that have always been available to table players. The bad thing about a slot club is that it confines your play. In other words, you must give most of your business to one or two casinos in order to accumulate award points. If you are a footloose player and enjoy gambling all around town, you may never accrue enough points in any one casino to redeem a prize.

Even if you never redeem any points, however, it's still a good idea to join. Joining a club gets you identified as a gambler on the casino's mailing list. Just for joining, and without gambling that first quarter, you will be offered discounts on rooms and a variety of other special deals. If you travel to Las Vegas regularly on business, join your hotel's slot club. Membership might make you eligible for deals on rooms and food that would otherwise not be available to you.

Video Poker

Never in the history of casino gambling has a new game become so popular so quickly. All across Nevada, casinos are reallocating game-table and slot space to video-poker machines. More people are familiar with poker than with any other casino game. The video version affords average folks an opportunity to play a game of chance and skill without going up against professional gamblers.

In video poker you are not playing against anyone. Rather, you are trying to make the best possible five-card-draw poker hand. In the most common rendition, you insert your coin(s) and push a button marked "deal." Your original five cards are displayed on the screen. Below the screen and under each of the cards pictured are "hold" buttons. After evaluating your hand and planning your strategy, designate the cards you want to keep by pressing the appropriate hold button(s). If you hit the wrong button or change your mind, most machines have an "error" or "erase" button, which will allow you to revise your choices before you draw. If you do not want to draw any cards (you like your hand as dealt), press all five hold buttons. When you press the hold button for a particular card, the word "hold" will appear over or under that card on the display. Always double-check the screen to make certain the cards you intend to hold are marked before proceeding to the draw.

When you are ready, press the button marked "draw" (on many machines it is the same button as the deal button). Any cards you have not designated to be held will be replaced. As in live draw poker, the five cards in your possession after the draw are your final hand. If the hand is a winner (a pair of jacks or better on most quarter machines and dollar machines), you will be credited the appropriate winnings on a credit meter on the video display. These are actual winnings that can be retrieved in coins by pressing the "cash-out" button. If you choose to leave your winnings on the credit meter, you may use them to bet, eliminating the need to physically insert coins in the machine. When you are ready to quit, simply press the cash-out button and collect your coins from the tray.

You do not have to know much about poker to play video poker. All of the winning hands with their respective payoffs are posted on or above the video display. As with other slot machines, you can increase your payoffs and become eligible for bonus jackpots by playing the maximum number of coins. Note that some machines have jackpots listed in dollars, while others are specified in coins. Obviously, there is a big difference between $4,000 and 4,000 nickels.

Quarter and dollar video-poker machines come in progressive and nonprogressive models. Nonprogressive machines will pay more on a full house (nine coins) and a flush (six coins) than will progressives (eight and five coins respectively). Progressives feature a grand jackpot that continues to build until somebody hits it. Nonprogressives usually feature a bonus jackpot for hitting a royal flush when playing the maximum number of coins.

In popular jargon, video-poker machines are labeled according to these different payoffs as "nine/six" or "eight/five" machines. Never play a progressive (eight/five) machine unless you are playing the number of coins required to win the grand jackpot. By playing less than the maximum number of coins, you disqualify yourself for the grand jackpot while subsidizing the jackpot's growth. Plus, you get a lower return rate than you would on a nonprogressive (nine/six). Also be aware that the grand jackpot for maximum coin play on a nonprogressive can sometimes be larger than the grand jackpot on a progressive. Always scout around before you play.

It should be noted that some casinos have begun to experiment with progressive and nonprogressive ten/six and nine/seven machines. The expected value of perfect play on these machines exceeds 100%.

In addition to straight draw poker, games with jokers or deuces wild are also available at many casinos. Jokers wild machines normally pay on a pair of kings or better, while deuces wild programs pay on three-of-a-kind and up. Casinos clean up on the wild card machines because very few players understand the basic strategy of proper play.

With flawless play, the house advantage on nine/six quarter and dollar machines ranges up from about 0.5%, and for eight/five machines and wild card programs, from about 3%. On nickel video-poker machines, the house advantage is about 5% to 10%.

Video-Poker Strategy

Each deal in a video-poker game is dealt from a fresh 52-card deck. Each hand consists of ten cards, with a random number generator or "black box" selecting the cards dealt. When you hit the deal button, the first five cards are displayed face up on the screen. Cards six through ten are held in reserve to be dealt as replacements for cards you discard when you draw. Each replacement card is dealt in order off the top of the electronic deck. The microprocessor "shuffles" the deck for each new game. Thus on the next play, you will be dealt five new and randomly selected initial cards, and five new and randomly selected draw cards to back them up. In other words, you will not be dealt any unused cards from the previous hand.

The Power of the Royal Flush   In video poker, the biggest payout is usually for a royal flush. This fact influences strategy for playing the game. Simply put, you play differently than you would in a live poker game. If in video poker you are dealt:

$$A\clubsuit \qquad Q\clubsuit \qquad 10\clubsuit \qquad A\spadesuit \qquad J\clubsuit$$

you would discard the ace of spades (giving up a sure winner) to go for the royal flush. Likewise, if you are dealt:

$$5\spadesuit \qquad A\spadesuit \qquad K\spadesuit \qquad Q\spadesuit \qquad J\spadesuit$$

you would discard the 5 of spades (sacrificing a sure spade flush) in an attempt to make the royal by drawing the 10 of spades. If you are dealt:

$$J\heartsuit \qquad Q\heartsuit \qquad K\heartsuit \qquad 4\heartsuit \qquad 6\clubsuit$$

draw two cards for the royal flush as opposed to one card for the flush. If you are initially dealt the following straight:

$$7\clubsuit \qquad 8\clubsuit \qquad 9\clubsuit \qquad 10\clubsuit \qquad J\diamondsuit$$

keep it on a nine/six or eight/five quarter or dollar machine. This particular hand occasions much debate among video-poker veterans. The 6 of clubs or the jack of clubs would give you a straight flush, while any other club would give you a flush. Your chances of improving this hand are 9 in 47, with a 5 in 47 chance of recapturing your straight with a drawn nonclub 6 or jack. It's a close call, but keeping the sure straight gets the nod (with an expected win of four coins for standing versus two and threefourths coins for drawing). If the same situation comes up on a nickel machine, however, take the gamble and draw.

The payoff for the royal flush is so great that it is worth risking a sure winning hand. The payoff for a straight flush, however, does not warrant risking a pat flush or straight.

Other Situations   If you are dealt:

Q ♦   A ♣   4 ♥   J ♠   4 ♣

hold the small pair except when you have a chance at making a royal flush by drawing one or two cards.

But, if you are dealt:

K ♦   A ♣   4 ♥   J ♣   3 ♠

hold the ace of clubs and the jack of clubs to give yourself a long shot at a royal flush. Similarly, if you are dealt:

K ♣   A ♣   4 ♥   J ♣   3 ♠

hold the ace of clubs, king of clubs, and jack of clubs.

Straight Poker   If you are playing straight poker (no wild cards), with a pair of jacks or better required to win, observe the following:

1. Hold a jacks-or-better pair, even if you pass up the chance of drawing to an open-end straight or to a flush. If you have:

Q ♣   4 ♠   6 ♠   2 ♠   Q ♠

or

Q ♥   9 ♦   10 ♣   J ♠   Q ♣

in each case, keep the pair of queens and draw three cards.

2. Split a low pair to go for a flush. If you are dealt:

2 ♦   4 ♣   4 ♦   8 ♦   10 ♦

discard the 4 of clubs and draw one card to try and make the flush.

3. Hold a low pair rather than drawing to an inside or open-end straight.

4. A "kicker" is a face card or an ace you might be tempted to hang onto along with a high pair, low pair, or three-of-a-kind. If you are dealt, for example:

5 ♣   5 ♦   8 ♠   10 ♠   A ♥

or

J ♣   J ♠   8 ♣   7 ♥   A ♦

or

2 ♣   2 ♠   2 ♥   8 ♠   A ♥

hold the pair or the three-of-a-kind, but discard the kicker (the ace).

Blackjack

Many books have been published about the game of blackjack. The serious gamblers who write these books will tell you that blackjack is a game of skill and chance in which a player's ability can actually turn the odds of winning in his favor. While we want to believe that, we also know the casinos wouldn't keep the tables open if they were taking a beating.

The methods of playing blackjack skillfully involve being able to count all the cards played and flawlessly manage your own hand, while mentally blocking the bustle and distraction of the casino. The ability to master the prerequisite tactics and to play under casino conditions is so far beyond the average (never mind beginning) player that any attempt to track cards is, practically speaking, exhausting and futile.

This doesn't mean that you should not try blackjack. It is a fun, fast-paced game that is easy to understand, and you can play at low-minimum-wager tables without feeling intimidated by the level of play. Moreover, most people already have an understanding of the game from playing "21" at home. The casino version is largely the same, only with more bells and whistles.

In a game of blackjack, the number cards are worth their spots (a 2 of clubs is worth two points). All face cards are worth ten points. The ace, on the other hand, is worth either 1 point or 11, whichever you choose. In this manner, an ace and a 5 could be worth 6 points (hard count) or 16 (soft count). The object of the game is to get as close to 21 points as you can without going over (called "busting"). You play only against the dealer, and the hand closest to 21 points wins the game.

The dealer will deal you a two-card hand, then give you the option of taking another card (called a "hit") or stopping with the two cards you have been dealt (called "standing"). For example, if your first two cards are a 10 and a 3, your total would be 13, and you would normally ask for another card to get more points. If the next card dealt to you was a 7, you would have a total of 20 points and you would "stand" with 20 (i.e., not ask for another card).

It makes no difference what the other players are dealt, or what they choose to do with their hands. Your hand will win or lose only in comparison to the hand that the dealer holds.

The dealer plays his hand last. This is his biggest advantage. All the players that go over 21 points, or bust, will immediately lose their cards and their bet before the dealer's turn to play. What this means in terms of casino advantage is that while the player has to play to win, the only thing the dealer has to do is not lose. Every time you bust, the casino wins. This sequence of play ensures a profit for the casino from the blackjack tables.

We recommend that you take the time to observe a few hands before you play. This will give you the opportunity to find a personable, friendly dealer and to check out the minimum-bet signs posted at each table. They will say something like: "Minimum bet $2 to $500." This means that the minimum wager is $2, and the maximum wager is $500. If you sit down at a blackjack table and begin to bet with insufficient cash or the wrong denomination chip, the dealer will inform you of the correct minimum wager, whereupon you may either conform or excuse yourself.

The Blackjack Table

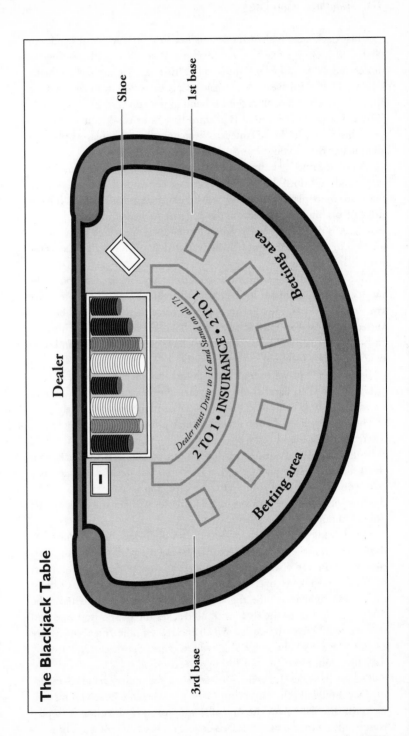

Shoe

1st base

Dealer

Betting area

Dealer must Draw to 16 and Stand on all 17s

2 TO 1 • INSURANCE • 2 TO 1

Betting area

3rd base

A blackjack table is shaped like a half circle, with the dealer inside the circle and room for five to seven players around the outside. Facing the dealer, the chair on the far right is called "first base." The chair on the far left is called "third base." The dealer deals the cards from first base to third, and each player plays out his hand in the same order.

The best possible position is at third base or as close to it as you can get. This gives you the advantage of watching the other players play out their hands before you play.

To buy in, find an empty seat at a table with an agreeable minimum wager and wait until the hand in progress is concluded. Though you can bet cash, most players prefer to convert their currency to chips. This is done by placing your money on the table *above* the bettor's box. Because blackjack is one of the many games in the casino in which the dealer is allowed to accept cash bets, he will assume that any money placed *in* the bettor's box is a wager.

Your dealer will take the cash, count out your chips, and push the money through a slot cut in the top of the table. Because he cannot give you change in cash, the total amount you place on the table will be converted to chips. You may at any time, however, redeem your chips for cash from the casino cashier. Once you have been given chips and have bet, you will be included in the next deal.

To confound a player attempting to count cards, many casinos deal blackjack with two to six decks shuffled together. This huge stack of cards is rendered manageable by dealing from a special container known as a shoe.

The dealer will shuffle the decks and may offer the cards to you to cut. Don't get fancy. Simply take off the top half of the deck and lay it beside the other half. Do this with one hand and never conceal the deck from the dealer. If you are playing with a large multiple deck, the dealer may offer you a plastic card stop. Place the card stop halfway or so into the deck, leaving the stop sticking out. The dealer will cut the deck at that point and put it into the shoe.

After he cuts a single deck, or puts the multiple deck into the shoe, the dealer will "burn" one or more cards by taking them off the top and putting them into the discard pile. This is yet another tactic to inhibit players from keeping track of cards dealt. Also to the advantage of the casino is the dealer's right to shuffle the cards whenever he pleases. Usually the dealer will deal from the shoe until he reaches the plastic stop card and then he will "break the deck," which means reshuffle and recut before dealing the next hand. In a single-deck game, the dealer will usually reshuffle about three-quarters through the deck.

Because the dealer always plays his hand last, you must develop your strategy by comparing your card count to what you assume (based on his visible card) the dealer has. The rule of thumb for most situations is to play your hand as if you know the dealer's down card has a value of ten. The principles governing when or when not to take a hit are known as "basic strategy" (chart page 309). If you elect to take a hit and go over 21 (bust), you lose. If you stand with your original two cards or take a number of hits without going over 21, you can sit back and relax for a few seconds while the dealer continues on around the table, repeating the same process with the other players. When the other players finish, the dealer exposes his "down" card and plays out his hand according to strict rules. He must take a hit on any total of 16 or less, and he must stand on any total of 17 or more. When he finishes his hand, the dealer goes from third base to first, paying off each winning player and collecting chips from the losers who didn't bust.

If you have more points than the dealer, then you win. If he has more points (or if you busted), then he wins. If there is a tie, neither hand wins. When you tie, the dealer will knock on the table above your bet to indicate that the hand is a tie, or a "push." You may leave your bet on the table for the next hand, or change it.

There is a way for you to win automatically, and that is to be dealt exactly 21 points in the first two cards. This can be done with an ace and any ten-value card. Called a blackjack, or a natural, this hand is an automatic winner, and you should turn your cards face up immediately. The dealer will look to see if he ties you with a blackjack of his own; this is one of the only times a dealer will look at his cards before all the players have played. If the dealer does not have a blackjack, he will pay you immediately at three-to-two odds, so your $5 bet pays off $7.50 and you keep your original wager. If the dealer has a blackjack too, then only you and any other players at the table with a natural will tie him. The rest lose their bets, and the next round will begin.

Nothing beats a natural. If the dealer has a 4 and a 6, then draws an ace, his 21 points will not beat your blackjack. A blackjack wins over everything and pays the highest of any bet in the game. Just as you can win automatically, you may lose just as fast. When your count goes over 21 and you bust, you must turn your cards over. The dealer will collect your cards and your bet before moving on to the next player.

Hitting and Standing

BASIC STRATEGY*											
The Dealer Is Showing:		2	3	4	5	6	7	8	9	10	Ace
Your Total is:	4–11	H	H	H	H	H	H	H	H	H	H
	12	H	H	S	S	S	H	H	H	H	H
	13	S	S	S	S	S	H	H	H	H	H
	14	S	S	S	S	S	H	H	H	H	H
	15	S	S	S	S	S	H	H	H	H	H
	16	S	S	S	S	S	H	H	H	H	H
S=Stand H=Hit											

*The correct term for the spots on playing cards is "pips."

When dealing, whether from the shoe or from a single deck in his hand, the dealer will give two cards to each player. Most casinos will deal both cards facedown, though some casinos, especially those that use large multiple decks, will deal both cards faceup. There is no advantage to either method. Most players are more comfortable with the secrecy of the facedown deal, but the outcome will not be affected either way. Starting with the player at first base, the dealer will give you cards to play out your hand. After the initial deal, you have two basic options: either stand or take a hit. If you are satisfied with your deal, then you elect to stand. If your cards were dealt facedown, slide them under the chips in the bettor's box with one hand, being careful not to touch your chips or conceal them from the dealer. If the cards were dealt faceup, wave your hand over the top, palm down, in a negative fashion, to signal the dealer not to give you another card.

Sometimes you will improve your hand by asking for another card. You signal for a hit by scratching the bottom of your cards toward you on the felt surface of the table. In a faceup game, scratch your fingers toward you in the same fashion. You may say, "Hit me," or "I'll take a hit," depending on the mood at your table but use the hand gestures also. Because of noise and distractions, the dealer may misinterpret your verbal request.

The card you request will be dealt faceup, and you may take as many hits as you like. When you want to show that you do not want another card, use the signals for standing. If you bust, turn your cards faceup right away so the dealer can collect your cards and chips. He will then go to the next player. There are times when the dealer stands a good chance of busting. At these times, it is a good idea to stand on your first two cards even though the total in points may seem very low. The accompanying basic strategy chart shows when to stand and when to take a hit. It is easy to follow and simple to memorize. The decision to stand or take a hit is made on the value of your hand and, once again, the dealer's up card, and is based on the probability of his busting. Although following basic strategy won't win every hand, it will improve your odds and take the guesswork out of some confusing situations.

SOFT HAND STRATEGY*										
The Dealer Is Showing:	2	3	4	5	6	7	8	9	10	**Ace**
You Have: Ace, 9	S	S	S	S	S	S	S	S	S	S,H
Ace, 8	S	S	S	S	S	S	S	S	S	S
Ace, 7	S	D	D	D	D	S	S	H	H	S
Ace, 6	H	D	D	D	D	S	H	H	H	H
Ace, 5	H	H	D	D	D	H	H	H	H	H
Ace, 4	H	H	D	D	D	H	H	H	H	H
Ace, 3	H	H	H	D	D	H	H	H	H	H
Ace, 2	H	H	H	D	D	H	H	H	H	H
S=Stand H=Hit D=Double Down										

*The charts reflect basic strategy for multiple-deck games. For single-deck games, a slightly different strategy prevails for doubling and splitting.

Basic strategy is effective because the dealer is bound by the rules of the game. He must take a hit on 16 and stand on 17. These rules are printed right on the table so that there can be no misunderstanding. Even if you are the only player at the table and stand with a total of 14 points, the dealer with what would be a winning hand of 16 points *must* take another card.

There is one exception to the rule: Some casinos require a dealer to take a hit on a hand with an ace and a 6 (called a "soft 17"). Because the ace can become a 1, it is to the casino's advantage for the dealer to be allowed to hit a soft 17.

Bells and Whistles

Now that you understand the basic game, let's look at a few rules in the casino version of blackjack that are probably different from the way you play at home.

Doubling Down When you have received two cards and think that they will win with the addition of one and *only* one more card, then double your bet. This "doubling down" bet should be made if your two-card total is 11, since drawing the highest possible card, a 10, will not push your total over 21 points. In some casinos you may double down on ten points, and some places will let you double down on any two-card hand.

To show the dealer that you want to double down, place your two cards touching each other faceup on the dealer's side of the betting box. Then place enough in the box to equal your original bet. Now, as at all other times, don't touch your chips once the bet is made.

DOUBLING DOWN										
The Dealer Is Showing:	**2**	**3**	**4**	**5**	**6**	**7**	**8**	**9**	**10**	**Ace**
Your Total Is: 11	D	D	D	D	D	D	D	D	D	H
10	D	D	D	D	D	D	D	D	H	H
9	H	D	D	D	D	H	H	H	H	H

H=Hit   D=Double Down

Splitting Any time you are dealt two cards of the same value, you may split the cards and start two separate hands. Even aces may be split, though when you play them, they will each be dealt only one additional card. If you should happen to get a blackjack after splitting aces, it will be treated as 21 points; that is, paid off at one to one and not three to two.

Any other pair is played exactly as you would if you were playing two consecutive hands, and all the rules will apply. Place the two cards *apart from each other* and above the betting box, so the dealer won't confuse this with doubling down. Then add a stack of chips equal to the original bet to cover the additional hand. Your two hands will be played out one at a time, cards dealt faceup.

You will be allowed to split a third card if it is the same as the first two, but not if it shows up as a later hit. Always split a pair of eights, since they total 16 points, a terrible point total. *Never* split two face cards or tens, since they total 20 and are probably a winning hand.

Some casinos will let you double down after splitting a hand, but if you're unsure, ask the dealer. Not all blackjack rules are posted, and they can vary from casino to casino, and even from table to table in the same casino.

SPLITTING STRATEGY

The Dealer Is Showing:	2	3	4	5	6	7	8	9	10	Ace
You Have: 2, 2	H	H	SP	SP	SP	SP	H	H	H	H
3, 3	H	H	SP	SP	SP	SP	H	H	H	H
4, 4	H	H	H	H	H	H	H	H	H	H
5, 5	D	D	D	D	D	D	D	D	H	H
6, 6	H	SP	SP	SP	SP	H	H	H	H	H
7, 7	SP	SP	SP	SP	SP	SP	H	H	H	H
8, 8	SP	SP	SP	SP	SP	SP	SP	SP	SP	SP
9, 9	SP	SP	SP	SP	SP	S	SP	SP	S	S
10, 10	S	S	S	S	S	S	S	S	S	S
Ace, Ace	SP	SP	SP	SP	SP	SP	SP	SP	SP	SP

S=Stand   H=Hit   SP=Split   D=Double Down

Insurance   When the dealer deals himself an ace as his second, faceup card, he will stop play and ask, "Insurance, anyone?" Don't be fooled. You're not insuring anything. All he's asking for is a side bet that he will have a natural. He must make the insurance bets before he can look at his cards, so he doesn't know if he has won or not when he asks for your insurance bets.

The insurance wager can be up to half the amount of your original bet. Place the chips in the large semicircle marked "insurance." As it says, it pays off two to one. If your original bet was $10 and you bet $5 that the dealer had a natural, you would be paid $10 if he actually did. Depending on your cards, you would probably lose your original $10 bet but break even on the hand. If the dealer does not have a ten-value card, you lose your $5 insurance bet, but your $10 bet still can win.

This sounds deceptively easy. Insurance is always a bad move for the basic-strategy player because the odds are against the dealer actually having a natural. You will lose this bet more often than you will win it, though the dealer may suggest it to you as a smart move. The dealer might also tell you to insure your own blackjack, though this should never be done. The odds are always against the insurance bet. When you insure your blackjack you can be paid off for it at one to one, as if it were 21 points, instead of the three to two that you would normally be paid for the blackjack. Even though you may occasionally tie with the dealer, you will more than make up for it with the three-to-two payoffs on the blackjacks you don't insure.

Avoiding Common Pitfalls

1. Always check the minimum bets allowed at your table before you sit down. Flipping a $5 chip into a $25-minimum game can be humiliating. If you make this mistake, simply excuse yourself and leave. It happens all the time.

2. Keep your bet in a neat stack, with the largest value chips on the bottom and the smallest on top. A mess of chips can be confusing should you want to double down, and your dealer will get huffy if he has to ask you to stack your chips.

3. Never touch the chips once the bet is down. Cheaters do this, and your dealer may assume you're cheating. It's too easy for a player to secretly up his bet once he's seen his cards or lower it if the cards are bad. Do not stack a double-down bet or split bets on top of the original bet. Place them beside the original bet and then keep your hands away.

4. Along the same lines, don't touch a hand if the cards are dealt faceup. Use the hand signals to tell the dealer that you stand or that you want a hit. Never move your cards below the level of the table, where the dealer can't see them. When you brush your cards for a hit, do so lightly so that the dealer won't think that you are trying to mark them by bending them.

5. Take your time and count your points correctly. The pace of the game in the casino can pick up to a speed that is difficult for a beginner. It's perfectly all right to take your time and recount after a hit. One hint: count aces as 1 first, then add 10 to your total. An ace and a 4 is equal to 5 or 15. Once you have this notion in your head, you won't make a mistake and refrain from hitting a soft hand. If you throw down an ace, a 10, and a 9 in disgust, for example, many dealers will simply pick up your cards and your bet, even though your 20 might have been a winning hand. If you are confused about your point total, do not be embarrassed to ask for help.

6. Know the denomination of the chips that you are betting. Stack them according to denomination, and read the face value every play until you know for sure which chips are which color. Otherwise you might think you are betting $5 when you are actually throwing out a $25 chip on every hand.

7. Be obvious with your hand signals to the dealer. The casinos are loud and busy, and the dealer may be distracted with a player. Don't leave any room for misinterpretation.

8. If cards fly off the table during the deal, pick them up slowly using two fingers. See number four, above.

9. Tip the dealer at your discretion if he or she has been friendly and helpful. One of the better ways to tip the dealer is to bet a chip for him on your next hand and say, "This one is for you." If you win, so does he. Never tip when a dealer has been rude or cost you money by being uncooperative. Then you should finish your hand and leave. Period.

Craps

Of all the games offered in casinos, craps is by far the fastest and, to many, the most exciting. It is a game in which large amounts of money can be won or lost in a short amount of time. The craps table is a circus of sound and movement. Yelling and screaming are allowed—even

encouraged—here, and the frenetic betting is bewildering to the uniniti-
ated. Don't be intimidated, however: The basic game of craps is easy to
understand. The confusion and insanity of craps have more to do with
the pace of the game and the amazing number of betting possibilities
than with the complexity of the game itself.

The Basic Game

Because it is so easy to become confused at a crowded and noisy craps
table, we highly recommend that beginning players take advantage of the
free lessons offered by most of the casinos. Once you understand the
game, you will be able to make the most favorable bets and ignore the rest.

In craps, one player at a time controls the dice, but all players will
eventually have an opportunity to roll or refuse the dice. Players take
turns in a clockwise rotation. If you don't want the dice, shake your head,
and the dealer will offer them to the next player.

All the players around the table are wagering either with or against the
shooter, so the numbers he throws will determine the amount won or
lost by every other player. The casino is covering all bets, and the players
are not allowed to bet among themselves. Four casino employees run the
craps table. The boxman in the middle is in charge of the game. His job
is to oversee the other dealers, monitor the play, and examine the dice if
they are thrown off the table.

There are two dealers, one placed on each side of the boxman. They
pay off the winners and collect the chips from the losers. Each dealer is in
charge of half of the table.

The fourth employee is the stickman, so called because of a flexible
stick he uses after each roll to retrieve the dice. His job, among other
things, is to supply dice to the shooter and to regulate the pace of the
game. When all bets are down, the stickman pushes several sets of dice
toward the shooter. The shooter selects two dice, and the stickman
removes the others from the table. From time to time, the stickman
checks the dice for signs of tampering.

The shooter then throws the dice hard enough to cause them to
bounce off the wall at the far end of the table. This bounce ensures that
each number on each die has an equal probability of coming up.

The Play　When it is your turn to throw the dice, pick out two and
return the other to the stickman. After making a bet (required), you may
throw the dice. You retain control of the dice until you throw a 7 ("seven
out") or relinquish the dice voluntarily.

Your first roll, called the come-out roll, is the most important. If you roll
a 7 or an 11 on your come-out roll, you are an immediate winner. In this
case, you collect your winnings and retain possession of the dice. If your
come-out roll is a 4, 5, 6, 8, 9, or 10, that number becomes "the point." A

marker is placed in the correspondingly numbered box on the layout to identify the point for all players at the table. In order to win the game, this number (the point) will have to be rolled again before you roll a 7.

Thus, if you roll a 5 on your first roll, the number five becomes your point. It doesn't matter how long it takes you to roll another 5, as long as you don't roll a 7 first. As soon as you roll a 7, you lose, and the dice are passed to another player.

Let's say 5 is your point, and your second roll is a 4, your third roll is a 9, and then you roll another 5. You win because you rolled a 5 again without rolling a 7. Because you have not yet rolled a 7, you retain possession of the dice, and after making a bet, you may initiate a new game.

Your next roll is, once again, a come-out roll. Just as 7 or 11 are immediate winners on a come-out roll, there are immediate losers, too. A roll of 2, 3, or 12 (all called "craps") will lose. You lose your chips, but you keep the dice because you have not yet rolled a 7.

If your first roll is 2, for example, it's craps, and you lose your bet. You place another bet and roll to come-out again. This time you roll a 5, so 5 becomes your point. Your second roll is a 4, your third is a 9, and then you roll a 7. The roll of 7 means that you lose and the dice will be passed to the next player.

This is the basic game of craps. The confounding blur of activity is nothing more than players placing various types of bets with or against the shooter, or betting that a certain number will or will not come up on the next roll of the dice.

ACTUAL ODDS CHART		
Number	Ways to Roll	Odds against Repeat
4	3	2–1
5	4	3–2
6	5	6–5
8	5	6–5
9	4	3–2
10	3	2–1

The Betting Of the dozens of bets that can be made at a craps table, only two or three should even be considered by a novice craps player. Keeping your bets simple makes it easier to understand what's going on, while at the same time minimizing the house advantage. Exotic, long-shot bets, offering payoffs as high as 30 to 1, are sucker bets and should be avoided.

The Line Bets: Pass and Don't Pass Pass and don't pass bets combine simplicity with one of the smallest house advantages of any casino game, about 1.4%. If you bet pass, you are betting that the first roll will be a 7 or 11 or a point number, and that the shooter will make the point again

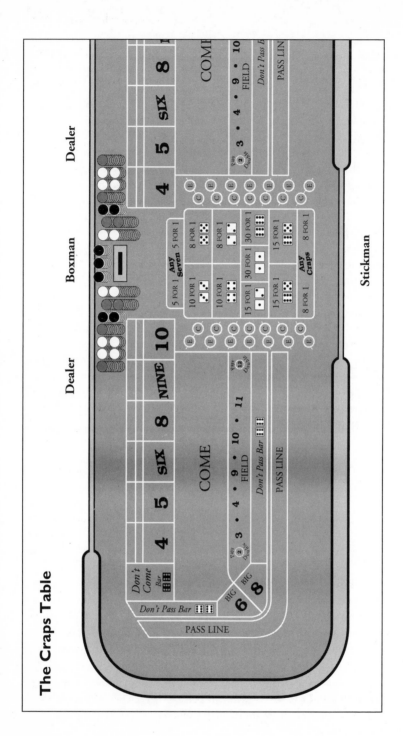

The Craps Table

before he rolls a 7. If you bet don't pass, you are betting that the first roll will be a 2, 3, or 12, or, if a point is established, that the shooter will seven out and throw a 7 before he rolls his point number again. The two and three are immediate losers, and the casino will collect the chips of anyone betting pass. A roll of 12, however, is considered a standoff where the shooter "craps out" but no chips change hands for the "don't" bettor. Almost 90% of casino craps players confine their betting to the pass and don't pass line.

Come and Don't Come   Come and don't-come bets are just like pass and don't-pass bets, except that they are placed *after* the point has been established on the come-out roll. Pass and don't-pass bets must be placed before the first roll of the dice, but come and don't-come bets may be placed before any roll of the dice *except* come-out rolls. On his come-out roll, let's say, the shooter rolls a nine. Nine becomes the shooter's point. If at this time you place your chips in the come box on the table, the next roll of the dice will determine your "come number." If the shooter throws a six, for example, your chips are placed in the box marked with the large six. The dealer will move your chips and will keep track of your bet. If the shooter rolls another six before he rolls a seven, your bet pays off. If the shooter sevens out before he rolls a six, then you lose. If the shooter makes his point (i.e., rolls another nine), your come bet is retained on the layout.

If you win a come bet, the dealer will place your chips from the numbered box back into the come space and set your winnings beside it. You may leave your chips there for the next roll or you may remove them entirely. If you fail to remove your winnings before the next roll, they may become a bet that you didn't want to make.

Don't come bets are the opposite of come bets. A 7 or 11 loses, and a 2 or 3 wins. The 12 is again a standoff. The don't come bettor puts his chips in the don't come space on the table and waits for the next roll to determine his number. His chips are placed *above* the numbered box to differentiate it from a come bet. If the shooter rolls his point number before he rolls your number, your don't come bet is retained on the layout. You are betting against the shooter; that is, that he will roll a seven first. When he rolls seven, you win. If he rolls your don't come number before he sevens out, you lose.

The come and don't come bets have a house advantage of about 1.4% and are among the better bets in craps once you understand them.

Odds Bets   When you bet the pass/don't pass, or the come/don't come area, you may place an odds bet *in addition* to your original bet.

Once it is established that the come-out roll is not a 7 or 11, or craps, the bettor may place a bet that will be paid off according to the actual odds of a particular number being thrown.

Note that the Actual Odds Chart shows the chances against a number made by two dice being thrown. For example, the odds of making a nine are three to two. If you place an odds bet (in addition to your original bet) on a come number of nine, your original come bet will pay off at even money, but your odds bet will pay off at three to two.

Because this would make a $7.50 payoff for a $5 bet, and the tables don't carry 50-cent chips, you are allowed to place a $6 bet as an odds bet. This is a very good bet to make, and betting the extra dollar is to your advantage.

To place an odds bet on a line bet, bet the pass line. When (and if) the point is established, put your additional bet behind the pass line and say, "Odds."

To place an odds bet on a come bet, wait for the dealer to move your chips to the come number box, then hand him more chips and say, "Odds." He will set these chips half on and half off the other pile so that he can see at a glance that it's an odds bet.

HOW NOT TO SHOOT CRAPS

On a recent visit to a downtown casino, one *Unofficial Guide* researcher pleaded with a Las Vegas friend to teach her how to play craps. Our Vegas friend not only outlined the basics, he also rattled off descriptions of all the various side bets and offered advice on when each was appropriate. By the time the lady was handed the dice, she was so apprehensive about remembering the rules that she forgot to pay attention to her throw. She hurled the dice with all her might right into a stack of chips in front of the boxman, scattering the house chips all over the table. The boxman and dealers sighed in annoyance but didn't complain as they put the table back in order. The other players were not pleased, however. And it only got worse when the flustered lady threw again, this time so worried about the boxman that she overthrew the table entirely, striking another player in the chest with the dice. Shortly after that, it was decided that she'd best stick with slot machines.

Craps Etiquette

When you arrive at a table, find an open space and put your money down in front of you. When the dealer sees it, he will pick it up and hand it to the boxman. The boxman will count out the correct chips and give them to the dealer, who will pass them to you.

A craps table holds from 12 to 20 players and can get very crowded. Keep your place at the table. Your chips are in front of you, and it is your responsibility to watch them.

After you place your bets, your hands must come off the table. It is very bad form to leave your hands on the table when the dice are rolling.

Stick to the good bets listed here, and don't be tempted by bets that you don't understand. The box in the middle of the layout, for example, offers a number of sucker bets.

Baccarat

Originally an Italian card game, baccarat (bah-kah-rah) is the French pronunciation of the Italian word for zero. The name refers to the value of all the face cards in the game: zero.

Because baccarat involves no player decisions, it is an easy game to play, but a very difficult game to understand. Each player must decide to make a bet on either the bank or the player. That's it. There are no more decisions until the next hand is dealt. The rules of playing out the hands are ridiculously intricate, but beginning players need not concern themselves with them, because all plays are predetermined by the rules, and the dealer will tell you exactly what happened.

All cards, ace through 9, are worth their spots (the 3 of clubs is worth three points). The 10, jack, queen, and king are worth zero. The easiest way to count points is to add all points in the hand, then take only the number in the ones column.

If you have been dealt a 6 and a 5, then your total is 11, and taking only the ones column, your hand is worth 1 point. If you hold a 10 and a king, your hand is worth zero. If you have an 8 and a 7, your point total is 15, and taking the ones column, your hand is worth 5. It doesn't get any simpler than this.

In baccarat, regardless of the number of bettors at the table, only two hands are dealt: One to the player and one to the bank. The object of the game is to be dealt or draw a hand worth nine points. If the first two cards dealt equal nine points (a 5 and a 4, for example), then you have a natural and an automatic winner. Two cards worth eight are the second best hand and will also be called a natural. If the other hand is not equal to or higher than eight, this hand wins automatically. Ties are standoffs, and neither bank nor player wins.

If the hands equal any total except nine or eight, the rules are consulted. These rules are printed and available at the baccarat table. The hands will be played out by the dealer whether you understand the rules or not.

The rules for the player's hand are simple. If a natural is not dealt to either hand, and if the player holds one, two, three, four, five, or ten (zero), he will always draw a card. He will stand on a total of six or seven. A total of eight or nine, of course, will be a natural.

The bank hand is more complicated and is partially determined by the third card drawn by the player's hand. Though the rules don't say so, the bank will always draw on zero, one, or two. When the hand is worth three or more, it is subject to the printed rules.

If you study a few hands, the method of play will be clear:

First Hand   The player's hand is worth three, and the bank's is worth four. The player always goes first. Looking at the rules for the player, we see that a hand worth three points draws a card. This time he draws a 9, for a new total of 12 points, which has a value of two. The bank, having four points, must stand when a player draws a 9. The bank wins four to two.

Second Hand The player's hand is worth six points, and the bank has two queens, for a total of zero. The player must stand with six points, while the bank must draw with zero. The bank gets another card, a 4. Player wins, six to four.

BACCARAT RULES

Player

When First Two Cards Total:	
1, 2, 3, 4, 5, or 10	*Draws a Card*
6 or 7	*Stands*
8 or 9	*A Natural—Stands*

Banker

Having:	Draws When Player's Third Card Is:	Does Not Draw When Player's Third Card Is:
3	1, 2, 3, 4, 5, 6, 7, 9, 10	8
4	2, 3, 4, 5, 6, 7	1, 8, 9, 10
5	4, 5, 6, 7,	1, 2, 3, 8, 9, 10
6	6, 7	1, 2, 3, 4, 5, 8, 9, 10
7	*Stands*	*Stands*
8 or 9	*Stands*	*Stands*

The Atmosphere

The casinos try to attract players by making baccarat seem continental and sophisticated. The section is roped off from the main casino, and the dealers are often dressed in tuxedos instead of the usual dealer's uniforms. Don't be put off by glamorous airs; everyone is welcome to play.

Because the house wants baccarat to be appealing to what they consider to be their upper-crust clientele, the table minimums are usually very high in baccarat—usually $20 to $2,000. This means that the minimum bet is $20, and the maximum bet is $2,000. Most of the players, however, will play with $25 and $100 chips.

Even the shuffle and deal of the deck is designed to perpetuate the feeling of the exotic. Elaborately cut and mixed by all three dealers, the cards are cut by one player and marked with the plastic card stop. The dealer will then separate the cards at the stop, turn the top card over, and discard, or burn, the number of cards equal to the face value of the upturned card. The cards are then placed in a large holder called the shoe.

The Play If the game has just begun, the shoe will be passed to the player in seat number one, who is then called the bank. Thereafter, whenever the bank hand loses, the shoe is passed counterclockwise to the

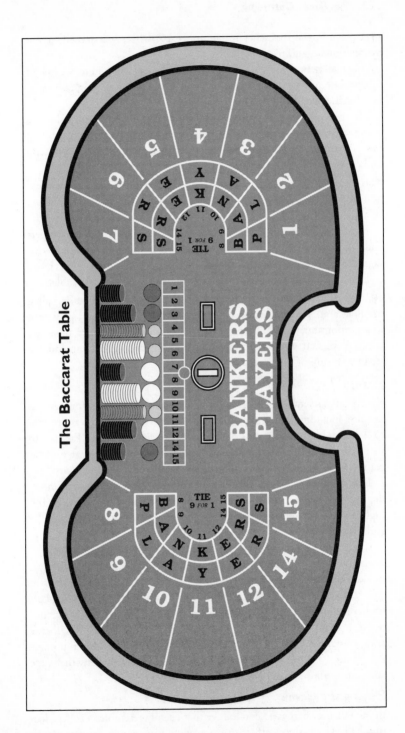

The Baccarat Table

next player, until it reaches seat number 15, where it is passed to seat number one again.

When all bets are down, one of the three dealers will nod to the holder of the shoe, who will then deal out four cards in alternating fashion—two for the player and two for the bank.

The player's hand is passed (still facedown) to the bettor who has wagered the most money on the player's hand. He looks at the cards and passes them back to the dealer. The dealer then turns both hands faceup and plays out the game according to the rules.

The Betting   In baccarat, you must back either the player or the bank. You do this by putting your chips in the box in front of you marked "player" or "bank." Once the bets are down, the deal will begin.

The house advantage on baccarat is quite low: 1.36% on player wagers and 1.17% on bank bets. Because the bank bet has such an obvious advantage, the house extracts a commission when you win a bank bet. This is not collected with each hand, but must be paid before you leave the table.

Minibaccarat   Some casinos have installed smaller baccarat tables, called minibaccarat. The dealers dress in the standard uniform and play with lower minimum bets. The games move more quickly, since there are fewer players. If you feel intimidated by baccarat, we recommend the smaller version of the game.

Keno

Keno is an ancient Chinese game. It was used to raise money for national defense, including, some say, building the Great Wall. Keno was brought to America by the thousands of workers who came from the Far East to work on the railroads during the 1800s. It is one of the most popular games in the Nevada casinos, though it is outlawed in Atlantic City.

This game has a house advantage of between 20% and 35% or more, depending on the casino—higher than any other game in Las Vegas. Too high, in fact, for serious gamblers. So if you're down to your last dollar and you have to bet to save the ranch, don't go to the keno lounge.

While keno is similar to bingo, the betting options are reminiscent of exacta horse-race betting. It is like bingo in that a ticket, called a blank, is marked off and numbers are randomly selected to determine a winner. And it is similar to exacta betting because any number of fascinating betting combinations can be played in each game. The biggest difference between keno and bingo and exactas is that in the other two, there's always a winner. In keno, hours can go by before anyone wins a substantial amount. The main excitement in keno lies in the possibility that large amounts of money can be won on a small bet.

Playing the Game

In each casino there is a keno lounge that usually resembles a college lecture hall. The casino staff sit in front while players relax in chairs with writing tables built into the arms. It is not necessary to sit in the keno lounge to play. In fact, one of the best things about keno is that it can be played almost anywhere in the casino, including the bars and restaurants. As in bingo, it is acceptable to strike up a conversation with your neighbor during a game, and because the winning numbers are posted all over the place, keno also offers the opportunity to gamble while absent from the casino floor.

Keno is one of the easiest games to understand. The keno blank can be picked up almost anywhere in any Nevada casino. On the blank are two large boxes containing 80 numbers: the top box with 1 to 40, and the bottom box with 41 to 80. Simply use one of the crayons provided with the blanks to mark between 1 and 15 numbers on the blank, decide how much you want to bet, and turn the blank in to a keno writer. The keno writer records your wager, keeping your original, and gives you a duplicate, which *you* are responsible for checking. The keno writer can be found at the front of the keno lounge. The keno runner is even easier to spot: she is usually a woman in a short skirt with a hand full of blanks and crayons. She will place your bets, cash in your blanks, and bring you your winnings. Of course, you are expected to tip her for this service.

The drawing of the winning numbers takes place in the keno lounge. When the keno caller has determined that the bets are in for the current round, he will close the betting just like the steward does at the racetrack. Then the caller uses a machine similar to those employed by state lotteries: a blower with numbered Ping-Pong balls. Ten balls are blown into each of two tubes. These 20 balls bear the numbers that will be called for the current round. The numbers, as called out, are posted on electronic keno boards around the casino. If any of the lighted numbers are numbers that you marked on your card, you "caught" those numbers. Catching four or more numbers will usually win something, depending on how many numbers you marked on your card. The payoffs are complicated, but the more numbers you guess correctly and the more money you bet, the greater your jackpot. Suffice it to say, however, that you are not paid at anything even approaching true odds. If, by some amazing quirk of fate, you win, you must claim your winnings before the next round starts or forfeit.

The Odds A "straight" or basic ticket is one where the player simply selects and marks a minimum of 1 number to a maximum of 8 to 15 numbers, depending on the casino. The ways to combine keno bets are endless and understandable only to astrophysicists. Any number can be played with any other number, making "combination" tickets. Groups of numbers can be combined with other groups of numbers, making "way" tickets. Individual numbers can be combined with groups of numbers, making "king" tickets. Then there is the "house" ticket, called different things at each casino, which offers a shot at the big jackpot for a smaller investment, though the odds won't be any better.

All of these options and the amounts that you are allowed to bet (usually from 70 cents up per ticket) will be listed in the keno brochures, which are almost as ubiquitous as the blanks. The payoffs will be listed for each type of bet and for the amount wagered. Keno runners and keno lounge personnel will show you how to mark your ticket if you are confused, but they cannot mark it for you. The only thing you really need to know about keno, however, is that the house has an unbeatable advantage.

The best strategy for winning at keno is to avoid it. If you want to play for fun (and that is the only rational reason to play), then understand that one bet is about as bad as another. Filling out a complicated combination ticket won't increase your chances of winning. If by some miracle you do win, accept the congratulations and the winnings, and then run, do not walk, to the nearest exit.

Roulette

A quiet game where winners merely smile over a big win and losers suffer in silence, roulette is very easy to understand. The dealer spins the wheel, drops the ball, and waits for it to fall into one of the numbered slots on the wheel. The numbers run from zero to 36, with a double zero thrown in for good measure. You may bet on each individual number, on combinations of numbers, on all black numbers, all red numbers, and many more. All possible bets are laid out on the table.

Special chips are used for roulette, with each bettor at the table playing a different color. To buy in, convert cash or the casino's house chips to roulette chips. When you are ready to cash out, the dealer will convert your special roulette chips back to house chips. If you want cash, you must then take your house chips to a casino cashier.

To place a bet, put your chips inside a numbered square or choose one of the squares off to the side. A chip placed in "1st 12," for example, will pay off if the ball drops into any number from 1 to 12. The box marked "odd" is not for eccentrics—it pays when the ball drops into an odd-numbered slot.

Roulette is fun to play, but expect to pay! The house advantage on most bets is a whopping 5.26%, and on some wagers it can be as high as 7%.

ROULETTE BET AND PAYOFF CHART

Bet	Payoff	Bet	Payoff
Single number	35 to 1	12 numbers (column)	2 to 1
Two numbers	17 to 1	1st 12, 2nd 12, 3rd 12	2 to 1
Three numbers	11 to 1	1–18 or 19–36	1 to 1
Four numbers	8 to 1	Odd or Even	1 to 1
Five numbers	6 to 1	Red or Black	1 to 1
Six numbers	5 to 1		

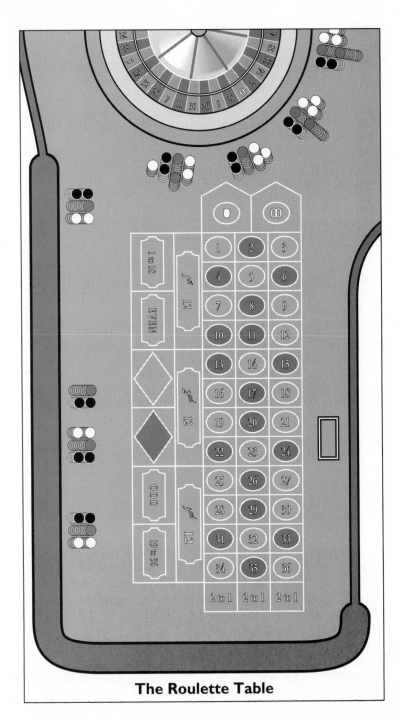

The Roulette Table

Part Four

Dining and Restaurants

Dining in Las Vegas

In little more than a decade, Las Vegas has become a dining destination of great distinction. Few cities can compete with the number of celebrated chefs who have transformed Las Vegas into an extraordinary dining mecca. And there is no end in sight.

MGM Grand is abloom with new restaurants: Michael Mina's **SeaBlue,** a splendid seafood concept; New York restaurateur Steve Hanson's more casual version of his New York award winner, **Fiamma Trattoria;** Tom Colicchio (Craftsteak) with his **'Wichcraft,** the New York sandwich shop like no other; **Diego Mexican** restaurant that showcases rare tequilas along with zesty cuisine; **Wolfgang Puck Bar & Grill,** a stunner, with California cuisine and California bungalow style; and **Shibuya,** a Japanese eatery named after the hip Tokyo district. The Mirage has added **Cravings,** an all-you-can-eat "dining experience" (a.k.a. buffet), designed by Adam Tihany. It is a remarkable change from the norm with almost all of the cooking made-to-order as diners watch. Each station has its own cook and individual style.

Soon to open is a branch of New York's **Carnegie Deli,** the official hangout of the guys and gals of Old Broadway who hunger for "real" corned beef and pastrami. On the way is Bobby Flay, who will open a **Mesa Grill** at Caesars Palace. It should be ready by the time you read this. Caesars Palace is movin' on up. The Forum Shops expansion includes a Florida favorite, **Joe's Seafood and Steakhouse** (expect humongous stone crab, in season).

California's **Bradley Ogden,** whose namesake restaurant at Caesars Palace is barely one year old, was already a hot ticket when it was named named "Best New Restaurant" at the 2004 James Beard Foundation Awards. It is the first time ever that a Las Vegas restaurant has been recognized in this distinguished category.

Isla at Treasure Island (T. I.) is Richard Sandoval's first Las Vegas venture. Sandoval, who owns Maya and other modern Mexican restaurants in New York, has created a hip, hot cafe, bar, and restaurant with Isla. Now based in California, Sandoval promises to be a regular presence at Isla. Napa's premier chef Thomas Keller (French Laundry, Bouchon) has opened a **Bouchon** bistro in the new Venizia tower at the Venetian; housemade charcuterie and bistro specialties in gorgeous surroundings with super patio dining.

And as new restaurants continue to bloom, older favorites such as **Emeril's Fish House** at MGM Grand are being refurbished and refreshed. Steve Wynn's **Wynn Las Vegas** opening April 28, 2005, has inked Daniel Boulud for a star turn, yet the always-innovative Wynn will continue to seek out promising young chefs who have star quality.

Just when it appears that the cavalcade of new restaurants has slowed down, the music of a new parade wafts over the mountains.

Subsidized Dining and the Free-Market Economy

There are two kinds of restaurants in Las Vegas: those that are an integral part of a hotel-casino operation, and those that must make it entirely on the merits of their food. Celebrity-run restaurants and gourmet rooms in the hotels are usually associated with the casinos. Their mission is to pamper customers who are giving the house a lot of gambling action. At any given time, many of the folks in a hotel restaurant are dining as guests of the casino. If you are a paying customer in the same restaurant, the astronomical prices you are charged help subsidize the feeding of all these comped guests. Every time you buy a meal in one of these places, you are helping to pay the tab of the strangers sitting at the next table.

This is not to say that the hotel restaurants do not serve excellent food or offer the best of service. On the contrary, some of the best chefs in the country cook for hotel-casino gourmet rooms. The bottom line, however, if you are a paying guest, is that you are taking up space intended for high rollers, and the house is going to charge you a lot of rent.

What has changed in the hotel-restaurant scene is the arrival of the celebrity chefs. They have created a demand for fine dining totally independent of their restaurant's relationship with the host hotel and casino. Expressed differently, before the advent of the big-name chefs, hotel restaurants catered primarily to guests of the hotel and patrons of the casino. These hotel restaurants, though excellent, provided convenience first and operated within the context of the casino's relationship with its customers. Generally speaking, and with a few exceptions, nobody went out of their way simply to dine in these places. Today, celebrity-run restaurants have immense drawing power, and patrons will haul themselves all the way across town just to have dinner in one of them. And although they still cater to high rollers and hotel guests, they function much more like an independent restaurant than did the hotel gourmet rooms of old.

Restaurants independent of casinos work at a considerable disadvantage. First, they do not have a captive audience of gamblers or convention-goers. Second, their operation is not subsidized by gaming, and third, they are not located where you will just stumble across them. Finally, they not only compete with the casino gourmet rooms, but also go head-to-head with the numerous buffets and bulk-loading meal-deals that casinos offer as loss leaders to attract the less affluent gambler.

Successful proprietary restaurants in Las Vegas must offer something very distinct, very different, and very good at a competitive price, and must somehow communicate to you that they are offering it. Furthermore, their offer must be compelling enough to induce you to travel to their location, forsaking the convenience of dining in your hotel. Not easy.

All of this works to the consumer's advantage, of course. High rollers get comped in the gourmet rooms. Folks of more modest means can select from among the amazing steak, lobster, and prime-rib deals offered by the casinos, or enjoy exceptional food at bargain prices at independent restaurants. People with hardly any money at all can gorge themselves on loss-leader buffets.

In many ways, Las Vegas restaurants are the culinary version of free-market economy. The casinos siphon off the customers who are willing to pay big bucks for food and feed them for free. This alters the target market for the independents and serves to keep a lid on their prices. Independents providing exceptional quality for such reasonable charges ensure in turn that buffets and meal-deals stay cheap. Ah, America, what a country!

So Many Restaurants, So Little Time

Dining options in Las Vegas, as noted above, have been shaped by the marketing strategies of the casinos. Before a gambler can wager any money, the casino has to get him through the front door. If what it takes are $3 steaks, buffets, and $1 shrimp cocktails, that's what the casino does. For those more attracted to eating than to gambling, this is a great boon to mankind.

Although there are hundreds of restaurants in Las Vegas, you will be able to sample only a handful during your stay. But which ones? Our objective in this section is to point you to specific restaurants that meet your requirements in terms of quality, price, location, and environment. No beating around the bush.

Buffets

Buffets, used by the casinos to lure customers, have become a Las Vegas institution. Like everything else, they come and go, but on average there are around 40 to choose from. The majority of casinos operate their buffets at close to cost or at a slight loss. A few casinos, mostly those with a more captive clientele (like the Las Vegas Hilton, the Mirage, and Caesars Palace), and the new breed of upscale spreads (Bellagio, Paris, Aladdin) probably make money on their buffets. **Café Lago,** the 24-hour "resort café" located in Caesars Palace ("coffee shop" is no longer hip), also serves up a buffet.

Cravings, the brilliant, new buffet concept at the Mirage, was designed by Adam Tihany. He counts among his credits Charlie Palmers' Aureole at Mandalay Bay, with its eight-story wine tower. Cravings is in a class of its own, with marble counters, graphics that change with the seasons, and stations that are self-contained "mini-restaurants," with chefs that cook food to order. Prices are midrange.

Almost all of the buffets serve breakfast, lunch, and dinner, changing their menus to some extent every day. Prices for breakfast range from less than $5 to $12. Lunch goes for $7 to $15, with dinner ranging between $8 and $32. Because most buffets operate as an extension of sales and marketing, there is not necessarily any relationship between price and quality.

BUFFET SPEAK	
Action Format	Food cooked to order in full view of the patrons
Gluttony	A Las Vegas buffet tradition that carries no moral stigma
Groaning Board	Synonym for a buffet; a table so full that it groans
Island	Individual serving area for a particular cuisine or specialty (salad island, dessert island, Mexican island, etc.)
Shovelizer	Diner who prefers quantity over quality
Fork Lift	A device used to remove shovelizers
Sneeze Guards	The glass/plastic barriers between you and the food

At breakfast, relatively speaking, there is not much difference between one buffet and the next (exceptions are the standout breakfast buffets at the **Orleans, Paris, Bellagio, The Mirage,** and the **Palms**). If your hotel has a breakfast buffet, it is probably not worth the effort to go somewhere else. When it comes to lunch and dinner, however, some buffets do a significantly better job than others.

If you are looking for upscale gourmet-quality food and a large variety to choose from, head straight for our top four buffets. If you're hankering for well-seasoned meats and vegetables, ethnic variety, and culinary activity, the other six will suffice nicely.

	LAS VEGAS'S TEN BEST BUFFETS		
Rank	Buffet	Quality Rating	Last Year's Ranking
1	Aladdin Spice Market Buffet	99	1
2	Bellagio Buffet	98	2
3	Paris Le Village Buffet	97	3
4	Mirage Cravings Buffet	95	not ranked
5	Rio Carnival World Buffet	93	7
6	Green Valley Ranch Feast	92	6
7	Texas Station Feast	90	5
8	Palms Fantasy Market	89	4
9	Orleans French Market Buffet	88	9
10	Sam's Town Firelight Buffet	86	8

Our top choice of Las Vegas buffets is the Aladdin Spice Market Buffet. It blends quality, variety, and a surprisingly attractive and cozy setting. There are Italian, Mexican, American, Middle Eastern (grape leaves, hummus, couscous, and carved lamb), and seafood (hot king crab is the specialty) serving stations, plus salads, desserts, and breads. Everything is fresh, tasty, and well stocked. Best of all, the Aladdin's buffet actually rates as a bargain compared to the other gourmet spreads at the megaresorts next door (Paris) and across the street (Bellagio).

The newest buffet in Las Vegas is the remodeled **Cravings Buffet at the Mirage.** The room sets a new standard in buffet aesthetics and crowd control (the stations are widely dispersed), while the food is gourmet quality and the prices (so far) seem to have been determined with value in mind. Innovative touches include dim sum for breakfast, a bagels-and-lox station, fried plantains, and an emphasis on seafood at lunch and dinner. You can avoid the lines at the cashier by sitting, eating, and paying at the 14-seat bar at the back.

Texas Station's Feast around the World Buffet is the best of the "bargain superbuffets." The room is spacious and efficient, the choices are manifold, and the prices are among the lowest in town. In addition to the Aladdin and Texas Station, **Paris, Palms, Rio, Fiesta, Gold Coast, Sunset Station, Green Valley Ranch, Main Street Station, Fiesta Rancho, Fiesta Henderson, Harrah's, Paris, Orleans, Cannery, Mirage,** and **Bellagio** all have the new-style "superbuffets." The **Rio** started the craze in 1993 with its huge room, action cooking, and separate serving islands for a vast variety of ethnic choices: American, Italian, Chinese, Mexican, and Mongolian barbecue, along with sushi, fish and chips, pizza, burgers, salads, and desserts; the Rio completely remodeled and upgraded **The Carnival World** in 2004. Aladdin and the Palms include excellent Middle Eastern stations.

The **Fiesta Rancho Festival** buffet is not as sprawling and various as the Rio's, but it has a monster rotisserie for barbecuing every kind of flesh known to man, specialty Cajun and Hawaiian selections, and Las Vegas's first and only coffee bar, serving espresso, cappuccino, and latte. **Texas Station** introduced a chili bar with nine selections and cooked-to-order fajitas; it also has good barbecue, Chinese, Italian, and lots of pizza. **Paris** has a made-to-order crepe station, and the Rio has an Oriental soup station.

Bellagio is the most expensive superbuffet—and is worth every penny. The quality, quantity, and variety of food is unsurpassed in Las Vegas history. Seafood galore, bread warm from the oven, creative salads, gourmet entrées, perfect vegetables—this joint has it all. Even at $13 for breakfast, $16 for lunch, and $25 for dinner ($33 Friday and Saturday), the Bellagio buffet barely breaks even. For the money, we like lunch here better than dinner.

Main Street Station is the only superbuffet downtown, served in one of the most aesthetically pleasing buffet rooms in town. Its cuisine has a distinct Hawaiian emphasis, which is where most of its patrons come from.

Harrah's buffet gets an A for effort, a B for quality, and a C for value. **Mandalay Bay's** buffet is expensive and odd; it's small, congested, and slow—there's something off about it. But **Treasure Island, Boulder, Green Valley Ranch, Sunset Stations, MGM Grand,** and **Luxor** are tried-and-true; you won't go wrong at any of these.

The buffet at **Paris** is an interesting set-up for Las Vegas buffets. The different buffet stations represent different regions of France, and the dining room has several intimate dining nooks and a view as well. Best of all, there's virtually no waiting. You check in with the host or hostess, they tell you when a table will be available, take your name, and you are free to explore until the designated time. When you return, a table is actually ready.

The **Palms** buffet is a meat-eaters paradise (brisket, corned beef and pastrami, pork, rotisserie chicken, turkey, and several kinds of ribs) and has a Mongolian grill, a good Middle Eastern section, and even some Jewish food (knishes and kugel). As a footnote, Bellagio, Main Street Station, Paris, Aladdin, **Sam's Town,** the Flamingo, Caesars Palace, the Mirage, Fiesta Henderson, the Golden Nugget, Sunset Station, the MGM Grand, and T. I. provide the most attractive settings for their buffets. The buffets at the Rio, Fiesta Rancho, Palms, Arizona Charlie's Decatur, and Texas, Palace, Sunset, and Boulder Stations are the favorites of Las Vegas locals. (Get the leftovers at no extra charge during lunch on Tuesdays.)

Seafood Buffets

Several casinos feature seafood buffets on Friday and sometimes on other days. The best of the seafood buffets is the **Rio's Village Seafood Buffet** (daily). The **Orleans'** seafood night is Monday, and the **Fremont's** and **Main Street Station's Seafood Fantasies** is on Sunday, Tuesday, and Friday.

The **Rio's** seafood buffet is the most expensive buffet, at $35, but the quality and variety of this piscatory repast are unbelievable, even for Las Vegas. Check it out: small lobster tails (dinner), peel-and-eat shrimp, Dungeness crab legs, Manila steamers, and oysters on the half-shell; seafood salads, chowders, and Mongolian grill; plus Italian, Mexican, and Chinese dishes, along with fried, grilled, broiled, breaded, blackened, beer-battered, and barbecued preparations. And if you have even a millimeter of stomach space left after the main courses, the dessert selection is outstanding.

The Fremont's and Main Street Station's seafood buffets are perennial favorites, strong in quality and popularity. Other worthwhile ocean spreads include those at the **Cannery** (Thursday), **Rampart** (Thursday), **Golden Nugget** (Friday), and **Suncoast** (Friday). The **Fremont's** Sunday, Tuesday, and Friday Seafood Fantasy isn't quite as extensive or expensive as the **Fiesta's,** but its quality and popularity are almost as strong.

Buffet Line Strategy

Popular buffets develop long lines. The best way to avoid the crowds is to go Sunday through Thursday and get in line before 6 p.m. or after 9 p.m. If you go to a buffet on a weekend, arrive extra early or extra late. If a large trade show or convention is in town, you will be better off any day hitting the buffets of casinos that do not do a big convention business. Good choices among the highly ranked buffets include **Texas Station,** the two **Fiestas, Main Street Station, Boulder Station, Gold Coast, Orleans, Suncoast, Silverton,** and **the Fremont.**

Some restaurants now use pagers to let diners know when their table is available. This gives you a bit more freedom to roam around while you wait, but many pagers have a fairly small range.

Champagne Brunches

Upscale, expensive Sunday champagne brunches with reserved tables, imported champagne, sushi, and seafood are making an impact on the local brunch scene. Although there are a plethora of value-priced champagne brunches, the big-ticket feasts attract diners who are happy to pay a higher tab for fancy food and service at a place that takes reservations so they can avoid a wait. In general, the higher the price of the brunch, the better the champagne served. **Bally's, Circus Circus,** and the **MGM** serve decent French champagne; California sparkling wine is the norm at the others. Reservations are accepted at all of the following:

- **Broiler Brunch,** Boulder Station (702) 432-7777
  Brunch at The Broiler restaurant at Boulder Station has been a sleeper for years. Here, you order your entree (eggs Benedict, crab cakes, shrimp, chicken, lamb) off the menu, which a server brings to the table, then help yourself to buffet offerings, such as salads, cold crab legs, ham, and prime rib, and made-to-order omelets and potato pancakes. $19.95 adults, $9.99 children ages 3 to 12. Available 10 a.m.–3 p.m.

- **Commanders Palace Jazz Brunch,** Desert Passage, Aladdin (702) 892-8272
  Toe-tapping jazz and a bit of New Orleans. Food selections ($35) are what you would expect from the Big Easy: not too many surprises, but always delicious. Specialties include eggs Sardou, pecan-crusted catfish, and grits with goat cheese served in a small copper pot (yum). Gracious service and heady drinks make this a popular brunch spot.

- **Gospel Brunch,** House of Blues, Mandalay Bay (702) 632-7777
  "Praise the Lord and pass the biscuits!" This is the most raucous and joyous Sunday brunch in town. A five-member group belts out the gospel tunes, and the food is soulful as well: fried chicken, skillet cornbread, jambalaya, turnip greens, made-to-order omelets, ham and prime rib, bagels and lox, smoked salmon, and banana-bread pudding. Purchase tickets at The House of Blues box office, adults, $41.50; children ages 7–11, $22.50. Two seatings, at 10 a.m. and 1 p.m.

- **The Steak House,** Circus Circus (702) 734-0410
  Elaborate ice carvings and decorative food displays are a tribute to the chef's cruise-line background. Featured are many breakfast items, steak and seafood, entrées, and salads. Adults, $25 (all-inclusive); children ages 6–12, $13. Three seatings: 9:30 a.m., 11:30 a.m., and 1:30 p.m.

- **Sterling Brunch,** Bally's Steakhouse (702) 739-4111
  The Sterling Brunch was the first of its kind. At $58 per person, plus tax (children under age 12, $30 plus tax), it's also the most costly, but there's no shortage of diners who love it, even at more than double its original price. The lavish selection of foods includes a host of breakfast items, freshly made sushi, real lobster salad, raw and cooked seafood, caviar, and French champagne. Pheasant and rack of lamb appear regularly. The dessert selection is awesome. Entrée selections change weekly. Available 9:30 a.m.–2:30 p.m.; reservations are required.

Bally's Sterling Brunch, though quite expensive, is by far the best brunch in town and, in our opinion, a fair value for the money if you are a big eater. Other good brunches include **Bellagio, Mirage, Aladdin, Main Street Station,** and **Gold Coast** (the best bargain brunch at $8).

Meal-Deals

In addition to buffets, many casinos offer special dining deals. These include New York strip, T-bone, and porterhouse steaks, prime rib, lobster, crab legs, shrimp cocktails, and various combinations of the foregoing, all available at giveaway prices. There are also breakfast specials.

While the meal-deals generally deliver what they promise in the way of an entrée, many of the extras that contribute to a quality dining experience are missing. With a couple of notable exceptions, the specials are served in big, bustling restaurants with the atmosphere of a high-school cafeteria.

Eating at closely packed formica tables under lighting bright enough for brain surgery, it is difficult to pretend that you are engaged in fine dining.

Our biggest complaint, however, concerns the lack of attention paid to the meal as a whole. We have had nice pieces of meat served with tired, droopy salads, stale bread, mealy microwaved potatoes, and unseasoned canned vegetables. How can you get excited about your prime rib when it is surrounded by the ruins of Pompeii?

Deke Castleman, co-author of this book and writer for the *Las Vegas Advisor,* doesn't believe that discount dining is about food at all. He writes:

Of course you're entitled to your opinion, and I'll fight to the death for your right to express it. But 'quality dining experience' is not really what Las Vegas visitors, IMHO ('in my humble opinion,' in Netspeak), are looking for when they pursue a $3 steak, a $5 prime rib, or a $10 lobster. To me what they're after is twofold: A very cheap steak, prime rib, or lobster, and damn the salad, vegetable, and Formica; and to take home a cool story about all the rock-bottom prices they paid for food.

Finally, it's hard to take advantage of many of the specials. They are offered only in the middle of the night, or alternatively you must stand in line for an hour waiting for a table, or eat your evening meal at 3:30 in the afternoon. In restaurants all over town, in and out of the casinos, there is plenty of good food served in pleasant surroundings at extremely reasonable prices. In our opinion, saving $5 on a meal is not worth all the hassle.

Because Las Vegas meal-deals often come and go, it is impossible to cover them adequately in a book that is revised annually. If you want to stay abreast of special dinner offerings, your best bet is to subscribe to the *Las Vegas Advisor,* a monthly newsletter that provides independent, critical evaluations of meal-deals, buffets, brunches, and drink specials. The *Las Vegas Advisor* can be purchased by calling (800) 244-2224. If you are already in town and want to pick up the latest edition, single copies are available at the **Gamblers Book Club** store at 630 South 11th Street, (702) 382-7555.

Steak Though specials constantly change, there are a few that have weathered the test of time. Our favorite is the 16-ounce porterhouse steak dinner at the **Redwood Bar & Grill** in the California, (702) 385-1222. A complete dinner, including relish plate, soup or salad, and steak with excellent accompanying potatoes and vegetables, can be had for about $15, excluding drinks, taxes, and tips. What's more, it is served in one of the most attractive dining rooms in Las Vegas. The porterhouse special, incidentally, does not appear on the menu. You must ask for it.

There's a great 16-ounce T-bone served in the coffee shop of the **Gold Coast** 24 hours a day for $11, (702) 367-7111. This big slab is accompanied by soup or salad, potatoes, onion rings, baked beans, garlic bread, and a glass of draft beer. For $8 this would be a deal *without* the steak.

Little Ellis Island, attached to the Super 8 motel on Koval Lane near East Flamingo Road, serves an excellent $5 steak dinner complete with crunchy rolls, salad, baked potato, and garlic bread. It's available 24 hours, but it's not on the menu, so you have to ask for it. **The Hard Rock Hotel** has a steak-and-shrimp special served 24 hours in the coffee shop for $10, (702) 693-5000.

Prime Rib The most readily accessible and one of the best prime-rib specials in a town full of prime-rib specials is available at the San Remo's **Ristorante del Flori** coffee shop for $6, (702) 739-9000. They offer a generous piece of meat, accompanied by good sides. The special is available 24 hours a day, and the restaurant is rarely crowded. Downtown, at the **California,** you can get a good cut of meat between 4 p.m. and 10 p.m. for $7; it comes with an all-you-can eat salad bar and cherries jubilee for dessert.

For $11–$17 more you can dine in comparative luxury with much less effort at **Sir Galahad's** at the Excalibur, (702) 597-7777. The prime rib is excellent and served tableside in huge slabs, accompanied by fresh salad/soup and excellent side dishes, including Yorkshire pudding. There is no hassle about getting a table if you arrive by 6:30 p.m.

Another good prime-rib and crab-leg special, when available, is at **Bally's** for $14, (702) 739-4111. **Jerry's Nugget** on Las Vegas Boulevard in North Las Vegas has a trio of prime-rib meal deals for $9, $15, and $30 (for the biggest piece of beef you've ever seen), (702) 399-3000.

Lobster and Crab Legs Lobster-and-steak (surf-and-turf) combos and crab-leg deals appear regularly on casino marquees around Las Vegas. **Pasta Pirate** at the California serves the best all-around shellfish specials, (702) 385-1222. Unfortunately, they are on-again, off-again. When on, they alternately feature a steak and lobster combo, a lobster dinner, or a king crab dinner, all for $13–$18, not including tax or gratuity. Entrées are served with soup or salad, pasta, veggies, garlic bread, and wine. The setting is relaxed and pleasant. Reservations are accepted.

In addition to the Pasta Pirate, an excellent crab special for $25 is routinely offered in the **Arriva Room** at the Gold Coast, (702) 367-7111. Another good one is the king crab and steak special served for $21 at **Roberta's** at El Cortez, (702) 385-5200. Though El Cortez is not the fanciest joint in town, the total restaurant experience is not a drawback, either: Roberta's is the best bargain gourmet room in town.

The perennial favorite of the steak and lobster deals (which tend to be of lesser quality than steak, prime-rib, and crab-leg meal-deals) is found at **Island Paradise Café** at the Stardust for $12, (702) 732-6111. Beware of buffets advertising lobster. Buffet lobsters have the consistency of rubber and have been known to leap tall buildings in a single bounce.

Shrimp Cocktails Shrimp cocktails at nominal prices are frequently used to lure gamblers into the casinos. Usually the shrimp are small (popcorn shrimp) and are served in cocktail sauce in a tulip glass. The best and cheapest (99 cents) shrimp cocktail can be found at the **Golden Gate,** a small downtown casino, which has been serving this special for more than 45 years. Other contenders are the **Four Queens, Arizona Charlie's,** and the **Lady Luck.**

Pasta and Pizza The **Pasta Palace** at Palace Station regularly runs half-price specials on excellent pasta entrées, and the **Pasta Pirate** at the California offers some of the best designer pasta dishes in town. The best play is to hit up pizza "satellite" outlets (fast-food counters attached to the Italian restaurants) at Boulder Station and Sunset Station for a quickie slice. You can also get a good slice of New York–style pizza at **Toscana's** at the Rio. At the Palms fast-food court is **Regina's Pizza,** an outlet of a 175-year-old Boston pizzeria, which has a great deal on excellent pizza: two slices and a drink for under $5.

Breakfast Specials Our favorite breakfast deal is the huge ham-and-eggs special at the **Gold Coast.** One of the best breakfasts you will ever eat, it would still be a bargain at three times the price. Both **Arizona Charlie's West** and **East** serve a $5 steak-and-eggs special at their coffee shops round the clock; this meal is the oldest and most reliable breakfast bargain in town. Other worthwhile breakfast deals include steak and eggs at the **Frontier** and the **San Remo** (24 hours), the ham-and-eggs breakfast at the **Horseshoe** (4 a.m.–2 p.m.) and the breakfast buffets at **Sam's Town,** the **Orleans,** and the **Palms.**

The Restaurants

Our Favorite Las Vegas Restaurants

We have developed detailed profiles for the best restaurants (in our opinion) in town. Each profile features an easily scanned heading that allows you, in just a second, to check out the restaurant's name, cuisine, Overall Rating, cost category, Quality Rating, and Value Rating.

Overall Rating The Overall Rating encompasses the entire dining experience, including style, service, and ambience, in addition to taste, presentation, and food quality. Five stars is the highest rating possible and connotes the best of everything. Four-star restaurants are exceptional, and three-star restaurants are well above average. Two-star restaurants are good. One star is used to denote an average restaurant that demonstrates an unusual capability in some area of specialization—for example, an otherwise immemorable place that has great barbecued chicken.

Cost Our expense description provides a comparative sense of how much a complete meal will cost. A complete meal for our purposes consists of an entrée with vegetable or side dish, and choice of soup or salad. Appetizers, desserts, drinks, and tips are excluded.

Inexpensive	$14 or less per person
Moderate	$15–$30 per person
Expensive	$30–$45 per person
Very expensive	$46 or more per person

Quality Rating   Beneath each heading appear a quality rating and a value rating. The quality rating is based expressly on the taste, freshness of ingredients, preparation, presentation, and creativity of food served. There is no consideration of price. If you are a person who wants the best food available, and cost is not an issue, you need look no further than the quality rating. The quality ratings are defined as:

★★★★★	Exceptional quality
★★★★	Good quality
★★★	Fair quality, you get exactly what you pay for
★★	Somewhat sub-par quality
★	Sub-par quality

Value Rating   If, on the other hand, you are looking for both quality and value, then you should check the value rating. The value ratings are a function of the overall rating, the price rating, and the quality rating:

★★★★★	Exceptional value, a real bargain
★★★★	Good value
★★★	Fair value, you get exactly what you pay for
★★	Somewhat overpriced
★	Significantly overpriced

Location   Next to the value rating is a zone number. This zone will give you a general idea of where the restaurant described is located. For ease of use, we divide Las Vegas into five geographic zones:

Zone 1	The Strip and Environs
Zone 2	Downtown
Zone 3	Southwest Las Vegas
Zone 4	North Las Vegas
Zone 5	Southeast Las Vegas and the Boulder Highway

If you are staying downtown and intend to walk or take a cab to dinner, you may want to choose a restaurant from among those located in Zone 2. If you have a car, you might include restaurants from contiguous zones in your consideration. (See pages 13–18 for detailed zone maps.)

Other Information   If you like what you see at first glance when you scan a particular restaurant's heading and location, you might move on to read the rest of the profile for more detailed information.

Our Pick of the Best Las Vegas Restaurants

Because restaurants are opening and closing all the time in Las Vegas, we have tried to confine our list to establishments with a proven track record over a fairly long period of time. Newer restaurants (and older restaurants under new management) are listed but not profiled. Those newer or changed establishments that demonstrate staying power and consistency will be profiled in subsequent editions. Also, the list is highly selective. Exclusion of a particular place does not necessarily indicate that the restaurant is not good, only that it was not ranked among the best in its genre. Note that some restaurants appear in more than one category.

THE BEST LAS VEGAS RESTAURANTS				
Name	*Overall Rating*	*Price Rating*	*Quality Rating*	*Value Rating*
Adventures in Dining				
8-0-8 (Hawaiian/French)	★★★½	Expensive	★★★★	★★½
Emeril's (New Orleans)	★★★	Expensive	★★★½	★★★½
Marrakech (Moroccan)	★★½	Moderate	★★★½	★★★½
American				
Craftsteak	★★★★½	Expensive	★★★★½	★★★
Spago	★★★★½	Moderate	★★★★½	★★½
Aureole	★★★★½	Very Exp	★★★★½	★★½
Renoir	★★★★½	Very Exp	★★★★½	★★½
Bradley Ogden	★★★★	Expensive	★★★★½	★★½
Wolfgang Puck Bar & Grill	★★★★	Moderate	★★★★	★★★★½
Rosemary's Restaurant	★★★★	Moderate	★★★★	★★½
Simon Kitchen & Bar	★★★½	Mod/Exp	★★★★½	★★½
Lucille's	★★★½	Expensive	★★★★	★★★★½
Olives	★★★½	Expensive	★★★★	★★★½
Neros	★★★½	Expensive	★★★★	★★½
Range Steakhouse	★★★	Expensive	★★★★	★★½
Redwood Bar & Grill	★★★	Moderate	★★★½	★★★★½
Grape Street Café	★★★	Moderate	★★★½	★★★½
Lawry's The Prime Rib	★★★	Expensive	★★★½	★★½
Magnolia Room†	★★★	Moderate	★★★½	★★½
Rainforest Café	★★★	Moderate	★★★½	★★½
Red Square	★★★	Moderate	★★★½	★★½
Top of the World	★★★	Mod/Exp	★★★½	★★½
Hugo's Cellar	★★★	Expensive	★★★½	★★★½
Kathy's Southern Cooking	★★½	Moderate	★★★½	★★★★½
Harley-Davidson Café	★★½	Moderate	★★★½	★½
Asian/Pacific Rim				
Ah Sin	★★★½	Mod/Exp	★★★★½	★★★½
China Spice	★★★½	Mod/Exp	★★★★	★★★★½

† not profiled

THE BEST LAS VEGAS RESTAURANTS (continued)

Name	Overall Rating	Price Rating	Quality Rating	Value Rating
Asian/Pacific Rim (continued)				
Malibu Chan's	★★★½	Moderate	★★★★	★★½
China Grill	★★★½	Moderate	★★★½	★★★½
Barbecue				
Lucille's	★★★½	Expensive	★★★★	★★★★½
Memphis Champion Barbecue	★★★	Inexpensive	★★★½	★★★★½
Sweet Georgia Brown's	★★★	Moderate	★★★½	★★★★½
Sam Woo Bar-B-Q†	★★½	Inexpensive	★★★	★★★½
Brazilian				
Samba Grill	★★★½	Moderate	★★★★	★★★½
Rumjungle	★★★	Expensive	★★★½	★★½
Brewpub				
Triple Seven Brewpub†	★★½	Inexpensive	★★★½	★★½
California-Continental				
Drai's	★★★★	Expensive	★★★★½	★½
Chinese (see also Dim Sum)				
Mayflower Cuisinier	★★★★	Moderate	★★★★	★★★★½
Pearl	★★★★	Expensive	★★★★	★★½
China Spice	★★★½	Mod/Exp	★★★★	★★★★½
Little Buddha	★★★½	Mod/Exp	★★★★	★★★
Noodles	★★★	Moderate	★★★★	★★★½
Ping Pang Pong	★★★	Moderate	★★★★	★★★★½
Peking Market	★★★	Moderate	★★★½	★½
Chang	★★½	Moderate	★★★½	★★★½
Chinese/French				
Mayflower Cuisinier	★★★★	Inexpensive	★★★★	★★★★½
Chinois	★★★	Moderate	★★★½	★★★½
Continental/French				
Alize	★★★★★	Expensive	★★★★★	★★½
Buccaneer Bay Club	★★★★½	Expensive	★★★★½	★★★½
Renoir	★★★★½	Very Exp	★★★★½	★★½
Bouchon	★★★★½	Expensive	★★★★	★★★★
Picasso	★★★★½	Very Exp	★★★★	★★½
Marche Bacchus/Bacchus Bistro	★★★★	Expensive	★★★★	★★★★
Andre's	★★★★	Expensive	★★★★	★★½
Mon Ami Gabi	★★★½	Mod/Exp	★★★★	★★★½

† not profiled

THE BEST LAS VEGAS RESTAURANTS (continued)

Name	Overall Rating	Price Rating	Quality Rating	Value Rating
Continental/French (continued)				
8-0-8	★★★½	Expensive	★★★★	★★½
Michael's	★★★½	Very Exp	★★★★	★★½
Fiore	★★★½	Expensive	★★★½	★★½
Bonjour French Restaurant	★★★	Mod/Exp	★★★½	★★½
Isis	★★★	Expensive	★★★½	★★½
Pinot Brasserie	★★★	Expensive	★★★½	★★½
Café Nicolle	★★½	Moderate	★★★½	★★½
Pamplemousse	★★½	Mod/Exp	★★★½	★★½
Burgundy Room†	★★½	Mod/Exp	★★★	★½
Creole/Cajun				
Commander's Palace	★★★½	Expensive	★★★★	★½
Voodoo Café and Lounge	★★★	Expensive	★★★½	★★½
Cuban				
Florida Café	★★★	Inexpensive	★★★½	★★★★½
Dim Sum (see also Chinese)				
Chang	★★½	Moderate	★★★½	★★★½
Mirage Noodle Kitchen†	★★½	Moderate	★★★½	★★½
Eclectic				
Cheesecake Factory	★★★	Inexp/Mod	★★★½	★★★★½
German				
Hofbrauhaus	★★★	Moderate	★★★½	★★★★½
Café Heidelberg	★★★	Moderate	★★½	★★★½
Greek				
Magnolia Room†	★★★	Moderate	★★★½	★★½
Tony's Greco Roman†	★★½	Moderate	★★★	★★★½
Hawaiian				
8-0-8	★★★½	Expensive	★★★★	★★½
Hawaiian Plantation House	★★★	Mod/Exp	★★★½	★★★
Indian				
Gaylord's	★★½	Expensive	★★★	★½
Indonesian				
Taste of Indonesia	★★★	Expensive	★★★½	★★★★½
Italian				
Circo (Osteria Del)	★★★★	Mod/Exp	★★★★½	★★½
Piero's	★★★★	Expensive	★★★★	★★½
Terrazza	★★★★	Mod/Exp	★★★★	★★½

† not profiled

THE BEST LAS VEGAS RESTAURANTS (continued)

Name	Overall Rating	Price Rating	Quality Rating	Value Rating
Italian (continued)				
Antonio's	★★★½	Moderate	★★★★½	★★★½
Panevino Ristorante/ Gourmet Deli	★★★½	Mod/Exp	★★★★½	★★★½
Fiamma Trattoria	★★★½	Mod/Exp	★★★★	★★★½
Stefano's	★★★½	Mod/Exp	★★★★	★★½
Trattoria del Lupo	★★★½	Moderate	★★★★	★★½
Ventano	★★★½	Moderate	★★★½	★★★★½
Piero's Trattoria	★★★½	Moderate	★★★½	★★½
La Scala	★★★	Moderate	★★★★	★★½
Anna Bella	★★★	Moderate	★★★½	★★★★½
Bootlegger	★★★	Mod/Exp	★★★½	★★★★½
Fellini's	★★★	Moderate	★★★½	★★★★½
Sazio	★★★	Moderate	★★★½	★★★★½
Bertolini's	★★★	Moderate	★★★½	★★★½
Magnolia Room†	★★★	Moderate	★★★½	★★½
Medici Café	★★½	Mod/Exp	★★★★½	★★★½
Il Fornaio	★★½	Moderate	★★★½	★★★½
Mama Jo's	★★½	Moderate	★★★	★★½
Japanese (see also Sushi)				
Ah Sin	★★★½	Moderate	★★★★½	★★★½
Blue Wave	★★★½	Moderate	★★★★	★★★★½
Makino Sushi Restaurant	★★★½	Moderate	★★★★	★★★★½
Shintaro†	★★★½	Moderate	★★★½	★★½
Noodles	★★★	Moderate	★★★★	★★★½
Tokyo	★★★	Moderate	★★★½	★★★½
Fuji	★★½	Inexpensive	★★★	★★★½
Korean				
Koreana	★★½	Moderate	★★★★	★★½
Lobster				
Alan Alberts	★★★	Expensive	★★★½	★★½
Rosewood Grille	★★★	Moderate	★★★½	★★½
Lobster House†	★★★	Moderate	★★★½	★½
Mediterranean				
Olives	★★★½	Expensive	★★★★	★★★½
Mexican				
Isla	★★★★½	Moderate	★★★★	★★★★½
Garduno's at the Palms	★★★	Inexp/Mod	★★★½	★★★½

† not profiled

THE BEST LAS VEGAS RESTAURANTS *(continued)*

Name	Overall Rating	Price Rating	Quality Rating	Value Rating
Mexican (continued)				
Garduno's Chili Packing Co.	★★★	Moderate	★★★½	★★★½
Middle Eastern				
Habib's	★★★	Moderate	★★★½	★★½
Haifa (kosher)†	★★½	Moderate	★★★½	★★½
Moroccan				
Marrakech	★★½	Moderate	★★★½	★★★½
Peruvian				
Inka	★★½	Inexpensive	★★★½	★★★½
Polish				
Polonez	★★½	Inexpensive	★★★½	★★½
Prime Rib				
Redwood Bar & Grill	★★★	Moderate	★★★½	★★★★½
Sir Galahad's	★★★	Moderate	★★★½	★★★★½
Lawry's The Prime Rib	★★★	Expensive	★★★½	★★½
Seafood				
Aqua	★★★★½	Expensive	★★★★½	★★½
SeaBlue	★★★★	Mod/Exp	★★★★	★★★½
Buzios	★★★½	Mod/Exp	★★★★	★★½
Kokomo's	★★★½	Very Exp	★★★★	★★½
Pasta Pirate	★★★	Moderate	★★★½	★★★★½
The Tillerman	★★★	Expensive	★★★½	★★½
Emeril's New Orleans Fish House	★★★	Expensive	★★★½	★★★½
The Broiler	★★½	Mod/Exp	★★★½	★★★½
Steak				
Craftsteak	★★★★½	Expensive	★★★★½	★★★
Delmonico	★★★★	Expensive	★★★★	★★½
Prime	★★★½	Expensive	★★★★½	★★½
Samba Grill	★★★½	Moderate	★★★★	★★★½
Kokomo's	★★★½	Very Exp	★★★★	★★½
Ruth's Chris Steak House	★★★½	Very Exp	★★★★	★★½
The Palm	★★★½	Very Exp	★★★½	½
The Steak House	★★★	Expensive	★★★½	★★★½
A. J.'s Steakhouse	★★★	Expensive	★★★½	★★½
Rosewood Grille	★★★	Moderate	★★★½	★★½
Alan Alberts	★★★	Expensive	★★★½	★★½

† not profiled

THE BEST LAS VEGAS RESTAURANTS (continued)

Name	Overall Rating	Price Rating	Quality Rating	Value Rating
Steak (continued)				
The Broiler	★★½	Mod/Exp	★★★½	★★★½
Yolie's †	★★½	Expensive	★★★½	★★½
Billy Bob's Steakhouse	★★½	Moderate	★★★	★★★½
Sushi (see also Japanese)				
Blue Wave	★★★½	Moderate	★★★★	★★★★½
Makino Sushi Restaurant	★★★½	Moderate	★★★★	★★★★½
Little Buddha	★★★½	Mod/Exp	★★★★	★★★
Chinois	★★★	Moderate	★★★½	★★★½
Tokyo	★★★	Moderate	★★★½	★★★½
Hamada of Japan†	★★½	Moderate	★★★½	★½
Thai				
Noodles	★★★	Moderate	★★★★	★★★½
Lotus of Siam	★★★	Mod/Exp	★★★½	★★½
Vietnamese				
Noodles	★★★	Moderate	★★★★	★★½
Pho Chien	★★★	Moderate	★★★½	★★★★½
Rooms with a View				
Alize	★★★★★	Expensive	★★★★★	★★½
Eiffel Tower Restaurant†	★★★½	Very Exp	★★★★	★½
Top of the World	★★★	Mod/Exp	★★★½	★★½
Voodoo Café and Lounge	★★★	Expensive	★★★½	★★½

LAS VEGAS RESTAURANTS BY ZONE

Name	Cuisine	Overall Rating
Zone 1: The Strip		
Ah Sin	Asian	★★★½
A. J.'s Steakhouse	Steak	★★★
Alan Alberts	Lobster/Steak	★★★
Alize	Continental/French	★★★★★
Andre's	Continental/French	★★★★
Antonio's	Italian	★★★½
Aqua	Seafood	★★★★½
Aureole	American	★★★★½
Bertolini's	Italian	★★★
Bootlegger	Italian	★★★

LAS VEGAS RESTAURANTS BY ZONE *(continued)*		
Name	**Cuisine**	**Overall Rating**
Zone 1: The Strip (continued)		
Bouchon	French Bistro	★★★★½
Bradley Ogden	American	★★★★
Buccaneer Bay Club	Continental	★★★★½
Buzios	Seafood	★★★½
Café Heidelberg	German	★★★
Chang	Chinese/Dim Sum	★★½
Cheesecake Factory	Eclectic	★★★
China Grill	Asian/Pacific Rim	★★★½
Chinois	Chinese/French/Sushi	★★★
Circo (Osteria Del)	Italian	★★★★
Commander's Palace	Creole/Cajun	★★★½
Craftsteak	American/Steak	★★★★½
Delmonico	Steak	★★★★
Drai's	California-Continental	★★★★
8-0-8	Hawaiian	★★★½
Emeril's New Orleans Fish House	Seafood/New Orleans	★★★
Fiamma Trattoria	Italian	★★★½
Fiore	Continental	★★★½
Florida Café	Cuban	★★★
Gaylords	Indian	★★½
Harley-Davidson Café	American	★★½
Hofbrauhaus	German	★★★
Il Fornaio	Italian	★★½
Inka	Peruvian	★★½
Isis	Continental	★★★
Isla	Contemporary/Mexican	★★★★½
Kokomo's	Seafood/Steak	★★★½
La Scala	Italian	★★★
Lawry's The Prime Rib	Prime Rib/American	★★★
Little Buddha	Chinese/Sushi	★★★½
Lotus of Siam	Thai	★★★
Marrakech	Moroccan	★★½
Michael's	Continental	★★★½
Mon Ami Gabi	Continental/French	★★★½
Neros	American	★★★½
Noodles	Chinese/Japanese/Thai	★★★
Olives	American/Mediterranean	★★★½
The Palm	Steak	★★★½
Pamplemousse	Continental/French	★★½
Panevino Ristorante/Gourmet Deli	Italian	★★★★½
Pearl	Chinese/Dim Sum	★★★★
Picasso	Continental/French	★★★★½

LAS VEGAS RESTAURANTS BY ZONE *(continued)*		
Name	**Cuisine**	**Overall Rating**
Zone 1: The Strip *(continued)*		
Piero's	Italian	★★★★
Piero's Trattoria	Italian	★★★½
Pinot Brasserie	French	★★★
Polonez	Polish	★★½
Prime	Steak	★★★½
Rainforest Café	American	★★★
Range Steakhouse	American	★★★
Red Square	American/Russian	★★★
Renoir	American/Continental	★★★★½
Rosewood Grille	Lobster/Steak	★★★
Rumjungle	Brazilian Rodizio	★★★
Ruth's Chris Steak House	Steak	★★★½
Samba Grill	Brazilian/Steak	★★★½
SeaBlue	Seafood	★★★★
Simon Kitchen & Bar	American	★★★½
Sir Galahad's	Prime Rib	★★★
Spago	American	★★★½
The Steak House	Steak	★★★
Sweet Georgia Brown's	Barbecue	★★★
Taste of Indonesia	Indonesian	★★★
Terrazza	Italian	★★★★
Tokyo	Japanese/Sushi	★★★
Trattoria del Lupo	Italian	★★★½
Voodoo Café and Lounge	Creole/Cajun	★★★
Wolfgang Puck Bar & Grill	American	★★★★
Zone 2: Downtown		
Andre's	Continental/French	★★★★
Burgundy Room†	Continental/French	★★½
Hugo's Cellar	American	★★★
Pasta Pirate	Seafood	★★★
Redwood Bar & Grill	American/Prime Rib	★★★
Stefano's	Italian	★★★½
Zone 3: Southwest Las Vegas		
Café Nicolle	Continental/French	★★½
Fellini's	Italian	★★★
Garduno's at the Palms	Mexican/Southwestern	★★★
Habib's	Middle Eastern	★★★
Makino Sushi Restaurant	Japanese/Sushi	★★★½
Malibu Chan's	Pacific Rim	★★★½
Mama Jo's	Italian	★★½
Marche Bacchus/Bacchus Bistro	French Bistro	★★★★

LAS VEGAS RESTAURANTS BY ZONE *(continued)*		
Name	**Cuisine**	**Overall Rating**
Zone 3: Southwest Las Vegas (continued)		
Mayflower Cuisinier	Chinese/French	★★★★
Pho Chien	Vietnamese	★★★
Ping Pang Pong	Chinese/Dim Sum	★★★
Rosemary's Restaurant	American	★★★★
Sam Woo Bar-B-Q†	Barbecue	★★½
Sazio	Italian	★★★
Top of the World	American	★★★
Zone 4: North Las Vegas		
Garduno's Chili Packing Co.	Mexican/Southwestern	★★★
Grape Street Café	American	★★★
Magnolia Room†	American/Greek	★★★
Zone 5: Southeast Las Vegas and the Boulder Highway; Henderson		
Anna Bella	Italian	★★★
Billy Bob's Steakhouse	Steak	★★½
Blue Wave	Japanese/Sushi	★★★½
Bonjour French Restaurant	French	★★★
The Broiler	Steak/Seafood	★★½
China Spice	Chinese/Asian	★★★½
Ferraro's	Italian	★★★
Fuji	Japanese	★★½
Hawaiian Plantation House	Hawaiian	★★★
Kathy's Southern Cooking	American	★★½
Koreana	Korean	★★½
Lucille's	Southern/Pit Barbecue	★★★½
Mama Jo's	Italian	★★½
Medici Café	Italian	★★½
Memphis Champion Barbecue	Barbecue	★★★
Ruth's Chris Steak House	Steak	★★★½
The Tillerman	Seafood	★★★
Ventano	Italian	★★★½

More Recommendations

The Best Bagels

Bagel Oasis   9134 West Sahara Avenue (702) 363-081. New York–style; baked fresh daily; large selection.

Harrie's Bagelmania   855 East Twain Avenue (at Swenson) (702) 369-3322. Baked on the premises; garlic and onion among the choices. Locals hangout.

The Best Bakeries

Albina's Italian Bakery   3035 East Tropicana Avenue in the Wal-Mart Center (702) 433-5400. Classic Italian pastries; baba au rhum, with and without custard; Italian and American cheesecakes; wide variety of cookies.

Chocolate Swan Two locations: Mandalay Place 3930 Las Vegas Boulevard South, Suite 201B; (702) 632-9366 and near *Mamma Mia* Box Office. Chocolates, pastries, cheesecakes, and frozen custard, many of which come with a wine or cordial recommendation.

Great Buns 3270 East Tropicana Avenue (at Pecos) (702) 898-0311. Commercial and retail; fragrant rosemary bread, sticky buns, and apple loaf are good choices. Regularly add new items.

Tintoretto Italian bakery, Canal Shops at The Venetian Hotel (702) 414-3400. International breads, cakes, and cookies. Charming European design and a patio perfect for people-watching.

The Best Brewpubs

Gordon Biersch Brewpub 3987 Paradise Road (Hughes Center) (702) 312-5247. Upbeat brewery restaurant with contemporary menu and surprisingly good food at reasonable prices.

Monte Carlo Pub & Brewery Monte Carlo (702) 730-7777. Located adjacent to the pool area in a faux-warehouse setting, this new brewpub offers six different beers and affordable food options. The beer is brewed right on the premises. Eighteen different pizzas are available, as well as sandwiches, pastas, and more.

Triple Seven Brewpub 200 North Main Street (Main Street Station) (702) 387-1896. Late-night happy hour with bargain brews and food specials. Open 24 hours.

The Best Burgers

Burger Bar Mandalay Bay Place, 3930 Las Vegas Boulevard (702) 632-9364. Burgers of every description, some outrageous.

Champagnes Café 3557 South Maryland Parkway (702) 737-1699. Classic half-pounder with creative toppings.

Kilroy's 1021 South Buffalo Drive (at West Charleston) (702) 363-4933. Half-pound burgers, choice of 15 toppings.

Lone Star Cheese, Bubba, Texas, Mexi, or Willie half-pounders on a toasted onion bun.

1290 East Flamingo Road (702) 893-0348

1611 South Decatur Boulevard (702) 259-0105

210 Nellis Boulevard (702) 453-7827

3131 North Rainbow (702) 656-7125

Tommy's Hamburgers 2635 East Tropicana Avenue (702) 458-2533. Good eat-in or carry-out burgers.

The Best Delis

Harrie's Bagelmania 855 East Twain (at Swenson) (702) 369-3322. Breakfast and lunch only. Full service bagel bakery and deli. On Tuesdays buy bagels by the dozen at half price. Pastrami and corned beef by the pound at half price.

Canter's Delicatessen at Treasure Island 3300 Las Vegas Boulevard South; (702) 894-6390. Sandwiches served on legendary sourdough rye bread, soups including signature barley bean, New York cheesecake, and a world-famous chocolate chip racetrack cake.

Samuel's Deli 2744 North Green Valley Parkway, Henderson (702) 454-0565. Full-service deli, bakery, and restaurant. Home cooking and giant matzo balls.

Siena Deli 2250 East Tropicana Avenue (at Eastern) (702) 736-8424. Italian spoken here: everything Italian and homemade. Excellent bread baked every morning. Siena bakes bread for many of the area's Italian restaurants. Local favorite for Italian grocery items.

Stage Deli The Forum Shops at Caesars (702) 893-4045. Las Vegas branch of New York's famous pastrami palace; enormous menu runs gamut of Jewish specialties, including triple-decker sandwiches named for celebrities, and 26 desserts. Open wide—the sandwiches are skyscrapers.

The Best Espresso and Dessert

Café Nicolle   4760 West Sahara Avenue, Suite 17 (at Decatur);   (702) 870-7675. Sidewalk café; cooling mist in summer.

Café Sensations   4350 East Sunset Road (east of Green Valley Parkway) (702) 456-7803. Scrumptious variety of baked goods, casual food, sandwiches, salads.

Chocolate Swan   Two locations: Mandalay Place 3930 Las Vegas Boulevard South, Suite 201B; (702) 632-9366 and *Mamma Mia* box office. Pastries, frozen custard, and much more.

Coffee Bean & Tea Leaf   4550 South Maryland Parkway; (702) 944-5029. California-based chain of speciality coffee houses.

Coffee Pub   2800 West Sahara Avenue, Suite 2A (702) 367-1913. Great breakfast and lunch location, imaginative menu.

Jitters Gourmet Coffee   Many varieties of coffees plus homemade muffins, sandwiches, brownies, truffles. Popular local hangout.

  2295 North Green Valley Parkway (702) 434-3112

  8441 West Lake Mead Boulevard (Summerlin location) (702) 256-1902

La Piazza   Caesars Palace (702) 731-7110. Caesars' bakers create pies, cakes, and cookies to eat in or take out.

Palio   Bellagio (702) 693-8160. Cafeteria-style coffee house with scrumptious pastries and casual eats—quiche, salads, and sandwiches.

Spago   The Forum Shops at Caesars (702) 369-6300. Wolfgang Puck's pastry chef crafts imaginative and sinful creations. Available all day in the café and at dinner in the dining room.

Starbucks Coffee Houses   Many area locations.

Tintoretto at **The Venetian**   Canal Shops at The Venetian (702) 414-3400

The Best Oyster and Clam Bars

Buzios   Rio (702) 252-7697. Oyster stews, cioppino, shellfish, and pan roasts. Table service or oyster bar.

Emeril's New Orleans Fish House   MGM Grand; (702) 891-1111

SeaBlue   MGM Grand; (702) 891-3486. Superior tuna tartare.

The Best Pizza

Bootlegger   7700 Las Vegas Boulevard South (702) 736-4939. Great selection; crispy, tender, homemade crust.

Metro Pizza   1395 East Tropicana Avenue (702) 736-1955. Fast service, generous with the cheese. Try the Old New York with thick-sliced mozzarella, plum tomatoes, and basil. Thick Ragu-style tomato sauce topping.

Spago   The Forum Shops at Caesars (702) 369-6300. Wolfgang Puck's regular specials include spicy shrimp, duck sausage, and smoked salmon with dill cream and golden caviar. Other toppings change frequently.

Venetian   3713 West Sahara Avenue (702) 876-4190. Old-time Las Vegas favorite; pizza with greens and olive oil (no cheese) is a popular item.

The Best Soup and Salad Bars

Paradise Garden Café   Flamingo Hilton (702) 733-3111. A good display at lunch; a large choice of seafood added at dinner.

Souper Salad   Moderate prices, many combinations, shiny clean, and inexpensive.

  2051 North Rainbow (702) 631-2604

  4022 South Maryland Parkway (702) 792-8555

Restaurants with a View

Alize Palms (702) 951-7000. At the top of the Palms, Alize's panoramic view includes portions of the Strip.

Circo Bellagio (702) 693-8150. Circo (full name Osteria Del) is adjacent to its pricier sister, Le Cirque. Tuscan fare with a view of Lake Como and Paris's Eiffel tower.

Eiffel Tower Restaurant Paris (702) 948-6937. Fancy French food in a drop-dead gorgeous setting that towers over the Strip. This is one spectacular view that encompasses the fountains at Bellagio.

Picasso Bellagio (702) 693-7223. Highly original food and glorious original artwork by Picasso. As good as it gets (since you can't eat in the Louvre!).

Voodoo Café Rio Hotel and Casino (702) 252-7777. At the top of the new Rio tower, Voodoo offers the mystique of New Orleans, a complete view of the city, Cajun/Creole cooking, and late-night lounge.

Restaurant Profiles

A. J.'S STEAKHOUSE ★★★

STEAK | EXPENSIVE | QUALITY ★★★½ | VALUE ★★½ | ZONE 1

400 East Flamingo Road; (702) 893-0703

Customers Visitors, locals **Reservations** Recommended, especially during conventions **When to go** Anytime **Entrée range** $22–$50 **Payment** VISA, MC, AMEX, DC, CB **Service rating** ★★★½ **Friendliness rating** ★★½ **Parking** Shopping-center lot, garage, valet **Bar** Attractive, full service **Wine selection** Excellent **Dress** Business casual **Disabled access** Same level as parking lot

Dinner Monday–Thursday, 5–11 p.m.; Friday and Saturday, 5–11 p.m.; Sunday, 5–10 p.m.

Setting & atmosphere Men's club atmosphere, with paneled boardroom (for large parties), polished oak barroom, and comfortable booths.

House specialties Black-bean soup; whole onion bread brought to table; porterhouse steak; New York sirloin steak; rib-eye steak; double filet mignon; whole Maine lobster; shrimp Alexander; huge strawberries with sabayon sauce.

Other recommendations Appetizer of broiled sea scallops wrapped in bacon, apricot chutney; double-cut prime rib; lamb chops; swordfish steak; lemon-oregano chicken. shrimp Alexander as an appetizer.

Entertainment & amenities Storage lockers for regular guests' wines.

Summary & comments Branch of Chicago-based steakhouse. Appetizers, salads, entrées, desserts all served in large portions. Everything à la carte, including side dishes. The dessert soufflés are a specialty but disappointing. Stick to selections from the pastry tray or the gorgeous fresh berries. Cigar smoking is encouraged in the dining room. Prime steaks, but a less-than-prime attitude.

AH SIN ★★★½

ASIAN/SUSHI | MOD/EXP | QUALITY ★★★★½ | VALUE ★★★½ | ZONE 1

Paris; 3655 Las Vegas Boulevard South; (702) 946-7000

Customers Visitors, locals **Reservations** Recommended **When to go** Anytime **Entrée range** $15–$30 **Payment** All major credit cards **Service rating** ★★★½ **Friendliness rating** ★★★★½ **Parking** Valet, garage **Bar** Full service **Wine selection** Good **Dress** Casual chic **Disabled access** Ground floor

Open 11 a.m.–midnight

Setting & atmosphere There are many parts to Ah Sin, all beautiful. Asian artifacts and artwork fill the room, cleverly dividing it, yet allowing open views. A sushi bar flows almost to the dining room. The Malaysian satay bar is another work of art and the first of its kind in Las Vegas.

House specialties Cantonese crêpes, the Ah Sin version of mu shu, freshly made on on oversized French irons; barbecue from the Chinese oven, including suckling pig, roast duck, chicken in the Ko Samet style, and Macao pork tenderloin; such appetizers as Peking stuffed chicken wings or Indochine foie gras; nigiri sushi and sashimi and the many special sushi rolls; seafood from live tanks; special teas.

Other recommendations Dim sum, Sarawak roasted duck salad, the noodle and rice dishes, the Mongolian lamb chops topped with sweet curried onions.

Summary & comments Ah Sin offers an exceptional selection of Asian dishes. All menu items are available wherever you choose to sit, including at the sushi bar. Desserts are offered at Ah Sin, but it's more fun to have dessert at Risqué, a late-night spot right above the restaurant. The dessert bar is separated from the club by a translucent glass wall. The range of desserts includes everything from made-to-order soufflés to flambéed desserts to such homespun favorites as banana fritters and rice pudding. Work off the indulgence at Risqué's billiard table.

ALAN ALBERTS ★★★

STEAK/LOBSTER | EXPENSIVE | QUALITY ★★★½ | VALUE ★★½ | ZONE 1

3763 Las Vegas Boulevard South, Epicenter Plaza, North of the MGM Grand; (702) 740-4421

Customers Visitors, locals **Reservations** Accepted **When to go** Anytime **Entrée range** $20–$42 **Payment** All major credit cards **Service rating** ★★★★½ **Friendliness rating** ★★★★½ **Parking** Lot **Bar** Full service **Wine selection** Excellent **Dress** Business attire, informal **Disabled access** Ground floor

Dinner Daily, 5–11:30 p.m.

Setting & atmosphere This self-named "vintage steakhouse" features beveled glass, fine wood paneling, and photo walls showcasing celebrities and stars of the glory days of Old Las Vegas. The dining room has comfortable, easy-to-get-into booths and expert, flattering lighting.

House specialties Prime Angus steaks and jumbo lobsters; a flavorful culotte steak seldom found elsewhere; crab cakes; osso buco; a 26-ounce rib eye; veal and lamb chops.

Other recommendations Grilled salmon on garlic spinach; oysters Rockefeller; delectable desserts, especially the tiramisu.

Summary & comments Tucked away in the corner of a strip mall, Alan Alberts is a pleasant surprise. Lobsters are fairly priced—choose one from the live tank. Average weight is 2½ pounds. Portions are generous. A meal could be made from appetizers.

ALIZE ★★★★★

FRENCH | EXPENSIVE | QUALITY ★★★★★ | VALUE ★★½ | ZONE 1

Palms Resort, 4321 West. Flamingo Road; (702) 951-7000; www.alizelv.com

Customers Visitors, locals **Reservations** Requested **When to go** Anytime **Entrée range** $23–market price **Payment** All major credit cards **Service rating** ★★★½

Friendliness rating ★★★★½ **Parking** Valet, garage, lot **Bar** Full service **Wine selection** Excellent **Dress** Upscale business attire **Disabled access** Elevator

Dinner Nightly, from 5:30 p.m.

Setting & atmosphere On the top floor of the Palms tower, Alize offers a spectacular view from most tables. Elegantly furnished and appointed, Alize is as romantic as it gets.

House specialties Such daily specials as monkfish loin and Maine lobster civet; lobster thermidor, superb Cervena venison tenderloin, sautéed veal sweetbreads with marinated wild mushrooms, artichoke salad with goat cheese, Roma tomato relish and ciboulette oil.

Other recommendations Andre's duck foie gras and black truffle tureen with Sauternes gelee and country-bread toast, the phyllo-wrapped baked pear salad and Roquefort cheese; the after-dinner cheese plate with imported and domestic cheeses (your choice) served from a trolley; the luscious desserts and soufflés.

Summary & comments Alize is the ultimate dream-come-true for owners Andre Rochat and Mary Jane Jarvis, who also own two Andre's restaurants.

ANDRE'S ★★★★

CONT/FRENCH | EXPENSIVE | QUALITY ★★★★ | VALUE ★★½ | ZONES 1 & 2

Monte Carlo Hotel, (702) 798-7151; www.andresfrenchrest.com
401 South Sixth Street, Downtown; (702) 385-5016

Customers Visitors, locals **Reservations** Necessary **When to go** Early or late **Entrée range** $30–$50 **Payment** VISA, MC, AMEX, DC **Service rating** ★★★½ **Friendliness rating** ★★★½ **Parking** Street, valet **Bar** Full service **Wine selection** Excellent **Dress** Sport coat, dressy **Disabled access** Ramps

Dinner Monday–Saturday, 6–9:30 p.m.

Setting & atmosphere Country French decor in a converted former residence in a historic part of the city. Elegant European decor at the Monte Carlo location.

House specialties Menu changes with the seasons. Sea scallops with duck foie gras, black truffle, and port wine en papillote; marinated salmon tartare with cucumber salad; Maryland blue crab cakes with citrus beurre blanc and escargot garlic butter; rabbit loin with spinach fettuccine Dijon; pavé of veal sautéed with morel mushrooms; variety of unusual fresh fish with imaginative sauces; filet of pork tenderloin stuffed with sun-dried fruit and nuts, served with apricot sauce. Memorable sweetbreads, soufflés, and pastries.

Other recommendations Ask if you can tour Andre's extensive wine cellar; vintages date back to 1830. The daily specials, especially the fish.

Summary & comments Chef/owner Andre Rochat is mostly in the kitchen of Alize, his gorgeous new dining room at the top of the Palms (spectacular view). He makes frequent forays into the dining room to visit with guests. He honors special requests if given 24-hour notice. Spectacular winemaker dinners (Thursday nights) several times a year. Ask to be put on the mailing list. Downtown location is closed the month of July.

Honors & awards *Wine Spectator* Award of Excellence; *Travel/Holiday* magazine award for many years; Ambassador Award of Excellence through 1987 (discontinued); DiRoNA Award.

ANNA BELLA ★★★

ITALIAN | MODERATE | QUALITY ★★★½ | VALUE ★★★★½ | ZONE 5

3310 South Sandhill Road at Desert Inn Road; (702) 434-2537

Customers Locals **Reservations** Suggested all week **When to go** Anytime **Entrée range** $16–$32 **Payment** VISA, MC, AMEX, DC **Service rating** ★★★½ **Friendliness rating** ★★★★½ **Parking** Shopping-center lot **Bar** Full service **Wine selection** Modest **Dress** Casual **Disabled access** Ground floor

Dinner Tuesday–Sunday, 4:30–10 p.m.

Setting & atmosphere A charming neighborhood restaurant with flower-bedecked booths, pink tablecloths, soft lighting, and a caring staff.

House specialties Homemade ravioli filled with wild mushrooms (not on the menu, but frequently available); fettuccine with fresh salmon in vodka sauce; cannelloni alla Romano; pollo alla Tony; osso buco; capellini gamberi puglia.

Other recommendations The flavorful homemade soups; a generous bowl or a green salad comes with entrées. Veal marsala; linguini with clams in a red or white sauce (try the pink sauce made from a mix of both); the classic angel-hair pasta with fresh tomato sauce, garlic, basil, and olive oil.

Summary & comments Anna Bella is a real find. The owners are always there, the service is friendly and caring, and the food is affordable for even modest budgets. Daily specials allow the chef to offer seasonal seafood and higher-end Italian dishes. Service can be slow at times, but be patient. The waitstaff is small, and most of the delicious food is cooked to order. Always a pleaser.

ANTONIO'S   ★★★½

ITALIAN | MODERATE | QUALITY ★★★★½ | VALUE ★★★½ | ZONE 1

Rio, 3700 West Flamingo Road; (702) 252-7777

Customers Visitors, locals **Reservations** Suggested **When to go** Anytime **Entrée range** $26–$50 **Payment** VISA, MC, AMEX, DC, D **Service rating** ★★★★½ **Friendliness rating** ★★★★½ **Parking** Lot, valet, garage **Bar** Full service **Wine selection** Excellent **Dress** Informal slacks and collared shirts for men **Disabled access** Through casino

Dinner Friday–Tuesday, 5–11 p.m.

Setting & atmosphere Marble accents, fresh flowers, elegant table appointments, and expert lighting highlight the comfortable dining room; domed ceiling replicates the sky. Enjoy drinks and Italian coffees before or after dinner in the comfortable lounge.

House specialties The chef's appetizer of the day; vitello al marsala, veal scallops with porcini mushrooms and marsala wine, a superior version of the classic dish; osso buco, the traditional braised veal shank, is presented à la the Rio chef. Daily specials such as oven-roasted pork loin with apricot port wine demi-glacé.

Other recommendations Lobster sautéed with delicate lobster sauce over capellini; pollo all' aglio e rosmarino. There's a small patio outside with its own moderately priced menu of soups, salads, and a dozen pastas. Cioppino. Tiramisu.

Summary & comments There are nice touches at Antonio's. A fruity olive oil for dunking is offered instead of butter—the imported breadsticks are habit-forming; a complementary liqueur is offered "to thank you for dining at Antonio's." A small private dining room for up to 12 is available. This attractive restaurant is a local favorite.

AQUA   ★★★★½

SEAFOOD | EXPENSIVE | QUALITY ★★★★½ | VALUE ★★½ | ZONE 1

Bellagio, 3600 Las Vegas Boulevard South; (702) 693-7223

Customers Visitors, locals **Reservations** A must **When to go** Avoid convention times **Entrée range** $32–$50; 5-course tasting, $75 (vegetarian, $55) **Payment** All major credit cards **Service rating** ★★★★½ **Friendliness rating** ★★★½ **Parking** Valet, garage **Bar** Full service **Wine selection** Extensive **Dress** Casual elegance **Disabled access** Ground floor

Dinner Daily, 5:30–10:30 p.m.

Setting & atmosphere Elegant yet relaxed decor with rich woods and fabulous fabrics. Window tables overlook the pool. Aqua is located away from the Bellagio restaurant corridor. The walk through the amazing Botanical Gardens is glorious—bring a camera.

House specialties Appetizers: a superb tartare of ahi tuna; a selection of chilled shellfish; sea scallops and domestic foie gras; black mussel soufflé. Entrées: Miso-glazed Chilean sea bass; porcini-crusted turbot; the comforting Maine lobster pot pie. An old-fashioned root-beer float, Aqua-style, served with warm chocolate-chip cookies or the Grand Marnier crème caramel for a memorable finish.

Summary & comments This San Francisco transplant wins raves for service, food, and decor. It's not easy to get a reservation if you're not staying at Bellagio, but it's worth any effort it takes to get one.

AUREOLE ★★★★½

AMERICAN | VERY EXPENSIVE | QUALITY ★★★★½ | VALUE ★★½ | ZONE 1

Mandalay Bay, 3950 Las Vegas Boulevard South; (702) 632-7401

Customers Visitors, locals **Reservations** Required **When to go** Anytime **Entrée range** $55–$75 prix fixe menus; 6-course tasting menu, $95; à la carte menu $10–$40 in lounge area only **Payment** All major credit cards **Service rating** ★★★★½ **Friendliness rating** ★★★★½ **Parking** Valet, garage **Bar** Full service **Wine selection** Outstanding **Dress** Casual elegance **Disabled access** Elevator

Dinner Daily, 6–11 p.m. lounge open (serving food) 5 p.m–1 a.m.

Setting & atmosphere A one-of-a-kind, four-story wine tower dominates the entrance to this exceptional restaurant. There are three dining rooms and the separate Swan Court with just 14 tables—all have a view of the waterfall and live swans.

House specialties Roasted duck pot-au-feu with foie gras; spiced tuna tartare; lobster chowder with grilled prawns; sautéed veal mignon with blue cheese lasagna; citrus-basted chicken; roasted pork Saltimbocca. (Some dishes are seasonal and may not be available.)

Other recommendations Thyme-roasted filet mignon; Colorado lamb chop with red-onion rings. Scrumptious desserts; homemade chocolates are served with coffee.

Summary & comments The wine tower is unique—the bottles are accessed by black-clad females who hoist themselves up to the various levels to remove the bottles. It's quite a show and a great photo op. Another wine first is Aureole's wine e-book, which enables patrons to order their favorite dinner wines in advance. All dining rooms offer prix fixe menus only, with an à la carte menu available in the lounge and bar area. Several multicourse tasting menus are available.

BERTOLINI'S ★★★

ITALIAN | MODERATE | QUALITY ★★★½ | VALUE ★★★½ | ZONE 1

The Forum Shops at Caesars Palace; (702) 735-4663

Customers Visitors, locals **Reservations** For large groups only **When to go** Always busy, especially Friday and Saturday evenings **Entrée range** $14–$29 **Payment** VISA,

MC, AMEX, DC, JCB **Service rating** ★★½ **Friendliness rating** ★★★½ **Parking** Hotel garage, valet **Bar** Full service **Wine selection** Good **Dress** Informal, casual **Disabled access** Ground floor

Open Sunday–Thursday, 11 a.m.–midnight; Friday and Saturday, 11 a.m.–1 a.m.

Setting & atmosphere The restaurant's beautifully decorated interior offers peaceful respite from the lively action of the dining patio. A colorful mural decorates one wall. There is a display of antipasto, a mesquite-fired pizza oven, an open kitchen, and a gelateria. Butcher paper–covered tables and crayons for doodling.

House specialties Focaccia and pizza made in a wood-burning oven. Carpaccio di manzo; insalata di pollo con pasta; gorgonzola and fontina pizza with roasted potatoes and rosemary; rigatoni with sausage ragout, tomato sauce, and mozzarella; angel hair pomodoro. Homemade ice cream as well as cakes, espresso, and cappuccino in the gelateria.

Other recommendations Salad with homemade mozzarella, tomatoes, and basil oil; prosciutto and smoked mozzarella with fig jam crostini and sun-dried tomato vinaigrette; roasted garlic, fresh spinach, béchamel, and mozzarella pizza; lasagna. Any of the new dishes, especially crusted chicken Romano with Gorgonzola sauce and the fazzoletto con funghi—a "handkerchief" of pasta enfolding spinach and ricotta cheese in a delicate wild mushroom sauce. Cappuccino crème brûlée.

Summary & comments The Sidewalk Café outside Bertolini's overlooks the Forum's bustling scene and the Roman fountain. It's an ideal spot for photos. The fountain can be noisy, but no one seems to mind—it's so pretty. Table turnover is good, but even with a busy day's wait, time goes quickly.

BILLY BOB'S STEAKHOUSE & SALOON   ★★½

STEAK | MODERATE | QUALITY ★★★ | VALUE ★★★½ | ZONE 5

Sam's Town, 5111 Boulder Highway; (702) 456-7777

Customers Visitors, locals **Reservations** Suggested **When to go** Anytime **Entrée range** $15–$40 **Payment** VISA, MC, AMEX, DC, D **Service rating** ★★★½ **Friendliness rating** ★★★½ **Parking** Valet, lot, garage **Bar** Full service **Wine selection** Good **Dress** Come as you are **Disabled access** Through casino

Dinner Sunday–Thursday, 5–10 p.m.; Friday and Saturday, 5–11 p.m.

Setting & atmosphere Stroll through the lovely climate-controlled park to Billy Bob's. The critters that chirp and peep are lifelike robotics; the trees and lush foliage are real. Mosey into the Western-themed Billy Bob's for a taste of the Old West and some mighty fine grub.

House specialties Beef is king at Billy Bob's: steaks and prime rib. The 28-ounce rib-eye is a huge favorite. Entrée prices include soup or salad and a selection from the potato bar. Desserts serve four to six. The Grand Canyon chocolate cake could serve a small army. The foot-long eclair is a dessert lover's fantasy.

Summary & comments Prepare to eat as if you were heading out for a day on the range. The setting and the prices make Billy Bob's a popular choice. At prime times, even with a reservation, there might be a wait. Have a drink in the saloon. After dusk, enjoy the laser light show complete with original music and a lifelike wolf who shows up on the mountain top.

BLUE WAVE   ★★★½

JAPANESE /SUSHI | MODERATE | QUALITY ★★★★ | VALUE ★★★★½ | ZONE 5

Green Valley Town Center, 4300 East Sunset Road (behind T.G.I.F.); (702) 947-2583

Customers Visitors, locals **Reservations** Accepted for 6 or more people **When to go** Anytime **Payment** All major credit cards **Service rating** ★★★½ **Friendliness rating** ★★★½ **Parking** Large lot **Bar** Full service **Wine selection** Modest **Dress** casual **Disabled access** Ground floor

Lunch Monday–Thursday, 11:30 a.m.–2:30 p.m., $13; Friday, 11:30 a.m.–3 p.m., $15; Saturday and Sunday, 11 a.m.–2:30 p.m., $15

Dinner Monday–Thursday, 5:30–9:30 p.m., $22; Friday–Sunday, 5–9:30 p.m., $24; holidays, 11 a.m.–midnight, $24; happy hour (bar only), daily, 5–7 p.m. Children 4–12 years, half price at all seatings.

Setting & atmosphere Blue Wave's decor, lighting and high-tech appointments reflect the owners wish that the eatery be thought of as a restaurant (an à la carte menu is also available) rather than a buffet, but it's hard to deny the stunning 120-foot buffet that dominates one side of the attractive dining room.

House specialties Snow crab legs, plump oysters on the half-shell, spinach and salmon salad, the surprising variety of soups, including black mussel, cream of carrot or pumpkin or tomato or corn; fried oysters; the terrific selection of sushi arranged in the display case like jewels—soft-shell crab roll, sea eel (anago) and freshwater eel (unagi), sea urchin (uni), hamachi, grilled tuna roll, temaki hand roll are just a sampling of the large selection.

Other recommendations The specials offered on various nights, prime rib, or lobster (tasty, but two bites at most of a small spiny lobster); the neat selection of fresh fruits and desserts. Small portions, so tasting many is not a problem. Don't pass on the pale Japanese cookies. They're like shortbread. The tiny lemon tarts are delicious. Tea or soft drinks are included with meals.

Summary & comments Trying to find the entrance (no signage) isn't easy. It's on the side, rather than the front where it would be expected to be. But it's a pretty sight with plants and flowers. Not everyone speaks fluent English here, yet the charm and manners of the staff conquer all. Patio dining when the weather permits. Opt for a table instead of a booth. Booths are small and narrow. The owners are aware of the problem and may have already corrected it.

BONJOUR FRENCH RESTAURANT   ★★★

FRENCH | MOD/EXP | QUALITY ★★★½ | VALUE ★★½ | ZONE 5

8878 South Eastern Avenue (Colonnade movie center at Pebble); (702) 270-2102

Customers Locals **Reservations** Weekends **Entrée range** $16–$24 **Payment** All major credit cards **Service rating** ★★★½ **Friendliness rating** ★★½ **Parking** Large lot **When to go** Anytime **Bar** Full service **Wine selection** Good **Dress** Casual **Disabled access** Ground floor

Open Tuesday–Friday, 11 a.m.–10 p.m.; Friday and Saturday 5:30 p.m.–10 p.m.

Setting & atmosphere Typically French, with checked tablecloths, rustic chandeliers, candlelight, and French music.

House specialties Rack of lamb with herb crust; salmon en croute on a bed of spinach and raisins with tarragon sauce; bouillabaise; mussels stuffed with garlic butter and paprika.

Other recommendations Potato-crusted sea bass on a bed of green lentils; roasted duckling brushed with lavender honey and lime glaze garnished with edible lavender flowers; seasonal specialties.

Summary & comments This charming neighborhood eatery has a loyal local following who take advantage of the four-course, prix-fixe mid-week special (Tuesday–Thursday).

It's a fine value. Marie and Bernard Calatayud are the congenial owners. She is the chef; he oversees the friendly, relaxed dining room.

BOOTLEGGER ★★★

ITALIAN | MOD/EXP | QUALITY ★★★½ | VALUE ★★★★½ | ZONE 1

7700 Las Vegas Boulevard South; (702) 736-4939

Customers Locals, some visitors **Reservations** Accepted **When to go** Anytime **Entrée range** $10–$28 **Payment** VISA, MC, AMEX, DC, D **Service rating** ★★★½ **Friendliness rating** ★★★★½ **Parking** Shopping-center lot **Bar** Full service **Wine selection** Large **Dress** Informal **Disabled access** Ground floor

Open Tuesday–Friday, 11 a.m.–11 p.m.; Saturday and Sunday, 3 p.m.–midnight; Monday, closed. Tavern open 24 hours.

Setting & atmosphere Turn-of-the-century decor, Italian style. Wonderful ancestral portraits decorate the walls. The full bar overlooks an informal dining room with fireplace. Two additional dining rooms offer comfortable banquettes, which are original to the previous location. The booths were relocated in the new location at the request of sentimental longtime patrons of Bootlegger. Twenty-two-hundred-square-foot tavern offers round-the-clock drinking opportunity and a late-night menu.

House specialties Complementary homemade appetizer panettis (small bread puffs) tossed with garlic, oregano, and oil, served with tomato-basil sauce. Homemade breads. Seafood diavolo; veal saltimbocca à la Blackie; and veal Lorraine with fresh mushrooms in a cream and wine sauce, named for the owners. Varied pasta menu, vegetarian menu, pizzas, and calzones. Biscuit tortoni and tartufo.

Other recommendations The seafood dishes are very good.

Summary & comments This venerable Italian restaurant is owned by Nevada's current lieutenant governor. The joint swings on the weekends with regular appearances by such Las Vegas stalwarts as Sonny King and his Show Biz amis. Entertainers in the golden era of Old Las Vegas. The New Hip Era show up regularly. The menu offers all of the Bootlegger faves. A politician's reputation may depend upon it, after all . . .

BOUCHON ★★★★½

FRENCH BISTRO | MOD/EXP | QUALITY ★★★★ | VALUE ★★★★ | ZONE 1

Venetian Hotel, 3355 Las Vegas Boulevard, Venezia Tower; (702) 414-6200

Customers Visitors, locals **Reservations** A must on weekends **When to go** Anytime **Entrée range** $16.95–$29.50 **Payment** All major credit cards **Service rating** ★★★★½ **Friendliness rating** ★★★★½ **Parking** Valet, garage **Bar** Full service **Wine selection** Very good **Dress** Upscale casual **Disabled access** Elevator

Breakfast 6:30–10:30 a.m.

Dinner 5–10:30 p.m.

Oyster Bar & Lounge 3 p.m.–midnight

Setting & atmosphere Designed to be the ultimate bistro, Bouchon is beautiful. Owner Thomas Keller and renowned restaurant/hotel designer Adam Tihany have created a setting with great appeal. This is bistro as an art form

House specialties Fresh seafood plateaus, grand plates with an assortment of freshly shucked raw items and shrimp and lobster. The superb oysters—selection changes with the season. Country paté served with cornichons and radishes. Roasted chicken with a ragout of wild mushrooms.

Other recommendations Bouchon mussels steamed in white wine, mustard, and saffron; steak frites, a pan-seared flat-iron steak with a heap of French fries. Frisée salad with bacon lardons, poached eggs, and warm bacon vinaigrette. Garlic sausage with French green lentils and garlic confit.

Summary & comments The most requested tables are on the outdoor terrace. Difficult to get, but worth a try. There are many á la carte options at moderate cost. Keller has added a hip new dimension to bistro dining.

BRADLEY OGDEN ★★★★

AMERICAN | EXPENSIVE | QUALITY ★★★★½ | VALUE ★★½ | ZONE 1

Caesars Palace, 3570 Las Vegas Boulevard South; (702) 731-7110

Customers Visitors, locals **Reservations** Suggested **When to go** Anytime **Entrée range** $29–$48 (changes daily with menu) **Payment** All major credit cards **Service rating** ★★★★½ **Friendliness rating** ★★★★½ **Parking** Valet, garage **Bar** Full service **Wine selection** Very good **Dress** Upscale casual **Disabled access** Ground floor
Lunch daily, 11:30 a.m.–2:30 p.m..
Dinner Sunday–Thursday, 5–11 p.m.; Friday and Saturday, 5 p.m.–midnight
Bar & Lounge Day menu, 2:30–5 p.m.; night menu, 5 p.m. until kitchen closes

Setting & atmosphere Elegance and simplicity. Soft lighting, beautiful table appointments and comfortable seating in the restaurant and the adjacent bar and lounge. Relaxed and inviting surroundings.

House specialties Menus change daily, but such signatures as the foie gras, Vintage Prime Summerfield Farms New York Steak, the seasonal oysters, the blue cheese soufflé appetizer (not to be missed), and the selection of artisan American cheeses are always in place. Noted chef/owner Bradley Ogden has dubbed his cooking "Farm Fresh American cuisine," buying exclusively from American producers and farmers.

Other recommendations Any of the fish and seafood dishes. Selection varies with the season, but is always exciting. Wood-grilled yellowtail with Dungeness crab leg and green onion pancake, roasted monkfish with mussels, grilled rack of lamb and barbecued lamb bacon, and clay pot Guinea hen with Kara Kara orange sauce are typical. Whimsical, delicious desserts—Carnival Jubilee with a snow cone, mini-funnel cake, ice-cream sandwich, sweet hot pretzel with a trio of fondue sauces, cotton candy; rhubarb upside-down cake with vanilla crème fraîche ice cream; and the intriguing chocolate childhood tasting.

Summary & comments Allow enough time to dine if seeing the Celine show is included (at least two hours). A prix fixe pre-theater menu is in the works. Except for the signature dishes, foods mentioned here may not be available. Lunch and bar menus also change daily. Cooking with Ogden is his son Bryan, graduate of the Culinary Institute of America. Bradley Ogden is the first Las Vegas restaurant to be named the nation's Best New Restaurant by James Beard Foundation. The award was received in 2004.

THE BROILER ★★½

STEAK/SEAFOOD | MOD/EXP | QUALITY ★★★½ | VALUE ★★★½ | ZONE 5

Boulder Station, 4111 Boulder Highway; (702) 432-7777

Customers Visitors, locals **Reservations** Suggested **When to go** Anytime **Entrée range** $16–$56 **Payment** VISA, MC, AMEX, DC, D **Service rating** ★★★½ **Friendliness rating** ★★★★½ **Parking** Valet, lot **Bar** Full service **Wine selection** Fair **Dress** Casual **Disabled access** Through casino

Brunch Sunday, 10 a.m.–2 p.m.

Dinner Sunday–Thursday, 5–10 p.m.; Friday and Saturday, 5–11 p.m.

Setting & atmosphere Comfortable, relaxed dining room with greenery, an exhibition kitchen, and a handsome soup and salad bar. Desert decor with style. A refrigerated showcase at the entrance displays the day's fresh fish and meat selection.

House specialties Fresh seafood, steaks, and prime rib. All entrées include the soup and salad bar, a choice of potatoes or rice, and vegetable or cole slaw. Fish selections are mesquite-grilled or broiled, baked, or sautéed. Most earn the American Heart Association heart symbol for being low cholesterol. Nonfat dressings and sour cream are available, too. Chicken, marinated in herbs and garlic, is cooked on the rotisserie. Sunday brunch is a fine value. Included are the soup and salad bar, dessert, and table service for the entrées.

Summary & comments Reservations should be made for dinner and Sunday brunch.

BUCCANEER BAY CLUB ★★★★½

CONTINENTAL | EXPENSIVE | QUALITY ★★★★½ | VALUE ★★★½ | ZONE 1

T. I., 3300 Las Vegas Boulevard South; (702) 894-7111

Customers Visitors, locals; hotel guests get preference; children under age 5 not allowed **Reservations** Accepted 7 days in advance **When to go** Avoid peak hours **Entrée range** $22–$60, higher for lobster **Payment** All major credit cards **Service rating** ★★★½ **Friendliness rating** ★★★★½ **Parking** Garage, valet **Bar** Full service **Wine selection** Small, but good **Dress** Sport jacket, upscale casual **Disabled access** Elevator

Dinner Daily, 5–10:30 p.m.

Setting & atmosphere Exotic decor and accessories gathered from all parts of the world. Restaurant overlooks the Pirates Village and Buccaneer Bay, scene of the "fight to the finish" sea battles between the British ship *Britannia* and the pirates' *Hispaniola*. It's a fierce, colorful encounter with dialogue to match.

House specialties Pyramid of fresh salmon filets atop a mound of mashed potatoes and fresh vegetables; Buccaneer clams casino; oysters (topped with smoked salmon and hollandaise); lobster bisque under a puff-pastry dome. Bay Club combination—filet mignon au poivre, breast of chicken Oscar. Pirate's Plunder—chocolate treasure chest filled with coconut rum mousse, white chocolate treasure map, and devil's rock cake. Menu changes seasonally.

Other recommendations Smoked salmon Napoleon; lobster ravioli; escargots in brioche; osso buco; veal Florentine; prime rib; Chilean sea bass with fruit salsa. Chocolate Frigate—pair of chocolate ships filled with frozen chocolate and walnut parfaits topped with coconut cookie sails.

Summary & comments The menu, geared to the pirate theme, changes seasonally. Some dishes listed above may not be available. The rousing sea battle takes place every hour and a half from 4 p.m. to 11:30 p.m. Diners experience the fun without the din and smoke. Request a window table for best view of the battle.

BUZIOS ★★★½

SEAFOOD | MOD/EXP | QUALITY ★★★★ | VALUE ★★½ | ZONE 1

Rio, 3700 West Flamingo Road; (702) 252-7697

Customers Visitors, locals **Reservations** Recommended for dinner **When to go** Anytime **Entrée range** $16–$36 **Payment** VISA, MC, AMEX, DC, D **Service rating**

★★★½ **Friendliness rating** ★★★½ **Parking** Valet, lot, covered garage **Bar** Full service **Wine selection** Very good **Dress** Casual **Disabled access** Through casino **Open** Daily, 11 a.m.–11 p.m.

Setting & atmosphere This popular seafood restaurant is a magnet to local business types. The new section has been cleverly added so that the original ambience is intact. The decor includes massive alabaster chandeliers and flowering plants suspended from the canvas-tented ceiling. Walls of glass allow a beautiful view of the sandy beach and pool. A comfortable counter à la Grand Central Station attracts diners who like to watch the seafood being prepared in the individual high-pressure steam kettles. The counter is a good choice for quick meals.

House specialties Buzios offers a selection of fresh oysters from Canada, Maine, and Washington State; clams; shrimp; and many hot seafood appetizers. Fish soups and stews such as bouillabaisse and cioppino; huge bowls filled with a savory assortment of denizens of the deep. Rockefeller-style prawns, clams, or oysters; lobsters from Japan, Finland, Great Britain, Germany, Iceland, and The Netherlands; a selection of fresh fish flown in daily. The irresistible Rio breads, baked in their own bakery in a European open-hearth oven, accompany all dishes. They're wonderful when used to mop up the broth from the fish soups and stews. Endless baskets are provided.

Other recommendations Seafood salads and pastas; the chicken and shrimp combination glazed with a tarragon and honey sauce; any preparation with Chilean sea bass.

Summary & comments Buzios, named for a small Portuguese fishing village, is the Rio's version. All entrées include a choice of salad or soup. On weekends and during conventions, even with reservations, there is sometimes a short wait for a table. Don't fret. For seafood aficionados Buzios is worth a brief delay. Or sit at the oyster bar; the savory pan roasts are quickly prepared.

CAFÉ HEIDELBERG

GERMAN | MODERATE | QUALITY ★★½ | VALUE ★★★½ | ZONE 1

610 East Sahara Avenue (behind Marie Callender's); (702) 731-5310

Customers Locals and German community **Reservations** Accepted **When to go** Anytime **Entrée range** $10–$16 **Payment** All major credit cards **Service rating** ★★★½ **Friendliness rating** ★★★★½ **Parking** Lot **Bar** No **Wine selection** Limited **Dress** Casual, neat **Disabled access** Ground floor

Lunch Daily, 11 a.m.–4 p.m.

Dinner Monday–Saturday, 4–10 p.m.

Setting & atmosphere Simple, clean café setting with patio chairs and tables separated from the Old World booth-lined dining room.

House specialties The generous hot schnitzel sandwich served only at lunch; the zeiger schnitzel (Gypsy schnitzel) pork cutlet topped with a Gypsy-inspired sauce and sautéed mushrooms, onions and wine sauce; the Bavarian plate, a sausage sampler of bratwurst, knockwurst, and Polish sausage.

Other recommendations Rouladen, thin slices of beef filled with onion, smoked bacon, and pickles, then rolled; schnitzel Holstein with fried egg and capers.

Summary & comments Good intentions and generous portions have made Café Heidelberg a success for many years. The lunch specials are good value; entrées include soup or salad and side dishes. When ordering the apple strudel, ask to have it warmed in the oven, not the microwave. A deli on the opposite side of the café sells all things German—meats, cheeses, groceries, and gift items.

CAFÉ NICOLLE   ★★½

CONTINENTAL | MODERATE | QUALITY ★★★½ | VALUE ★★½ | ZONE 3

4760 West Sahara Avenue; (702) 870-7675

Customers Locals **Reservations** Strongly suggested **When to go** Anytime **Entrée range** $9–$30 **Payment** VISA, MC, AMEX, DC **Service rating** ★★★½ **Friendliness rating** ★★★½ **Parking** Shopping-center lot **Bar** Full service **Wine selection** Excellent **Dress** Informal, casual **Disabled access** Ground floor

Open Monday–Thursday, 11 a.m.–10 p.m.; Friday and Saturday, 11 a.m.–11 p.m.; Sunday, closed

Setting & atmosphere Restaurant and European-style outdoor café with cooling overhead mist in summer and heat lamps in winter. Bright, cheerful interior on two levels, with cozy corners for intimate dining.

House specialties Spinach pie; variety of egg dishes; calamari appetizer; osso buco with wine sauce; blue-crab cakes; Atlantic salmon cakes. Scallops Nicolle baked with white wine, paprika, and butter; lamb chops à la Grecque; filet mignon with béarnaise sauce. Same menu all day and evening, plus lunch and dinner specials on blackboard.

Other recommendations Selection of salads, including garlicky Caesar with garlic bread. Selection of pastas, such as penne arrabbiata. Variety of fresh seafood. Spicy veal stew with fettuccine; chicken Française; daily specials. Entrée and dessert crêpes; tiramisu; pecan pie. Cappuccino; espresso; caffe latte.

Entertainment & amenities Live entertainment nightly except Sunday in the bar-lounge area.

Summary & comments This is a longtime local restaurant with a strong local following.

CHANG   ★★½

CHINESE/DIM SUM | MODERATE | QUALITY ★★★½ | VALUE ★★★½ | ZONE 1

Gold Key Shopping Center, Strip and Convention Center Drive; (702) 731-3388

Customers Visitors, locals **Reservations** Suggested **When to go** Anytime **Entrée range** $7–$36 **Payment** VISA, MC, AMEX, CB, DC **Service rating** ★★★½ **Friendliness rating** ★★★★½ **Parking** Shopping-center lot **Bar** Full service **Wine selection** Fair **Dress** Casual **Disabled access** Ground floor

Open Daily, 10 a.m.–midnight
Dim sum Daily, 10 a.m.–3 p.m.

Setting & atmosphere Chang is filled with Chinese art and artifacts, artistic sand-blasted glass, live plants, comfortable booths, and lazy Susan tables for large parties.

House specialties Excellent assortment of dim sum, including the seldom-seen-here Chinese cruller. The sizable dim sum menu offers items not available elsewhere, such as the large, steamed shark's fin dumpling served in a bowl. Bite into it over the bowl, for the delicious dumpling contains not only bits of seafood and mushrooms, but also shark's fin soup. New dumplings include sweet rice enclosed in a steamed bun and piquant Chinese sausage spiral-wrapped in flaky pastry. Peking-style pork cutlet (called Mandarin here); jumbo crystal prawns; half or whole steamed chicken with ginger sauce; crispy beef—a spicy dish of shredded beef; and eggplant Szechuan cooked with ground pork and red chili peppers are all fine choices.

Summary & comments Chang shines during the day when owner Hing is on the premises. She is friendly and helpful and never minds answering questions, even when the restaurant is busy. Service in the evening is friendly, but reserved. Special dishes are always available for Chang's Asian customers. Adventurous eaters are welcome to ask what's available.

CHEESECAKE FACTORY ★★★

ECLECTIC | INEXP/MOD | QUALITY ★★★½ | VALUE ★★★★½ | ZONE 1

The Forum Shops at Caesars Palace; (702) 792-6888

Customers Visitors, locals **Reservations** For large parties only **When to go** Anytime **Entrée range** $8–$18 **Payment** VISA, MC, AMEX, DC, D **Service rating** ★★★½ **Friendliness rating** ★★★★½ **Parking** Valet, garage, lot **Bar** Full service **Wine selection** Fair **Dress** Casual **Disabled access** Ground floor

Open Monday–Thursday, 11:15 a.m. (after the first Atlantis show)–11:30 p.m.; Friday and Saturday, 11:15 a.m.–12:30 a.m.; Sunday, 10:15 a.m.–11:30 p.m.

Setting & atmosphere Patio dining that's perfect for people-watching. The Egyptian-themed dining room has impressive brick-red pillars that reach from the first floor to the second-floor dining room; the ceiling is a series of exquisite murals; lush foliage thrives among the cheesecakes.

House specialties American and ethnic specialties—Vietnamese shrimp rolls; quesadillas; a terrific selection of appetizers, pizzas, and meal-size salads, especially the Beverly Hills pizza salad, Chinese chicken salad, and herb-crusted salmon salad. Chicken Madeira is a most requested dish. The monster Factory Burrito Grande, filled with chicken, cheese, rice, onions, and peppers, and topped with guacamole, salsa, and sour cream accompanied by black beans and rice; fresh lump meat crab cakes or grilled skirt steak; jumbo hamburgers or omelets; scrumptious desserts in addition to the scrumptious cheesecakes—at least 30 or more flavors.

Summary & comments The eclectic menu is so large it's spiral-bound. Portions are more than generous. Share a dish rather than forego the cheesecake. This is no time to order the light version—opt for the real thing and share it. Not to be overlooked is the huge, warm apple dumpling topped with billows of whipped cream. True believers order it with two scoops of vanilla ice cream.

CHINA GRILL ★★★½

ASIAN | MODERATE | QUALITY ★★★½ | VALUE ★★★½ | ZONE 1

Mandalay Bay, 3950 Las Vegas Boulevard South; (702) 632-7777

Customers Visitors, locals **Reservations** Accepted **When to go** Anytime **Entrée range** $26–$49 **Payment** All major credit cards **Service rating** ★★★½ **Friendliness rating** ★★★★½ **Parking** Valet, self **Bar** Full service **Wine selection** Excellent **Dress** Casual **Disabled access** Ground floor

Dinner Daily, 5:30–midnight

Setting & atmosphere Highly original furnishings and lighting and contemporary art and accessories make a dramatic statement at China Grill. It all works.

House specialties Lamb spareribs in a spiced plum sauce; duck pancakes; sake-cured salmon rolls; mahi mahi with amazing lobster mashed potatoes; Shanghai lobster; sizzling whole fish; lobster pancakes. New dishes were being added as of press time.

Other recommendations Asian antipasto; crispy duck with caramelized black vinegar sauce; grilled 38-ounce porterhouse steak with a kimchi dressing; China Grill banana split—enough for a crowd.

Summary & comments Unlike its New York original, the sound level here allows conversation. The comfy lounge is a fine place for relaxing. Food portions are sized to be shared. Dishes arrive as cooked, not all at once, but it's not a problem unless you don't want to share.

CHINA SPICE   ★★★½

CHINESE/ASIAN | MODERATE | QUALITY ★★★★ | VALUE ★★★★½ | ZONE 5

Green Valley Ranch Station, 2300 Paseo Verde Parkway, Henderson; (702) 617-7777

Customers Locals, hotel guests **Reservations** Accepted **When to go** Anytime **Entrée range** $9.95–market price **Payment** All major credit cards **Service rating** ★★★½ **Friendliness rating** ★★★½ **Parking** Valet, garage, lot **Bar** Full service **Wine selection** Good **Dress** Casual **Disabled access** Elevator, ground floor

Dinner Sunday–Thursday, 5–10 p.m.; Friday and Saturday, 5–11 p.m.

Setting & atmosphere High-tech decor that surrounds the room like a spaceship, yet is hip and appealing. China Spice is small; the menu is large.

House specialties Peking duck á la the chef—scallion pancakes, cucumbers, scallions, and hoisin sauce, for a moderate price; heart-healthy dishes; minced chicken in lettuce wraps, Singapore chicken salad, vegetarian lettuce wraps, and soups and vegetable chow fun. Pan-fried pot stickers with a hot ginger-soy dipping sauce. Wok-fried fresh Dungeness crab.

Other recommendations The combination seafood served in a crispy "bird's nest," a fried-potato basket. Crispy-fried garlic chicken; honey-glazed walnut prawns. Dishes from the menu designed for the hotel's Asian clientele. Have an adventure. The pan-fried squid with shrimp paste is delish.

Summary & comments Adjacent to China Spice is Sushi+Sake. Ask nicely and the sushi master just might oblige by sending sushi to China Spice.

CHINOIS   ★★★

CHINESE/FRENCH | MODERATE | QUALITY ★★★½ | VALUE ★★★½ | ZONE 1

The Forum Shops at Caesars Palace; (702) 737-9700

Customers Visitors, locals **Reservations** Recommended **When to go** Avoid conventions **Entrée range** $16–$30 **Payment** VISA, MC, AMEX, DC, D **Service rating** ★★★★ **Friendliness rating** ★★★★½ **Parking** Valet, garage, lot **Bar** Full service **Wine selection** Excellent **Dress** Casual **Disabled access** Ground floor and elevator

Open Daily, 11 a.m.–9 p.m.

Setting & atmosphere Enchanting Asian decor by Barbara Lazaroff, the wife and partner of Chinois owner Wolfgang Puck. All the Asian art and artifacts are from her own private collection. Steps on the dramatic staircase to the upstairs banquet and party room are emblazoned with bits of wisdom in English and Chinese. A waterfall trickles down the stone wall. Both the café and dining room blaze with ribbons of color that, according to Lazaroff, "energize the viewer."

House specialties Hog Island oysters on the half-shell; satays; noodles; wok-charred salmon; incredible short ribs; and crispy sesame-crusted pork loin. The sushi-bar area includes table seating—sushi selection is extensive and excellent. The menu includes many signature dishes from Puck's Chinois on Main in Santa Monica, California— Shanghai lobster, whole sizzling catfish, and grilled Mongolian lamb. A small vegetarian menu is now available, and the chef will adapt other dishes upon request. Service is family style. Entrées are sized to share. Asian-influenced desserts are by the award-winning Spago pastry chef. Have one of the cold premium sakes served in a wine glass, but sip slowly—this is heady stuff.

Summary & comments Chinois is another winner for Puck. The view is wonderful, but it can be noisy when the Trojan horse across the way at FAO Schwarz speaks his piece. The outdoor patio is a fine place for people-watching. Soon to come: a late-night club on the second floor.

CIRCO (OSTERIA DEL) ★★★★

ITALIAN | MOD/EXP | QUALITY ★★★★½ | VALUE ★★½ | ZONE I

Bellagio, 3600 Las Vegas Boulevard South; (702) 693-8150

Customers Visitors, locals **Reservations** Recommended **When to go** Anytime **Entrée range** $12–$36 **Payment** All major credit cards **Service rating** ★★★½ **Friendliness rating** ★★★½ **Parking** Valet, garage **Bar** Full service **Wine selection** Excellent **Dress** Upscale casual **Disabled access** Through casino

Lunch Daily, 11:30 a.m.–2:30 p.m.

Dinner Daily, 5:30–10:30 p.m.

Setting & atmosphere Circo is a delight. At once whimsical and vibrant, the decor is pure fun. Booths, tables, and hideaway corners with a view of the fountains are wonderful. Linger over an espresso and enjoy the action in this homespun but chic haven.

House specialties Pizzas and homemade focaccia breads; home-style Tuscan food inspired by Egidiana Maccioni, matriarch of the New York family that owns the popular Le Cirque; papardelle with a Chianti-braised duck sauce and wild mushrooms; grilled hanger steak with caramelized onions and steak fries; satisfying Tuscan fish soup with lobster, prawns, calamari, monkfish, clams, and mussels. Half orders are a good starter.

Other recommendations Napoleon of grilled portobello mushroom layered with zucchini, crispy potato, goat cheese, and green tomatoes—a vegetarian's dream come true. The sensational desserts.

Summary & comments This elegant Italian restaurant is not as grand as the adjacent Le Cirque, but it's every bit as inviting, and there's super views of the fountain from most tables. Mario Maccioni, son of the founders, directs both restaurants.

COMMANDER'S PALACE ★★★½

CREOLE/CAJUN | EXPENSIVE | QUALITY ★★★★ | VALUE ★½ | ZONE I

Desert Passage at the Aladdin, 3667 Las Vegas Boulevard South; (702) 892-8272

Customers Visitors, locals **Reservations** Suggested **When to go** Anytime **Entrée range** $15–$39; 7-course tasting menu, $85 **Payment** All major credit cards **Service rating** ★★★½ **Friendliness rating** ★★★½ **Parking** Valet, garage **Bar** Full service **Wine selection** Very good **Dress** Upscale casual **Disabled access** Ground floor

Brunch Sunday, 11 a.m.–2:30 p.m.

Lunch Daily, 11 a.m.–2:30 p.m.

Dinner Daily, 6–11 p.m.

Setting & atmosphere Like the original in New Orleans, Commander's Palace is handsome and large, yet at the same time intimate. Divided into spacious dining rooms that flow naturally into one another, the size is minimized. Locals favor the wine room with its candle-lit fireplace and wine walls. The very Southern garden room is just right for ladies who lunch.

House specialties Tasso shrimp Hemican, flash-fried and coated with Crystal hot sauce beurre blanc; the trio of small cups filled with real turtle soup, murky, wonderful gumbo and a soup of the day; pan-roasted gulf oysters with a confit of artichokes; Creole seasoned filet mignon, grilled and served over a warm smashed potato; lamb chops so thick and tender; grits and goat cheese that will make a believer out of anyone who hasn't tried the Southern staple; Louisiana pecan-crusted gulf shrimp. Any of the desserts, but especially the Creole bread pudding soufflé with a heady bourbon sauce; tiny French Quarter Beignets, dusted with powdered sugar, served with a café au lait dipping sauce. The price fixed Sunday Jazz Brunch, a toe-tapping delicious event.

Summary & comments Brad Brennan, the youngest working member of the illustrious New Orleans restaurant family, is always available to chat about New Awlins. Service can sometimes be slow, but the food is always pleasing. Don't expect Café Diablo made tableside. The fire department wouldn't allow it, so there's an exhibition dessert station where diners may gather to watch the flames. The shortest way to reach CP is through the Aladdin casino. It's a long walk through Desert Passage.

CRAFTSTEAK ★★★★½

AMERICAN/STEAK | EXPENSIVE | QUALITY ★★★★½ | VALUE ★★★ | ZONE I

MGM Grand Studio Walk; (702) 891-7318

Customers Visitors, locals **Reservations** Recommended **When to go** Anytime **Entrée range** $26–$49 **Payment** All major credit cards **Service rating** ★★★★½ **Friendliness rating** ★★★★½ **Parking** Valet, garage **Bar** Full service **Wine selection** Excellent **Dress** Casual **Disabled access** Ground floor

Open Daily, 5:30–10 p.m.

Setting & atmosphere Smashing decor, almost a clone to chef/owner Tom Colicchio's acclaimed Craft eatery in New York City, but larger. Colicchio strives for simplicity and quality and can describe the reason for every design component, from the exotic-wood floor to the bronze-and-wood tables with butcher-block elements. The same approach defines the bar and lounge.

House specialties Braised, roasted, and grilled foods; a terrific selection of seasonal side dishes and vegetables; roasted or smoked sweetbreads; grain-fed and grass-fed New York strip steaks; lobster braised in butter.

Other recommendations Braised veal breast or boneless short ribs, quail for an appetizer or main course, duck leg confit. Any of the nostalgic desserts. Anyone remember hot milk cake? The pastry chef does. The roasted peaches are divine and so are toasted-oat waffles with lavender honey-butter and the cinnamon pull-apart brioche.

Summary & comments Smokers can dine in the lounge or at the bar. Executive Chef Chris Albrecht worked with Colicchio at Craft and Gramercy Tavern. Menus change seasonally, so some of the dishes mentioned above may not be available. Valet service for Studio Walk restaurants is available nearby the MGM Grand Arena.

DELMONICO ★★★★

STEAK | EXPENSIVE | QUALITY ★★★★ | VALUE ★★½ | ZONE I

Venetian Hotel, 3355 Las Vegas Boulevard South; (702) 414-3737

Customers Visitors, locals **Reservations** A must **When to go** Avoid conventions **Entrée range** $25–$49 **Payment** VISA, MC, AMEX, DC, D **Service rating** ★★★★ **Friendliness rating** ★★★★½ **Parking** Valet, garage **Bar** Full service **Wine selection** Excellent **Dress** Upscale resort wear **Disabled access** Ground floor

Lunch Daily, 11:30 a.m.–2 p.m.

Dinner Sunday–Thursday, 5:30–10:30 p.m.; Friday and Saturday, 5:30–11 p.m.

Setting & atmosphere Expert lighting sets off the handsome decor highlighted with rich woods and fine fabrics. A separate cigar lounge and bar adjoins the dining room. A chef's table in a private room gives a full view of the kitchen. Must be reserved in advance.

House specialties Dry aged beefsteaks; lobsters from the live tank and fresh fish; roasted, double-cut pork chop with walnut-glazed sweet potatoes; New Orleans–style veal picatta with Louisiana crawfish vegetable slaw; the side dishes—especially the addictive truffle oil-and-Parmesan homemade potato chips.

Other recommendations Grilled creole rack of lamb; baked oysters casino; grilled smoked-salmon flatbread with Maytag white cheddar cheese; Caesar salad, served tableside for two; cornmeal-fried Alabama rock shrimp with mixed greens, avocado, and rémoulade dressing.

Summary & comments It's not surprising that owner Emeril Lagasse has infused the menu with strong Creole influences. Getting a reservation for prime dinner hours is not easy, but if you're willing to dine late or early you may get lucky. (Even with a reservation, diners must confirm by 3 p.m. on reservation day.) A private kitchen table is open to those who order a tasting menu, with an optional wine-pairing offered.

DRAI'S   ★★★★

CALIFORNIA/CONT. | EXPENSIVE | QUALITY ★★★★½ | VALUE ★½ | ZONE 1

Barbary Coast Hotel;,3595 Las Vegas Boulevard South; (702) 737-0555

Customers Visitors, locals **Reservations** Requested **When to go** Anytime **Entrée range** $29–$49 **Payment** VISA, MC, AMEX **Service rating** ★★★★ **Friendliness rating** ★★★★½ **Parking** Valet **Bar** Full service **Wine selection** Very good **Dress** Upscale casual or business attire **Disabled access** Ramp

Dinner Daily, 5:30–midnight

Setting & atmosphere Drai's features a cutting-edge contemporary dining room designed by the owner, Victor Drai. The handsome lounge is designed like a library in a grand home. Filled bookcases cover one wall. The pattern on the faux leopard skin banquettes is repeated on the china and gift tins of cookies. Live plants somehow thrive in the soft lighting of the lounge and the dining room. It's all very appealing. Original art, mostly nudes, are on every wall. A private elevator in the casino transports diners to the lower level, where Drai's is located.

House specialties A large variety of fresh fish and seafood (expertly cooked), including soy-glazed Chilean sea bass, delicate escolar, and Lake Superior whitefish; in season, jumbo langoustine, prepared a variety of ways; calf's liver cut into strips, sautéed with balsamic vinegar and roasted shallots; grilled free-range chicken with roasted garlic and crispy, perfectly cooked French fries; the house signature mashed potatoes in three flavors; briny Willipa Bay oysters from the Northwest; the irresistible chocolate soufflé—order when ordering dinner to avoid a delay.

Other recommendations Rich, creamy soups made without dairy products; terrine of foie gras; frog legs; the vegetarian selection; the whitefish in phyllo dough appetizer.

Summary & comments Drai's has become a hip, hot spot for those who like the nightlife. Dine first, then segue into another world. Wednesday through Saturday Drai's becomes an after-hours nightclub—cool and crowded.

8-0-8 ★★★½

HAWAIIAN/FRENCH | EXPENSIVE | QUALITY ★★★★ | VALUE ★★½ | ZONE I

Caesars Palace, 3570 Las Vegas Boulevard South; (702) 731-7110

Customers Locals, visitors **Reservations** Accepted **When to go** Anytime **Entrée range** $16–$60 **Payment** All major credit cards **Service rating** ★★★½ **Friendliness rating** ★★½ **Parking** Valet, garage, lot **Bar** Full service **Wine selection** Good **Dress** Casual **Disabled access** Ground floor

Dinner Sunday, Monday, and Thursday, 5:30–10:30 p.m.; Friday and Saturday, 5:30–11 p.m.

Setting & atmosphere This newest Caesars dining gem was conceived by Hawaii's premiere chef, French transplant Jean-Marie Josselin. The small dining room and bar glow with special lighting (flattering to everyone). The island influence is everywhere, in the furnishings and appointments. Yet it's not hokey—it's relaxing and lovely.

House specialties Josselin has created an à la carte menu of original specialties with his own island twist. A chilled seafood platter includes seasonal fish and seafood—a typical variety includes Kumamoto oysters, sashimi, sesame poke, shrimp, lobster, and clams (market price). The deconstructed ahi roll is as gorgeous as it is delicious—fusion cooking at its best. Wok-stirred fried lobster, porcini-crusted ahi, miso-crusted Chilean sea bass; any of the terrific appetizers. Desserts are choice. More masterful fusion.

Summary & comments Caesars continues to update and revamp this veteran hotel. It's trendy without being chichi, the food and setting are wonderful. Josselin shows up frequently and is always friendly.

EMERIL'S NEW ORLEANS FISH HOUSE ★★★

SEAFOOD/NEW ORLEANS | EXPENSIVE | QUALITY ★★★½| VALUE ★★★½ | ZONE I

MGM Grand, 3799 Las Vegas Boulevard South; (702) 891-7777

Customers Visitors, locals **Reservations** Strongly suggested **When to go** Avoid convention times **Entrée range** $18–$56; prix fixe, $75 with wine pairing **Payment** VISA, MC, AMEX, DC, D **Service rating** ★★★★½ **Friendliness rating** ★★★★½ **Parking** Valet, lot, covered garage **Bar** Full service **Wine selection** Excellent **Dress** Upscale casual **Disabled access** Through casino

Lunch Daily, 11 a.m.–2:30 p.m.

Dinner Daily, 5:30–10:30 p.m.

Oyster Bar/Café Daily, 11:30 a.m.–10:30 p.m.

Setting & atmosphere "A bit of New Orleans" is the way award-winning chef/owner Emeril Lagasse describes his beautiful restaurant. The main restaurant is comfortable and handsome, with fine appointments and accessories. The separate courtyard dining room is French Quarter pretty with a faux balcony and louvered shutters. Masses of real plants and a stone floor complete the illusion.

House specialties The five- to eight-course "tasting" dinner is a fine way to sample small portions of many dishes, prix fixe at $75; some are special recipes being considered for the menu. Emeril's lobster cheesecake with Creole-spiced tomato coulis; the house Louisiana Choupiquet caviar; the "lobster dome," a whole lobster shelled and served with roasted potatoes, onion marmalade, and lobster sauce and covered with a puff pastry dome; Louisiana campfire steak served on a cedar plank on a bed of country-style mashed potatoes and drizzled with warm rémoulade and Emeril's homemade Worcestershire sauce.

Summary & comments Emeril's is an exciting restaurant that personifies the "new Las Vegas." The faithful, drawn by Emeril's success on the Food Network, regularly fill his Las Vegas eateries.

Honors & awards Emeril's is the recipient of many dining awards, including "Best Southeast Regional Chef"—The James Beard Foundation; "One of the Top 25 Chefs in the Country"—*Food & Wine* magazine; "American Express Fine Dining Hall of Fame"— *Nation's Restaurant News.*

FELLINI'S ★★★

ITALIAN | MODERATE | QUALITY ★★★½ | VALUE ★★★★½ | ZONES 1 & 3

5555 West Charleston Boulevard; (702) 870-9999
Stratosphere, 2000 Las Vegas Boulevard; (702) 383-4859
Sam's Town, 5111 Boulder Highway (702) 456-7777

Customers Visitors, locals **Reservations** Suggested **When to go** Anytime **Entrée range** $16–$28 **Payment** VISA, MC, AMEX, D **Service rating** ★★★★ **Friendliness rating** ★★★★ **Parking** Lot **Bar** Full service **Wine selection** Good **Dress** Upscale casual **Disabled access** Ground floor

Dinner Monday–Thursday, 5–10 p.m.; Friday and Saturday, 5–11 p.m.

Setting & atmosphere Inviting decor and lighting, comfortable seating, fresh flowers, a European-style dessert table, and congenial management that welcomes everyone as if they were longtime friends.

House specialties Warm spinach salad served in an edible Parmesan cheese basket; bouillabaisse (when available); arrabbiata con melanzane (penne pasta in a spicy sauce with grilled eggplant); New Zealand and California mussels in a tomato and white-wine sauce; bistecca Fiorentina (the famous steak of Florence); Tuscan-style grilled chicken breast with little pillows of polenta.

Other recommendations The breads and desserts (all made on the premises); homemade contuccini (small biscotti), served with a glass of Italian dessert wine, Vin Santo—dunk the hard cookies in the wine, as they do in Tuscany.

Summary & comments Fellini's chef-partner Chaz LaForte spent four years in Tuscany refining his skills. He frequently comes out of the kitchen to talk with diners. Live piano music is played at just the right level. Fellini's has a strong local following. The Stratosphere location offers a smaller menu, casual fare.

FIAMMA TRATTORIA ★★★½

ITALIAN | MOD/EXP | QUALITY ★★★★ | VALUE ★★★½ | ZONE 1

MGM Grand, 3799 Las Vegas Boulevard South; (702) 891-7600

Customers Visitors, locals **Reservations** A must on weekends and holidays **When to go** Avoid convention times **Entrée range** $17–$44 **Payment** All major credit cards **Service rating** ★★★½ **Friendliness rating** ★★★★½ **Parking** Valet, garage **Bar** Full service **Wine selection** Very good **Dress** Upscale casual **Disabled access** Main valet, garage

Dinner 5:30–10:30 p.m.

Setting & atmosphere This first Las Vegas venture for New York restaurateur Stephen Hanson is a moe casual version of Fiamma New York. A cheerful fireplace near the bar adds a comforting touch. Separate dining rooms that flow together give a more intimate touch to this sizeable Italian restaurant.

House specialties The all-time favorite Florentine-style charcoal-grilled, dry-aged porterhouse for two carved in the kitchen and reassembled; braised short rib-filled ravioli with just-enough meat an da drizzle of wine sauce; swordfish marinated in olive oil, then grilled and topped with puttanesca sauce; al dente fusille with tiny green peas, San Daniele proscuitto, and truffle butter.

Other recommendations Any of creamy risotto that change each day; the char-grilled octopus appetizer, carpaccio of big-eye tuna with capers, Ligurian black olives, shaved fresh fennel, and citrus oil. The wonderful selection of housemade pastas made on an Italian pasta machine as big as small cottage. Simply marvelous. The irresistible pastries, especially the hot-from-the-fryer Amoretti doughnuts with a creamy center.

Summary & comments Adventurers can order a multicourse tasting dinner. Pricey, but wonderful.

FIORE   ★★★½

CONTINENTAL | EXPENSIVE | QUALITY ★★★½ | VALUE ★★½ | ZONE   I

Rio, 3700 West Flamingo Road; (702) 252-7777

Customers Visitors, locals **Reservations** Suggested **When to go** Anytime except during conventions **Entrée range** $22–$50 **Payment** VISA, MC, AMEX, DC, D **Service rating** ★★★★ **Friendliness rating** ★★★★½ **Parking** Lot, garage, valet **Bar** Full service **Wine selection** Excellent **Dress** Dressy, informal **Disabled access** Ground floor

Dinner   Thursday–Monday, 6–11 p.m.

Setting & atmosphere Handsome exhibition kitchen filled with cookware. Elegant table appointments. Climate-controlled cigar terrace for smokers. A fine selection of cigars.

House specialties Dill and grappa-cured salmon with blinis; limestone lettuce with marinated shiitake mushrooms and lemon avocado oil; charred tuna carpaccio; Dungeness crab cake with diablo sauce; breast of quail salad; Moroccan-spiced chicken in phyllo. The menu changes every seven to ten days, so specialties are always changing.

Other recommendations Pizzas from the wood-burning ovens; any of the nightly rotisserie offerings, including roast lamb; hand-carved New York strip; duck or chicken; whole salmon (portioned). Different woods used for grilling include cherrywood, almond, olive, and mesquite. Edible flowers garnish dishes; Dom Perignon tops sorbets (doused tableside by captain). Twenty fine wine selections by the glass.

Summary & comments Fiore is a departure from the Rio's usual moderately priced restaurants. There is much that's new and exciting here; menu changes are constant.

FLORIDA CAFÉ   ★★★

CUBAN | INEXPENSIVE | QUALITY ★★★½ | VALUE ★★★★½ | ZONE   I

Howard Johnson Hotel, 1481 Las Vegas Boulevard South; (702) 385-3013

Customers Cuban community, locals, HoJo guests **Reservations** No **When to go** Anytime **Entrée range** $5–$15 **Payment** VISA, MC, AMEX, DC **SERVICE RATING** ★★★ **Friendliness rating** ★★★½ **Parking** Lot **Bar** Wine and beer **Wine selection** Small **Dress** Casual **Disabled access** Yes

Breakfast Daily, 7–11 a.m.
Lunch Daily, 11 a.m.–4 p.m.
Dinner Daily, 4–10 p.m.

Setting & atmosphere Colorful Cuban paintings adorn the walls, but it's still a coffee shop at heart.

House specialties Cuban-American food at value prices; Cuban breakfast eggs, stuffed potatoes, sweet plantains, and toast; croquettes; corn ramales; fresh seafood; real Cuban sandwiches, pressed thin in a special grill. All entrées include side dishes.

Other recommendations Classic arroz con pollo, chicken with yellow rice; marinated leg of pork; Cuban pizzas; the many Cuban desserts. A meal could be made from the à la carte side dishes.

Summary & comments Very little English is spoken here, but the staff is accommodating, and the menu descriptions are clear.

FUJI ★★½

JAPANESE | MODERATE | QUALITY ★★★½ | VALUE ★★★½ | ZONE 5

3430 East Tropicana Avenue; (702) 435-8838

Customers Locals **Reservations** Accepted, required on weekends **When to go** Anytime **Entrée range** $9–$17 **Payment** VISA, MC, AMEX, DC, JCB **Service rating** ★★★½ **Friendliness rating** ★★★½ **Parking** Large lot **Bar** Beer and wine only **Wine selection** Fair **Dress** Informal, casual **Disabled access** Ground floor

Lunch Tuesday–Friday, 11:30 a.m.–2 p.m.

Dinner Tuesday–Sunday, 4:30–10 p.m; closed Monday

Setting & atmosphere Small family-style restaurant with 2 teppan tables, booths, and traditional seating.

House specialties All the basic Japanese fare is available: sushi, tempura, sukiyaki, teriyaki. Combination dinners also available.

Other recommendations Tall or large diners will find a table more comfortable than the small booths.

Summary & comments Moderate prices, a caring staff, and good food make Fuji a popular local dining option. Children are treated like honored guests.

GAYLORD'S ★★½

INDIAN | EXPENSIVE | QUALITY ★★★ | VALUE ★½ | ZONE 1

Rio, 3700 West Flamingo Road; (702) 252-7777

Customers Visitors, locals **Reservations** Weekends **When to go** Anytime **Entrée range** $12–$24 **Payment** All major credit cards **Service rating** ★★★ **Friendliness rating** ★★★½ **Parking** Valet, garage, large lot **Bar** Full service **Wine selection** Small **Dress** Casual chic **Disabled access** Ground floor

Lunch Daily, 11 a.m.–2:30 p.m.

Dinner Nightly, 5–11 p.m.

Setting & atmosphere Beautiful Indian art and artifacts, etched-glass windows designed to emulate lace. Splendid carved teakwood elephants guard the entrance.

House specialties Tandoori salmon; tandoori breads; vegetarian appetizers (the samosas and pakoras are terrific); Bombay chicken wings (hot, hot); Royal feast combination dinners; chicken or lamb curries.

Other recommendations The large variety of meatless specialties; prawn vindaloo (jumbo prawns prepared in a spicy hot sauce); chicken tikka masala (mesquite-broiled chicken in a mild tomato-butter sauce).

Summary & comments Gaylord's has the makings of a fine Indian restaurant, but has not yet found its way. Unlike their San Francisco branch, the service and food are uneven. On a good night the food is what it's supposed to be. But hey, this is Las Vegas, so take a chance. It just might be wonderful.

GARDUNO'S AT THE PALMS   ★★★

MEXICAN | INEXP/MOD | QUALITY ★★★½ | VALUE ★★★½ | ZONE 3

Palms, 4321 West. Flamingo Road; (702) 942-7777

Customers Visitors, locals **Reservations** No **When to go** Anytime **Entrée range** $8–$17 **Payment** All major credit cards **Service rating** ★★★½ **Friendliness rating** ★★★★½ **Parking** Valet, lot, parking garage **Bar** Full service **Wine selection** Good **Dress** Casual **Disabled access** Ramp

Sunday Margarita Brunch 10 a.m.–3 p.m. ($12)

Lunch Monday–Friday, 11 a.m.–2 p.m. (except holidays)

Dinner Sunday–Thursday 11 a.m.–10 p.m.; Friday and Saturday, 11 a.m.–11 p.m.

Setting & atmosphere Upscale Mexican chic. Two patios for outdoor dining, dining rooms on two levels, both with views. Garduno's casino perimeter is ringed with oversize, elegant planters. Mexican art and artifacts throughout. The Blue Agave oyster and chile bar gives diners a view of the chefs at work.

House specialties The sizzling fajitas, including a vegetarian version; pastas with Mexican flair—green chile Alfredo, Cajun shrimp and red chipotle chicken. The award-winning Blue Agave pan roasts (voted best new dish by the National Restaurant Association), king crab, lobster, scallop, shrimp, or the house roast—lobster, crab, and shrimp.

Other recommendations Homemade tamales, the relleno combo, green chile Caesars salad, steak enchiladas, the chunky burritos and chimichangas, and the zesty guacamole prepared tableside. Each server has a unique version. Diners can add their own touches or eliminate any ingredient they don't want. Fun to watch and delicious.

Summary & comments Garduno's at the Palm offers more than tasty food. There's a seemingly endless selection of margaritas, tequilas, and mockaritas. Have the fried ice cream for dessert. It's a sweet conversation piece.

GARDUNO'S CHILI PACKING CO.   ★★★

MEXICAN | MODERATE | QUALITY ★★★½ | VALUE ★★★½ | ZONE 4

Fiesta Hotel, 2400 North Rancho Drive; (702) 631-7000

Customers Visitors, locals **Reservations** Not accepted **When to go** Anytime **Entrée range** $9–$15 **Payment** VISA, MC, AMEX, DC, D **Service rating** ★★★½ **Friendliness rating** ★★★½ **Parking** Valet, lot **Bar** Full service **Wine selection** Good **Dress** Informal **Disabled access** Ground floor

Open Sunday, 10 a.m.–3 p.m. (brunch, 11. a.m.–3 p.m.) and 4–10 p.m.; Monday–Thursday, 11 a.m.–10 p.m.; Friday and Saturday, 11 a.m.–11 p.m.

Setting & atmosphere Colorful, appealing Mexican decor with many plants and beautiful artifacts. This large restaurant has been cleverly divided, which makes it intimate.

House specialties Hatch chiles, grown only in the Mesa Valley of New Mexico, are used exclusively. Baskets of fresh sopaipillas accompany entrées. The honey on the table is for pouring over the puffy pillows of dough. Spicy chili verde served in a huge bowl. Guacamole prepared tableside; fresh avocados are mashed, then lime juice, spices, chiles, and seasonings are added to your taste. Tortillas are handmade the old-fashioned way. Posole soup rich with hominy, pork, and red chiles. Any of the fajitas.

Summary & comments The food is authentic and good. Daily lunch specials are large enough to be an early dinner. The Sunday margarita brunch is a fine value and a good way to get to know the Garduno style of Mexican cooking.

GRAPE STREET CAFÉ   ★★★

AMERICAN | MODERATE | QUALITY ★★★½ | VALUE ★★★½ | ZONE 4

Summerhill Plaza, 7501 West Lake Mead Boulevard; (702) 228-9463

Customers Locals **Reservations** Accepted **When to go** Anytime **Entrée range** $8–$24 **Payment** VISA, MC, AMEX **Service rating** ★★★½ **Friendliness rating** ★★★★½ **Parking** Lot **Bar** Wine and beer **Wine selection** Excellent **Dress** Informal **Disabled access** Ground floor

Open Sunday and Tuesday–Thursday, 11 a.m.–10 p.m.; Friday and Saturday, 11 a.m.– 11 p.m. Dinner specials available from 4 p.m.

Setting & atmosphere The 90-seat dining room has brick walls, polished concrete floors, hand-forged wrought-iron tables and chairs (available for sale), a counter facing the kitchen, and a wine bar. Adjacent to the dining room is the wine cellar sales room and a take-out counter. Grape Street is a very homey place with a San Francisco feel.

House specialties Any of the daily specials; the grilled goat cheese and portobello mushroom "Philly" sandwich; the exceptional chopped salad; any of the entrée-sized salads; linguine with Brie; the plate-sized pizzas with creative toppings, or make up your own; the tapas appetizer (roasted garlic and vegetables, Greek meatballs, olives, and goat cheese); the salmon burger.

Other recommendations The reasonably priced dinner specials served after 4 p.m., which include a house salad and side dishes; the succulent rack of lamb includes English-style mint sauce; chocolate fondue with fruit and cake for dipping, big enough for two.

Summary & comments Grape Street is a delightful, informal eatery with caring owners. An outdoor patio seats 50. It's always busy. At least 50 wines are always available by the glass. Wines from the cellar are available with meals for just $6 over the retail price. The take-out counter sells pâtés, imported cheeses, and a variety of prepared dishes that would be ideal for a picnic. Live music every Thursday night includes everything from Flamenco to jazz to steel drums to folk and acoustic.

HABIB'S   ★★★

MIDDLE EASTERN | MODERATE | QUALITY ★★★½ | VALUE ★★½ | ZONE 3

Sahara Pavilion, 4750 West Sahara Avenue; (702) 870-0860

Customers Visitors, locals **Reservations** Accepted **When to go** Anytime **Entrée range** $11–$22 **Payment** VISA, MC, AMEX **Service rating** ★★½ **Friendliness rating** ★★★½ **Parking** Shopping-center lot **Bar** Beer and wine only **Wine selection** Poor **Dress** Casual **Disabled access** Ground level

Lunch Monday–Saturday, 11:30 a.m.–3 p.m.

Dinner Monday–Saturday, 5–10 p.m.

Setting & atmosphere Located in the restaurant corridor of a popular neighborhood shopping center, this attractive, small restaurant has gained a loyal local following. A mist-controlled outdoor patio allows for al fresco dining even in warm weather. The area is filled with beautiful plants.

House specialties Middle Eastern appetizers and salads; chicken, ground beef, and beefsteak kabobs; many Persian specialties.

Other recommendations Tabbouleh salad so fresh the parsley tastes just-picked; the eggplant appetizer, borani; hummus; torshi, a mixture of pickled, aged vegetables; zereshk polo, a seasoned chicken-breast kabob prepared with barberries and fragrant spices that are then mixed with rice.

Summary & comments Habib's menu is not large, but it is filled with exotic, delicious dishes that, except for the Middle Eastern starters and salads, have unfamiliar names. The waitstaff is happy to explain the food to the best of their ability. At least two of the special Persian dishes listed separately on the menu are available each day. Habib's is the only Persian restaurant in Las Vegas; the Middle Eastern dishes are a concession to his sizable following of Middle Eastern customers. Photos of the dishes are included with the menu, enabling diners unfamiliar with the cuisine to see what the finished dish looks like. A selection of American dishes has been added, giving Habib's a broader base of diners. A Habib market is a new addition. A good place to buy exotic foods and gifts.

HARLEY-DAVIDSON CAFÉ ★★½

AMERICAN ROAD FOOD | MODERATE | QUALITY ★★★½ | VALUE ★½ | ZONE 1

Strip at Harmon; (702) 740-4555

Customers Mostly visitors **Reservations** Accepted **When to go** Anytime **Entrée range** $8–$22 **Payment** All major credit cards **Service rating** ★★★ **Friendliness rating** ★★★★ **Parking** Garage and lot **Bar** Full service **Wine selection** Fair **Dress** Casual **Disabled access** Ground floor

Open Daily, 11 a.m.–midnight

Setting & atmosphere Hog heaven for Harley fans. This place is a kick. It's home to Harley Davidson memorabilia, past, present, and future, including one-of-a-kind H-D bikes and famous movie bikes. A special section celebrates Las Vegas entertainment legend Ann-Margret. A 1,500 pound H-D Heritage Softail Classic Bike bursts through the café's facade. What a sight!

House specialties Harley Hog sandwich, Carolina pulled pork covered in barbecue sauce with two sides; a chunky chicken pot pie overflowing with a pastry crust; a veggie wrap (would you believe it?) with grilled veggies in a sundried tomato wrap; the café's homestyle meat loaf, a thick slab covered in brown gravy; barbecued baby-back ribs. Sweet things, too—Reese's chocolate peanut-butter pie topped with chocolate ice cream, a warm chocolate-chip Toll House cookie swimming in hot chocolate sauce with a scoop of English toffee crunch ice cream.

Summary & comments The adjacent, fully loaded merchandise store is a treasure of Harley Davidson merchandise. Be patient; there's usually a line of fans waiting to get their turn. The store is open daily, 10 a.m.–11 p.m. Have fun, ya hear?

HAWAIIAN PLANTATION HOUSE ★★★

HAWAIIAN | MOD/EXP | QUALITY ★★★½ | VALUE ★★★ | ZONE 5

10940 South Eastern Avenue (near Horizon Ridge); (702) 990-6341

Customers Visitors, locals **Reservations** Recommended **When to go** Anytime **Entrée range** $8–$30 **Payment** All major credit cards **Service rating** ★★★½ **Friendliness rating** ★★★★½ **Parking** Large lot **Bar** Full service **Wine selection** Modest **Dress** Casual **Disabled access** Ground floor

Lunch 11 a.m.–2:30 p.m.

Dinner 5:30–10 p.m.

Pauhana (means done for the day) 10:30 p.m.–2:30 a.m.

Setting & atmosphere Aloha life reincarnated. Partner Norman Schuhardt spent many years in Hawaii. His affection for the Islands comes through in the colorful decor, music, and mellow staff.

House specialties Island-style appetizers (pupus) that are satisfying and delicious. Big Island barbecue dishes such as the Huli Huli roasted chicken basted with five-spice teriyaki sauce. Maui onion soup with Puna goat cheese croutons. Crispy ginger-duck salad with Asian vegetables. Any of the fresh island fish, grilled or blackened.

Other recommendations The value-priced plates ($8 or $10) served at lunch that include macaroni salad and steamed rice and a choice of shoyu chicken or grilled mahi mahi or pork and cabbage and more. The combination plates served at dinner. Shellfish and pasta selection. The island drinks—sip the heady brews slowly. Pineapple upside down cake or hula pie.

Summary & comments Hawaiian Plantation House is a congenial place. A children's, or Keiki, menu offers pizza, mac and cheese, coconut shrimp, and other kid favorites. Dessert is included. The late-night Pauhanamenu is a smaller version of the dinner carte.

HOFBRAUHAUS ★★★

GERMAN | MODERATE | QUALITY ★★★½ | VALUE ★★★★½ | ZONE 1

4510 Paradise Road; (702) 853-2337

Customers Visitors, local German community, beer enthusiasts **Reservations** Requested for main dining room **When to go** Anytime **Entrée range** $8.95–$25.95 **Payment** All major credit cards **Service rating** ★★★½ **Friendliness rating** ★★★½ **Parking** Valet, large lot **Bar** Limited **Wine selection** Small **Dress** Casual **Disabled access** Ramp

Hours 11 a.m. until; specials served until 5 p.m.

Setting & atmosphere A mini-replica of Munich's Hofbrauhaus that required permission from the German government. The main dining room is where the action is. Communal tables and oompah bands flown in monthly put the din in diner, yet the crowds love it. Comely frauleins dressed in dirndls hoisting as many as eight steins without a tray.

House specialties Tennis-ball-sized dumplings that accompany the pork stew and a few other braised dishes; sauerbraten that can be on the dry side—the beer makes it easier to go down. Roasted chicken and potato pancakes. Pretzels baked throughout the day. The dough is shipped in containers from Germany, shaped and baked in the kitchen. Weiner schnitzel. Tender, tasty spaetzle.

Other recommendations Crisp apple strudel, not too sweet, just delicious.

Summary & comments Take advantage of the discount coupons available in most hotels and taxis. Those seeking German food in more bucolic surroundings can request to sit in the faux gardens behind the main dining room. A monitor, sans sound, shows the action in main room. The attractive gift shop is worth a look-see. Prices are fair, and there are many specials.

HUGO'S CELLAR ★★★

AMERICAN | EXPENSIVE | QUALITY ★★★½ | VALUE ★★★½ | ZONE 2

Four Queens Hotel, 202 Fremont Street; (702) 385-4011

Customers Visitors, locals **Reservations** Strongly recommended **When to go** Anytime but Friday and Saturday **Entrée range** $26–$56 **Payment** VISA, MC, AMEX, DC, D **Service rating** ★★★½ **Friendliness rating** ★★★★½ **Parking** Indoor garage, valet **Bar** Full service **Wine selection** Very good wine list **Dress** Informal, tie and jacket suggested **Disabled access** Elevator to cellar

Dinner Daily, 5:30–11 p.m.

Setting & atmosphere Unique cellar location, comfortable lounge, warm bar, and gracious hostess. Booths provide privacy; noise at minimum. Cozy cocktail lounge serves pâté, cheese, crackers, and very large drinks.

House specialties Variety of breads, including lavosh crackers. Waiter creates salad of choice from selection on the cart wheeled to your table. Steaks and prime rib; duck flambé anise; snapper en papillote with shallots and white wine; medallions of lobster with white wine, crushed red pepper, sun-dried tomatoes, and mushrooms.

Other recommendations Appetizer for two of beef tenderloin medallions; marinated swordfish, breast of chicken, and jumbo shrimp cooked at the table on sizzling granite slab. Imaginative preparations of veal and chicken; rack of lamb Indonesian.

Entertainment & amenities Hostess presents a fresh rose to female guests. Sorbet is served in a miniature cone. Chocolate-dipped fruits with whipped cream are presented before dessert order is taken.

Summary & comments A most popular downtown restaurant. On weekends the Cellar is packed. Expert wine steward to assist you with selection. Don't let the little cone of sherbet served between courses throw you—it's a house signature. A consistent local favorite, in spite of too-high prices.

IL FORNAIO ★★½

ITALIAN | MODERATE | QUALITY ★★★½ | VALUE ★★★½ | ZONE I/HENDERSON

New York–New York, 3790 Las Vegas Boulevard South; (702) 740-6969

Green Valley Ranch, 2300 Paseo Verde Drive, Henderson; (702) 617-7777

Customers Visitors, locals **Reservations** Suggested for dinner **When to go** Anytime **Entrée range** $10–$22 **Payment** VISA, MC, AMEX, CB, JCB **Service rating** ★★★½ **Friendliness rating** ★★★★½ **Parking** Valet, garage **Bar** Full service **Wine selection** Small, but good **Dress** Informal **Disabled access** Ground floor

Open Daily, 8:30 a.m.–midnight

Setting & atmosphere Upscale, upbeat contemporary decor. Rich woods and natural stone and marble accents. Dine on the outdoor patio with a view of the flowing brook and people-watch as you dine. Faux trees add an almost real touch of nature.

House specialties Carpaccio with shavings of Italian cheese, capers, and baby arugula; Tuscan tomato-and-bread soup; the meal-sized salad of mixed greens, rotisserie chicken, apple wood-smoked bacon, and shaved Parmesan; the selection of thin-crusted pizzas baked in the wood-fired oven. Eat at the bar and watch as they're assembled and baked. The herbed chicken roasted on the wood-burning rotisserie and served with vegetables and roasted potatoes; the 22-ounce certified Angus porterhouse marinated in olive oil and rosemary, served with Tuscan white beans and sautéed spinach; the remarkable breads, baked on the premises, served with all meals.

Other recommendations Any of the homemade pastas, especially the ravioli filled with spinach, Swiss chard, pine nuts, and basil, with baby artichokes; grilled fresh salmon; veal scallopini with baby artichokes and lemon; elbow macaroni with chicken breast, fresh broccoli, and sun-dried tomatoes.

Summary & comments The success of New York–New York has brought an enormous amount of business to Il Fornaio. Dine during off hours for the most relaxing experience. Patio dining is the most requested. It can be noisy, so opt to dine in the lovely dining room. Take home the remarkable Il Fornaio European breads. They're sold in Il Fornaio's retail bakery/coffee house just a few doors from the restaurant. The new location at Green Valley Ranch in Henderson is more upscale, less crowded. Outdoor dining, handsome Tuscan decor.

INKA ★★½

PERUVIAN BISTRO | INEXPENSIVE | QUALITY ★★★½ | VALUE ★★★½ | ZONE 1

2797 South Maryland Parkway; (702) 731-0826

Customers Visitors, locals **Reservations** No **When to go** Anytime **Entree range** $8–$16 **Payment** All major credit cards **Service rating** ★★★★½ **Friendliness rating** ★★★★½ **Parking** Large lot **Bar** Full service **Wine selection** Interesting **Dress** Casual **Disabled access** Ground floor

Open From 11 a.m. (same menu)

Setting & atmosphere Pure Peruvian, from the tapestry paintings to the punched tin accents and the photos. All of the staff is from Peru, much of the food is shipped from Peru. Inka is large and colorful—even the humor is an import (read the rules of the house on the menu).

House specialties Most of the dishes are variations on the same theme—seafood, salads, fish, and meats (well done). Most of the meats are marinated and skewered. Inka's paella is a generous plateful of seasoned rice studded with scallops, fish, shrimp, and calamari.

Other recommendations Baked scallops covered with a crisp layer of Parmesan cheese; chicha, a sweetened soft drink made from purple (almost black) corn, flavored with cinnamon and clove.

Summary & comments A whimsical, humorous staff offers caring service and corny repartee. Eat here 3 times and you get to dance with a waiter who will also teach you to speak Spanish (dinner time only). The cool bar serves appetizers. Don't expect the same dish on a second visit—Inka boasts that "our food is so homemade that it never tastes the same." Only the fun is always the same.

ISIS ★★★

CONTINENTAL | EXPENSIVE | QUALITY ★★★½ | VALUE ★★½ | ZONE 1

Luxor, 3900 Las Vegas Boulevard South; (702) 262-4773

Customers Visitors, locals **Reservations** Suggested **When to go** Anytime **Entrée range** $26–$49 **Payment** VISA, MC, AMEX, DC, D **Service rating** ★★★★½ **Friendliness rating** ★★★★½ **Parking** Lot, valet **Bar** Full service **Wine selection** Excellent **Dress** Dressy, informal **Disabled access** Elevator

Dinner Friday–Tuesday, 5:30–11 p.m.; closed Wednesday and Thursday

Setting & atmosphere Exact replicas of the statues guarding the entrance to the pharaohs' tombs dramatically flank the entrance to Isis. Glass-enclosed Egyptian artifacts separate the comfortable booths. A statue of Isis is the focal point of this lovely dining room.

House specialties Poached oysters over creamed spinach with a touch of Pernod; baked shrimp filled with crab and mushroom duxelle; Sonoma greens with warm goat cheese and walnut dressing; beef Wellington; lobster tail en croute with seafood mousse and white zinfandel sauce. Baked Egypt (pyramid-shaped baked Alaska); specialty coffees, Ramses's Torch and Flaming Sceptor.

Other recommendations Grenadine of veal sautéed with sorrel and dry vermouth sauce; Red Sea sesame chicken with lobster tahini; seafood ravioli in chive and lobster sauce; Dahibeyeh Delight (barge-shaped chocolate mousse with raspberry filling).

Entertainment & amenities Romantic harpist performs at restaurant's entrance.

Summary & comments Unusual menu cover decorated with illustrations of Egyptian stone carvings is just one of the original touches at Isis.

ISLA ★★★★½

CONTEMP. MEXICAN | MODERATE | QUALITY ★★★★ | VALUE ★★★★½ | ZONE 1

T. I., 3300 Las Vegas Boulevard South; (702) 894-7349

Customers Visitors, locals **Reservations** Suggested for weekends **When to go** Anytime **Entrée range** $10–$25 **Payment** All major credit cards **Service rating** ★★★★½ **Friendliness rating** ★★★★½ **Parking** Valet, garage **Bar** Full service, excellent tequila list **Wine selection** Interesting and good **Dress** Casual **Disabled access** Valet or elevator

Open 11 a.m.–11 p.m.

Setting & atmosphere Hot, new Mexican Isla is a comfort zone just off the casino. Sophisticated decor without pretense. The patio bar is designed for those who want a bit of people-watching with their cocktails and light noshes.

House specialties Made-from-scratch guacamole from a cart brought tableside. Try the lobster guacamole studded with bits of lobster, achiote passion fruit, and serrano chiles. Pulled pork tamale with sweet and spicy chipotle sauce; the Sandoval family dish—roast pork pipian, lean pork tenderloin marinated in tamarind sauce. Slices of the roast pork are arranged atop a bed of crushed sweet corn and encircled with a rich pumpkin-seed puree.

Other recommendations Crispy empanadas filled with shredded beef, toasted pine nuts, and dried cherries; the delicious trio of corn masa cakes with various toppings; crispy rock shrimp tacos laced with chipotle rouille, a Mexican spin on the garlicky mayonnaise; the huitlacoche dumpling served with the spiced chicken breast.

Summary & comments Garbed in an eye-catching gown, the statuesque tequila goddess gives diners a crash course in tequila. The selection of original Mexican dishes is unique and outstanding. The names may be familiar, but the food is original and wonderful.

KATHY'S SOUTHERN COOKING ★★½

AMERICAN | MODERATE | QUALITY ★★★½ | VALUE ★★★★½ | ZONE 5

6407 Mountain Vista Street; (702) 433-1005

Customers Locals **Reservations** Suggested, especially for groups of 6 or more **When to go** Anytime **Entrée range** $12–$23 **Payment** VISA, MC, AMEX, D **Service rating** ★★★½ **Friendliness rating** ★★★½ **Parking** Shopping-center lot **Bar** Wine and beer only **Wine selection** Limited (house wine) **Dress** Informal **Disabled access** Ground floor

Open Tuesday–Thursday, 11 a.m.–8:30 p.m.; Friday and Saturday, 11 a.m.–9:30 p.m.; Sunday, 1–7:30 p.m. Same menu. Closed Monday.

Setting & atmosphere Casual, down-home dining room with 46 seats. One wall is painted with a mural of a paddle wheeler on the Mississippi River.

House specialties Gumbo; catfish; "gravy dinners"—smothered pork chop, steak, or chicken with rice or mashed potatoes, slabs of cornbread, and a side dish from a selection of black-eyed peas, red beans and rice, greens, and more.

Other recommendations Oxtails; shrimp Creole; barbecued beef and spareribs; étouffé, sweet-potato pie. Kathy's spareribs are huge, with a zesty sauce that will make you tingle. Hearty, wholesome fare.

Summary & comments The owner of this family operation, Kathy Cook, presents authentic selections from Mississippi and Louisiana kitchens "like Mama used to make." Comfortable, with a "you all" kind of friendliness. Park in shopping center and walk through to Mountain Vista Street (no access from shopping center).

KOKOMO'S ★★★½

SEAFOOD/STEAK | VERY EXPENSIVE | QUALITY ★★★★ | VALUE ★★½ | ZONE 1

The Mirage, 3400 Las Vegas Boulevard South; (702) 791-7111

Customers Visitors **Reservations** Required; high rollers and hotel guests get preference; reservations available 7 days in advance **When to go** Anytime **Entrée range** $35–$65 (à la carte) **Payment** VISA, MC, AMEX, DC, D **Service rating** ★★★★½ **Friendliness rating** ★★★½ **Parking** Lot (long walk), valet **Bar** Full service **Wine selection** Good choices **Dress** Casual **Disabled access** Ramp

Dinner Daily, 5–10:30 p.m.

Setting & atmosphere Magnificent tropical decor—waterfalls, streams, lush foliage, orchids, and other exotic flowers—brings the South Pacific to the Strip. Tables are well spaced for privacy.

House specialties Red onion soup with Monterey Jack and Parmesan cheeses. Shaved fried onions; steaks; chops and ribs; grilled rib-eye with sautéed red onions and tricolor pepper sauce. Crème brûlée; peanut-butter cheesecake; chocolate mousse; bread pudding.

Other recommendations Orange roughy caprice; veal and salmon combo; baked oysters in a smoked-salmon crust; sea bass Montego; lobster Mediterranean style; grilled Polynesian swordfish; broiled breast of chicken basted with honey mustard; extra-thick lamb chops. English trifle; marshmallow brownie cheesecake; apple torte with cinnamon ice cream; taco shell delight; raspberries with Grand Marnier crème; chocolate sinful pâté with pecan brandy sauce.

Summary & comments Imaginative chefs and decor combine to create a memorable lunch or dinner in this romantic room. Peaceful and romantic, Kokomo's is a sleeper. One of the best-kept secrets in town.

KOREANA ★★½

KOREAN | MODERATE | QUALITY ★★★★ | VALUE ★★½ | ZONE 5

2447 East Tropicana Avenue; (702) 458-6869

Customers Locals **Reservations** Suggested weekends **When to go** Anytime **Entrée range** $12–$20 **Payment** VISA, MC **Service rating** ★★★½ **Friendliness rating** ★★★★½ **Parking** Lot **Bar** Wine and beer **Wine selection** No **Dress** Casual **Disabled access** Ground floor

Lunch Monday–Friday, 11 a.m.–2:30 p.m. (except holidays)
Dinner Daily, 11 a.m.–midnight

Setting & atmosphere Minimalist decor (there isn't any) does not detract from the good food served in this neat and clean, small Korean eatery.

House specialties Dinners cooked at the table, by the server, on an electric grill. Price includes a number of side dishes—cooked seaweed, not-too-fiery kimchi, spinach, cucumbers and seaweed, bean sprouts, a bowl of salad, and slightly vinegared rice. The marinated rib-eye is a good choice.

Other recommendations Selections from the à la carte menu: steamed black cod in a spicy sauce, shredded beef brisket noodle soup, broiled fish, the casserole dishes.

Summary & comments Good, moderately priced food without any frills. Service is caring. English is limited, but somehow questions get answered.

LA SCALA ★★★

ITALIAN | MODERATE | QUALITY ★★★★ | VALUE ★★½ | ZONE 1

1020 East Desert Inn Road (a few blocks east of the Strip); (702) 699-9980

Customers Visitors, locals **Reservations** Suggested weekends **When to go** Anytime **Entrée range** $11–$28 **Payment** All major credit cards **Service rating** ★★★★½ **Friendliness rating** ★★★★½ **Parking** Lot **Bar** Full service **Wine selection** Good **Dress** Upscale casual **Disabled access** Ground level

Lunch Monday–Friday, 11:30 a.m.–2 p.m.

Dinner Daily, 5–10 p.m.

Setting & atmosphere Recently refurbished, La Scala is a cheerful, pretty room that belies its history with many previous owners.

House specialties The daily specials listed on a reader board (the fresh fish is the most expensive), any of the homemade pastas, the buffalo carpaccio, calamari, and pescolini fritti— deep-fried squid or smelts with a spicy marinara sauce, pansanella alla Toscana—Tuscan bread salad with a Chianti vinegar dressing, lumachi Tirolesi—baked escargots irolo-style.

Other recommendations The five-course tasting dinner (two-person minimum) that lets the chef show off his culinary talent. Lamb chops with fresh artichoke; Melanzane alla Parmigiana, a more delicate take on the standard eggplant fave; homemade cappellacci pasta filled with lobster and crab in a bisque-like sauce.

Summary & comments The new owners have reclaimed the reputation of the former Vesuvio and its venerable Joe Pignatello, Old Blue Eyes' favorite chef, but the melody lingers on with the savvy owners and chef of La Scala.

LAWRY'S THE PRIME RIB ★★★

AMERICAN/PRIME RIB | EXPENSIVE | QUALITY ★★★½ | VALUE ★★½ | ZONE 1

4043 Howard Hughes Parkway; (702) 893-2223

Customers Visitors, locals **Reservations** Requested **When to go** Anytime but convention times **Entrée range** $25–$40 **Payment** All major credit cards, JCB **Service rating** ★★★★½ **Friendliness rating** ★★★★½ **Parking** Valet, lot **Bar** Full service **Wine selection** Good **Dress** Business attire **Disabled access** Ground floor

Dinner Sunday–Thursday, 5–10 p.m.; Friday and Saturday, 5–11 p.m.

Setting & atmosphere Elegant but not intimidating, Lawry's reflects the founder's philosophy that a restaurant should be "believable, understandable, and appeal to all." The dramatic "silver" carts brought to the table so the beef can be carved as you watch are actually made of hammered stainless steel. A handsome separate bar is a fine place for before- or after-dinner drinks.

House specialties Prime rib, and not much else, has kept diners happy since the original Lawry's The Prime Rib opened in Beverly Hills, California, in 1938. All prime-rib dinners include a spinning salad bowl, Yorkshire pudding, mashed potatoes, and whipped cream horseradish. Four cuts of prime rib are offered. Add twin lobster tails to a prime-rib dinner for an additional $16.95.

Other recommendations The fresh fish of the day—expertly prepared in the kitchen, accompanied by seasonal vegetables; the nostalgic creamed spinach or creamed corn. The selection of homespun desserts, especially the deep-dish apple pie with caramel sauce and the coconut banana cream pie.

Summary & comments How can a restaurant survive that's devoted almost exclusively to prime rib in a town filled with inexpensive prime-rib deals? Very well, indeed. Lawry's Las Vegas opened with a rush that's never stopped. For prime-rib devotees, it's the ultimate luxurious temple of beefdom. Consistent food and service.

LITTLE BUDDHA ★★★½

CHINESE/SUSHI | MOD/EXP | QUALITY ★★★★ | VALUE ★★★ | ZONE 5

Palms, 4321 West. Flamingo Road; (702) 942-7778

Customers Locals, celebs, visitors **Reservations** Suggested weekends **When to go** Anytime **Entrée range** $13–$24 **Payment** All major credit cards **Service rating** ★★★½ **Friendliness rating** ★★★★½ **Parking** Valet, garage, lot **Bar** Full service **Wine selection** Small but good **Dress** Casual chic **Disabled access** Ground floor

Open Daily, 5:30 p.m. until

Setting & atmosphere Soft lighting and elegant, laid-back decor. A handsome sushi bar was recently added. Have a drink at the bar. It's the place for conversation and making new friends.

House specialties Lettuce wraps with a generous amount of chicken, not minced, but sliced into chunks. Wok-fried salt-and-pepper calamari; crispy chicken spring rolls with a sweet chili sauce. Pork loin with pineapple-and-mango sauce; seabass and salmon harlequin pave, an original dish from chef Jean Paul; filet mignon cooked teppanyaki style. Duck confit with orange sauce—a succulent fall-off-the-bone duck leg served with baby bok choy.

Other recommendations Sesame-crusted ahi tuna; red-fire curry shrimp with cilantro rice. The banana and mango phyllo roll, the caramelized lemon tart, or crème brûlée desserts.

Summary & comments After a slow start, a new manager and a new executive chef have turned this Paris (France) transplant around. The super sushi is available at the sushi bar or at a table. The dinner menu is also offered at the sushi bar.

LOTUS OF SIAM ★★★

THAI | MOD/EXP | QUALITY ★★★½ | VALUE ★★½ | ZONE 1

Commercial Center, 953 East Sahara Avenue; (702) 735-3033

Customers Locals, visitors **Reservations** Not required **When to go** Anytime **Entrée range** $8–$20; lunch buffet, $10; market price **Payment** VISA, MC **Service rating** ★★½ **Friendliness rating** ★★★★½ **Parking** Lot **Bar** No **Wine selection** Good **Dress** Casual, dressy **Disabled access** Ground floor

Lunch Monday–Friday (buffet and menu), 11:30 a.m.–2:30 p.m.
Dinner Daily, 5:30–9:30 p.m.

Setting & atmosphere Attractive, though modest, decor; teak tables and comfortable chairs. Thai paintings and accessories.

House specialties Beef jerky, Nissan style—crisp yet tender marinated beef served in a spicy sauce. Nam kao tod—minced, tart sausage mixed with crispy rice, ginger, peanuts, and lime juice. Green papaya salad with or without crab; salmon Panang—charbroiled fresh salmon, served Thai-style with a creamy curry sauce.

Other recommendations Long-grained sticky rice steamed and served in small bamboo baskets; the generously sized satays. Ask the owner to design a special menu of Nissan dishes for your party. The seasonal soft-shell, crispy prawns are outstanding. Shells are edible—chew carefully.

Summary & comments The Nissan specialties featured here come from the Northwestern corner of Thailand, bordering Laos. These dishes are both hotter and more highly seasoned than most Thai food, but the chef/owner will temper the heat to suit your taste. Gentle, caring service and exceptional, if little-known, Thai dishes make Lotus of Siam a fine choice when you've jostled through quite enough surf 'n' turf buffets, thank you. Service can be slow, especially on the weekends.

LUCILLE'S ★★★½

SOUTHERN/BARBECUE | MODERATE | QUALITY ★★★★ | VALUE ★★★★½ | ZONE 5

The District at Green Valley Ranch, 2245 Village Wal Drive; (702) 257-7427

Customers Locals, visitors **Reservations** No **When to go** Anytime **Entrée range** From $14.95 **Payment** All major credit cards **Service rating** ★★★ **Friendliness rating** ★★★★½ **Parking** Large lot **Bar** Full service **Wine selection** Modest **Dress** Casual **Disabled access** Ramp

Hours Sunday–Thursday, 11 a.m.–11 p.m.; Friday and Saturday, 11 a.m.–midnight

Setting & atmosphere The legend of Lucille and her life with grandma "in a tiny little nothing of a place on a back road," is a fairy tale concocted by the California family who owns this funky barbecue restaurant and four more in California. It's designed to look like a roadside restaurant before fast food took over the country's landscape.

House specialties Humongous portions of tasty appetizers, salads, Bunyan-sized barbecue dinners, and many specialities. The buttermilk biscuits are warm, tender, and like everything else at Lucille's—bigger than life. Sandwiches and burgers on homemade buns or baguettes. The dinosaur-sized beef ribs are awesome.

Other recommendations The fried pork chop or barbecued rib-tip appetizer large enough for two or three people; Lucille's onion straws. The best old-fashioned banana pudding ever, served in a pint-sized wide-mouth Mason jar—the pudding is made from scratch and assembled when ordered; the peach cobbler with a biscuit crumb topping.

Summary & comments Live jazz and blues Friday and Saturday nights. Take-home boxes are a way of life at Lucille's. Order the full rack of ribs for just a few dollars more and share dinner. Kids love Lucille's. Call ahead and they'll tell you how long the wait is or come early and shop Las Vegas' newest mall. It's designed for walking and sight-seeing.

MAKINO SUSHI RESTAURANT ★★★½

JAPANESE | MODERATE | QUALITY ★★★★ | VALUE ★★★★½ | ZONE 3

Renaissance Center, Decatur near Flamingo; (702) 889-4477

Customers Asian community, locals **Reservations** Groups of 6 or more only **When to go** Anytime **Entrée range** Fixed buffet price ($14–$22) **Payment** VISA, MC **Service rating** ★★★½ **Friendliness rating** ★★★½ **Parking** Large lot **Bar** Wine and beer (license due any day) **Dress** Casual **Disabled access** Ground floor

Lunch Monday–Friday, 11 a.m.–2:30 p.m., $14; Friday–Sunday and holidays, 11:30 a.m.–3 p.m., $15

Dinner Monday–Thursday, 5:30–9:30 p.m., $22; Friday, 5:30–9:30 p.m.; Saturday, 5–10 p.m.; Sunday and holidays, 5–9 p.m., $24. Seniors (65 and older) with ID get a 20% discount at dinner only. Youngsters under five feet tall eat for half-price. Children under two years of age eat free.

Setting & atmosphere Simple, pleasant Japanese decor. The dining room is surrounded by food stations. The food stations are captivating, especially the sizeable sushi, sashimi, and nigiri sushi area.

House specialties More than 40 varieties of sushi made as you watch (a supply is always ready) by a cadre of sushi chefs who work nonstop. More than 12,000 pieces of sushi are made most days. Hot and cold salads, some include seafood. A remarkable selection of hot seafood and Japanese specialties, including roast chicken, noodle dishes, sukiyaki, and much more. The food selections change daily. The largest selection is at dinner, when mountains of snow crab legs, shrimp, and other pricey seafood are added. Mikino offers a spectacular selection of fresh fruits and desserts. The almond cookies, more like French sugar cookies, are exceptional.

Summary & comments If you enjoy serving yourself, Makino is a fantastic deal. You'll not find a more appealing array of foods. Salads and desserts are presented on white porcelain platters. Everything is appealing and tasty. This is no ordinary buffet. Before making your choices take the time to walk all of the stations. It would be nigh impossible to taste all of the foods, so hone in on your favorites. Except for the array of sushi the food is put out in small amounts and replaced as needed. The sushi alone is worth more than what it costs for this no-limits Japanese feast.

MALIBU CHAN'S ★★★½

PACIFIC RIM | MODERATE | QUALITY ★★★★ | VALUE ★★½ | ZONE 3

Promenade Center, 8125 West Sahara Avenue; (702) 312-4267

Customers Locals **Reservations** Suggested for prime times **When to go** Anytime **Entrée range** $10–$40 (changes with menu) **Payment** VISA, MC, AMEX, D **Service rating** ★★★½ **Friendliness rating** ★★★★½ **Parking** Lot **Bar** Full service **Wine selection** Good **Dress** Upscale casual **Disabled access** Yes

Dinner Daily, 5 p.m.–2 a.m.

Setting & atmosphere Colorful, high-energy, California-style café and sushi bar with contemporary art and decor. An open kitchen gives some diners a view of the action.

House specialties Generously sized starters (a few could be a light meal), salads, and entrées. Among the favorites are the garlic shrimp pizza; chicken wings laced with Thai sweet-soy glaze; Tokyo ravioli pot stickers; and live Manilla clams. The rack of lamb is basted with sesame, soy, and ginger; scampi Asia is a new twist on the Italian classic.

Other recommendations Sesame-crusted salmon with Thai cucumber salsa; seared duck breast; basil–lemon grass shrimp; Chilean sea bass with a potato crust; sushi.

Summary & comments This high-powered local hangout serves very good, albeit pricey, food and sushi. The happy-hour sushi menu (11 p.m. until closing) is a terrific value. Though the sushi menu is shorter during this time, prices are considerably less.

MAMA JO'S ★★½

ITALIAN | MODERATE | QUALITY ★★★ | VALUE ★★½ | ZONE 3 & 5

8427 Lake Mead Boulevard
1000 North Green Valley Parkway; (702) 719-6262

Customers Locals **Reservations** Suggested **When to go** Anytime **Entrée range** $12–$30 **Payment** All major credit cards **Service rating** ★★★ **Friendliness rating** ★★★½ **Parking** Large lot **Bar** Full service **Wine selection** Small **Dress** Casual **Disabled access** Ramp

Lunch Monday–Saturday, 11 a.m.–3 p.m.

Dinner Sunday–Thursday, 3–9 p.m.; Friday and Saturday, 3–10 p.m.

Early-bird specials Monday–Thursday, 4:30–6 p.m.

Setting & atmosphere Spacious, simply furnished, a good old-fashioned family style Italian with a separate bar for adults.

House specialties Mama's cuisine, red sauce and all, on such standards as veal Milanese, lasagna Bolognese, and eggplant Parmigiana. Fish soup bowls with a choice of flavored broth.

Other recommendations Savory pizzas, mix-and-match pastas, subs and sandwiches (panini).

Summary & comments Good wholesome food in pleasant surroundings that will please those who like their Italian food familiar and plentiful. Call ahead for wheelchair access to Lake Mead location.

MARCHE BACCHUS / BACCHUS BISTRO ★★★★

FRENCH BISTRO | MOD/EXP | QUALITY ★★★★ | VALUE ★★★★ | ZONE 3

2620 Regatta Drive, #106; (702) 804-8008

Customers Locals **Reservations** Suggested weekends **When to go** Anytime **Entrée range** Dinner $18–$27 **Payment** All major credit cards **Service rating** ★★★★½ **Friendliness rating** ★★★★½ **Parking** Large lot **Bar** Full service **Wine selection** extensive **Dress** Casual **Disabled access** Ground floor

Brunch 10–11 a.m., baguette and coffee

Lunch 11 a.m.–4 p.m.

Dinner 5–9 p.m.

Early-bird specials Monday–Thursday, 4:30–6 p.m.

Setting & atmosphere Walk through the wine shop to the adjacent bistro, or dine on the terrace with its gorgeous view of Regatta Lake (man-made). Simply furnished, this neighborhood eatery is an escape from the cares of the day. After one visit, you're welcomed by owners Agathe and Gegoire Verge as if you're members of the family.

House specialties Plum moules frites; mussels cooked in white wine, served with a mountain of crisp French fries. Traditional cassoulet with duck confit and navy beans and Toulouse and garlic sausages is served year-round, or the regulars get grumpy.

Other recommendations This inviting Summerlin bistro and wine shop is a late-night haven for Strip chefs who come here to unwind. Dine late and you might find yourself rubbing elbows with a few celebrity chefs.

Summary & comments Good wholesome food in pleasant surroundings that will please those who like their Italian food familiar and plentiful. Call ahead for wheelchair access to Lake Mead location.

MARRAKECH ★★½

MOROCCAN | MODERATE | QUALITY ★★★½ | VALUE ★★★½ | ZONE 1

3900 Paradise Road; (702) 736-7655

Customers Visitors, locals **Reservations** Suggested; required on weekends **When to go** After 6:30 p.m. for belly dancers; busy during conventions **Entrée range** 6-

course complete dinner, $30 **Payment** All major credit cards **Service rating** ★★★½ **Friendliness rating** ★★★½ **Parking** Shopping-center lot **Bar** Full service **Wine selection** A Moroccan red and French white by the glass or bottle; Mondavi and Jordan, plus imported wines **Dress** Informal, casual **Disabled access** Ground floor **Dinner** Daily, 5:30–11 p.m.

Setting & atmosphere Simulated desert tent with servers in native garb. Brass tables, floor pillows, and benches for seating maintain the illusion. Diners eat with their hands.

House specialties Shrimp scampi; harira soup; Moroccan-style chicken in light lemon sauce; flambé lamb brochette. Multicourse fixed-price dinner, which does not include couscous. Pastilla, a flaky chicken pie, normally a dinner course, is served for dessert at Marrakech.

Entertainment & amenities Belly dancers undulate and undulate, pausing only to have greenbacks thrust into their costumes.

Summary & comments Las Vegas version of Moroccan food in an Arabian Nights setting. Belly dancing is competent but often intrusive. It's not authentic, but it's fun.

MAYFLOWER CUISINIER ★★★★

CHINESE/FRENCH | MODERATE | QUALITY ★★★★ | VALUE ★★★★½ | ZONE 3

4750 West Sahara Avenue; (702) 870-8432

Customers Locals, some visitors **Reservations** Suggested **When to go** Anytime **Entrée range** $8–$22 **Payment** VISA, MC, AMEX, DC, D **Service rating** ★★★½ **Friendliness rating** ★★★★ **Parking** Shopping-center lot **Bar** Full service **Wine selection** Upscale **Dress** Casual to semi-dressy **Disabled access** Ground floor **Lunch** Monday–Friday, 11 a.m.–3 p.m.

Dinner Monday–Thursday, 5–10 p.m.; Friday and Saturday, 5–11 p.m.; Sunday, closed

Setting & atmosphere Two-level, 100-seat dining room; tastefully decorated in pink with contemporary black lacquer accents and handsome wall hangings. Choose from the main-level dining room or the more private mezzanine, or dine on the mist-cooled patio.

House specialties Roast duck salad with plum vinaigrette; roast duck and goat cheese quesadilla with salsa topping; chicken pot-stickers with peanut-basil sauce; grilled lemongrass chicken salad; Cornish game hen à la Chinoise; grilled tenderloin of beef with Mongolian sauce; Mayflower shrimp in pineapple-apricot sauce with scallion noodles.

Other recommendations Ginger chicken ravioli with scallion-Szechuan sauce; hot-and-sour soup; Mongolian grilled lamb chops with cilantro-mint sauce; grilled ahi tuna with Dijon-lime sauce; stir-fried chicken in plum wine with lychee nuts. Imaginative desserts that change seasonally.

Summary & comments Chef/owner Ming See Woo and manager Theresa, her daughter, created this fine cross-cultural restaurant. The new bar is ideal for a pre-dinner drink. An excellent fusion of Chinese and other cuisines.

MEDICI CAFE ★★½

ITALIAN | MOD/EXP | QUALITY ★★★★½ | VALUE ★★★½ | ZONE 5

Ritz-Carlton, 1610 Lake Las Vegas Parkway, Henderson; (702) 567-4700

Customers Visitors, locals **Reservations** Recommended **When to go** Anytime **Entrée range** $14–$34 **Payment** All major credit cards **Service rating** ★★★★½ **Friendliness rating** ★★★★½ **Parking** Valet, lot **Bar** Full service **Wine selection** Good **Dress** Upscale casual **Disabled access** Elevator **Breakfast** Daily, 7 a.m.–10 p.m.

Lunch Daily, noon–3 p.m.

Dinner Nightly, 6–10 p.m.

Setting & atmosphere Tuscan-themed, spacious dining room with elegant appointments and decor. Earthy and beautiful, Medici Cafe offers a view of the Florentine gardens: a sumptuous scene.

House specialties The portobello carpaccio appetizer with oven-cured tomatoes, with truffled vinaigrette and frisée salad; lobster two ways (a whole, split Maine lobster and potato-lobster pot pie); bone-in New York steak with herbed French fries; seasonal daily specials..

Other recommendations Roasted chicken with caramelized vegetables; red wine-braised short ribs; and pan-flashed striped sea bass with baby artichokes. The terrific selection of desserts: pineapple confit with mango ice cream and tapioca pudding, roasted pear with dried-apricot compote, a martini glass filled with passion-fruit panna cotta, and lychee ice cream topped with a miniature savarin.

Summary & comments Ritz-Carlton's Tuscan theme is a delight. Have a meal and visit the gardens and the Pontevecchio bridge. Visit Monte Lago Village on Lake Como. Not yet complete, Casino Monte Lago is open and the shops are coming along.

MEMPHIS CHAMPION BARBECUE ★★★

SOUTHERN BARBECUE | INEXPENSIVE | QUALITY ★★★½ | VALUE ★★★★½ | ZONE 5

2250 East Warm Springs Road, Warm Springs; (702) 260-6909

Santa Fe Station Hotel, 4949 North Rancho Drive (at Craig, next to Nellis Air Force Base)

Customers Visitors, locals **Reservations** Advised on weekends and holidays **When to go** Anytime **Entrée range** $12–$22 (includes sides) **Payment** All major credit cards **Service rating** ★★★½ **Friendliness rating** ★★★★½ **Parking** Large lot **Bar** Full service **Wine selection** Modest, beer selection good **Dress** Casual **Disabled access** Ramp, ground floor

Lunch Sunday–Thursday, 10 a.m–4 p.m.

Dinner Sunday–Thursday, 11 a.m.–10 p.m.; Friday and Saturday, 11 a.m.–10:30 p.m.

Setting & atmosphere Down-home comfort with ranch-house decor. Plenty of Southern memorabilia, including the street sign from the town where owner Mike Mills grew up.

House specialties Real pit barbecue perfected by the owner. He's still using the family recipe that he continually tweaks. Southern fried dill pickle appetizer—much too good. It may sound crazy, but these pickles are addictive. Mama Faye's Down Home Supper, named for Mill's mother. A whopping platter for four that could easily feed more. Included are a rack of ribs, beef brisket, hot links, one whole chicken, four sides, and rolls.

Other recommendations Barbecued pork shoulder, blackened rib-eye, charbroiled shrimp, the half-pound burgers, sandwiches from the pit—the Southern catfish sandwich is a good choice. A large selection of combination plates.

Summary & comments The Santa Fe Station location has a blues and jazz lounge that fits right in with the zesty food. Featured are John Earl and his BoogieMan band. Mike Mills is a legendary pit barbecue master. He's won four World Championship Cook-offs at the annual competition in Memphis and many more. Read the legend on the menu. Lunch prices are smaller and so are the portions. Dinner menu is available all day.

MICHAEL'S ★★★½

CONTINENTAL | VERY EXPENSIVE | QUALITY ★★★★ | VALUE ★★½ | ZONE 1

Barbary Coast Hotel, 3595 Las Vegas Boulevard South; (702) 737-7111

Customers Visitors, locals **Reservations** Difficult, but starts taking reservations at 3:30 p.m. **When to go** Whenever you can get a reservation **Entrée range** $26–$49, à la carte **Payment** All major credit cards **Service rating** ★★★★½ **Friendliness rating** ★★★★½ **Parking** Parking garage, valet **Bar** Full service **Wine selection** Excellent **Dress** Sport coat, dressy **Disabled access** Small staircase

Dinner Daily, 2 seatings at 6 and 9 p.m.

Setting & atmosphere Comfortable chairs in intimate table settings. Deep carpeting and romantic lighting create a luxurious room in the rococo style of early Las Vegas.

House specialties Rack of lamb bouquetière; live Maine lobster; veal chop Florentine; fresh Dover sole.

Other recommendations Shrimp cocktail served atop an igloo of ice, illuminated from within. All meats are prime.

Entertainment & amenities Complementary petits fours, chocolate-dipped fruits, and fancy fresh fruits are presented after dinner. Old Las Vegas lives at this opulent signature of the past.

Summary & comments If you're staying at a Strip hotel, the casino can help with a reservation. Early diners have a better chance of securing a table than those who like to dine at prime time. The menu (strictly à la carte) is a high-priced view of the Las Vegas of yesteryear.

MON AMI GABI ★★★½

CONT/FRENCH | MOD/EXP | QUALITY ★★★★ | VALUE ★★★½ | ZONE 1

Paris, 3655 Las Vegas Boulevard South; (702) 944-GABI

Customers Visitors, locals **Reservations** Requested for dining room, not accepted for patio **When to go** Anytime **Entrée range** $26–$49 **Payment** VISA, MC, AMEX, DC **Service rating** ★★★½ **Friendliness rating** ★★★½ **Parking** Garage, valet **Bar** Full service **Wine selection** All French wines **Dress** Upscale casual **Disabled access** Yes

Lunch Daily, 11:30 a.m.–3 p.m.

Dinner Sunday–Thursday, 5–11 p.m. Friday and Saturday, 5 p.m.–midnight

Setting & atmosphere Handsome brasserie with black leather booths and tables. The main dining room leads to a wonderful, plant-filled patio and a marvelous sidewalk café with a view of the Strip.

House specialties Steak frites, thin-sliced steak and French fries; an excellent selection of seafood and hors d'oeuvres; many hot seafood appetizers; the daily special listed on the blackboard; filet mignon and New York strip are among the regular steak selections.

Other recommendations Crêpes; omelets and sandwiches served at lunch; plates of seafood, le coquillage, with mussels gribiche (mussels with caper mayonnaise).

Entertainment & amenities The restaurant is child-friendly, accepts take-out requests, and features banquet dining with fixed-price gourmet meals.

Summary & comments Mon Ami is a charming dining place. everyone wants to dine at the sidewalk café, but you'll have to come early to get a table (there are no reservations for the café). The frites are curly fries, not steak fries, but they're crisp and good; so what if they're not authentic? Everything else is right on the mark. And for those whose dinner isn't complete without a good bottle of wine, a separate list of fine reserve wines has just been added.

NEROS ★★★½

CONTEMP. AMERICAN | EXPENSIVE | QUALITY ★★★★ | VALUE ★★½ | ZONE I

Caesars Palace, 3570 Las Vegas Boulevard South; (702) 731-7731

Customers Visitors, locals **Reservations** Requested **When to go** Anytime except convention times **Entrée range** $26–$50 **Payment** All major credit cards **Service rating** ★★★★½ **Friendliness rating** ★★★★½ **Parking** Valet, garage, lot **Bar** Full service **Wine selection** Excellent **Dress** Business attire **Disabled access** Ground floor

Dinner Daily, 5:30–11 p.m.

Setting & atmosphere Softly lit, with comfortable booths and tables, Neros is a fine example of understated elegance.

House specialties Cut-to-order steak tartare with toasted brioche, waffled potato chips, and a garnish of pansies; pan-seared foie gras with 100-year-old balsamic vinegar; roasted beet and wild green salad; smoky Vidalia onion soup with herbed goat cheese crouton; glazed, whole roasted Sonoma squab with parsnip puree; grilled swordfish with pan-fried risotto cakes.

Other recommendations Pan-roasted free-range chicken atop truffled mashed potatoes; rack of Colorado lamb with creamy Parmesan polenta; grilled Pacific salmon with French de Puy lentils; the splendid desserts, especially the delectable fallen chocolate soufflé.

Summary & comments A prime steak house with a contemporary menu of upscale fare.

NOODLES ★★★

CHINESE/JAPANESE/THAI | MODERATE | QUALITY ★★★★ | VALUE ★★★½ | ZONE I

Bellagio, 3600 Las Vegas Boulevard South; (702) 693-7111

Customers Visitors, locals **Reservations** No **When to go** Anytime **Entrée range** À la carte $15–$28 **Payment** All major credit cards **Service rating** ★★★½ **Friendliness rating** ★★★½ **Parking** Valet, lot **Bar** Full service **Wine selection** Good **Dress** Casual **Disabled access** Ground floor

Open Daily, 11 a.m.–3 a.m.

Setting & atmosphere Follow the marble floor with Chinese brass inlays that represent bits of Asian wisdom into this wonderful eatery. There's an open kitchen, a wall of artifacts, and the hustle and bustle of an authentic noodle kitchen.

House specialties Oodles of slurpy, authentic noodle dishes from China, Vietnam, Thailand, and Japan and authentic Hong Kong–style barbecue dishes, reasonably priced. There's a long list of appetizers and many different teas.

Summary & comments Noodles is small, only 88 seats, so it's tough to get in at prime times, but it's open long hours so you're bound to get in sometime. This is a favorite stop for Bellagio's Asian clientele. Find the Baccarat bar, and you'll find Noodles.

OLIVES ★★★½

AMER/MEDITERRANEAN | EXPENSIVE | QUALITY ★★★★ | VALUE ★★★½ | ZONE I

Bellagio, 3600 Las Vegas Boulevard South; (702) 693-7223

Customers Visitors, locals **Reservations** Accepted **When to go** Anytime **Entrée range** Lunch, $16–$25; dinner, $22–$40 **Payment** All major credit cards **Service rating** ★★★½ **Friendliness rating** ★★★★½ **Parking** Valet, garage **Bar** Full service **Wine selection** Eclectic **Dress** Casual **Disabled access** Ground floor

Lunch Daily, 11 a.m.–2:45 p.m.

Dinner Daily, 5–10:45 p.m.

Setting & atmosphere Intricate mosaic tiling, a sculpted wood ceiling, an open kitchen, and an outdoor patio with a view of the lake.

House specialties The menu changes regularly but always includes a risotto with a wild mushroom ragu; the signature butternut squash tortellini with brown butter, sage, and Parmesan cheese; the savory spit-roasted chicken on a crisp mashed-potato cake; individual pizzas with a flatbread-like crust; and grilled sirloin with shiitake glaze. Typical of the daily specials is the pan-seared, maple-glazed Hudson Valley foie gras.

Other recommendations Cod cake with lobster rémoulade and Boston baked beans; chocolate falling cake; roasted banana tiramisu; any of the wonderful sandwiches served only at lunch.

Summary & comments Olives at Bellagio bears no resemblance to the Boston original, but it does have the same warmth and expert staff; many are from the Boston Olives. These Olives veterans have re-created the essence and spirit of the original. Try for a terrace table, but don't be disappointed if it's not available. Everyone wants one (terrace seating cannot be reserved).

PAMPLEMOUSSE ★★½

CONTINENTAL/FRENCH | MOD/EXP | QUALITY ★★★½ | VALUE ★★½ | ZONE 1

400 East Sahara Avenue; (702) 733-2066

Customers Visitors, locals **Reservations** Required **When to go** Avoid conventions **Entrée range** $18–$24 **Payment** VISA, MC, AMEX, DC, D **Service rating** ★★★½- **Friendliness rating** ★★★★½ **Parking** Street, lot **Bar** Beer and wine only **Wine selection** Excellent **Dress** Upscale casual **Disabled access** Ground floor

Dinner Tuesday–Sunday, 6–10 p.m.; Monday, closed

Setting & atmosphere Country French. Attractive wine cellar at entrance to dining room. Restaurant has no menu; waiters recite the day's offerings and describe each dish.

House specialties Duckling dishes; medallions of veal prepared with baked apples; special seafood dishes in season—mussels, monkfish, salmon; assorted desserts, all delicious.

Other recommendations Dinner begins with a fine assortment of fresh vegetables (crudités) served from a handsome basket with an individual crock of house vinaigrette.

Summary & comments Waiters will give prices when reciting menu only if asked. Ask, so there are no surprises when the check arrives. One of the few independent off-Strip restaurants to maintain food prices.

PANEVINO RISTORANTE/GOURMET DELI ★★★½

ITALIAN | MOD/EXP | QUALITY ★★★★½ | VALUE ★★★½ | ZONE 1

246 Via Antonio, east of Las Vegas Boulevard on Sunset; (702) 222-2400

Customers Visitors, locals **Reservations** Recommended **When to go** Anytime **Entrée range** $14–$36 **Payment** All major credit cards **Service rating** ★★★★½- **Friendliness rating** ★★★★½ **Parking** Large **Bar** Full service **Wine selection** Upscale casual **Dress** Business casual **Disabled access** Ground floor

Lunch Daily, 11:30 a.m.–4:30 p.m.
Dinner Daily, 11:30 a.m.–10:30 p.m.

Setting & atmosphere Designed by owner Anthony Marnell, Panevino's red travertine walls were custom-quarried in Italy. A spectacular curved glass wall shapes the view of the Las Vegas skyline. Italy's finest artisans contributed their best to this gorgeous restaurant.

House specialties Pastas, breads, and pastries baked daily. Farfalline Contadina, bow tie pasta in a creamy pesto sauce with grilled chicken; risotto pescatore, arborio rice slowly cooked with fish stock, fresh fish, clams, mussels, calamari, and shrimp, in a light, spicy tomato sauce; pollo alla brace, grilled boneless chicken breast prepared with olive oil, garlic, red pepper and rosemary and served with roasted potatoes; filetto al Pepe Nero, a ten-ounce filet mignon sautéed with shallots in black peppercorn and brandy sauce with corn-mashed potatoes.

Other recommendations Riviera-style lobster salad; pizza and stuffed focaccia from the wood-burning oven; strozzapreti Emiliani, twisted pasta with fava beans and dried tomatoes in a veal reduction sauce topped with chopped filet mignon and goat cheese.

Summary & comments Panevino is located in Marnell's corporate office business complex. There is plenty of signage on Sunset Road, but the entrance is easy to miss, so stay alert. Adjacent to Panevino Ristorante is a delightful gourmet deli featuring homemade soups, sandwiches, salads, and other casual Italian eats. Eat in or take out. Prices are reasonable, the staff is congenial, and this is the prettiest deli outside of Italy.

PASTA PIRATE ★★★

SEAFOOD/PASTA | MODERATE | QUALITY ★★★½ | VALUE ★★★★½ | ZONE 2

California Hotel, 12 East Ogden Avenue; (702) 385-1222

Customers Visitors, locals **Reservations** Suggested **When to go** Anytime **Entrée range** $12–$40 **Payment** VISA, MC, AMEX, DC, D **Service rating** ★★★½ **Friendliness rating** ★★★½ **Parking** Garage, valet **Bar** Full service **Wine selection** Adequate **Dress** Casual **Disabled access** Ground floor

Dinner Daily, 5:30–11 p.m.

Setting & atmosphere Small restaurant with waterfront motif featuring tin walls, a brick floor, fishnets, neon signs, and an open kitchen.

House specialties Pasta and seafood; Alaskan king crab legs; scampi; baby lobster tails; and marinated sesame lobster brochettes. A glass of wine is included with all entrées.

Other recommendations Filet mignon with prawns; live Maine lobster; rigatoni Romano; cavatelli with broccoli; penne Diana; Cajun tuna.

Entertainment & amenities Piano player entertains between bar and dining room entrances, 6–11 p.m.

Summary & comments The Pasta Pirate offers an imaginative menu at moderate prices. Consistently good food and prices.

PEARL ★★★★

CHINESE | EXPENSIVE | QUALITY ★★★★ | VALUE ★★½ | ZONE 1

MGM Grand, 3799 Las Vegas Boulevard South; (702) 891-7380

Customers Visitors, locals **Reservations** Suggested **When to go** Anytime **Entrée range** $12–market price **Payment** All major credit cards **Service rating** ★★★★½ **Friendliness rating** ★★★★½ **Parking** Valet, parking garage **Bar** Full service **Wine**

selection Very good **Dress** Business attire, casual chic **Disabled access** Ramp
Dinner Daily, 5:30–11 p.m.

Setting & atmosphere Arguably the most beautiful Chinese dining room in Las Vegas. Sleek and inviting, the tall booths offer privacy and a view of the dining room. A private dining area adjacent to the wine cellar is in great demand, especially by parties of six or more. Expert lighting and gorgeous appointments.

House specialties Multicourse tasting menu; pricey, but worth it. Pearl's family style menus for two or more—six or more courses for a fixed price. Spider-prawn dumplings, minced tiger prawns and pine nuts in lettuce petals; deep-fried shiitake mushrooms glazed with spicy black vinegar. The live fish and seafood selection; Dungeness crab meat baked in the shell; crisp fried squab; wok-fried filet of venison and asparagus, Cantonese-style.

Other recommendations The signature Asian bouillabaisse, spiced king crab legs with chili and garlic, the steamed Maine and Australian lobster tasting. Maine lobster fried rice, braised young Thai eggplant with chili-plum sauce, star anise lamb chops with braised string beans. The tableside tea service orchestrated by a "tea butler."

Summary & comments Dining at Pearl is relaxing and satisfying. It's elegant, inviting, and a terrific departure from the usual Chinese restaurant.

PHO CHIEN ★★★

VIETNAMESE | INEXPENSIVE | QUALITY ★★★½ | VALUE ★★★★½ | ZONE 3

3839 West Sahara Avenue; (702) 873-8749

Customers Asians and locals **Reservations** No **When to go** Anytime **Entrée range** $8–$22 (complete dinner); lobster at market price **Payment** VISA, MC **Service rating** ★★★ **Friendliness rating** ★★★★½ **Parking** Lot **Bar** No **Wine selection** No **Dress** Casual **Disabled access** Ground floor

Open Monday, Tuesday, Thursday, and Friday, 10:30 a.m.–9 p.m.; Wednesday, 10 a.m.–3:30 p.m.; Saturday and Sunday, 10:30 a.m.–10 p.m.

Setting & atmosphere New owners have cleaned up this storefront Vietnamese restaurant, but it's no beauty. The owner provides the friendly atmosphere and speaks understandable English. Come for the food, not the setting—though very clean, your surroundings will be rather spare.

House specialties Sautéed shrimp and spareribs; Vietnamese egg rolls; noodle soup with steak and brisket; curried chicken with steamed rice; beef satay with rice or egg noodle soup; beef with lemon grass.

Other recommendations Charbroiled pork and vegetable rolls; grilled shrimp wrapped with sugar cane; the selection of noodle soups.

Summary & comments The food is far prettier than the premises, and it's very good. This is not capital "D" dining, but if you're in the mood for a delicious, inexpensive meal served quickly, this is the place. There is not much English spoken here.

PICASSO ★★★★½

FRENCH/SPANISH | VERY EXPENSIVE | QUALITY ★★★★ | VALUE ★★½ | ZONE 1

Bellagio, 3600 Las Vegas Boulevard South; (702) 693-7223

Customers Visitors, locals **Reservations** A must **When to go** Anytime you can get a reservation **Entrée range** Prix fixe only, $80 or $90 **Payment** All major credit cards **Service rating** ★★★★½ **Friendliness rating** ★★★★½ **Parking** Valet, self **Bar** Full service **Wine selection** Excellent **Dress** Casual elegance, jackets recommended **Disabled access** Elevator

Dinner Thursday–Tuesday, 6–9:30 p.m; Wednesday, closed

Setting & atmosphere Arguably the most beautiful dining room in Las Vegas. A treasure of original Picasso artworks adorn the walls. The flower displays throughout the restaurant are exquisite. A wall of windows gives most tables a full view of the dancing fountains.

House specialties Selections on both the five-course degustation and the four-course prix fixe change regularly according to the whim of the chef. The warm lobster salad, sautéed foie gras, roasted Atlantic turbot, and seafood sausage—a plump casing filled with chunks of seafood—appear often. The roasted pigeon (squab) is outstanding. Chef Julian Serrano, formerly of Masa's in San Francisco, sometimes offers a sensational amuse bouche (entertainment for the mouth), a tiny potato pancake topped with crème fraîche and osetra caviar. It's worth asking for—beg if you have to.

Summary & comments This exceptional restaurant is grand yet unpretentious. Allow enough time to enjoy the experience. After dinner have a drink on the terrace. Where else but in Las Vegas can you have a view of Lake Como as well as one of the Eiffel Tower? Chef Julian Serrano was named the "Best Chef in the Southeast 2002" by the James Beard Foundation. Serrano is the first Las Vegas chef to win a Beard award.

PIERO'S ★★★★

ITALIAN | MODERATE | QUALITY ★★★★ | VALUE ★★½ | ZONE 1

355 Convention Center Drive; (702) 369-2305

Customers Visitors, locals, conventioneers **Reservations** Required **When to go** Anytime **Entrée range** $20–$36 (higher for lobster) **Payment** VISA, MC, AMEX, DC, D **Service rating** ★★★★ **Friendliness rating** ★★★★ **Parking** Valet, lot **Bar** Full service **Wine selection** Excellent **Dress** Business casual **Disabled access** Ground floor

Dinner Daily, 5:30–9 p.m.

Setting & atmosphere Many softly lit booths and alcoves for guests desiring privacy. There are two private dining rooms for 12 to 20 people; a banquet room that can accommodate up to 250; a piano bar; and a much larger kitchen. The excellent waitstaff specializes in Old World–style service.

House specialties Osso buco Piero; zuppa di pesce, a seafood "soup" filled with lobster, clams, mussels, shrimp, calamari, and scallops; whole roasted kosher chicken as good or better than Mama used to make; any dish with Provimi veal; the Italian pastas with French-influenced sauces; the 25-ounce New York steak; stone crab claws or cakes of Maryland blue crab, in season.

Summary & comments Celebrities and sports figures always make their way to Piero's, as do Las Vegas power brokers, who consistently dine here. Dom Perignon, Cristal, Grand Cordon champagnes, and $400 bottles of Montrachet are the norm at Piero's. Quirky owner Freddy Glusman divides his time between Piero's and his new Piero's Trattoria. The Trattoria is partnered with Glusman's two sons—two charming young men with nary a quirk between them.

PIERO'S TRATTORIA ★★★½

CONTEMP ITALIAN | MODERATE | QUALITY ★★★½ | VALUE ★★½ | ZONE 1

225 Hughes Center Drive (Paradise Road); 892-9955

Customers Locals and celebs **Reservations** Advised for weekends **When to go** Anytime **Entree range** $15–$50 **Payment** All major credit cards **Service rating** ★★★½ **Friendliness rating** ★★★★½ **Parking** Large lot **Bar** Full service **Wine selection** Very good **Dress** Informal **Disabled access** Ground floor

Lunch Monday–Friday, 11 a.m.–3 p.m.

Dinner Nightly, 5:30–10:30 p.m.

Setting & atmosphere Club-like and comfortable. At least one of the young owners is always on premises. Business types fill the bar after office hours. Excellent bartenders who know all of the locals. For a quick meal eat at the counter and watch the chefs in action.

House specialties Contemporary Italian, seafood, and steaks. Portions are very generous. Everything from salads to pastas to steaks can be ordered in half portions. The eggplant and chicken appetizer or the steak salad could be a meal. Wild-mushroom pasta—split an order and one entrée for a terrific dinner.

Other recommendations Crunchy-crusted pizzas with innovative toppings, fried portobello mushroom appetizer, grilled salmon, the crisp fried calamari. There are always surprises here.

Summary & comments A trendy restaurant for all ages, Piero's Trattoria reflects the restaurant background of the family—papa Freddie Glusman owns the venerable Piero's, a prime place for celebrity watching. Yes, there are "A" tables, but this place is so friendly everyone feels at home.

PING PANG PONG ★★★

CHINESE | MODERATE | QUALITY ★★★★ | VALUE ★★★★½ | ZONE 3

Gold Coast Hotel, 4000 West Flamingo Road; (702) 247-7272

Customers Locals, Chinese community **Reservations** Suggested for weekends **When to go** Anytime except Chinese New Year **Entrée range** $10–$30 **Payment** All major credit cards **Service rating** ★★★½ **Friendliness rating** ★★★★½ **Parking** Valet, parking garage, lot **Bar** Full service **Wine selection** Small **Dress** Casual **Disabled access** Ground level

Dinner Daily, 5 p.m.–3 a.m.

Setting & atmosphere An open-sided, round pagoda that overlooks the casino, with typical Chinese decor—red accents for good luck, Chinese lanterns, and comfortable seating.

House specialties The fish and seafood selection from the live tanks (pricey); San Pan tiger prawns; Cantonese roast duck or tea smoked duck (a generous half for little money); kung pao chicken, the authentic Szechwan prep with fire-roasted chiles; wrinkled green beans; pan-toasted mixed seafood noodles—hiding under the noodles is a generous amount of seafood.

Other recommendations The small selection of dim sum are value priced and delicious. The custard tarts are made fresh every evening. Noodle soups, a meal in a bowl, especially the ba bao—Mandarin noodles topped with a spicy shrimp sauce and peanuts, curry-flavored Singapore rice noodles and the calamari rice noodles.

Summary & comments Ping Pang Pong is owned by Kevin Wu, who also owns the upscale Chinese, Royal Star at the Venetian. Many of Ping Pang Pong's dishes were created by Wu who was determined to set the same standards here that apply to the pricey Royal Star. He's reached his goal.

PINOT BRASSERIE ★★★

FRENCH | EXPENSIVE | QUALITY ★★★½ | VALUE ★★½ | ZONE 1

Venetian Hotel, 3355 Las Vegas Boulevard South; (702) 414-8888

Customers Visitors, locals **Reservations** Requested at dinner **When to go** Avoid conventions **Entrée range** $12–$22 (lunch); $25–$60 (seafood) (dinner) **Payment** VISA, MC, AMEX, DC, D **Service rating** ★★★½ **Friendliness rating** ★★★★ **Parking** Valet, garage **Bar** Full service **Wine selection** Good **Dress** Upscale casual (dinner) **Disabled access** Ground floor

Lunch Daily, 11:30 a.m.–3 p.m.

Dinner Daily, 5:30–10:30 p.m.

Setting & atmosphere Authentic French brasserie decor, with comfortable booths and tables. The owners scoured flea markets and design centers in Paris to achieve this warm and inviting atmosphere. Everything from the lamps to the beautiful wood facade (rescued from an old hotel) are authentic.

House specialties Fresh seafood—the shellfish platter for two is especially terrific, as are the steamed mussels with shallots, garlic, and wine; traditional French onion soup gratinée with a thick crust of melted cheese; rotisserie pork rack with pommes Anna; pan-seared breast of duck; and cote du boeuf for two—a hearty grilled beef chop with roasted portobello mushrooms, roasted potatoes, onion rings, and red-wine shallot sauce.

Other recommendations The daily plat du jour (plate of the day) that could be a classic cassoulet, lamb shank pot-au-feu, bouillabaise, grilled veal chop, or a Sunday surprise, known only to the chef (for adventurous diners only). The desserts are scrumptious—order the chocolate soufflé when you place your entrée order.

Summary & comments A small café outside the Brasserie is a fine place to people-watch and enjoy a casual meal. They serve seafood, appetizers, sandwiches, salads, and some entrées—but it's plenty to choose from. Seafood is not inexpensive here, but this is a rare Las Vegas occurrence of truly getting what you pay for; just expect the higher tab. As in France, meals are a leisurely occurrence at Pinot, especially so if the restaurant is busy. But with such carefully chosen surroundings and lush food, you might gladly while away an entire day here, anyway.

POLONEZ ★★½

POLISH | MODERATE | QUALITY ★★★½ | VALUE ★★½ | ZONE 1

1243 East Sahara Avenue at Maryland Parkway; (702) 369-1556

Customers Locals **Reservations** No **When to go** Anytime **Entrée range** $10–$20 **Payment** Major cards **Service rating** ★★★½ **Friendliness rating** ★★★½ **Parking** Large lot **Bar** Full service **Wine selection** Small **Dress** Casual **Disabled access** Ramp

Open Daily, 7 a.m–10 p.m.

Setting & atmosphere A large bar dominates the small dining room. Beyond the dining room is very good Polish deli with appealing displays and European foodstuff, meats, cheeses, and groceries.

House specialties All things Polish—stuffed cabbage, bigos (hunter's stew), barley and other sausages, a variety of pierogi and borscht.

Other recommendations The Polish platter, a sampling of Polish sausage, barley sausage, pierogi, and stuffed cabbage (golabki); the pork tenderloin with Polish mushrooms.

Summary & comments Polonez is a B movie with live characters and Polish food. Intentions are good, and if you don't mind a little European schtick you'll have a fine time. Just don't ask about lunch and dinner hours. It's like a Marx brothers routine. Some of the authentic Polish dishes are gone (not enough demand), but the classic dishes remain.

PRIME ★★★½

STEAKHOUSE | EXPENSIVE | QUALITY ★★★★½ | VALUE ★★½ | ZONE 1

Bellagio, 3600 Las Vegas Boulevard South; (702) 693-8484

Customers Visitors, locals **Reservations** Requested **When to go** Avoid convention times **Entrée range** $26–$54 **Payment** All major credit cards **Service rating** ★★★★½ **Friendliness rating** ★★★★½ **Parking** Valet, self **Bar** Full service **Wine selection** Excellent **Dress** Casual elegance, jackets preferred **Disabled access** Elevator

Dinner Daily, 5:30–10:30 p.m.

Setting & atmosphere Dazzling chocolate and powder-blue carpets and wall hangings in a setting seldom seen for a steakhouse—it's gorgeous. In keeping with Bellagio's fine-arts policy, there's plenty of original art to view here. Have a drink at the elegant bar and take it all in.

House specialties Prime, aged steaks and seafood; herb-crusted rack of lamb; roasted rib-eye steak for two; caramel-roasted pork loin. A choice of a variety of sauces and excellent side dishes.

Summary & comments Prime is on the lower level of the shopping corridor beside Picasso. Both restaurants get their share of lookers, but the staff keeps them from disturbing diners. It's hard to resist this rare steakhouse with impeccable service.

RAINFOREST CAFÉ ★★★

AMERICAN | MODERATE | QUALITY ★★★½ | VALUE ★★½ | ZONE 1

MGM Grand, 3799 Las Vegas Boulevard South; (702) 891-8580

Customers Visitors, locals **Reservations** No **When to go** Anytime **Entrée range** $12–$15 **Payment** All major credit cards **Service rating** ★★½ **Friendliness rating** ★★★½ **Parking** Valet, garage **Bar** Full service **Wine selection** Good **Dress** Casual **Disabled access** Through casino

Open Breakfast served every day, 8–11 a.m. Entrées served every day, 10:30 a.m. until closing: Monday–Thursday and Sunday, until 11 p.m.; Friday and Saturday, until midnight

Setting & atmosphere Whimsical and wonderful—a faux tropical paradise with live birds, animatronic animals (elephants, leopards, gorillas), and butterflies. The retail shop, designed to entice kids, includes a talking tree that's home to a slinky, talking python, Julius Squeezer, and there's a pond filled with scary alligators. The café is a marvel of simulated and natural effects.

House specialties Amazon flatbreads that look suspiciously like pizzas; meat loaf; fried chicken; barbecued ribs; kid's choices; chicken pot pie; vegetable lasagna.

Other recommendations Daily fish special; mini–hot dogs on mini-buns; chicken tidbits; pastas; selection of wild desserts; exotic spirited and nonspirited beverages.

Summary & comments Themed restaurants are common in Las Vegas, but Rainforest Café has better food than most, and a wonderful theme. However, calling the

Rainforest Café for information can be a maddening experience. To get a real person, defeat the long, long taped litany of information by pushing 0. Per Rainforest Café's instructions, the café cannot be accessed through the MGM switchboard.

RANGE STEAKHOUSE ★★★

AMERICAN | EXPENSIVE | QUALITY ★★★★ | VALUE ★★½ | ZONE 1

Harrah's, 3475 Las Vegas Boulevard South; (702) 369-5000

Customers Visitors, locals **Reservations** Requested **When to go** Avoid conventions **Entrée range** $16–$25 **Payment** VISA, MC, AMEX, DC **Service rating** ★★★½ **Friendliness rating** ★★★★½ **Parking** Valet, lot **Bar** Full service **Wine selection** Very good **Dress** Upscale casual **Disabled access** Elevator

Dinner Sunday–Thursday, 5:30–10:30 p.m.; Friday and Saturday, 5:30–11:30 p.m.; bar open until 2 a.m.

Setting & atmosphere Enter the glass-enclosed elevator to the second floor, and the adventure begins. The blue sky turns to sunset by the time the restaurant comes into view. Range's tiered dining room (3 levels) affords every table a splendid view of the Strip. The decor is a fine mix of rough-hewn wood and polished copper and brass with splashes of forest colors.

House specialties Steaks; slow-roasted prime rib; veal, beef, pork, and lamb chops; the signature swordfish; lobster, shrimp, and Alaskan king crab legs; free-range chicken; a bone-in filet mignon. Signature dishes are marked on the menu with the Range brand.

Summary & comments Harrah's has undergone a dramatic change; no sign of the former hotel remains. The Range is a prime example of the direction the hotel has taken. An elegant lounge and bar serves light snacks. An ideal spot for viewing the action on the Strip.

RED SQUARE ★★★

AMERICAN/RUSSIAN | MODERATE | QUALITY ★★★½ | VALUE ★★½ | ZONE 1

Mandalay Bay, 3950 Las Vegas Boulevard South; (702) 632-7777

Customers Visitors, locals **Reservations** Suggested on weekends **When to go** Anytime **Entrée range** $19–$40 **Payment** VISA, MC, AMEX, DC **Service rating** ★★★½ **Friendliness rating** ★★★½ **Parking** Valet, garage **Bar** Full service **Wine selection** Vodka's the drink here **Dress** Casual **Disabled access** Ground floor

Dinner Daily, 5:30 p.m.–midnight; bar open Sunday–Thursday until 2 a.m., and until 4 a.m. Friday and Saturday

Setting & atmosphere More American than Russian, this comfy dining room with "Russian-inspired" decor and a large bar with a top that's partly a slab of ice is neat.

House specialties Updated Russian classics: stroganoff; chicken Kiev and caviar; rack of lamb; crab and arugula angel-hair pasta; Chilean sea bass.

Other recommendations The frozen-ice bar offers more than 100 frozen vodkas and infusions, plus martinis and Russian-inspired cocktails.

Summary & comments Another winning concept from the China Grill creators. There are some dining limits; ask when you make your reservation. Adventurers can don a provided coat for a visit to the Walk-In Box, home to numerous vodkas. Glass enclosed, this is one chilly experience that's worth a nip of frostbite.

REDWOOD BAR & GRILL ★★★

AMERICAN/PRIME RIB | MODERATE | QUALITY ★★★½ | VALUE ★★★★½ | ZONE 2

California Hotel, 12 East Ogden Avenue; (702) 385-1222

Customers Visitors, locals **Reservations** Suggested **When to go** Early evening **Entrée range** $16–$25 **Payment** VISA, MC, AMEX, DC, D **Service rating** ★★★½ **Friendliness rating** ★★★★½ **Parking** Hotel lot and valet **Bar** Full service **Wine selection** Good **Dress** Informal **Disabled access** Ground floor

Dinner Daily, 5:30–11 p.m.

Setting & atmosphere Country English furnishings and a fireplace make for comfortable dining. A quiet room where service is efficient and gracious.

House specialties Caesar salad; steak Diane; chicken with apricot sauce. Porterhouse steak special: 16 ounces for $14 includes soup or salad, potatoes, vegetable, dessert.

Other recommendations Soup du jour such as seafood chowder; Australian lobster tail; fresh fish; roast prime rib; veal Oscar; steak and lobster.

Entertainment & amenities Piano music nightly.

Summary & comments Excellent value. Prime-rib portion is succulent, generous, and cooked as ordered. Although part of a locally owned group of five hotels, the Redwood Bar & Grill maintains its cozy individuality in both decor and service. Outstanding value.

RENOIR ★★★★½

FRENCH/AMERICAN | VERY EXPENSIVE | QUALITY ★★★★½ | VALUE ★★½ | ZONE 1

The Mirage, 3400 Las Vegas Boulevard South; (702) 791-7111

Customers Visitors, locals **Reservations** A must **When to go** Whenever a reservation is available **Entrée range** $35–$80 **Payment** VISA, MC, AMEX, DC **Service rating** ★★★★½ **Friendliness rating** ★★★★½ **Parking** Valet; garage **Bar** Full service **Wine selection** Excellent **Dress** Jackets required for men **Disabled access** Ramp

Dinner Tuesday–Sunday, 6–10 p.m.; closed Monday

Setting & atmosphere Exquisite silk fabrics, brightly colored tapestries, and rich wood are a perfect foil for Renoir and art by other French impressionist painters.

House specialties A superb braised shortrib without a drop of fat served with a red-wine sauce you won't believe; slow-baked salmon; cream of lobster soup with wild mushrooms and lobster fricassee; Napoleon of house-smoked salmon with ahi tuna and osetra caviar.

Other recommendations Cave Creek escargots with roasted garlic ravioli; tenderloin of veal; a five-course tasting menu; any one of the irresistible desserts. Menus change with the seasons.

Summary & comments Flawless food and service in a divine setting, yet it's not terribly pretentious. A genuinely welcoming staff adds to the charm and your comfort level. Overall, Renoir offers a high-ticket meal, but then it *is* exceptional dining.

ROSEMARY'S RESTAURANT ★★★★

AMERICAN | MODERATE | QUALITY ★★★★ | VALUE ★★½ | ZONE 3

8125 West Sahara Avenue, Summerlin; (702) 869-225
Rio, 3700 West Flamingo Road; (702) 777-2300

Customers Visitors, locals **Reservations** Recommended **When to go** Anytime **Entrée range** $18–$30 **Payment** All major credit cards **Service rating** ★★★★ **Friendliness rating** ★★★★½ **Parking** Large lot **Bar** Full service **Wine selection** Very good **Dress** Upscale casual **Disabled access** Ground level

Lunch Monday–Friday, 11:00 a.m.–2:30 p.m. (Summerlin location only)
Dinner Daily, 5:30–10:00 p.m.

Setting & atmosphere A comfortable bar separates the street side from the attractive dining room. Simple, effective decor with gauzy drapes and local artwork, all appealing. An open kitchen gives a view of the chefs.

House specialties Roasted rack of lamb with black-olive mashed potatoes and arugula, crispy skin striped bass, pepper-grilled New York strip, grilled veal chop with soft cheesy grits, Texas barbecued shrimp.

Other recommendations Salmon tartar, butternut squash soup, wilted spinach salad, brick chicken, seared scallops, any of the side dishes.

Summary & comments Chef/owner Michael Jordan was formerly the executive chef for Emeril's at MGM Grand. With the opening of Rosemary's on Sahara and the new Rosemary's at the Rio, he and his chef/wife Wendy are a peerless culinary team. Wendy oversees the Sahara location; Michael cooks at the Rio.

ROSEWOOD GRILLE ★★★

LOBSTER/STEAK | MODERATE | QUALITY ★★★½ | VALUE ★★½ | ZONE 1

3339 Las Vegas Boulevard South; (702) 792-9099

Customers Visitors **Reservations** Strongly recommended **When to go** Anytime **Entrée range** $19–$30, higher for lobster and stone crab **Payment** All major credit cards **Service rating** ★★★½ **Friendliness rating** ★★★½ **Parking** Lot behind restaurant **Bar** Full service **Wine selection** Excellent **Dress** Informal **Disabled access** Ground floor

Dinner Daily, 4:30–11:30 p.m.

Setting & atmosphere Muted lighting, large booths, seating for 200. This always-busy restaurant still retains its Old World charm.

House specialties Live Maine lobster in humongous sizes. Dinner includes salad and potatoes.

Other recommendations Lobster and steak combination; beef chop; beef-eaters brochette; scampi; stone crabs; broiled salmon Charlotte; tournedos Scandia; lobster ravioli; chicken with strawberries in Cointreau. Strawberries with Dom Perignon for two; café Mozart.

Summary & comments Restaurant stocks a week's supply of large and extra-large lobsters (up to 25 pounds). Price (3-pound minimum) changes with the market. Lobster prices are typically $17–$25 per pound, depending on availability.

RUMJUNGLE ★★★

BRAZILIAN RODIZIO | EXPENSIVE | QUALITY ★★★½ | VALUE ★★½ | ZONE 1

Mandalay Bay, 3950 Las Vegas Boulevard South; (702) 632-7408

Customers Boomers and Gen-Xers **Reservations** Suggested for dinner **When to go** Anytime **Entrée range** $15–$25 (rodizio, $36) **Payment** VISA, MC, AMEX, DC, D **Service rating** ★★★ **Friendliness rating** ★★★★½ **Parking** Valet, garage **Bar** Full service **Wine selection** Small **Dress** No overly funky clothes, no hats. A blazer or collared shirt must be worn with jeans. **Disabled access** No

Dinner Monday–Thursday, 5:30–11 p.m.; Friday and Saturday, 5:30 p.m. to last seating (usually 9 p.m.)

Setting & atmosphere Wild jungle-like setting with soaring ceilings, an open fire pit, and a wall of fire. This place really rocks, though dinner hours are less frenetic.

House specialties Unlimited quantities of meat, fish, and poultry with many accompaniments and sauces for a fixed price. The cost is about half the adult price for kids ages 12 and under.

Other recommendations À la carte appetizers—Jamaican-spiced chicken skewers; coconut shrimp; jerk spiced chicken wings and Bahamian conch fritters; Honolulu Caesar salad; banana leaf seabass; baby-back pork ribs.

Summary & comments There are so many rules and restrictions here, you need a guide to get you through without mishap. On weekends, parties of eight or more have two hours in which to dine. There is a cover charge after 11 p.m. Still, Rumjungle is a cool spot for the younger (but over 21) set who find the dancing fire wall and pulsating dance floor a kick.

RUTH'S CHRIS STEAK HOUSE

STEAK | VERY EXPENSIVE | QUALITY ★★★★ | VALUE ★★½ | ZONES 1 & 5

3900 Paradise Road; (702) 791-7011

4561 West Flamingo Road; (702) 248-7011

Customers Visitors, locals **Reservations** A must **When to go** Avoid convention times **Entrée range** $45–$65 **Payment** All major credit cards **Service rating** ★★★★½ **Friendliness rating** ★★★★½ **Parking** Lot **Bar** Full service **Wine selection** Excellent **Dress** Informal **Disabled access** Ground floor

Lunch *Paradise:* Monday–Friday, 11 a.m.–4:30 p.m. *Flamingo:* Not open for lunch.

Dinner *Paradise:* Daily, 4:30–10:30 p.m.; *Flamingo:* 4:30 p.m.–3 a.m.

Setting & atmosphere Plush with dark cherry woods and beveled glass windows. Comfortable cocktail lounge.

House specialties Prime steak, cooked to order and served sizzling with butter (steaks may be ordered dry).

Other recommendations Besides excellent steaks, the restaurant offers veal chops, lamb chops, fresh salmon, and an outstanding variety of potatoes and vegetables. The Lyonnaise and hash brown potatoes are addictive.

Summary & comments Wine selection includes Dom Perignon and Louis Roederer Cristal. Ruth's Chris serves only prime beef. The check for two, however, can be steep; everything is à la carte, but portions are large enough to be shared. There is no service charge for sharing. The new Proprietor's Reserve private dining room can seat up to 45. There's a new, attractive garden room at the Paradise location. A late-night supper menu is available at the Flamingo location, along with entertainment from 10 p.m.— mostly jazz, some pop classics.

SAMBA GRILL

BRAZILIAN/STEAK | MODERATE | QUALITY ★★★★ | VALUE ★★★½ | ZONE 1

The Mirage, 3400 Las Vegas Boulevard South; (702) 791-7111

Customers Visitors, locals **Reservations** Recommended **When to go** Anytime **Entrée range** Prix fixe, $29; à la carte, $16–$25 **Payment** All major credit cards **Service rating** ★★★½ **Friendliness rating** ★★★★½ **Parking** Valet, garage **Bar** Full **Wine selection** Good **Dress** Upscale casual **Disabled access** Ground floor, ramp

Dinner Sunday–Thursday, 5:30–10:15 p.m. (last seating); Friday and Saturday, 5:30 p.m.–1 a.m.

Setting & atmosphere Vibrant colors and colorful booths and appointments capture the theme of this Brazilian steakhouse. Remember Fiesta chinaware? The same palette of colors is found here.

House specialties The Rodizio Experience: unlimited servings of marinated meats, poultry, and fish for a fixed price. Dinners include a bottomless bowl of Samba salad, side dishes of creamed spinach, black beans and rice, fried bananas (plantains), Cuban-style potatoes, and a basket of Brazilian breads. À la carte selections include the side dishes, but the meats are grilled, not cooked on a spit.

Other recommendations À la carte appetizers, especially Nuestra duck tamales and awesome coconut prawns; freshly made juices by the glass or pitcher—mango, passion fruit, grapefruit, and orange. The delectable rice pudding laced with fresh pineapple; a huge banana split for two that could easily serve four.

Summary & comments The jewel-like bar is a nice place for a drink and appetizers. Samba Grill is a terrific restaurant with prices right out of the past.

SAZIO ★★★

ITALIAN | MODERATE | QUALITY ★★★½ | VALUE ★★★★½ | ZONE 3

Orleans, 4500 West Tropicana Avenue; (702) 948-9501

Customers Visitors, locals **Reservations** Accepted **When to go** Anytime **Friendliness rating** ★★★★½ **Service rating** ★★★½ **Entrée range** $8–$19 **Payment** All major credit cards **Parking** Valet, garage, lot **Bar** Full service **Wine selection** Limited **Dress** Casual **Disabled access** Ramp

Lunch Daily, 11 a.m.–2 p.m.

Dinner Daily, 5 p.m.–10:30 p.m.

Setting & atmosphere Large framed "paintings" in the style of Andy Warhol dominate the various dining rooms. Featured are likenesses of local movers and shakers. Retro ceiling lights cast beams of color. Comfortable booths circle the rooms; stylish chairs and tables complete the sleek design.

House specialities Spit-roasted loin of pork, lightly seasoned with rosemary and garlic; spit-roasted chicken Diablo, brushed with hot mustard, herbed bread crumbs and a peppercorn sauce. Sicilian Capresé salad—generous slices of tender, fresh mozzarella and roasted peppers Siciliano, topped with garlic bread crumbs—the roasted peppers can be ordered separately; Tuscan-style mussels, a generous portion for a small price; swordfish picatta, topped with lemon, herbs, and capers. Apple crumble à la mode and the chocolate lovin' spooncake for dessert. (Desserts are the only weakness on the menu.)

Summary & comments Sazio is a terrific value. Portions are equally generous, especially the spit-roasted pork. Wines are priced right, too. This is Old Las Vegas revisited. Nothing fancy, just good tasty food at affordable prices, in a most pleasant setting.

SEABLUE ★★★★

SEAFOOD | MOD/EXP | QUALITY ★★★★ | VALUE ★★★½ | ZONE 1

MGM Grand, 3799 Las Vegas Boulevard South; (702) 891-3486

Customers Visitors, locals **Reservations** Suggested weekends **When to go** Anytime **Entrée range** Market price, but $24 average **Payment** All major credit cards **Service rating** ★★★½ **Friendliness rating** ★★★★½ **Parking** Valet, garage **Bar** Full service **Wine selection** Very good **Dress** Upscale casual **Disabled access** Main entrance

Dinner 5:30 p.m. until

Setting & atmosphere A large circular aquarium filled with glimmering small fish captivates as diners approach SeaBlue, chef/owner Michael Mina's latest concept. A sizeable raw bar almost fills one side of the dining room. There is booth seating here, too. SeaBlue puts into play a new Mina concept based on seafood. With cascading water walls and other special effects, SeaBlue's decor is magic.

House specialties Small plates that can be a meal (think tapas). There 3 choices in each category, mix and match as you will, marking off what you want on the list provided. Choose up to ten. The remarkable salad has a glorious mix of ingredients. The superior tuna tartare served with mini pita breads (Mina's mother's recipe).

Other recommendations Orange-glazed chicken cooked in Moroccan clay casserole (tajine); no cream or butter is used in any of the dishes (excluding dessert). The fruit de mer is an abundance of seasonal shellfish nestled with hand-cut fettuccine. Dessert fruit soups, Italian granita, cookies, ice creams, and fruits are refreshing and delicious.

Summary & comments Mina's passion for seafood was fired when he was part of the team that developed Aqua in San Francisco. He remains the managing chef at Aqua at Bellagio and of Nobhill at MGM Grand.

SIMON KITCHEN & BAR ★★★½

AMERICAN | MOD/EXP | QUALITY ★★★★½ | VALUE ★★½ | ZONE 1

Hard Rock Hotel, 4455 Paradise Road; (702) 693-5000

Customers Locals, celebs, visitors **Reservations** Recommended **When to go** Anytime **Entrée range** $18–$34 **Payment** All major credit cards **Service rating** ★★★½ **Friendliness rating** ★★★★½ **Parking** Valet, garage, large lot **Bar** Full service **Wine selection** Good **Dress** Upscale casual **Disabled access** Ground level

Brunch: Saturday and Sunday, 11:30 a.m.–3 p.m.
Dinner Sunday–Thursday, 5:30–10:30 p.m.; Friday and Saturday, 6–11 p.m.

Setting & atmosphere Casual and contemporary with eclectic decor and cool furnishings and appointments. Small intimate rooms that open to the dining room give privacy and a view of the patio and pool area.

House specialties A colossal crab cake with young papaya Asian slaw; meat loaf with garlic mashed potatoes; the 20-ounce bone-in rib-eye steak. Shellfish platters with chilled oysters, clams, mussels, shrimp crab claws, and Maine lobster can be ordered for diner.

Other recommendations Roasted sea bass with quinoa, currants, and pine nuts; Kerry's chicken curry; spit-roasted chicken with Tuscan fries. Warm-from-the-oven cookies and milk; chunky peanut butter cookies sandwiched with grape jelly and ice cream; twice-baked banana bread with tempura bananas and brown sugar ice cream; or a "mountain" of pink cotton candy.

Summary & comments Chef/owner Kerry Simon has opened many acclaimed restaurants, including a few with über chef Jean-Georges Vongrichten. This is the first on his own and he's put his heart into it. Restaurant consultant Elizabeth Blau is his partner. Some menu items change regularly, but the signatures remain.

SIR GALAHAD'S ★★★

PRIME RIB | MODERATE | QUALITY ★★★½ | VALUE ★★★★½ | ZONE 1

Excalibur, 3850 Las Vegas Boulevard South; (702) 597-7777

Customers Visitors, locals **Reservations** Suggested **When to go** Less crowded weekdays **Entrée range** $17–$35; prix fixe, $40 **Payment** VISA, MC, AMEX, DC, D

Service rating ★★★½ **Friendliness rating** ★★★½ **Parking** Large lot, valet, garage **Bar** Full service **Wine selection** Good **Dress** Casual **Disabled access** Elevators

Dinner Sunday–Thursday, 5–10 p.m. (last seating); Friday and Saturday, 5–11 p.m. (last seating)

Setting & atmosphere English castle; waitstaff in costume of days of King Arthur. Prime rib served from large, gleaming steel and copper cart and sliced to order by skilled carvers tableside.

House specialties Prime rib, prime rib, and prime rib served with beef barley soup or a garden salad, plus mashed potatoes, creamed spinach, and whipped cream horseradish.

Other recommendations Appetizers such as mushrooms Cliffs of Dover. Chicken à la reine; fresh fish of the day.

Summary & comments Prime rib plus Yorkshire pudding, creamed spinach, mashed potatoes, and beef barley soup or green salad is a very hearty meal. Top it off, if you can, with English trifle or mud pie.

SPAGO ★★★★½

AMERICAN | MODERATE | QUALITY ★★★★½ | VALUE ★★½ | ZONE 1

The Forum Shops at Caesars Palace; (702) 369-6300

Customers Visitors, locals **Reservations** Recommended for dinner; not accepted for lunch **When to go** Anytime except during busy conventions **Entrée range** $16–$27 in the café; $25–$42 in the dining room **Payment** VISA, MC, AMEX, DC, D **Service rating** ★★★½ **Friendliness rating** ★★★★½ **Parking** Garage, valet **Bar** Full service **Wine selection** Excellent **Dress** Informal, casual **Disabled access** Ground floor

Open *Café:* Daily, 11 a.m.–11 p.m.
  Restaurant: Daily, 6–9:30 p.m.

Setting & atmosphere There are two separate dining rooms. The casual café offers a fine bird's-eye view of The Forum Shops from the comfort of a European-styled sidewalk setting. The restaurant inside is an eclectic mix of modern art, wrought iron, and contemporary tables and chairs and booths. Each Sunday in the café from about 2:30 p.m. to 6:30 p.m., a jazz band entertains. A private banquet room is available for parties up to 100. A small private room within the restaurant can seat up to 20.

House specialties *Café*—Wolfgang Puck's signature pizzas; imaginative sandwiches on homemade bread; salads; pastas; and frequently, a supertasty meat loaf with port wine sauce, grilled onions, and garlic potato puree. *Restaurant*—exquisite appetizers; pastas; grilled veal chop with dried cherry-wild rice and sage hollandaise; big-eye tuna with couscous; salmon encrusted with almonds and ginger. Menus in the café and restaurant change daily. Desserts are sensational. Menus change daily; signature dishes always available.

Summary & comments Recently refurbished and updated, Spago has a new look. The café has been enlarged and the bar is a busy centerpiece. Locals, who've always considered Spago a favorite now have their home parties catered by the restaurant. Owner Wolfgang Puck surrounds himself with the best staff, the best ingredients, the best of everything. One caveat—on very busy nights the dining room noise level can make conversation difficult. But the people-watching is terrific.

THE STEAK HOUSE ★★★

STEAK | EXPENSIVE | QUALITY ★★★½ | VALUE ★★★½ | ZONE 1

Circus Circus, 2880 Las Vegas Boulevard South; (702) 734-0410

Customers Visitors, locals **Reservations** Required **When to go** Weekdays **Entrée range** $15–$25; brunch: $12 for children, $25 for adults **Payment** All major credit cards **Service rating** ★★★½ **Friendliness rating** ★★★½ **Parking** Garage, lot, valet **Bar** Full service **Wine selection** Good **Dress** Informal **Disabled access** Ramps

Brunch Sunday, 9:30 a.m., 11:30 a.m., and 1:30 p.m. seatings

Dinner Monday–Friday, 5–11 p.m.; Saturday, 5 p.m.–midnight

Setting & atmosphere Wood-paneled rooms. The small dining room is decorated like a manor-house library. A mesquite-fired broiler in center of main room creates a cozy atmosphere. Glass refrigerator case displays over 3,000 pounds of aging meat.

House specialties Thick steaks; black-bean soup; giant baked potato.

Other recommendations Shrimp, crab, and lobster cocktails; Caesar salad; grilled chicken.

Summary & comments Consistently high quality and service. Don't be fooled by the children running around the lobby. Inside the Steak House, the atmosphere is adult, and the food is wonderful. Patio dining has less din.

STEFANO'S ★★★½

SOUTHERN ITALIAN | MOD/EXP | QUALITY ★★★★ | VALUE ★★½ | ZONE 2

Golden Nugget, 129 East Fremont Street; (702) 385-7111

Customers Visitors, locals **Reservations** Required **When to go** Avoid convention times **Entrée range** $26–$50 **Payment** All major credit cards **Service rating** ★★★½ **Friendliness rating** ★★★½ **Parking** Garage, valet **Bar** Full service **Wine selection** Very good **Dress** Sport coat **Disabled access** Elevators

Dinner Sunday–Thursday, 6–10:30 p.m.; Friday and Saturday, 5:30–10:30 p.m.

Setting & atmosphere A bright room with hand-decorated cabinetry, custom tile and Venetian chandeliers. Italian murals grace the walls.

House specialties Agnolotti, fresh mussels; veal scallopini Stefano (with prosciutto, asparagus, and mozzarella); chicken Sorrentino; osso buco; veal chop with porcini mushrooms and mascarpone cheese.

Other recommendations Roasted peppers; carpaccio; cioppino; capellini frutti di mare; fresh fish; daily specials. Chocolate pasta with vanilla ice cream, almonds, strawberries, and honey sauce; crème brûlée; tiramisu.

Entertainment & amenities The staff breaks into classical Italian songs throughout the meal. You will, too.

Summary & comments Dishes presented with flair. A happy dining experience.

SWEET GEORGIA BROWN'S ★★★

BARBECUE | MODERATE | QUALITY ★★★½ | VALUE ★★★★½ | ZONE 1

2600 East Flamingo Road; (702) 369-0245

Customers Visitors, locals **Reservations** Suggested **When to go** Anytime **Entrée range** $14.95–$29.95 **Payment** All major credit cards **Service rating** ★★★½ **Friendliness rating** ★★★★½ **Parking** Valet, large lot **Bar** No **Wine selection** No **Dress** Dressy casual **Disabled access** Ground floor

Lunch 11 a.m.–4 p.m.; buffet, Monday 11 a.m.–3 p.m., Sunday all day

Dinner Daily, 4–11 p.m.

Setting & atmosphere After a devastating fire destroyed their longtime H&H Barbecue location on the Westside, the Hicks family regrouped and opened Sweet Georgia Brown's Southern Cuisine on the site of a former Italian supper club. The decor remains the same: a little tired, yet pleasant. This genteel family has high standards. The staff dresses well and gives caring service.

House specialties Patriarch Hicks' original barbecue sauce, developed when he couldn't find one that suited his taste. It's good. An appetizer sampler plate with crisp catfish finger, meaty pork rib tips, and the zesty hot wings is a meal.

Other recommendations The daily buffet (except Saturday) that includes just about the entire menu. The side dishes that accompany most meals. Smothered dishes, hearty and filling; liver and onions; the peach cobbler with vanilla ice cream.

Summary & comments A surfeit of food that can be shared. Portions are more than generous. Á la carte service can be slow, so have a tall glass of the sweet lemonade and relax.

TASTE OF INDONESIA ★★★

INDONESIAN | MOD/EXP | QUALITY ★★★½ | VALUE ★★★★½ | ZONE 1

5700 West Spring Mountain Road, #A; (702) 365-0888

Customers Locals **Reservations** Weekends **When to go** Anytime **Entrée range** $7.50–$14.99 **Payment** All major credit cards **Service rating** ★★★½ **Friendliness rating** ★★★★½ **Parking** Lot **Bar** Ask server for current selection **Wine selection** Limited **Dress** Informal **Disabled access** Ground floor

Dinner 11 a.m.–10 p.m.; closed Sunday

Setting & atmosphere A small island-themed eatery with pleasing homestyle decor. The husband-and-wife owners, Ryan and Melania, are betting that an Indonesian restaurant, the first and only one in Las Vegas, will beat the odds. They celebrated their first anniversary January 2004.

House specialties Rijstaffel (rice table), a complete dinner with 13 courses for a modest fixed price. A vegetarian rijstafel is also offered. A variety satays are wonderful. These grilled skewers are the real thing. The flavors are distinctive, yet not too hot. Spicy dishes are marked.

Other recommendations All of the rice plates, potato fritters stuffed with ground been and scallions.

Summary & comments Desserts are not tempting, but there's so much here that is, it's hardly an issue.

TERRAZZA ★★★★

ITALIAN | MOD/EXP | QUALITY ★★★★ | VALUE ★★½ | ZONE 1

Caesars Palace, 3570 Las Vegas Boulevard South; (702) 731-7110

Customers Visitors, locals **Reservations** A must **When to go** Avoid conventions **Entrée range** $20–$40 **Payment** VISA, MC, AMEX, DC, CB, D **Service rating** ★★★★ **Friendliness rating** ★★★★½ **Parking** Valet, garage **Bar** Full service **Wine selection** Excellent **Dress** Business attire **Disabled access** Ground floor

Dinner Daily, 5:30–10:30 p.m.

Setting & atmosphere Italian rustic design carried throughout the various dining rooms, each with its own unique decor. Terrazza's design is open and inviting. An outdoor patio for warm-weather dining gives a splendid view of the new Palace Tower and the grand swimming pools.

House specialties Fat, homemade pappardelle pasta with wild mushrooms and truffle oil; risottos that change each day; rack of lamb, Roman style; a succulent pan-fried veal chop; thin, crisp focaccia filled with robiola cheese and drizzled with truffle oil; seared salmon with a light mustard sauce. Desserts: Triestine-style chocolate mousse with zabaglione; warm mascarpone tortine with coffee ice cream; Italian blood orange flan with pear, Barolo, and assorted berries.

Other recommendations Any of the seasonal daily specials.

Summary & comments Terrazza in the new Palace Tower has replaced the older Primavera. The main dining room is adjacent to Terrazza's lounge, where diners may have a before-dinner drink. Restaurants in the Palace Tower offer elegant dining away from the din of the casino.

THE TILLERMAN   ★★★

SEAFOOD | EXPENSIVE | QUALITY ★★★½ | VALUE ★★½ | ZONE 5

2245 East Flamingo Road; (702) 731-4036

Customers Visitors, locals **Reservations** Requested **When to go** Early evening **Entrée range** $20–$50 **Payment** VISA, MC, AMEX, DC, D **Service rating** ★★★½ **Friendliness rating** ★★★½ **Parking** Lot **Bar** Full service **Wine selection** Excellent **Dress** Informal, casual **Disabled access** Ramp

Dinner Sunday–Thursday, 5–10 p.m.; Friday and Saturday, 5–11 p.m.

Setting & atmosphere Attractive, airy main dining room with balcony seating. Hanging plants, wood paneling, beautiful live trees. Menu presented on scroll. Servers memorize orders without taking any notes. Ten to fifteen fresh fish listed daily.

House specialties Seafood fresh from California, the Gulf of Mexico, the Atlantic. Pacific salmon, Chilean sea bass, Florida snapper.

Other recommendations Prime steaks; Tillerman pasta Portofino. Fresh homemade pastries.

Summary & comments One of the most popular Las Vegas seafood restaurants. A new owner has made many improvements. For the first time since opening, the Tillerman accepts reservations.

Honors & awards *Wine Spectator* Award of Excellence for many years.

TOKYO   ★★★

JAPANESE/SUSHI | MODERATE | QUALITY ★★★½ | VALUE ★★★½ | ZONE 1

Commercial Center, 953 East Sahara Avenue; (702) 735-7070

Customers Visitors, locals **Reservations** Accepted **When to go** Anytime **Entrée range** $11–$20 **Payment** All major credit cards **Service rating** ★★★½ **Friendliness rating** ★★★½ **Parking** Large lot **Bar** Full service **Wine selection** Fair **Dress** Informal, casual **Disabled access** Ground floor

Dinner Daily, 5–10 p.m.

Setting & atmosphere Newly decorated interior—tatami room, sushi bar.

House specialties Small hibachi grills for those who wish to cook their own dinner. Shabu shabu also available.

Other recommendations Combination, special, and deluxe dinners, all modestly priced; a wide selection is available.

Summary & comments A family-run restaurant—very popular with the locals. Tokyo is a terrific value.

TOP OF THE WORLD ★★★

AMERICAN | MOD/EXP | QUALITY ★★★½ | VALUE ★★½ | ZONE 3

Stratosphere Tower, 2000 Las Vegas Boulevard; (702) 380-7711

Customers Visitors, locals **Reservations** Required **When to go** Anytime **Entrée range** $16–$25 **Payment** VISA, MC, AMEX, DC, D **Service rating** ★★★★½ **Friendliness rating** ★★★½ **Parking** Valet, garage, and lot **Bar** Full service **Wine selection** Excellent **Dress** Upscale casual **Disabled access** Elevator

Lunch 11 a.m.–3 p.m., every day

Dinner Sunday–Thursday, 6–11 p.m.; Friday and Saturday, 6 p.m.–midnight

Setting & atmosphere Without question, Top of the World offers one of the most beautiful views of the city. The restaurant revolves as you dine, giving a panoramic spectacle of the surrounding mountains. The dining room is handsomely designed with inlaid tables, fine woods and brass, and copper accents. There are no bad tables.

House specialties San Francisco–style cioppino; chicken quesadilla soup; charbroiled portobello mushrooms with Marsala demi-glace; Sonoma Valley rack of lamb; Santa Fe–style rotisserie chicken.

Other recommendations Tequila-lime shrimp, served on a bed of linguini; almond-crusted salmon; the towering vacherin dessert; the signature bread pudding made with egg bread.

Summary & comments The food is secondary to the view, which is simply spectacular, but the food is very good. Arrive before sunset and watch one of the best free shows. Be aware that there is a $15 food minimum. It's an easy amount to reach in this strictly à la carte room. The fine service and the view enhance any meal.

TRATTORIA DEL LUPO ★★★½

ITALIAN | MODERATE | QUALITY ★★★★ | VALUE ★★½ | ZONE 1

Mandalay Bay, 3950 Las Vegas Boulevard South; (702) 740-5522

Customers Visitors, locals **Reservations** Suggested **When to go** Anytime **Entrée range** $16–$25 (lunch), $20–$42 (dinner) **Payment** All major credit cards **Service rating** ★★★½ **Friendliness rating** ★★★★½ **Parking** Valet, garage **Bar** Full service **Wine selection** Good **Dress** Upscale casual **Disabled access** Through casino

Lunch 11:30 a.m.–5 p.m., every day

Dinner Sunday–Thursday, 5–11 p.m.; Friday and Saturday, 5 p.m.–midnight

Setting & atmosphere Designed by the renowned restaurant specialist Adam Tihany, Lupo features laid-back Italian rustic decor with vaulted ceilings, an open exhibition kitchen, and a handsome bar for imbibing or dining as the centerpiece of the dining room.

House specialties Prosciutto-wrapped monkfish with artichokes, peas, and fava beans; seared Tuscan-style porterhouse steak with caramelized fennel and lemon. The marvelous breads and pizzas; homemade charcuterie, pastas, and grilled fish. Heavenly desserts.

Summary & comments Yet another winner for Wolfgang Puck. Executive chef Mark Ferguson came to Lupo from Spago after a tour of Italy. His spin on such classic dishes as the Tuscan porterhouse is super. The bar attracts local power brokers who like nothing better than to observe the scene from the lofty barstools. Noisy and energetic, Lupo is a cool dining place.

VENTANO ★★★½

ITALIAN | MODERATE | QUALITY ★★★½ | VALUE ★★★★½ | ZONE 5

191 Arroyo Grande; Henderson; (702) 944-4848

Customers Visitors, locals **Reservations** Weekends **When to go** Anytime; lunch hour is busy **Entrée range** $12–$24 **Payment** All major credit cards **Service rating** ★★★★ **Friendliness rating** ★★★★½ **Parking** Large lot **Bar** Full service **Wine selection** Good **Dress** Casual **Disabled access** Ramp

Lunch Daily, 11 a.m.–4 p.m.

Dinner Nightly, 5–10:30 p.m.

Oyster Bar Daily, 11 a.m.–11 p.m.

Lounge Open 24 hours

Setting & atmosphere Rustic Italian with a spectacular view. The wraparound terrace for al fresco dining has an unobstructed view of the mountains and the surrounding area. Late-night dining is available in the comfy smoking lounge.

House specialties Grilled shrimp (½ pound) served on a hot "stone," redolent of garlic, herbs, and fresh lemon; this well-priced specialty is available at lunch and dinner. Lobster bisque served in a bread bowl; Sicilian rice balls; riatoni Portofino; fettuccine cartoccio (shrimp, mussels, and clams baked in a paper bag); osso buco agnello (a tasty spin on the usual veal shank); and costolette di Maiale (spareribs slowly cooked in honey and vinegar).

Other recommendations Spiedini and scampi, the Italian version of surf and turf; scarpariello, roasted chicken with sausage and vegetables; the pizzas and sandwiches served at lunch; and the pan roasts at the oyster bar (some oyster bar specialties are offered in the dining room).

Summary & comments Ventano is a lively, friendly place with affable owners. No pretensions, just good food at reasonable prices.

VOODOO CAFÉ & LOUNGE ★★★

CREOLE/CAJUN | EXPENSIVE | QUALITY ★★★½ | VALUE ★★½ | ZONE 1

Rio, 3700 West Flamingo Road; (702) 252-7777

Customers Visitors, locals **Reservations** Suggested **When to go** Anytime **Entrée range** $27–$49 **Payment** VISA, MC, AMEX, DC, D **Service rating** ★★★½ **Friendliness rating** ★★★★½ **Parking** Valet, garage, lot **Bar** Full service **Wine selection** Excellent **Dress** Sportscoat or dress shirt with collar for men; no shorts, sneakers, T-shirts, or jeans **Disabled access** Elevator

Open Daily, 5–11 p.m.

Setting & atmosphere Voodoo decor, black walls accented with splashes of color, comfortable booths and tables, and a spectacular view from atop one of the city's tallest buildings. With its location west of the Strip, the view of the action is the absolute best.

House specialties Crawfish and blue-crab cakes; frog legs d'Armond; baked oyster sampler with Rockefeller, Bienville, and tasso toppings; spicy, boiled Louisiana crawfish; Voodoo gumbo; the house salad with cane-syrup vinaigrette; fresh tuna Napoleon; soft shell crab Lafayette.

Other recommendations Cajun rib eye; catfish Bayou Teche (pan-fried catfish topped with crawfish étouffée); a seafood plate of cornmeal-crusted fried oysters, shrimp, crawfish, and catfish.

Summary & comments It took a while for Voodoo to hit its stride, but now this colorful eatery and late-night hangout offers some very tasty food. The lounge features bartenders who do tricks while mixing drinks. In the past they performed flaming tricks, tossing the fiery libations from glass to glass, but those spoilsports at the fire department put out their fire.

WOLFGANG PUCK BAR & GRILL ★★★★

AMERICAN | MOD/EXP | QUALITY ★★★★ | VALUE ★★★★½ | ZONE 1

MGM Grand, 3799 Las Vegas Boulevard South; (702) 891-3019

Customers Visitors, locals **Reservations** Suggested **When to go** Anytime **Entrée range** $13–$29 **Payment** All major credit cards **Service rating** ★★★★½ **Friendliness rating** ★★★★½ **Parking** Valet, garage **Bar** Full service **Wine selection** Very good **Dress** Casual **Disabled access** Ground floor

Open Monday–Friday, 11:30 a.m.–11:30 p.m.; Sunday, 11:30 a.m.–10 p.m.

Setting & atmosphere A celebration of America, this restaurant takes us back to early California and its laid-back style. Relaxed and beautiful decor with a flavor reminiscent of Puck's first restaurant. It's lovely.

House specialties The boneless rib-eye, a succulent pleaser served with crushed red potatoes and onion rings; pizzas with newly created toppings. Ditto the pastas and the calzone.

Other recommendations Starters and salads that could be a light meal; calf's liver with leeks and pancetta; the special fish of the day; duck bratwurst with mascarpone polenta; braised lamb osso buco with orzo pasta.

Summary & comments Menus change all the time, but the favorites always remain. Open just a short time, Puck's is already a hipster's hangout.

Part Five

Shopping and Seeing the Sights

Shopping in Las Vegas

The most interesting and diversified specialty shopping in Las Vegas is centered on the Strip at the **Fashion Show Mall** (call (702) 874-1400), **Grand Canal Shoppes at the Venetian** (call (702) 414-4500), and the **The Forum and Appian Way Shops at Caesars Palace** (call (702) 893-4800). These three venues, within walking distance of each other, collectively offer the most unique, and arguably the most concentrated, aggregation of upscale retailers in the United States. In fairness, it should be noted that The Forum Shops and the Grand Canal Shoppes are not your average shopping centers. In fact, both are attractions in their own right and should be on your must-see list even if you don't like to shop. Both feature designer shops, exclusive boutiques, and specialty retailers. Fashion Show Mall, by comparison, is plain white-bread, with no discernible theme but a great lineup of big-name department stores.

At the intersection of Las Vegas Boulevard and Spring Mountain Road, the Fashion Show Mall is anchored by **Saks Fifth Avenue, May Company, Neiman Marcus, Macy's, Nordstrom, Bloomingdales', Lord & Taylor,** and **Dillard's,** and contains over 100 specialty shops, including four art galleries. There is no theme here—no Roman columns or canals with gondolas. At the Fashion Show Mall, shopping is king. And although there is no shortage of boutiques or designer shops, the presence of the big department stores defines the experience for most customers. The Fashion Show Mall is the place to go for that new sport coat, tie, blouse, or skirt at a reasonable price. The selection is immense, and most of the retailers are familiar and well known. To underscore its name, the mall stages free fashion shows most afternoons.

The Forum Shops is a *très chic (et très cher)* shopping complex situated between Caesars Palace and the Mirage. Connected to the Forum Casino in Caesars Palace, The Forum Shops offers a Roman market–themed shopping environment. Executed on a scale that is extraordinary even for Caesars, The Forum Shops replicate the grandeur of Rome at the height of its glory. Nearly 100 shops and restaurants line an ancient Roman street punctuated by plazas and fountains. Dozens of new retailers and eateries populate the new three-story, 175,000-square-foot Appian Way expansion. Though indoors, clouds, sky, and celestial bodies are projected on the vaulted ceilings to simulate the actual time of day outside. Statuary in The Forum is magnificent; some is even animatronic.

The Grand Canal Shoppes are similar to The Forum Shops in terms of the realistic theming, only this time the setting is the modern-day canals of Venice. Sixty-five shops, boutiques, restaurants, and cafes are arrayed along a quarter-mile-long Venetian street flanking a canal. A 70-foot ceiling (more than six stories high) with simulated sky enhances the openness and provides perspective. Meanwhile, gondolas navigating the canal add a heightened sense of commerce and activity. The centerpiece of the Grand Canal Shoppes is a replica of St. Mark's Square, without the pigeons.

A fourth major Strip shopping venue is **Desert Passage**, a 450,000-square-foot shopping and entertainment complex at the Aladdin (call (702) 866-0710). The venue recreates street scenes from real and imaginary North African and eastern Mediterranean towns in a shopping concourse that stretches around the periphery of the hotel and casino. The bazaars and shop facades sit beneath an arched ceiling painted and lighted to simulate the evening sky. Overall, although the replication is effective, it falls a little short of the Forum Shops but gives the Grand Canal Shoppes a run for the money. Like the Grand Canal Shoppes, Desert Passage offers primarily upscale boutique shopping, but more of it, with 144 shops and restaurants compared to the Canal Shoppes' 65.

At Paris is **Rue de la Paix,** 31,000 square feet of upscale French boutique shopping. Modest in size by Las Vegas shopping standards, the Rue de la Paix re-creates a Paris street scene with cobblestone pavement and winding alleyways.

Mandalay Place, a mall with over 40 boutiques and restaurants, also serves as the pedestrian connector linking Mandalay Bay and Luxor. The retailers seem more diverse and selectively chosen than at many other venues, making the shopping interesting even for those not hooked on shopping. There's a great wine shop with very affordable selections, a bookstore specializing in Las Vegas lore, a barber spa and retail shaving emporium for men, and a chocolate shop, among many others. Among the restaurants is the Burger Joint, featuring a $60 hamburger dressed with truffles. Fortunately, there are also less foo-foo burgers at reasonable prices.

Another Strip shopping venue is the **Showcase,** adjacent to the MGM Grand. Although most of the 190,000-square-foot shopping and entertainment complex is devoted to theme restaurants, a Sega electronic games arcade, and an eight-plex movie theater, there remains space for a number of retail specialty shops. Practically next door is the **Hawaiian Marketplace,** an 80,000-square-foot mall. Though the theme is Polynesian, the mall's restaurants and retailers are an eclectic lot ranging from **Wahoo's Fish Tacos** to **Mrs. Fields Cookies,** and from **Tropical Jewelers** to the **Las Vegas Tobacco Company.**

There are three large neighborhood malls in Las Vegas: the **Boulevard Mall** (call (702) 732-8949), the **Meadows** (call (702) 878-4849), and the **Galleria at Sunset** (call (702) 434-0202). The Boulevard Mall, with 122 stores anchored by **Sears, JC Penney, Marshalls, Dillard's,** and **Macy's,** is on Maryland Avenue, between Desert Inn Road and Flamingo Road. The Meadows, featuring the same department stores (except for Marshalls), has more 73 stores spread over two levels. The Meadows is situated between West Charleston Boulevard and the Las Vegas Expressway (US 95) on Valley View. The third mall, Galleria at Sunset, at 1300 Sunset Road, offers 130 stores and restaurants with **Dillard's, JC Penney, Robinsons-May,** and **Mervyns California** leading the lineup. Because the three malls target locals, and because locals also have access to area discount shopping, the malls offer lowball prices to stay competitive. You won't have the choice available at Fashion Show Mall, but if you can find what you're looking for, it will probably be cheaper.

Neonopolis, downtown's first entertainment and shopping complex, opened at Fourth and Fremont Streets in 2002. Anchored by **Gillian's,** Neonopolis also features a 14-screen movie complex, a games arcade, and a couple of dozen specialty shops, including a **Frederick's of Hollywood.** If you're downtown, it's worth a few minutes to check out the vintage neon signs on display at Neonopolis. Also downtown is **Las Vegas Premium Outlets,** an $85-million, 120-store outlet mall. A clone of other Premium Outlet malls, featured brands include **AIX Armani Exchange, Ralph Lauren, Kenneth Cole, Lacoste,** and **Coach.** The mall is situated just to the west of downtown, between downtown and I-15. It's a bit far from downtown to walk but is only a short cab ride away. From I-15, the mall entrance is off Charleston Boulevard.

Another large discount shopping venue has materialized about five miles south of Tropicana Avenue on Las Vegas Boulevard, near the Blue Diamond Road exit off I-15. Just north of Blue Diamond Road is a **Belz Factory Outlet** mall (call (702) 896-5599), with 155 stores. Belz, like The Forum Shops, doubled its size in 1998. Promotional literature listing the individual shops is available in almost all hotel brochure racks. The easiest way to reach the outlets is to drive south on I-15 to Exit 33, Blue Diamond Road. Proceed east on Blue Diamond to the intersection with Las Vegas Boulevard. Turn left on Las Vegas Boulevard to the Belz mall. For those without transportation, Las Vegas Citizen's Area Transit

(CAT) operates a bus route that connects the various Strip and suburban shopping centers. Fare is $1.25 in residential areas and $2 on the Strip. Service is provided daily from 10:35 a.m. to 6:30 p.m. For more information on CAT, call (702) 228-7433.

About an hour southwest on I-15 in Primm, Nevada, is **Fashion Outlet Mall** (call (702) 874-1400), offering themed dining and 100 outlet stores. You'll find **Williams-Sonoma, Pottery Barn, Versace, Brooks Brothers, Calvin Klein, Tommy Hilfiger, Escada, Kenneth Cole, Banana Republic, Baby Guess, LeSportsac,** and **Last Call from Neiman Marcus,** among others. The mall is adjacent to the Primm Valley Resort and Casino.

Unique Shopping Opportunities

Wine and Liquor Though not centrally located, **Lee's Discount Liquors** (call (702) 269-2400) on South Las Vegas Boulevard just south of Blue Diamond Road offers the best selection of wine, liquor, and beer within easy access of the Strip. Unless your hotel is south of Tropicana, take I-15 to the Blue Diamond Road exit and then head south on South Las Vegas Boulevard. If your hotel is south of Tropicana you're just as well off taking South Las Vegas Boulevard the whole way.

Art Las Vegas is a great place to shop for contemporary and nontraditional art and sculpture, with galleries in the Fashion Show Mall, The Forum Shops, and the Grand Canal Shoppes. Do not, however, expect any bargains.

Gambling Stuff As you would expect, Las Vegas is a shopping mecca when it comes to anything gambling related. If you are in the market for a roulette wheel, a blackjack table, or some personalized chips, try the **Gamblers General Store** at 800 South Main, (call (702) 382-9903, or (800) 322-CHIP outside Nevada). For books and periodicals on gambling, we recommend the **Gamblers Book Club** store near the intersection of South 11th Street and East Charleston, (call (702) 382-7555).

If you have always wanted a slot machine for your living room, you can buy one at **Showcase Slot Machines,** 4305 South Industrial Road, (call (702) 740-5722). Possession of a slot machine (including video poker and blackjack) for personal use is legal in the following states:

Alaska	Minnesota	Texas
Arizona	Nevada	Utah
Arkansas	New Mexico	Virginia
Kentucky	Ohio	West Virginia
Maine	Rhode Island	

Another group of states will allow you to own a slot machine providing the machine is fairly old (how old depends on the state). In New Jersey, Pennsylvania, New York, and South Dakota, the machine must have been manufactured before 1941. In the following states and the District of Columbia, the required age falls somewhere between 20 and 42 years:

California	Kansas	New Hampshire	South Carolina
Colorado	Louisiana	New Jersey	South Dakota
Delaware	Maryland	New York	Vermont
Florida	Massachusetts	North Carolina	Washington
Georgia	Michigan	North Dakota	Washington, D.C.
Idaho	Mississippi	Oklahoma	Wisconsin
Illinois	Missouri	Oregon	Wyoming
Iowa	Montana	Pennsylvania	

In all other states, the possession of any type of slot machine is illegal.

Head Rugs   The next time you go to a Las Vegas production show, pay attention to the showgirls' hair. You will notice that the same woman will have a different hairdo for every number. Having made this observation, you will not be surprised that the largest wig and hairpiece retailer in the United States is in Las Vegas. At 953 East Sahara Avenue about five minutes away from the Strip, **Serge's Showgirl Wigs** inventories over 7,000 hairpieces and wigs, made from both synthetic materials and human hair. In addition to serving the local showgirl population, Serge's Showgirl Wigs also specializes in assisting chemotherapy patients. A catalog and additional information can be obtained by calling (702) 732-1015.

Ethnic Shopping   At the southwest corner of Spring Mountain and Wynn Roads is Las Vegas Chinatown Plaza with 30 outlets, (call (702) 221-8448). This location offers Asian theme shopping and restaurants.

Authentic African products, including sculpture, art, pottery, baskets, jewelry, musical instruments, and attire, can be found at **African & World Imports** in the Boulevard Mall at 3680 South Maryland Parkway, (call (702) 734-1900).

For Native American art, crafts, books, music, and attire, try the **Las Vegas Indian Center** at 2300 West Bonanza Boulevard (call (702) 647-5842). And 25 minutes north of Las Vegas in Moapa, Nevada, you'll find the **Moapa Tribal Enterprises Casino and Gift Center** (call (702) 864-2600). Take I-15 north to Exit 75.

Zoot Suits   No kidding. For the coolest threads in town, try **Valentino's Zootsuit Collection: Vintage Apparel & Collectibles** at the corner of South Sixth Street and Charleston. If you only want to zoot up for a special occasion, rentals are available (call (702) 383-9555).

Costumes   **Halloween Experience** at 5800 South Valley View features thousands of costumes, masks, and accessories year round. The showroom is open Monday through Friday to the public and on weekends by special arrangement (call (702) 740-4224). For "sex-theme" apparel and costumes, try **Bare Essential Fantasy Fashions** at 4029 West Sahara (call (702) 247-4711). You'll find everything from dresses to G-strings. There's even a large selection of "bare essentials" for men. Some merchandise would be at home in suburbia, but some is strictly XXX. And speaking of XXX, that goes for sizes too.

Shoes   If you have feet a helicopter could land on, you might want to check out **Leonard's Wide Shoes,** 3999 South Las Vegas Boulevard (call (702) 895-9993). Leonard's specializes in W-I-D-E sizes, 5 to 13EE for women, and 6 to 18 (6E) for men. If smoking stunted your growth, increase your height with custom-made platforms, boots, and high heels from **Red Shoes,** 4011 West Sahara, Unit 1 (call (702) 889-4442). For a great selection of cowboy boots, try **Cowtown Boots,** 2989 Paradise Road (call (702) 737-8469).

Seeing the Sights

Residents of Las Vegas are justifiably proud of their city and are quick to point out that it has much to offer besides gambling. Quality theater, college and professional sports, dance, concerts, art shows, museums, and film festivals contribute to making Las Vegas a truly great place to live. In addition, there is a diverse and colorful natural and historical heritage. What Las Vegas residents sometimes have a difficult time understanding, however, is that the average business and leisure traveler doesn't really give a big hoot. Las Vegas differs from Orlando and Southern California in that it does not have any bona fide tourist attractions except Hoover Dam. Nobody drives all the way to Las Vegas to take their children to visit the Guinness Book of Records exhibit. While there have always been some great places to detox from a long trade show or too many hours at the casino, they are totally peripheral in the minds of visitors. Las Vegas needs a legitimate, nongaming tourist draw, but the strange aggregation of little museums, factory tours, and mini–theme parks is not it.

In 1993, the opening of the MGM Grand Hotel and Casino and Grand Adventures Theme Park brought Las Vegas a little closer to penetrating the consciousness of the nongambling traveler, but, alas, the park was a dud. It limped along for eight years before shutting down in 2001. During the 1990s, Circus Circus opened a smaller theme park, Adventuredome, behind its main casino. For the most part, the new theme parks have made little impression on either the locals or the tourists. From 1997 through 2000, a number of Strip casinos, including Caesars Palace, the Stratosphere, New York–New York, the Sahara, and the Las Vegas Hilton, opened new attractions. They are, by and large, imaginative, visually appealing, and high-tech. Some, like the Hilton's *Star Trek* attraction, would stand out as headliners in any theme park in the country. Others, while not up to Disney or Universal Studios standards, represent a giant leap forward for Las Vegas. Clearly, the competition learned a few things from MGM Grand's theme-park flop.

Adventuredome at Circus Circus

To further appeal to the family market targeted by the MGM Grand Adventures Theme Park, Circus Circus opened a small but innovative amusement park in August of 1993. Situated directly behind the main hotel and casino, the park now goes by the name of Adventuredome. Architecturally compelling, the entire park is built two stories high atop the casino's parking structure and is totally enclosed by a huge glass dome. From the outside, the dome surface is reflective, mirroring its surroundings in hot tropical pink. Inside, however, the dome is transparent, allowing guests in the park to see out. Composed of a multilayer glass-and-plastic sandwich, the dome allows light in but blocks ultraviolet rays. The entire park is air-conditioned and climate-controlled 365 days a year.

The park is designed to resemble a classic Western desert canyon. From top to bottom, hand-painted artificial rock is sculpted into caverns, pinnacles, steep cliffs, and buttes. A stream runs through the stark landscape, cascading over a 90-foot falls into a rippling blue-green pool. Set among the rock structures are the attractions: a roller coaster, a flume ride, an inverter ride, and Chaos, a spinning amusement that hauls riders randomly through three dimensions. There are also some rides for small children. Embellishing the scene are several life-sized animatronic dinosaurs, a re-creation of an archeological dig, a fossil wall, and a replica of a Pueblo cliff dwelling. There is also a small theater featuring magic and illusion. Finally, and inevitably, there is an electronic games arcade.

Adventuredome's premier attractions are the **Canyon Blaster,** the only indoor, double-loop, corkscrew roller coaster in the United States; the **Rim Runner,** a three-and-a-half-minute water-flume ride, and **Chaos,** a verticle Tilt-A-Whirl on steroids. Canyon Blaster and Rim Runner wind in, around, and between the rocks and cliffs. The flume ride additionally passes under the snouts of the dinosaurs.

Guests can reach the theme park by proceeding through the rear of the main casino to the entrance and ticket plaza situated on the mezzanine level. Circus Circus has changed the admission policy so many times we have lost track. You can choose between paying for each attraction individually ($4–$6) or opting for an all-inclusive day pass ($22). For exact admission prices on the day of your visit, call (702) 794-3939.

Bellagio Attractions

The big draw at the Bellagio is the **Gallery of Fine Art Exhibition,** which hosts temporary traveling exhibits. Tickets usually run about $15 for adults, $12 for children. For information, call (702) 693-7871.

Bellagio's free outdoor spectacle is a choreographed **water-fountain show** presented   on the lake in front of the hotel (which stretches the length of three football fields); Monday through Friday, every half hour from 3 p.m. until 7 p.m.; and Saturday and Sunday every half hour from noon to 7 p.m. The five-minute production uses 1,200 fountains that blast streams of water as high as 200 feet. Almost 5,000 white lights and musical accompaniment by Sinatra, Pavarotti, and Strauss, among others, complete the picture. It's pleasant and fairy-like, but not necessarily something you should go out of your way to see. Also, Bellagio's dramatic three-story, glass-domed botanical garden is a quiet oasis.

Las Vegas Hilton Attractions

The Hilton offers an attraction called *Star Trek: The Experience.* You enter through a museum of *Star Trek* TV/movie memorabilia and props en route to a 16-minute *Klingon Encounter* that culminates in a four-minute space-flight simulation ride. The Hilton ride differs from other simulation attractions in that the field of vision seemingly surrounds the guests. In 2004, a sister *Star Trek* attraction, *Borg Invasion 4-D,* was added. In this one, the Borg attack your spaceship and chase you to an escape spacecraft (actually a theater) where you see a 3-D movie in which your spacecraft helps defeat the Borg. The special effects are good, but the plot is a little fuzzy to anyone not already familiar with the Borg. All you need to know really is that the Borg drill out your brain and inhabit your body. You can purchase tickets for each attraction individually or opt for a ticket that covers both.

Upon returning from your mission to far-flung reaches of the galaxy, you are welcomed back to this planet at the gift shop. The History of the Future Museum is a self-guided exhibit that you can enjoy at your own pace. Besides the museum, the *Klingon Encounter,* the *Borg Invasion,* and the gift shop, *Star Trek: The Experience* includes an electronic-games arcade, a restaurant, and a lounge.

Although the visuals on the simulator ride are a little fuzzy by modern standards, the overall experience, including *Borg Invasion 4-D* (which offers several neat twists and surprises), earns *Star Trek* a first-place ranking among Las Vegas's attractions. Not wanting to detract from your enjoyment of *Star Trek,* we're not going to tell you what happens. Suffice it to say that it's extremely well done, and the total experience gives most Disney or Universal attractions a good run for their money. Both *Klingon Encounter* and *Borg Invasion 4-D* are approximately 22 minutes long. Each experience is complete with live interaction. The best times to see *Star Trek: The Experience* and *Borg Invasion 4-D* are on weekdays from 12:30 to 2 p.m. or after 4:30 p.m. If you happen to go when there is not much of a line, take time to check out the chronological history of the universe. The history show is open 11 a.m. to 11 p.m. daily. Admission is $30, including tax. You can purchase tickets three days in advance only at the *Star Trek* box office (at entrance). *Hint:* the entrance from "Deep Space Promenade" is free. For information, call (702) 732-5111 or (888) GO-BOLDLY.

Luxor Attractions

The Luxor offers two continuously running, gated (paid admission) attractions inside the pyramid on the level above the casino. Designed by Douglas Trumbull, creator of the *Back to the Future* ride at Universal Studios, *In Search of the Obelisk* (in the Egyptian ruins) consists of two motion simulators: a runaway freight elevator that gives you the unusual (and disconcerting!) sensation of plummeting a fair distance, and a runaway tour tram in the bowels of a subterranean world. The second attraction, a seven-story IMAX 3-D theater with a 15,000-watt sound system, runs 24 hours a day and costs about $10.

Mandalay Bay Attractions

The big draw at Mandalay Bay is the **Shark Reef** aquarium featuring sharks, rays, sea turtles, venomous stonefish, and dozens of other denizens of the deep playing house in a 1.3-million-gallon tank. If you don't like fish, separate exhibits showcase rare golden crocodiles and pythons. Something for everybody, you might say. The Shark reef audio tour is open daily from 10 a.m. until 11 p.m. Admission is about $16 for adults and $10 for children 12 and under. Additional information is available at (702) 632-4555.

MGM Grand Attractions

The MGM Grand hosts a **tri-story 5,345-square-foot lion habitat** that houses up to five of the big cats. The lions are on duty from 11 a.m. until 10 p.m. daily and admission is free. There is also, of course, an MGM Lion logo shop and the opportunity (for $20) to be photographed with a lion.

Mirage and T. I. Attractions

Not only are the Mirage and T. I. attractions of top quality, they are also free. The two biggies are the **pirate battle at Treasure Island** and the **exploding volcano at the Mirage.** The disco naval battle takes place every 90 minutes, weather permitting, beginning at 4 p.m., with the last performance at 10 p.m. (11:30 p.m. on warm-weather-month Fridays and Saturdays). In 2003, as part of an image makeover, T. I. wrote the British out of the script (they always lost anyway) and replaced them with "a group of sexy women" called "The Sirens," who now fight the pirates. In the new production, the pirates are apparently so disconcerted by all the leg and cleavage that they do not put up a very robust fight. The best vantage points are along the rope rail on the entrance bridge to the casino. On weekdays, claim your spot 15 to 20 minutes before show time. On weekends, make that 35 to 45 minutes. If you do not insist on having a *perfect* vantage point, you can see most everything just by joining the crowd at the last minute. If you are short, or have children in your party, it's probably worth the effort to arrive early and nail down a position by the rail.

The volcano at the Mirage goes off about every 15 minutes from dusk until midnight, if the weather is good and the winds are light. In the winter, when it gets dark earlier, the volcano starts popping off at 6 p.m. Usually, because of the frequency of performances (eruptions?), getting a good, rail-side vantage point is not too difficult. If you want to combine the volcano with a meal, grab a window table at the second-floor restaurant in the Casino Royale across the street. Dinner here costs $10 to $20, though, so these are not cheap seats.

The Mirage has some of *Siegfried and Roy's* white tigers on display in a well-executed, natural habitat exhibit. In addition to the tigers, the Mirage maintains a nice dolphin exhibit. Both are open daily, 11 a.m. to 5:30 p.m. (the Secret Garden tigers retire at 3:30 p.m., however). The exhibit costs $12. (Children ages 10 and under get in free.) For the price of admission you can also take in the **Secret Garden** next to the dolphin habitat, and a small zoo with Siegfried and Roy's white and Bengal tigers, white lions, an Indian elephant, and more. For more information about Mirage, call (702) 791-7111. For more information about Treasure Island, call (702) 894-7111.

Paris Las Vegas Attractions

The big draw at Paris is, of course, the 540-foot-tall replica of the **Eiffel Tower.** Requiring ten million pounds of steel and over two years to erect, the Las Vegas version is a little more than half the size of the original. Just below the top (at 460 feet) is an observation deck accessible via two ten-passenger glass elevators. It costs a stiff nine bucks to ride, but that's just the beginning of the story. You must first line up to buy tickets. Your ticket will show a designated time to report to the escalator (that's right: *escalator*. You must take an escalator to reach the elevators). If you're late you'll be turned away, and there are no refunds. The escalator will deposit you in yet another line where you'll wait for the elevator. The elevators run from 10 a.m. until 1 a.m. except when it's raining.

Though all this hopping from line to line is supposed to take 5 to 20 minutes, we found 40 to 60 minutes more the norm. Here's the rub. The observation deck holds less than 100 persons, and once someone gets up there they can stay as long as they want. Hence, when the observation deck is at max capacity, nobody can go up unless someone comes down. Because the tower affords such a great view of Bellagio across the street, gridlock ensues several times nightly while people squeeze on the observation overlong to watch Bellagio's dancing-waters show. If accessing the observation platform seems like too much work, take the separate elevator that serves the restaurant and bar on the 11th floor of the tower. You don't need reservations to patronize the bar, but you must be nicely dressed, i.e., jackets recommended for men and absolutely no jeans, T-shirts, tank tops, or sandals. The bar is open nightly from 5 p.m. until midnight.

Sahara Attractions

The newly renovated and expanded Sahara has its own entry in the raging simulator-ride craze. Called **Speedworld,** the attraction draws its inspiration from Indy car racing. You can elect to drive an Indy car in an interactive simulated race, or alternatively, you can strap in as a passive passenger for a 3-D, motion-simulator movie race. The interactive racecars respond exactly like a real racecar to braking, acceleration, and steering control. You can even choose between driving a manual or automatic (recommended) transmission. Your race pits you against other drivers and lasts about eight minutes.

There are several racecourses to choose from, ranging from an easy oval to a simulated Grand Prix course through the streets of Las Vegas. You start by choosing a racecourse and then proceed to a video orientation briefing where you learn how to get into the car, adjust the seat and steering wheel, turn on the engine and work the transmission, accelerator, and brakes. While none of the above is especially complicated, most people require a little coaching or assistance when they actually get into their car.

Once your race begins, driving the course at high speed demands intense concentration. If you have a simulated crash, you will be directed to the simulated pits for repairs. The visuals on the screen in front of your car are reasonably good, but come to you at numbing speed. If you are sensitive to motion sickness, the Indy car simulator will leave your stomach spinning.

In our opinion, you need to race once just to understand how everything works. After you get the hang of it, you will enjoy the experience more and also be more competitive. Start out on a simple course with an automatic transmission and work up to more demanding courses. After each race you will be given a computer-generated report that tells how you finished, and it provides some comparative information on your general performance. Each race you drive costs $10, while the 3-D movie costs $5.

Speed, the roller coaster at the Sahara, opened in June of 2000. You race down 1,350 feet of track, including one 360-degree loop and a harrowing 224-foot climb straight up a tower. From the tower's top, you'll roll *backwards* back to the starting point. The round-trip takes 48 seconds. Special electromagnetic fields slingshot riders from 0 to 40 mph and again from 35 to 70 mph in two seconds flat. Yikes! Speed is flat out the fastest roller coaster in town, and is open from 11 a.m to 11 p.m. every day. Rides cost about $10 each or $13 all day, call (702) 737-2111 on the day you go.

Stratosphere Attractions

The Stratosphere Tower stands 1,149-feet tall and offers an unparalleled view of Las Vegas. You can watch aircraft take off simultaneously from McCarran International Airport and Nellis Air Force Base. To the south, the entire Las Vegas Strip is visible. To the west, Red Rock Canyon seems practically within spitting distance. North of the Tower, downtown glitters beneath the canopy of the Fremont Street Experience. By day, the rich geology of the Colorado Basin and Spring Mountains merge in an earthtone and evergreen tapestry. At night, the dark desert circumscribes a blazing strand of twinkling neon.

A 12-level pod crowns the futuristic contours of three immense buttresses that form the Tower's base. Level 12, the highest level, serves as the boarding area for the **High Roller,** a roller coaster; **X Scream,** a dangledaddy; and the **Big Shot,** an acceleration/free-fall thrill ride. Levels 11 and 10 are not open to the public. An outdoor observation deck is Level 9, with an indoor observation deck directly beneath it on Level 8. Level 7 features a 220-seat lounge, and Level 6 houses an upscale revolving restaurant. Levels 4 and 3 contain meeting rooms, and the remaining levels—1, 2, and 5—are not open to the public.

The view from the Tower is so magnificent that we recommend experiencing it at different times of the day and night. Sunset is particularly stunning, and a storm system rolling in over the mountains is a sight you won't quickly forget. Be sure to try both the indoor and outdoor observation decks.

The rides are a mixed bag. The first roller coaster was such a snoozer that the Stratosphere re-engineered it only two months after it opened and then closed it indefinitely because of "technical problems." When the coaster is working, it basically lumbers around the circumference of the pod. Visibility, the only thing this coaster has going for it, is limited by the tilt of the tracks, the safety restraints, and other people in the car. All sizzle and no steak, this ride only works in the press release. The newer ride, X Scream, is not much better.

Where the High Roller is hype at best, the Big Shot is cardiac arrest. Sixteen people at a time are seated at the base of the skyward projecting needle that tops the pod. You are blasted 160 feet straight up in the air at 45 mph and then allowed to partially free-fall back down. At the apex of the ascent, it feels as if your seatbelt and restraint have mysteriously evaporated, leaving you momentarily hovering 100-plus stories up in the air. The ride lasts only about a half-minute, but unless you're accustomed to being shot from a cannon, that's more than enough.

If you're having difficulty forming a mental image of the Big Shot, picture the carnival game where macho guys swing a sledgehammer, propelling a metal sphere up a vertical shaft. At the top of the shaft is a bell.

If the macho man drives the sphere high enough to ring the bell, he wins a prize. Got the picture? OK, on the Big Shot, you are the metal sphere.

In X Scream, you ride in a large gondola attached to a huge steal arm. The arm dangles the gondola over the edge of the Tower, then releases it to slide forward a few feet as if the gondola is coming unglued from the arm. All and all, it's pretty dull. *Note:* Stratosphere has announced a fourth and final ride for the Tower: Let's hope it puts this one to shame.

The elevators to the Tower are at the end of the shopping arcade on the second floor of the Stratosphere, above the casino. Tickets for the Tower can be purchased at the ticket center in the elevator lobby on the second floor or at various places in the casino. Tower tickets cost about $9. Packages including the Tower and the rides run $25. You can purchase individual tickets for the rides at a cost of $4–$15, in addition to your Tower admission.

Expect big crowds at the Tower on weekends. Once up top, the observation levels are congested, as are the lounge, snack bar, rest rooms, and gift shops. If you want to try the rides, expect to wait an additional 20 to 40 minutes for each on weekends. When you've had your fill of the Tower and are ready to descend, you'll have another long wait to before boarding the elevator. However, if you walk down to the restaurant (you'll take the emergency staircase; ask an attendant where to find it), you can catch the down elevator with virtually no wait at all. If you must see the Tower on a weekend, go in the morning as soon as the Tower opens.

Another way to see the Tower without a long wait is to make a reservation for the **Top of the World** restaurant. To be safe, reservations should be made at least two weeks in advance. When you arrive, inform the greeter in the elevator lobby that you have a dinner reservation and give him your confirmation number. You will be ushered immediately into an express elevator. The restaurant is pricey, but the food is good and the view is a knockout, and you do not have to pay the $9 Tower admission. If you want to try the Big Shot or the High Roller, purchase ride tickets before taking the elevator to the restaurant. Finally, be aware that most folks dress up to eat at the Top of the World.

On weekdays it is much easier to visit the Stratosphere Tower. Monday through Thursday, except at sunset, the wait to ascend is usually short. Waits for the rides are also short. Tower hours are Sunday to Thursday, 10 a.m.–1 a.m., and Friday and Saturday, 10 a.m.–2 a.m. For more information, call (702) 380-7777.

Venetian Attractions

Like New York–New York down the Strip, it can be argued that the entire Venetian is an attraction, and there's a lot to gawk at even if you limit your inspection to the streetside Italian icons and the Grand Canal

Shoppes. But there's more. The Venetian is host to the first **Madame Tussaud's Wax Museum** in the United States. Covering two floors and 28,000 square feet, the museum is about half the size of the original London exhibit. Approximately 100 wax figures are displayed in theme settings. Some, like Frank Sinatra and Tom Jones, were central to the development of the entertainment scene in Las Vegas. The museum opens daily at 11 a.m. Admission is $20 per adult, and $10 per child.

The Venetian also hosts the **Guggenheim Heritage Museum,** which presents rotating exhibits from the Guggenheim collection. In 2004, the museum showcased nineteenth- and twentieth-century masterpieces in *A Century of Painting: From Renoir to Rothko.* Admission is $15 for adults, $12 for seniors and Nevada residents, $11 for students with ID, and $7 for children ages 6–12. Admission discount coupons are routinely available in the hotel lobby. A portable audio guide is included in the price of ticket. For additional information, call (702) 414-2440 or visit **www.venetian.com.** Museum hours are 9:30 a.m.–8:30 p.m. daily.

The Venetian entry in the ride category is **Time Traveler,** featuring your choice of four different films that each take you on a 10-minute odyssey through space and time. Admission is $9 for one ride, $12 for two, and $18 for three. Hours are 10 a.m. to 11 p.m., Sunday through Thursday, and 10 a.m. to midnight, Friday and Saturday. For additional information, call (702) 414-1000.

A Word about Strip Roller Coasters

There are now four roller coasters on the Strip. After careful sampling, we have decided that, although shorter, the **Canyon Blaster** at **Adventuredome** offers a better ride than the more visually appealing **Manhattan Express** at **New York–New York.** The Canyon Blaster is tight and oh-so-smooth. The Manhattan Express, on the other hand, goes along in fits and starts, all of which are jerky and rough. It does, however, provide a great view of the Strip as it zips in and out of the various New York–New York buildings.

Speed, at the Sahara, lives up to its name, but is overpriced at $10. The other coaster, the High Roller at the Stratosphere, is a dud.

Free Stuff

In addition to free attractions described earlier, two other "attractions" worthy of your consideration are the **Fremont Street Experience** and the Rio's **Masquerade in the Sky.** The Fremont Street Experience is an electric light show produced on a futuristic canopy over the Fremont Street pedestrian concourse downtown. Shows begin at 4 p.m. and run about once an hour through 10 p.m. on weekdays, and midnight on weekends. The show at the Rio is a sort of musical Mardi Gras parade complete with floats, acrobats, musicians, and dancers, all circling the casino suspended from a track on the ceiling (who thinks this stuff up?). Both shows are free. A third free attraction is the **water-and-laser show** at Caesars Palace at the Forum Shops. This production, staged on the hour daily beginning at 10 a.m., combines animatronic statues and fire drama. The Tropicana hosts **Air Play,** in which slot machines serve as a makeshift stage for acts performed by singers, dancers, and aerialists who spin and fly inches above the machines; show times are daily at 11 a.m. and 1, 3, 5, 7, and 9 p.m. Outdoor productions at Bellagio, T. I., and the Mirage (all described earlier) are also free of charge.

Really Expensive Thrills

For $94 to $3,000 you can fly a foot off the ground at the **Richard Petty Driving Experience.** Here you can get behind the wheel of a 600-horsepower NASCAR Winston Cup style stock car. The Driving Experience is located at the Las Vegas Motor Speedway. Call (702) 643-4343 or visit **www.1800bepetty.com** for additional information.

Other Area Attractions

The local visitor guides describe nearby attractions and sites pretty honestly. If you have children, try the **Scandia Family Fun Center,** (702) 364-0070, for miniature golf and the **Lied Discovery Museum,** 23(702) 382-5437, for a truly rewarding afternoon of exploration and enjoyable education. Right across the street from the Lied is the **Las Vegas Natural History Museum,** (702) 384-3466. The **Wet 'n' Wild** water theme park, (702) 737-3819, may be the best place in Las Vegas for teens and is also good for preschoolers. Look for Wet 'n' Wild discount coupons in the local visitor guides.

Near scenic Red Rock, a curious side trip just outside of Las Vegas is **Bonnie Springs Old Nevada.** This rustic recreation of an Old West town features several trinket stores, a saloon, two museums, a restaurant, petting zoo, and guided horse rides. The hoot, though, that goes with this holler are the low-budget, scratch-your-head melodramas. The kicker is the real, live Western hanging that takes place at noon, 2:30, and 5 p.m. "You can't hang me sheriff!" "Why not?!" "Cause yer wife'll miss me!" Cost to get in—$7 per carload weekdays, $10 on weekends; (702) 875-4191. Real rope, real fun.

Adults who wax nostalgic over vintage automobiles should check out the **Auto Collection at the Imperial Palace,** (702) 731-3311, where more than 200 antique and historically significant vehicles are on display. Part of a much larger collection, these automobiles are rotated periodically to keep the exhibit fresh. Seeing the collection is well worth the admission price of $6.95, $3 for seniors and children under 12, though discount coupons are readily available in the local visitor guides and at the Imperial Palace casino.

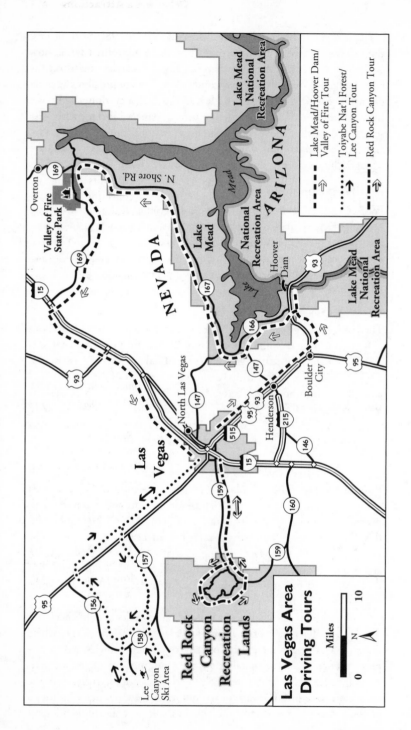

Las Vegas Area Driving Tours

Miles

N

0   10

Red Rock Canyon Recreation Lands

Lee Canyon Ski Area

Las Vegas

NEVADA

ARIZONA

Lake Mead

Lake Mead National Recreation Area

Lake Mead National Recreation Area

Lake Mead National Recreation Area

Valley of Fire State Park

Overton

North Las Vegas

Henderson

Boulder City

Hoover Dam

N. Shore Rd.

Mead

- - → Lake Mead/Hoover Dam/ Valley of Fire Tour
····→ Toiyabe Nat'l Forest/ Lee Canyon Tour
-··-→ Red Rock Canyon Tour

The Liberace Foundation and Museum, (702) 798-5595, on East Tropicana Avenue is one of Las Vegas's most popular tourist attractions. Housed in multiple buildings and enlarged in 2002, the exhibit chronicles the music, life, and excesses of Liberace. Though possibly the most professionally organized and well-presented celebrity museum in the United States, it's definitely more fun if you are a Liberace fan ($12, adults; $8, children ages 5 and up and seniors).

If you've come to pay tribute to the King, you'll find his most elaborate temple at the **Elvis-a-Rama Museum,** (702) 309-7200; 3401 Industrial Road. The gift shop sells every kind of Elvis kitsch imaginable, and the museum has a moderately decent collection of Presley memorabilia. If you still want more, stick around to catch an impersonator show in the museum's theater (see profile for **The King in Concert** in Part Two).

Adjacent to the MGM Grand is the **Showcase,** a shopping, dining, and entertainment venue with a giant Sega arcade, an eight-screen movie complex, and the World of Coca-Cola—a 150-foot Coke bottle housing two elevators.

Natural Attractions near Las Vegas

In the Mexican Pavilion of Epcot at Walt Disney World, tourists rush obliviously past some of the most rare and valuable artifacts of the Spanish colonial period in order to take a short, uninspired boat ride. Many Las Vegas visitors, likewise, never look beyond the Strip. Like the Epcot tourists, they are missing something pretty special.

Las Vegas's geological and topographical diversity, in combination with its stellar outdoor resources, provides the best opportunities for worthwhile sight-seeing. So different and varied are the flora, fauna, and geology at each distinct level of elevation that traveling from the banks of Lake Mead to the high, ponderosa pine forests of Mount Charleston encompasses (in 90 minutes) as much environmental change as driving from Mexico to Alaska.

Red Rock Canyon, the **Valley of Fire,** the **Mojave Desert,** and the **Black Canyon of the Colorado River** are world-class scenic attractions. In combination with the summits of the **Spring Mountains,** they comprise one of the most dramatically diversified natural areas on the North American continent. So excuse us if we leave coverage of the Guinness World of Records Museum to the local visitor's guides.

Driving Tours

For those who wish to sample the natural diversity of the Las Vegas area, we recommend the following driving tours. The trips begin and end in Las Vegas and take from two hours to all day, depending on the number of stops and side trips. The driving tours can conveniently be combined with picnicking, hiking, horseback riding, and sight-seeing. If you have the bucks ($70–$200 per person, depending on the package), we also recommend taking one of the air/ground tours of the Grand Canyon.

1. Mount Charleston, Kyle Canyon, Lee Canyon, and the Toiyabe National Forest *4 to 6 hours*

If you have had more than enough desert, this is the drive for you. Head north out of Las Vegas on US 95 and turn left on NV 157. Leave the desert and head into the pine and fir forest of the Spring Mountains. Continue up Kyle Canyon to the Mount Charleston Inn (a good place for lunch) and from there to the end of the canyon. Backtracking a few miles, take NV 158 over the Robbers Roost and into Lee Canyon. When you hit NV 156, turn left and proceed to the Lee Canyon Ski Area. For the return trip to Las Vegas, simply take NV 156 out of the mountains until it intersects US 95. Turn south (right) on US 95 to return to Las Vegas. If you start feeling your oats once you get into the mountains, there are some nice short hikes (less than a mile) to especially scenic overlooks. If you are so inclined, there is also horseback riding, and there are some great places for picnics.

2. Red Rock Canyon Scenic Loop *1½ to 3 hours*

Red Rock Canyon is a stunningly beautiful desert canyonland only 20 minutes from Las Vegas. A scenic loop winds among imposing, rust-red Aztec sandstone towers. There is a visitor center, as well as hiking trails and picnic areas. With very little effort you can walk to popular rock-climbing sites and watch the action. From Las Vegas, head west on Charleston Boulevard (NV 159) directly to Red Rock Canyon. The scenic loop is 13 miles (all one-way), with numerous places to stop and enjoy the rugged vistas. The loop road brings you back to NV 159. Turn left and return to town via Charleston Boulevard.

3. Lake Mead and the Valley of Fire *5 to 8 hours*

This drive takes you to the Lake Mead National Recreation Area and Valley of Fire State Park. How long the drive takes depends on how many side trips you make. If you plan to visit Hoover Dam during your visit, it will be convenient to work it into this itinerary. The same is true if you wish to tour the Ethel M (as in Mars bars) Chocolate Factory and Cactus Garden.

Head south out of Las Vegas on US 95/93 (detour west on Sunset Road to visit the Chocolate Factory and Cactus Garden), continuing straight on US 93 to Boulder City. From Boulder City continue to the Hoover Dam on US 93 (if desired) or turn left on the Lakeshore Scenic Drive (NV 166) to continue the drive. Travel through the washes and canyons above the lake until you reach the Northshore Scenic Drive (NV

147 and NV 167). Turn right, continuing to the right on NV 167 when the routes split. If you wish, you can descend to the lake at Callville Bay, Echo Bay, or Overton Beach. If you are hungry, Callville Bay and Echo Bay have restaurants and lounges. Overton Beach has a snack bar, but Echo Bay has the best beach.

Near Overton Beach, turn left to NV 169 and follow signs for Valley of Fire State Park. Bear left on NV 169 away from Overton. Valley of Fire features exceptional desert canyon scenery, a number of panoramic vistas, unusual and colorful sandstone formations, and Indian petro-glyphs. A short two-mile scenic loop makes it easy to see many of the valley's most interesting formations. If you have time, take the road past the visitor center and climb to the Rainbow Vista overlook. From here a new highway accesses some of the most extraordinary terrain in the American Southwest. After the loop (and any other detours that interest you), continue west on NV 169 until it intersects I-15. Head south to return to Las Vegas.

Hoover Dam

Hoover Dam is definitely worth seeing. There is a film, a guided tour, and a theater presentation on the Colorado River drainage, as well as some static exhibits. Try to go on a Monday, Thursday, or Friday. Arrive no later than 9 a.m., when the visitor area opens, and do the tour first ($10, $8 seniors, and $5 students). After 9:30 a.m. or so, long lines form for the tour, especially on Tuesdays, Wednesdays, Saturdays, and Sundays. The dam is closed to visitors at 5 p.m. A ban on visitors inside the dam, initiated following 9/11, was subsequently lifted, but there are security checkpoints on US 93 leading to the dam.

Other than chauffeured transportation, there is no advantage in going to Hoover Dam on a bus tour. You will still have to wait in line for the tour of the dam and to see the other presentations. If you are the sort of person who tours quickly, you probably will have a lot of time to kill waiting for the rest of the folks to return to the bus.

The Canyons of the Southwest

Las Vegas tourist magazines claim **Bryce Canyon** (400 miles round-trip; (435) 834-5322) and **Zion Canyon, Utah** (350 miles round-trip; (435) 772-3256), as well as the **Grand Canyon, Arizona** (call (520) 638-7888) as local attractions. We recommend all of the canyons if you are on an extended drive through the Southwest. If your time is limited, however, you might consider taking one of the air day-tours that visit the canyons from Las Vegas. Running between $100 and $400 per passenger, the excursions follow one of two basic formats: air only, or air and ground combined. Some tour companies offer discounted fares for a second person if the first person pays full fare. Also, discount coupons are regularly available in *What's On* and *Today in Las Vegas,* distributed free of charge in most hotels.

Almost all canyon tours include a pass over **Lake Mead** (call (702) 293-8906) and **Hoover Dam** (call (702) 294-3523). The trip involving the least commitment of time and money is a round-trip flyover of one or more of the canyons. A Grand Canyon flyover, for example, takeoff to touchdown, takes about two hours. While flying over any of the canyons is an exhilarating experience, air traffic restrictions concerning the Grand Canyon severely limit what air passengers can see. Flying over the other canyons is somewhat less restricted. If you want to get a real feel for the Grand Canyon particularly, go with one of the air/ground excursions. The Grand Canyon is many times more impressive from the ground than from the air.

The air/ground trips fly over the Grand Canyon and then land. Passengers are transferred to a bus that motors them along the rim of the canyon, stopping en route for lunch. Excursions sometimes include one or more of the other major canyons in addition to the Grand Canyon, and they last from seven to ten hours. Many flights offer multilingual translations of the tour narrative.

All of the aircraft used will feel very small to anyone accustomed to flying on big commercial jets. Most of the planes carry between 8 and 20 passengers. The captain often performs the duties of both flight attendant and pilot. Each passenger usually has a window, though some of the windows are pretty small. Cabin conditions for the most part are spartan, and there is not usually a toilet on board.

Because small aircraft sometimes get bounced around and buffeted by air currents, we recommend taking an over-the-counter motion-sickness medication if you think you might be adversely affected. The other thing you want to do for sure is to relieve your bladder *immediately* before boarding. If you go on an early-morning excursion, take it easy on the coffee and juice during breakfast.

Part Six

Exercise and Recreation

Working Out

Most of the folks on our *Unofficial Guide* research team work out routinely. Some bike; some run; some lift weights or do aerobics. Staying in hotels on the Strip and downtown, it didn't take them long to discover that working out in Las Vegas presents its own peculiar challenges.

The best months for outdoor exercise are October through April. The rest of the year it is extremely hot, though mornings and evenings are generally pleasant in September and May. During the scorching summer, particularly for visitors, we recommend working out indoors or, for bikers and runners, very early in the morning. If you do anything strenuous outside, any time of year, drink plenty of water. Dehydration and heat prostration can overtake you quickly and unexpectedly in Las Vegas's desert climate. For outdoor workouts in Las Vegas comparable to what you are used to at home, you will deplete your body's water at two to three times the usual rate.

Walking

Primarily flat, Las Vegas is made for walking and great people-watching. Security is very good both downtown and on the Strip, making for a safe walking environment at practically all hours of the day and night. Downtown, everything is concentrated in such a small area that you might be inclined to venture away from the casino center. While this is no more perilous than walking in any other city, the areas surrounding downtown are not particularly interesting or aesthetically compelling. If the downtown casino center is not large enough to accommodate your exercise needs, you are better off busing or cabbing to the Strip and doing your walking there.

If you are walking the Strip, it is about four miles from Mandalay Bay on the south end to the Stratosphere on the north end. Because the topography is so flat, however, it does not look that far. We met a number of people who set out on foot along the Strip and managed to overextend

427

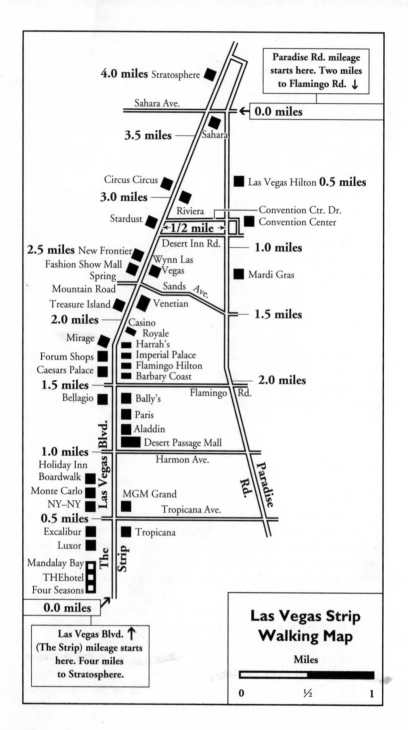

4.0 miles Stratosphere ■

Sahara Ave.

← **0.0 miles**

Paradise Rd. mileage starts here. Two miles to Flamingo Rd. ↓

3.5 miles — ■ Sahara

■ Las Vegas Hilton **0.5 miles**

Circus Circus ■

3.0 miles — ■

Stardust ■ Riviera ■

Convention Ctr. Dr.
■ Convention Center

←**1/2 mile**→

Desert Inn Rd. **1.0 miles**

2.5 miles New Frontier ■
Fashion Show Mall ■ Wynn Las ■
Spring Vegas
Mountain Road Sands *Ave.*
Treasure Island ■ ■ Venetian

■ Mardi Gras

2.0 miles — Casino
Royale ■
Mirage ■ ■ Harrah's
Forum Shops ■ ■ Imperial Palace
Caesars Palace ■ ■ Flamingo Hilton
1.5 miles — ■ Barbary Coast
Bellagio ■ Flamingo Rd.

1.5 miles —

2.0 miles

■ Bally's

■ Paris

■ Aladdin

■ Desert Passage Mall

1.0 miles — Harmon Ave.

Holiday Inn
Boardwalk ■
Monte Carlo ■ ■ MGM Grand
NY–NY ■ Tropicana Ave.
0.5 miles —
Excalibur ■ ■ Tropicana
Luxor ■

Mandalay Bay ▫
THEhotel ▫
Four Seasons ▫

0.0 miles ↗

Las Vegas Blvd.

The Strip

Paradise Rd.

Las Vegas Blvd. ↑ (The Strip) mileage starts here. Four miles to Stratosphere.

Las Vegas Strip Walking Map

Miles

0   ½   1

themselves. Check out our Strip walking distance map before you go, and bear in mind that even without hills, marching in the arid desert climate will take a lot out of you. Finally, carry enough money to buy refreshments en route and to take a cab or bus back to your hotel if you poop out or develop a blister.

Running

If you stay on the Strip, you will have more options than if you stay downtown. Those of us who are used to running on pavement ran on the broad sidewalks of Las Vegas Boulevard South. These runs are great for people-watching also, but are frequently interrupted by long minutes of jogging in place at intersections, waiting for traffic lights to change. Our early risers would often run before 7:30 a.m. on the now-defunct Desert Inn golf course. This was the best (and safest) running in town, with good footing, beautiful scenery, and no traffic. Suffice it to say, however, that course managers were less than overjoyed to see a small platoon of travel writers trotting off the 18th fairway. If you run on a golf course, stay off the greens and try to complete your run by 7:30 a.m. In addition to area golf courses, the Las Vegas Hilton and Mandalay Bay each have a jogging circuit.

If you stay downtown, you must either run on the sidewalks or drive to a more suitable venue. Sidewalks downtown are more congested than those on the Strip, and there are more intersections and traffic lights with which to contend. If you want to run downtown, particularly on Fremont Street, try to get your workout in before 10 a.m.

For those who dislike pounding the blacktop, sneaking onto golf courses, or exercising early in the morning, a convenient option is to run on the track at the university. Located about two miles east of the Strip on Harmon Avenue, **UNLV** offers both a regulation track and some large, grassy athletic fields. Park in the dirt lot near the tennis courts if you do not have a university parking sticker. For more information, call (702) 895-3177. A more expensive alternative is the posh **Las Vegas Sporting House** at 3025 Industrial Road (located directly behind the Stardust Hotel), which has both an indoor and outdoor track. The charge is a hefty $15 to $20 a day (depending on hotel), or $50 a week, but the fee includes the use of all club facilities. Call (702) 497-7822.

If you have a car and a little time, two of the better off-road runs in the area are at **Red Rock Canyon,** out Charleston Avenue, 35 minutes west of town. Red Rock Canyon Conservation Area, managed by the U.S. Bureau of Land Management, is Western desert and canyon scenery at its best. Spectacular geology combined with the unique desert flora and fauna make Red Rock Canyon a truly memorable place. Maps and information can be obtained at the visitor center, on site.

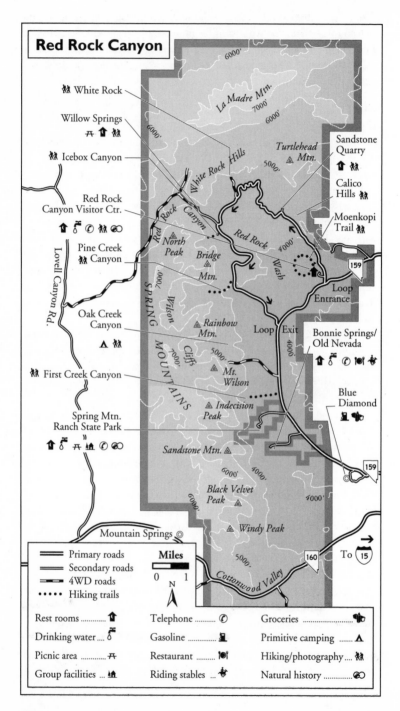

Red Rock Canyon

White Rock

Willow Springs

Icebox Canyon

Red Rock
Canyon Visitor Ctr.

Pine Creek
Canyon

Oak Creek
Canyon

First Creek Canyon

Spring Mtn.
Ranch State Park

Lovell Canyon Rd.

La Madre Mtn.
7000'
6000'
6000'

White Rock Hills

Turtlehead Mtn.
5000'

Sandstone
Quarry

Calico
Hills

Moenkopi
Trail

Red Rock Wash
4000'

Red Rock Canyon

North Peak

Bridge Mtn.

Wilson Cliffs

Rainbow Mtn.

Loop Entrance

Loop Exit

Bonnie Springs/
Old Nevada

Blue
Diamond

159

Mt. Wilson

Indecision Peak

SPRING MOUNTAINS
7000'
5000'

Sandstone Mtn.

6000'
4000'

159

Black Velvet Peak
6000'

4000'

Mountain Springs

Windy Peak

5000'

160

To 15

Miles

0   1

N

— Primary roads
═ Secondary roads
▭ 4WD roads
•••• Hiking trails

Rest rooms .... 🚹
Drinking water ....
Picnic area ....
Group facilities ...

Telephone .... ✆
Gasoline ....
Restaurant ....
Riding stables ..

Groceries ....
Primitive camping ...... ▲
Hiking/photography ....
Natural history ....

Cottonwood Valley

One two-mile round trip, the **Moenkopi Loop,** begins and ends at the visitor center. A three-mile circuit, the **Willow Springs Trail,** begins at the Willow Springs Picnic Area and circles around to Lost Creek Canyon. Both routes are moderately hilly, with generally good footing. The Moenkopi Loop is characterized by open desert and expansive vistas, while the Willow Springs Trail ventures into the canyons. The Willow Springs Trail is also distinguished by numerous Indian petroglyphs and other artifacts. Both trails, of course, are great for hiking as well as for running.

Finally, if you want to hook up with local runners, you can join the Las Vegas Track Club for a weekly run to **Tule Springs** (north of downtown on US 95) or many other area locations. For a current schedule or additional information, call the Running Store at (702) 898-7866 or the Runner's Hotline at (702) 594-0970.

Swimming and Sunbathing

Swimming, during warm-weather months, is the most dependable and generally accessible form of exercise in Las Vegas. Most of the Strip hotels and a couple of the downtown hotels have nice pools. Sometimes the pools are too congested for swimming laps, but usually it is possible to stake out a lane.

If the pool at your hotel is a funny shape or too crowded for a workout, there are pools more conducive to serious swimming at the **Las Vegas Sporting House** on Industrial Road, at the **Las Vegas Athletic Club** on Flamingo Road, and in the **McDermott Physical Education Complex** of UNLV.

For those who want to work on their tans in style, the **Mirage, Tropicana, Mandalay Bay, Venetian, Paris, Monte Carlo, MGM Grand, Treasure Island, Caesars Palace, Rio, Las Vegas and Flamingo Hiltons, Alexis Park, Palms, Green Valley Ranch, Hard Rock Hotel, Bellagio, Aladdin,** and **JW Marriott Las Vegas,** among others, have particularly elegant facilities. Hotels with above-average pools include the **Luxor, New Frontier, Riviera, Harrah's, Imperial Palace,** and **Sahara.** If you are staying in a place where the swimming is not very interesting, try the **Wet 'n' Wild** water theme park near the Sahara on the Strip.

Be forewarned that sunbathing in Las Vegas can be dangerous. The climate is so arid that you will not feel yourself perspiring: perspiration evaporates as soon as it surfaces on your skin. If there is a breeze, particularly on a pleasant fall or spring day, you may never feel hot, sticky, or in any way uncomfortable until you come out of the sun and discover that you have been fried.

You can really get zapped in a hurry if you do not protect yourself properly, and even those who already have a good tan need to be extra careful. We recommend using twice the block you use in nondesert areas.

If in Delaware, for example, you use a SPF-4 lotion, use at least a SPF 8 in Las Vegas. Come out of the sun frequently to check yourself, and be careful not to fall asleep in the sun for an extended period.

Health Clubs

If you can get by with a Lifecycle, a StairMaster, or a rowing machine, the fitness rooms of most major hotels should serve your needs. Fortunately, local health clubs welcome visitors for a daily ($15 to $20) or weekly ($30–$50) fee. All of the clubs described here are coed.

The most luxurious (and expensive) club is the **Las Vegas Sporting House,** located close to the Strip at 3025 Industrial Road. Open 24 hours a day, the club offers racquetball, squash, tennis, basketball, volleyball, exercise equipment, and aerobics. For information and rates, call (702) 497-7822. The **Las Vegas Athletic Clubs,** with five locations, offer much the same activities and services as the Sporting House, though not all features are provided at each location. The Las Vegas Athletic Clubs depend more on local patronage than on visitors; their facilities are commodious but less luxurious than those at the Sports Club, and fees are at the lower end of the range. While reasonably convenient to the Strip, only the West Sahara club is within walking distance. For rates and additional information call:

Las Vegas Athletic Club	**Las Vegas Athletic Club**	**Las Vegas Athletic Club**
5200 W. Sahara Avenue	3315 Spring Mountain Rd.	E. Flamingo at Sandhill Rd.
(702) 362-3720	(702) 364-5822	(702) 451-2526
Las Vegas Athletic Club	**Las Vegas Athletic Club**	
2655 S. Maryland Pkwy	S. Maryland Parkway	
(702) 733-1919	at Tropicana	
	(702) 798-5822	

The **24 Hour Fitness** centers, with three locations, run an excellent aerobics program and have an extensive weight and exercise facility. While the facilities are good and the use fees midrange, the locations are a little remote for most visitors staying on the Strip or downtown.

24 Hour Fitness	**24 Hour Fitness**	**24 Hour Fitness**
S. Eastern near Sahara	S. Valley View, half a mile	Cheyenne and Rainbow
(702) 641-2222	south of Sahara	(702) 656-7777
	(702) 368-1111	

Aerobics

A number of health clubs offer coed aerobics on a daily basis. Daily or weekly rates are available. For additional information, see the preceding Health Clubs section.

Free Weights and Nautilus

Almost all of the major hotels have a spa or fitness room with weight-lifting equipment. Some properties have a single Universal machine, while others offer a wide range of free-weight and Nautilus equipment. Hotels with above-average facilities for pumping iron are the **Las Vegas Hilton, Bellagio, Venetian, Caesars Palace, Golden Nugget, Mirage, Paris, Regent Las Vegas, Monte Carlo, MGM Grand, Luxor,** and **T. I.**

For hardcore power lifters and bodybuilders, try **Gold's Gym**. Gold's is coed and offers daily, weekly, and monthly rates for use of its Nautilus and free weights ($20, $35, and $70, respectively). Contact them at any one of their five locations: West, (702) 877-6966; East, (702) 451-4222; North, (702) 646-4609; South, (702) 914-5885; and Summerlin, (702) 360-8205.

Racquetball, Squash, and Handball

Visitors are welcome at most local racquet and health clubs. **Sports Club–Las Vegas** and the **Las Vegas Athletic Clubs,** among others, provide good court facilities. For additional information see the preceding Health Club section.

Golf

Peak season for golf in Las Vegas is October through May. The other four months are considered prohibitively warm for most golfers, and greens fees are reduced at most courses during the summer. Certain courses also have reduced rates for locals and for guests staying at hotels affiliated with the golf course. Morning tee times are always more difficult to arrange than afternoons. Call the starter one day before you wish to play. Same-day phone calls are discouraged. In summer, most courses and driving ranges stay open until at least 7:30 p.m. In winter and early spring, temperatures drop rapidly near sundown, so always bring a sweater or jacket. Las Vegas has an elevation of 2,000 feet and is considered high desert. Take this into account when making club selections.

Golf Course Ratings

Quality rating	★★★	Championship, challenging
	★★	Playable, suitable for all caliber golfers
	★	Preferred by beginners and casual golfers
Value rating	I	A good bargain
	2	A fair price
	3	Not a good bargain

Note: Quality and value ratings are abbreviated as *QV Rating* in the following listings.

Important Note Quite a few outstanding courses are not listed, including **Shadow Creek Country Club,** privately owned by Mirage Resorts, Inc., and played only by their special guests. Built at a cost of nearly $40 million and looking more like a North Carolina layout bordered by cathedral pines than a traditional desert course, Shadow Creek was named by *Golf Digest* as the finest new course in the United States in 1990. The ultimate accolade was bestowed when the same magazine listed Shadow Creek as the eighth best golf course in the United States, an unprecedented honor for a course less than five years old. **The Tournament Players Club,** open to guests of JW Marriott Las Vegas at Summerlin, is currently the host course for both the Las Vegas Senior Classic and the Las Vegas Invitational. Other than La Costa Resort, this is the only course in the United States to host both men's professional tours. The Summerlin course was designed by architect Bobby Weed with assistance from player/consultant Fuzzy Zoeller and is rated by both *Golf Digest* and *Golfweek* magazines as the second best course in Nevada, behind Shadow Creek. Many current professional athletes are members, including pitcher Greg Maddux (Chicago Cubs), and golfers Jim Colbert, Robert Gamez, and Bob May. **Canyon Gate Country Club** was designed by noted architect Ted Robinson and is a championship golf course in every sense, with lush, narrow fairways, outstanding bentgrass greens, and an eclectic scattering of fairway bunkers and mounds. Management was taken over in 1992 by the elite company ClubCorp International (CCI). Frequently ranked as one of the top five courses in Nevada, the **Las Vegas Country Club** is one of the hosts for the Las Vegas Invitational Men's PGA tournament. Beautifully conditioned, with recently planted bentgrass greens. It's not available to the public, although a few tee times are reserved daily for high-rolling guests staying at the Las Vegas Hilton. Eventually, **Lake Las Vegas** will be a $3.8 billion residential community surrounding a private, 320-acre lake. Its $19 million Southshore Golf Club was designed by Jack Nicklaus, and the hilly terrain includes a combination of manicured turf, Bermuda grass, bentgrass greens, and desert flowers, plants, and trees. For six years, **Spanish Trail Country Club** was a host of the Las Vegas Invitational PGA tournament. This 27-hole complex designed by Robert Trent Jones, with undulating fairways, heavy bunkering, a number of water hazards, and fast, bentgrass greens, can play havoc with less-than-accomplished golfers. In just its second year of operation, **Sunrise Golf Club** was a host course of the Las Vegas Invitational PGA tournament, and Chip Beck humbled it with a 59. It was only the second time in history a player had broken 60. With 54 holes and the city's largest driving range, Sunrise has become Las Vegas's most accommodating and affordable private club. Set to open shortly after press time, **Greens of Las Vegas** re-creates 24 of the most famous greens in the world, allowing players to putt on holes from Hilton Head's Harbour Town, Augusta National, and Britain's Turnberry, St. Andrews, and Royal Dornoch.

Angel Park Golf Club

Established 1989
Address 100 South Rampart Boulevard, Las Vegas, NV 89128
Phone (702) 254-4653 **Web site** www.angelpark.com
Status Public/municipal course

TEES

Palm Course

Championship 6,530 yards, par 70, USGA 72.6, slope 130
Men's 5,857 yards, par 70, USGA 69.8, slope 120
Ladies' 5,438 yards, par 70, USGA 68.6, slope 112

Mountain Course

Championship 6,722 yards, par 71, slope 128
Men's 6,235 yards, par 71, slope 117
Ladies' 5,751 yards, par 71, slope 116

Fees Nonresident, January 30–April 30: Monday–Thursday, $125; Friday–Sunday and holidays, $145; twilight, $75 weekday and $80 weekend. May 1–31: Monday–Thursday, $95; Friday–Sunday and holidays, $125. Clark County residents: Monday–Thursday, $65; Friday–Sunday and holidays, $75; twilight, $45. May 1–May 31: Monday–Thursday, $60; Friday–Sunday and holidays, $70; twilight, $70 weekday and $75 weekend. Club rental: nonresident, $50; resident, $45. Shoe rental, $20.

Facilities Pro shop, night-lighted driving range and 18-hole putting course, putting green, restaurant, snack bar, bar, tennis courts, and walking track nearby.

QV Rating ★★ 2

Comments Angel Park, a good, functional golf complex, is rapidly becoming one of the most successful public golf facilities in the United States. Its courses are well designed—by Arnold Palmer, no less—and the sophisticated 18-hole putting course, complete with night lighting, sand traps, rough, and water hazards, is a popular attraction even for non-golfers. Angel Park has matured and become lush and attractive. Both courses are crowded year-round.

Bali Hai

Established 2000
Address 5160 Las Vegas Boulevard, Las Vegas, NV 89119
Phone (888) 397-2499 **Web site** www.waltersgolf.com
Status Public

TEES

Championship 7,002 yards, par 72, USGA 73.0, slope 130
Men's 6,619 yards, par 72, USGA 70.2, slope 125
Ladies' 6,174 yards, par 72, USGA 68.6, slope 113

Fees September–May: weekdays, $245; weekends, $295; 9-hole weekdays (after 3:30 p.m.), $169; 9-hole weekends (after 3:30 p.m.), $195. June–August: weekdays, $175; weekends, $195; 9-hole weekdays (after 1 p.m.), $125; 9-hole weekends (after 1 p.m.), $150, or (after 3 p.m.), $199.

Facilities Pro shop, tropical boutique, driving range, putting green, snack bar, restaurant, full locker facilities, caddies, fore-caddies.

QV Rating ★★ 3

Comments In real estate, location is everything, and the only reason Bali Hai commands these outrageous greens fees is its location on the Strip next to Mandalay Bay. It also strives for luxury, with caddies and a pro shop selling tropical plants. Designed in a tropical theme, Bali Hai features water everywhere, with an island green, endless tropical flora, and vast expanses of black "coral" and white sand. No island golf course, even in the South Pacific, looks anything like this, and for a reason: Bali Hai is undeniably beautiful, but that does not make it a great or even good course, and better golf can be had for less, even with the taxi fares.

Bear's Best

Established   2002
Address   11111 West Flamingo Road, Las Vegas, NV 89135
Phone   (866) 385-8500   **Web site**   www.bearsbest.com
Status   Public
TEES
  Gold 7,194 yards, par 72, USGA 74.0, slope 147
  Blue 6,628 yards, par 72, USGA 71.3, slope 130
  White 6,043 yards, par 72, USGA 68.3, slope 122
  Red 5,043 yards, par 72, USGA 68.7, slope 116

Fees   High season, $195–$235. Low season, $75–$100. Club rentals, $60.
Facilities   Pro shop, driving range, putting green, restaurant, full locker facilities.
QV Rating   ★★★   3
Comments   The first of several Bear's Best courses, this is a unique tribute by Jack Nicklaus, a.k.a. the Golden Bear, to himself. Here Nicklaus has recreated holes from his favorite original designs, but unlike most tribute or replica courses, including Vegas's Royal Links, the holes were specifically chosen to fit the desert setting. As a result, this is one of the best of these gimmicky layouts in the world, and all the holes are very good, giving fans an opportunity to play holes from Nicklaus's most acclaimed public courses, such as Cabo del Sol, Palmilla, and Castle Pines, along with very private ones from Desert Mountain, Desert Highlands, and PGA West.

Black Mountain Golf and Country Club

Established   1959
Address   500 Greenway Road, Henderson, NV 89015
Phone   (702) 565-7933   **Web site**   www.golfblackmountain.com
Status   Semiprivate
TEES
  Championship 6,550 yards, par 72, USGA 71.2, slope 123
  Men's 6,223 yards, par 72, USGA 69.8, slope 120
  Ladies' 5,518 yards, par 72, USGA 71.6, slope 120

Fees   Nonresidents: weekdays, $55 for 18 holes. Weekends, $75 for 18 holes. Seniors (over 63), $45 Tuesday and Thursday, excluding holidays. Carts mandatory on weekends and included in all fees. Club rentals, $40.
Facilities   Pro shop, clubhouse, driving range, putting green, restaurant, snack bar, and bar.
QV Rating   ★   1
Comments   Black Mountain is set amidst the Henderson hills, 20 minutes from the Strip. Many who prefer walking to riding play here, as it's one of the few area courses that don't require electric carts during the week. Many bunkers and unimproved areas off fairways make for tough recovery shots, but nobody said the game was supposed to be easy. A good course for beginning and intermediate golfers and juniors.

Boulder City Municipal Golf Course

Established   1972; back 9 completed 1986
Address   1 Clubhouse Drive, Boulder City, NV 89005
Phone   (702) 293-9236
Status   Public

TEES

Championship 6,542 yards, par 72, USGA 70.2, slope 110
Men's 6,120 yards, par 72, USGA 68.3, slope 103
Ladies' 5,458 yards, par 72, USGA 66.4, slope 110

Fees $50 for 18 holes ($40 without cart); $35 for 9 holes ($30 without cart).
Facilities   Pro shop, driving range, putting green, restaurant, snack bar, and bar.
QV Rating   ★★   1

Comments   Just 20 minutes away from Las Vegas, in the one municipality in Nevada that forbids legalized gambling, this pleasant course is relaxing, accommodating to all-level golfers, and just ten minutes away from Hoover Dam. Walking is permitted.

Craig Ranch Golf Course

Established   1963
Address   628 West Craig Road, North Las Vegas, NV 89030
Phone   (702) 642-9700
Status   Public

TEES

Championship 6,100 yards, par 70, USGA 66.8, slope 105
Men's 5,432 yards, par 70, USGA 64.6, slope 100
Ladies' 5,221 yards, par 70, USGA 67.4, slope 100

Fees $18 without cart 18 holes, $26 with cart; $10.50 without cart 9 holes, $14.50 with cart. Club rentals, $10 ($6 for 9 holes).
Facilities   Pro shop, driving range, putting green, and snack bar.
QV Rating   ★★   1

Comments   A short public course with over 11,000 trees and perhaps the smallest greens in the state. A good course for beginning and intermediate golfers, with only one water hazard and three out-of-bounds holes.

Desert Pines Golf Club

Established   1997
Address   3415 East Bonanza Road, Las Vegas, NV 89101
Phone   (702) 366-1616   **Web site**   www.waltersgolf.com
Status   Public

TEES

Championship 6,810 yards, par 71, USGA 70.4, slope 122
Men's 6,464 yards, par 71, USGA 66.8, slope 112
Ladies' 5,873 yards, par 71, USGA 69.4, slope 116

Fees   Nonresidents: $135 for 18 holes, $85 twilight, Monday–Thursday; $175 for 18 holes, $100 twilight, Friday–Sunday and holidays (cart included).
Facilities   Pro shop, driving range, putting green, snack bar, and restaurant.
QV Rating   ★★   3

Comments   Desert Pines is a 6,810-yard course on Bonanza Road between Mohave and Pecos Roads. Inspired by the Pinehurst courses in North Carolina, its fairways and greens are flanked by trees, some already as tall as 40 feet. Instead of rough, developer Bill Walters laid down 45,000 bales of red-pine needles imported from South Carolina.

Desert Rose Golf Course

Established 1960
Address 5483 Club House Drive, Las Vegas, NV 89122
Phone (702) 431-4653
Status Public/municipal course
TEES
 Championship 6,511 yards, par 71, USGA 69.6, slope 117
 Men's 6,135 yards, par 71, USGA 69, slope 114
 Ladies' 5,458 yards, par 71, USGA 69, slope 119

Fees Nonresidents: 18 holes; $69 on weekday, $89 on weekends and holidays (cart included). Twilight $49 weekdays, $59 weekends. Nonresidents: $32 (no cart) 9 holes (before 7 a.m. or after 3:30 p.m.), $42 (cart included) 9 holes. Club rentals, $30.
Facilities Pro shop, driving range, 3 putting/chipping greens, restaurant, banquet room, snack bar, and bar.
QV Rating ★ 2
Comments With a name change (formerly Winterwood) and much moving of dirt, former PGA tour star Jim Colbert has created a functional public golf course that gets a lot of play year-round. A good course for recreational golfers, Desert Rose has fairly wide-open fairways with just a few out-of-bounds holes. Men must wear collared shirts.

Highland Falls Golf Club

Established 1992
Address 10201 Sun City Boulevard, Las Vegas, NV 89134
Phone (702) 254-7010 **Web site** www.suncitygolf.com
Status Semi-private
TEES
 Championship 6,512 yards, par 72, USGA 71.2, slope 12
 Men's 6,017 yards, par 72, USGA 68.6, slope 11
 Gold 5,579 yards, par 72, USGA 67.1, slope 112
 Ladies' 5,099 yards, par 72, USGA 68.2, slope 115

Fees Nonresidents of Sun City: $130 for 18 holes, $60 after 2 p.m.
Facilities Pro shop, driving range, putting green, 2 chipping greens, luncheon area, patio for outside dining, and bar.
QV Rating ★★ 2
Comments A testing layout designed by Hall of Famer Billy Casper's company, Casper-Nash Associates. Bentgrass greens with 328 Bermuda fairways overseeded with rye. More undulations than most desert courses, with several demanding holes. No one broke par for the first six months after opening. Schedule your tee time at least seven days in advance.

Las Vegas Golf Club

Established 1949
Address 4300 West Washington Avenue, Las Vegas, NV 89107
Phone (702) 646-3003
Status Municipal course
TEES
 Championship 6,319 yards, par 72, USGA 70, slope 112

Men's 5,917 yards, par 72, USGA 68.1, slope 105
Ladies' 5,250 yards, par 72, USGA 69.9, slope 112

Fees Nonresidents: weekdays; $69 before noon, $49 after noon. Weekends; $89 before noon, $69. Club rentals, $20 for 18 holes.

Facilities Pro shop, night-lighted driving range, putting green, restaurant, snack bar, bar, and beverage-cart girls who patrol the course.

QV Rating ★ 1

Comments Popular public course and site of many local amateur tournaments. Formerly owned and managed by Senior PGA star Jim Colbert. A good course for recreational golfers, it offers fairly wide-open fairways and not a lot of trouble so play should move briskly. Tee times are always in great demand.

Las Vegas National

Established 1961
Address 1911 East Desert Inn Road, Las Vegas NV 89109
Phone (800) GO TRY 18 or (702) 796-0013 (tee-time service and other reservations)
Status Public (privately owned)

TEES

Championship 6,815 yards, par 72, USGA 72.1, slope 130

Men's 6,418 yards, par 70, USGA 70.2, slope 121

Ladies' 5,741 yards, par 72, USGA 72.9, slope 127

Fees $75–$95.
Facilities Pro shop, night-lighted driving range, putting green, snack bar, and bar.
QV Rating ★★★ 2

Comments A championship course that has at one time co-hosted the Tournament of Champions, the Sahara Invitational, and the Ladies' Sahara Classic. Excellent variety of holes, with good bunkering and elevation changes uncharacteristic of a desert course. Better for intermediate and advanced golfers. No longer has any affiliation with the Sahara Hotel.

Las Vegas Paiute Resort

Established 1995
Address 10325 Nu/Wav Kaiv Boulevard, Las Vegas, NV 89124 (US 95 between Kyle Canyon and Lee Canyon turn-off to Mount Charleston)
Phone (702) 658-1400   **Web site** www.lvpaiutegolf.com
Status Public

TEES

Snow Mountain

Tournament 7,158 yards, par 72, USGA 73.9, slope 125
Championship 6,665 yards, par 72, USGA 71.2, slope 120
Ladies' (white) 6,035 yards, par 72, USGA 74.5, slope 129
Ladies' (red) 5,341 yards, par 72, USGA 70.4, slope 117

Sun Mountain

Tournament 7,112 yards, par 72, USGA 73.3, slope 130
Championship 6,631 yards, par 72, USGA 70.9, slope 124
Ladies' (white) 6,074 yards, par 72, USGA 74.8, slope 131
Ladies' (red) 5,465 yards, par 72, USGA 71, slope 123

Fees Monday–Sunday; $95–$165; twilight (seasonal)$95; includes unlimited balls and cart.

Facilities Pro shop, driving range, 2 putting greens, restaurant, snack bar, and bar with gaming.

QV Rating ★★ 2

Comments The first of what is planned to be a 72-hole resort golf complex, the courses are Pete Dye designs, without the fangs. Director of Golf Johnny Pott, who enjoyed a fine career on the PGA tour, assures us that all caliber golfers can enjoy the course and survive.

Legacy Golf Club

Established 1989

Address 130 Par Excellence Drive, Henderson, NV 89014

Phone (702) 897-2187

Status Public (privately owned)

TEES

  Championship 7,233 yards, par 72, USGA 74.9, slope 136
  Men's 6,744 yards, par 72, USGA 72.1, slope 128
  Ladies' 5,340 yards, par 72, USGA 71, slope 120
  Resort 6,211 yards, par 72, USGA 69.1, slope 118

Fees 18 holes (no 9-hole rate): weekdays, $135; weekends, $150. Summer rates (June 18–September 3): weekdays, $65; weekends, $90. Twilight rates vary. All greens fees include mandatory carts. Club rentals, $50.

Facilities Clubhouse, pro shop, driving range, chipping facility, putting green, restaurant, snack bar, and bar.

QV Rating ★★★ 2

Comments Legacy is a mixture of rolling fairways and target golf. Championship tees require long carry on tee-ball to clear desert mounding. Located at the southeastern tip of Las Vegas, Legacy has quickly become a favorite of intermediate and advanced golfers. Course plays host to a number of mini-tour professional events.

Los Prados Country Club

Established 1985

Address 5150 Los Prados Circle, Las Vegas, NV 89130

Phone (702) 645-4523; pro shop, 645-5696 **Web site** www.losprados-golf.com

Status Semiprivate

TEES

  Championship 5,350 yards, par 70, USGA 64.8, slope 103
  Ladies' 4,474 yards, par 70, USGA 64.4, slope 104

Fees Nonresidents, $40–$65; residents, $25–$50. Club rentals, $30.

Facilities Pro shop, putting green, restaurant, snack bar, and bar.

QV Rating ★ 2

Comments Los Prados is a good course for beginners, intermediates, and families. Executive-length, with many short par-fours. Like most real-estate developments in which golf is secondary to property values, the emphasis of the builders was on homesites rather than the design of the course. Not very accessible from the Strip, nearly a 25-minute drive.

Painted Desert

Established 1987

Address 5555 Painted Mirage Way, Las Vegas, NV 89129

Phone   (702) 645-2568 (tee-time service); (702) 645-2570 (pro shop)
Web site   www.americangolf.com
Status   Public (privately owned)
TEES
  Championship 6,840 yards, par 72, USGA 73.7, slope 136
  Men's 6,323 yards, par 72, USGA 71, slope 128
  Ladies' 5,711 yards, par 72, USGA 73.0, slope 127

Fees   Monday–Thursday, $130; twilight rate, $80. Friday–Sunday, $170; twilight rate, $85. Regular club rentals, $40; deluxe clubs, $50; twilight rentals half price. Twilight 1:30 p.m. until March 31, 2:30 after.
Facilities   Pro shop, driving range, putting green, snack bar, and bar.
QV Rating ★★   2

Comments   Target course designed by renowned architect Jay Morrish, Tom Weiskopf's partner. Lush fairway landing pads and well-manicured greens, but make certain you're on target. The rough is pure waste-area. Course gets heavy traffic, primarily from intermediate and advanced golfers. A sprinkling of beginners can really slow things down on this course.

Palm Valley Golf Club (formerly Sun City Summerlin)

Established   1989
Address   9201-B Del Webb Boulevard, Las Vegas, NV 89128
Phone   (702) 363-4373
Status   Semiprivate
TEES
  Championship 6,849 yards, par 72, USGA 72.3, slope 127
  Gold 5,757 yards, par 72, USGA 67.5, slope 119
  Men's 6,341 yards, par 72, USGA 69.8, slope 124
  Ladies' 5,502 yards, par 72, USGA 70.7, slope 119

Fees   Nonresidents: before noon, $45; after noon and weekends, $60. Carts included. Club rentals, $40.
Facilities   Pro shop, driving range, 2 putting greens, luncheon area, and bar. Additional facilities for members.
QV Rating ★★   2

Comments   A demanding layout in a retirement community. Rolling, wide-open terrain, heavy bunkering, and bentgrass greens. The course will close to public play when membership fills from the 3,100 homeowners in the community..

Reflection Bay

Established   1998
Address   75 MonteLago Boulevard, Henderson, NV 89011
Phone   (877) 698-4653   **Web site**   www.lakelasvegas.com
Status   Resort public
TEES
  Black 7,261 yards, par 72, USGA 74.8, slope 138
  Blue 6,862 yards, par 72, USGA 73.0, slope 134
  White 6,391 yards, par 72, USGA 71.2, slope 130
  Gold 5,891 yards, par 72, USGA 69.6, slope 128
  Red 5,166 yards, par 72, USGA 70.0, slope 127

Fees   Public guest: weekday $165, twilight $120; weekend $190, twilight $130. On-property guest: weekday $135, twilight $120; weekend $160, twilight $130.

Facilities Pro shop, driving range, putting green, snack bar, restaurant, full locker facilities, Nicklaus Flick Golf School, resort hotel.

QV Rating ★★★ 2

Comments Expensive but worth it. On *Golf Magazine's* Top 100 You Can Play list shortly after opening, this is simply one of the best public courses in the nation, and vies with the twice-as-expensive Shadow Creek as the top course in Nevada. This is the public course in the Lake Las Vegas residential community, and along with the adjacent private South Shore Club, hosted the Wendy's Three Tour Challenge several times. A stunning combination of hilly desert, fraught with ravines and boulders, and waterfront "coastal" holes on the state's largest man-made private lake, with gorgeous water features throughout, including streams and waterfalls. On one hole, golfers step across stones in the stream to putt out. A strategic design thinking players will enjoy, and an aesthetic wonder that all golfers will love. This is Las Vegas's must-play course. Also on the property is Falls Golf Club by acclaimed designer Tom Weiskopf.

The Revere at Anthem

Established 1999
Address 2600 Evergreen Oaks Drive, Henderson, NV 89052
Phone (702) 259-GOLF or (877) 273-8373
Status Public

TEES
 Red 7,143 yards, par 72, USGA 73.6, slope 139
 Blue 6,590 yards, par 72, USGA 70.8, slope 131
 Black (Ladies') 5,305 yards, par 72
 White (Ladies') 5,941 yards, par 72

Fees Nonresidents: $150, Monday–Wednesday; $180, Thursday–Sunday.
Facilities Fully stocked clubhouse and snack bar.
QV Rating ★★ 2

Comments About 20 minutes from the Strip in the southeast Las Vegas Valley, this new course was designed by Billy Casper and Greg Nash. Built in a natural canyon, the course is both secluded and intimate, as well as challenging to all skill levels. Tee times, which must be reserved by credit card, can be made up to a year in advance.

Rio Secco Golf Club

Established 1997
Address 2851 Grand Hills Drive, Henderson, NV 89052
Phone (888) 867-3226   **Web site** www.playrio.com
Status Resort semiprivate

TEES
 Championship 7,332 yards, par 72, USGA 73.6, slope 127
 Blue 6,946 yards, par 72, USGA 70.2, slope 121
 Middle 6,375 yards, par 72, USGA 69.0, slope 115
 Forward 5,778 yards, par 72, USGA 70.3, slope 118

Fees Weekday, $85–$125; weekend, $100–$195. Lodging and golf packages with significant discounts are frequently offered by The Rio All-Suite Casino Hotel, especially through the hotel's Web site, at times of low room occupancy.
Facilities Pro shop, driving range, putting green, snack bar, restaurant, full locker facilities, Butch Harmon Golf School.
QV Rating ★★★ 2

Comments   The best of Las Vegas's pure desert-style courses, the course is set amid 240 acres of dramatic canyons and features six holes down in the canyons, six on relatively level plateaus, and six that roller coaster through a rugged setting of desert dry washes. Variety, beauty, and strategic design highlighted by 88 bunkers make this a challenging but beautiful course. Traditionally available only to guests of the Rio and local residents, the course now accepts Harrah's guests and limited outside play. It is also home to celebrity instructor Butch Harmon, whose prize pupil, Tiger Woods, frequently plays here and holds the course record with a stunning 63.

Royal Links

Established   1999
Address   5995 East Vegas Valley Road, Las Vegas, NV 89142
Phone   (888) 397-2499   **Web site**   www.waltersgolf.com
Status   Public
TEES
  Royal 7,029 yards, par 72, USGA 73.7, slope 135
  Gold 6,602 yards, par 72, USGA 71.2, slope 131
  Ruby 5,864 yards, par 72, USGA 69.3, slope 123
  Emerald 5,142 yards, par 72, USGA 69.8, slope 115

Fees   September–April, weekdays $225, weekends $250. Twilight (after 2:30 p.m.) weekdays $135, weekends $155. Club rentals, $60.
Facilities   Pro shop, driving range, putting green, restaurant, English pub, full locker facilities, caddies.
QV Rating   ★★   3
Comments   Royal Links sets out to emulate 18 holes from British Open venues in England and Scotland. In many ways the course succeeds, with excellent representations of links bunkering, exposure to fierce winds, and even authentic rough and gorse. But nearly every course represented is actually on the ocean, something that cannot be replicated in the desert, and the re-creations are far from exact. As a result, the course is more fun the less you know about the real thing. For instance, the famous Postage Stamp hole from Royal Troon, the shortest hole on the British Open rota, is copied here, but for some reason the elevation is way off, the bunkering is different, and architect Perry Dye saw fit to add a pond to the famously dry hole. The very expensive layout is mainly worth playing as a novelty if you've never been and never intend to visit the English courses.

Shadow Creek Golf Club

Established   1990
Address   3 Shadow Creek Drive, Las Vegas, NV 89030
Phone   (877) 209-9897   **Web site**   www.shadowcreek.com
Status   Resort public
TEES
  Championship   7,239 yards, par 72, USGA 71.0, slope 115
  Regular 6701 yards, par 72, USGA 68.9, slope 113
  Forward 5985 yards, par 72, USGA 69.2, slope 114

Fees   Monday–Thursday $500, includes caddie and round-trip limo transportation; must be a guest of a Mirage/MGM casino hotel to play, weekends invited guests only.
Facilities   Pro shop, driving range, putting green, restaurant, full locker facilities, caddies.

QV Rating ★★★ 3

Comments Shadow Creek is widely rated as not just the best course in Las Vegas, but among the best in the country. It is ranked 31st in the nation, including privates, by *Golf Magazine*, and 10th among public courses. Shadow Creek is better considered barely public, with the nation's highest greens fees, and those allowed only from Monday–Thursday, with weekends reserved for VIPs and high-rolling gamblers. Nonetheless, when the required lodging and dining are thrown in, Shadow Creek falls in the same price range as Pebble Beach and Pinehurst Number Two, and offers a far more luxurious experience than either. The course is always empty and meticulously maintained, the caddies excellent, and the layout is both gorgeous and fun to play. An engineering marvel that transported a classic, heavily wooded Carolina-style parkland layout to the desert, it is rumored to be the most expensive course ever built, having cost about $38 million in the 1980s. The finishing three holes are as memorable and dramatic a close as you will find in the golf world.

Siena Golf Club

Established 2000
Address 10575 Siena Monte Avenue, Las Vegas, NV 89135
Phone (888) 689-6469; golf shop (702) 341-9200
Web site www.sienagolfclub.com
Status Semiprivate

TEES
Gold 6,816 yards, par 72, USGA 71.5, slope 129
Black 6,538 yards, par 72, USGA 70.2, slope 126
Blue 6,146 yards, par 72, USGA 68.5, slope 123
White 5,639 yards, par 72, USGA 66.3, slope 115
Green 4,978 yards, par 72, USGA 68.0, slope 112

Fees January–May: weekdays, $139; weekends, $169; special twilight rates available.
Facilities Pro shop, driving range, putting green, snack bar, restaurant, full locker facilities.
QV Rating ★★ 1

Comments A sleeper course in the Summerlin residential community, Siena welcomes outside play and is one of the region's best buys, especially with the bargain replay option. The course showcases extensive rock outcroppings and water features, including cascading waterfalls around the 18th green. All four par-3s are unique and notable, including "sunken Treasure," a gorgeous island green. Well-separated tees offer the right challenge for every player.

Other Las Vegas Area Golf: Primm and Mesquite

As expensive as golf is in the Las Vegas area, even with discounts for residents, it is no surprise many locals drive an hour to play in these nearby towns. The surprise is the quality of the golf there, which many feel is better than any of the Vegas courses, with the exceptions of Shadow Creek and Reflection Bay.

Primm

The three major casino hotels in Primm, **Buffalo Bill's,** the **Primm Valley Resort,** and **Whisky Pete's,** are all owned by MGM Grand/Mirage Resorts, which also owns the 36-hole **Primm Valley Golf Club.** These properties and courses are significantly less expensive than their Las Vegas counterparts, and all offer golf and lodging packages.

Las Vegas's Shadow Creek proved that uber-designer Tom Fazio could work in the desert as well as, or better, than any designer, but it wasn't a desert course. Fazio filled the void in his resume with these two courses in Primm, which virtually every golfing local will tell you are more than worth the drive to play. Both are ranked in the Top 100 You Can Play by *Golf Magazine,* an honor reserved for just four facilities in the country with multiple Top 100 courses.

The two courses are quite different, but both exceptional. **The Lakes'** layout puts wide, lush, rolling, carpet-like fairways in the flat desert setting, but employs much more water, in the form of large man-made lakes, ponds, meandering creeks, even waterfalls. **The Desert** course is longer and utilizes more of its natural surroundings, but still features wall-to-wall grass, unlike many limited turf target-style desert designs. This is the longer layout, with elaborate sculpted bunkering, built into the rolling ridges alongside the fairways to make them more visually prominent. The routing was designed to intentionally showcase surrounding views of the deserts and mountains, and like its partner, is gorgeous. Call (800) 386-7867 or visit **www.primmvalleyresorts.com.**

Mesquite

About the same distance from town but in the opposite direction lies Mesquite, another frontier-style casino town that is becoming well known for golf. There is one major golf resort here, but the main attraction is a more idiosyncratic daily fee complex.

Si Redd's Oasis Resort Casino   This 1,000-room casino hotel is much more family oriented than those in Vegas, with a fun park featuring go-carts and the like, numerous pools, tennis, and other diversions, including 45 holes of golf. The original **Palms** course is Mesquite's oldest, and features a benign front with nine relatively flat holes lined with palms. The back takes a Mr. Hyde turn, with razor-thin fairways and precipitous elevation changes that make it extremely challenging while offering great views. The marquee layout here is the Arnold Palmer–designed **Oasis** course, which is unusual in that almost every fairway runs dead straight. Normally this would be grounds for criticism, but Palmer makes it work by using radical drops and climbs and elaborate bunkering to force players to place shots, even without doglegs. In fact, the Oasis is one of Palmer's very best works. There is also a 9-hole par-three course at the resort. Call (800) 21-OASIS or visit **www.oasisresort.com.**

Wolf Creek at Paradise Canyon   In one of the area's more bizarre tales, Dennis Rider, a local real-estate developer, acquired 1,000 acres of rugged desert topography and decided to build his own course without prior experience, which he did, designing it mostly from the seat of his bulldozer. This improbable success story is not just good, but great. Some critics have gone so far as to call it the best pure desert course ever built, laid out through a series of impressive slot canyons and along the namesake Wolf Creek. It fits the landscape like a glove, in the style of early Scottish and Irish courses, with the course made to fit the land rather than the reverse modern method. Although only two years old, Wolf Creek opened to such local accolades that Rider immediately built its neighbor, Falcon Ridge, which is a little more gimmicky, with greens cut from the face of limestone cliffs, but no less visually appealing. There is currently no lodging on site, although Rider is working on that. Call (866) 252-4653 or visit **www.playthewolf.com.**

Outdoor Recreation

Bicycling

Ask any cyclist in Las Vegas about the on- and off-road riding nearby and you'll probably hear two kinds of comments. First, why pedaling in the desert is such a treat: excellent surface conditions; the option of pancake-flat or hilly riding; beautiful stark scenery any time of year, and cactus blossoms in March and April; the possibility of spying raptors or jack rabbits or wild burros as you pedal; the unbelievably colorful limestone and sandstone formations . . .

Unfortunately, newcomers to desert and high-elevation biking often recall only these comments and not the "Be sure to carry—" warnings, which fellow riders usually provide after they've gotten you all revved up. So read the following and remember that bikers are subject to those very same conditions—heat and aridity—that make the desert so starkly beautiful.

Biking Essentials

1. Time of Day   Desert biking in late spring, summer, and early fall is best done early or late in the day. Know your seasons, listen to weather reports, and don't overestimate your speed and ability.

2. Clothing   Ever see someone perched on a camel? What was he wearing? Right, it wasn't a tank top and Lycra shorts. The point is protection—from the sun during the day, from the cold in the morning and evening. And if you don't use a helmet, wear a hat.

3. Sunscreen   In the desert, even well-tanned riders need this stuff.

4. Sunglasses   The glare will blind you without them.

5. Water   The first time we rode in the desert, we carried as much water as we would have used on a ride of comparable distance in the eastern United States. Big mistake. Our need for water was at least twice what it normally would be in New York or Alabama. We were thirsty the entire trip and might have gotten into serious trouble had we not cut our ride short.

You already know that you will need extra water, but how much? Well, a human working hard in 90°F temperature requires ten quarts of fluid replenishment every day. Ten *quarts*. That's two-and-a-half gallons—12 large water bottles, or 16 small ones. And with water weighing in at eight pounds per gallon, a one-day supply comes to a whopping 20 pounds.

In other words, pack along two or three bottles even for the shortest rides. For longer rides, we carry a large Camelbak water carrier along with two bottles of water on the bike frame and a third stuffed inside the mesh of the Camelbak.

In the desert, the heat is dry, and you do not notice much perspiration because your sweat evaporates as quickly as it surfaces. Combine the dry heat with a little wind, and you can become extremely dehydrated before realizing it. Folks (like us) from the East tend to regard sweating as a barometer of our level of exertion (if you are not sweating much, in other words, you must not be exercising very hard). In the desert, it doesn't work that way. You may never notice that you are sweating. In the desert you need to stay ahead of dehydration by drinking more frequently and more regularly and by consuming much more than the same amount of exercise would warrant in other climates. Desert days literally suck the water right out of you, even during the cooler times of the year.

6. Tools   Each rider has a personal "absolute minimum list," which usually includes most of the following:

tire levers	chain rivet tool
spare tube patch kit	spare chain link
air pump or CO_2 cartridges	spoke wrench
allen wrenches (3, 4, 5, and 6 mm)	6-inch crescent (adjustable-end) wrench
small flat-blade screwdriver	

7. First-Aid Kit   This too is a personal matter, usually including those items a rider has needed due to past mishaps. So, with the desert in mind, add a pair of tweezers (for close encounters of the cactus kind) and a snakebite kit. Most Las Vegas bikers have only seen snakes at the zoo or squashed on the highway, but you'll feel better if you pack one (the kit, that is) along.

Road Biking

Road biking on the Strip, downtown, or in any of Las Vegas's high-traffic areas is suicidal. Each year an astoundingly high number of bikers are injured or killed playing Russian roulette with Las Vegas motorists. If you want to bike, either confine yourself to sleepy subdivisions or get way out of town on a road with wide shoulders and little traffic.

There are a number of superb rides within a 30- to 40-minute drive from downtown or the Strip. The best is the **Red Rock Canyon Scenic Loop ride,** due west of town, which carves a 15.4-mile circuit through the canyon's massive, rust-colored, sandstone cliffs. The route is arduous, with a 1,000-foot elevation gain in the first six miles, followed by eight miles of downhill and flats with one more steep hill. One-way traffic on the scenic loop applies to cyclists and motorists alike. Although there is a fair amount of traffic on weekends, the road is wide and the speed limit is a conservative 35 miles per hour. If you park your car at the Red Rock Canyon Visitor Center, take careful note of when the area closes. If you are delayed on your ride and get back late, your car might be trapped behind locked gates.

A second ride in the same area follows State Route 159 from the town of Blue Diamond to the entrance of Red Rock Canyon Scenic Loop Drive and back again, approximately eight miles. From Blue Diamond the highway traverses undulating hills, with a net elevation gain of 193 feet on the outbound leg. In general, the ride offers gentle, long grades alternating with relatively flat stretches. Cliff walls and desert flora provide stunning vistas throughout. Traffic on NV 159 is a little heavy on weekends, but the road is plenty wide, with a good surface and wide shoulders. In the village of Blue Diamond there is a small store.

Another good out-and-back begins at Overton Beach on Lake Mead, northeast of Las Vegas, and ascends 867 feet in eight miles to the visitor center at the Valley of Fire State Park. (You can, of course, begin your round trip at the visitor center, but we always prefer to tackle the uphill leg first.) Geology in the park is spectacular, with the same red sandstone found in the cliffs and formations of the Grand Canyon. There are no shoulders, but traffic is light and the road surface is good. Since the route runs pretty much east-west, we like to schedule our ride in the afternoon so that we will have the setting sun at our back as we coast down to the lake on the return leg. Another good option is an early-morning ride with the sun at your back as you ascend and high in the sky as you return.

Dressing for a bike ride in the canyons and high country around Las Vegas is a challenge. In early December, when we rode the Red Rock loop, it was about 62° F in town and about 10° F cooler in the canyon. We started out in Lycra bike shorts and polypro long-sleeve windbreakers. By the time we completed the six-mile uphill, we were about to die of heat prostration. On the long, fast downhill, we froze.

Our recommendation is to layer on cooler days so that you can add or shuck clothing as conditions warrant. On warm days try to bike early in the morning or late in the afternoon and wear light clothing. Always wear a helmet and always, always carry lots of water. If you are not used to biking in arid climates, take twice as much water as you would carry at home, and drink *before* you get thirsty.

There is no place on any of these routes to get **help with a broken bike.** You should bring an extra tube and a pump and know how to fix flats and make other necessary adjustments and repairs. Water is available at Blue Diamond and at the Red Rock and Valley of Fire visitor centers, but no place else. Always replenish when you have the opportunity.

Mountain Biking

Las Vegas, most unexpectedly, has become a mountain-biking destination. Southwest of Las Vegas on NV 160 is Cottonwood Valley, with over 200 miles of single track and double track for all skill levels. There are five named loop trails, two named out-and-backs, and miles of unnamed trails and unpaved roads. Trail surface is mostly packed sand (good traction) with loose rock and a little soft sand. Trails on the north side of NV 160 are mellower in general, though there's some advanced riding below the east face of Wilson Cliffs. If it's your first time in the area, start with the figure-8 Mustang Trail. Almost all single track on good surface, this trail over rolling high desert offers moderate climbs, gradual descents, and great views of the Red Rock cliffs and valleys. A number of trails branch off Mustang if you want to lengthen your ride or opt for more advanced terrain.

On the south side of NV 160, the rides require more climbing. The showcase trail is the Dead Horse Loop, 14 miles of intermediate to advanced single track. Site of NORBA races, the route climbs to an overlook, with a stunning view of Las Vegas in the distance, and then drops off the mountain in a blue-cruiser known locally as the three-mile smile. Out-and-backs and additional loops connecting to Dead Horse serve up more technical climbs and descents.

There are two ways to reach Cottonwood Valley. The fastest is to go south on I-15, exiting onto NV 160 and heading west 16 miles to the Mustang Trailhead parking lot (on the right) or 17 miles to the Cottonwood Valley Trailhead on the left. You can also go west out of town on Charleston Boulevard, which becomes NV 159. Take NV 159 until it intersects NV 160 south of Blue Diamond. Turn right on NV 160 for five to six miles to the parking lots.

Southeast of Las Vegas near Boulder City, Hoover Dam, and Lake Mead is Bootleg Canyon, primarily an advanced skill level mountain-bike park. Though mostly known for its full-body-armor downhills and jumps, the parks also serves up some technical cross-country, great views of Boulder City, and, on the backside, Lake Mead. Though hard to get really lost, the layout, with lots of crisscrossing trails, is confusing to many bikers riding there for the first time. A lot, if not most, of the riding is hard core, as are the riders who hang here. Surface is packed dirt or sand and a lot of rock, much of it loose. Trails, carved into the side of the hill, are frequently not level. Our advice is to try riding Cottonwood Valley first. If Cottonwood doesn't offer enough challenge, try Bootleg Canyon. To get there from Las Vegas, take NV 93 to Boulder City. Turn left at the light onto Buchanan Boulevard, and then left onto Canyon Road. Continue beyond where the pavement gives way to dirt to the Bootleg Canyon parking lot situated between two hills. Usually there are freebie maps of the park in a box at the parking lot, but if possible, team up with locals who know the terrain.

If you're not used to riding in the high desert, you won't believe how much water you consume. We recommend a full Camelbak plus as many water bottles as you can carry on the frame. Rental bikes, unfortunately, generally come with only one water holder. If you can jam an extra water bottle into the deep pouch on your Camelbak, you'll be glad you did. Wind, almost always howling out of the west, is a factor at both biking destinations, so much so that trails are generally laid out on a north/south axis with as little east/west as possible. Even so, tackling a tough climb into a headwind will probably be part of your Nevada biking baptism. Finally, almost all of the riding is exposed. If you want shade, bring an umbrella.

Other area rides include the Bristlecone Pine Trail in Lee Canyon on Mount Charleston, about an hour northwest of Las Vegas. Though just under 6 miles in length, this loop trail is at altitude with a 700 feet rise and fall in elevation. Take US 95 north and then follow NV 157 for 17 miles up into the mountains until you see a dirt road where you can turn off and park.

Good bikes are available for rent at **Escape Adventures,** 8221 West Charleston Boulevard, (call (702) 596-2953 or visit **www.escape adventures.com**). Helmets, bike racks, water bottles, Cottonwood Valley trail maps, and other gear are likewise available for rent or sale. Escape also offers guided mountain-bike tours daily, with trails chosen based on the skill level of the group. If you book a tour, Escape will pick you up at your hotel or one close by.

Another option is to rent a bike from **Blue Diamond Bike Outpost** (call (702) 875-4820 or visit **www.bikeoutpost.com**), in the little desert town of the same name. Blue Diamond is off NV 159 about three miles north of the intersection with NV 160. Located on the east end of Cottonwood Valley, you can actually get on the trail outside the back door of the shop. That said, you have to bike quite a way uphill and west to access the popular loop trails. Even if you don't access the Valley from Blue Diamond, however, stop there and purchase one of their trail maps; it's not as well labeled, but easier to follow than Escape Adventure's

maps. In addition to rentals and repairs, Blue Diamon
runs free guided rides on most Sunday mornings.

In addition to the foregoing, many mountain bikers ri
scenic loop at Red Rock Canyon (described under road bik
448–449). Call (702) 875-4820.

Hiking and Backpacking

Hiking or backpacking in the desert can be a very enjoyable experience.
can also be a hazardous adventure if you travel unprepared. Lake Mead
ranger Debbie Savage suggests the following:

*The best months for hiking are the cooler months of November through
March. Hiking is not recommended in the summer, when temperatures
reach 120°F in the shade. Never hike alone and always tell someone
where you are going and when you plan to return. Carry plenty of water
(at least a half gallon per person) and drink often.*

*Know your limits. Hiking the canyons and washes in the desert
often means traveling over rough, steep terrain with frequent elevation
changes. Try to pick a route that best suits your abilities. Distances in the
desert are often deceiving. Be sure to check the weather forecast before
departure. Sudden storms can cause flash flooding. Seek higher ground if
thunderstorms threaten.*

*Essential equipment includes sturdy walking shoes and proper clothing.
Long pants are suggested for protection from rocks and cactus. A hat, sunscreen, and sunglasses are also recommended. Carry a small daypack to
hold such items as a first-aid kit, lunch, water, a light jacket, and a flashlight.*

Canyons and washes often contain an impressive diversity of plant
life, most easily observed during the spring wildflower season. Desert
springs are located in some of the canyons and support a unique community of plants and animals. They are often the only source of water
for many miles around. Take care not to contaminate them with trash or
other human wastes. Along similar lines, understand that desert soils are
often very fragile and take a long time to recover if disturbed. These surfaces are recognizable by their comparatively darker appearance and
should be avoided whenever possible.

Poisonous animals such as snakes, spiders, and scorpions are most
active after dark and are not often seen during daylight hours by hikers.
Speckled rattlesnakes are common but are not aggressive. Scorpion
stings are no more harmful than a bee sting, unless you are allergic. Black
widow spiders are shy and secretive and are most often found around
man-made structures. Watch where you place your hands and feet and
don't disturb obvious hiding places.

The Las Vegas area offers quite a diversity of hiking options. Trips that
include a choice of canyons, lakes, desert, mountains, or ponderosa pine
forest can be found within an hour's drive of Las Vegas.

...creation Area, an hour southeast of Las ...king experiences, although there are few ... in the NRA are Lakes Mead and ...sert. Ranger-guided hikes are offered ...ngs cover six to eight miles and are ...you prefer to explore on your own, ...to the most popular areas are available at ...dmission fee of $5 per vehicle is good for five ...ion, call (702) 293-8907.

...Rock Canyon National Conservation Area contains some ...he most rugged rock formations in the West. Only 40 minutes from Las Vegas, Red Rock Canyon offers loop as well as out-and-back trails of varying lengths. (See map on page 430.) The short Moenkopi Loop originates at the visitor center, and it takes a little more than an hour to walk over undulating terrain in a broad desert valley. Other popular short hikes include out-and-backs to Lost Creek (three-tenths of a mile, one-way), Icebox Canyon (one-and-three-tenths miles, one-way), and Pine Creek Canyon (one mile, one-way), leading to the ruins of a historic homestead near a running creek surrounded by large ponderosa pine trees. Our favorite trail, and certainly one of the most scenic, is the out-and-back Calico Tanks Trail, which winds up through a narrow canyons to a tinaja, a circular canyon or "tank," that forms a natural lake. The hike is a stunner, even in hot dry months when there's little or no water in the tank, and ends at the top of the canyon with a knock-out view of Las Vegas on the distant valley floor.

Altogether there are nineteen trails, four rated easy, five rated easy-to-moderate, nine rated moderate, and one classified as difficult. Distances range from three-fourths of a mile to six miles. Estimated hiking times are one–two hours for most trails (30 minutes for the shortest and three hours for the longest). Most of the easy and easy-to-moderate trails are pretty level. Elevation gain for moderate and difficult trails ranges from 300 feet to 1,700 feet. Maps and hiking information are available free when you pay your entrance fee and for sale in the Visitor Center. For more information, call (702) 363-1921, or check out **www.redrock canyon.blm.gov.**

The Toiyabe National Forest, high in the mountains 40 minutes northwest of Las Vegas, provides a totally different outdoor experience. The air is cool, and the trails run among stately forests of ponderosa pine, quaking aspen, white fir, and mountain mahogany. Hikes range in distance from one-tenth of a mile to 21 miles, and in difficulty from easy to very difficult. Most popular are the Cathedral Rock Trail (two miles round-trip), which climbs 900 feet to a stark summit overlooking Kyle Canyon, and Bristlecone, a five-mile loop that traverses the ridges above the Lee Canyon Ski Area. Though the distances of these loops are not

Recreation

d Bike Outpost

Recreation

451

e the paved

ing, pages

great, the terrain is exceedingly rugged, and the hikes are not recommended for one-day outings unless you begin very early in the morning and are used to strenuous exercise at high elevations. For additional information, call (702) 738-5171.

The Valley of Fire State Park, 45 minutes northeast of Las Vegas, rounds out the hiking picture. This park features rock formations similar to those found in the Grand Canyon, as well as a number of Indian petroglyphs. The *Las Vegas Advisor* compares hiking the Valley of Fire with being "beamed" onto another planet. Trails traverse desert terrain and vary from seven miles to a half-mile in length. Visitors should check in at the visitor center before they begin hiking. The park fee is $5; for more information, call (702) 397-2088.

Guided Hikes and Tours

Rocky Trails (call (702) 869-9991, or visit **www.rockytrails.com**) offers guided tours to the natural sites described above as well as to Death Valley, the Grand Canyon, Bryce Canyon, and Zion National Park. Guests are picked up at their hotel and transported in modern Suburbans or vans. Lunch or dinner is included. Expeditions to the Valley of Fire, Red Rock Canyon, Death Valley, and the Grand Canyon last six to ten hours and cost $89 to $499 per adult.

Rock Climbing and Bouldering

The Red Rock Canyon National Conservation Area is one of the top rock-climbing resources in the United States. With over 1,000 routes, abundant holds, and approaches ranging from roadside to remote wilderness, the area rivals Yosemite in scope and variety for climbers. Offering amazing diversity for every skill level amidst desert canyon scenery second to none, the area is less than a 40-minute drive from Las Vegas.

Though there is some granite and limestone, almost all of the climbing is done on sandstone. Overall, the rock is pretty solid, although there are some places where the sandstone gets a little crumbly, especially after a rain. Bolting is allowed but discouraged (local climbers have been systematically replacing bolts on some of the older routes with more modern bolts that blend with the rock). There are some great spots for bouldering, some of the best top-roping in the United States, a lifetime supply of big walls, and even some bivouac routes. Climbs range in difficulty from nonbelayed scrambles to 5.13 big-wall overhangs. You can climb year-round at Red Rock. Wind can be a problem, as can most of the other conditions that make a desert environment challenging. Having enough water can be a logistical nightmare on a long climb.

Red Rock Guide by Joanne Urioste describes a number of the older routes. Newer route descriptions can be obtained from **Desert Rock Sports** in Las Vegas (call (702) 254-1143). Desert Rock Sports can also help you find camping and showers and tell you where the loose rock is. Offering climbing shoe rentals, the store is at 8201 West Charleston, conveniently on the way to the canyon from Las Vegas. The **Powerhouse Rock Gym** (call (702) 254-5604) is next to Desert Rock Sports and offers excellent indoor climbing and showers. Guides and/or instruction are available from Desert Rock Sports or from **Sky's the Limit Climbing School and Guide Service** (call (702) 363-4533 or (800) 733-7597). Sky's the Limit also teaches courses in winter mountaineering, avalanche awareness, and cross-country skiing. Most Sky's the Limit guides are UIAGM/IVBV/AMGA accredited and certified.

River Running

The Black Canyon of the Colorado River can be run year-round below Hoover Dam. The most popular trip is from the tailwaters of the dam to Willow Beach. In this eleven-mile section, canyon walls rise almost vertically from the water's edge, with scenery and wildlife very similar to that of the Colorado River in the Grand Canyon above Lake Mead. There are numerous warm springs and waterfalls on feeder streams, presenting the opportunity for good side-trip hikes. Small beaches provide good rest and lunch sites. Bighorn sheep roam the bluffs, and wild burros can often be seen up the canyons. The water in the river, about 53°F year-round, is drawn from the bottom of Lake Mead and released downstream through the Hoover Dam hydroelectric generators.

Under normal conditions, the Black Canyon is a nice flatwater float trip with a steady current to help you along. There are places along the river such as Ringbolt Rapids and The Chute that are named for falls and rapids long since covered up and flattened out by the voluminous discharge of water from the dam. There is nothing remaining on the run in the way of paddling challenges beyond a few swells and ripples. The Black Canyon is suitable for canoes, kayaks, and rafts. Motorized craft cannot be launched below the dam but can come upstream to the dam from Willow Beach or from other marinas farther downstream. The trip takes about six hours, including side trips and lunch, for a canoe or kayak, and about three and one half hours for a commercial motorized raft.

There are several ways you can get into serious trouble. The put-in below the dam is rocky and slippery. More than few boaters have accidentally launched their boat before they climbed aboard, while others have managed to arrive in the river ahead of their boat. Once underway, it's important to keep your group close together. With the water temperature at 53°F, you want to pluck people our of the river post haste in the event of a capsize. When you go ashore to explore, pull your boat way up out of the water and tie it to something sturdy. If at the dam they happen to crank up an extra generator or two while you're off hiking in a side canyon, it's possible for the river to rise several feet, sweeping any unsecured boats and equipment downstream.

For the most part, the eleven-mile run from the dam to Willow Beach does not require any prior paddling experience. On most days, you could practically float to the take out, with breaks for lunch and exploring, in five hours. The exception, and it's a big one, is when headwinds blow up the canyon from the west. Though headwinds of less than ten miles an hour won't affect the paddling situation much, winds of 10–18 miles an hour require more experience and advanced boat handling skills. If the weather service predicts headwinds in excess of 18 miles an hour, cancel the trip, even if it means losing your permit fee. When the wind is high, it can blow you upstream, making forward progress grueling or impossible, and can whip up crosscurrents as well as waves up to three feet high. Chances of capsize grow exponentially with wind speed, and rescue efforts become correspondingly more difficult.

Private (noncommercial) parties must obtain a launch permit from:

Black Canyon/Willow Beach River Adventures
Phone (702) 293-8204
Fax (702) 294-4464
www.blackcanyonadventures.com

The launch permit costs $10 per person and is required to launch from below Hoover Dam. A $3 per person National Park Service entrance fee is also required. Only 30 boats are allowed to launch from below the dam each day, so weekends sell out well in advance. On weekdays, it's sometimes possible to get a permit on short notice. Permits can be obtained on a first-come, first-serve basis six months in advance. The permits and fees apply to a specific date and are nonrefundable, though space available, the permitting authority will try to assign you an alternate date in the event of bad weather, high winds, or other mitigating circumstances. There are, however, no guarantees.

The application can be downloaded from the above Web site, or, alternatively, you can phone and request that the application be faxed or mailed to you. Completed applications can be submitted by e-mail or fax. When your permit is approved, it will be e-mailed, faxed, or mailed to you along with directions, put-in/take-out instructions, and salient information about the river. Also included is information on canoe and kayak rentals, transportation of rented boats, and shuttle arrangements.

The best time to run the Canyon is in the fall through December. The spring is prettiest, with new green foliage seen on the beaches and in the side canyons. The spring, along with January and February, tend to be the windiest times of year, however. Summers are hot, and the canyons tend to hold the heat. The water, however, provides some natural cooling. Canoers and kayakers can make the run in one day or alternatively camp overnight in the canyon en route. Commercial raft trips are one-day affairs.

If you don't have your own equipment, you can rent canoes as well as one- and two-person kayaks from **Down River Outfitters** in nearby Boulder City (call (702) 293-1190, or visit **www.downriver outfitters.com**). The kayaks are the preferred craft but unfortunately don't come with spray skirts. This means essentially that every time you take a paddle stroke, 53° F water drips off the paddle into your lap. Canoes are drier, but slower, and more affected by wind. In addition to providing equipment, Down River Outfitters also transport you and your boat to the river. At the end of the run, they pick you up at Willow Beach and drive you back to your car. Canoe and two-person kayaks run $42 per person for one-day trips; one-person kayaks, $50. Call or visit the outfitter's Web site for booking procedures and rates for multiday trips. In addition to granting permits, Black Canyon/Willow Beach River Adventures also operates guided, motorized raft trips, with guest transportation provided from the Strip and downtown. No permit is required for these trips.

The raft outing is unlike most commercial river trips. First, the rafts are huge, accommodating more than two dozen guests. Secondly, the trip is entirely passive, no paddling or anything else required. The rafts motor up from Willow Beach in the morning and pick up their passengers at the put-in below the dam. From there, it's a scenic, narrated three hours or so float back to Willow Beach, where guests are loaded up and transported back to their cars or delivered to their Las Vegas hotel. The trips run $73 for adults, $70 for children ages 12–15, and $45 for children ages 5–11. For transportation from your Las Vegas hotel, add $33.

There is little protection from the sun in the canyon, and temperatures can surpass 110°F in the warmer months. Long-sleeve shirts, long pants, tennis shoes, and a hat are recommended minimum attire year-round. Be sure to take sunscreen and lots of drinking water.

Snow Skiing

The Lee Canyon Ski Area is a 45-minute drive from Las Vegas. Situated in a granite canyon in the Spring Mountain range, the resort provides three double chair lifts servicing ten runs. Though the mountain is small and the runs short by Western standards, the skiing is solid intermediate. Of the ten runs, seven are blue, two are black, and there is one short green. Base elevation of 8,510 feet notwithstanding, snow conditions are usually dependable only during January. Because of its southerly location and the proximity of the hot, arid desert, there is a lot of thawing and refreezing in Lee Canyon, and hence, frequently icy skiing conditions. If the snow is good, a day at Lee Canyon is a great outing. If the mountain is icy, do something else.

Snowmaking equipment allows the Lee Canyon Ski Area to operate from Thanksgiving to Easter. There is no lodging on-site and only a modest coffee shop and lounge. The parking lot is a fairly good hike from the base facility.

Skis can be rented at the ski area or from **Las Vegas Ski and Snowboard Resort** at the resort lodge. For information on lift tickets or snow conditions, call the ski area office at (702) 385-2SKI, and for summer event info at Lee Canyon, call (702) 593-9500.

Horseback Riding

The closest horseback riding outfitters are in the Red Rock Canyon area half an hour west of Las Vegas. Riding is allowed on only a couple of trails in the Red Rock National Conservation Area, but there's a lot of riding to be found just outside the Conservation Area. **Red Rock Riding Stables** (702) 875-4191; **Old West Tours,**(702) 798-7788; and **Cowboy Trail Ride** (702) 387-2457, are all located within a four- to ten-minute drive from Red Rock Canyon.

A great place for horseback riding is Kyle Canyon in the Toiyabe National Forest northwest of Las Vegas. Quarter horses with Western saddles can be rented spring through fall for one-and-a-half- to two-hour daytime rides at $69 to $89. The scenery is spectacular, with mountain vistas, ponderosa pine forests, and 300,000 acres to explore. Guides are available. Advance payment and reservations are required. For information or reservations, call **Mount Charleston Riding Stables** at (702) 387-2457.

For a real *City Slickers* experience, try **Sandy Valley Ranch** (call (702) 726-3998, or visit **www.sandyvalleyranch.com**). Located 45 minutes southwest of the Strip, the ranch is isolated from towns, roads, and just about everything else. You can follow existing trails or blaze new ones in 300 square miles (yes, that's square miles) of sage and mesquite rangeland. The terrain varies from flat valleys to foothills to canyons and mountains. Guest horses are carefully screened for responsiveness, gentleness, patience, and compatibility with other horses. The ranch offers overnight camping in sturdy, platform-mounted tents; excellent dinners in a modern but rustic dining hall; buckboard rides; and guided trail rides. Most fun of all, however, is playing with cattle (you'll want to take some home!). You can participate in an actual round-up where you scour the plains and canyons in search of cattle to herd back to the corral, or you can join friendly competitions in the rodeo arena. Here, you are timed to find out how quickly you can gather up an unwieldy herd of cattle and get them all into a small corral. Other competitions include cutting out a designated steer or bull from the herd and ushering him into the corral. The veteran cowboys at the ranch teach, coach, and cheerlead. Incredibly, with the help of the pros, most greenhorns (including guests who have never been on a horse) learn to do all of this in the space of an afternoon outing. At night after a meal of ribs, beans, salad, fresh fruit, and cobbler, new buckaroos join ranch hands around a crackling fire for songs, jokes, stories, and sometimes a visit from cowboy poet Al Marquis. Partial-day outings run from $60 to $350. All include preliminary training, a trail ride, and working with the cattle. The more expensive outings include a meal, cowboy skills games, and an evening campfire. The ranch also provides transportation from Las Vegas hotels.

Fishing

The Lake Mead National Recreation Area offers some of the best fishing in the United States. Lake Mead is the largest lake, with Lake Mohave, downstream on the Colorado River, offering the most diverse fishery. Largemouth bass, striped bass, channel catfish, crappie, and bluegill are found in both lakes. Rainbow and cutthroat trout are present only in Lake Mohave. Remote and beautiful in its upmost reaches, Lake Mohave is farther from Las Vegas but provides truly exceptional fishing. Bass and trout often run three pounds, and some trout weigh ten pounds or more. Willow Beach, near where the Colorado River enters the pool waters of Lake Mohave, is where many of the larger trout are taken.

LAKE MEAD BAIT AND TACKLE, BOAT RENTAL, FUEL, AND SUPPLIES	
Callville Bay Resort	(702) 565-8958
Cottonwood Cove Resort	(702) 297-1464
Echo Bay Resort	(702) 394-4000
Lake Mead Resort	(702) 293-2074 or (800) 752-9669 for reservations
Overton Beach Resort	(702) 394-4040
Lake Mohave Resort (AZ)	(928) 754-3245
Temple Bar Resort (AZ)	(928) 767-3211

Lake Mead, broader, more open, and much closer to Las Vegas, has become famous for its stripers, with an occasional catch weighing in at over 40 pounds. Bass fishing is consistently good throughout Lake Mead. The Overton Arm (accessed from Echo Bay or Overton Beach) offers the best panfish and catfish action.

Because Lakes Mead and Mohave form the Arizona/Nevada state line, fishing license regulations are a little strange. If you are bank fishing, all you need is a license from the state you are in. If you fish from a boat, however, you need a fishing license from one state and a special use stamp from the other. Fortunately, all required stamps and licenses can be obtained from marinas and local bait and tackle shops in either state.

Nonresidents have the option of purchasing one- to ten-day fishing permits in lieu of a license. Permits are $18 for one day and $69 for annual, and apply to the reciprocal waters of Lake Mead and Lake Mohave only. In addition to the permit, a special use stamp costing $3 is required for those fishing from a boat, and a $10 trout stamp is necessary to take trout. In addition, a $10 stamp is available for fishing with two rods. Youngsters age 12 years and under in the company of a properly licensed, permitted, and stamped adult can fish without any sort of documentation.

Sixteen-foot, aluminum, fishing boats (that seat five) can be rented on both lakes by the hour (about $30 with a two-hour minimum), by the half-day (four hours for about $50), or by the day (about $100). Bass boats, houseboats, and pontoon craft are also available. Rods and reels rent for about $5 for four hours or less and about $12 a day.

Pleasure Boating, Sailing, Water Skiing, and Jet Skiing

Lake Mead and Lake Mohave are both excellent sites for pleasure boating, water skiing, and other activities. Both lakes are so large that it is easy to find a secluded spot for your favorite boating or swimming activity. Rock formations on the lakes are spectacular, and boaters can visit scenic canyons and coves that are inaccessible to those traveling by car. Boats, for example, can travel into the narrow, steep-walled gorge of Iceberg Canyon in Lake Mead or upstream into the Black Canyon from Lake Mohave.

First-timers, particularly on Lake Mead, frequently underestimate its vast size. It is not difficult to get lost on the open waters of Lake Mead or to get caught in bad weather. Winds can be severe on the lake, and waves of six feet sometimes arise during storms. In general, there is no shade on the lakes, and the steep rock formations along the shore do not make very hospitable emergency landing sites. When you boat on either lake, take plenty of water, be properly dressed and equipped, and be sure to tell someone where you are going and when you expect to return.

Most of the resorts listed under "Fishing" rent various types of pleasure craft and water-skiing equipment, and two of them, the Overton Beach Resort on Lake Mead and the Callville Bay Resort, rent personal watercraft. In addition, at Callville Bay on Lake Mead and Cottonwood Cove on Lake Mohave, luxury houseboats are available for rental. The boats sleep up to ten adults and have fully equipped galleys and heads. For rates and other information concerning houseboats, call (800) 255-5561 or (800) 752-9669.

Relaxation and Rejuvenation

Following a vigorous day's exercise, Las Vegas offers numerous ways to relax, including a wide choice of health spas. The spas offer everything from massage to exotic body wraps. Each spa is different but, in addition to workout equipment, these spas generally have tanning facilities, skin treatments, and steam rooms.

Most spas are open to the public, but some cater only to hotel guests. A tourist staying in one of the larger hotel-casinos should have access to on-site spa facilities. Check the following listing for phone numbers and access information.

LAS VEGAS HEALTH SPAS

Spas Open to the Public

Aladdin	The Elemis Spa at Aladdin	(702) 785-5555
Alexis Park	Alexis Park Health Spa	(702) 796-3300
Caesars Palace	The Spa at Caesars Palace (Sun.–Thu.)	(702) 731-7776
Excalibur	Royal Treatment Spa	(702) 597-7772
Flamingo	Flamingo Health Spa	(702) 733-3533
Hard Rock Hotel	The RockSpa	(702) 693-5554
Harrah's	Harrah's Spa	(702) 369-5189
Hyatt at Lake Las Vegas	Spa Moulay	(702) 567-1234
Imperial Palace	Health and Fitness Center	(702) 731-3311
Las Vegas Hilton	The Spa at the Las Vegas Hilton	(702) 732-5648
Luxor	Oasis Spa	(702) 730-5724
Mandalay Bay	Spa Mandalay	(702) 632-7220
MGM Grand	The MGM Grand Spa (Mon.–Thu.)	(702) 891-3077
Monte Carlo	The Spa at Monte Carlo	(702) 730-7596
New York–New York	The Spa at New York–New York	(702) 740-6955
Paris Las Vegas	Spa by Mandara	(702) 946-4366
Rio	The Spa at Rio (Mon.–Thu.)	(702) 252-7779
Riviera	Executive Fitness at the Riviera	(702) 794-9441
T. I. at the Mirage	T. I. Health Spa (Mon.–Thu.)	(702) 894-7472
Tropicana	Tropicana Spa	(702) 739-2680

Spas for Hotel Guests Only

Bally's	The Spa at Bally's	(702) 967-4366
Bellagio	Spa Bellagio	(702) 693-7472
Caesars Palace	The Spa at Caesars Palace(Fri.–Sat.)	(702) 731-7776
Four Seasons	Four Seasons Spa	(702) 632-5302
Golden Nugget	The Grand Court	(702) 385-7111
Mirage	The Spa at the Mirage	(702) 791-7427
Rio	The Spa at Rio (Fri.–Sat.)	(702) 252-7779
T. I. at the Mirage	T. I. Health Spa (Fri.–Sun.)	(702) 894-7472
The Venetian	Canyon Ranch SpaClub	(702) 414-3600

Suggested Reading

Bass, Thomas. *Eudaemonic Pie*. Houghton Mifflin, 1985. The fascinating story of physicists from the University of California–Santa Cruz who invent a computer to beat the casinos at the game of roulette. A hilarious, true-life adventure.

Castleman, Deke. *Las Vegas*. Compass American Guides, 2003. A well-written guide to Las Vegas and its environs. This book is long on anecdote and history. If you take only one other book to Las Vegas, take this one. A very enjoyable read. Castleman has also authored an excellent guide to the entire state of Nevada.

Castleman, Deke. *Whale Hunt in the Desert—Secrets of Las Vegas Superhost Steve Cyr and His High Rollers*. Huntington Press, 2004. Castleman's rare access to hosts and high rollers enabled him to pen the definitive, never-before-told, behind-the-scenes story of the catering to Las Vegas's heaviest high rollers, known as whales.

Dancer, Bob. *Million Dollar Video Poker*. Huntington Press, 2003. Bob Dancer tells the story of how he rose from an obscure scuffler to become the best known and most successful video poker player and writer in the world.

Demaris, Ovid and Ed Reid. *Green Felt Jungle*. Trident Press, 1963. When first published, this was a highly sensational exposé of Las Vegas—its mobsters, rackets, and prostitution. Lively reading . . .

Mezrich, Ben. *Bringing Down the House: The Inside Story of Six MIT Students Who Took Las Vegas for Millions*. Free Press, 2002. A fascinating and illuminating look at team blackjack players and the casino security systems that try to stop them.

Nestor, Basil. *The Unofficial Guide to Casino Gambling*. Wiley, 2001. Every game has an optimal strategy. So, if you want to win more, this is the book to check out first.

Orkin, Mikael. *Can You Win?* W. H. Freeman and Company, 1991. A discussion of the real odds for casino gambling, sports betting, and lotteries, including winning strategies and computer odds.

Rubin, Max. *Comp City: A Guide to Free Las Vegas Vacations*. Huntington Press, 1994. A practical and often hilarious guide to taking advantage of every possible comp and freebee.

Scott, Jean. *More Frugal Gambling*. Huntington Press, 2003. Dubbed the "Queen of Comps" by CBS's *48 Hours*, Jean Scott is the most successful low roller in the country. This is the sequel to her best-selling *The Frugal Gambler*—full of thousands more tips on getting everything you want from casinos without losing your shirt.

Shaner, Lora. *Madam—Inside a Nevada Brothel*. Huntington Press, 2003. Author Shaner worked for five years as a full-time madam at Sheri's Ranch, the nearest legal brothel to Las Vegas. This is her compelling account of the sex-for-money culture, complete with a how-to section for potential brothel customers.

Silberstang, Edwin. *The Winner's Guide to Casino Gambling*. Signet, 1980. The basic primer on casinos in simple, easy-to-understand language. A difficult subject made simple and fun.

Whitney, Branch. *Hiking Southern Nevada*. Huntington Press, 2000. Whitney details 50 adventures-on-foot within an hour's drive of the bright lights of Las Vegas.

Hotel Index

Restaurant Index

Subject Index